# SUBMARINE

# SUBMARINE

## An anthology of first-hand accounts of the war under the sea, 1939–1945

EDITED BY JEAN HOOD

CONWAY

*For George Hunt, Mario Rossetto,*
*Volkmar König and Aart Hopman*

A Conway Maritime book

© Jean Hood, 2007
© Foreword Rear Admiral D. J. Cooke, MBE, 2007

First published in Great Britain
in 2007 by Conway,
an imprint of Anova Books Company Limited,
10 Southcombe Street,
London W14 0RA
www.anovabooks.com
www.conwaymaritime.com

British Library Cataloguing in Publication Data:
A catalogue record for this book is available from the British Library

ISBN: 9 781844 860463

Editing and design by DAG Publications Ltd

Printed by MPG Books Ltd, Bodmin

To receive regular email updates on forthcoming Conway titles,
email conway@anovabooks.com with Conway Update in the subject field.

**Endpaper illustration:**
View through the periscope of USS *Nautilus*
after she has torpedoed the Japanese destroyer
*Yamakaze*. (Conway Picture Library)

# Contents

# Foreword

## by Rear Admiral D. J. Cooke, MBE

### Rear Admiral Submarines,
### Commander (Operations) and COMSUBNORTH

I feel very privileged to have been invited to contribute the foreword to this anthology of wartime submariners' stories. These stories represent a wealth of experience drawn from the majority of the submarine-operating nations of the Second World War, and certainly from all of the major participants. There has been a considerable amount written, particularly in recent years, about the technical aspects of submarines in that war, and understanding the technology is a key element in understanding the operational successes and failures of the submarine conflict. An equally critical element, however, is the human factor, without which the technology is to no avail. It is in painting a vivid human picture, particularly of the sea-goers, that Jean Hood's book has been so successful and has struck a chord with me that I believe will be echoed with my fellow submariners of all nationalities.

I joined my first submarine, HMS *Oberon*, just over thirty years after the end of the Second World War. During the next twenty years I served in both conventional and nuclear-powered submarines, being fortunate enough to command one of each type. I am now equally fortunate to be Head of the Royal Navy's Submarine Service, and the NATO Commander Submarines North. Throughout my career, in whatever capacity I have been serving, I have felt strongly that one of the most important single factors that distinguishes submariners from other seafarers is the knowledge that he (or indeed she, in many navies now) is a member of a very special family. It is not just a national family either, but very much an international community with instinctive bonds based, not only on professionalism and training, but on common experiences of living in one of the most challenging environments in which man chooses to operate – underwater. It has rightly been said that it is only as a team that submariners can successfully survive these challenges, because however good the rest of the ship's company may be it only takes one of them to sink a submarine; there is no margin for complacency or error, and that is *before* you throw in the best efforts of the enemy to further complicate your life.

The conventional submarines in which I served were very similar in many ways to the later wartime boats, with the notable exception of not being on the receiving end of determined anti-submarine attacks with deadly weapons. Nuclear submarines are bigger, faster and deeper-diving but still surprisingly cramped, and their patrol endurance is ultimately limited by the amount of food carried and the stamina of the crew; there are striking examples of their wartime forebears enduring patrol lengths, in far greater discomfort, that rival or exceed those of modern nuclear boats. Regardless of the period or of the type of submarine, what does not seem to have changed much about submariners is their characters and personalities. The excerpts in this book are taken from a very broad cross-section of submariners, from those who are among the best-known and most successful commanding officers to those who were relatively unsung and best-known only to their shipmates but who were fundamental to the safe and successful operation of their submarines. What shines through, regardless of nationality, victor or vanquished, is their professionalism, good humour, sheer competence often under the most demanding of circumstances, and above all their sense of belonging to this unique international family.

The submarine community is a great club, into which no one can buy his way. Membership can only be earned, and once a submariner you are always a submariner. I derive great pride from being part of that club, and I believe that every other member, young or old, shares that sentiment. Jean Hood's book illustrates better than many why we are so proud of belonging to the submarine family. We never forget that we share a common heritage based on what our predecessors of all nationalities accomplished, and she brings that heritage vividly to life.

Finally, let no one forget the price that submariners paid for their achievements in the Second World War; to give only a few examples, in their respective submarine services the Royal Navy suffered 38% casualties (the equivalent figure for the whole of the RN was just under 8%, exceeded only by the 43% casualties of Bomber Command), the US Navy suffered 22%, and the German Navy a staggering 85%. The vast majority of those casualties were deaths, rather than losses as prisoners of war.

This book is testimony to their remarkable and courageous achievements, and I commend it to you.

# Introduction

'You would never have got me in one of those things!'
'I couldn't believe there was so little room.'

Such statements sum up the general reaction of ordinary visitors – as opposed to nostalgic submariners – to the handful of Second World War submarines now preserved as museums around the world. Clambering with difficulty through a succession of bulkhead openings, men, women and children stare at the narrow bunks and peer into the cramped wardroom, the tiny galley from which the cook fed upwards of thirty men, and the minuscule alcove that passed for the captain's cabin. They pull faces at the primitive hygiene facilities, look bewildered at the innumerable pipes, handwheels and gauges, and they file past the huge diesels, now mercifully cold and silent – all wondering how any crew could have coped with a peacetime patrol of a few days, let alone the eighty days or more that some submariners endured during hostilities.

They have never been privileged to see the boat ready to sail, with every space crammed full of food, torpedoes and other stores, nor heard the order for 'Diving Stations!' that preceded the shutting of the conning tower hatch to seal the crew in their narrow cylinder as the submarine submerged. They may be able to imagine the individual smells of sweat, sewage, diesel, damp clothes and cabbage, but they cannot combine them, and, though technology may allow the tour guide to provide the 'ping' of enemy Asdic and the explosion of a depth charge, it in no way conveys the shuddering anguish of a submarine under attack, much less conjures up the human fear that had to be suppressed for the sake of discipline and morale. As the visitors emerge, thoughtful, perhaps even humbled and a little emotional, into the fresh air and daylight at the end of the tour and look back at the old 'steel coffin', their sense of relief cannot begin to approach that of the crew when the submarine surfaces, light pours down from the open hatch and the airflow to the throbbing diesels starts to clear the foetid atmosphere.

All this, and much worse, was the wartime experience of the submariner irrespective of the flag under which he served, and this book has one very simple aim: to allow the submariners who served in the Second World War to tell their own stories, regardless of rank, nationality and, above all, wartime allegiance. Those stories range from the extremely funny to the dramatic and the deeply moving. Not everyone I approached was willing to take part. Ill health has taken its toll, and some veterans have memories that are too painful to be reopened. Several contributors understandably declined to share their experiences of the darkest moments – the loss of friends and comrades – preferring to write about the lighter side of submarine life, and when it comes to making the best of a bad job, there can be few more resourceful characters than submariners.

The accounts are taken from a variety of sources, including interviews with living veterans. To those who suggest that after more than sixty years memories are too unreliable I would say that names, dates and places may fade a little but can be re-established from other sources. Even if stories, like fishermen's catches, grow a little with repeated retelling, the experience itself remains clear. Accounts written during and just after the war can also have deficiencies, usually the result of imperfect information at the time, the influence of propaganda or the simple subjectivity that affects everyone. A dozen witnesses to the same incident yesterday may give the police a dozen different stories today, without anyone telling a single lie.

The structure of the book, to some extent, reflects the subject matter. Treat the first four chapters as a 'working-up patrol', starting with a periscopic sweep. Men of various nationalities describe how they found themselves in the service and how they adjusted to it, speaking frankly about the fear they felt. Commanders and crewmen talk about the role of the commanding officer, his influence and the critical decisions he had to make, and they offer examples of just what it meant to be operational.

In the second chapter they explain how the boats worked and describe their own duties, from routine greasing jobs in the engine room and working the commander's periscope to firing a torpedo and operating a deck gun. The third chapter provides a frank and often funny look at life on board – food, hygiene, medical dramas and home-made entertainment, before the fourth chapter brings home the deadly perils of mines, depth charges, equipment failure, ramming, foul weather and so-called 'friendly fire' that faced the submariners of every nation during the conflict. Thereafter, the events unfold year by year, with each year subdivided into theatres of war – North Sea, Baltic and Arctic; Atlantic; Mediterranean; Indian Ocean and Pacific – as the conflict becomes truly global. Each of those seven chapters commences with a brief overview that is designed to provide a context for the accounts that follow rather than offer a synopsis of the naval war as a whole. The chapter for 1945 is followed by a short Epilogue that looks at the high price paid by the submarine flotillas.

War makes enemies of men who, in other circumstances and despite the barriers of language and culture, might have found enough common ground for friendship, yet in encounters between captors and prisoners humanity often triumphed: many submariners speak with gratitude of their treatment by the crew of the enemy ship. As must be expected, some accounts betray bitterness towards the opposing side, but in post-war years many former enemies have come together to talk over their shared experiences, and lasting friendships have been formed. This collection is a contribution to that reconciliation.

# Acknowledgements

First and foremost, let me thank the submarine veterans from around the world who, in person, by telephone, letter, third-parties or email, so generously contributed their fascinating and vivid memories of the Second World War and by so doing made this a very special and personal book to write. They are: Earl Beegle, Cyril Bowden, Commodore Brian Cleary, RAN, Retd, Louis Corrolleur, Ezio Cozzaglio, Peter de Jong, Stephen Dearnley, OAM, Albert Dempster, William Fong, Alfred Fraedrich, Billy Grieves, Korvettenkapitän Reinhard Hardegen, Robert Haughney, Lieutenant-Commander Aart Hopman, Kapitän Alwin Hullmann, Captain George Hunt, DSO*, DSC*, Volkmar König, Yoshio Nakano, Comandante Sergio Parodi, Dr Wolfgang Pohl, Carlo Pracchi, Comandante Mario Rossetto, Ammiraglio Elio Sandroni, Commander Donald 'Pete' Sencenbough, Captain 1st Rank, Retd, Konstantin Sergeev, Finn-Christian Stumoen, Nickolay Leontievich Tolokonnikov, Yoshio Uchikado and George Woodward.

To that list should be added Robert Lagane, Etienne Schlumberger, Max Shean, DSO, RANVR, Retd, and Ian Fraser, VC, for their kindness in allowing me to use extracts from their autobiographies, together with Francis Louis and Charles Bernard for providing material. Several people kindly allowed me to use accounts written by family members: John de Majnik and Juanita Ironside, Ton Biesemaat, Helen Clark and Madame Deschamps.

I am also grateful to Talkback Thames and, of course, the publishers in various countries who have given permission for extracts to be reproduced from a wide range of books and articles. Full details of those books will be found in the Bibliography.

There are a large number of additional people without whom this book simply would not exist: the friends and contacts around the world who have assisted in so many ways – but particularly in helping me to find submariners willing to recount their experiences, checking my translations from the languages I can read, translating from those beyond my abilities, explaining or correcting technical jargon, and extending friendship and hospitality. To say that I am grateful is a gross understatement, and the inclusion of their names is a very small reward for their assistance, which was in some cases far above and beyond anything I could have hoped, much less expected:

Italy: Dr Maurizio Brescia, Dr Enrico Cernuschi, Cesare Manstretta, Ammiraglio Dulio Ranieri, Retd; Poland: Tomasz Kawa, Andrej Bartelski; France: Contr'Amiral Jehan Marion, Retd, Jean Mémain; Russia: Lieutenant-Commander Kirill Lysenko,

Retd, Dina Akhmetzianova, Lee Steele; Japan: Mrs Katja Boonstra, Akira Tsurukame; Australia: Norman Williams; Norway: Commander Ola Bøe Hansen; Britain: Ron Hiseman, John Harland, Richard Hughes; Germany: Klaus Mattes; USA: Vince O'Hara, Pete Birse. I only hope I have not accidentally missed out anyone – and, if I have, that they forgive me.

There are, of course, the institutions who have assisted: Commander Jeff Tall, Debbie Corner and George Malcolmson at the Royal Navy Submarine Museum; my old friends Barbara, Anne and Louise at Lloyd's Register of Shipping; the National Archives; The Imperial War Museum's Department of Documents and Sound Archive; the BBC; the US Submarine Veterans Inc; the Submariners Club of St Petersburg; and the Verband DeutscherUbootfahrer. I must thank John Lee and Alison Moss at Conway, and David and Tony at DAG Publications. I also want to offer special thanks to Stephen Dent for his help and moral support; to John Jordan and Jak Mallman-Showell for enlarging my understanding of the conflict in the Pacific and the Battle of the Atlantic respectively; to Fred West for checking the translations of commands and technical jargon; to my father-in-law, George, who did his National Service in submarines; to my son, Adrian, for his assistance with the science; to Judy, Peter and Sarah for so obligingly living equidistant from central London and the National Archives, and to my husband George without whom …

My final thanks go to Rear Admiral D. J. Cooke, MBE, Rear Admiral Submarines, Commander (Operations) and COMSUBNORTH, who was so enthusiastic about contributing the foreword. I am very grateful to him because it is appropriate that such a senior officer in an advanced modern navy, in which submarines are now the capital ships, should pay tribute to the courage and resource of the Second World War veterans of so many nations and recognise the close ties of shared dangers, privation and resourcefulness that bind all submariners together.

# Glossary

| | |
|---|---|
| 3×AK | 3 × äusserste Kraft: three times extreme power. A submarine going 'Full Ahead' is not using the maximum power the engine can produce. 3×AK – there is no 2×AK – is ordered in emergencies only and, by the addition of the electric motors at full power, may give the submarine an extra two or three knots for a brief time in order to escape before diving (German) |
| Aldis lamp | Hand lamp used for signalling |
| Barking mad | Crazy |
| Bawl out | To reprimand, loudly and angrily |
| Billet | Patrol sector assigned to a submarine |
| Boards | The plates forming the deck above the battery compartments and other tanks |
| Bollocking | A severe reprimand (slang) |
| Boom | A floating barrier, usually across a harbour entrance |
| Bouillabaisse | Fish stew |
| Bounced | Caught by surprise |
| Bug | Translation of Mücke, colloquial name for FuMB 25 radar detector |
| Bump off | Murder |
| Cant | Italian bomber aircraft |
| Casing | Upper deck of a submarine, unpressurised, open to the sea and covering the pressure hull and external tanks. |
| Chernikeef log | An instrument used to measure nautical speed and distance travelled |
| Clobbering (receiving a) | Being hit, as in bombed |
| COMSUBPAC | Commander Submarines Pacific (US Navy) |
| CPO | Chief Petty Officer (US Navy) |
| CSAF | Commander Submarines Asiatic Fleet |
| Dead reckoning | Calculation of position based on data such as distance run, speed and course, as opposed to using celestial observations |
| Degaussing | Procedure to demagnetise the hull of a ship as protection against mines |
| Depot ship | Each submarine flotilla had a depot ship, which provided support and accommodation for the boats and their crews |

| | |
|---|---|
| | between patrols. |
| Do his nut | Become very angry |
| Dog watch | The 24-hour day at sea was divided into 7 watches: 5×4hrs and 2×2hrs, dog watches (1600–1800 and 1800–2000) |
| Dory | A small flat bottomed boat |
| Dove | Past tense of dive (US) |
| DSEA | Davis Submarine Escape Apparatus |
| Eel | Torpedo (German) |
| Emergency Flank Speed | US term equivalent to the German term 3×AK: absolute maximum speed, obtained by coupling up both diesels and motors. This can only be done for short bursts |
| ERA | Engine Room Artificer |
| ETA | Estimated Time of Arrival |
| Exec | Executive Officer |
| Fine on | At a narrow angle to, as in 'fine on the port bow' |
| Fish | Torpedo |
| Fix / take a fix | Position; calculate one's position |
| Fly | Translation of Fliege, colloquial name for FuMB 24 radar detector |
| Folboat | Collapsible canoe used by commandos and other special operators |
| Four-pipe | Four-funnelled |
| Fruit machine | A manual calculator used in a torpedo attack |
| Group down | Motors coupled in parallel, for higher speed |
| Group up | Motors coupled in series, for slower speed |
| Hank | To pull |
| Harbour stations | Posts taken by the crew when the boat sails |
| HE | Hydrophone Effect, the sound made by propellors, etc., which can be passively detected by hydrophones |
| Head for the barn | Go home, return to base |
| Heads | Lavatory |
| HEDA | High Explosive Delayed Action |
| Hydrophone | Externally mounted microphone used to pick up the sound of other vessels |
| Hydroplanes | Horizontal rudders which are adjusted to allow the boat to dive |
| IMC | The circuit used in US Navy submariners for internal communication |
| Jimmy | 1st Lieutenant (Royal Navy) |
| Jitters, to have the | Feel afraid or anxious |
| Kingstons | Valves on the underside of internal ballast tanks |
| Kipper | Torpedo |
| Loading line | Line painted on a hull to indicate the maximum draft to |

which a ship can be loaded. This, and therefore the amount of cargo, varies in different temperatures and between salt and fresh water. A loading line consists of several lines, one of which is WNA, or Winter North Atlantic

| | |
|---|---|
| Mariscom | Submarine command (Italian navy) |
| Mess, to | To eat with, etc; no messing, however, means 'without hesitation or argument' |
| Metox | Receiver designed by the Germans to detect Allied radar transmissions, but with poor discrimination and nullified by the deployment of centimetric radar after March 1943 |
| Mole | A pier |
| MTB | Motor Torpedo Boat |
| OOD | Officer of the Deck |
| PDQ | Immediately – 'pretty damned quick' |
| Pierhead jump | An appointment at very short notice |
| Pig | Translation of the Italian 'maiale', the nickname given to their torpedoes by the frogmen of the Decima Flottiglia MAS |
| Pitometer log | Device for calculating distance travelled |
| Planesman | Crew member whose duties include operating the hydroplanes |

Sectional drawing of a British T-Class submarine.

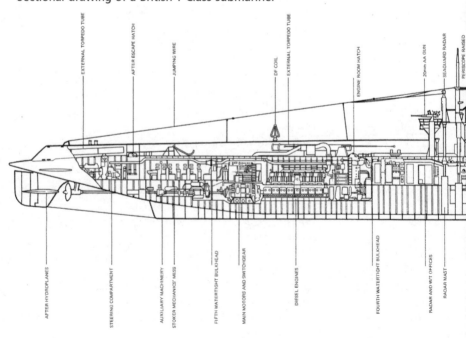

| | |
|---|---|
| Plank owner | In the US Navy, a member of the boat's original crew |
| PO | Petty Officer |
| R&R | Rest and recuperation |
| RANVR | Royal Australian Naval Volunteer Reserve |
| Relative Bearing | The direction, measured clockwise in degrees, from the bow of the narrator's own submarine |
| RNR | Royal Naval Reserve |
| RNVR | Royal Naval Volunteer Reserve |
| Shears | Periscope supports |
| SJ | An early form of surface search radar installed on US submarines and son relaced by Planned Position Indicator (PPI) |
| SOB | Son of a bitch (US slang) |
| Sounder | A device with which to measure the depth to the sea bed |
| Sounding / to take soundings | Measuring/measure the depth to the seabed |
| SSS | A distress call in Morse code, indicating that the transmitting vessel has been attacked specifically by a submarine |
| Steerage way | Making just enough speed, relative to the current, to keep the submarine answering the helm |
| Stem | Bow |

he galley, which is not shown, was opposite the radar
d W/T offices.

The spaces in the bottom of the boat were tanks containing either oil fuel, lubricating oil, fresh water or salt water.

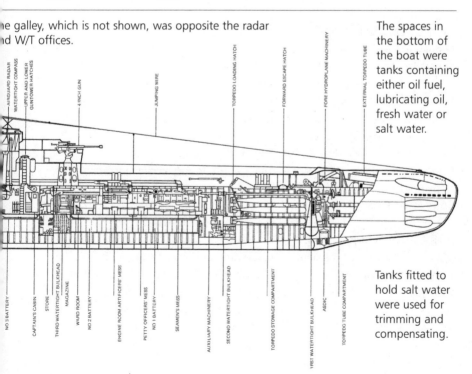

Tanks fitted to hold salt water were used for trimming and compensating.

| Stop bolt | The stop bolt keeps the torpedo in the correct position in the tube so that the required speed, depth and gyro data can be set before it is fired |
| Stop the rot | Prevent things from getting worse |
| SUE | Signal Underwater Explosion |
| Supermarina | Italian Admiralty |
| Swain | Contraction of boatswain |
| Swept channel | Route patrolled by minesweepers to keep it safe |
| Tanks (to do the tanks) | To learn how to escape from a submarine underwater by using Davis Submarine Escape Apparatus; the training was carried out in a deep tank of water |
| TBT | Target-bearing transmitters |
| TDC | Torpedo Data Computer (US Navy) |
| Tenente | 1st Lieutenant in the Italian Navy |
| Tiffy | Royal Navy slang for an engine room artifiicer |
| Tinfish | Torpedo |
| Trim | A submarine is trimmed when it is level |
| Trimmed down | Running on the surface but with as much as possible of the boat submerged. |
| TTC | Torpedo data computer |
| Wardroom | Compartment for the officers |
| WO | Wach Offizier (I, II, III, etc.) Officer of the Watch (German) |

## NAVAL NOMENCLATURE

**Kongelige Norske Marine:** Royal Norwegian Navy

**Koninklijke Marine:** Royal Netherlands Navy

**Kriegsmarine:** German Navy (at the time)

**Marine Nationale:** French Navy. However, between 1940 and 1942 a distinction is made between the vessels of the Vichy Marine and the Free French, **Forces Navales Françaises Libres** (FNFL)

**ORP:** Oret Rzeczypospolitej Polskiej (Ship of the Polish Navy)

**Regia Marina:** Italian Navy (as it was called prior to Italy becoming a republic post-war)

**Royal Navy:** British Navy

## A NOTE ON DECORATIONS

It is a peculiarly British tradition to list civil and military decorations after the names of the recipients, and this extends to many Commonwealth countries; therefore such decorations are shown. In the case of British awards to submariners of allied nations, the decorations have not been shown; nor have awards made by other countries to their own and foreign nationals.

# An All-Round Look

The submarine was a controversial weapon, often considered an unchivalrous, stealthy killer sneaking around under the waves, sinking much larger vessels at will and at little risk to itself. For that same reason it became such a valuable addition to the world's navies, some fifteen* of which were involved, to a greater or lesser extent, in the submarine war between 1939 and 1945:

**Allies:** Great Britain, France, USA, USSR, Poland, The Netherlands, Norway, Greece and Brazil. **Axis:** Germany, Italy, Japan, Finland, Romania and Yugoslavia.

With all the advantages of stealth that the ability to submerge gave them, Second World War submarines *were* nevertheless vulnerable, particularly in the aftermath of an attack on anything but unprotected merchantmen or while on the surface, and they became more so as the war progressed. The German submariners ended up suffering a horrific casualty rate of around 80%; in percentage terms the US Navy losses were higher in submarines than in any other arm of their navy. Only one Norwegian boat was sunk – with all hands – but she accounted for 33% of their operational submarine strength at the time. Yet for all that it was a service which, for the most part, enjoyed the highest morale.

Little wonder that, whatever their nationality, whatever their motives for joining the service, and whatever the fortunes of war, submariners of every rank saw themselves as a breed apart, an elite, even a microcosm. Some had gained their experience in the service before the start of the war; others came straight from civilian life; more than a few transferred from surface ships, both naval and merchant, with all the attendant culture shock.

## A SERVICE UNLIKE ANY OTHER

**Lieutenant-Commander Ian Fraser, VC, Royal Navy**; from *Frogman VC*

It was in the *Sahib* that I came to experience to the full what I had already partly felt in myself and observed in others: the enormous pride that

---

* Brazilian submarines operated, on the Allied side, in home waters. In addition, Latvian and Estonian submarines were taken over by Germany at the very start of the war; Danish boats were scuttled. It should, however, be remembered that different countries joined the war at different times; some withdrew before the end; and others changed sides or divided their loyalties. A number of governments-in-exile put their boats under Royal Navy operational command, but those submarines still flew their own flags and were crewed and commanded by their own nationals, usually with a British liaison officer on board.

submariners have in being just submariners. I have sailed with men who thought nothing floated on the surface of the sea to compare with a destroyer; I have messed with men who would glory in the strength and the wonder of a battleship; I was at one time carried away by the enthusiasm of men who raced over the waves in forty-knot motor torpedo boats. All this, in my judgement, is nothing when set beside the pride of the submariners.

This is something quite different from what land-lubbers sometimes refer to as 'love of the sea' or what Admirals at school speech days will describe as 'belief in the proud tradition of the Queen's Navy'. All that, though it is never in practice alluded to, is taken for granted – even if it be a rather grand assumption. No. The submariners' pride is a pent-up feeling, a consciousness of being one of a tightly-knit band of men cut off from most of the normal naval experience and living pent-up lives in incredibly cramped quarters, embarked on missions that are dangerous in themselves before ever a glimpse is had of an enemy. The submariner – in wartime, at any rate, and even to a certain extent in peacetime – is in danger from the moment his boat dives below the surface. A surface-craft may sail many thousands of miles without encountering anything more abnormal than a heavy storm or a thick fog; if anything goes wrong, seriously wrong, there is usually a fair bit of time to get the boats out, and usually a fair bit of time to get into those boats. If anything goes wrong with a submarine, there is only the rather laborious escape hatch as the way out … With such inescapable facts tucked away subconsciously, the submariner sets about forgetting all about them: but they are there, hovering about below the surface of the mind as the submariners' own craft moves about below the surface of the seas. Among men who find themselves in such circumstances, it would be unnatural not to find a special kind of bond being forged …

**Stoker George Woodward, Royal Navy, HMS *Thule***

I was nearly 18. I'd a brother on destroyers – *Ivanhoe* – and that got sunk in 1939 and he got off it, and he went to another one, *Intrepid*, [lost in 1943]:, and he was lucky: he got off it. And I volunteered for submarines; they seemed safer than surface ships.

**Luitenant ter Zee 1 Peter de Jong, Koninklijke Marine, then Exec, *O.24***

From a small boy we used to go on holidays to some small islands up the north of Holland, and I found the sea was beautiful, and I saw ships, and from a small boy onwards I wanted to become an admiral. I had a cousin who was in the navy and I became a midshipman. I was 16 at the time. I had been very quickly through the schools. At 19 I was lieutenant 3rd Class and I came out to the Dutch East Indies, and there I sailed on destroyers the whole time. The navy had a system where, after you were an officer for about a year, you could choose what sort of thing you wanted to specialise in. I always had a mathematical sort of mind. I thought I'd become a gunner, artillery. So I put in for gunnery school. And then the answer came back and it was the submarine school. I didn't dislike that at all because it had two big advantages. First, you got your own boat quite early while all your friends were still on a big ship, and, second, you were paid extra. You got a slight extra payment for being so many hours submerged. So I went to the submarine school. I was two years at Surabaya on the submarine, and I reached the stage, when I was a young Number 1, that I went to the Rotterdam Dry Dock. They were building a series of seven submarines …

## Outside ERA's Mate Cyril Bowden, Royal Navy, HMS *Virtue*

They started to conscript people into submarines because we'd lost, I think, nearly two-thirds of the submarine fleet. They bore the brunt from 1940. After I had finished my training I went down to Devonport and it was packed, absolutely packed with people, sailors, because half the dockyard had been knocked down, bombed. It took a right clobbering in 1942, I think it was. There were all these people coming in, and there was nowhere to put them. We were all mustered in the morning and the Drafting Petty Officer said: 'Now, draft sheets. You've got two choices: either tank landing craft or submarines.'

I said: 'What pays the most money?' and he said: 'Submarines.' I said: 'Well put me down for that then.'

From there I went to Portsmouth and did the tanks [learned how to escape from a submarine underwater], and then I stood by the boat in Barrow in Furness. It was being built; it was in the water, being fitted out, and of course the idea was, if you could be there, standing by and seeing it all, it was far better than reading about it or seeing it in a classroom. I knew that boat from back to front.

My wife's mother wouldn't allow us to get married before I went on the boat – she'd already lost one son in submarines, so she didn't want her daughter marrying a submariner.

You always got the odd one who didn't want to be on submarines. Not many, just the odd one or two. I never saw any, but I believe there were. If you got venereal disease you were out straightaway, no messing, because discipline had to be spot on, which it was.

We were more lackadaisical than the surface craft, yes, but only for the fact that you couldn't do anything … You couldn't swing your arms around and that kind of thing. So you dressed accordingly – but, at the same time, every order had to be obeyed at that moment, and before if you could! And you always repeated that order straight away. Your mate's life was in your hands. If you made a mistake you'd kill him as well as yourself, and everyone with him.

You thought you were different to anybody else and you thought you were special. You felt special because you did things right. In my opinion, if you've got a submarine crew, including the captain and the officers, petty officers and seamen, you have the finest form of socialism ever invented. If that was applied today, as a submarine crew, you wouldn't go wrong.

### Sub-Lieutenant Robert Lagane, Marine Nationale; from *Cinq Ans Dans le Brouillard*

Complete with uniforms and equipment for every operational, climatic and formal eventuality that a young officer might face, Midshipman Robert Lagane joined his first ship, the *Jeanne d'Arc*, at Brest in 1939. The French cruiser was then sent to patrol in the waters around Puerto Rica, Jamaica, the French Antilles, Aruba and Venezuela.

Saturday April 6 1940, anchored at Fort-de-France. Bursting with excitement as usual, Lieutenant de Vaisseau Marche exploded into the midshipmen's quarters.

'Lagane! Get your "whites" on. At once! Get into the captain's launch. You're off to the Admiralty. You'll be told what you'll be doing!'

At 1000, surrounded by a selection of his staff, Admiral Robert received me. *Knock, enter, salute, take off cap, remove right glove if your superior offers his hand, sit down if he invites you to …* Naval etiquette was followed to the letter. I learned of my appointment to the Admiralty's signal office.

At midday I had the unexpected surprise of being given a seat at the Admiral's table, right at the far end and on the understanding that I would be seen and not heard. The Admiral High Commissioner presided; he boasted about his rose gardens. The Rear-Admiral was a man of the world; he collected old postage stamps. The captain of the *Jeanne*, for his part, was mad keen on photography.

I was present at a dazzling display of eloquence on subjects that jumped from the delights of the Black Sea to the charms of the lovely little Pauline; the shimmer on the wings of Brazilian butterflies and on the sea in the Bay of Along; features of gothic cathedrals and melon cloches; not forgetting the comparative merits of a 1934 Château Petrus and a 1921 Margaux. In other words the very model of the amazing conversation to be found in the senior officers' wardroom.

During the afternoon, Commander Antoine of the 15th Submarine Flotilla turned to this signal station officer:

'Good day, Midship. I understand that you have volunteered for submarine service. If you are free, I will send you to Trinidad tomorrow.'

'Yes, sir.'

At 0630, in my whites, complete with sword and white gloves, and accompanied by a sailor who carried my kit, I presented myself at the gangway of the *Iris*, moored with her sister ships *Vénus*, *Cèrés* and *Pallas*.

Alone, lost in thought, a shaggy-haired, bearded sub-lieutenant with a pipe clenched between his teeth was pacing up and down the deck. He wore blue shorts, a shabby khaki shirt, no socks and tatty leather sandals.

Before coming aboard, I introduced myself at a distance.

'My respects, sir. Enseigne de Vaisseau [Sub-Lieutenant] Lagane, reporting to the *Iris*.'

Thus addressed he stopped, considered me with a pitying look, took his pipe a few centimetres from his mouth and replied.

'You can stick your respects up your arse, Midi. Along with all your equipment, your trunk, your sword and your white gloves. You can keep one uniform for going ashore, and I mean one, and you can make yourself comfortable on the wardroom bench which will be your private kingdom in this rust-bucket. You can put your gear in the drawer under the bench; you'll just have to shove up the stuff that's already there. And get a move on: harbour stations in twenty minutes. We weigh at 0730. Oh, I forgot. I'm Dégé and I'm the Number Three. Number Two is below. He's waiting for you so he can trim the boat ...'

Two days at sea taught me that life in a surface ship was a world away from that of the submariner. Here, it was relaxed and coarse within a family atmosphere, while at the same time making no compromises whatsoever where safety is concerned.

For example, no more of the segregation by rank that led to the Jeanne having five separate dining rooms – and five different menus – for the five levels of officer on board: admiral, commander, senior officers, junior officers and midships. Here there was the one table for the commander (CC 4 stripes); the Exec (LV 3 stripes); 3rd Officer (EV 1ière Classe, two stripes) and the midship (EV 2ième Classe, one stripe).* There was only one menu: that for the whole crew.

The quality of the grub was one of the attractions of a career in submarines. The regulations laid down 'a protein-rich diet accompanied by milk rations', in order to prevent any risk of anaemia caused by the lead in the batteries and by

* The stripes do not correspond to Royal Navy ranks.

carbon dioxide. These two measures meant a doubling or even tripling of the standard food allowance. And the serving of three-star menus every time if the supply-chief-petty-officer was able to justify the orders ...

One of my first surprises was to hear that every order involving a change of activity was immediately followed by an order to have a snack.

## Midshipman Volkmar König, Kriegsmarine, *U-99*

By the time Volkmar König was eligible for active service. German U-boats were operating out of bases along occupied France's Atlantic coast, including Lorient in Brittany.

This was the first time they put midshipmen aboard submarines going out to sea, so I was proud like a Spaniard. I had a friend – we were both at artillery school in Kiel – and we got this command to join the 7th Submarine Flotilla at Lorient, and we said: 'On our way to Lorient we could visit our parents. No one will notice if we come one day later. We will stop somewhere and we will meet in Bremen on the train.'

When I came to the station in Bremen there was an extra train, a special train because it was war and so many were on leave ... I said to myself: 'I'll go on board the first train and walk through the train. If he is not on there I get off the train at Osnabruck and wait for the second train and join him there.' But our train stopped on the way to Cologne because there was engine trouble and so the other train overtook the train I was on, and he arrived in Lorient sooner than I did and he went aboard *U-47* (Prien), and this boat was sunk with all hands on the next patrol. In theory, I might have gone on board of Prien if I had been there on time, if I had not stopped over in Paris. I couldn't board a train in Paris because some line was broken due to snowfall ... so I had a day in Paris.

So it was Paris in the snow in February, '41 and the sister of a friend was secretary to some navy staff and she said: 'If you are tired I have a hotel room and you can put your head down on my pillow.' So when I was lying down, very tired, I said: 'Silly: it is once in a lifetime you are in Paris and you are sleepy. Now get up!' So I walked all day through Paris. At that time life in Paris was wonderful, there was nothing happening. I was walking all day long, through Paris in my navy uniform. The French were so glad the war was over and the communists were gone ... When I finally arrived in Lorient the next day I went aboard *U-99*, the boat of Kretschmer: this was something! I was 20 and he was 28. He was the Old Man, that's quite a difference. And I admired him for his intelligence and for his audacity and for his courage and for his calculation, but he was not chummy with his subordinates; he was Authority. In later years he talked much more than when he was young, when he was 'silent Otto'.

*U-99* was known as the 'horseshoe boat'. These two horseshoes on the conning tower of *U-99* came up from the bottom of Kiel Bay at the end of an anchor manoeuvre. When the anchor came up and was cleaned with water there was one horseshoe on an anchor fluke, and this was reported to the captain on the conning tower. And then they they shouted up to the captain: 'There's another horseshoe on the other fluke!' The captain shouted back, "Where's the horse?" But because of this rather unbelievable event there was an absolute confidence in the safety of the boat and the crew from that moment. Nothing will ever happen to us. Those two horseshoes were welded to the conning tower.

I was excited the first time we went to action stations because it was an experienced crew: so many depth-charge attacks, so many ships, so many patrols – was routine for them and if you are engulfed as a newcomer there it's very easy. If they all had been on their first patrol it would have been different for me, and not so easy, but they were used to all this, it was routine for them, so it's something that's routine for you as well, more or less.

I was excited, too, the first time the boat dived.

## Comandante Mario Rossetto, Regia Marina

Having found myself on the losing side at the end of the conflict, I don't want to say simply that my government of that time was wrong to undertake the enormous events for which we were completely unprepared, facing a more powerful enemy and allied to an ill-fated (iniquitous) regime.

In the years leading up to the conflict, the propaganda had a massive influence above all on the younger generations. I myself was born in 1915, just before Italy's entry into the First World War. I entered the Naval Academy in 1933, emerged in 1936 and at the outbreak of the Second World War I was a sub-lieutenant. I had grown up, therefore, in a particular climate in which, along with fascism, the Motherland was extolled, memories of the glories of Rome and her empire were revived; we spoke contemptuously about the great powers who had built up their great empires in the preceding century when Italy, fragmented into so many small states, grew in importance on the world stage only through the greatness of her artists and scientists.

Steeped in that propaganda, we consented, even enthusiastically, to play our part even though we had not made a conscious choice.

In the navy, we young men saw the opportunity to make our mark in its smaller branches. The large surface fleet, although completed while the war was already going on, would not have been comparable to that of England which at that time dominated the Mediterranean – which the propaganda, harking back to the history of Rome, defined as Mare Nostrum. Young officers serving in small ships had the opportunity to get noticed. That was particularly true of submarines which, although more dangerous, were more coveted perhaps as a result of the publicity given to the exceptional achievements of the German U-boats.

### Stoker Reginald Bucke, Royal Navy; from 13107 IWM Sound Archive 9223/3

They might have been a bit envious of you, in so much perhaps as you got a bit more glory than they did. And of course a few more shillings a day. No, as submariners we never envied anyone else, whether it was a soldier in a tank or whether it was the ordinary sailor in an ordinary ship or even aircraftsmen, we never envied anybody else. We used to think we was better off – whether the word is safer I don't know, but we used to think we was better off ... The submariners were a class apart.

### Wireless Operator Finn-Christian Stumoen, Kongelige Norske Marine, *Utsira*

Of all those who escaped from an occupied country to join his chosen side, Finn-Christian Stumoen probably had the longest journey.

I had been all round the world before I came into the Navy. After school, because my father had a farm, I worked on the farm for about a year and then I got fed up. I said I wanted to go to sea, and I went to sea in Norway's biggest passenger ship, as a potato peeler ... That was my life before the war. I stayed at home for a year after the war broke out, before I escaped, because I had to finish Navigation School and radio school. The Germans allowed the Navigation School to continue because they took all the pupils for the navy. So when I finished at the school I had to escape, or they would have taken me. And of course it was the death penalty for trying to escape Norway in those days. So you had to do it right! I said: 'Well, here we go.'

I put on my skis and in the night I skied over to Sweden. I used most of the night: I started at nine o'clock at night and walked towards the Swedish border. I had a star at that time, Arcturus, and that star was standing in the east all night. So as long as I kept that right ahead and walked – there was no path – towards Sweden I was alright. If it had been overcast I would have tended to go in a circle and that would have been very bad. It was a tough job but it was quite exciting to do it.

From Stockholm I flew to Helsinki and from there by train to Leningrad. On the train again, to Odessa. Over the Black Sea in a cruise ship to Istanbul. From there, train all through Turkey to Alexandretta. Here I got on board an English freighter bound for Port Said.

Half way down the Mediterranean we were attacked by a Syrian Vichy plane. He managed to drop a bomb in hatch No. 1 ... Another hour, an Italian Dornier came in but dropped his bombs 100 yards away. We arrived at Port Said fully loaded with water ...We were sent aboard the troop transport *Empress of Asia*. This was in Aden. There we met Prince Philip. He was also on his way to England. From Aden we went to Durban, Cape Town, Trinidad and New York.

So we got to New York and we were stationed in a lovely hotel, just by Grand Central Station and I applied to get into the Norwegian Air Force. I was all ready to go up to Toronto, but then I got a telephone call to say, no, you are going on to a ship as wireless operator. Here I went aboard a tanker, *Svenor*, as Third Mate and Telegraphist. We should load oil and go to England. And when we came to England I was taken into the Navy. I ended up in Troon, in Scotland, on the minelayers.

I was on minelayers when the first Norwegian submarine was sunk, the Uredd. You can't help thinking about how the water comes in, and you sit there and you die slowly, you drown slowly. I shiver when I think of it. There's no way out and the water's coming nearer and nearer. I can't think of anything worse.

Then my ship, *ML-210*, was mined outside Somme, a small town in France. I had been sent down to Plymouth that trip. Lucky me: five men were killed. The man who relieved me fell out through the hole made by the mine – he did survive, though.

That's how I got into submarines: because my ship had gone down.

## Korvettenkapitän Reinhard Hardegen, Kriegsmarine

Despite a legacy of injuries sustained in a flying accident in 1936, which should have prevented his ever being posted to submarines, Reinhard Hardegen became one of Germany's ace commanders.

I spent four years in the Seefliegerei [naval air arm] and at the outbreak of war I was a pilot. I was only transferred to the U-boat division in '39 and then I spent six months training. Afterwards I went to the torpedo-testing unit and was involved in target practice with submarine torpedoes. That was very important for me because it gave me a lot of practical experience of firing torpedoes. Then I went through my commander's course. The II WO* of *U-124* had to leave his boat because he had broken his hand, so I got a pierhead jump** and took over the duties of II WO. I made two patrols with *U-124* as a WO. The I WO was somewhat younger than me but I did my job, which was important for me insofar as after two patrols I received my active service

---

* 2nd officer of the watch: zweiter Wachoffizier, colloquially called Zwo-WO (pronounced Zvo-vo).
** Royal Navy slang meaning 'was posted at very short notice'.

badge: I would be offered a boat on active service, not a training boat. I knew the commander [Georg Wilhelm Schultz] well: we had been together at the naval academy as midshipmen, and after the first patrol I had asked him if I might do a second patrol with him. He was pleased to have a WO who had been through the commander's course and passed. So I made those two patrols and then I went to Kiel to commission a new boat, *U-147*, and I made one patrol in her. I went up around England – she was a small boat [Type IID] – and in the spring of '41 I took over *U-123*. She was a large boat [Type IXB]. I made a number of patrols in her: to Africa, Freetown, and up to Greenland, two patrols to America, and at the end of August 1942 I handed her over to my I WO, Horst von Schroeter – who also won the Knight's Cross and who went on to become a Vice Admiral in the Bundesmarine. I came ashore at the end of August and never went back to sea. I held various commands at home. First of all I was a training instructor at the Torpedo School and later in the Torpedo Weapons Department where new types of torpedo were developed.

As far as the war goes, we did our duty. Okay, when we sank ships, when we scored our successes, we were pleased about it, but I have also rescued crews (I put one crew on a neutral Swiss ship) if that was possible. On one occasion there was a solitary chap … a boat floated past – and we had him on board with us, and the only thing he moaned about was the fact that he'd had a couple of tins of cigarettes, and of course, he had left them behind in the lifeboat instead of bringing them with him. And you can't smoke in a submarine. He was very sad about that because he was a heavy smoker and wasn't allowed to smoke on board. But when we were depth-charged, then he was really frightened. 'Why so? They're your friends, not mine.' It was the English doing it, and he was an Englishman.

### Chief Electrician Yoshio Nakano, Imperial Japanese Navy, *I-165*

I joined the Japanese Imperial Navy in 1934. I was 17 years old. I first became a crew member on the cruiser Kirishima. The senior crew, named Mr Mizumoto, from the same hometown (Kagoshima) suggested me to become a submariner. So, I went to the Submarine School. After graduation, I joined *RO-42*, then on *I-165* from 1940. I was in charge of the electric department such as battery-related work.

*RO-42* was not too good. It was small and crowded. However, *I-165* had a very advanced engine and had long cruising distance and high speed (20 knots). The battery was very good. In my four years' service, it seldom gave us trouble.

Once fresh vegetables and fruit ran out, it was a canned food every day. As I had to work on a hot (sometimes 50 to 60 degrees Centigrade) battery room, I often lost my appetite. When you eat canned food only, your gums start to bleed due to the lack of vitamins and minerals. Ever since then, I hate canned food even today. Accommodation was poor for both *RO-42* and *I-165*, but I did not worry much as I was still young and strong.

## CONFRONTING FEAR

Submarine crews may have been proud, and they were certainly brave, but they were not immune to fear, and that went for both officers and men.

### Stoker George Woodward, Royal Navy, HMS *Thule*

We had to go through a minefield. We was landing agents. That's a bit scary. If you're in the control room you know what's going on, but in the engine room you haven't an idea. That's the worst part about it. If you don't know anything, your mind starts working. I was in the forward pump space and you're on your own. All you've got are six valves, an indicator, and you just sit there and you have to either Flood or Pump. You're on your own, you don't know what's happening, and every little noise …Whereas if you're with somebody it helps.

The first thing you get in a submarine is 'Black smoke on the horizon.' Soon as we used to hear that we knew we would go to diving stations. When the torpedoes actually go and you hear the explosion, I felt sorry. I used to have butterflies in my stomach, but whether everybody is the same as me, I don't know. It's being human, you don't like killing people, no matter who they are.

### Captain William Ruhe, US Navy, *S-37*; from *War in the Boats*

William Ruhe was a young engineering officer, only just out of college, when he volunteered to join the US Navy's submarine service so he could see some action. In August 1942 he joined *S-37*, an ancient, broken-down boat, known to her crew as 'the rusty old sewer pipe'. However, she already had the distinction of being the first US submarine to sink a Japanese destroyer.

I'd begun having the shakes from the moment the *37* had been ordered to close Lunga Roads. An irrational and growing sense of fear had begun to invade my body, making me shiver and sweat. Reporting the sighting of the sub to the captain had taken much self control, along with a tight gripping of the bridge combing to support my rubbery legs. I couldn't let the captain detect signs of nervousness either in my voice or in my body.

For the first time in the war, I felt really scared. The captain's bland reaction to my report only heightened my anxiety. Too casually, he said, 'That's the *S-41*. I was wondering when we'd start seeing her.'

The captain swung his binoculars back to the 37's port quarter but couldn't spot the dark blob, that I could see quite clearly with my better night vision. Even the lookouts hadn't spotted the dark anomaly on the ocean's surface.

My estimate of the range to the submarine following the 37 was five to six thousand yards and no more. Still, I couldn't see her bow wake through my binoculars. I stared hard for many minutes, feeling that the friendly, or enemy, submarine must be closing the 37 at a speed a bit higher than the 37's.

If it was the S-41, a less battered boat, she would make a knot or more than the 37. So I felt that if it was the S-41 following the 37, the lookouts would soon make her out and set my fears to rest.

But if it was the Japanese sub, the one Bobby had seen a day ago, she'd be a newer boat and able to make as high as seventeen knots. Thus she should close the 37 to torpedo-shooting range in less than an hour.

The thought made me shake even more violently. So much so, in fact, that I weakly lowered myself down into the conning tower and crouched in the back of the tiny cubicle in the most shadowed part so as to be unnoticeable by the quartermaster or anyone climbing from the control room up to the bridge.

I watched the luminous minute hand on the conning tower clock moving ahead inexorably slowly, and had decided to go back up to the bridge after thirty minutes to see if the submarine trailing the 37 had moved dangerously closer.

As the minutes agonizingly passed, there were no reports from the bridge that a submarine back aft had been sighted. Was the captain feeling that I was slipping a cog by imagining that there was an actual enemy threat right behind the 37? In times of high tension, a few false reports could be expected. They were the nature of war itself. And the fellow making a false report was always a bit suspect.

I climbed back to the bridge a few minutes before thirty minutes had elapsed and looked for the dark blob on the port quarter. It was still there and didn't look much closer, except that I was now able to make out a white sliver of a bow wake in front of the dark blob. When I told the captain that 'the sub is still following us but is now a little closer', my throat was so dry that I had difficulty mumbling the words. I added, 'She looks close enough now to get off a long-range torpedo shot, Captain.'

In a barely audible murmur the captain merely acknowledged my report with a 'Thank you.' Thanks, for what?

How else could I alert the captain that we might have an enemy sub within firing position? So I told the captain of my foreboding.

He laughed tolerantly. Again he indifferently swept the seas off the 37's port quarter with his binoculars. He couldn't see the sub, but just then a lookout sang out, 'I have a submarine in sight to port, about thirty degrees off our stern.'

'Does she look like the *S-41*?' the captain casually asked.

'Perhaps,' the lookout guessed.

I wasn't relieved by the lookout's sighting. Nor were my nerves steadied by the captain's lack of concern for what we might be getting into – either from the trailing sub, the warships that were still shelling the airfield, or perhaps even from the Japanese bombers which had begun dropping loud, crashing bombs in great numbers, in the area of Henderson Field.

I couldn't stay on the bridge and let any of the men see my shivering body, so I returned to the back of the conning tower to get a grip on myself. And to think.

How had this feeling of terror overcome me? Was I feeling real fear or was I letting an overanxious imagination get the better of me? Was I physically exhausted or even a little sick? Perhaps I had the flu or some sort of tropical fever that caused me to be irrational and to sweat and shake violently.

I certainly had lots of time to think about how badly my body was reacting to the situation. I had nothing to distract my mind. It was a sure formula for building up a good case of the nerves. 'I've got to do something, not just sit here,' I thought. But I felt rooted to the spot, unable to move until the radiant hands of the clock had moved ahead another thirty minutes.

After just twenty minutes I could no longer delay going topside.

The sub was still there back on the quarter and a little closer. But it continued to be more of a dark blob than a silhouette of a sub's conning tower and shears.

'It's the *41*,' the captain reassured me, even before I observed that the sub looked to be a little bit closer.

Then at 0503 the dark blob disappeared from the ocean's surface in a mass of luminescent whitish foam. I stared even harder through my binoculars at the spot where the submarine had submerged, expecting to see the wakes of a couple of torpedoes heading for the *37* from the spot where the sub had gone down. I was convinced that the blob was not the *41*-boat. But the seas remained dark and menacing.

At about the same time, the booming of shell-fire and the crashing of bombs stopped and deep silence enveloped the *37*. The noise of the two diesels suddenly sounded deafeningly loud. Almost automatically, the captain ordered, 'Slow to one-third speed.' That was hardly the right command if a torpedo was about to be shot at the *37*.

Nothing happened in the next few minutes as the first light of dawn crept into the eastern sky. There were no returning warships, no Marine fighters overhead, no sign of an unfriendly submarine, and the Japanese bombers had left the area. The Jap warships had apparently retired on a course that took them to the north of Savo Island.

The 37 coasted ahead before turning back towards Cape Esperance and she zig-zagged radically to spoil the aim of a lurking submarine.

My heart slowed down. I stopped my infernal sweating and was suddenly conscious of having steady legs. I also recalled that the captain had made no attempt to exchange recognition signals by blinker gun with the unidentified submarine that had followed the S-37 for several hours.

As the 37 headed back toward her station south of Savo Island, I still believed that my fears were justified. Perhaps when the S-41 left station to head home, her patrol summary would tell something about her response to the Lunga Roads incident.

Even though I experienced this episode of uncontrolled fear, I was determined to remain on the 37 and see her back to the States after this patrol.

### Outside ERA's Mate Cyril Bowden, Royal Navy, HMS *Virtue*

Panic, yes, that happened once. We were out on patrol and it was very early doors … This was one of the first times we'd dived. Now this stoker petty officer – well, to me he was an old man, he'd be in his thirties probably – and as soon as we dived he tried to get out. He went for the conning tower hatch. Someone – I was in the engine room then, so I don't know if it was the captain – hit him. Of course he was discharged straightaway because that's what you were discharged for, that and if you got seasickness very bad.

Nobody can tell you that they've never been seasick, because they have. If you've been a long time at sea you get it once or twice but usually you get over it. But some people are subject to it very bad. It was the cook, he was seasick, and he'd got to feed the skipper. As well as us … He used to get seasick when he was standing on the dock. The first patrol I went on was out in the North Sea, which was way past Lerwick, Norway way, and we were on toast [reduced to living on toast], I think. That was terrible. Of course, the skipper didn't go much on this.

### Fregattenkapitän Reinhard 'Teddy' Suhren, Kriegsmarine; from *Teddy Suhren, Ace of Aces*

After a successful career as both Torpedo Officer and Commander during the war, Suhren became Führer der Unterseeboote in Norway.

One day my oldest staff officer told me that one of the Kommandants had confided to him that he felt psychologically incapable of having the courage to attack. In short he was a coward. Without making a great song and dance about it I tried in private to talk this Kommandant around. All he needed to do was to get control of himself at the first onset of nerves, and everything else would then follow of its own accord. He was very surprised, and had difficulty getting his head round what I was saying; in the course of our conversation I described how nervous I was before each attack – as I had already repeatedly told the pupils of the ULD [Submarine Training Division]. In his eyes I was a man who knew no fear. My God! I could only reassure him that in my experience there was no Kommandant, in fact no soldier at all, who hadn't had the jitters before every attack, wondering whether their number was about to come up or not. His fears therefore were absolutely normal. Before I sent this Kommandant off on a new mission I arranged a codeword with him. Should he find himself again in a dilemma and be unable to make decisions, he should transmit this code-word to me, and I would then call him straight back on some pretext or other. But the opposite happened. The Kommandant carried out an exemplary patrol, torpedoed two freighters and two destroyers and came back to Narvik bursting with pride. He was very taken aback when I told him that he had to come ashore because I needed him as chief of staff of a flotilla. He said of course – quite reasonably – that he had now got over his failings and would be very successful in the future. I wouldn't be moved. I knew from experience that this kind of Kommandant most probably wouldn't return from his next patrol. Just to prove the point to themselves and everyone else, they usually gambled the lot on a single card in a state of high elation: 'They can't get me.'

### Secondo Capo Mechanista Carlo Pracchi, Regia Marina, *Velella*

They've found us. The Asdic pings follow one after another until they get the echo …They're like whip-lashes against the hull, and when they get an instantaneous echo, they know they have hit the bullseye.

The sounds are coming from starboard, midships. Thuds in the water, three at a time, and a few seconds later you hear three rumbles followed by the inevitable shaking. Sound source from 10 o'clock and then from 7 o'clock, and louder thuds. It sounds as if every gauge in the control room is shattering. All the valves are shut down.

The glass of the depth gauge breaks. From the telephone comes the voice of someone shouting 'Engines … signal leaks or other faults.' We get the boards up to look at the water-level in the bilge tanks. I can see water running down the sides … I look up. In the meantime the bombs go off. I look up again to see where that water is coming from. I can see from the cracks that fortunately it is the varnish peeling off! Higher up I can see drips on the heads of the rivets in the frames. I touch one with my finger, and water runs down my arm. Then we get another depth charge, and the drips start to run down by themselves. That earlier charge exploded underneath and brought us up; this one went off overhead, and pushed us down. Machine room crew informs: no damage.

Forward, with a lunatic grin on his face M.N. shows me a rope with knots: he has been keeping a tally of the bombs with it. The main relays shut down. The lights have just gone. We'll have to use the emergency lighting.

I feel my leg cramp up, then the tingling starts, then shaking. Maybe I'm tired after these hours of tension. I try to snatch a bit of rest sitting down on the centre of the aft bulkhead door of the [salvage] box called by the name of the inventor: Garitta Girolami-Arata-Olivati ... The effect on my legs doen't stop; I use my arms to try to suppress it, holding my knees. It makes no difference ... I try to stop just one knee from trembling, but it carries on and only makes my arms shake. In desperation I say: 'Bloody hell I'm just panicking.' I can't get myself out of it ... I really panic.

**Konteradmiral Erich Topp, Kriegsmarine, *U-552*; from *Fackeln über dem Atlantik***

In 1940 Topp was a Kapitänleutnant about to take command of his second submarine.

On 4 December 1940 in Hamburg, *U-552* was commissioned at the Blohm and Voss Shipyard.

We were off on our first patrol – already in the North Sea – when I noticed that my Obersteuermann [CPO navigator], until then a lively, good-humoured chap, was silent and looked pale. He was on watch, so I got into conversation with him and asked him why he was so quiet. He didn't want to say anything but I pressed him hard and finally he said to me:

'Sir, it's not important. I just left something behind.'

'What was it you forgot?'

After hesitating for a while, he told me that every time he went out on a war patrol he took his wife's wedding garland which he kept under a glass dome, as is common in many middle-class families, and this time he had forgotten it. I sensed that along with that charm he had also left at home his belief in a happy and successful patrol.

I gave the order to put back, we fetched the talisman and the Obersteuermann was fully operational again, and remained so throughout the whole patrol.

## CAPTAIN IN THE CONTROL ROOM

A huge responsibility rested on the commanding officer's shoulder, not just because he was the captain and had to make the decisions, often in a split second and based on imperfect information, but because he was usually the only one who could see what was going on. Most were very young, compared with the commanders of surface ships, and to have command of a submarine in one's mid-twenties was not unusual, particularly in the latter stages of the war. Submarines were often said to be a young man's game.

### Torpedoman Billy Grieves, US Navy, USS *Thresher*

Every skipper who ever took a boat out on patrol was repeatedly faced with these life-or-death decisions …

And when the boat was being rocked by depth charges and the lives of 80 men hung in the balance, it was up to the skipper to maintain his focus and give the orders to get his boat free and home safely into port. Because on a submarine there is one man who cannot escape for an instant the onerous grasp of responsibility for the safety, and performance, and the morale of his boat. He is the Skipper. It is the most lonesome, overwhelming responsibility God ever placed on a man.

On numerous occasions during the war, after a prolonged or successful attack, as I walked through the narrow passageway past the tiny cubicle known as the Captain's Cabin, I was fiercely tempted to stop and put my head in and say, 'Good job, Skipper, thanks a lot.' But it wouldn't have been appropriate then, would it? Because the crew would have accused me of being patronizing. Or, worse yet, trying to make Chief on my first cruise. And so the years passed. And then in 1991, the submarine convention was held in San Antonio. And the first Skipper's Brunch was set into motion. On the day of the general member-ship meeting, about 300 guys assembled in a large meeting room. But the entire front row of seats was reserved. It was reserved for skippers, and there were about 45 or 50 of them there. When the meeting opened, Joe McGrievy, the coordinator, took the floor and called off each skipper's name together with his boat. When his name was called, the skipper stood and faced the audi-ence. And when all were standing, the crowd snapped to its feet as one man and I have never heard such loud, enthusiastic, prolonged applause from a group that size in my life time. As the skippers marched out to their breakfast the applause continued to the last man. And then it came to me: these were the thank yous that were never said. These were the congratulations that were never offered.

## Korvettenkapitän Reinhard Hardegen, Kriegsmarine

It was a case of first among equals. You are not the lord of the submarine, that's wrong. As commander, I was just the commander and the success of the boat represented the success of the whole crew, not of any one person. I was fortunate in having a well-built boat from a Bremen shipyard and a fine, experienced crew. So it was teamwork and as a team we enjoyed success. Of course [as commander] you have to make decisions, that's true, but right from the start I had precise orders about where I must go, as well as locating convoys. In combat I had to make my own decision. Then I couldn't get any instructions from Head-quarters because in that situation tactical decisions have to be taken at the scene, not far away on shore. Off America I sank many single ships, travelling alone, as well, of course, as various ships in convoy. And during every patrol I had my fair share of depth charges dropped by ships and aircraft, as well as gunfire – a bit of everything. Through it all I was lucky, so I came home in one piece.

Few COs, however, faced the problem which Lieutenant Karnicki, commanding the Polish submarine *Sokol*, confronted in 1941.The submarine was under Royal Navy operational control, but she had been handed over to the Poles and flew the Polish flag.

## Luitenant ter Zee 1 Peter de Jong, Koninklijke Marine, O.24

We met in Dundee to start with and then we met up again in the depot ship *Maidstone* in Gibraltar. Borys Karnicki was the captain of one of the U-Class boats that you [the British] built; I was the No.1 of *O.24* at the time, and we met up at the bar of the *Maidstone* and he said he had been in trouble. He had been busy torpedoing ships at Naples when he had got caught in an anti-submarine net and he had been working backwards and forwards but he couldn't get out and his battery was getting low. He hadn't got a cutting knife – we had sharp knives at the bow to cut through a net. He hadn't got that and he felt that he might have to surface and then they would be taken prisoner.

But then he said: 'Peter, I had a problem. We were not at war with Italy! I was sure we would be shot as pirates. So then I thought about it and called the crew together and said, "I, Borys Karnicki, captain of the *Sokol*, hereby declare war on Italy."'

And that is a funny thing. If you are a naval officer in charge of your ship, and you cannot reach your admiral or your ambassador, and you have to do something, if you announce it to the whole crew officially then it is the law. As soon as you surface, the law is gone …

'Now listen,' he said to his crew, 'if we are forced to surface and we are taken prisoner then you must insist that your captain told you you were at war and you must be treated as prisoners of war under the rules of Geneva. And I myself will talk myself out of it.'

We, the Dutch, had a legal government in London and our government had put our navy, for operations, at the disposal of the British Navy and so they operated the Navy.

## Lieutenant-Commander Alastair Mars, DSO, DSC; from *Unbroken*

Lieutenant-Commander Mars, commanding first *Unbroken* and then *Thule*, was a good example of a successful and exacting commander who inspired the confidence, respect and even the affection of his crew. Mustering the crew of *Unbroken* for the first time, he left them in no doubt of what he expected of them.

'... We have two jobs – to be successful and to survive. To achieve these I need every ounce of loyalty and strength you can give me. Remember that I am the sole arbiter of what is good for you, and my orders are to be obeyed implicitly. You may expect work, work and more work. If any of you joined submarines to get away from discipline, you are in for shocks. You will learn more discipline with me than you dreamed of – the proper sort of discipline – self-discipline ...

One final thing. What was good enough in other submarines will not be good enough here. Nothing is 'good enough' for me. I'm going to have the best, and only the best – and you're going to give it to me ...' Later, when walking through the ship, I noticed that in every mess had been pinned up copies of a newspaper advertisement for Mars Bars. It said, as I remember: 'Nothing but the best is good enough for Mars.'

## Stoker George Woodward, Royal Navy, HMS *Thule*

Mars – we used to call him Mars Bars, or Marvellous – was a good skipper. He used to get us together and say 'Even I make mistakes, so if you make a mistake, admit it and we can always put it right, and if there's something wrong tell us everything that you know.'

And when we'd sink boats, he always picked up the survivors – he wouldn't leave them in the water. It was a bit foolish in some ways, because you're leaving yourself open, but he was that kind of chap. We had more prisoners than crew one time. I think it were the second patrol in the Pacific. He even picked one chap up and he had shrapnel in his chest and one leg was shattered. He didn't leave him in the water, even like that ... The coxswain, well he wasn't a doctor but he was as good as a doctor, had the hacksaw out of the engine room and sawed the leg off, just above the knee. And it was just like being in a butcher's shop. It was ever so clean, but he actually died. I saw his little face, and I'll never forget that.

The prisoners were kept mostly in the fore end where the torpedoes were but we had to take them to the toilet because there's valves everywhere and they might sabotage the ship.The skipper used to interrogate them. He used to keep the ones he thought would be useful and then he used to capture a junk and put them on and get rid of them. We used to go to gun action, and we used to ram some [vessels]. The engineering officer used to work out if the bows were strong enough to sink them. This is the type of chap Mars was: he thought about people as well and he wouldn't go to gun action if he thought he could sink it in some other way, and that's what he did. They hadn't got many big ships left. They got small stuff, keeping to the coast and we used to have to go in to get them; there wasn't room to dive, but we had to go in close to get them because they'd got rice on board. We also got depth charged while we had prisoners aboard. Being depth charged is not very comfortable when the enemy is not many feet above you and travelling at speed. It is like standing in a station and an express train comes by. And then you get the explosion of the depth charges.

A sense of humour was no disadvantage to a commander.

**Seaman Jack Casemore, Royal Navy, HMS *Unbeaten*;**
from *Even More Submarine Memories*

Jock Bernie joined *Unbeaten* in the summer of 1941 in Malta. I think he had been on the Upright before he came to us and I believe he was a survivor of the Unity which had been rescued by one of our own convoys in the North Sea. He was short, scruffy and had hair and a beard which was grey to fair and his beard stuck out at right angles to his face; but at the Asdic set he was faultless. On being attacked he would give a running commentary on what the destroyers were doing even telling when the depth charges had hit the water intermingled with lots of funny comments that helped to ease the tension in the boat. He was also a very good caricature artist and if something out of the ordinary happened in the course of a day, that night a cartoon would go up on the notice board. For example, one day in the summer of 1941 suddenly 'Captain in the Control Room' was called. Teddy Woodward jumped from his bunk, he was in the nude but wrapped a towel around himself and started the attack. Half way into the attack the towel fell from him, but he carried on the attack naked. That evening Jock's cartoon went up on the notice board with the caricature of Teddy dancing round the periscope with the biggest genitals imaginable. We all thought that Jock had gone too far and that he would get a telling off by the skipper, but no, Teddy loved it and I believe he kept all the cartoons that Jock did.

Cramped, spartan and uncomfortable inside, submarines went out on patrol ready to torpedo, shoot or even ram enemy vessels; they operated in every theatre: from the bitter cold of the Arctic to the heat of the Indian Ocean; from the clear waters of the Mediterranean in summer to the wild storms of the grey North Atlantic. They penetrated shallow harbours and estuaries, crossed oceans, attacked shore installations, sank troopships and warships, laid mines, decimated enemy merchant shipping, supported their own convoys, blockaded ports, carried cargo, dropped off agents, provided intelligence and even transported troops. Sometimes the operation went more or less to plan; on other occasions there might be a nasty surprise in store.

On return to base, every submarine commander submitted a patrol report to the flotilla commander on return to base. In addition to basic information such as position and weather, it contained a detailed description of the submarine's offensive, defensive and intelligence-gathering activities and comments about the performance of the boat and its weapons and anything else the CO wished to bring to the attention of superior officers. This was then studied and commented upon by the flotilla commander. Some reports are purely objective; others display the personality of the CO and his literary talents.

## Captain George Fawkes, Captain (S), 8th Flotilla, based at Algiers; from ADM199/1855

Dolfyn left Algiers on 20 July [1943] for a patrol of the northern end of the Straits of Messina. On the afternoon of 26 May she daringly decided to investigate Santa Maria anchorage.

## Luitenant ter Zee, Henri van Oostrom Soede, Koninklijke Marine, *Dolfyn*; from his Patrol Report, ADM199/1855

1650. While passing Ustica, investigated Santa Maria anchorage. Present, one small tug of 200 tons, one apparently unarmed small MTB, no depth charges being visible and no torpedo starboard side. In order to make sure no torpedo was carried on the port side, I decided to close. As the MTB. was moored at a very sharp angle to the coast, I had to come very close inshore. A torpedo was seen to be carried, whereupon the plan for a gun action was abandoned. I had overestimated the distance from the coast, however, and while turning away at 1700 grounded at slow speed on the rocks. Tried to force the ship over the shallow rocks using more speed but came high to 20 feet. Blew main tanks; manned machine-gun and 3-inch gun to keep MTB. at a distance in case ship did not get clear of shallow water straight away. Kept MTB covered with machine-gun fire, doing damage and preventing crew from slipping their cable. Gun did not bear. Within 30 seconds of opening the hatch, a light machine-gun on a hill ashore, range approximately 400 yards, opened fire which was uncomfortably accurate. This was joined in about a minute by two heavy machine-guns at the other side of the bay, at rather longer range and not so accurate, only one hit being obtained on the conning tower. As the ship was by now in deep water, recalled the gun crew and dived.

1706. At periscope depth. It was reported that there were two wounded. Sub-Lieutenant Brakema, R. Neth. N., had been hit in the back while going down the hatch, while A/PO Henneveld had been shot through the thigh. The conduct of Henneveld merits high praise. He was in charge of the medicine chest and did not report his own wound till after he had taken care of Sub-Lieut. Brakema.

Ordered to proceed to Malta with her casualties, *Dolfyn* was escorted into the harbour, where she landed both men as walking wounded. The following day, Lieutenant-Commander van Oostrom Soede resumed his patrol.

**Captain George Fawkes, Captain (S), 8th Flotilla, based at Algiers;**
from ADM199/1857

The report of the 6th Mediterranean patrol carried out by the French Submarine *Casabianca* (Capitaine de Frégate L'Hermimier) is forwarded herewith together with my remarks ...

2. *Casabianca* left Algiers on 27 July, returning on 7 August, after successfully landing a large quantity of stores in Corsica, not without incident ... I would point out that the term 'run aground' as used in the report means that *Casabianca* felt her way inshore until her bow touched at the selected landing point, and should not be taken literally.

**Capitaine de Frégate Jean L'Herminier, Marine Nationale, *Casabianca*;**
from Patrol Report, ADM199/1857

On passage to landing point. The *Casabianca* having sailed from Algiers at 1900 on 27 July, 1943, after a normal passage, arrived in position, dived, at 0430 on 30 July, 10 miles from Cape Rosso and the Isle of Gargalo. After taking a fix, she steered a course towards point 'A' on Gradelle Beach. At 1452 on a bottom of 31 metres, approximately 500 metres from the beach, the ship's head to North.

I made my last periscope reconnaissance 1½ hours before resting her on the bottom, and continued by estimation and sounding, in order to avoid the risk of being sighted from shore.

PUT TO THE TEST OF A REAL ENEMY ATTACK

We lower: – two 'dories' for a preliminary reconnaissance of the beach and for towing the rubber dinghies. 14 rubber dinghies for carrying the material. At 2250, I surfaced.

The sight is hallucinating. The coast looms up before us at a distance of 500 yards. The Gulf of Porto stretches out to starboard, and the southern shore closes us in astern. Beaches A and B stand out white. We make our way at dead slow speed, to run aground between the rocks which spread out to port and starboard. In dead silence the Commando lowers the two dories and starts to inflate the first of the rubber dinghies.

At 2300, the enemy opens fire on us. Shots seem to come from all sides. Automatic arms open fire. Rounds whistle overhead, others striking near at hand.

Everyone went down below in the greatest calm. Meanwhile I put both engines fast astern. By a miracle nobody is wounded. But the two dories dragged on their painters, which unshipped. The rubber dinghies are still on the casing, so we waited until we were clear of the bay before securing them.

PASSAGE FROM THE GULF OF PORTO

While we were opening the range from shore, the enemy continued to fire. All the emplacements in the district are certainly on the alert owing to all the noise. I decided to leave that area and try my luck again at Curza Point the following night. I intend to use the same hiding places as the previous time, as they are already known by the patriots, and reconnaissance would tell whether they had been discovered by the enemy. At midnight on the 30th, we are steering a course towards Curza Bay at 16 knots.

LANDING IN THE BAY OF CURZA

After our usual approach, we were lying on the bottom one mile from the landing point at 1522 on 31 July.

Surface at 2235/31 July. The Commando prepares its landing gear while I steer course towards the westerly end of Saleccia beach in order to run aground as near to shore as possible. The experience of the night before has made us very wary. The 1st Lieutenant asked my permission to command the Commando. I acquiesce voluntarily. We run aground about 400 metres from the rocky westerly end of the beach, where we hope to hide some of the material in the same place as at the beginning of July. The Commando sets out under the command of the 1st Lieutenant. It consists of two trains, that of the 1st Lieutenant and that of the English who were sent to watch the landing by their own organisation at Algiers. The 1st Lieutenant is equipped with a short range R/T set, and after a brief reconnaissance, informed us that all is clear. So we start landing the rubber dinghies.

Owing to the loss of the dories, we lower the iron dinghy belonging to the *Casabianca*. We thought that it would be possible to employ it as a form of relay. We would anchor 100 metres from the beach, where a pulley could be made fast to haul out the dinghies. But its anchorage was not sufficient for this. It was finally employed to tow the rubber dinghies, and ⅔ of the material was landed in this manner on the first night.

The lack of a reception committee once more forced us to dispose of the material by our own means. It was not without apprehension that I sent 25 hands of my crew ashore in order to complete the operation as quickly as possible.

At 0500 on 1 August, we are lying on the bottom, waiting to finish the operation on the following night. During the day I left the English captain and a sailor ashore, so as not to lose time in reconnoitring the beach. Equipped with a '38' R/T set, he should begin calling us up at 2300, from the Eastern end of Saleccia beach. It was not possible to hide any more material in the first place.

At 2235, surfaced and then grounded at 200 metres from the beach. Contact made with the party ashore. All is well. The landing and disposing of the rest of the material is carried out by 30 men of the *Casabianca* under command of the 1st Lieutenant.

About 11 tons of material were landed and hidden at point A on the night of 31 July / 1 August. About 6 tons at point B. As these points were well known to the head of the patriots, I did not consider it necessary to land the agent, who only knew the area around the Gulf of Porto.

The submarine did not escape entirely unscathed, as L'Herminier recorded after the war in his book *Casabianca*.

### Capitaine de Frégate Jean L'Herminier, Marine Nationale; from *Casabianca*

At 0700 hours on 7 August we were zigzagging our way on the surface into the Bay of Algiers. Bellet and I were on deck, enjoying the pleasant early morning air and congratulating ourselves on having escaped from Gradella Cove without casualties. The group of men preparing the rubber boats for launching had been working just where we were standing when the fusillade had begun – on the foredeck under our gun. Suddenly Bellet examined the bridge-plates more attentively.

'Look at this hole here, sir!' he exclaimed. 'To port, halfway up the bridge.'

Looking more closely I could see the hole a bullet from an enemy machine gun had made in the plating. Here was 'tangible evidence' – as they say in the detective stories – of our encounter with the enemy.

When we got back to port, that was one repair we refused to have done. We didn't want to lose that plate. We just framed the hole with a horseshoe for luck. I imagine that the *Casabianca* was the only submarine ever to wear such a decoration.*

## THERE BUT FOR THE GRACE ...

**Seaman Jack Casemore, Royal Navy;** from *Even More Submarine Memories*

One of the most emotional things that happened to me one day in the summer of 1941, July or August, was on returning to Lazoreto Base after a rather trying patrol. We had been in harbour for about two days and had heard that *Union* was overdue and had been sunk. Some of our crew were detailed to empty the lockers of the seamen and stokers of *Union* and stow each individual's items in their kitbags so that a new boat coming from England could use their lockers.

About four of us from *Unbeaten* were given the job and on cutting the locks off started to put their belongings into their kitbags. On opening the lockers we were confronted with photographs and letters from their wives, girlfriends and mothers as well as their personal clothing and mementos that these friends of ours had in their lockers; one could not help reading some of the letters and wondered how this poor bastard had died. Would we on the *Unbeaten* very soon face the same fate and would some other submariner then be stowing – *my* personal things in *my* kitbag?

* But see pages 23 and 189.

# Operating the
# Second World War Submarine

Irrespective of navy, class, purpose and size, all submarines worked on the same scientific principles, starting with a steel-framed, steel hull, circular in cross-section in order to resist water pressure when submerged. Additional strength was provided by watertight bulkheads that divided the hull into individual compartments accessed through watertight steel doors. A much thinner outer casing protected external fitments including any external tanks: it was not required to withstand pressure, and water was able to pass freely through it. A second pressurised compartment, the conning tower, was constructed above the control room and entered from the pressure hull via a watertight steel hatch. It led up to the bridge and gave access to gun positions. Except in an emergency evacuation underwater, a submarine's forward and after hatches were usually sealed during patrols.

With the ballast tanks, both internal and external, empty, the submarine had positive buoyancy and floated on the surface. If the main vents at the top of the tanks were opened, water entered the ballast tanks through flooding holes in the external tanks and kingston valves in the internal tanks. The boat then took on negative buoyancy and could submerge or dive. To reverse the procedure, the upper valves were closed and blowers expelled the water. Rear Admiral Corwin Mendenhall recalled that on war patrols it was usual for US boats to run with the kingstons permanently open – riding the vents – to ensure swift submergence and avoid any valve malfunctions that would increase diving time.

In 1939 almost every submarine was powered on the surface by diesel engines directly connected to the propellers and underwater by electric motors, the batteries of which were recharged by the diesels when the boat was surfaced. Diesel-elecric boats, such as the new British U-Class, were coming on stream, and in these boats the propellers were at all times driven by the motors. The diesels were used to generate electricity while the boat ran surfaced and, as before, to recharge the batteries.

**Korvettenkapitän Peter Cremer, Kriegsmarine**; from *U-Boat Commander*

Cremer commanded *U-333*, a Type VIIC – generally described as the workhorse of the Kriegsmarine – which came into service from the end of 1940.

Strictly speaking, they were not pure 'under-sea-boats' but submersibles which, for shorter or longer periods, were kept 'hovering' over a watery abyss.

If this period were exceeded they were obliged to surface to gasp for air and charge the batteries. How and why, we shall see in a moment.

The U-boat has a double hull, a strong inner and a thin outer one. The inner, called the pressure hull, contains all the functional elements such as the command system in the control room, the engines, the underwater weapons, the W/T office, and space for the crew who live a boxed-in existence between all these things. The steel pressure hull is strong enough to withstand the water pressure which, for every 10 metres of depth, increases by 15 pounds per square inch, or one atmosphere. The boat is designed for a maximum diving depth, and if it exceeds this it is crushed like an egg shell. The limit of the diving depth is governed by the strength of the pressure hull. The diving depths of the different U-boat types in the Second World War ranged theoretically between 50 and 250 metres. In fact they were exceeded at times until the frame members began to crack.

The considerably thinner outer hull, which with its superstructure gives the boat its shape, mainly contains the ballast or diving tanks. For the outer hull water pressure presents no problem. When submerged, the ballast tanks are flooded and the inside pressure equals the pressure of the surrounding water. When the boat is surfaced the bottom of the ballast tank is open and air, kept in from above, prevents the water entering. The boat is floating on an air bubble. To dive, the air is allowed to escape at the top through vents. Water takes its place – the boat sinks and disappears. To surface again, one method is to blow out the tanks with compressed air. This might make the boat come up unnecessarily quickly, using up a lot of compressed air, and hence electrical energy, in the process. The other way is to proceed dynamically and steer the boat to the surface with the hydroplanes; here the diesel engines take over the work, expelling the water from the tanks with their exhaust gases. This latter, however, was not the usual way of surfacing. (The horizontal hydroplanes, fore and aft, work as in an airship, steering the boat up and down.)

So-called trimming tanks within the pressure hull, whose water content can be adjusted to bring about and compensate weight changes, hold the boat in equilibrium – hovering in the ideal neutral buoyancy state – so that it maintains its diving depth and neither tends to rise nor sink. But a U-boat is easier to keep in balance when it is moving. Control is easily lost when it is stopped and it can slowly sink to the sea-bed. At times, then, the boat is so sensitive that even a small change of weight, such as the movement of one man from bow to stern, is enough to throw it out of balance. When it is being hunted and lies still so as not to betray its presence by pumping or flooding, with consequent noises, it must be properly trimmed or 'balanced'. Its weight changes continually, through the consumption of fuel oil and fresh water alone, and at times the change is quite sudden (as after the firing of torpedoes), when it becomes lighter by a matter of tons and must be quickly stabilised so as not to surge upward and betray itself, particularly as on such occasions it is only at periscope depth. The preservation of the trim, the balancing out of the stability, calls for a whole system of pumps, circuits, valves, hand-wheels and more – and practice in their use.

The U-boat is propelled in two ways. Above water by diesel engines, below water by electric motors. On the surface the diesels charge the batteries. When submerged, the diesels cannot be used because they consume fresh air. The electric motors derive their energy from the batteries which are heavy and bulky, limited in size only by the narrowness of the boat. Under heavy loads their energy is soon exhausted and the boat is obliged to surface to recharge them. The same holds for the fresh air, which diminishes underwater and must be replenished. Those, in broad outline, are the strengths and weaknesses of the serviceable diving-boat types with which we had to deal in the Second World War.

The submerged U-boat is connected with the upper world by a periscope, a telescope 14 metres long that can be raised and lowered. There is an attack periscope with an all-round view, its disadvantages being a dead angle immediately above the boat, but in addition there is a periscope for aerial targets which covers this sector. For a close observer above water its comparatively large head makes it more easily recognised. In naval German we called the periscope Spargel (asparagus). Periscope depth, that is the diving depth at which a periscope could be extended above the surface, was between 12 and 14 metres. The upper edge of the conning tower, the highest point of the boat, was then about 6 metres below water.

## ENGINES AND ELECTRICS

When the submarine dived, the diesel engines had to be shut off quickly.

**Stoker, later Outside ERA's Mate, Cyril Bowden, Royal Navy, HMS *Virtue***

Those engines did thousands and thousands of miles. We had the occasional breakdown which we could repair, but as long as one engine was alright you could still charge the batteries, but if both engines went, you'd had it. There was very little that went wrong with a diesel engine. These were Paxman 6RXS. I always remember the name, I had it right in front of me more often than not. Sometimes we had to scrape the white metal because if the white metal went in the bottom of the camshaft, I believe it was, it used to melt and you had to make it smooth. It were a terrible job.

When you were on watch your eyes never left that square red light just up the end of the engines; you always kept your eye flicking on that, and on all the dials at the back of the engine measuring the oil pressure, because that had to kept at a certain level. You never let that go down.

Red light meant you were on the way down, diving, and you'd got to get the engines off immediately. You flicked a lever and you jumped straight for the muffler valve and spun that shut because that was what controlled the seawater what was keeping it cool. Now you were dived, now your work started. Just imagine the heat that that generated. All the dials on the back of the engines going up and up. You could pump distilled water around the engines. You carried distilled water in a tank. The temperature could be 120, 130 degrees, and you were working away, taking it in shifts. Someone would come along and give you a spell off. Because it was very hot. But that was the only way to cool them down, and if you didn't cool them down you'd ruin them. Normally the seawater would be going all round their jackets keeping them cool.

As a stoker, I stood my watch in the engine room and did anything that needed doing, like making square sennets for the pistons – you take 8 strands of string and some grease, you weave them and make it come out square, and you put that in the cylinder. It acts like a washer to stop the oil coming out.

### Electrician 1st Class Bob Haughney, US Navy, USS *Threadfin*

USS *Threadfin* was one of the US Navy's new *Balao*-Class fleet submarines which entered service in the latter part of the war. Constructed from high tensile steel, instead of mild steel, and with thicker pressure hull plating they could dive to 400 feet, an increase of 100 feet over the *Gato*-Class. While the older boats were popularly known as thin-skinners, the *Balao*-Class were called thick-skinners, and the change in technology was a closely guarded secret. They incorporated other advances with which the crews had to get to grips.

In 1944 I received orders to report to the *Threadfin* but I never set a foot on the boat. Instead I received orders to report to the Westinghouse Plant in E Liberty PA, where they were building the controls for the main panels for the *Threadfin*. After I finished there I was sent to Ridgeway, PA to the Elliott Co. plant where they made the motors and generators for the *Threadfin*. The motors were a new design that did away with reduction gears. On reporting back to Portsmouth, NH, I was sent to New London to learn about the electric torpedoes, which were new. The *Threadfin* was ready to sail and I had not met most of the crew, and was considered the new man on the boat. So far I knew only a few of the crew and wondered if all the schooling was worth the while – but I was wrong.

On one patrol we were under heavy depth charging and the main floating panel moved too much and punctured a water line, and at 600 feet water came in under quite a pressure. We could not afford to loose the main control panels, so when we were able to stop the water flow someone had to enter them and check them out, and that was me.

On another patrol while being depth charged smoke began to come out of the left panel, so I ordered it to be pulled clear, which meant we now ran on only one screw, so I could enter and check the damage. I realized later that I never did ask permission to pull the left panel clear, but no one questioned me why I did. I was able to make the repairs after the depth charging stopped.

Another time they woke me up and told me that the electric torpedo was running in its tube and the Captain wanted it checked. I asked the torpedo men to pull it and disconnect the head so it would not explode while I worked on it. I found that the wiring was badly burnt, so we were not to use it until we returned to base.

The only time that I went topside in daylight was when the Captain wanted to know what we could do if we spotted a torpedo coming towards us. He said that immediate speed was important and putting extra engines on line was not quick enough. As we had control over the number of engines and batteries for power we had to answer what they wanted quickly. One dark night we surfaced among the Jap fleet that was heading towards our fleet. The Captain wanted flank speed plus 10 percent, which we gave him.

## TRIMMING AND WATCHKEEPING

A submerging submarine did not just sink: already in motion, it was driven down, using horizontal rudders – hydroplanes. In emergency, the boat would execute a 'quick dive' (official US Navy term), 'immersione rapida' (Regia Marina), 'crash dive' (Royal Navy), 'plongée de catastrophe' (Marine Nationale) or 'Alarmtauchen' (Kriegsmarine). The skill was in diving to the required depth and then catching the trim – essentially levelling out by pumping water between the compensating tanks to balance the submarine.

### Luitenant ter Zee 1 Peter de Jong, Koninklijke Marine, commanding O.24

At the end I could run full speed ahead on both diesel engines and if there was an air alarm you could be at 20 feet in 40 seconds. If you made [the boat] 10 tons too heavy forward and 10 tons too heavy in the middle, then you went down very quickly. You could catch your trim at 30 metres. That was pretty good.

## Stoker George Woodward, Royal Navy

It [also] entailed going round with the oil can because the rockers in the engine weren't fed, we had to do it with an oil can at the top and we had to take barometer readings every hour, take temperature recordings to make sure everything was running alright. Then we had a separator, because as you're running on the surface in a submarine, you're using the diesel, so you have to let water in to compensate for the diesel you're using. It goes into the diesel tank, actually, and shoves the diesel out, and the diesel comes to the engine room and it has to be separated in case there's water in it. You have different duties. You have a diving station; that's the place you've got to go when the klaxon goes, and then you have a patrol routine when you're on the surface. So, you're not only dealing with engines, you've got different jobs besides.

We had a pump in the engine room and when we dived we had to look after that. Inside, you've got compensating tanks and they're all lettered from 'A' right through the alphabet. And they're all connected to a main line. In the front end, there's a pump there, a six-valve, and in the engine room there's a pump there, and all them tanks are connected to that line. And if they wanted to pump something to a particular tank they'd say 'open A inboard vent' and they'd ring me to pump up forward, whatever, into that tank. If you dive in an estuary you've got fresh water in your tanks. When you go out to sea the water's heavier, so you've got to have compensating tanks. So's you can compensate the weight. But they do say, in theory, if you're on the ocean bed, if the submarine's at perfect trim, you should be able to lift it. I don't know if it's true.

I had to take her out on the first dive. The first time they've got no furniture – bunks and things like that – what there is, is 56lb weights and what you have to do is keep moving these weights around to get the trim. They knew the weight of the furniture.

## Commander Edward Young, DSO, DSC, RNV(S)R, Royal Navy; from *One of Our Submarines*

In 1940, Lieutenant Edward Young, RNVR, was appointed to his first submarine, the small and venerable *H.28*, based at Harwich and commanded by Lieutenant M. R. G. Wingfield. Within a day of leaving to patrol in the North Sea, he embarked on his first periscope watch.

'Up periscope,' I said, trying to make it sound like an order I had been giving for a long time. First, following the standard periscope drill, I had a quick look all round in low power. Satisfied that no ships or aircraft were close to us, I followed this by a slow, careful search in high power of one quarter of the horizon. As I turned the periscope, my panoramic eye, seemingly pivoted a few inches above the gently heaving water, sometimes obscured as a wave lapped over the top lens, moved slowly across the empty edge of the grey horizon, looking for the masthead or the breath of smoke that might announce the approach of a target. Then another all-round sweep in low power to make sure that nothing had crept up behind me. Then 'down periscope'. Then again 'up periscope', a quick all-round sweep, and a thorough examination of the next ninety degrees of horizon. Training carefully along the misty coastline, I could not help thinking it was rather amusing, almost impudent, that we two-score [40] Englishmen should be living, sleeping and eating here, so close, and so invisible, to the enemy.

At least we hoped we were invisible. All the time, when you were keeping periscope watch, you had to take care that you were not showing more than a few inches of periscope. If the planesmen did not keep to the exact periscope depth of thirty feet, whether from lack of skill or attention, or because the boat was not properly trimmed, you might find the periscope sticking up several feet out of the water, with the danger of being sighted through some shore-watcher's telescope. You could correct this by having the periscope lowered a little and bending down to keep your eyes still on the eyepiece, but the constant arching and straightening of the back was tiring. Much better see to your trim …

### Luitenant ter Zee 1 Aart Hopman, Koninklijke Marine

As a sub-lieutenant in 1941 on the somewhat older Dutch submarine *K. XV* commissioned in 1933, Aart Hopman offers a useful overview of how the crew was employed and of some of the features of his boat which were common to most submarines. Crew sizes, of course, varied between types of boat: the huge French *Surcouf* carried a complement of 118; the US Fleet Submarine of the *Tambor*-Class, 60; the German Type VII U-boat, 44; the British U-Class, 33. Not all had the same equipment. Net-cutters, for example, were not universally fitted, and the number, location and arrangement of torpedo tubes also differed significantly.

There were generally about 38 crew members:

The captain had in a small cabin on the aft-battery, closed by a curtain. Also on the aft-battery were the three watch officers and the engineer officer and sometimes some army passengers.

There were about eight persons who had day duties and were always available: The CO, the engineer officer and his chiefs for the diesel and electric battery system, the boatswain and the torpedo chief, plus the cook and the steward.

Then we had three watch-officers, to man the three deck watches, in my case all from the Merchant Navy: the exec, the navigator and the subbie.

On every watch there was one electrician in the control room, and three diesel men in the engine room. Five deck personnel were available in the control room: signalman, torpedoman and three seamen. The seamen acted as helmsman, and another two, while underwater, operated the hydroplanes. On the surface they acted as lookouts on the periscope wave breaker.

Several seamen were specialised in gunnery, signals and later sonar/radar.

In the early days of the war the boat had a listening device, hydrophones, built in on starboard and port bow. They were passive and very useful to hear ships in the distance, but identification was some guesswork.

So, travelling to or from the patrol area there was the watch officer and two lookouts on the bridge, six men in control and another three in the Engine room. The others were busy with daily routine or at the right time slept. My captain insisted on proper sleep, for in his opinion, 'There was nothing so dangerous as a sleepy man on duty'.

Of course we had no radar or sonar in those days and relied mainly on good eyesight and quick reaction. Later sonar and radar were installed.

The boat had a net-cutting saw with jumping wire running aft, from the bow (to allow the submarine to pass under obstacles such as nets without its super-structure getting caught or tangled up), an 88mm gun and two 40mm machine-guns which were later taken away and replaced by a single 20 mm Oerlikon gun.

We had four 21-inch torpedo tubes in the forward torpedo compartment and two in the aft torpedo compartment.

Above the forward battery room, and outside the pressure-hull, was the compartment for circa 12 chiefs and POs and a twin-torpedo deck tube set which could be trained. Later the latter was dumped as too dangerous, and as an unnecessary hole in the hull. Above the control room was the conning tower and the periscopes were used from that lofty position.

Inside the pressure hull, we had the all-important trim tanks – fore, middle and aft – and the pipe lines. Also some fuel tanks and a drinking water tank: 11 tons for circa 30 days for our crew of 38 men. We managed! On long journeys fuel could be stored in the main tanks.

We had two 8 cyl. 4-stroke Diesel MAN engines, two propellers and two batteries of 112 cells ...

We had pressure bulkheads with oval doors and grip-handles to close these doors. Very slow and cumbersome. We were at the most rather old fashioned even in those days.

About 12 men slept on the forward battery and another 20 in the forward torpedo compartment. Army passengers were distributed according to rank and room. Some room was always found for their equipment. There were two toilets to starboard in the engine room (one for officers and one for the crew – there was a difference in those days). Later on a tank was built underneath the toilets, because, while the boat was under attack, these toilets could not be used and a submarine might be, and often was, hunted for up to 24 hours.

During the whole of my submarine time we never wore a life-jacket. Obviously or somehow, we were expendable.

Until the arrival of radar, the eyes of the submerged submarine – assuming that it had not gone deep – were its periscopes.

The *K. XV* series boats had three periscopes (no radar and no Asdic).

A day periscope, a night periscope to catch all available light and an attack periscope, very small and thin, hoping that it was difficult to detect.

From the moment of alert and alarm stations, the captain observed the approach of the suspected enemy ship, identified and considered the angle of sight, possibly spoiled by camouflage, and he estimated the speed of approach, possibly spoiled by zigzagging. He considered how many torpedoes: one, two or a spread of three. Some thrift had to be used according to our high command ashore: if possible one torpedo per enemy ship. Such an order seems to have existed, or it might have been some form of joke!

The attack happened underwater, coordinated from the conning tower above the control room by the captain and his assistants, for instance the subbie or signalman or both, who read the angle of the periscope to the course of the submarine, and the captain controlled the periscope. The subbie also helped to deduce the speed of advance and other information from the captain's sightings about the target. Some gadgets were designed during those days to help the sharp and agile minds of these early submariners.

Orders were given in the silence of the boat from conning tower to control room, clearly heard and as normal always repeated (to make sure) and some orders went from control room if necessary onwards to the torpedo compartments (that connection was also quite primitive).

## ACTION STATIONS

**Torpedo Gunner's Mate J. C. Brighton, Royal Navy;**
from the Papers of J. C. Brighton, Imperial War Museum

A torpedo was really a miniature submarine with a two hundred and fifty horsepower motor and a speed of forty to fifty knots. It had two propellers on a single tail shaft, each revolving in an opposite direction. The length of a torpedo was, as near as I can remember, around twenty-four feet. Submarine torpedoes were all twenty one inches in diameter and weighed about one and a half tons.

The body of the torpedo was divided into sections. The forward section was the warhead, containing about seven hundred and fifty pounds of explosive. Also, in a watertight pocket in the head, was a device called a 'pistol' which carried the detonator and primer. This device set off the main explosive when the torpedo struck the target, or was triggered magnetically when it came under the influence of a steel-built vessel. The head was bolted to the air vessel. This was the main part of the body and was made from specially toughened steel. It was charged with compressed air to a pressure of up to three thousand pounds per square inch. Next, aft of the air vessel, was the balance chamber. This was a watertight compartment containing, among other things, the depth-keeping mechanism. Briefly, the depth-keeping unit consisted of a pendulum which was designed to keep the torpedo running level. To keep the torpedo at its set depth there was a hydrostatic valve. The depth at which the torpedo was to run was set on this hydrostatic valve, depending on the draught of the target, and could be set or altered from outside the torpedo tube. In simple terms, the action of the depth-keeping mechanism was as follows: the pendulum swung forward if the torpedo tried to nose-dive and swung aft if it tried to surface. The movement of the pendulum weight was transmitted to an air-operated motor, called a servomotor, in the tail of the torpedo. This servomotor was connected to the two horizontal rudders on the tail fins and brought the torpedo level. The hydrostatic valve came into operation if the torpedo rose above, or sank below, the set running depth and, by linkage with the pendulum weight, sent a signal to the servomotor for correction on the horizontal rudders. The depth-keeping mechanism usually worked efficiently, as depth and roll recorders were fitted to practice torpedoes to monitor their performance.

The steering of the torpedo was handled by means of vertical rudders. These were operated by an air-operated steering motor which was controlled by a relay valve mounted on a gyroscope in the buoyancy chamber. In other words, the torpedo had to remain on a steady course in relation to the spinning gyroscope. If it deviated from its course, the relay valve would operate and give steering corrections, via the steering motor, to the vertical rudders.

The fuel used in torpedoes was shale oil and the fuel tank held four gallons. A variety of oil types was used as lubricant for the engine and various valves which controlled the accurate running of the system. The engine was a four cylinder (radial) type and the air/fuel mixture entered the induction ring via the generator.

The torpedo is fitted with side lugs which rest on runners inside the torpedo tube to prevent the torpedo from turning. On the top of the torpedo was a steel block, called a 'top block'. When the torpedo was loaded into the tube, the top block butted against an air-operated stop which was known as the 'top stop'. A spring-operated stop also entered the tube at the rear of the top block and the torpedo was prevented from moving in any direction until the firing gear was operated. Great care was essential when loading the torpedoes. Settings had to be checked and the propeller had to be lined up to ensure that the engine pistons were in the correct position for starting. The main body of the torpedo had to be a fairly tight [fit], as any small object could jam the torpedo in the tube. In wartime, this would be disastrous and was a TGM's nightmare. I wonder how many submarines have been lost by this happening? It was called a 'hot run' and happened, not infrequently, in peacetime. However, with practice torpedoes and no enemy to worry about, it was usually not too serious: it was mainly a case of gases from the torpedo engine leaking into the tube and flaking out the tube crews. This could be cleared by surfacing the boat and, hopefully, removing the torpedo by firing another air impulse. Torpedoes fired for practice were fitted with collision heads or blowing heads which gave the torpedoes positive buoyancy at the end of a run so they floated on the surface for easy recovery. In wartime, the warheads gave the torpedoes negative buoyancy and, when the set range had been run off mechanically, air was automatically shut off and the torpedo sank.

When a torpedo left the tube, the sequence was as follows: The torpedo was fired from the tube by air impulse. When the 'tube firing lever' was operated, the 'air-operated top stop' was immediately lifted, allowing the air impulse to launch the torpedo forward. On top of the torpedo was a projection called an 'air lever'. This was knocked aft by another projection inside the tube. The action operated valves in the torpedo, admitting air (at a pressure of three hundred pounds per square inch) to the torpedo engine, the gyroscope and the fuel and oil bottles. Initially, then, the torpedo was started with a cold air/fuel mixture. On the generator there was a device known as the 'ignition delay gear'. This was a kind of breech-block which held three cartridge-like igniters, fired by three hammers. Before the torpedo was loaded into the tube, these hammers were cocked and prevented from falling by a setting on the gearing which connected mechanically with the engine. (As I remember it, the setting was ten revolutions.) The igniters would be fired as the engine revolved, the fuel/air gas ignited in the generator and passed on to the ignition ring of the engine. The thought of a torpedo, with engine running, jammed inside a tube, while in contact with the enemy, is too horrible to contemplate. It could, and probably did, happen. There would be no survivors to tell the tale. In my experience, in peacetime, it happened on at least two occasions with practice torpedoes. This could have been caused by faulty firing gear, by insufficient air impulse or by some small object jamming the torpedo in the tube.

The torpedoes were always known as 'fish'. The firing gear was a collection of devices designed to launch the torpedo from the tube by air pressure, but the air impulse could not be allowed to follow the torpedo from the tube, as this would cause large bubbles on the surface which could easily have been seen by the enemy. To avoid this, an automatic inboard venting system had been arranged. This came into operation as soon as the torpedo had been given its initial launch forward by the air impulse. An air-operated valve operated automatically, allowing the air impulse to be diverted to an open tank, called the 'AIV tank', under the tubes. In addition to the air, a quantity of water had to be taken into the boat to make up for the weight of the torpedoes which had been fired. Induction of the correct amount is achieved by very careful calibration of the time the AIV cock remains open, and is done automatically.

Perched on the seat at the top and rear end of the tubes was my position at the firing panel with the firing levers (six on *Porpoise*). The three fore-endsmen in the tube space attended to the alteration of torpedo settings and carried out any emergency instructions. During an attack the crew would be at their stations throughout the boat and, no doubt, offering up a silent prayer that it would be a successful attack and that any counterattack would be unsuccessful. In the fore-ends the tubes would be ready for firing, and the safety pins removed from the firing levers. The captain, in the Control Room, would decide the time interval between the firing of each torpedo, and this would be passed by 'phone to an officer in the fore-ends. He passed the order to the TI and then timed the intervals by stop watch. At the order 'Fire!', the firing lever for that particular tube would be pulled back, held back for two or three seconds, then replaced. The officer would then call out the timing for the rest of the salvo. Up on my perch I would be offering my brand of prayer that the tube apparatus and torpedoes would perform well. As I pulled the firing lever I would hear the lifting of the top stop, the hiss of the small firing valve, the opening of the large firing valve, the hiss of the impulse cut-off valve, the opening and closing of the water non-return valve, the closing of the large firing valve and the automatic inboard valve opening to allow the air impulse to vent back into the AIV, bringing with it enough water to compensate for the lost weight of the torpedo, then shutting off. The sequence was repeated when each tube was fired. It was quite noisy in the fore-ends, with air and water sounds, but in the remainder of the boat there was a bit of a shudder when each tube fired and a build-up of air pressure. Inwardly, I would offer a prayer of thanksgiving that the torpedoes were safely away. Everyone would be waiting for the sound of a fish striking the target. The length of the wait depended on the range involved. It could be several minutes. The sound made by a torpedo striking would also depend on the distance, and the target could be a few miles away.

Almost all submarines had one or more deck guns, which could be used in surface assaults on small targets, thus saving valuable torpedoes for stealthy attacks on larger or heavily armed vessels.

**Lieutenant Corwin Mendenhall, later Rear Admiral, US Navy;**
from *Submarine Diary, the Silent Stalking of Japan*

USS *Sculpin* left Pearl Harbor on her seventh patrol on 24 May 1943, bound via Midway for Honshu Island, north of Tokyo. On 9 June she damaged the Japanese light carrier *Hiyo*. Three days later they had their first sight of Japan. After a few uneventful days they had moved 50 miles east and away from the coast.

19 June. At 0128 radar reported a contact to the southwest at 8,000 yards. During thirty minutes of tracking *Sculpin* closed to a range of 6,700 yards. From the bridge we could see that the contact was quite small. (In that latitude, at that time of year, there was never complete darkness during the night.) The radar operators were learning the technique of estimating a target's size from the pip characteristic on the radar screen. After an additional thirty minutes of tracking *Sculpin* submerged to continue closing. At 0314, with a range of 1,000 yards, the captain decided to use guns against the fishing-patrol boat.

Gun crews were called to stations, and at 0325 *Sculpin* surfaced to begin the attack. The 3-inch gun commenced firing at a range of 500 yards. Continuing to close, the 20-mm gun opened fire, then at 50 yards the .50-caliber machine guns. In thirty minutes the target was on fire and sinking, and *Sculpin* broke off the action and retired to the east at best speed. We submerged at daybreak for daylight patrol along the Kiska traffic lane.

Another fishing-patrol boat came into sight to the southwest in mid-afternoon. This one was similar to the boat sunk earlier in the day and had an impressive array of unusual radio antennae. After watching the boat for almost an hour, the captain decided to hit this one with guns just as we had done earlier in the day. So with a fog bank for concealment, *Sculpin* surfaced, closed to 400 yards on radar information, and commenced firing the 3-inch gun as we pulled out of a fog bank.

After forty minutes of 3-inch and 20-mm pounding, the target was awash and on fire. The name on the stern of the boat was Miyashiyo Maru. We ceased fire and the captain moved *Sculpin* closer until her bow almost touched the target. A boarding party led by George Brown, with Joe Defrees and three crewmen, looking like pirates with knives tucked in their belts and .45 caliber pistols in their hands, waited on *Sculpin's* bow, ready to board the Jap and take the guns mounted on the bow, stern, and on top of the wheelhouse.

A long swell was running, making it difficult to step directly across the space to the deck of the wallowing Japanese boat. Each man timed his jump over the gap that opened and closed with the swells. Joe Defrees was the last to jump, and, being a short individual and overanxious to get on board the Jap, he mistimed his jump, making a grand splash as he hit the water.

There were some Japs in the water, too, clutching pieces of timber, some hiding behind the hull of their boat. Our men on the bow were shooting at them. I went forward to stop them from taking any more potshots at the Japs.

Our other concern was that Joe might be crushed between *Sculpin* and the other boat. But Joe was more concerned that someone might shoot him, and yelling, 'Don't shoot me! Don't shoot me!', he made record time swimming to *Sculpin's* stern, to be hoisted aboard by helping shipmates. He was still clutching his .45 automatic, with his Bowie knife in his belt, as he ran, thoroughly soaked, back to the bow, intent on getting aboard the Japanese boat. By that time the boarding party had returned, so Joe missed being able to brag about boarding a Jap ship.

The boarding party brought back one wooden dummy gun from the bow, two rifles that they found near the wheelhouse, and a piece of radio equipment from the radio room. The fire raging in the interior of the boat made it impossible to get to the real machine gun on top of the wheel-house.

With the boarding party safely aboard, *Sculpin* pulled clear to patrol the Kiska traffic lane.

## JACKS OF ALL TRADES

Operating a submarine required the crew to be competent in a variety of essential tasks.

### Outside ERA's Mate Cyril Bowden, Royal Navy, HMS *Virtue*

When I went to be Outside ERA's Mate, I used to do gun action and that was no joke. You got absolutely drowned. They used to keep the boat under pressure, and then all of a sudden they used to let it go and it would bob up and the hatch would open and all the water would come in. Of course, you were standing there; you'd got to take it. You wanted every second to get onto the gun. On the V-Boat, and the U you only had ropes. You had to get over, swing down and on to the gun that way. I had to be one of the first out because at the front of the submarine there were what they called ready-use lockers, two of them, either side of the gun. Inside there would be shells, ready – I had to kick the lockers open, get the shells out and pass them to the cook. The whole thing had changed in the submarine service: all the gunnery ratings had gone. So you had one gun layer and a trainer, that was the only seamen ratings you got. Then you'd got a radar wallah on the sights, the cook on the gun and me passing the shells to him, and that was the way it had to be because there was nobody else to do it.

Greasing was very important. Every moveable part that you could get at inside had to be done at least once a day. When you got in harbour that's when your work really started because then you had to go and do all the outside greasing, the hydroplanes, the lot, every moving part, with non-floatus grease. That was grease that wouldn't float, so it wouldn't come off. It was rather a mucky job, but it had to be done.

I had to work the periscopes as well for the skipper. So you do get a rapport between yourself and the Old Man because you knew how he was going to act, more or less. He would never speak as we are speaking now. He'd say: 'Up'. That was all, right down your ears, and when he wanted you to slow down he would say 'whoa', and you got to know that. I must have been doing something right because your papers were done every year ending: *satisfactory, very good* … and I got on mine *very good, superior* which was the highest accolade that I could have got. But at the same time, if I'd have been in the surface fleet, skimmers as we called them, I would have sat for my Leading Stokers. But you had to pass a test, and I was never ashore that long.

Taking it by and large, I enjoyed my stint in submarines. I had more good times than bad times.

Carrying sufficient fuel for long patrols was made possible in several ways, not all them ideal. The simplest was to put fuel in some of the water tanks, which left the crew short of water. The Germans developed the Milchkühe – the 'milk-cows' – supply submarines which could refuel and resupply submarines in the South Atlantic; a number of Italian boats performed a similar function for their compatriots – commanders were forbidden to attack enemy shipping until the refuelling mission was completed. The US Navy's solution created a new and dangerous job – the Fuel King.

## MOMM 2nd Class Earl A. Beegle, US Navy, who served as Fuel King on the USS *Tilefish*

The newer submarines which patrolled the Pacific Ocean during the Second World War were equipped with reserve fuel oil tanks called 'Fuel Ballast Tanks'.

The FBTs were saddle tanks welded to the exterior of the pressure hull. Before each patrol the three FBTs were converted from the normal function as regular ballast tanks to the mission of carrying thousands of gallons of diesel fuel. This was to supplement the regular fuel tanks. The tanks provided fuel for the five diesel engines on the submarine.

Usually a first class or a second class petty officer from the Motor Machinist (engineer) division was selected to be 'The Fuel King'. The king was responsible for fuelling the sub in port; he kept track of the amount of diesel and lubricating oil used each day. He had many other assigned duties which included keeping the Engineer Officer informed daily regarding the status of fuel used the previous day and fuel and lubricating oil available for future use ...

The submarine routinely, when travelling to and after reaching the assigned operating area, pumped fuel out of the fuel ballast tanks first. When the two saddle tanks, which made up an FBT, were emptied, the tanks had to be converted back to the primary mission of normal ballast tank use.

Converting the tanks was a dangerous operation. It was dangerous because the task almost always took place after dark. It was also dangerous because the sub many times was patrolling very near the Japanese main islands. So near that often the lights of automotive vehicles, as well as cities and villages, could be clearly seen a short distance away. The danger of being detected by enemy aircraft or shore battery installations as the sub ran on the surface was always anticipated. To help to keep detection low the submarine would ballast down to where very little of the outline of the sub could be seen.

The Fuel King and an assistant were required to go outside the sub and proceed to the area in the superstructure where the FBT huge vents to be [re-] converted were located. It was, as previously mentioned, dark and the team carried flashlights with red covers over the lenses to prevent the light from shining toward the enemy shore. In addition, the team carried a large bucket and large heavy-duty wrenches to be used in the tank conversions. It was necessary to go down into the superstructure to where the tank vent system was located. Because the sub was running partially submerged the two men would often be soaked by the cold sea water sloshing around in the superstructure.

The tank vents were disconnected from the hydraulic operating system to prevent the tanks when carrying fuel from leaking which would betray the location of the submerged sub. The disconnection took place prior to the patrol. In addition to the vent linkage, a thick steel spacer was inserted in the vent line and bolted into the correct position to insure no fuel leakage during depth charge or bombing by the enemy. The spacer was bolted in place using multiple heavy stainless steel nuts. During the conversion at sea the huge nuts were taken off each stud and carefully placed in the large bucket to prevent loss in the some-times rough seas. The heavy steel spacer was removed and secured to prevent its loss. The vent linkage was reinstalled and the heavy nuts previously removed were firmly locked down over the vent cover to enable the vent to open and close in a normal ballast tank operation. The same procedure was performed for the opposite saddle tank. During fuel removal for the diesel engines the saddle tanks would be configured to draw fuel equally from each tank to prevent a 'list' from occurring. After the FBT was converted back to seawater the submarine submerged much faster because seawater is heavier than fuel oil.

Conversion of FBTs took place three times during a normal war patrol. The procedure took approximately 30–40 minutes for a pair of tanks. Each Fuel King Team was aware that if the enemy threatened an attack on the submarine, forcing the boat to 'crash dive', to prevent loss of the sub plus 75–80 men inside, the crew could not hesitate submerging in order for the team to struggle out of the superstructure and attempt to get back inside the boat prior to the dive. It would mean a real cold attempt to swim to shore and none of us ever wanted to be shark bait.

I never heard of a team being left behind on the surface. I never heard of a team receiving medals for bravery or any letters of commendation being placed in the team's service records for successful completion of their dangerous tasks. After all – we were members of a unique group of men which made up 'THE SILENT SERVICE'.

## SPECIAL OPERATIONS

Submarines for specialised operations were either adapted, as in the case of transporting *siluri a lenta corsa* (the Italian human torpedoes otherwise known as chariots) or purpose-built, such as minelayers and midget submarines.

### Sub-Lieutenant Ruari McLean, DSC, British Liaison Officer, FNFL *Rubis*; from *Half Seas Under*

Much vital work was carried out by mine-laying submarines operating both defensively to guard the approaches into friendly harbours and offensively in laying minefields in areas frequented by the enemy. Serving first as a French and then a Free French submarine, the *Rubis* held the Allied record: 683 mines in 28 operations.

We had to lay our mines in three groups of ten, ten and twelve, in positions a mile apart, in the shipping lane about two miles offshore. Our orders permitted us to lay them submerged or on the surface at night, or dived by day, and the Captain had decided to lay them submerged by day. After that, we were permitted about two days 'tourisme' (as the Captain said), in which to look for torpedo targets, before returning to Dundee.

Having dived at 0300 we went to action stations at 0745. At 0800 we began to lay the first group of mines. The Captain and Brunet were in the kiosk, the Captain at the periscope and Brunet plotting on the chart the exact position and time of each lay. The Captain shouted 'Mouillez un!', a button was pressed in the control room; a slither and a 'ting' like a ticket-collector's punch, outside the pressure hull, indicated that the mine had gone; 'Première mine mouillée' was shouted up the control room. 'Mouillez deux', 'Deuxième mine mouillée' 'Mouillez trois!' And so on. Casey, Green and I were sitting in the wardroom, out of everyone's way. The submarine was moving slowly forward at about two knots. Each mine, on being released was supposed to go to the bottom, where, after six minutes or so, a soluble plug would dissolve and then the mine itself would rise on a cable to a preset depth, and become live, to be detonated by the breaking of one of its horns.

The first 'paquet' of ten mines was successfully laid. The Captain said the weather was perfect, and while we proceeded along the coast to our next position, hands went to breakfast.

**Prince Junio Valerio Borghese, Regia Marina**; from *Sea Devils*

... two submarines, the *Gondar* and the *Scire*, were being thoroughly transformed into 'assault craft transports'. With this object three steel cylinders had been placed on deck (two aft and one forward), having the same pressure resistance as the submarines themselves, and designed for carrying the two-man torpedoes; the gun was removed, since there was now no room for it; further modifications were introduced in connection with the ventilation of the batteries of the two-man torpedoes and the flooding and exhaust systems of the cylinders themselves. I had other improvements, which my experience suggested, carried out on the conning tower, which became smaller and more slender, so as to render the unit less conspicuous when surfaced; with the same object, after prolonged comparative tests to discover which colour was least visible at night, I decided upon a pale, greenish tint, which proved to be the most suitable for camouflaging the submarine by blending its appearance with that of the night sky.

**Lieutenant-Commander Max Shean, DSO, Royal Navy**; from *Corvette and Submarine*, describing the X-Class of midget submarines

There was an air compressor driven from the motor. One attack periscope, ten feet long, was mounted in a dome amidships. The periscope was to be raised only when necessary, and would be visible only at short range, the top being little thicker than a finger. Here, the watchkeeper could stand with six feet headroom. Elsewhere there was four and a half feet. A second, short periscope was also mounted in the dome. This could be used to watch the diver and for navigation only when at the surface, though not necessarily in full buoyancy. A Browne's gyro compass, one magnetic compass, and a Chernikeef log to measure speed and distance travelled, completed the navigation facilities.

Initially there was a hydrophone fitted on the short periscope. This did not function well, and was removed. External sounds, if they were loud, could be heard from within, without special equipment. Weak sounds could often be heard by holding a wooden hammer shaft with one end against the pressure hull, and one ear against the other. However reliable this method was, it gave no sense of direction. Nevertheless, it was very useful, and required a certain skill, as possessed by some ERAs.

There was enough flat space on the cover boards above the batteries forward for one, or at a pinch two men, to lie down and to sleep. In the control room was another space on the port side where a man could thread his legs between pipes and pumps to stretch out, with his head under the chart table. This was where the CO would take his rest as and when he could leave his post, not that he left it by much. It took but one step to reach the periscope once he had extricated himself. For all the inconvenience of this bunk, the few odd hours, or even minutes, which I was to spend in this position, were golden.

Cooking appliances consisted of a carpenter's double boiler glue pot, and an electric kettle. We did not really cook, but heated prepared food. For ventilation there was a Protosorb canister with circulating fan and two small cylinders of oxygen, but mostly we breathed the air we dived with, and it became stale with the passage of time.

Overall length was fifty-two feet, diameter five feet ten inches, and surfaced displacement thirty tons. Maximum speed on diesel was six knots, five or less when submerged, but not for long before the batteries would be exhausted; two knots was an economical speed. Range on diesel was one thousand miles.

## HIDE AND SEEK

At the start of the war, apart from spotting it on the surface, the only way to find a submarine was by using Asdic. The apparatus sent out ultrasonic sound waves with a range of about a nautical mile. When they struck an object, an echo in the form of a 'pinging' noise was sent back, allowing the position of the submarine to be calculated. Submarines as well as surface ships were fitted with Asdic but tended to use it passively for listening to Asdic operations through the hydrophones. These could detect so-called Hydrophone Effect (usually abbreviated HE): the sound made by propellers and engines, alerting the operator to the presence of other vessels. German U-boats learned the value of silent running and 'hiding' in dense layers of water; their Italian allies suffered from the excessive noise produced by their boats.

An experienced hydrophone operator could frequently identify another vessel from the speed and sound of its propellers, and the Asdic operator in HMS *Unbroken* showed an even more sensitive ear. At the time of the incident in question he had been 'imprisoned' in the forward torpedo compartment on a charge of disobeying an order.

### Lieutenant-Commander Alastair Mars, DSO, DSC*, Royal Navy; from *Unbroken*

I was in the ward-room when Petty Officer Lee arrived to say: 'Cryer says he can hear Asdic impulses.'

I frowned. 'I thought he was for'ard in the torpedo compartment?'

'He is, sir.'

'Do you mean to tell me he can hear supersonic Asdic waves without a set?'

'He says he can hear them, sir.'

I hurried to the control-room. 'Hear anything on the Asdic?'

'No, sir.'

Cryer's gone round the bend ... Maybe there's a defect on the set ... But surely Cryer can't hear Asdic impulses with the naked ear? ...

I turned to Lee. 'Cryer. Do you think he's mad?'

'Looks all right, sir.'

'No wild eyes or waving arms?' 'No, sir.'

Richards was officer of the watch. 'Bring her up,' I said. 'Twenty-six feet ...'

As we tilted upwards there was a shout from Jones on the Asdic : 'HE red one-two-oh.'

Cryer was right!

'Diving stations!'

I trained the periscope on the bearing of the HE, and as the glass broke the surface I gasped. 'It's the biggest bloody tanker you've ever seen!'

Although the tanker was well protected, *Unbroken* sank her. Cryer was recalled to duty immediately afterwards.

### Capitaine de Frégate Etienne Schlumberger, FNFL / Marine Nationale; from *L'Honneur et Les Rebelles de la Marine Française, 1940–1944*

If no landmarks were to be seen, a submarine had three ways to fix her position: dead-reckoning, sounding and celestial observations.

At that time there was no electronic aid to navigation. That was done with a sextant, and the trouble with that was that you had to be able see both a star and the horizon at the same time. It was too dangerous to surface by day to observe the sun because of German air patrols. At night, you couldn't see the horizon. There was only one way round this: take bearings at dawn and dusk; you still need to be able to spot the occasional star among the clouds.

Well, we did have a sounder to measure the depth to the seabed, but its noise could betray our position. So at night we navigated by dead reckoning; at dawn, weather permitting, we fixed our position by star sight; by day we were once again back to dead-reckoning with the watch; at dusk by another star sight. When entering a fjord we used the periscope and, as far as possible, the sounder. (We had two periscopes: one with small optics used during an attack: the attack periscope; and another, much larger, the watch periscope.)

## WHAT'S IN A NAME

The US Navy named most of its submarines after fish, which led to some very famous boats bearing commonplace names, Halibut being a prime example. The Poles looked to their wildlife – for example the *falcon* (*Sokol*) – for inspiration; the French and Italians between them commemorated national heroes, colonial possessions, jewels and classical deities. German boats were famously identified by U numbers; Japanese by I, RO and HA in descending order of size; most Dutch submarines were known by their numbers, prefixed by O or K, where O stood for *Onderzee*, indicating that the boats were intended for operation in home waters and K for *Kolonien*, denoting submarines based in the Dutch East Indies.

So many new  British submarines were projected by 1940 that the custom of naming them was dropped, and they were identified simply by numbers. Prime Minister Winston Churchill wanted the practice reinstated and at the very end of 1942 he  wrote to Admiral Sir Dudley Pound, the First Sea Lord, pointing out that nothing had come of his assurance that all submarines, like surface ships, would all be named. The result was a frantic scramble for the dictionary by COs in search of appropriate names – which had to begin with the letter of the boat's class. The little U-Class boats were numerous, but so many words beginning with U had only negative meanings. Nevertheless, the commanders were diligent, and so names such *Unbroken*, *Uproar*, *Upholder*, *United*, *Unruly*, *Ultor* (from the statue of Mars Ultor in Rome) *Unique* and, with charming understatement, *Unshaken* and *Unruffled*, quickly established themselves.

But whether named or numbered, a submarine soon wormed its way into the hearts of its crew.

# Life On or Under the Ocean Waves

Living conditions were at best primitive. A submarine leaving on patrol carried provisions and a full load of torpedoes; the crew fitted around that, and while North Sea and Mediterranean patrols might only last a couple of weeks, submarines in the Atlantic, Indian and Pacific Oceans were at sea for much longer. It was far from unknown for food to run short. Refrigerators, where fitted, allowed a limited amount of fresh food to be carried along with the vegetables that soon went rotten in the clammy environment. While water for drinking and hygiene was invariably in short supply, there was no lack of moisture in the pressure hull, the result of sweat, condensation and seawater pouring through the conning tower hatch.

Depending on the class of boat in which they served, men slept on the battery boards that formed the floor, among the torpedoes, in closely packed hammocks or in bunks. There was no personal space: more often that not, a man coming off watch climbed into a bunk only just vacated. The captain possessed a tiny, curtained-off area euphemistically called a cabin; his officers slept in the ward-room.

Many submariners have written and spoken feelingly of the conditions they endured, day in, day out: frozen in the Arctic and the North Atlantic; boiled in the hotter latitudes; frequently damp; reeking of diesel; choking on foul air and chlorine gas given off by batteries. Days of boredom could give way in a split second to a call to action stations; the adrenaline rush of an attack was often followed by hours of unrelieved battering by depth charges. Yet the one quality that rarely seems to have failed was a sense of humour, however sardonic or resigned. They needed it.

**Captain First Rank Viktor Korzh, USSR Navy; *L-21*;**
from *Red Star under the Baltic*

Life aboard a Soviet submarine operating in Baltic temperatures was particularly arduous. In March 1945 Lieutenant Viktor Korzh sailed from the Finnish base of Turku on *L-21*.

Day had dawned, and the Finnish ice-breaker *Gutsy* had diligently broken up the thick ice in the harbour and provided us with a towing-rope. There was still not even a hint of spring. The temperature was fifteen degrees below zero.

Jerked by the taut rope, our boat pulled away from the pier. Snow-covered islands glided by. Blocks of ice collided and somersaulted in the churning wake of the ice-breaker. They thudded and rubbed against the sides of the boat. The noise was so great that it was impossible to talk to one another.

We encountered some Finnish fishermen. They were riding little sledges. Their stocky little horses ran merrily over the hard crust of ice. It was some-what strange to see such a conveyance out at sea. We asked the ice-breaker to stop. The fishermen drove up to the very edge of the ice. We struck up a conversation. It turned out that they were getting sprats to be smoked. They generously shared their catch with us. The sprats were not sturgeon, of course, and neither were they sterlet, but the ratings nevertheless feasted pleasurably for two days on fish soup and fried fish.

They had put me up in a head of department's cabin. There were two bunks in it. Dolgopolov had obligingly allowed me, as senior man, to take the lower one. The bunks were attached to the ship's side. Although the ship's hull was lined with compressed cork, a frosty vapour blew from it and coated every-thing with a thick layer of rime. There was a portable electric heater in our cabin. It gave out such a heat that your jacket would start to steam and you would turn over on to your other side. The warmed-up jacket would melt the frost on the inside of the hull, and then freeze to it, and the cold penetrated even through fur. You could stand it for not more than ten minutes without changing position. With the door closed, the temperature in the cabin rapidly rose to over forty degrees (we had a thermometer hanging above the table). When you switched off the electric heater, twenty minutes later your teeth were chattering. So you would sleep like a clockwork toy – in perpetual motion, constantly turning over, switching the heater on then switching it off, opening or closing the cabin door. Nikolai Sergeievich called this 'automatic temperature control'.

### Stoker George Woodward, Royal Navy, HMS *Thule*

My first boat was a training boat, actually, *H.33*, and after I had done my training I went on the HMS *Thule*. I served in that from when it was brand new until when the war was finished. On the *Thule* everything was hydraulic but on the *H.33* everything was hand operated – all the main vents were hand operated.

On the *H.33* we only had one toilet and that was right at the stern, and everybody on the boat could see you were on the toilet. But on the *Thule* we had two, both amidships just after the control room, and a wash-hand basin so you could actually have a wash. On the *H.33* there were no bunks – you had to sleep on the battery boards. In the *Thule* there were bunks but not for everyone. You used to wake the chap to come on duty and you used to go into that bunk. And we didn't carry all the stuff. You used depot ships in those days and we only used to take a toothbrush and underwear with us out to sea. There weren't room to put anything. You didn't see daylight but if the submarine were on the surface you could volunteer to ditch gash at night. But it's a good life and it does you good to rough it; it makes you appreciate it when you see the blue sky and you get fresh air.

Lord Nuffield used to give us five bob a day when we come on leave, and when we were at Devonport when *Thule* was being built we used to go down to Torquay. Well, it was out of bounds, only Americans and aircrews could go – but they let submariners go. They wouldn't let ordinary ratings go because of fighting.

We did a lot of time out in the Far East, and temperatures out there were hot; we had temperatures of 135 to 140 degrees Fahrenheit. All you had on was a pair of shorts. But we used to have sweaters. Even in the Far East in the engine room, sometimes you used to have to wear sweaters to save catching cold. Temperatures were 130, perhaps 140 F, and we had the engines running as well but we had cold air coming down.

## Sub-Lieutenant Dr Wolfgang Pohl, Kriegsmarine, *U-581*

We had very, very little space for us, and many of my friends have asked me – during the war and after – 'how could you survive in the submarine? It must have been terrible; I never would have gone there.' And I always answered: 'First, we were very young, and, also, as young boys in the Hitler Youth we were very well drilled.' I was in the younger group of the Jungvolk, and we were drilled and taught to withstand any difficulties. At the end I told my friends: 'do you think that to die in a hole, in an icy hole in Stalingrad in 30 or 40 degrees below, without any food, without any care taken by the doctors, wounded and with three of four shots of the gun is better? I think this is worse than submarine warfare. 'Of course we were in a narrow iron coffin, but we had the feeling we were doing the best for our country.'

When we had free time we went to our bunks. We had only one bed for two persons. It was very important to sleep because there was much difficulty with stress. We were there in winter time, near Iceland, and Greenland and north of Ireland; weather was bad and we had storms. When we were on watch in the conning tower in bad weather time, it lasted only four or five minutes and we were totally wet, and then we stood there for four hours in wet conditions, cold. When we came back down through the conning tower into the boat we just peeled off our dress and went into our bunk to sleep. But the fact is, in submarine warfare we didn't get any influenza. There were no bacteria and there were hardly any influenza conditions.

We were a very compact friendly band of brothers. It was quite okay. Of course there was someone who was very close to you and another who was neutral, but I had a very good first officer of the watch, Heinrich Russ, and he became my friend. He was older than I; he belonged to the crew of 1936, the Olympia crew [so called because the 1936 Olympic Games had been held in Berlin], and he was an excellent human being.

### Luitenant ter Zee 1 Aart Hopman, Koninklijke Marine, *K. XV*

There was of course the problem of foul air. Coming to the surface, it was necessary to fill up the depleted battery, and the air for the diesels was sucked through our ventilation pipes by partly closing the watertight door between control room and engine room. It worked very well.

Another problem was the temperature in the boat: we had no air-conditioning or heating, and in the tropics it was very hot in the boat; we sweated like pigs. In the cold climate areas we dressed in whatever and stopped the airflow going through the conning tower hatch. The men inboard could feel the pressure change on the ears. We had the oilskins on in bad weather, the lookouts stood either side of the Pericope gulf-breaker, ready to disappear into the hatch.

The story goes that two subs, from opposite countries, saw each other and just waved. What could one do? The weather even in summer can be very bad and cold up there. Coming from a watch, out of the oilskins and wet and miserable; into your bunk and sleep, the great healer and provider.

When it came to toilets, in the early days, we had only a very small tank under the toilet and that was a problem while under enemy attack. Closed up in watertight compartments, a bucket became useful. Later on a tank was fitted and the refuse blown into the forever-patient ocean, or so we accepted the problem in those days. Loo-paper is a pest and gets stuck into the valves. We washed with our hands and washed our hands thoroughly, but, even as young and agile as we were (very few of the crew were above 30 years of age), lack of exercise and bad food promoted constipation and resultant piles.

The seamen crew saw daylight, but some of the engine room crew went down below after leaving harbour and came out again on arrival. We had an arrangement for airing the crew, while on passage. Smoking was allowed in the control room, in the airflow of the diesels.

### Electrician 1st Class Bob Haughney, US Navy, USS *Threadfin*

Life on the submarine was much, much better than on the First World War destroyer I was on, and, incidentally, we gave England about 50 of those destroyers.

The newer submarines [the *Balao*-Class thick-skinners] were air conditioned, not because they wanted us to be particular, but in the North Atlantic
we'd not been air conditioned and were at 40 below zero. It was like raining all
the time from the sweating and what with water on the skin of the ship and the
warmth from the engines – everything was damp in the boat. They learned the
submarines had to be air conditioned to get rid of that moisture. Incidentally,
that moisture which we took out of the air we used to take showers with.

We were able to make our drinking water from the seawater also.

The only time we went ashore was when we were bounced off the bottom
and we damaged some of the controls underneath the submarine and we had
to go into drydock. They put us up in the Royal Hawaiian Hotel [Pearl Harbor]
for R&R. That was a big hotel and I'd be lying on the bed, looking up and I'd
say: 'You know, that ceiling looks so far away.' When I was on the submarine I
was on top of a torpedo and the ceiling was about six inches from my face.
Sleeping wasn't any problem. I guess I was not the excitable type. We kept the
lights very dull because there were all these men sleeping. If you wanted to
read or anything, or study courses … In the kitchen and in the compartment
next to it they had some tables and the fellas could go up there and read, play
cards, or something like that, but they wouldn't go into the battery rooms
because that's where the bunks were, or the torpedo rooms.

## Korvettenkapitän Reinhard Hardegen, Kriegsmarine

We had English uniforms which we acquired at Lorient – they were khaki
uniforms and we wore them inside the boat. Up on the bridge we had leather
gear, and in the winter we wore thick pullovers and leather trousers with
oilskins over the top. Apart from that, nobody wore any uniform – this was
more practical gear.

## Wireless Operator Alfred Conrad Wernard, Kriegsmarine;
from IWM Sound Archive 18573

Personally, I can't speak for other people, I was seasick solidly for six weeks and
it got to a stage where you said to yourself: why can't I die? You feel that bad,
you really do. And you have to be on duty mind you … The main problem was
seasickness which I didn't overcome until – it might raise a giggle now – one
old seadog – he waited six ruddy weeks watching me being seasick – never said
a thing. Until he said: swallow a bit of bacon on a bit of string [and] pull it up
again. Well after swallowing that bacon and him extracting it on that piece of
string I was as sick as a dog. I thought I was going to die, in fact I wished I could
die. I felt that bad – but the very next day I wasn't seasick.

# THE FLOATING RESTAURANT

With submarines spending so long at sea, and often with nothing happening, it is little wonder that meal times were so important, even though the men often left their hearty appetites on shore, to be reclaimed on return from patrol.

## Comandante Mario Rossetto, Regia Marina, then 1st Officer, *Enrico Tazzoli*

When I was the tenente in the *Enrico Tazzoli* and responsible for making preparations for the missions, I asked Commander Fecia di Cossatto how many days of patrol were anticipated and what stock of foodstuffs I should get on board. Up till then, the longest patrol had lasted about fifty days. Moreover, because these patrols had been in the South Atlantic, usually in bad weather, which spoilt appetites and led to less than the normal amount of rations being eaten, the senior officers I asked for advice recommended that I didn't take any extra stock. (The surplus would have to be given back on our return, anyway.)

We left from Betasom [the Italian base at Bordeaux] for the Caribbean.

The outward voyage took about a month and we didn't come across a single target to attack. We didn't even find any in the Caribbean itself, between the islands and the coast of Brazil. Our Commander now decided to switch to the area east of Trinidad (where we actually found a pair of ships to sink) but in the meantime, through frequent checks on our stock levels, we realised that there wasn't going to be enough food for the length of the patrol, which had been extended beyond what had been expected. The immediate consequence was a reduction in the daily ration. That reduction, which was rigorously applied, put the whole crew on an enforced diet. In eighty days I lost six kilos, going from 75 kilos at departure to 69 when we returned.

This diminution of rations obliged us to seek other sources of food. At sea, of course, you can try stocking up on fish. And so it was that one day, having spotted an empty life-raft, the relic of a steamer sunk long before (but without any clues to help us identify from where it had come), we approached it and made it fast to our boat. Now we noticed that there was a fair quantity of fish around the raft, eager to eat the molluscs that were thriving on the submerged part. A couple of sailors went down into the raft and by reaching into the water easily got hold of a good number of these fish (of modest size) which were clearly not expecting to be caught and which calmly carried on with their meal. The catch was passed, one at a time, to another sailor who despatched them by crushing their heads with a pair of pliers.

When the 'miraculous' fishing expedition was over a good proportion of the best fish was put aside and used for at least three meals for the whole crew; we had no means of preserving any more for longer and we could not have caught any more of them.

The food supply ran out, allowing us one last meal from the last tin of meat, when we reached the rendezvous with the minesweeper in the safe route at the mouth of the Gironde. A few hours later, on arrrival at the Betasom base, a great big steaming meal – which Comandante di Cossato had ordered without a word to any of us – awaited the starving crew, even though 5pm was a most unusual time for a banquet.

When we Italians are looking unsuccessfully for something, we say 'we can see it with binoculars'. In a submarine, obviously, we say 'we can see it through the periscope'.

So it was that, a fortnight into one patrol, when the crew wanted to celebrate the August festival with a banquet, given the scarcity of rations they thought of seeing it through the periscope. So it became a 'virtual banquet', commemorated in a menu specially designed for the occasion. [See images]

Subsequently, Rossetto was given command of the *Giuseppe Finzi*, also operating in the Atlantic out of Bordeaux. His rank failed to intimidate the submarine's cook.

I enjoy eating onions but I do not like finding them in soup or broth, especially when they are a bit tough. The cook we had on the *Finzi* loved using onions in the soup which was usually served in the evening. One day I asked Ganci, the cook, not to put onions in the soup, but come the evening, there they were once more. Summoned again, the cook justified himself by saying that onions were an essential ingredient, and he carried on using them. Then I asked Ganci to at least strain my soup. My words fell on deaf ears.

Seeing the stubbornness of the cook I summoned the petty officer in charge of provisions and ordered him to confiscate every remaining onion.

## Comandante Sergio Parodi, Exec, Regia Marina, *Delfino*

Our food, notwithstanding it was tinned, was very good, if I well remember.

One or two days before our departure for patrol, we tried to buy fresh provisions on the market; the most part of them were potatoes, vegetables, lemons and season fruits, salted-meat and bacon, eggs and other victuals which could stay fresh for some days in a submarine where the space for refrigerators was rather scarce.

I still remember the brand 'Motta' – still existing and to-day producing no more toasted tinned coffee, but many kinds of sweet and 'panettoni'.

When the submarine was on patrol, the very important order shouted by the second in command was 'Fondo alla pasta!' This order, given as soon as the submarine surfaced, divided the day in two halves: the one was silent while the submarine navigated submerged with a good part of the crew resting. During the second part, the submarine was patrolling on the surface, the diesel engines were roaring in accordance with the waves and the people on the bridge, with the maximum attention, looked into the darkness of the night: the importance of radar was not understood by Italy's most important chiefs.

Of course the order 'fondo alla pasta' was given only if no enemy was suspected near the submarine. Otherwise instead of pastasciutta the submariners would have had depth-charges!

### Captain George Hunt, DSO*, DSC*, Royal Navy, HMS *Ultor*

Because HMS *Ultor* was a small submarine we only had thirty-six crew. There was nobody to cook on board, so one of the stokers volunteered to be the cook. Frank Surridge really did a fantastic job; he got a Distinguished Service Medal. In peacetime we used to get what were called 'submarine comforts', which turned out to be some rather nice soup and one or two extra tins of 'herrings in tomato sauce' and that sort of thing. But during the war we had to just muddle in with everybody else, and we just got what we could. We were never hungry. When we got alongside the depot ship I took Surridge in to the chief cook and asked him to 'teach him to make bread'.

So he used to make bread when we were on patrol quite often. That was very good. There's not too many men that can make bread, I mean not too many stokers! And he was so uncomplaining and so cheerful with everybody and so hard-working, his galley was always spotless. Just as if he was looking after one of his engines.

We finally did get a cook. Well, he was rated as a cook. He had a cook's badge on his arm. But he just didn't fit in a submarine. I had him for three months, and I decided I wasn't going to keep him – I got fed up with him, he was hopeless. He didn't get on with the crew, he didn't get on with me either. So we went back to our old stoker, Surridge, and the 'cook' was returned to the depot ship. What would we have done without bangers and mash [sausages served with mashed potato] and herrings in tomato sauce?

### Lieutenant-Commander B. Romanowski, Polish Navy, commanding ORP *Dzik*; from Patrol Report 23 December to 13 January 1944, North Aegean, ADM199/1853

8TH MEDITERRANEAN WAR PATROL, ATTACHED TO 1ST FLOTILLA, BEIRUT.
On the night of 8 January pursued a two-masted schooner and opened fire at 800 yards. A full moon provided excellent illumination but the sea was quite rough. We fired 21 rounds of HEDA and obtained six hits. The schooner mean-

while kept a steady course doing about six knots. We went alongside, boarded her without opposition, as her crew had apparently abandoned ship, and destroyed her with one demolition charge. She was the Greek '*Eleni*' carrying a cargo of 30 cows, fresh provisions, ammunition, pistols, several bags of mail and sacks of warm clothing. Unfortunately we were unable to take anything as she was still under way and the sea was rough; we could not even take a calf which had been killed during the gun action and would have been a welcome addition to our larder.

### Lieutenant Konstantin Sergeev, USSR Northern Fleet, *K-21*

*K-21* fired at the *Tirpitz* on 5 July 1942 while the German battleship was involved in the attack on convoys PQ.17 and QP.13. Having heard explosions, Captain Lunin claimed to have hit the target, but German records have no mention of any damage to the ship, leading to a post-war conclusion that the torpedoes probably exploded prematurely. The submarine and her crew became heroes in the Soviet Union. The attention they attracted subsequently brought the officers a meal to remember.

Once, at the end of 1943, after our 10th patrol, Captain Lunin and Executive Officer Arvanov called the whole of the crew together and warned that our submarine would be visited by some Americans from the United States Naval Mission. In order to be ready for the visit we had to finish some repair work; put everything in order; lock the wireless room and the sonar room; put on clean clothes, stay at our battle stations, and answer any questions properly – no data about weaponry, equipments, rate of sailing, diving depth was to be given; that was classified information! It seemed that the Americans generally wanted to see the celebrated Captain Lunin who had attacked the famous German battleship *Tirpitz*, and, of course, they were also interested in the renowned submarine *K-21* itself and its crew.

Executive officer Arvanov assigned me to be the duty officer that day. At the appointed time the Americans came to the pier – they were Rear Admiral Olsen and three officers: a doctor, a mechanical engineer and an evident intelligence officer, a tall handsome guy with a little dandified moustache. He had the rank of lieutenant-commander and spoke Russian perfectly.

The rear admiral, tall and stout, red-faced, had a high fur-cap with a tin eagle on his head, and the officers were all wearing service caps, black overcoats and very long grey woollen scarves.

The Americans were accompanied by the chief of staff of the Northern Fleet, Rear Admiral Fyodorov, whom I had known since the Battle of Stalingrad.

Lunin met them on the pier, reported to Rear Admiral Fyodorov, introduced himself to the Americans and invited them to the submarine. The first who stepped down to the control room of the submarine was Fyodorov, and then something slightly embarrassing happened. I reported to Fyodorov:

'Comrade Rear Admiral, the duty officer of the submarine, Lieutenant Sergeev!'

Fyodorov said: 'Report to the American admiral.'

I waited for Admiral Olsen to step down to the control room and reported to him (in Russian): 'Comrade Admiral, the duty officer of the submarine, Lieutenant Sergeev!' Then Fyodorov who stood by my side, said quietly as a joke: 'You said Comrade? He's not a Comrade to you; he represents the global bourgeoisie.'

I felt awkward and told Fyodorov: 'He doesn't understand Russian, anyway.'

The American admiral grinned mischievously and suddenly said in incorrect but quite understandable Russian: 'I understand Russian!' Everyone burst out laughing, I was thoroughly embarrassed, and Arvanov told me: 'Go to your compartment six, comrade!'

The Americans examined the submarine very carefully; they went through all the compartments from the bow to the stern, asked a lot of questions. The translators were the staff translator of the Northern Fleet and the American lieutenant-commander, who tried all the locked doors, from the sealed compartments to the officers' cabins and even the heads. In compartment VI, near the starboard, the crew's dismantled bunks had been stacked and covered with sailcloth. The American officer nosed about there for a long time, eager to know what was hidden under the sailcloth. Finally he ran up to it, pulled it off, saw that there were only bunks there and rushed away from the compartment. In the control room he suddenly stopped a sailor, the steersman Panfilov, who was the shortest guy in the whole crew – his height was about 160 centimetres. He became interested in how old Panfilov was. It seemed that he thought that Panfilov was under age. Misha had to get his red seaman's pocketbook (a small notebook which every sailor had in his pocket – and still does; it contains all the data about the sailor and describes his duties in different types of combat actions) from his pocket and prove his legal age.

Needless to say that after surveying the submarine our guests were invited to the wardroom. Our Stores did not stint on such an occasion. Having seen the spread, our visitors brightened up noticeably. As it became clear a little later, this was in no way down to the foreign delicacies which our Stores gave us but to the traditional Russian food – vodka, caviar, mushrooms, herring and onions, sauerkraut and rye (black) bread. And when boiled potatoes and fried rockfish were served up, the guests went into pure raptures and waited impatiently for the opportunity to have a mouthful after every toast.

On our part the toasts were generally raised to the landing of Allies in Europe in the not-too-distant future, and, on their part, to our great combat successes and battle victories. The toasts were numerous, and the guests got blind drunk. We had to hoist the American admiral up the vertical ladder of the mineloading-hatch door with a rope tied under his arms and using a pulley. The doctor stepped on his long scarf while going up the ladder. Jerking his head, he pulled his leg off the rung and crashed down. Only the intelligence officer stayed absolutely sober as a judge, though he drank more than anybody. He also returned all the thanks.

When the guests had left, the officers of the submarine sat down at the table in the wardroom. It turned out that the distinguished guests were a long way from having eaten and drunk all the delicacies the Stores gave us. This was probably because a lot of spirit had been added to their wine – through some misunderstanding, of course!! So everybody was satisfied by the visit – both the guests and the hosts. The norms of international naval courtesy and hospitality were fulfilled a hundred per cent and even more.

## Lieutenant-Commander Zenji Orita, Imperial Japanese Navy; from *I-Boat Captain*

I did my best to make sure my crew received good food, which was harder to do in a shipyard than at sea. Japanese submariners, like American ones, ate very well at sea. A typical menu consisted of boiled rice (sometimes fresh, sometimes tinned), 'umeboshi' (pickled plums), 'takuan' (pickled horse-radish), and 'nori' (dried seaweed). These were on the mess tables in plenty at all three meals. 'Miso-shiro' was always served for breakfast. This is a soup much favored by Japanese. It contains dried onions, fresh spinach, and added vitamin extracts.

Lunch and dinner were a little more elaborate. For about the first 10 days at sea we enjoyed fresh meat and vegetables. We ate broiled fish, beefsteak, pork cutlets and 'tempura' (shellfish or vegetables, dipped in batter and fried). When fresh food supplies were exhausted, we would have tinned vegetables, fruit, fish, beef, pork, chicken, broiled eels, tomato stew, ham salad, fish in soy sauce, and soup. We ate plenty of eggs, fresh at first, then powdered. And much, much rice.

For evening snacks there were dried biscuits and sometimes milk or noodles, or 'zenzai' (beans cooked in sweet fashion for a treat) and tinned fruits. We drank very little coffee, but lots of green tea. Our average daily intake was 3,300 calories, far above the Japanese national average. It was high in protein, but I think it lacked in fats.

At Rabaul, while I was there, submarine crewmen used to take rice, cigarettes and soap ashore to the native villages and trade these for fresh fruit. Once in a while, when the crew was very tired, I would allow an issue of sake or whiskey. Overdrinking was strictly not tolerated.

## Luitenant ter Zee 1 Aart Hopman, Koninklijke Marine, then Luitenant ter Zee 3, *K. XV*

We had no fridges and laughed with some kind of jealousy about the Yanks and their ice cream.

We had the first three to five days some form of fresh food and continued onwards with tinned vegetables, often rice and corned beef à la cook's fancy.

The tins of veggies were marked by paper stuck around the tins and that paper often loosened up – became soggy – and in that case we had mixed veggies à la chef de cuisine. In fact the cook was a wizard, a magician.

The crew was allowed one bottle (750ml) a day per man, of course if available. These bottles took a lot of room, but the crew was very inventive to oblige. Don't forget the water was chlorinated to keep the bugs out. It worked. As officers we got a glass of red wine (some form of vinegar) which we generally poured into our glass of water next to the meal to drink the mixture. It became a habit and once I did so automatically aboard a French ship much to the disgust of the Captain. After explanation, he accepted the excuse and I got a new glass to approve, sniff and roll (not spit) his special and excellent choice. Needless to say that our wine aboard the submarines was arranged by the men ashore.

Every night at nightfall, the change of the dogs,* the dirtbin (rubbish bin) was carried by two men from the forward torpedo compartment over the battery compartments to the control room, hoisted to the bridge (the bathtub) and dumped, hoping that by daylight all evidence would have disappeared.

## Torpedo Gunner's Mate J. C. Brighton, Royal Navy;
from the Papers of J. C. Brighton, Imperial War Museum

As for food, we always had a well stocked refrigerator. In the larger submarines, before we went to sea bags of spuds, oranges or any fruit available were stacked, mainly in the fore-ends. There were plenty of tinned foods. In fact, with a good cook, such as the one we had in *Porpoise* (Fred Crossley), we had very good menus. Of course, under the stresses and strains of our particular way of life, appetites were rarely hearty. One great problem was the shortage of drinking water. Any thoughts of a daily wash had to go by the board. Twice

---

* Dog-watches.

a day, I filled a milk tin with water. This was for cleaning the teeth and, after rinsing out the mouth, it was used to saturate a sweat rag which gave me a refreshing wipe down. Likewise, the cook could not be too fussy when preparing food. I remember settling down one night to a meal of rabbit, all nicely cooked. The Chief Stoker was praising the cook for the quality of the stuffing. The cook modestly accepted the praise. It turned out that the stuffing represented the last meal the rabbit had enjoyed on this earth, but it never lived to digest it! Most of us (all those served with a portion of the body), found that we had been served with stuffing.

### Stoker George Woodward, Royal Navy, HMS *Thule*

We had to travel from Trincomalee across the Indian Ocean to the Malacca Straits which is quite a good way, and we used to have to have diesel in our water tanks so we could get there and back again. So we were very short of water.

### Lieutenant-Commander Boleslaw Romanowski, Polish Navy, ORP *Dzik*; from Patrol Report No. 4, 5–20 August, ADM199/1853

Our main complaint is about the inferior quality of the water obtained from the Torpedo Depot, as it contained a great quantity of salt.

Attitudes to alcohol varied between the different navies. The British maintained their long-standing tradition of serving rum; the Dutch and the Americans banned it (though the rule may have been relaxed for officers in Dutch colonial submarines). The French and Italians regarded wine as an essential; the Japanese greatly restricted it.

### Torpedo Gunner's Mate J. C. Brighton, Royal Navy; from the Papers of J. C. Brighton, Imperial War Museum

During the worst days of the siege of Malta, Allied submarines ran a 'magic carpet' bringing in supplies.

Many and varied were the stores we took to Malta. Bags of mail were always stuffed in every nook. Sometimes we carried hundreds of Sten and Bren guns. These were in individual rubber bags and stuffed in spare places in the mine casing among the stores carried on the rails which were open to the sea. We once took on board several cartons of cans of ale. There were twelve cans to a carton. The fore-endsmen and I considered that we were entitled to a can or two of beer as much as anyone ashore in Malta, so we reserved a couple of cartons for ourselves. When the time came for the celebration, we each selected a can according to whether we preferred a light or a dark ale, settled down in the fore-ends with our rum rations already inside our belts, lit up fags and were all set for a short session of bliss. Guess what was inside those bloody cans? Metal polish! The cans were genuine beer cans with all the usual lettering, marked Export Only, and as properly sealed as the real stuff. We did not complain to the authorities, however …

The fore-endsmen were a particularly fine bunch: Leading Seaman Griffiths, Leading Seaman Cummings, Able Seaman Falford and Able Seaman Gerard. All good lads. On one occasion, I thought a couple of fore-endsmen were behaving in a strange manner. Their eyes were glazed, their speech was slurred and they smelt strongly of liquor. I didn't think they had access to extra rum, knowing that they always drank their eighth of a pint when issued. They had none bottled, so there must have been a leak in some other way. I had a hunch that there was something going on in the torpedo-tube space. This was the foremost compart-ment in the boat, the space taken up by the rear halves of six torpedo tubes, plus valves and equipment to operate the torpedo tubes, forward tanks, and forward hydroplane gear, etc. It was a very confined space. It was also very dark and evil-smelling. Cunningly concealed and suspended right forward was a pair of pants or a vest containing some kind of sloppy mush, with a tin underneath to catch the liquor as it percolated through. Sadly, I had to commit this concoction to the gash bucket, without even a taste, but did nothing more. Later, one of them gave me the recipe: Open up a large pumpkin, take out the pulp, stuff with brown sugar and leave to mature. Hang in a muslin bag and drink the liquor as it leaves the main bulk. This was called Marrow, or Pumpkin, rum.

* * *

Our skipper was a heavy smoker. Normally in submarines, there were no restrictions on smoking with the boat on the surface, except for a period during the charging of the batteries, and then only in certain places. While dived, however, smoking was strictly taboo. With Bennington in *Porpoise*, and later in *Tally-Ho*, he always allowed a smoke about noon and again just before surfacing at dusk. Word would be passed by Tannoy: 'One each apiece all round.' The air would become blue but very soon would be filtered through our lungs. Such a break was a Godsend and we blessed 'Old Benny' for his consideration.

### Torpedoman Billy Grieves, US Navy, USS *Thresher*

After the attack on Pearl Harbor, the Hawaiian Islands were placed under martial law. The islands were blacked out and every bar, every nightclub was shut down. You couldn't buy a drink anywhere. A '6:00 p.m.' curfew was rigidly enforced, everybody off the streets. And there was another restriction: every white woman, or I should say, every woman who was not a citizen of the islands, was packaged aboard the *Lurline*, the *Monterey*, the *Mariposa* and the *Matsonia* and shipped back to the States. The battleship fleet was on the bottom and the airforce was decimated on the ground and the islands could no longer defend themselves.

These restrictions proved a source of great irritation to submariners returning from two months on war patrol. Especially the married men, who expected their wives to be there greeting them. One machinist's mate was overheard to say, 'When this thing is over, I'm going straight home and the second thing I'm going to do is lay down my sea bag.'

But submariners are resourceful; and torpedoes run on compressed air and grain alcohol. The alcohol was contaminated by the addition of croton oil so the 'fish' could run on it but the torpedomen couldn't drink it. So it had to be redistilled.

This was done in an ordinary soup pot called a tureen, which the cooks furnished, and a hot plate. The 'pink lady', as torpedo alcohol was called, was poured into the pot. Then a soup bowl was placed in the center of the liquid. The lid was inverted and placed on the pan and ice cubes were placed in the lid. The heat was kept low to keep the temperature below 160 degrees so as not to boil off the contaminates. The alcohol turned to steam, struck the lid and dripped down into the bowl as clear, 190 proof alcohol. This was commonly called 'gilly'.

When a submarine returned to port from two months war patrol, the crew was sent on two weeks rest leave at the Royal Hawaiian hotel on Waikiki Beach. But with no bars, and girls and night life, it could only be called a rest. Two weeks of monotony. What to do? Let's run off some 'gilly'.

*Thresher* was on leave at the Royal and the islands were blacked out. The Royal Hawaiian was not air conditioned so the rooms were kept cool by opening the patio doors facing the beach. This meant that the lights must be turned out at night.

So we set up the 'still' in the bathroom with the door closed. There were six of us crammed into the small room. Don Meek was running the 'still'. The hot plate was taped to the tub near the wall and the water valves. There was no ice to be had so the 'Doc' supplied a rubber tourniquet tube which, when we cut off the ends, was fitted over the nozzle of the tub and circulated cold water over the inverted lid. The water spilled back into the tub. The procedure was slow but, drip by drip, the clear 'gilly' dripped into the bowl. Then we took turns mixing a shot of pure grain with grapefruit juice and drinking it down.

As time went on the bathroom became filled with cigarette smoke and the effects of the 'gilly' became evident. The flowing water, spilling off the lid, began to seep down on the hot plate. Then there were sparks. Meek, grabbing 'Gunner' Lewis's arm for support, reached over and touched the pot. 'Gunner' bounced off the wall. 'You sonofabitch!', he shouted. And Meek yelled back, 'Hold still, godammit!' and he touched the pot again. When 'Gunner' bounced off the wall again, we opened the door and, through a rectangular wall of cigarette smoke, we emerged into the bedroom.

But improvisation is a way-of life for submariners. When things broke down at sea there was no one else to call on. And the 'First Class' in charge of the torpedo room had the key to the 'pink lady'.

### Comandante Mario Rossetto, Regia Marina, *Giuseppe Finzi*

Commander Dominici who commanded the *Finzi* two years before me came from Piedmont and loved the local wine. At that time Piedmont wine was part of his submarine's supplies.

Naturally, as part of the preparations before leaving on a mission it was necessary to take on board all the food and drink necessary for the length of the patrol as planned – and with a certain amount extra in case circumstances demanded that the boat stay at sea for longer than envisaged. If on return to base it turned out that the patrol had lasted for fewer days than the supplies were intended for, it was necessary to return to the stores a surplus quantity corresponding to the number of days that had been saved. Any discrepancy – on the minus side – would be charged to the submarine.

Everyone on the *Finzi* remembers that Comandante Dominici, being a lover of Piedmont wine, allowed the whole crew to drink rather more of it than the normal ration. On return to port after patrols, therefore, it would have been necessary to pay the difference. However, to avoid this the commander had got into the habit of claiming in his official reports that the lack of bottles was owing to the fact that during the missions 'many bottles had been found to be empty as a consequence of the corks popping'.

The justification had been accepted, but the Stores withdrew the fine Piedmont wine as being 'unsuitable for the demands imposed by long patrols'. They had replaced it with Tuscan wine, which is itself, moreover, pretty fine.

### Sub-Lieutenant Ruari McLean, DSC, British Liaison Officer, FNFL *Rubis*; from *Half Seas Under*

1941 SPRING

I soon realised that I had been very lucky in being posted to *Rubis*. Of all the allied submarines in Dundee, she had the best chef, and there was vin rouge every day; not as a luxury, but as a normal French ration. I do not know where it came from, or what genius of a victualling officer managed to secure a constant supply of it, but I do know that although we sometimes sailed without mines, we never sailed without vin rouge ...

30 JUNE 1942

We returned to Portsmouth, not Dundee, and were quartered in HMS *Dolphin*, otherwise Fort Blockhouse. My French officers were made very welcome, but it was a bit like St Paul's Cathedral, not the sort of place in which they could ever feel at home. After fourteen days (most of which they spent on leave in Dundee) we prepared for another patrol in the Bay of Biscay. We were due to sail from Blockhouse at 1900.

At the last moment there was a hitch, which looked like developing into a crisis. The red wine had not arrived. It had been promised from London, and signals had flashed to and fro between victualling yards, but at 1800 we still had no wine. We had never yet sailed without it. The crew were looking very glum.

At 1830 there was still no wine. At 1845, a look-out came running to report that three barrels had been sighted on the jetty at HMS *Vernon*, about a mile away across the harbour. He thought they were being lowered into a boat. We dashed to the walls of the fort, and saw a motor-boat actually under way, labouring towards us, with the barrels visible. I had to go to Captain (S) and request permission for our sailing time to be postponed by half an hour to enable us to take the wine on board. It had to be siphoned out of the barrels into our tanks. Permission was granted – the first time, perhaps, that a submarine's sailing had ever been postponed in *Dolphin* in order to take on wine.

Finally at 1930, with all French faces beaming, we sailed ...

## CLEANLINESS IS NEXT TO GODLINESS ...
## BUT NOT IN A SUBMARINE

Dealing with the inevitable consequences of eating and drinking was a perennial problem on all submarines, made worse when under attack. The toilets, known as 'heads' (a centuries-old term referring to the very foremost part of a sailing ship which acted as an open-air lavatory for the crew), were usually inconveniently situated, sometimes very public and invariably hard to operate successfully.

### Torpedoman Billy Grieves, US Navy, USS *Thresher*

About a week into the patrol, all fresh water showers were shut down. Fresh water was for drinking and cooking only. And operating near the equator with long periods under attack or rigged for silent running, bodies perspired constantly. The 'jock itch', a severe rash on both sides of the groin, was an occupational disease with submariners. The engineers used diesel oil to try to keep it in check and the torpedomen used alcohol, but nothing worked. But this was tolerated because we knew that the salt water and sun at the Royal Hawaiian on Waikiki cured everything.

But we were allowed one sink full of water to wash down our entire body and shave. We called this a 'Marine bath'. On large surface ships, Marines were part of the ship's company. In port, when liberty started after a day's work, sailors took a shower and put on a clean uniform. But Marines, it was said, only washed their face, dabbed some after-shave under their arms, and went ashore. This was called a 'Marine bath' because, as everybody knows, Marines are filthy.

Then there were the 'heads', the sea-going lavatories. All the enlisted men's heads discharged directly overboard. The head had two sections, the upper and lower chamber, which was separated by a flapper valve. Even on the surface and tied up to the dock, the head was below the water line and it was necessary to manipulate seven valves in proper sequence to blow the head overboard. At sea and submerged, this required a lot more pressure.

The head had two compartments, one above the other, and separated by a flapper valve. To use a head, one first opened a sea-stop and then a sea-valve allowing salt water to fill the upper chamber of the bowl to the proper level. Then, when finished, a lever on the right side of the steel bowl and connected to the flapper valve, was pulled, emptying the bowl into the lower chamber. Then he stood up in the tiny compartment and faced the head. On the bulkhead to his left were two gauges, one registering outside sea pressure at the current depth, the other registering pressure in a tank connected to the lower chamber of the head and used to blow the head. A lever above the gauges was then pushed outboard to pressurize the tank 50 pounds above sea pressure. (I used a hundred.) The 'discharge' valve was a long lever which the man pulled across his belly to open the lower chamber to sea. Then, while simultaneously opening the 'discharge' valve with his right hand, he pulled the air tank lever with his left, admitting air pressure to the lower chamber and blowing the contents overboard.

But there was one more step that should not be omitted. Connected to the flapper valve on the left side of the bowl, was a pedal, which when depressed, guaranteed the seal between the upper and lower chambers. And it happened. Every now and then it happened. The guy was in a hurry, or preoccupied, and he didn't put his foot on the pedal. Then a loud stream of profanity emanated from the head, the door slammed open into the passageway, and the guy backed out with a vicious look on his face – and a piece of toilet paper on his ear.

But this was a noisy procedure and not permitted when rigged for silent running or under attack. And one thing we learned; there are no chemical laxatives nearly as effective as a good close depth charge attack. Those heads got pretty full sometimes.

## Comandante Sergio Parodi, Exec, Regia Marina, *Delfino*

I remember that submarine *Delfino* was transformed, in a few days, into a cargo submarine transporting gasoline and explosives for our Army that was fighting at El Alamein, towards the end of the year 1942.

All spaces available on *Delfino* were needed for gasoline and ammunitions; also the toilet places were considered useless for the crew and, naturally, at disposal for anti-tank mines. The ballast tank No. 2 was transformed into a kind of hold necessary for stowing about 25 tons of gasoline put in 10-gallon containers.

In return, the ballast tank No. 2 was reinforced to resist an hydraulic pressure of about 100 feet, as if the enemy destroyers could not take care of Italian submarines in navigation under 100 feet depth.

The voyage between Taranto and Buerat El Hsun (at the bottom of Sirte Gulf) needs about three days of surface and immersion navigation, because our route was very near to Malta. It was obvious that the crew needed something that could replace the toilet, even if many members of it were rather constipated because of the very restricted movement a submarine crew can get.

An urgent palaver occurred among the second in command (myself), the Chief Engineer and the Master-at-Arms. It was decided that the most convenient place to have a toilet was in the engine room (more ventilated), near the astern bulk head: in this place it was necessary to open a hole in the plates under which to put an empty big oil-drum. The plate was to be furnished, around the hole, with a foot-stool. Now, we arranged a very functional Turkish toilet. Before using the Turkish toilet, the big oil-drum had to be filled with sea water and, poured onto the surface, a little naphtha or diesel of our engines. Each night, soon after the surface navigation, the 'Serpante di bordo' (the man of the crew directed to clear the toilets) had to pump in other small drums, everything that was floating on the big oil-drum, using a small hand pump. Some other men, ordered by the Master-at-Arms, had to carry the small drum filled with the 'substance', into the control room, where the same, with a rope, was lifted on the bridge, and at last the substance finished at sea.

After the first night the Master-at-Arms hurried to tell the Tenente [Exec] that something was going wrong. The Tenente arrived immediately in the Turkish toilet and saw that something which floated in the big oil-drum was much bigger than the gun-pipes of the hand-pump. The Tenente had little time to lose in the matter and ordered a handle of 'frettazzo' (big broom) to be brought quickly to the engine room. As soon as it arrived he said to Serpante: 'Adesso rompili (now break them!)'.

The Serpante soon had the 'Serpante indemnity' doubled!

One day before the arrival at Buerat El Hsum the sea was rough with a strong southern wind. The *Delfino* was pitching and rolling so heavily that the Master-at-Arms thought, very prudently, to have the small oil-drum half-filled in order to avoid dirtying the [floor]plates. The first small drum passing through the conning tower had almost reached the bridge when the lookouts sighted two destroyers coming towards the *Delfino*.

Immediately the crash-dive signal was given; the man who pulled up the small drum did the only thing he could do: loosened the rope attached to the drum half-filled with excrement: The Tenente, half way up the conning tower, hearing the crash-dive signal, stopped his ascent and began his descent – that was hastened by the crash onto his head of the small drum loosened from the bridge. Luckily the nights were still cold, and the Tenente before going on the bridge had put on a heavy wool cap. This and the weight of the half-filled drum prevented the Tenente smelling worse than a Turkish toilet.

The Tenente very philosophically returned to the bridge, certain that the fresh air and the sprays of seawater would soon carry away the bad smell.

### Secondo Capo Mechanista Carlo Pracchi, Regia Marina, *Velella*

When the submarine was on the surface, there was the opportunity to pee al fresco, but that, too, had its problems, particularly when the sea was running high and the watch was in a jovial mood.

I went into the control room and from the foot of the conning tower ladder I shouted, 'Bridge!'

'What is it?' they replied.

'Permission to come up.'

'What for?'

'I need a slash.'

After a pause, there came the reply:

'Okay, come up.'

As I came up into the realm of the lookouts who, along with the helmsman and the officers, were all muffled in helmets, fur jackets and boots, I heard someone say about me:

'Well just look at the state of him!'

As a matter of fact, as I'd been in the engine room, I was stripped to the waist and wearing a pair of PE shorts, the sort with the blue stripe.

'Be very careful: it's rough out here.'

I started to do what I had to do; I held on tightly with my left hand and, with my right hand I tried to aim to leeward, while looking up in the hope of spotting a few stars. Then, out of the blue, I was struck by a powerful cascade of water which just went on and on.

That bunch of bastards, instead of keeping the waves on the bow, had changed course to get a laugh at my expense. When the wave had passed, I coughed and spat to clear my lungs and then I went back to what I had to do, but my penis, which I had been holding in my right hand had … retreated …

I'll get my own back on them when they come down to the engine-room wanting to dry their clothes. I'll burn the lot!

## Commander Edward L. Beach, US Navy; from *Submarine*

It seems that, months before the war started, USS *Skipjack* (SS184) had submitted a requisition for some expendable material essential to the health and comfort of the crew. What followed was, to the seagoing Navy, a perfect example of how to drive good men mad unnecessarily. For almost a year later *Skipjack* received her requisition back, stamped 'Cancelled – cannot identify material.' Whereupon Jim Coe, skipper of the *Skipjack*, let loose with a blast which delighted everybody except those attached to the supply-department of the Navy Yard, Mare Island, California.

This is what he wrote:

USS *Skipjack*

SS184/L8/SS36-1

June 11, 1942

From:   The Commanding Officer.

To:      Supply Officer, Navy Yard, Mare Island, California.

Via:     Commander Submarine, Southwest Pacific.

Subject: Toilet Paper.

Reference: (a) (4608) USS *Holland* (5184) USS *Skipjack* reqn. 70-42 of 30th July 1941

(b) SO NYMI cancelled invoice No. 272836.

Enclosure: (A) Copy of cancelled invoice.

(B) Sample of material requested.

1. This vessel submitted a requisition for 150 rolls of toilet paper on July 30, 1941 to USS *Holland*. The material was ordered by *Holland* from the Supply Officer, Navy Yard, Mare Island, for delivery to USS *Skipjack*.

2. The Supply Officer, Navy Yard, Mare Island, on November 26, 1941, cancelled Mare Island invoice No. 272836 with the stamped notation 'Cancelled – cannot identify.' This cancelled invoice was received by *Skipjack* on June 10, 1942.

3. During the 11 months elapsing from the time of ordering the toilet paper and the present date, the *Skipjack* personnel, despite their best efforts to await

delivery of subject material, have been unable to wait on numerous occasions, and the situation is now quite acute, especially during depth charge attack by the 'back-stabbers'.

4. Enclosure (B) is a sample of the desired material provided for the information of the Supply Officer, Navy Yard, Mare Island. The Commanding Officer, USS *Skipjack* cannot help but wonder what is being used in Mare Island in place of this unidentifiable material, once well known to this command.

5. *Skipjack* personnel during this period have become accustomed to the use of 'ersatz', i.e., the vast amount of incoming non-essential paper work, and in so doing feel that the wish of the Bureau of Ships for reduction of paper work is being complied with, thus effectively killing two birds with one stone.

6. It is believed by this command that the stamped notation 'cannot identify' was possibly an error, and that this is simply a case of shortage of strategic war material, the *Skipjack* probably being low on the priority list.

7. In order to co-operate in our war effort at a small local sacrifice, the *Skipjack* desires no further action to be taken until the end of current war, which has created a situation aptly described as 'war is hell'.

J. W. COE

It is to be noted that Jim Coe was wrong in one particular; it had been only ten and a quarter months. But his letter, carrying in it all the fervour and indignation of a man who has received mortal hurt, achieved tremendous fame.

We also heard that it had achieved rather remarkable results back in Mare Island, although this was mostly hearsay. But one result was extremely noticeable indeed: whenever *Skipjack* returned from patrol, no matter where she happened to put in, she received no fruit, no vegetables and no ice-cream. Instead, she received her own outstandingly distinctive tribute – cartons and cartons of toilet paper.

**Lieutenant-Commander Alastair Mars, Royal Navy, HMS *Thule*;**
from 6th War Patrol Report, ADM199/1867

There has been one consistent source of irritation which has produced insanitary conditions upon occasion. This is the quality of the toilet paper supplied. It resembles wallpaper more than anything else, and has a detrimental effect on the mechanism of the heads. On many occasions, ERAs have had to be employed on stripping and cleaning the flap and intermediate valves of heads which had become clogged with paper, thus causing floods of stinking water.

If a thinner and more soluble type of paper were supplied this extremely unpleasant work would become unnecessary.

The complaint received short shift from the Captain of the 4th Flotilla, Ben Bryant:

The moan about heads paper is not new; it is a question of supply and has been fully dealt with by Admiral (Submarines). The blocking of the heads mechanism would probably be avoided if the time-honoured submarine practice of rolling the paper into a ball was more generally practised.

## PASSING TIME

### Stoker George Woodward, Royal Navy, HMS *Thule*

I used to do embroidery. We had the women from the WVS come along from Campbeltown, and they'd learn us how to embroider. I used to be able to stem stitch.

We used to make little submarines. We used to have a piece of brass and a file. And then we'd keep the place tidy and clean – all the brasswork we used to clean until it'd shine. We did have a record player on board and some records. In Ceylon a singer came along. Her name was Cherry Lind and I never heard of her since, but she sat on the conning tower steps and she sang *One Fine Day* from *Madam Butterfly*, and we were all round her, and if ever I hear that it takes me back. Sometimes we'd have a sing-song. One of the songs was called *Underneath the Surface* and it was based on *Underneath the Arches*:

Big ships we never cared for,
Destroyers they can keep.
There's only one place that we know,
That is deep down deep.

*Chorus:*
Underneath the surface
We dream our dreams away,
Underneath the surface,
On battery-boards we lay.

There you'll always find us
Tired out and worn,
Waiting for the Coxswain to wake us
With the sound of the Klaxon horn,

Then we all get busy,
The Tiffies and the 'Swains'

Working vents and blows and hydroplanes
And when the panic's over
We'll get it down again,
Underneath the surface
We dream our dreams away.

They used to have a newspaper on board: the *Good Morning*, specially published by the *Daily Mirror*. When we left harbour we used to collect papers and each morning we had a paper. And one morning me mother was in it, and me sister, and some of the local pubs.

When I was in the Far East I was 21, and I was out for three days, because it's a tradition in the navy you have 'sippers' [a drop of everyone's rum ration] on your 21st birthday – and it's rum as well! In fact I don't drink, but you had to then because it was the tradition. And every time they gave me a drink of water it tasted like rum. I've never drunk any since. I wasn't in trouble because in a submarine you can get away with it. I was in a bunk at the back in the stokers' mess. It wasn't my fault! My shipmates covered for me saying I was not very well, and they covered my watches.

In the big ships they used to give you it 'two-and-one': two of water, one of rum, mixed, whereas in the subs they used to give it to you neat. I didn't actually have it because you used to be able to get 3d a day if you didn't have your rum.

When they dropped the bomb on Hiroshima we didn't set sail – we should have set sail with agents. The following two nights we had dances. The *Thule* had it on the first night and the second submarine had it on the next night. And the Swan Brewery at Fremantle put the beer on and everybody could have free beer. At that particular time in Australia they used to shut the pubs at 6 o-clock at night but they used to have shops where they sold wine. People used to come down to the boats to look round and invite us to their homes.

**Lieutenant-Commander Max Shean, Royal Navy;**
from *Corvette and Submarine*

The *Daily Mirror* produced a newspaper especially for submariners. Called *Good Morning*, it was supplied in month bundles, not dated but sequentially numbered. This was important in order that the comic strips like 'Jane' and 'Zeke' would appear in logical sequence. There were features on submariners and their families, and pictures of the 'Windmill' girls, who were famous throughout Britain and, I should think, the world. The Windmill Theatre in London presented a variety show with emphasis on shapely girls: most Aussie servicemen attended at least one Windmill show during London leave at some time.

'Jane' was also a national institution. Like the Windmill girls, she frequently managed to lose her clothes, but acted with propriety none the less. 'Zeke' was an anthropologist, or something like that, and during this particular month's issues had one single ambition, to capture a prehistoric animal and so to be made a Fellow of the Zoological Society.

One morning, Joe was allowed to distribute that day's 'Good Morning' throughout the messes in Syrtis. All seemed to be happy until members of each mess came to the wardroom with a complaint. 'Something is wrong with this issue, Sir. Yesterday, Jane was about to do something or other, and today she is on about something entirely different.' The fact was that Joe, in his eagerness to help, had issued the wrong number. I don't suppose many news-papermen have produced next week's news today.

Another time-passer was to play games on paper; a popular one being 'Hang the Man', in which one player thinks of a word which the other player must guess, letter by letter, losing a point for each incorrect guess. The points are scored by progressively drawing a gallows with rope and stick-man, ten pencil strokes in all. We spent so much time at this, it became nearly impossible to hang anybody, until Terry 'hung' his first lieut, Joe, with the word 'ZekeFZS', considered to be of doubtful validity.

## Luitenant ter Zee 1 Peter de Jong, Koninklijke Marine, Commander, O.24

If you are in enemy waters and you are on the surface you've got to be ready as captain if the phone goes Captain on the bridge! But if it's night and you sit reading you don't see a thing if you come up; it takes about 20 minutes to get used to the darkness. So we had red light. You try to read a book in the red light! It's dreadful. But you can't sit awake the whole night. So what I did, I used to play patience – pictures, you *can* see. If you start doing that for two days you start thinking, what is the chance it works? So I started figuring with some mathematics of my younger years, and I came to a sort of result. I was not happy with it ... and I decided there was only one way to test it, and that was to play 1,000 games. And I kept a record. I was on a very long patrol, 60 days, and when we came near Fremantle, home, I was at 956 or something near that. So that was a shame: I haven't got my thousand games ... So, there's always got to be an officer on board, and if you've been at sea for just over 60 days you want to go to the shore for a change. But to the obvious surprise of my officers I said 'You can go ashore tonight when we're alongside: I'll stay on board.' They must have thought: he's lost his mind, and off they went. I finished my 1,000 games berthed in Fremantle.

## Sub-Lieutenant Ruari McLean, British Naval Liaison Officer, FNFL *Rubis*; from *Half Seas Under*

Bridge had formerly meant for me a green baize-topped card-table in my mother's Oxford drawing-room, a folding wooden cake-stand with three tiers (bread-and-butter, scones, and sponge cake), the heavy silver tea-pot, and new packs of cards. They never played with a pack unless it was brand new, those serious, silent North Oxford, afternoon friends.

In the *Rubis*, things were slightly different. '*On joue un bridge?*' asked Rousselot after lunch one day. '*Père McLean, vous savez jouer?*' I explained that I knew the rules but had never played regularly. '*Vous jouez Culbertson, ou non?*' asked Dubuisson. 'I, er, well, that is to say ...' Well, at least I knew who Culbertson was. It appeared that Dubuisson was a Culbertson fan, the Captain not. A green cloth was fetched from the Captain's cabin and thrown over the wardroom table, two extremely greasy old packs of cards produced from a locker, and half-a-dozen bottles of Whitbread's Light Ale ordered up from the 'cellar'. Rousselot, Dubuisson, Hémar and I sat down. The submarine, steady at sixty feet below the surface, slowly puttered on towards the enemy coast at two knots. The gyro-repeater in the adjacent control room produced a constant but erratic click-click in the otherwise silent boat.

I was told the names of the suits in French (*trèfles, diamants, coeurs, piques,* and *atout* for trumps) and current conventions explained. Then we started.

Yes, bridge in the *Rubis* was very different from the bridge I had watched in North Oxford. My mother's friends were tight-lipped during play. They never criticised their partners openly, let alone cursed them. They never shouted, roared with laughter or tore their hair. The officers of *Rubis* did all that, and told me that I played like a child, like a dead body, like ordure, like filth, and like many other things that I have never yet succeeded in finding in any dictionary. After every game, they turned on me, venting their sarcasm and wit, only about half of which, perhaps luckily, I understood. If I wasn't learning bridge very quickly, I was certainly adding to my French vocabulary.

We played for a penny a hundred, and the Captain wrote down the results after each session in a little green note-book. My debts rose twice as fast as anybody else's, but gradually the curve flattened: I began to notice that I was not always on the losing side. I also noticed that although Dubuisson played by Culbertson (and constantly referred to Culbertson's *Golden Book*) the Captain ignored Culbertson, and much to Dubuisson's disgust, nearly always won – because he read his opponents' minds and faces like pages of large type.

By the end of the patrol, it was less certainly a catastrophe to be partnered with me; and occasionally they would even say: '*Il sait apprécier un jeu main-*

*tenant, ce McLean'* or *'Le perfide Albion'*; and once, after, the Captain and I had won a rubber, he rubbed his hands and said in a surprised tone: *'Il joue vachement bien, le père McLean.'*

We played bridge every day on this patrol, and I would have expected it to replace our tea-time arguments. But they loved talking, and not a day passed without a passionate controversy. Once we got in a great bother because we could only remember the names of six of the Seven Dwarfs (Walt Disney's *Snow White* had been in Dundee over Christmas).

### Lieutenant Konstantin Sergeev, USSR Navy, Northern Fleet, *K-21*

Submariners of all navies knew how to make the most of their time ashore, though not all flotilla bases had the opportunities offered by Murmansk to Soviet Russia's Northern Fleet.

Nobody knew why the officers' club, housed in the Northern Fleet Culture Centre at the Polyarnoye naval base was named the Capernaum but everyone loved that place. Only the political officers never called it that name. They used to simply say 'the officers' club'. Fifty years later I found this name in the Gospel of Matthew. In a Biblical encyclopaedia it said that Capernaum was a city in Judea, Galilee, the favourite place of Jesus Christ. It can be translated as 'the village of consolation'.

It was a cheerful and comfortable place to relax. There was a small bar where one could drink and get a bite to eat, a dance hall with a little five-piece jazz band, a pool table, comfortable foyers and lounges. The Fleet Centre included a well-stocked library; you could see excellent performances of the Northern Fleet theatre, concerts by naval bands and visiting artists, and various films, Soviet and foreign (American, English and some others). For example, in 1943 we were watching such films as *Sun Valley Serenade*, *That Hamilton Woman*, *Waterloo Bridge*, *In Old Chicago*, *His Butler's Sister* and so on. American and English Naval Missions in Polyarnoye also featured films in the Fleet Centre for their officers, but we watched them too. The jazz-band at the Capernaum, made up of professional performers, quickly took popular melodies from films and performed them in dance rhythm to the public's great delight. So, the Capernaum gave the opportunity of good, civilized and cheerful leisure to a young (or not-so-young) officer when off duty.

I cannot forget one particular night's leave. We were in dock at Rosta on the opposite shore of Kola bay to our home base of Polyarnoye. There wasn't an officers' club in Rosta, although there was quite a good culture centre. But it had its Capernaum in Murmansk. There was also the Interclub there, that is to say, the club for the sailors of foreign (Allied) merchant ships coming to

SUBMARINE

Murmansk as part of the convoys. Our officers did not visit the Interclub, it was uninteresting there. After successful voyages, foreign sailors used to celebrate heavily, all the more so because vodka in the USSR cost pennies when compared to whisky and similar products in their countries. To say nothing of the prostitutes who used to go there in search of excitement and money! Savage fights for various reasons, including national and racial, were frequent there. Anyway, we did not go to the Interclub. The Murmansk Capernaum was, of course, differerent from the Capernaum in Polyarnoye. As the saying goes, there's no place like home (East or West, home is best). But there was no pick-and-choose. Come to that, Murmansk was much bigger than Polyarnoye; it was a city, a regional centre, with corresponding opportunities and facilities for relaxation and entertainment. That's why, being under repair in Rosta, we always tried to get to the Murmansk Capernaum if the opportunity came up.

Easier said than done. It was five or six kilometres from Rosta to the centre of Murmansk, and there was no regular service then as there is now. In summer, when it was daylight and warm, it was a pleasant enough walk along the shore of Kola Bay. But in winter, when it was dark and cold almost day and night, and when a cutting wind with driving snow was blowing, such a trip down the snow-bound road required lots of strength and optimism. Yet we were young, so we had enough.

Our captain was summoned to Polyarnoye for some reason, and after supper the senior, executive officer Uzharovsky let our senior mechanic, Ivan Ivanovich Lipatov, and, after some hesitation, me, go to Murmansk Capernaum. We got ready in a flash, polished our boots, sewed clean collars to our jackets and went into the road leading to Murmansk. We were lucky – almost at once we were picked up by an empty lorry coming back from Vaenga (it is called Severomorsk now) to Murmansk. We got into the back and rushed along the road, holding on to the cab and bending double to get a little protection from the sharp onshore wind.

When we entered the city, the lorry turned off and we had to jump down from it. And we had a nasty surprise – when jumping down to the road in the dark, Ivan Ivanovich hurt his heels badly. I jumped successfully, and helped him to his feet, but he could not walk. There were no passing cars; waiting for them on the road was a waste of time and it was a kilometre or so to go to the Capernaum. In addition, one small fact emerged – the wife of his friend (a mutual acquaintance who was working late that day and could join us late in the evening only) would be waiting for Ivan Ivanovich at the Capernaum. For that reason, the friend had asked Ivan Ivanovich to meet his wife and to escort her to the Capernaum. The wife herself had just come to Murmansk from somewhere out in the sticks, and she did not have any acquaintances in the city. The situation was desperate. I offered to give Ivan Ivanovich a piggy-back, he climbed up, and we (that is, me!) started for the Capernaum. It was really good that the streets of Murmansk were poorly lit, and we did not meet patrols or acquaintances. The spectacle was extraordinary.

I have never been so tired in my life – before or after that – as on that evening. When we reached Capernaum, I was just shattered. My legs were giving way, the sweat was pouring off my forehead and getting into my eyes.

As always there were a lot of people near the lighted entrance to the Capernaum – officers and girls who were eager to get inside. When I let Ivan down, they burst out laughing. It was the first time that an officer had come to the Capernaum riding another one who, in addition, was his subordinate. A lot of people were acquainted with us. The audience was really enjoying it.

Ivan Ivanovich quickly found the person he was to look after – she was standing in the appointed place and stamping her frozen feet – and we got into the Capernaum. Ivan Ivanovich went nimbly enough, but I could hardly get up the stairs holding on to the handrail.

Having had a drink and a snack in the little bar, we got to the dance hall. Somewhat recovered from the effect of his unsuccessful jump, Ivan Ivanovich, had livened up and he danced with his female companion, looking at me smugly. His reckless flirtation with a stranger was noticed by the company at once and interpreted as the beginning of a serious infatuation. And the lady, who had found herself among a group of the elite – officers wearing magnificent uniforms with gold epaulettes and decorations – was also dancing with great pleasure with this courteous and handsome cavalier.

As for me, I could not recover even after being at the bar. My legs were still shaking; I was knackered; everyone who knew how much I loved dancing was taken aback by my miserable face and lethargic behaviour.

Meanwhile, the news of how I got my chief to the Capernaum quickly got round those who knew us well (they represented the majority) and those who didn't. The most witty congratulated me on a 'wise career move' and foretold rapid promotion. And I was so tired that I just could not tell them to get lost, or explain that I could not have abandoned my chief and fellow comrade in the cold dark street while I went dancing at the Capernaum. So it turned out to be one night's leave that I will never forget.

**Rear Admiral Corwin Mendenhall, US Navy Retd, Exec, USS *Pintado*;** from *Submarine Diary – The Silent Stalking of Japan*

The long-established ceremony of Crossing the Line became the initiation rite for seamen who were crossing the equator for the first time.

24 December–1 January 1945. An hour past noon of the twenty-fourth our escort reversed course to return to Saipan. *Pintado's* cooks were busily preparing a magnificent Christmas dinner from supplies that Jerry Mitchell had been able to scrounge from the tender at Saipan.

The twenty-fifth was like almost any other day for men who had been away from home as long as *Pintado's* had been. George Murray organized a very nice Christmas service in the crew's mess from 1000 to 1100. We sang every Christmas song we could think of and said a few prayers. George gave an inspirational talk. The microphone was there, so everything was broadcast throughout the boat. The men on watch appreciated that. The skipper later complimented us, so we must have done justice to the occasion.

George and Robbie gloated over the presents that their families had sent them ahead of time so they would have them on Christmas. The rest of us weren't that well organized, nor had our families realized that we would be away from the mailman for so long.

Everyone was excited in anticipation of crossing the Equator. That would happen on the twenty-sixth. Only seventeen of the ship's complement had been across that line, so we shellbacks were telling the polliwogs about the dread things they would experience and making plans to initiate them.

On Christmas Day *Pintado* passed to operational control of Commander Task Group 71.9 (CTG 71.9) in Brisbane, and we radioed a request for an escort to accompany us while passing Manus Island. There was quite a concentration of Allied navy ships in that vicinity, and we didn't want *Pintado* to be mistaken for an enemy.

*Pintado* crossed the Equator at longitude 148°15′E on the twenty-sixth. The time was 0357, so only the watch and the navigator were up to note the time of crossing.

At sunrise we sighted the light carrier *Hoggatt Bay*, with two DE escorts, to the southeast at fifteen miles and exchanged recognition signals and call signs. A short time later our destroyer escort, *DE-635*, moved in, exchanged signals, and joined *Pintado* to accompany us as we passed Manus. We were never close enough to see the island.

*Pintado's* crossing-the-equator ceremonies were quite a show. Surprisingly, Brant, our old-time navy man, had never been across. He was on the bridge in dress uniform, carrying a long glass and watching to see that no seagulls soiled our decks. Ed was there in a full suit of long underwear with a bucket and swab, keeping the decks clean. We had Jerry decked out in a mess jacket, cook's hat, and apron – nothing else – and he was kept busy running between the galley, pantry, and bridge, bringing coffee and sandwiches. He would stagger up the ladder to the bridge with many cups of coffee, then the recipient of the coffee would take one sip and toss the coffee over the side with a 'too hot,' or a 'too sweet,' or a 'too cold,' and order him to bring a good cup.

Robbie was racing around the engine rooms wearing nothing hut a jock strap and rain hat, shining valves. Bonny was in the galley with binoculars, looking for smoke. Gerry, in a complete set of long underwear and another of rainclothes, was sweating in the radio shack, listening on radio headphones. We really gave them a merry runaround. Everyone had a good time.

Then, for the initiation, I was the Royal judge, so I put on a wing collar and bow tie, a pair of swimming trunks, dark sunglasses, a black beret, and a pair of boots. We dressed Red Hill up as King Neptune with some unraveled rope as hair, a fancy white robe that appeared from somewhere, and a makeshift crown. The Queen wore an outfit of women's underwear that was found in a bale of cleaning rags. She looked quite curvy, with balls of twine in the bra. Among King Neptune's court were the Royal Navigator, the Chaplain, the Doctor, the Baby, and the Chief of Police, all dressed in their own imaginative creations.

Each polliwog was required to appear before the Royal judge and plead, on his knees, his innocence of some goofy infraction. I would assign a sentence. The Royal Barber, with a large paintbrush, might start working the polliwog over with heavy grease, paint, syrup, and various evilsmelling liquids. Polliwogs were blindfolded when the Royal Doctor moved in to look at their teeth, squirt bitter liquid in their mouths, and feed them a piece of cake made with soap powder, garlic, salt, and other awful-tasting things.

The initiation was a workout for both the shellbacks and the polliwogs. Everyone had a great time unwinding and laughing at the antics. A run on the showers took place when everything was over, and no one had a problem sleeping that night.

At sunset our escort departed, and *Pintado* headed toward Vitiaz Strait to go east around the eastern extremity of New Guinea.

The beautiful Southern Cross and Scorpio were rising higher and higher in the southern sky as we moved south, a nightly reminder that *Pintado* was getting nearer and nearer to Australia. The North Star had long since disappeared below the horizon.

While proceeding through Vitiaz Strait we sighted numerous merchantmen, tugs, and aircraft. At one time a sizeable convoy passed, headed north. *Pintado* was in the submarine safety lane, and they recognized that we were friendly.

## PETS AND PESTS

A number of submarine crews kept pets, particularly aboard the French boats. The most famous was Bacchus, a mongrel belonging to the French minelayer *Rubis*.

**Sub-Lieutenant Ruari McLean, DSC, British Naval Liaison Officer,**
**FNFL *Rubis*; from *Half Seas Under***

Bacchus has been the mascot of the French submarine *Rubis* for nearly five years. Five years in a submarine – including two and a half years of war – and when I saw him last Thursday he was chasing the harbour master's cat down the road like a young greyhound.

He is always the last to come on board, and the first off, but he's never missed the boat yet. Some of the crew say he's getting old, but I've not noticed it. His coat is as glossy, his short legs and long tail are as active as you could wish.

I wonder how many people in France remember seeing him in the days before the war? For the *Rubis* was one of the show submarines of the French fleet, and during the summer she used to visit resorts along the coast of France, especially those of Brittany and Normandy. Thousands of citizens came on board her, and they must all have seen Bacchus. Do you remember a black and white smooth-haired mongrel with short legs and a longish black tail; a mongrel with the wisest, the most intelligent head and eyes you have ever seen, and a quite pathetic weakness for sugar?

Yes, I wish he could write his autobiography. He's seen the world, has Bacchus, and only he knows what frolics he's had in the various Mediterranean, North Sea, and Atlantic ports he's visited. He enjoys himself ashore like any sailor.

As for our adventures at sea, well, he conducts himself just like the 40 other Frenchmen on board – with complete sang-froid. Once when we were being hunted with depth-charges, his nonchalance was a perfect example – if example were needed – of how a Frenchman behaves under fire. He seemed to realise that his duty was to keep as quiet as possible – for the slightest noise might be picked up by the enemy's hydrophones – and Bacchus lay down and very sensibly went to sleep.

Bacchus has not yet got, as some ship's dogs have, a hammock of his own. He usually sleeps in the bunk of a certain Petty Officer Electrician. This man, who belongs to the Midi and has a beautiful long beard, has taken particular care of Bacchus since he came aboard as a puppy. Bacchus recognises him, more than anybody else, as his real master; although of course the chef, who gives him his food, comes a close second in his affections.

If we are on the surface, and rolling about in a rough sea, it is amusing to watch Bacchus, quite unperturbed, adjusting himself on his sea legs to the boat's motion. Sometimes he stands with his forepaws on the bottom rungs of the conning-tower ladder, asking to be carried up; but he is allowed on deck only when we are in British coastal waters. As for looking through the periscope, Bacchus is not over-ambitious, and leaves this to the Captain.

People often ask: Doesn't the lack of air when we are submerged affect Bacchus? The answer is: not more than the rest of us. And it is because he always puts up with it so well, and never shows a sign of objecting, or does anything but wag his tail, that he so well deserves the medal with which he has been decorated. Of course, he is very much petted on board. He always comes along to the wardroom after lunch and after dinner, when the officers are drinking coffee, to beg for sugar. He lets himself be ragged, be made to sit up, stand up, shake hands, be tormented and tantalised and laughed at, for he knows, at the end, he'll eat sugar out of the hands of every one of us.

I suppose Bacchus is in a way better off than the other Frenchmen who are here. He doesn't smoke or drink, so doesn't miss his Gaulois, his Pernod and Dubonnet. Whether his thoughts ever turn to a Mrs Bacchus in Brest, or Cherbourg, or Bizerte, I cannot say …

**Stoker Reginald Bucke, Royal Navy, HMS *Otus*;** from IWM Sound Archive 9223/3

HMS *Otus* was attached to the 10th Flotilla at Malta at a time when the island was under sustained attack.

Obviously the dogs as well as the local population were having a very bad time in food likewise so we congregated a lot of dogs of all breeds and sizes. Now the captain in his wisdom said we couldn't maintain all these dogs. Apart from perhaps the odd ship's pet. So, therefore, this 40 or 50 dogs had to be shipped back to the mainland, because where we were based was rather like a peninsula, to let these poor things free. They shipped them back three or four to a local boat which is called a *Dhaisi* – oar-propelled boats very much like the gondola, propelled by an upright oar. They were shipped back to the mainland, and on reaching the mainland put on shore, but immediately swam back – which was about 300 yards – which caused a lot of merriment with all the sailors and officers watching either from on top of their building or on top of their submarines watching these things swim back, and one can well imagine these dogs of various shapes and sizes dog-paddling back. So they decided to give up, let the poor dogs try and maintain themselves, and the Britishers of course aren't willingly cruel to animals so we had to put up with them. But what saved the situation at that particular moment was, the air-raid warning went. The Germans were coming over again, so everyone had to scurry either to their guns or to their shelters accompanied by the dogs.

Not all the livestock to be found on submarines was quite so welcome.

### Yoshio Uchikado, Imperial Japanese Navy, *RO-61*

I joined the Japanese Imperial Navy in June 1937. I was 15 years old. Then I studied at the Submarine School and became a member of *RO-61* in 1940. I was in charge of radio communication. Japanese Imperial Navy submarines had three classes. I, RO, HA, depending on their size. I is the largest and HA is the smallest. I think our submarine *RO-61* was quite good for our task, even though we lacked a radar and a sonar.

Food was pretty good. Of course fresh vegetables soon went away and we had to survive with canned food. Accommodation was not good. Very crowded. We had a lot of cockroaches in our submarine. When we did not have battle, we spent our time to catch and kill cockroaches. We had some rats too. One time when oxygen in the submarine became so thin, we found many rats who could not run because of the lack of oxygen. We easily caught many rats.

### Captain William J. Ruhe, US Navy, Retd, sub-lieutenant, *S-37*; from *War in the Boats*

But, first things first. Neither Billy, Tex, nor I wanted to spend another day in the company 'of millions of cockroaches' that prowled around and over us at all hours. 'Millions' seemed a gross exaggeration until we swung into action to wipe out the vast hordes of 'curious, busy little brown fellas'.

Tex had promised to go to the tender and get a tankful of 'gas' to eliminate 'the little devils'. Billy and I stayed aboard the *37* as part of the in-port watch section, and waited for Tex's return. After supper he showed up and said that no gas to kill the roaches was available on the tender. So he'd gone into Brisbane to a hardware store and 'confiscated' a drum of Flit. The store owner had assured him that Flit was ideal for killing insects of all types. ('But were roaches insects? They seemed more like animals.') Tex then delivered a handwritten note to the owner that said, 'There is an immediate need for an insecticide for the control of cockroaches on the USS *S-37*. I am therefore authorized to officially requisition one container of Flit for the US Navy; signed Lieutenant R. B. Lander, USN.'

This seemed a foolish ploy, except that the store owner graciously donated a drum of Flit to Tex and used his truck to have it delivered to the *37's* main deck. As Tex noted, 'He acted as though I was doing him a big favor by letting him deliver his Flit to a US submarine.'

Tex had also brought along two Flit guns. So Billy and I went to work. The after battery room was evacuated. After which, Billy and I wearing oilskins, rubber gloves, and gas masks entered the compartment with our Flit guns. Tightly sealing the crew's messing compartment and where the crew had their food prepared –

a rather ideal spot for breeding roaches – we started soaking the cork insulation that lined the inside of the hull. This produced immediate havoc. The little silver-winged fellas popped out of their hiding places as their bodies were seared by the atomized spray of Flit from our guns. In the throes of great agony, they jumped to the deck and scurried around trying to find the lowest point in the compartment. It would have been the drains, but we'd plugged those. So they dove into the rectangular channel that indented the compartment's deck and that was the means for holding the canvas covering over the batteries. More and more roaches piled into the channel fighting their way towards the channel's bottom until it was filled to overflowing with little dead bodies.

At this, Billy and I stopped the spraying and retreated to the wardroom. When Tex was told about the mayhem we'd committed, he seemed doleful about a future without the little wanderers to playfully distract him from the 37's vengeance. Tex then had the thought that we could get a good estimate of how many cockroaches had just been killed. He found a small wooden match box and carefully measured it in order to calculate its cubic-inch volume. Then he sent Billy and me aft, with our gas masks, so Billy could fill the matchbox with little dead bodies while I measured the dimensions of the channel. Deriving statistics and understanding their significance was a major pastime on submarines. Statistics were always of great interest, even for the dumbest subjects: Do submariners produce more girls than boys? What percentage of the crew drink tea? Are athletes the best submarine skippers? What's the average collar size of torpedomen?

When we got back to the wardroom Tex dumped 'the little devils' out of the box and carefully counted them. After this, he figured how many dead cock-roaches there were to the cubic inch. He took my dimensions for the channel and converted them to the cubic-inch volume of the roaches' resting place. Finally, he announced the number of dead cockroaches in the overflowed channel: 'Over four million!'

## THE WRONG PLACE TO BE ILL

Rats, cockroaches and lice may have been unpleasant inconveniences; medical emergencies, such as appendicitis, during a patrol were serious matters.

**Yeoman 1st Class Albert Dempster, US Navy, USS *Crevalle***

We were starting out on our second war patrol on 30 December 1944 and we stopped in Exmouth Gulf to refuel and then proceeded to our operating area making contact with a RO-Class Japanese submarine on 7 January, firing two torpedoes but both prematured at the same spot. Made contact with a small sailboat – sanpan hull, two masts – and fired two 20mm rounds but occupants did not come and hid, destroyed it with 20mm and continued on to operating area.

I started feeling sick and they were pretty sure it was appendicitis. The Pharmarcist Mate lst Class Fred Loos was treating me with the sulfa drug and morphine for a couple of days and studying on operating in case they couldn't get permission to transfer me to another submarine returning to Australia. After three or four days, on 11 January broke radio silence and contacted Task Force Commander requesting to rendezvous with USS *Cabrilla* – who was returning to Australia – to transfer an acute appendicitis case. Permission was granted and we proceeded to rendezvous and on 12 January transferred me via rubber boat with TM2c Vincent Pace USNR as pilot. They had the rubber boat on deck and hoisted me up the ladder by rope (banging my head against the ladder) and then submerging the sub down until the rubber boat was afloat. The reverse procedure was taken by the *Cabrilla* when I arrived there. The whole transfer only took about 45 minutes. The *Cabrilla* was submerged while the *Crevalle* was hoisting me up and the *Crevalle* was submerged while the *Cabrilla* was taking me aboard. The Cabrilla submerged with Vince Pace in the rubber boat and left him floating until the Crevalle surfaced and picked him up. Both submarines were never on the surface at the same time.

After return of Pace, *Crevalle* proceeded to its operating area to complete War Patrol 2. While I was on the USS *Cabrilla* the Pharmarcist's Mate aboard the *Cabrilla*, Irv Rothenburg, gave me morphine, sulfathiazole, and orange juice and packed me with ice cubes, and one day I had a bowel movement which really stunk up the after battery crew's bunking section including blood and whatnot. Upon arrival in Fremantle on 23 January I was able to walk and was transferred to the submarine tender sick bay for observation. The Squadron Medical Officer in his evaluation wrote in his endorsement 'The rendezvous with the USS *Crevalle* on 12 January via rubber boat was well done. The recovery of this man is another triumph for sulpha drugs, the Squadron Medical Officer having diagnosed the case as a ruptured appendix which responded to treatment with sulfathiazole.'

I am now 85 years of age and so far I have not had any trouble as far as my appendix is concerned. I did have a medical doctor at the submarine base in New London, Ct. wanting to operate to see just what happened but I declined the offer.

### Luitenant ter Zee 1 Peter de Jong, Koninklijke Marine, *O.24*

We'd been shaken up a bit in the Mediterranean by depth charging and been back to Scotland for a refit, and then we were sent out to Colombo. Rommel was too near the Suez Canal so we couldn't go through the Suez Canal: we had to go round the Cape of Good Hope, and we got to Freetown on our way to Cape Town, and one of those German pocket ships was in the South Atlantic and we were told to keep a lookout for her as well. We couldn't signal to anyone.

There was one man on board who got terribly ill, 40 Celsius. We had on board what we called a paper doctor. You started off with how he looked, and you had then to turn to such-and-such a page, and eventually you hoped to come to what was wrong. Now the captain and I did that, and we got along quite far in the book, and then we split. He thought it was A and I thought it was B. That wasn't too dangerous, but the therapy was practically opposite.

Well we had to do something, because if we didn't do anything he would die anyway. So we decided to do it democratically. All the officers started from scratch and they all put down what they thought he had. And it was a majority for appendicitis, and a serious one. So we took all the stuff out of the ice machine and only made ice and put a pack of ice on that place. And then we came to Cape Town, and half an hour before Cape Town we were allowed to signal and warn. I must say they did it beautifully because we came alongside and the ambulance and the doctor and the nurse were all there, and he went straight to the operating table. The surgeon came on board later on, and said 'Well, you were absolutely right. It couldn't have lasted much longer, but what you did was absolutely the right thing ...' And he survived, because 'democratically' we had decided that he had appendicitis.

There is a dreadful story, not on my boat, but on a friend of mine's. One of the engineers flattened the last two-thirds of his finger and it had to be taken off but we didn't have anything to disinfect wounds and things. So what do we do? The engineer who operated said: 'Look, first you must have some skin to put over the stump.' So he circled it round, cut in, folded it back. He had only a huge pair of scissors that he had sterilised in boiling water, and he did it beautifully.

### Stoker George Woodward, Royal Navy, HMS *Thule*
Actually, we lost one rating [on 16 November 1944]. We had to bury him at sea in the Malacca Straits and we thought he'd got cholera at the time – his name was Tony [Thomas] Acton, he was from Ireland. But, since, looking back, I think it wasn't cholera, I think it was Legionnaire's Disease. We were the very first submarine to have a dehumidifier on, and it used to fetch the water out of the air, and we were short of water when we were in the Far East. We used to use this water to wash and clean teeth. You didn't hear about Legionnaire's Disease in those days ... Because we were the first submarine to have a dehumidifier we had scientists aboard when they first put it on. The Dutch had got them, and the Americans, but we were the first British submarine.

**Lieutenant-Commander Alastair Mars, Royal Navy, commanding HMS**
*Thule*; from Patrol Report, ADM199/1867

19 NOVEMBER

During the forenoon it was reported that the Chief Stoker had been taken sick in the night with similar symptoms to those of the late Stoker Acton. As the former had helped look after the dead man, I suspected a contagious or infectious disease in lieu of heat exhaustion. In my efforts to put a finger on the right thing, I found that B.R.36 (The Small Ship's Medical Handbook) was virtually useless. Inside the cover it is clearly stated that the book is for vessels which are always within reach of a base Medical Officer. It is suggested that something more comprehensive and more detailed is required. Finally, I decided that Cholera (not mentioned in B.R.36) was a possibility ...

**Fregattenkapitän Reinhard 'Teddy' Suhren, Kriegsmarine, *U-48*;**
from *Teddy Suhren, Ace of Aces*

Our Kommandant, Kapitänleutnant ['Vati'] Schultze, was a really kind-hearted man. On the way back on the occasion of our first assignment, we had a sick man on board. An engine mechanic was rolling about and groaning away in his bunk with stomach ache. In response to questions he only whimpered. I couldn't make head nor tail of it. 'Vati' gave orders for one bunk in the officer's mess to be vacated; one of the WOs had to move out so that his bunk could become a make-shift sick-bay! 'Not me,' I explained with feeling – I couldn't stand this kind of playing for sympathy; there's no way I was prepared to make a sacrifice of that sort! So it was up to our Number 2, the noble Otto Ites. At first, it must be said, he protested feebly, 'But I need to get my beauty sleep too!' Then however he changed places. Every morning when I prodded the sick man a great wail arose – always the same! And 'Vati' Schultze sat there, beating up eggs in stout out of the kindness of his heart to make a special invalid's diet. What a nice man he was! Between the Orkneys and the Shetlands I had an idea. 'Otto,' I said, 'As soon as the Obersteuermann goes on watch, we'll be alone in the mess. I'm going to start spinning a yarn about how dangerous it's getting. And we'll see how quickly our so-called invalid gives up your bunk.' And that was what happened. As Otto appeared in the mess, where the crewman was having a good sleep in the bunk, he noticed my worried expression. 'What's up, Teddy?' 'Otto,' I muttered, with a sideways glance at the bunk, 'we're just entering the North Sea. There's trouble in store. Only 50m deep, and all mined. Just think of it; we've had a signal that Tommy has mined the whole North Sea. What if we cop it? I'm staying right here by the tower.' 'I'm coming right away too. I wouldn't fancy being left inside to drown if we hit a mine.' Pause. There were sounds of stirring in the bunk. Otto looked at me. 'You're right, Number 1,' he answered anxiously. 'Where's my escape-gear? Best to put a lifejacket on too ...' – and with that off we went. It wasn't long before we saw our invalid nimbly up and about, with lifejacket and escape-gear under his arm, standing in the control-room. He'd raised his eyes heav-enwards to the main hatchways, obviously with a view to getting out! 'Look, Otto, now you can sleep in your own bunk again with a clear conscience.'

## Prince Junio Valerio Borghese, Regia Marina; *Scirè*; from *Sea Devils*

On the night of 18–19 December 1941, the Decima Flottiglia MAS of the Italian Navy executed a famous raid on the British naval base at Alexandria. Three slow-speed torpedoes and four two-man crews were transported close to Alexandria by the converted submarine *Scirè*, commanded by Prince Junio Valerio Borghese.

The first to go up were the two leaders of the reserve crews, Feltrinelli and Spaccarelli. Their job was to open the cylinder doors, to save the operators the fatigue of doing so.

One by one, de la Penne and Bianchi, Marceglia and Schergat, Martellotta and Marino, covered from head to foot in their black suits, their movements encumbered by their breathing gear, went up the ladder and disappeared into the darkness of the night and the sea. I submerged to the bottom ...

Inside the submarine we waited for the sounds of blows struck against the deck, the agreed signal to be made when the doors of the cylinders, now empty, had been closed and the reserves were ready to be taken aboard again. When at last we heard them, I surfaced. Feltrinelli told me, in a voice broken by emotion, that as he could see no sign of Spaccarelli, he had gone astern to look for him: by pure chance he had stumbled against something soft on deck; he had discovered by groping (for we must not forget that the scene took place underwater at night) that it was the missing Spaccarelli, who seemed lifeless. I instantly sent up two other divers, who had been kept ready for any emer-gency; Spaccarelli was lifted up and lowered down the ladder into the interior of the submarine. I descended to the bottom again and began to head for home, following precisely the same course which had proved to be safe during my approach.

The unfortunate Spaccarelli was forthwith relieved of his mask, breathing set and diver's suit and put to bed; he was quite blue in the face, his pulse was imperceptible and he was not breathing; he showed every normal symptom of having been drowned.

What was to be done? The mission's surgeon was not much use to us in this extremity, for he himself was the victim. I arranged for two men to give him continuous artificial respiration; I rummaged in the medicine chest and had him injected with the contents of all the phials that, judging from the description of the ingredients, seemed capable of exercising a stimulating action on the heart and circulation; others gave him oxygen (the air aboard was emphatically unsuitable in this case); all the resources of our extremely slender store of medicaments and of our still slenderer knowledge of medicine were brought into play in the attempt to achieve what appeared to be an utter impossibility, the resuscitation of a dead man.

Meanwhile the *Scirè*, with this dramatic episode taking place aboard her, slipped along the sea-bed, further and further away from Alexandria ... I continued on my course of withdrawal, remaining submerged, for the zone we were now crossing had been notified as constituting the minefield. After three and a half hours' continuous artificial respiration, a number of injections and some applications of oxygen, our surgeon, who had till then shown not the smallest sign of life, drew his first wheezing breath; it was a deep, hoarse sound, resembling a death-rattle. But it meant he was alive and we could save him! A few hours later, in fact, though his condition was still serious, he got back the use of his voice and was able to tell us that while he was making a terrific effort to close the starboard cylinder door, which stubbornly resisted every attempt he made, the effects of the oxygen he was breathing and those of water pressure at the depth involved had caused him to faint; luckily he fell on deck and did not slip overboard, as might very easily have happened, for there were no rails or bulwarks to the vessel (they had been removed to prevent the mine-cables from catching on them) ...

On the evening of the 21st, as soon as we had docked at Port Lago, we took Spaccarelli ashore to the local naval hospital. He was now out of danger but still required a good deal of attention in consequence of the severe shock he had experienced.

# Every Man's Hand Against You

The standard anti-submarine weapon remained the depth charge, which could be thrown from a surface ship or dropped by an aircraft. It contained explosive and a fuze set to what was believed to be the submarine's diving capability. Once a submarine was picked up on the Asdic, it would be relentlessly attacked with the intention of either sinking it at depth or forcing it to the surface. The Germans invented the *pillenwerfer* or Submarine Bubble Target, usually abbreviated to SBT, literally bubbles which could be released at intervals to fool the hunters' Asdic, encouraging them to bomb the wrong area. Eventually, experienced Asdic operators learned to differentiate between the echo returned from a bubble and one given off by a submarine. Newer classes of submarines with stronger pressure hulls were able to dive to safer depths, and for these there was a fortuitous window of opportunity before the hunters caught on.

Then there was the human element: destroyer and corvette captains, in particular, became more expert, hunting in groups and forcing submarine captains to look for strategies to survive depth charging or avoid being picked up in the first place. Taken with all the other innovations in submarine detection, it became, for the Axis forces, an unequal struggle.

Tethered or hydrostatic, magnetic or contact, mines accounted for many losses, even after boats underwent degaussing. During the war, claims of 'kills' were reported; afterwards, historians matched missing submarines against claims of successful attacks. Those boats still unaccounted for had to be presumed lost to the horned menace which, for example, sank something like 22 British and 35 German submarines. To survive a mine was a rare piece of good luck.

The anti-submarine net was a precaution taken to guard valuable targets such as warships anchored at their bases and the entrances to harbours. Secured to buoys, they hung down like underwater curtains. Some submarine classes were fitted with net cutters, serrated blades curving up from the bow, while jumping wires were designed to prevent the superstructure becoming fouled in the nets. Several submarines involved in high-speed escapes simply smashed through nets, and special forces with their midget submarines and human torpedoes found other ways. If the nets did not extend to the sea bed, it was possible to go under; hydraulic lifts could raise them, and cutters could also be employed. If the nets did not enclose the target completely, there would be a gap somewhere.

Such were the enemy's main active and passive defences. Submarines found plenty of problems closer to home. Systemic failures of technology, notably torpedoes, could change a boat in a few seconds from predator to defenceless prey and leave crews almost afraid to go into action because of the likelihood that they would be let down in the final moments of attack. Investigations, carried out only after significant numbers of angry and vociferous COs had complained, revealed torpedoes set to run too low, torpedoes breaking the water like porpoises, premature detonation and ineffective pistol or magnetic detonators. The problem was most acute in the German and US submarine fleets and drove commanders to distraction. The Germans were more fortunate than the Americans in that Admiral Dönitz was comparatively swift to take up their cause. It was only in early 1943, when Rear Admiral Charles Lockwood became COMSUBPAC at Pearl Harbor, that his commanders' concerns first began to be taken seriously, and even later before Admiral Christie, his opposite number at Fremantle, conceded that there was a critical problem with torpedoes.

Another risk that all submarines ran was that of being rammed, sometimes quite deliberately as a last resort.

Careless talk also cost lives: at a conference in June 1943, US Congressman Andrew J. May revealed that Japanese depth charges were set to explode at a depth well short of that to which US boats were diving. The Japanese were not slow to take advantage of that information.

Boats trying to refit or repair to get back to sea were sometimes frustrated by shortages in spare-parts (this was a particular problem for foreign submarines serving with the Royal Navy), dockyard procedures that seemed to take no account of the fact that the world was at war, and, particularly in the case of the Allied 10th Flotilla at Malta, unrelenting air attack.

But of the home-grown concerns, mistaken identity was one of the most distressing, and it accounted for more than a handful of submarines lost, as well as instances of damage and alarming near-misses. Misunderstandings between patrolling aircraft and returning submarines, and submarines operating close together, could and did happen, as did misunderstandings with surface ships and accidental collisions.

Finally there was the weather which, at its worst, could leave a crew cold, wet, sick and exhausted.

A submarine was never safe. Nobody could ever relax.

## DEPTH CHARGES

### Sub-Lieutenant Stephen Dearnley, Royal Navy, HMS *Universal*

Life became more interesting in August 1943 when I was sent as spare crew to HMS *Maidstone*, the depot ship based at the North African port of Algiers.

While there I sailed as extra hand on patrol in *Universal*, a little U-Class subma-rine. The Allies had landed in Sicily and we were patrolling the sea between the Italian coast and Corsica. It was an eventful patrol, especially after we sank a well-escorted tanker off La Spezia and were heavily counter-attacked. Because sound is so much louder under water it was a noisy affair – being depth-charged is like sitting in a tin garbage bin while someone belts the outside with a sledge hammer – and we had gone deep to shake off our pursuers. We reached 160 feet OK but when we tried to catch a trim and level out the boat just kept on going down and down, past its designed diving depth of 200 feet. All of us in the control room watched in silence as the deep-diving gauge wound on to 220 – 250 – 280 feet and I waited, very frightened, for the final cataclysmic moment when the pressure hull would collapse on us like a crushed eggshell. As a last desperate measure the CO ordered a short blast of high-pressure air into the two main ballast tanks. Normally this would be a suicidal measure because once tanks had been blown at that depth the air in them would expand as the boat began to come up and its ascent would accel-erate to the point where we would either break surface or have to vent a tell-tale bubble of air. Not a good idea when there were a number of hungry escort vessels waiting for us up top. Blowing main ballast stopped the descent at 297 feet and we started to rise again a few feet at a time. Suddenly, with an almost perceptible bump, we came up to 285 feet and stayed there. It took a little while to realise that we had risen under a layer of water of lesser density, either fresher or warmer than the rest, and we were bobbing there like a child's helium balloon against the ceiling. It was also a perfect hiding place from the ships hunting above as their sonar signals would be refracted harmlessly away by the density layer. It was a very fortunate set of circumstances and, for me, third time lucky – the near miss in the Manchester blitz, being sunk in *Fitzroy* the year before, and now this.

## MINES

**Comandante Mario Rossetto, Regia Marina, *Giuseppe Finzi*; returning to Betasom, the Italian base at Bordeaux, after an Atlantic patrol**

When the submarines went back to the base they had to meet with mine-sweepers to be escorted along the security course to the harbour entrance. But Allied planes every night threw magnetic mines that lay on the sea bottom, to explode when a ship passed over. The bombs had a characteristic: the explo-sion device was regulated to explode after an established number of ships' passages. The mine-sweepers' task was to go along security courses so many times, until no active mines were left.

Well, when on the morning of 18 April 1943, *Finzi* began to sail in the wake of a minesweeper, and the crew already tasted home air after nearly three months, just under the deck a big explosion made us hold our breath. I looked at the sea's surface to see if the boat was sinking, or not. To my great relief I verified that my old and dear submarine was explosion proof, and we went safe and sound to Betasom.

My gratitude to my *Finzi* was raised again when, some time after I knew that the German submarine *U-526* caused the explosion of a magnetic mine and sank, leaving only 12 survivors: it happened on 14 April coming back to Lorient in a situation similar to mine.

**Capitaine de Frégate Etienne Schlumberger, FNFL, *Junon*;**
from *L'Honneur et Les Rebelles de la Marine Française, 1940–1944*

When you hit a mine it explodes when one of its antennae is broken. The mine is tethered to a cable held on the bottom by a piece of ballast and submerged around 3 metres from the surface … In a submarine we draw well over three metres. Before our mission we had passed a cable around our hull to make sure that there was nothing a mine cable could catch on to. The propellers and hydroplanes were protected. However, it's always unpleasant, when you are submerged, to hear a cable scraping along the length of the hull. Any little projection on a submarine could hook a mine which would shatter and explode against us. The end would be swift and certain. There were also mines which became detached and could be found floating on the surface. It gives you a nasty feeling and you have to hope that the bow wave carries them away.

## TORPEDOES, AMMUNITION AND OTHER DEFECTS

**Admiral I. J. Galantin, US Navy, Retd;** from his Introduction to *Submarine Diary*

Still, we should never forget that the skippers who carried the war to the enemy in the lonely, disheartening, early months of war had, in Admiral Nimitz's words, 'held the lines against the enemy while our fleets replaced losses and repaired wounds'. They had few of the technological assets that we who came later could exploit, but they did have the one technical advantage that made everything else possible – good quality diesel engines … Pushed time and again beyond design limits, they made it possible to go the great distances of the Pacific, to make high-speed runs to close a target, or to evade counterattack.

However, too often after attacks were made they were frustrated by a grossly imperfect weapon. Our Mk-14 torpedo compared to the Japanese Type 95 as follows:

For the US – a 500lb warhead propelled by a smoky, wake-producing turbine to a range of 4,500 yards at 46 knots, or to 9,000 yards at 31 knots.

For Japan – a 900lb warhead propelled at 49 knots to 6,000 yards by a wakeless, oxygen-fueled engine.

But the Mk-14 did not perform as advertised. Its story deserves the label of major scandal that went too long uncorrected. It had three defects: running too deep, premature explosion, and a faulty contact exploder. Each of these defects hid the existence of the others.

When Lu Chappell and other frustrated skippers complained of torpedoes running under their targets and the Bureau of Ordnance in Washington took no action, the submarine force commanders took matters into their own hands. Running depth was corrected first, then the Mk VI magnetic exploder was discarded, and finally a more reliable contact exploder was designed and installed. It took almost two years of combat before our submarines went to war with effective torpedoes. In my own war patrols in command of *Halibut*, in late 1943 I sank a ship simply because two torpedoes punched twenty-one-inch holes in the side of a freighter. On another attack we hit the light cruiser *Nachi*, and she got home with one of our unexploded fish sticking in her side.

### Admiral I. J. Galantin, US Navy, Retd; from *Take Her Deep*

Another hazard to which all submarines were vulnerable was a 'hot run' when a torpedo failed to fire out of its tube. On 10 July 1943, following the receipt of orders based on an Ultra decrypt, 'Pete' Galantin, commanding USS *Halibut*, found the Japanese aircraft carrier *Unyo* (alternatively spelt *Junyo*) off Truk.

Eighteen minutes after our first shot had crippled our victim, Robbie mashed down the firing switch for No. 4 tube. But we did not feel the shudder which normally signalled the impact of air under 300 pounds pressure forcing the torpedo out of its tube. Instead, the forward room reported, 'Torpedo not ejected! Running hot in tube!'

As torpedo officer, Jack Barrett rushed forward to get precise information on our casualty: the torpedo tube's stop bolt had lifted, and the fish had moved forward enough to have its starting lever tripped. Its turbine was running, but it remained in the tube. With the pressure of our depth and motion through the water against its nose, it could not propel itself clear of the tube.

A 'hot run' was literally that; without the cooling of seawater rushing by its afterbody and with its contra-rotating propellers spinning madly in a void, the alcohol-fueled turbine would gain speed and heat until it could fly apart or melt, damaging the torpedo tube as well. To prevent this, an overspeed governor would in time cut off power.

But a big question remained: how far out of the tube did the warhead protrude? On the underside of the warhead was a recess containing the impeller that armed the exploder. Was it clear of the surrounding tube so that the impeller was free to turn? As a torpedo sped toward its target, the vanes of the impeller would be driven by the rushing seawater, arming the exploder after the torpedo had traveled a safe distance, some 400 yards, from the submarine. Were we pushing through the water a torpedo whose exploder mechanism was slowly turning, turning into an armed position where a sudden shock might actuate it?

I was angry. We had been given a once-in-a-lifetime opportunity, a chance to sink one of Japan's most important warships, and we had bungled it. What was wrong – our organization, our training, or me? I would have to find out. Possibilities raced through my mind, but this was no time for recriminations or self-doubt. It was not yet sunrise; we faced a whole day of Japanese search and attack; and we had no more torpedoes.

A look at the destroyer shows her swinging our way. I give orders loud and fast. 'All ahead full! Take her deep! Go to 300 feet! Use negative! Rig for depth charge!' In the forward room torpedoman Emil Ade and his gang work desperately to get the fish, now idle, back into its tube.

As we pass eighty feet going down, a second destroyer, which I had not seen, rumbles directly over us. Perhaps he has seen our periscope or our wake and was trying to ram, for the expected depth charges do not come.

Once our tail is safely deep, Jack Hinchey noses *Halibut* down more steeply, and we look longingly at the BT for sign of a friendly thermal layer under which to hide. Not till we're near 300 feet do we find one. Going still deeper, we rig for silent running, shut down all unnecessary noise producers. Instinctively, without orders, we talk in subdued tones, step carefully and quietly when we move. The accidental clatter of a dropped wrench rings out like a village fire bell, bringing glares to the culprit from the eyes of startled shipmates. Some men not needed on watch lie quietly but sweatily in their bunks. They are not necessarily the ones who are most frightened. Most others prefer to sit wedged in some corner where they can have the reassurance of contact with shipmates.

Two depth charges are dropped by No. 1 destroyer. We can tell it is she because her screw noises are different, a higher-pitched zum-zum, zum-zum, zum-zum. The explosions have a larger bang and shake us more than any we have previously endured. They are close. Their whoomp-whoomps slam into us without the telltale click-click which comes from charges exploding farther away.

Some locker doors fly open, spilling tools, spare parts, even clothing on the deck. Loose-fitting deck plates jump several inches high and fall in crazy patterns on their frames. Loosened dust and particles of dirt sift through the air, already hot and humid. In the manoeuvring room Chief Braun and his electrician's mates, Grisanti and Mitchell, watch their meters grimly, listen for ominous arcing, sniff for the odour of burning insulation in the vital electrical control cubicle. A massive circuit breaker pops open. Grisanti shoves his control lever to neutral while Allan Braun braces himself clear of dangerous live leads. With gloved hands, he forces the circuit breaker shut. Sweat pours from his bowed head and spatters on the floor plate.

In the maze of the pump room's machinery and piping, Phil Carano struggles to control a leak on the discharge side of the trim pump. He curses when he slips on the wet, slimy floor plate and cuts his shin against a pipe flange.

I wondered what effect the explosions were having on our reluctant torpedo. Then I realised that as long as I could wonder, they were having none. Obviously the torpedo had not armed; it had not exploded even though exposed to full sea pressure at 360 feet and to the overpressure of depth charging.

There was no way to sight the torpedo or to tell just how far out of the tube it extended. If pressure from our forward motion had forced it back far enough, perhaps closing the muzzle door against it would push it back into the tube. Tudor Davis cranked the door's operating shaft until it would go no farther. He could feel the door coming up hard against the fish, but it would not budge. Apparently the tube's stop bolt had dropped into place behind the torpedo's guide stud, preventing any rearward motion. Somehow it had to be lifted.

Trying to be oblivious to the sounds of ships overhead and to depth charges, Ade and his men worked swiftly but carefully The normally sacrosanct interlocks had to be disconnected. These were safety devices designed to prevent firing unless shutter and outer door were properly aligned, and to prevent muzzle and breech doors from being open at the same time.

The procedure was lengthy. The impulse stop valve was closed, and all air was bled off the firing valve. Working in the cramped space outboard of the tube, Jack Perkins and Ed Bertheau removed the No. 4 tube shutter bar interlock. Next the interlock disconnect flag was unlocked and disengaged. Now a stout line could be secured to the stop rod. Hauling back on it, the stop bolt was retracted.

In the forward room Jack Barrett took the phone and spoke to yeoman Snell in the conning tower. 'Snell, tell the captain we've got the stop bolt up, and will try to force the fish back with the outer door. But we'd like an up-angle on the boat and maybe a little more speed would help.'

'OK,' I said. 'Tell them to stand easy till we give them the word.'

'Foss, search all around, and tell me what you've got.'

The destroyers were in the vicinity, but unsure of our location. We could hear them echo-ranging for us. There were now three of them in the search. Sometimes one would slow his screws or lie-to so that he could listen with his passive sonar. They were co-ordinating their efforts well.

When all three were once more moving and echo-ranging, we made our move. Not knowing what the rest of the day would bring, it was best to boat our stubborn fish now.

'Jack, give us a three degree up-angle. Tell the manoeuvring room to build up turns slowly to two-thirds.'

As our bow lifted and our speed slowly increased, Davis and Bertheau cranked on the muzzle door. They could feel the resistance as it pressed on the nose of the warhead. 'A little more angle would help.'

'Control, give us a five degree up-bubble.'

Cranked hard, the muzzle door slowly pushed the fish back into the tube and seated itself against the knife edge of the tube. With the torpedo safely on board, we slowed down and resumed our cautious evasion. Diagnosis of our casualty and examination of the fish would have to wait.

**Lieutenant-Commander B. Romanowski, Polish Navy, ORP *Dzik*;** from Report of 8th Mediterranean War Patrol, 23 December to 13 January 1944, ADM199/1853

*Dzik* was operating in the northern Aegean and based at Beirut as part of the 1st Submarine Flotilla.

After firing torpedoes on 7 January the top Stop Bolt of No. 1 tube did not return to position. The second reload went too far into the tube and started a 'hot run'. After rear door had been closed the torpedo forced open the bow cap and left the ship. It was then seen to run straight for about 100 yards and then circled and zigzagged round the ship. It was then quite difficult to keep away from the torpedo, but it soon disappeared.

**Lieutenant-Commander Jerzy ('George') Koziolowski, Polish Navy, ORP *Sokol*;** from 6th Mediterranean War Patrol 4–22 November 1943

There were three cases within two patrols of gun-action being broken, when the enemy was damaged and disabled, due to the same cause: defective ammunition. The defective ammunition (shell being loose on the cartridge) requires extremely careful handling. Jamming of the gun had happened after firing 36, 24 and 20 rounds. The physical strain on the part of the loader must be accounted for as a human factor; besides, slow, careful loading is hardly possible under an enemy's fire, and delays considerably the rate of fire.

The jamming of the gun takes away all confidence which a Commanding Officer must have in his armament. Surfacing at close range, for gun action against an armed target, thus gaining an initial surprise and a possible hit with the first round, becomes impossible. Bearing possible jamming of the gun in mind, gun action must start at long range, for 'safe' diving in case of jamming – this requiring more ammunition and longer time, with doubtful results.

**Lieutenant de Vaisseau Houbaud, Marine Nationale,** *Achille*;
from Patrol Report, 18–28 April 1940, ADM199/18

Patrol in these latitudes at this season imposes a great strain on the battery, and only new batteries would be able to stand up to the work. These patrols do not by any means make the best use of the high speed and great cruising radius of 1,500-ton submarines. Their silhouette is far too visible and the engine exhaust is so noisy as to render a withdrawal to seaward essential while charging. The chain of the wireless masts are particularly noisy while dived and it is submitted that the masts and chains should be disembarked, or at least the chains. The port tail clutch has a noisy spot on each revolution; consequently when attempting to evade, submarine proceeded at 80 revolutions starboard screw, port motor stopped. The following gear is also very noisy: the compass, lubricating pump, ballast pumps and hydroplanes. It is not considered practicable to stop the compass, which is of the Anschuts type, has no stand-by setting and is very awkward to restart and line up.

The fragility of the external fuel tanks is considered to be a grave disadvantage. The G.16 microphone equipment was of the greatest value in contributing to the safety of the submarine while dived.

## RAMMING

**Captain George Hunt, DSO\*, DSC\*, Royal Navy**; as told to the editor, and **Commander Jeremy Nash, OBE, DSC**; from *All Round Look,* 2001–2

At this time, George Hunt was First Officer and Jeremy Nash Armament Officer, HMS *Proteus*

JEREMY NASH: In the spring of 1940 the 4th Submarine Flotilla, including *Proteus*, with their splendid depot ship HMS *Medway*, was moved from Hong Kong to Alexandria, re-designated 1st flotilla and prepared for the expected entry of Italy into the war. After two pretty uneventful patrols, *Proteus* returned to Portsmouth for a much needed refit before returning to the Med. under her new CO, Philip Francis, to start a year which proved busy, exciting and pretty successful.

GEORGE HUNT: *Proteus* was a very successful submarine with 17 ships sunk to her credit and commanded by Lieutenant Commander Philip Francis, DSO. I enjoyed my time with him. The highlight of my last patrol in that boat was an exciting ramming match with the Italian destroyer *Sagittario*.

It was a very dark and squally night with torrential downpours. The officer of the watch got the captain on the bridge because he had seen what he suspected was a U-boat on the surface. Whether it was because he suggested that it was a U-boat or not I don't know, but they both did think it was a U-boat.

JEREMY NASH: *Proteus* was on patrol just to the west of the Ionian Islands when the [radar] operator reported a contact, range 4,000 yards. To reduce our silhouette and bring the stern tubes to bear, Lieutenant-Commander Francis turned stern on to this contact and, two minutes later, could make out a dark smudge. From its size he judged it to be an enemy submarine and so fired both tubes at it. No hits, and the target continued on its course. Though the range by this time was only about a thousand yards, the enemy appeared to be oblivious of our presence, so Francis went hard-astarboard and fired two of the bow tubes as soon as they would bear. Still no hits, so 'gun action stations' was ordered.

GEORGE HUNT: He was in the process of turning, so he fired two torpedoes at it, from his stern tubes, which was all he'd got there. Then he realised after a brief interval that, with an ever-increasing bow wave, the ship ahead – that they thought was a U-boat – was obviously a destroyer. That being the case, he certainly hadn't got time to dive and get clear, and so he decided that the only thing to do was to stay on the surface and meet the ship absolutely head-on. It was at this point that he ordered 'Gun action stations.' We had our for'ard hydroplanes turned out, ready for diving, and so of course they stuck out to a certain extent there at the bow.

JEREMY NASH: As armament officer, I left the fore-ends and dashed up on to the bridge to join my captain peering through our binoculars. To my consternation I suddenly realised that I could make out a mast and funnel. I remember saying, rather like a nervous schoolboy, 'Please sir, that's not a submarine – it's a destroyer.' Simultaneously Francis, too, realised this, and that the enemy had at last woken up and was turning towards us. He also realised instantly that there was no time for us to dive, so he coolly turned *Proteus*, bows on to the rapidly approaching enemy. So exactly did he judge it that, when the destroyer hit us, her stem was only a couple of feet from our own. There was a flash of steel on steel, she bounced slightly to starboard and passed down our port side almost rubbing the paint off our ballast tanks. It was almost uncanny; her guns were still trained fore and aft; no one shouted or fired a shot – in fact I don't remember seeing anyone at all as we stood mesmerised for a few moments. As soon as she was clear astern we dived as quickly as we could, expecting a real bollocking.

GEORGE HUNT: Neither the destroyer nor we, I may say, fired a shot. We were just too enthralled, I suppose, with the idea that we were going to be ramming one another. But I wasn't on the bridge so I don't know what passed through their minds. But I do know that I was very conscious of the drama! I was down below and second-in-command and in the control room, and I did call up the voice pipe to the captain. I reminded him that we were running on main motors, not the engines, and that amps were pouring out of the battery and we were going to have a heck of a job to replace them before we dived, because we had been charging the batteries and now he was using up all the power that we'd got!

He said, 'You wouldn't be worrying about the so-and-so box, if you were up here.'

So I said, 'Well, what's going on?'

And he ordered 'Collision stations!' I didn't ask anything else after that.

So we went to collision stations and there was a sort of thump and a few bangs and we did hit one another, but it was a sort of glancing blow, more or less. So the captain then decided to dive right away because the destroyer was fast disappearing.

What had happened was that, as the destroyer came down our side, the hydroplane sticking out went through her side, broke off and fell into her engine room! The hydroplanes are mounted on a trunnion, an axle if you like, so they work in concert; well, this was also broken off and couldn't work any more, so we had no for'ard hydroplanes. We had a heck of a lot of water coming in because the bolts that were holding down the trunnion of the two hydroplanes all sheared off, leaving eight one-and-a-quarter-inch holes in the pressure hull!

One of my jobs, of course, was to trim the submarine when we dived, and I was in the control room battling the trim with no for'ard hydroplanes – as I realised very quickly from reports and so on – and the water coming in. The engineer officer rushed along to assess the situation in the tube space and see what had happened. I mean it was fairly obvious with these solid bars of water coming in that the bolts had been sheared up top. So they produced bungs of wood very quickly and hammered them in. There was no great drama down below.

JEREMY NASH: When on the surface at night, we always kept our foreplanes turned out to save a few precious seconds should we have to dive in a hurry. Now the first thing we heard as we tumbled down the conning tower was from the second coxswain, 'Foreplanes jammed, sir'. Then came a report from the tube space forrard of a bad leak. This came from the foreplanes' mechanism hull gland, and we realised then that the port foreplane must have taken the brunt of the collision. Meanwhile, as George Hunt (later of *Ultor* fame) got the boat under control using the afterplanes alone, the Asdic operator trained his set astern to pick up the HE of our assailant. Then came his surprising report 'Target stopped, sir'. It dawned on us then that our strong and heavy foreplane must have sliced open the hull of the Italian destroyer and that she was probably in worse shape than we were – possibly sinking, we hoped. We were in no condition to continue our patrol, so set course for Alexandria, where we arrived without further incident to learn that our opponent was the small Italian destroyer *Sagittario*, which had managed to limp back to harbour. I doubt whether many people recognised the crossed tin openers, which I designed for our Jolly Roger – but that is what the emblem is supposed to be.

GEORGE HUNT: It took us about a week to get back to Alexandria by slow stages. And when we got alongside the depot ship, we discovered that another submarine, a sister submarine in every respect, had just had a battery fire and couldn't go to sea so we were given her for'ard hydroplanes which fitted ours exactly.

That had happened mid-February 1942. Very much later, in 1944 when I was on my way back to the UK in command of *Ultor*, we called in at Algiers – by this time Italy, having surrendered, were our co-belligerents. I went on board the depot ship and contacted the chief yeoman of signals because I had seen a whole lot of destroyers lying in pens over in the corner of the dockyard. One of them, he said, was the *Sagittario*, so I got a boat, went over to her and said: 'Is there anybody on board when they rammed a submarine in the Aegean in February 1942?'

And the engineer officer said: yes, he was. And he said: 'We sank the submarine.' So I said: 'Well, you didn't, actually.' But then we talked about the whole incident, and he took me to the quarterdeck where they'd mounted a bit of our port for'ard hydroplane on a little plaque with a notice underneath it saying they'd sunk this 'sommergibile' as they called it.

JEREMY NASH: There was a rather delightful sequel to this story. In 1951, I was driving Teredo in the Malta squadron and we went over to Sicily for a week's exercises with the Italian Navy. On the Friday evening, there was the customary party in their officers' club ashore and I found myself chatting to a very nice Italian of about my age about the war – rather as if it had been an exciting football match. He told me that he had served in a destroyer called the *Sagittario*. 'Really?' I responded. 'Were you in her when she collided with a British submarine one dark night off the coast of Greece?' 'Oh yes,' he replied proudly, 'We sank her!' With a laugh I said 'Oh no you didn't – I was in her and here I am.' Instead of being disappointed, my delightful companion called out to the others, 'Look! My friend is alive! I thought he was dead. More drinks!'

## SPARES AND REPAIRS

**Captain First Rank Viktor Korzh, USSR Navy, S-7;**
from *Red Star under the Baltic*

During the winter of 1941–2, with Leningrad under siege, engineer submariner Viktor Korzh and the crew of *S-7* were desperate to get their submarine ready for sea. Soviet submarines had been driven out of ice-free bases such as Tallinn by the Germans and lay immobilised in the ice either at Kronstadt or, like the *S-7*, at Leningrad, where the river Neva provided a difficult exit to the Gulf of Finland.

There was a great deal to be done on the inside of the ship. But all the same this was still not the most difficult area: everything was accessible to the gaze; everything could be touched by the hand. It was worse with the underwater part of the hull. We had no dry docks in Leningrad. All the jobs on the hull were carried out on the spot. Our divers got the rough end of the stick. We hacked a hole in the ice. In the piercing wind, Leading Seaman Piskunov put on his protective suit, lowered himself into the black water. The last that I could see were his fingers, reddened by the frost, gripping the glassy-smooth ice. But then they too disappeared into the ice-hole. Leading Seaman 1st Class Golenko was 'standing on signal'; he straightened the rubber hose and the signal rope. Petty Officer Viktor Yurkevich sat with earphones on his head and a microphone at his lips. Both were freezing cold, blue with it. Not far from them two ratings were rotating the handles of the air pump.

The diver reported that one of the blades of the starboard propeller was missing entirely, while the other two were badly bent, and that the casing of the stern hydroplanes was damaged. Yurkevich ordered him to move over to the port side. Golenko started to carry the hose over there and suddenly he shouted out: 'Watch out, Petty Officer!'

'Don't yell!' the Petty Officer quietened him down. 'You'll scare the diver.' And meanwhile he was already speaking into the microphone as calmly as he could: 'Piskunov, come up. Come up, I tell you.' But his calmness did not last long, and the Petty Officer raised his voice: 'I'm telling you, drop everything! No, no-one's dragging you. It's the hose catching on the ice. Come up as fast as you can. But be careful: keep your eye on the ice!'

The boat moved under the pressure of the ice. The hawsers' steel cables tightened and started to screech. The ice-hole beside the ship was closing up before our very eyes. They scarcely had time to haul the diver up out of it. The commotion brought Ramazanov running:

'Stop work immediately!'

For a couple of days he would not allow the divers under the ice. And then once more, taking it in turn, they began to go off into the cold dark water. They removed the heavy propellers from the shafts. The sailors winched them up onto the deck. The propellers were so warped they were a dreadful sight to see. We began to rack our brains: what could be done with them? There were few spare propellers in the brigade; each one was accounted for.

Luckily for us, at this juncture Osip Grigorievich Briansky, in former days a leading designer at a shipbuilding plant, came to us from the front line. After suffering from concussion, he had a spell in hospital, and was then assigned to the navy, where he was really in his element. Put in charge of the workshops, Briansky, on Ramazanov's orders, set about getting the gas-welding of non-ferrous materials up and running. They got the equipment from a local factory, the carbide from the shipbuilding plant where Briansky used to work, and the oxygen from another local firm.

But for a long time the job did not progress too well. The copper seals turned out to be full of bubbles; fragile. We tried everything under the sun! For the lower layer we tried brick, asbestos, poronite and ceramics. All to no avail. 'Nothing will work without graphite,' said Ramazanov. 'Go and look for some!'

But where were we to find it in the besieged city? We ransacked our own establishment: all the boats and the floating bases. None anywhere. We did the rounds of the neighbouring factories. None there! We found it in a place where it might have been the least expected – in the Alexander Nevsky Monastery. Who could have brought these heavy black slabs there and for what reason? They had evidently taken it to be coal and had wanted to use it for fuel. But it wouldn't burn ...

The graphite was brought to Smolny. The welding went right. The seam came out even and strong. Earlier we had tried to straighten out each propeller blade, no matter how badly warped. Then we plucked up our courage: we simply cut off the distorted part and welded on a new piece. But, of course, there still remained plenty of problems with the propellers. A propeller needs to be rectified against a template, each blade polished, and then given its proper balance. Using files, the ratings were working the intractable copper by hand, until it acquired the necessary shape.

## Admiral I. J. Galantin, US Navy, Retd, then lieutenant-commander, USS *Halibut*; from *Take Her Deep*

I was greatly concerned by the poor performance of the shipyard. Jack Hinchey and Joe Galligan were finding more and more delay and inefficiency in the repair and reinstallation of components for their departments. We found material in our reduction gear casings that looked suspiciously like sabotage. The main electric power control cubicle was being shock mounted, and the insulation of some of its wiring was strangely damaged. Welding was often improper; numerous flaws had to be chipped out and reworked. Pumps were not meeting their test requirements. An overhaul that should have taken no more than 90 days was clearly going to run over 100. When I turned to Kraut Dettmann for help he put all the pressure he could on management, but to little avail. The company's ship superintendent seemed powerless to get cooperation from the foremen of the various trade unions.

It was the last straw when Ray Stewart reported that we had almost sealed a workman in our forward fresh water tank. Fortunately he had looked inside before the manhole cover was bolted in place. A yard workman was in the tank, sleeping blissfully amid fumes of alcohol.

My frustration and bitterness overflowed in a letter I wrote home: 'It has been one discouragement and disappointment after another. In peacetime we used to gripe about overpaid civilian workmen and their workmanship, but those days were bliss compared to these. The power, the selfishness, the indifference, the lack of patriotism the unions now show is nauseating. It is disheartening to see what contemptible selfishness we are fighting to preserve. If the same slow, inefficient labor prevails throughout the country as here, think how many days the war is being prolonged, how many lives are being thrown away.' As our days in the yard counted down there was impatience and eagerness to be done with shop visits, with pressure tests, with measurements and inspections. There was only desire to trade the noise, confusion, and dirt which had overflowed *Halibut* for the quiet, orderly, clean life of the sea.

## Capitaine de Frégate Etienne Schlumberger, FNFL; from *L'Honneur et Les Rebelles de la Marine Française, 1940–1944*

At the end of 1941, Etienne Schlumberger was appointed second in command of the Free French submarine *Junon*, attached to the 9th Submarine Flotilla at Dundee.

So there we were in the wet dock at the Caledonian Shipyard. Sometimes the maintenance work went well, at other times less so. But we could exert a little pressure on the workers. They considered that battery charging was dangerous because of the risk of giving off hydrogen and the consequent danger of explosion. We lived with the same risk every day when recharging at sea; smoking was absolutely forbidden. The shipyard workers saw the opportunity for a bonus if they worked on board during recharging. And so we would tip off the best workers as to when we would be recharging ...

But sometimes it didn't go so well. On one occasion the crane operators went on strike just as we were about to load our torpedoes, a delay which contributed to our missing the *Tirpitz* (and probably saved our lives). Another time, the boat was being careened in drydock. Meeting the completion schedule was vital; we needed a high tide to get her out because of her draught: the tide had to be very high. The workers went on strike. I was all in favour of getting the crew to paint the hull but was forbidden to do so because it might lead to a general strike. So I asked to speak to the workers. That was agreed; we got together. I told them: 'We are a long way from home. We are here to fight; but you, you can go home every night.' They understood that I was speaking from the heart and they went back to work. The boat was able to leave on the next high tide.

Another problem: nuts and bolts, etc. Our screws were metric. The British use a different thread – Whitworth – based on inches. For example, British bolts don't fit French nuts. To replace clutch screws we had to use some bolts taken from the airlock in the heads.

**Commander M. B. St-John, DSC, Royal Navy, *L.26*; from *All Round Look***

In one of his essays Francis Bacon stated, 'Adversity is not without comforts and hopes', and in the Second World War, I began to realise the truth of this assertion. As a Lieutenant aged 24, I had been appointed early in 1941 to my first command, an ancient but cell-preserved relic of the First World War, HM Submarine *L.26*, undergoing an extensive refit in North Yard at Devonport.

One day there walked into our dock-side office a singular and striking character who might have stepped out of a Joseph Conrad adventure. Lean, with hunched shoulders and short crinkly hair receding in a widow's peak, he had engaging brown eyes which advertised a ready wit and generosity of spirit; a nose, squashed down into a short upper lip, shouted ANZAC, above a jutting underslung jaw which, in contrast to the eyes, implied a degree of belligerence. This rugged countenance was perpetually on the verge of a grin when not actually grinning.

'You the Skipper? I'm Kerr, your new Engineer Officer,' he said as he crushed my hand to pulp in one of the largest mitts I had ever seen. Flinching,

I made him welcome and put him in the picture concerning the refit.

Lieutenant (E) Gilbert Kerr, RNR, to give him his correct style, became 'Digger Kerr' from that moment ... He had come hot foot into the Submarine Service from the Merchant Navy with a Chief's Certificate in marine diesels and a burning ambition to get his teeth into the enemy. It soon became clear that he knew more about the technicalities of our refit than the dockyard hierarchy but, being ignorant of British naval dockyard practice, he unfortunately did not hesitate to point out their shortcomings, in broad and picturesque Australian terms with disastrous consequences. Added to the dockyard officers' 'we couldn't care less' attitude, the entrenched, obstructive and ridiculous demarcation rules, ruthlessly applied by the dockyard 'mateys', were beyond his comprehension. Their self-serving attitude in wartime drove him barking mad. He was continually blowing his top to the extent that he often drove them off the job and eventually their union representatives on to the Admiral Superintendent's door step. There they joined the fortissimo diapason of complaint, in full flow from the dockyard officers.

It was tricky for me as his CO, for he was invariably right and how could I explain the arcane, antediluvian practices that had, for generations, obstructed and debilitated our naval yards? For him, they were simply unbelievable.

It was inevitable that the Admiral Superintendent sent for me and, in no uncertain terms, ordered me to stop the rot. Having delivered this bottle, he had recourse to another more congenial sort – Plymouth Gin – over the consumption of which he bemoaned the imponderable problem of the dockyard's appalling lack of morale and asked me, somewhat desperately I thought, if I had any constructive suggestions. I hadn't.

I duly summoned Digger and, doing my best to overcome the handicap of our disparate ages (he was four years my senior, for those in their twenties a significant difference), and gave him strict orders that in the event of any future trouble he was to keep his mouth shut and report to me personally.

It seemed I had succeeded in getting the message across to this free-ranging and, as yet, not very well known spirit, for all became peace on his front if not in general. For this was happening in the midst of the Nazis' saturation bombing of Plymouth and Devonport, certainly in retrospect, one of this submariner's more rugged war experiences. Day and night, the HE and incendiary bombs rained relentlessly down and, without fail, the dockyard 'mateys' took to the hills, leaving the naval personnel from the barracks and those standing by ships refitting (like ourselves) to act as air-raid wardens and fire-fighters ...

As I was far from confident that Digger's good behaviour would last, I kept a closer than usual watch on proceedings in the dry dock where *L.26* lay. Thus it was that, with the boat in sight of our office window, I was frequently glancing up to ensure play was fair. Sure enough and, as I feared, the moment of truth eventually came. They were replacing the hull-plates over the engine-room, a very critical operation, and there was Digger on the dockside, clearly in hot conflict with the Engineer Afloat's pompous and obstructive foreman. Grabbing my cap I dashed across but was too late. As I drew near I heard him shout, point blank in to the foreman's face: 'You f...ing well make me sick', whereon he opened his large mouth and was copiously sick over the foreman's trousers and boots. It was a stunning performance and I dare say that never, since Nelson with his blind eye at Copenhagen, has the Navy enjoyed such success from the disobedience of a superior's order. The dockyard 'mateys' present were turned to stone, months agape, whilst those of my crew, lucky to be present, fell about in rapturous merriment. Digger had won. Game, set and match. We never had another spot of bother completing our refit, for the dockyard could not do enough to satisfy our every whim – anything to hasten our departure ...

## MISTAKEN IDENTITY

**Lieutenant de Vaisseau Houbaud, Marine Nationale, *Achille*;**
from Patrol Report, ADM199/1857

At 2230, 19 May 1940, the French submarine *Achille* surfaced and set course to return to Dundee, having completed her North Sea patrol. At 0830 the following day she passed a mine to starboard; three hours later she spotted another to port.

0840. Sighted an aeroplane astern at about 500 metres. Tried to send out a recognition signal, but failed. Dived to 30 metres.

While still at a depth of 25 metres four or five bombs in succession fell exceedingly near, causing havoc on board; lamps burst, windows broke, battery terminals were loosened. Went down to 40 metres ...
1056. Surfaced.
1925. Anchored at King George V wharf.

The principal damage caused by the bombardment was the following:
All the hydrophones and supersonic sounder put out of action.
Partial shifting of the main battery.
Fracture of several air service junctions, all internal, fortunately.
Leakage of fuel from the external tanks.
Breakage of a large number of lamps, air gauges and ammeters, dislocation of a batter supply breaker.
Breakage of all the bridge windows and navigation lights.
Magnetic compass upset.

The crew has undergone these successive bombardments with praiseworthy composure ...

An investigation produced the following RAF report dated 21 May 1940.

BOMBING ATTACK ON THE FRENCH SUBMARINE *ACHILLE* AT 0825 ON 20 MAY, 1940

1. I have investigated this incident and submit the following remarks.

2. The attack was carried out by Hudson aircraft 'O' of No. 233 Squadron.

3. This aircraft took off at 0340 on the 20th May to carry out the first sorties of the L.5 anti-submarine patrol. On reaching the area of patrol, the navigator found the wind to be zero, the surface of the sea entirely smooth.

4. At 0927 hours ... a dark object was sighted approximately 10 miles on the port beam. The Captain of the aircraft turned towards it but was unable to make any accurate observations owing to the dazzle of the early sun on the glass-like surface of the sea. The submarine was seen to submerge. After flying for another 4 or 5 minutes and arriving over the place where the submarine had dived, a well defined oil track was seen on the smooth water.

An attack was carried out by stick bombing with three 250lb anti-submarine bombs released by automatic distributor. No hits or indication of damage were observed ...

5. No recognition signals were observed from the submarine.

6. The position was calculated to be ... definitely well to the North of the northern limiting line of the 'no bombing' area.

7. Upon arrival at a landfall, calculations showed the actual position where the attack was made to be ... well INSIDE the 'No Bombing Area' and 64 nautical miles from where the Captain and Navigator believed themselves to be ...

12. It is requested that you will cause to be conveyed to the Captain of the French submarine '*ACHILLE*' my most sincere regrets for the danger and inconvenience caused to himself, his crew and his craft.

It would be very much appreciated if I could be informed on the next occasion when the *ACHILLE* comes into these waters in order that I may have the opportunity of calling and making personal apologies.

(Signed) Charles Breese
Air Vice Marshal
Commanding, No. 18 Group.

## Luitenant ter Zee 1 Peter de Jong, Koninklijke Marine

There was a habit that if, you came from patrols in Norway, the boats signalled: 'ETA such-and-such, RAF permitting.'

## WEATHER

**Ammiraglio Elio Sandroni, Regia Marina, *Perla***

Those who have never sailed in a submarine know that you can always evade the effects of heavy weather (Force 8) by submerging. Easy, isn't it? But those who say so are overlooking a small detail: for several reasons, this means of escape isn't always an option ... and if it is not possible to submerge, what can a poor submarine do when caught in a squall or worse, in a storm? There is only one answer: keep rolling. And when the sea is in a bad mood, submarines really do roll, far more than the majority of surface ships.

I'm going to tell you about some incidents which occurred on the R Smg *Perla* in which, as a midshipman, I was the Navigation Officer on passage from Massaua to Bordeaux, which lasted 82 days, going round Africa and passing 200 miles south of CGH ...

14 March 1941 found us 120 miles north of Cape Amber, the northernmost tip of Madagascar and we decided to pass to the east of the island to reach Point 'A' (Lat. 35° S Long. 50° E.) where we had a rendezvous with the German auxiliary cruiser, *Atlantis* ... En route to the rendezvous, *Perla* followed the coast of Madagascar at a distance of about 50 miles out. However, on 17 March, after a couple of days of generally calm sailing, the barometer began to fall and towards evening the Force 5 wind unexpectedly dropped. Almost immediately an extremely strong southerly wind sprang up which quickly brought up a heavy sea. The *Perla* was definitely in the middle of an equatorial typhoon.

Towards 1200, it became increasingly difficult to keep the bows to a sea which was raising something like 10 metre waves, so the course was altered in order to run before the sea or keep it on the stern quarter. The waves hung over us, breaking into wild horses; the spray slashed visibility.

The furious force of the wind tore strips of sea from the breakers, and in concert with the beating rain, whipped air and water together, making it hard to use the binoculars. The watch on the bridge, firmly secured by safety lines, were simply unable to scan their sector of the horizon. So as not to be completely submerged by the high waves that swept the conning tower, they kept having to cling on to different rails to counter the dangerous rolling of the boat and were forced to take shelter as best they could behind the periscope shears. The weather was most certainly cyclonic.

The sea was mountainous and waves arrived from every direction. Luckily the barometer began to rise slowly, but the sea, though slightly calmer, still ran high. Anyhow, we resumed our original course, proceeding directly for Point 'A'. We managed to make only a few solar observations to verify the dead reckoning.

After having been reprovisioned by the *Atlantis*, the *Perla* proceeded towards the Cape of Good Hope.

During daylight on 4 April the weather took a turn for the worse. A strong wind blew up from the SW with frequent squalls. The two hours on watch on the bridge became increasingly exhausting and hard to bear. Unfortunately, the pump for the toilet we used when running submerged was only working erratically, so it was necessary to set up in their place two drums with a drop of diesel to serve as latrines for the men.

The barometer was plunging. The sea and the wind rose throughout the day until they reached storm-force with a Force 9 sea. At 2100, unable to face the waves, the *Perla* steered towards the land to keep the heavy seas astern. Next day, though the sea remained stormy, the submarine was forced to alter course to avoid getting any closer to the coast and, above all, the enemy shipping lanes. We held a course with the sea on our bows, en route for the Cape of Good Hope.

We reached the point where two oceans meet!

At 2300 on 7 April we passed Cape Agulhas at a distance of 200 miles. Running half-speed ahead and with the ballast and diving tanks and the double bottom empty for maximum buoyancy, the *Perla* proceeded towards Point 'B' (Lat. 25° S. Long. 20° W.) for the rendezvous with a German supply vessel on a course that kept the sea on the port quarter.

Those on the bridge were fascinated by the terrifying beauty of the angry sea and a sky that was ravaged by massive thunderclaps. The lookouts on the bridge, while drenched by the breakers, were saturated with oxygen in the ozone-rich air, and rode the waves in a state of euphoria, because it really was a case of the *Perla* riding the storm. And the continuous, unpredictable see-saw caused by the veering from side to side combined with the rolling and pitching, to the accompaniment of the rhythmic roar of the engines, the scream of the wind and the thundering seas, assailing the boat with indescribable violence.

Living conditions below, even when the submarine was running with the sea astern or on the stern quarter, were stressful, and for that reason the strict rule that reserved the bridge for the watch was relaxed a little: one pair at a time, the men were allowed to come up to recover in the fresh air and smoke a cigarette. Inside the boat, the men were dry; they did not suffer the cold, nor were they lashed by the ocean's angry spray; they ran no risk of being swept away by a wave. Nevertheless, many of them envied those on watch on the bridge ...

The *Perla*, sailing on the surface in a Force 9, at the mercy of high seas, behaved like a wild horse. While I was in my bunk I asked the Engineer-

Lieutenant, Leo Bacchini, if there was any danger of the *Perla* breaking in two, as her hull creaked dreadfully whenever she found herself poised on the crest of a wave. Bacchini smiled at me and told me to have no fear and not be frightened. Then I turned over and tried to go to sleep. The sharp and unexpected lurching forced men to move around as little as possible to avoid being hurled against the bulkheads, and making life harder for those on duty. The engineers had to keep checking the running of the engines to avoid breakdowns when the stern was out of the water and the propellers, turning in empty air, sent their rpms off the scale. The electricians were constantly monitoring the battery compartments to check that no acid was escaping from the batteries; from the conning tower hatch as well as the engine inductions, a torrent of water poured in, heavily occupying the control room watch who had to pump continuously to get rid of it.

The helmsman had his hands full keeping the right course in spite of the strong 'coming to' of the boat ...

In heavy weather one of the most important problems that had to be addressed was that of providing meals and the requisite cooking of the food which was prepared in the auxiliary engine room in a large electric pressure-cooker which was set up on an apparatus with cardanic suspension. Unfortunately, due to an unexpected problem with the watertight seal of the lid and the cardanic suspension, the pressure-cooker had to be hung from the ceiling on a steel cable, with a seaman checking that nothing spilled out amidst all the trouble caused by the rolling and pitching. In a high and confused sea, hot food inevitably gave way to the famous caponata: into the big pot went biscuits which were steeped in water – quite possibly seawater – to which was added tuna in oil, onion (if there was any), anchovies, olive oil, capers and a drop of vinegar. The cook rolled up his sleeves and, having washed his hands, did his utmost to mix the various ingredients.

The meal was served into the mess tins using a large ladle. You ate the slop with a spoon and sat down, trying to hold yourself steady by bracing your legs against one of the bulkheads.

Another problem to be overcome in heavy weather was that of measuring the altitude of the stars and the sun with a sextant to calculate the position. At my 'Stop!' a sailor beside me repeated the command to another seaman, usually the RT or signalman, who was at the chronometer in the RT cabin. I really was fighting a battle to stay on my feet, take care that the sextant mirrors did not get wet and that I did not lose sight of the stars through the monocular.

In rough conditions, anything that hasn't been secured can become a missile capable of serious damage. I remember how some locker bolts gave way, unleashing articles of clothing, bottles, tools and materials, shoes and toiletries which rolled and ricocheted around the deck forcing the crew to demonstrate amazing agility to avoid injury.

The fore and aft torpedo rooms are areas which really put their personnel to the test. In these two end compartments, the oscillation caused by the boat's pitching is so much greater that time spent in them is a real ordeal. Anyone who doesn't manage to anchor himself to a support runs the risk of being thrown against the sides or even the ceiling, while those who have to move around must choose the precise moment when the floor seems stable between the end of one oscillation and the start of the next.

For the men in the torpedo rooms it's like being on a roller-coaster without being able to see where the track is going. Talking of roller-coasters reminds me of our Chief Torpedoman, Albino, a cheerful fellow from Trieste, who always had a decent bottle of wine in his hand and swigged it when the sea was being difficult.

Not everyone in the submarine enjoyed the same conditions: there were the privileged ones who, on duty, were stationed in the compartment sandwiched between the Control Room and the Engine Room. That area, which included the auxiliary room, also used as sleeping accommodation for part of the crew, is well ventilated by the flow of air given off by the engines which, even though very humid, is a relief to those who can take advantage of it. The unending rolling of the submarine is also hard on men when they are on a long patrol.

The vomit of those crew members who hadn't managed to conquer the dreaded seasickness, overflow from the bilges, the acridity of diesel fumes, toilets, the smell of unwashed bodies, the imperfect system for emptying the toilets, the occasional upsetting of a drum filled with urine and excrement, the feeble ventilation resulting from the poor condition of the extractors – all threatened to make the air unbreathable at any moment.

The crew was divided into two watches, taking four-hour turns of duty; the bridge lookouts and the helmsman, however, enjoyed four hours off and two hours on. To get away from the nauseous atmosphere, the ones off watch tried to find themselves a nook in the auxiliary room with the draught.

Sleeping, even for those who didn't stand a watch, was a case of wishful thinking if they didn't manage to strap themselves into their bunk with their legs wide apart. I remember that once, having climbed up to the edge of my bunk, I was thrown out of the alcove by a sudden and violent roll. Luckily I landed on the open desk of the officers' wardroom, which was strewn with hoods belonging to the lookouts, and that softened the impact and reduced the damage to some bruising …

That brings to mind, with a touch of great sadness,* the accident that happened to my dear friend and fellow midshipmen, Biagio Gallio, the submarine's armament officer. Following a powerful roll, a massive wave overwhelmed the sail. Beneath the force of so much water, Gallo's safety line broke and he was dragged and battered across most of the length of the platform, from his post on the right to the left across the periscope shears. Just as Gallo was being washed under the stanchion and in danger of going overboard, the aft lookout on the port side, who, fortuitously, was fairly strong, managed to grab him by his jacket and hold on to him long enough for him to be pulled to safety with the help of the second lookout ...

When our commander thought that the sea and the wind had subsided a little, he judged that the submarine had headed into a fairly calm area, and he ordered submersion with all due precautions. The contrast from proceeding on the surface to proceeding submerged was astonishing. In a few dozen seconds the men went from a kind of hell and chaos created out of noise, crashing, banging, discomfort, nausea and the limits of physical effort, into a silent world where they could at last enjoy some refreshing rest. At a depth of 60 metres, perfectly trimmed and with the motors going slow ahead, the boat was more or less stable. The majority of the crew voluntarily decided against a cold meal, preferring to get some sleep because the need for rest was paramount. The only ones who stayed awake were those in charge of the boat.

**Korvettenkapitän Peter Cremer, Kriegsmarine, *U-333*;**
from *U-boat Commander*

After a failed attack (see pages 236–8), *U-333* continued on her cruise at the start of 1942.

Richer by that experience, and not exactly in joyful mood, we continued the journey. The weather showed its most unfriendly side: sky dark, water as grey as lead. Not for nothing does the loading line 'Winter North Atlantic' on the sides of merchant ships allow for lighter loading than in the peaceful summer. But the U-boat was up to the neck in it and had to take everything as it came, including the heavy storm that dragged on without ceasing for over a week, during which the wind backed and veered between SW and NW, screaming and howling up to hurricane strength. Within a few hours on 8 January an enormous sea developed which threatened to smash everything, and we met squalls which tore the combs from the wave tops. Visibility closed in, rain alternated with snow, sleet and hail. As far as the eye could see there were only rolling hills with strips of foam coursing down their sides like the veins in

* Sadness, because Gallio did not survive the war.

marble. On the surface, the U-boat literally climbed the mountainous seas, plunged through the wave crests, hung for a moment with its stem in the empty air and plunged down the other side into the trough of the waves. When it buried its nose, the screws in the stern seemed to be revolving in air. Then the stern dropped down, the screws disappeared in the maelstrom and the exhaust broke off with a gurgle.

In the hard thumps *U-333* shuddered in every frame member like a steel spring. Striking high up in front against the conning tower and from behind into the open bridge screen, the seas smothered us and we had to shut the conning-tower hatch for a while to prevent foundering.

Wet to the skin despite oilskins and sea-boots, the bridge watch were scarcely able to hold the heavy binoculars with their clammy hands. Wedged between periscope supports and bridge casing, they all hung on by safety belts and swivels, which did not prevent the sea tearing away a lookout during the continuing storm and hurling him to the deck, with serious injury to his eye.

Seen from below, the waves were as high as houses; they struck the deck like an avalanche and swept away the few things they could seize on. Fenders and lines under the outer casing disappeared, supports cracked like match-wood. The boat listed up to 60 degrees – as the pendulum in the control room showed – so that it seemed one could plunge one's bare hands in the water, then righted itself like a self-righting doll, owing to its low centre of gravity, only to tip over immediately to the other side. It was uncanny at night when the black hills rose and fell under a starless sky, phosphorescent combers rolled up and fell away. Far and wide, not a sign of a ship.

Wind Force 8 was the least, then the storm rose to Force 10, and in breath-taking squalls reached a full 11 to 12: a hurricane! The Beaufort scale ends at 12: wind speeds of over 65 knots, air filled with foam and spray … sea completely white, all distant visibility ceases, wave lengths 300 metres and more …

The inside of the boat was like a dice cup with everything whirling about. Those who had something to do groped from support to support. Sleeping was hardly possible; one just dozed. Those lying in the hammocks swayed to and fro like washing hung to dry; those in the wire bunks buckled themselves in. Anything lying on the tables had long since fallen off despite the surrounding fiddles, more than half our crockery was also long since broken; here metal would have been more practical than china. Nothing would stay put on the cooker, including, of course, hot food. The air in the boat was thick with smells and cold as well, but still more tolerable than after a long period submerged.

North Atlantic winter! In such weather waging war stops of its own accord because everyone has enough on his hands without it – even when we unexpectedly sighted a tanker about 3,000 metres away. I tried to keep contact and went on to a parallel course to attack after nightfall, it being impossible to attack straight away because of the high seas and colossal swell. Wind Force 10. At one moment the tanker was on a mountainous wave, the next she had disappeared into the valley. Then I lost sight of her altogether. Snowfall and visibility between 1,000 and 100 metres. Later, in the afternoon, when we encountered one another again the tanker at once turned towards me. This captain was no greenhorn either. Snow squalls separated us again. I tried a run-in again at high speed, but had to break off as the breaking seas threatened to carry away the bridge watch. Heaved-to, to ride out the hurricane, that meant marking time, making little more than one knot.

The same thing happened the following day when a steamer appeared dimly through a curtain of snow, disappeared in the rhythm of the sea, reappeared and again disappeared. I turned towards her but could not get close and the steamer ran off in front of my nose. When I tried to follow her at still higher speed the sea tore a lookout from his metal safety belt and wounded him.

So it went on, day after day. Between times, when it could no longer be endured, I ordered 'all hands to diving stations' and went to the cellar. The wild movements diminished, but at 40 metres the boat was still rocking and it was only at 50 metres that it lay still. We cleared, up. The cook brought a delicious-smelling stew to table and everyone fell to. Eat and sleep, hear nothing, see nothing. Music – ? No music at any price! It would have been a source of noise. The crew needed rest.

When we surfaced again, after some hours, the captain enjoyed the privilege of opening the conning-tower hatch and being the first to get wet. Now he was standing again on the bridge, a towel knotted round his neck, and the water ran in through the top of his oilskins and out again at the bottom. To wipe dry the dripping binoculars was hardly possible and there was little point in using them. In that weather there was no need to look at the sky; not an aircraft was to be seen. Eventually the storm abated, the snow squalls ceased and the sun even appeared again for a few minutes.

# 1939

In 1938 Hitler had assured Grossadmiral Erich Raeder that there would not be a war with Britain before 1943. Had that proved the case, Kapitän zur See – later Grossadmiral – Karl Dönitz might by that time have had the 300 U-boats which he regarded as essential to strangle Britain's supply lines: 100 on patrol, 100 on passage and 100 at their bases at any one time. In the event, on the day war broke out he did not even have one-fifth of that total. Both France (77 submarines) and Britain (69) were numerically superior to Germany's 65. In all cases, not every submarine was operational, immediately available or even suitable for the particular war that would be fought. Germany's 57 operational submarines included few ocean-going boats for the vital Atlantic campaign, and torpedoes were to be plagued by faulty fuzes. None the less, until improvements in anti-submarine warfare forced the U-boats to behave more like submarines and less like motor torpedo boats with diving capability, many were disproportionately effective. French boats were fast, but had a complex torpedo firing system. Those that had the opportunity to do so, proved themselves useful. British submarines built in the run-up to the war – the S- and T-Classes – were versatile and effective, while the small U-Class, initially designed as unarmed boats for A/S training, were reliable and manoeuvrable, ideal for a Mediterranean campaign.

Less than twelve hours after the official start of the Second World War, a submarine opened hostilities when *U-30*, commanded by Oberleutnant zur See Fritz-Julius Lemp, torpedoed the US-bound British liner *Athenia* some 250 miles north-west of Ireland, in contravention of Prize Regulations. The loss of the *Athenia* and the deaths of more than a hundred of her passengers and crew caused anger and indignation on both sides of the Atlantic and serious embarrassment to the Germans.

Even before the declaration of war, every one of the 43 available German U-boats had been sent out into waiting positions in remote areas of the Atlantic and strategic sectors around Britain, farther into the Atlantic towards Gibraltar or up into the Baltic. That was an untenable situation, and a system of reliefs had to be instituted to allow the submarines to return home, refuel, reprovision and repair, and to give the crews a rest. In the early months of the war, the number of U-boats in the Atlantic was sometimes more of a token presence than a strength. As a result they obtained much of their initial successes operating alone against single targets rather than in coordinated action against the convoys which had begun to be formed within a few days of the commencement of hostilities. For the forseeable future there was no possibility of the Allies escorting convoys throughout their voyages, and those approaching or leaving Britain could count on protection only for the first or last stage of the voyage. The U-boats in the Atlantic, therefore, lurked mainly in the Southern and Western Approaches.

On 17 September, Kapitänleutnant Otto Schuhart, commanding U-29, torpedoed the aircraft carrier HMS *Courageous*, and although the total British merchant tonnage sunk in the early weeks of the war (before 23 September French merchant ships were not allowed to be sunk) was not spectacular, it was a warning of what might be achieved if sufficient submarines could be built.

The penetration of the British anchorage at Scapa Flow and the sinking of HMS *Royal Oak* with the loss of 800 lives by Korvettenkapitän Günther Prien and U-47 came as the greatest shock to the Allies in 1939 and confirmed that the Admiralty's decision to sink more blockships in vulnerable channels was correct.

However, British mines laid in the Channel and Royal Navy warships fitted with Asdic to some extent redressed the situation, with nine U-boats sunk by the close of the year. *U-36* was the first to be lost to submarine attack when torpedoed off Kristiansand by HMS *Salmon* on 4 December, the prelude to an exceptional fortnight for the S-Class boat in the North Sea. Allied submarines suffered only one loss before the end of the year, and that was a tragic case of mistaken identity.

In terms purely of submarines, the Allies comprised France and Britain, though the latter's crews might include Empire and Dominion personnel. Then, on 20 September the Polish submarine *Wilk* was escorted into Rosyth after escaping from the Bay of Gdansk, weathering air attack and evading German destroyers. On 14 October a second Polish submarine, *Orzel*, completed an epic evasion. A month later, the Polish Government In Exile agreed to place its navy under Royal Navy operational control, the first of several such agreements with occupied countries over the coming months and years.

By the end of 1939, neutral ships in French and British waters were being threatened, and the German tally of victims in the early weeks of 1940 would have been vastly higher if Dönitz could have conjured up enough U-boats to take on the convoys in the wolf-pack formations in which he had such faith. British submarines operating in the North Sea around Norway and Holland, by contrast, were largely occupied in intelligence-gathering. French boats had been deployed off the coast of West Africa to keep an eye on a number of German tankers and freighters which had taken refuge in the creeks at the outbreak of war and were strongly suspected of resupplying U-boats.

The few British and French submarines in the Mediterranean at this time had little enough to do, and the Indian Ocean and the Far East presented merely the possibility of intercepting an occasional German merchantman. However, on 29

September the French submarine *Poncelet*, patrolling north of the Azores, captured the German merchant ship *Chemnitz*, which was flying the neutral Norwegian flag in an attempt to get home.

During the first months of the war the German Supreme Naval Command ordered Dönitz to send three U-boats down to Gibraltar and one of these (*U-26*) penetrated into the Mediterranean. It failed to sink anything, and Dönitz decided against further such missions for the moment. The Atlantic would remain the priority.

## NORTH SEA, BALTIC AND ATLANTIC

### Adolf Schmidt, Kriegsmarine, *U-130*

Adolf Schmidt had been wounded in an aerial attack while boarding another of Lemp's victims, the *Fanan Head*, eleven days after the sinking of the *Athenia*, and Lemp – who had carried out the rest of his patrol with strict adherence to the spirit as well as the letter of the law – obtained permission to land him at Reykjavik. The following testimony was given on 15 January 1946 at Nuremburg.

I, Adolf Schmidt, Official Number N 1043-33T, do solemnly declare that:

I am now confined to Camp No. 133, Lethbridge, Alberta.

On the first day of war, 3rd September, 1939, a ship of approximately 10,000 tons was torpedoed in the late hours of the evening by the *U-30*. After the ship was torpedoed and we surfaced again, approximately half an hour after the explosion, the Commandant called me to the tower in order to show me the torpedoed ship. I saw the ship with my very eyes, but I do not think that the ship could see our U-boat at that time on account of the position of the moon. Only a few members of the crew had an opportunity to go to the tower in order to see the torpedoed ship. Apart from myself, Oberleutnant Hinsch was in the tower when I saw the steamer after the attack.

I observed that the ship was listing. No warning shot was fired before the torpedo was launched. I myself observed much commotion on board the torpedoed ship. I believe that the ship had only one smoke stack.

In the attack on this steamer one or two torpedoes were fired which did not explode, but I myself heard the explosion of the torpedo which hit the steamer.

Oberleutnant Lemp waited until darkness before surfacing.

I was severely wounded by aircraft 14th September, 1939.

Oberleutnant Lemp shortly before my disembarkation in Reykjavik, 19th September, 1939, visited me in the forenoon in the petty officers' quarters where I was lying severely wounded.

Oberleutnant Lemp then had the petty officers' quarters cleared in order to be alone with me.

Oberleutnant Lemp then showed me a declaration under oath according to which I had to bind myself to mention nothing concerning the incidents of 3rd September, 1939, on board the *U-30*.

This declaration under oath had approximately the following wording: 'I, the undersigned, swear hereby that I shall keep secret all happenings of 3rd September, 1939, on board the *U-30*, from either foe or friend, and that I shall erase from my memory all happenings of this day.'

I signed this declaration under oath, which was drawn up by the Commandant in his own handwriting, very illegibly with my left hand.

Later on in Iceland when I heard about the sinking of the *Athenia*, the idea came into my mind that the *U-30* on the 3rd September, 1939, might have sunk the *Athenia*, especially since the Captain caused me to sign the above-mentioned declaration.

Up to today I have never spoken to anyone concerning these events.

Due to the termination of the war I consider myself freed from my oath.

### Outside ERA Julien Deschamps, Marine Nationale, *Psyché*

At the start of the war, the French coastal submarine *Psyché* was based at Oran as part of the 2nd Escadrille; from www.sous-mama.org

We returned to Casablanca on 10 September, mooring at the end of the Lyautel jetty near the sailing club. As soon as we had arrived, the paintbrushes came out and everyone got painting. We left no trace of her number nor any copper: everything was black. After a quick trip to the showers, we loaded food and fuel for fifteen days, our maximum, and at night we sailed, along the Moroccan coast, from north to south. On the evening of the 16th, the captain called us all together in the after ends and made a little speech:

'We are the first French submarine to carry out a war patrol. I trust I can rely on you just as you can rely on me.' When we were at harbour stations, only the captain knew the destination. He was getting orders directly from the Admiralty, and given that we were off Morocco, it was generally agreed it was the Azores, the Cape Verde Islands or the Canary Islands.

We patrolled or took station at the mouth of every bay or port at fixed times. When we took on food it was not possible to embark more than two days' worth of fresh food. The fridge was too small; bread didn't last more than two days before turning green and hairy. So after two days we only had tinned food to eat. Every evening we took a quinine tablet as a precaution against malaria, and every two days, tea with rum. We were dived for 250 hours a month, and the temperature could get up to 67 degrees [C] around the motors. It goes without saying that we dressed lightly and that every movement made us sweat. We also had a few unwanted passengers: rats, but I was lucky because they had decided to make themselves at home on the port side whilst my bunk was on the starboard side. They particularly liked to get into a middle bunk where they nibbled the feet of the occupant without waking him. A team had been assembled to catch them, comprising an officer, the Chief ERA and five leading seamen including myself.

We spent some seventeen hours a day submerged and if there was time at night we took it in turns to smoke a cigarette in the conning tower. The snorkel didn't exist at that time, and during a long dive we had to use the auxilite to purify the air. We spent most of the time lying down because it was forbidden to wander around to avoid spoiling the trim. One man at a time was able to go forward just to get the food … We usually ate sitting down on the deck or the lower bunks. There was a shortage of water, too, and you weren't allowed to shave or wash during the last days of a patrol.

On 14 October 1939 we were proceeding towards the Canaries with provisions for fourteen days. These patrols usually went off well. One day off Porto Cruz the torpedo petty officer made a mistake or gave the wrong order and the submarine surfaced instead of coming to periscope depth as had been ordered. She broke surface in the middle of a fishing fleet which quickly shot off without waiting to find out what was going on. The captain found suitable words of praise for the torpedo petty officer.

The patrols went on in the same fashion: on the surface at night and looking for traffic; identifying and observing vessels; sending messages to Casablanca. Some vessels were intercepted at gunpoint but allowed to proceed after their identity had been checked. One day, around 0500 I was in the conning tower when the signalman reported there was smoke ahead to port. I scrambled down the conning tower into the control room and made for my post aft. We were already diving. Suddenly I heard a strange noise and saw a beret caught up in the toothed wheels of the driving wheel of the aft hydroplanes. I tugged it free and threw it in the dustbin. Unfortunately, that beret had managed to bend the shaft of a gear wheel and the hydroplanes were stuck in that dive position. By telephone, the control room asked us to operate the hydroplanes by hand, and at speed 3 we could not change the angle of dive and we went down to 50 metres with the bow at a steep downward angle. The inclinometer had gone past its maximum reading. Our pet dog, Casa, didn't manage to keep his feet and tumbled into the next compartment. Loose articles fell; a glass which fell out of a locker cut one of the mechanics. I said to myself, 'We're for it now', and I don't think I was the only one thinking it. We went to 60 metres, a depth close to the safe maximum for [this class of] submarines.

The *maître mécanicien* (chief ERA) managed to shut off the air manifold. It must be remembered that the accident happened as the submarine was diving and so the air valves were open. As a matter of urgency the tanks were blown and the submarine came up like a cork ... I don't need to mention that we all gave a massive sigh of relief.

Unable to dive again, we returned to Casablanca on the surface with increased vigilance. We had to go into dock. That gave us a chance to check the safety equipment, and we had a few unpleasant surprises. The lead seals of the ballast under the keel were completely jammed, and the cable attached to the telephone buoy* was rusting away. If we had needed to use either of them, they would not have worked.

### Fregattenkapitän Reinhard 'Teddy' Suhren, Kriegsmarine, *U-48*; from *Teddy Suhren, Ace of Aces*

On 5 September, *U-48*, commanded by Kapitänleutnant Herbert 'Vati' Schultze, sank two vessels in the western Channel, the first of them the British freighter *Royal Sceptre*. Teddy Suhren was 1 WO or 1st Lieutenant at the time.

Events come in pairs. The waves had scarcely closed over the Royal Sceptre, and their boats were bobbing about near us, when the look-out again reported, 'Freighter sighted ahead!' We laid a course towards it, and as soon as we could make out its name (it was the English freighter *Browning*, a 5,000-tonner of the Lamport and Holt line, out of Liverpool) it immediately sent boats to meet us. We couldn't believe our eyes when we heard a great wailing borne across on the wind. In the first boat sat stout 'black mommas', who were reaching up their little babies to us and howling fit to break a heart of stone. The tears ran down their faces. It was a heart-rending scene, as they pleaded for their lives and for their children. We weren't prepared for all that. What did they take us for? 'Vati' Schultze, who had a particularly kind heart and was very likely thinking of his own twins, looked at me helplessly, despite his determination as Kommandant. 'Good God, what on earth do we do now?' In my usual impulsive way I blurted out, 'No way am I prepared to torpedo it!' Schultze replied immediately, 'No more am I.' But what now? After a short pause for thought he announced. 'The poor things are quite obviously caught up in the war against their will. We'll send them back to their ship. They can pick up the survivors from the Royal Sceptre and carry on with their voyage.' Either my English

---

* The lead seals existed to allow a crew trapped on the bottom to jettison some of the ballast thereby achieving sufficient positive buoyancy to bring the boat to the surface. The telephone buoy could be released from inside the submarine to allow rescuers to make contact with trapped survivors.

wasn't of the best, or they were in a state of shock. Thinking that their hour had come they didn't at first dare go back on board for fear that we'd blow them sky-high. In vain did we try to make ourselves understood; they didn't trust us. But the moment we slowly turned away and shouted to them 'Don't make use of your radio!' they hurried to make their way back again; and across the water drifted loud and clear their spiritual, 'Jesus come back to me'. It all went according to plan. They didn't radio, continued on their course, and made it into port three weeks later in South America with the survivors of the *Royal Sceptre*.

After the sinking of the British freighter *Winkleigh* on 8 September we received orders to return home. As well as the *Winkleigh* we had just disposed of the British freighter *Firby*, also a 5,000-tonner. The Captain had come on board and was close to tears. We were very moved, particularly when we discovered the cause of his distress. Against his wife's advice he had taken his son on the trip and was now desperate that our boat should do something to help him. 'Take him with you,' he pleaded. With the best will in the world that wasn't possible under the circumstances, but 'Vati' Schultze hit on a solution. We sent out a plain-text radio-signal: 'To Mr Churchill – We just sank the British steamer *Firby*. Please safe [sic!] the crew!' and added our latitude and longitude. Naturally this compassionate message got noticed, and the crew of the *Firby*, together with the Captain's son, were soon rescued by the British.

**Lieutenant-Commander H. P. de C. Steel, Royal Navy, HMS *Triton*;** testimony given at the Board of Inquiry into the circumstances of the loss of HMS *Oxley*; ADM178/194

I surfaced at about 5 minutes to eight on the evening of 10th September and fixed the position of the ship Obrestad Light 067°, Kvassiem Light 110°. That position put me slightly west and south of my patrol billet which was No. 5. My intention for the night was to patrol to the southward on a mean course of 190° and in order to get on that line I steered 170° zigzagging 30°, 15° each side of the mean course at about three to four knots, slow on one engine, charging on the other. The submarine was trimmed down. Before I went below I gave orders to the Officer of the Watch that if he saw a merchant ship he was to keep clear of her and in any case attempt to get end on. At the time there was one merchant ship coming south well away on my port quarter, and that was the only ship in sight at the time. The officer of the watch took over and I went below. Actually, we could not see this ship on the port quarter with the naked eye – only with binoculars.

Shortly before nine o'clock I was in the control room and there was a message from the bridge: Captain on the bridge immediately. I went straight up. The night was dark and there was a slight drizzle and I could see nothing except the shore lights. The Officer of the Watch informed me that there was a submarine fine on the port bow which for the moment I could not see. The ship was swinging to starboard and the officer of the watch was in charge. The signalman was sent for. In fact I am not certain whether he followed me up. I then made out through binoculars an object very fine on the port bow and I gave orders for the bow external tubes to stand by – Nos. 7 and 8 tubes.

At the same time the crew went to diving stations. I broke the charge and got on the main motors at once and it was at this moment that I recognised the object as a submarine. I took the ship and kept *Triton* bows on. From what I could see I appeared to be on a broad track, I should say about 120 degrees, and the object was steering in a north-westerly direction. It occurred to me that it might be *Oxley* and I dismissed the thought almost as soon as it crossed my mind because earlier in the day I had been in communication with *Oxley* and I had given her my position accurately, which was two miles south of my billet, No. 5, and *Oxley* had acknowledged this, and I had also given him my course which was at the time 154°. By this time the signalman was on the bridge and I gave him the bearing of the object or the submarine. I told him not to make any challenge until he got direct orders from me. He knew the challenge and the reply. I then ordered the challenge to be made as soon as my sights were on and I knew the armament was ready, and the signalman made it slowly. No reply was received. After about 20 seconds I ordered the challenge to be made again. During this time I had been studying the submarine very closely indeed. She was trimmed down very low and I could see nothing of her bow or shape and the conning tower did not look like *Oxley's*, and I could not see any outstanding points of identification such as periscope standards, etc.

Accordingly, I ordered the second challenge to be made; received no reply to the second challenge. Receiving no reply to the second challenge, I made a third challenge again after a short interval. Receiving no reply to the third challenge I fired a grenade which burst correctly. I did not see the grenade actually burst although I knew it had burst because of the light as I had my eyes fixed on the submarine. By this time I was completely convinced that this was an enemy submarine. I counted fifteen to myself like this: and-one, and-two, and-three ... When I had counted fifteen to myself I gave the order to fire; No. 7 and No. 8 tubes were fired at three-second intervals. About half a minute after firing, indeterminate flashing was seen from the submarine. This was unreadable and stopped in a few seconds. The Officer of the Watch also saw this. It gave me the impression that somebody was looking for something with a torch – it was certainly not Morse code. Very shortly afterwards, a matter of a few seconds after the flashing had stopped, one of my torpedoes hit. I told the

Officer of the Watch, Lieutenant. H. A. Stacey, to fix the ship, and he fixed the ship as follows: Obrestad Light 035° Egero Light 105°. This fix placed the ship 6.8 miles 189° from No. 5 position, which put me 4¼ miles inside my sector. I took the bearing of the explosion and proceeded towards the spot at once. The sea was about 3 and 2. Very soon we heard cried for help and as we came closer we actually heard the word 'Help'. There were three men swimming. I manoeuvred the ship to the best of my ability to close the men and kept Aldis lights on. Lieutenant Stacey and Lieutenant Watkins attached lines to themselves and dived in the sea which was covered in oil and succeeded in bringing Lieutenant Commander Bowerman and Able Seaman Gukes to safety. The third man who afterwards transpired to be Lieutenant Manley, RNR, was seen swimming strongly in the light of an Aldis when he suddenly disappeared and was seen no more.

No blame was apportioned to HMS *Triton*; *Oxley* was found to have been out of position and her watchkeeping had been at fault.

### Kapitänleutnant Otto Schuhart, Kriegsmarine, *U-29*; from IWM Sound Archive 2358

Kapitänleutnant – later Kapitän zur See – Schuhart was on his first war patrol when on 17 September he sank HMS *Courageous*, earning himself and his men the Iron Cross.

I found the *Courageous* accidentally. It was a fine Sunday afternoon in the Atlantic west of the Channel and I was watching there for merchant ships. It was my intention to return to Wilhelmshaven this evening because we were short of oil. At 4 o'clock in the afternoon, one of my sailors announced smoke. That must be a merchant ship. Our position was very good to attack the ship and I submerged. After half an hour I could see the merchant ship and saw that the merchant ship had a flag. But I didn't know the nationality of the ship and we were forbidden to attack neutral ships and we were allowed only ships when we knew the nationality. Therefore I had to wait, then to emerge and to stop the ship by artillery or by gunnery. But some minutes before emerging I saw an aeroplane flying round the ship. I was very angry, for under these circumstances it was impossible for me to emerge and I must wait until the aeroplane was away. Half an hour later I saw a bridge – the first moment I didn't know what that could be. I looked through my periscope and suddenly it was my idea it must be a carrier. The carrier approached my boat but the distance was so far that it was impossible for me to shoot. I think there were three or four miles. I kept in contact, and that was my fortune. I could see nothing from the carrier but suddenly I saw the bridge again above the horizon. I could look out only for seconds, fearing the aeroplanes could observe my periscope. The carrier had high speed and it was good for me; I had not to wait so long.

I fired three torpedoes, they were the last torpedoes I had, and after firing the torpedoes I ordered my chief engineer to go to depth. After one minute, nearly one minute, we heard an enormous explosion. After the explosion of the torpedoes we were attacked by the destroyer. The noise of the depth charges was enormous – it was the first we had heard them but we kept our heads for we were sure to have had a great success. The next day we heard by English radio that we had sunk the carrier *Courageous* and we were very proud of our success, but I knew too well that it was not unmerited, but that we were well trained for this task and that we had only done our duty.

**Commander Borys Karnicki, Polish Navy, then a kapitan marynarki (lieutenant) of ORP *Wilk*; interviewed on 23 December 1939; from IWM Sound Archive 236010\***

The war began for us on 1 September, at 5:40 in the morning, when artillery explosions from Gdansk were heard, and half an hour later we were attacked by German planes. The commanding officer, commander [Boguslaw] Krawczyk, immediately gave the order to sail. We proceeded to sea, and submerged after leaving the port. During this day and the following days, we saw squadrons of German planes flying low over the sea and proceeding towards Gdynia and the port on the Hel Peninsula. We had an unimpeded view of German destroyers in action against our coastal defence battery from the base on Hel, and our destroyer '*Wicher*'. We had absolutely no chance of attacking the Germans because of the high speed of the enemy vessels and the order we had follow. This was the difficult task of laying mines in the areas where the larger and smaller enemy vessels were operating. During the minelaying, we were forced to interrupt the operation because of depth-charge attacks. At night, we saw the Naval Base burning on the Hel Peninsula, and enormous explosions just on its tip, probably at the Laskowski coastal defence battery and also at Jastarnia [the neighbouring town]. Our anti-aircraft artillery fired as well.

With no chance of reaching the base at Hel, because of burning oil from the damaged destroyer *Gryf* which, after a long fight, succumbed to Luftwaffe planes, we had to leave the Gulf and proceed to new operating sectors. During the passage through the enemy lines of the Kriegsmarine, we were repeatedly attacked with depth charges. After failing to escape from the hunt, the CO decided to go down to the seabed. We turned off all the mechanical equipment

---

\* The recording is believed to have been made by the BBC for its Polish service. The escape of the *Wilk* and the other ORP submarine, *Orzel*, had been a secret until this time.

and slowly began to go down. We were very deep when we stopped. The situation was wretched. The pressure was so high that we couldn't open so much as a drawer or any door. The complete silence was interrupted by water rushing into the motor compartments. Probably, one of the bombs damaged the valve of the exhaust system. We thought we had lost the enemy. But after two hours of silence, a new series of depth charges shattered the boat. We were certain this was the end. It was probably the oil, from the damaged tanks, which came to the surface and pinpointed our position to the enemy.

By 8:00 in the evening there was no air to breathe. For our own safety we couldn't turn the ventilation on. The air became awful. We had to make a decision what to do next. The boat was prepared for surfacing, the call to action stations went out, the gun-crew was ready to fight it out with the enemy on the surface. At 8.15 the submarine slowly began to come up ...

We surfaced. There was nobody around. The sea was calm, full moon; from the Hel Peninsula enormous explosions sounded. The submarine's leaking oil was seen behind her. Our fears proved true: the ballast tanks were damaged. Because of the damaged gyrocompass, the CO decided to direct the boat northbound based on the Pole Star. At night, we threw out the oil from the damaged ballasts. To starboard, port and ahead we saw lights of the enemy vessels. By morning, we had managed to jettison the oil and prepare the boat for submersion. We spent the following days in other areas of Baltic, as ordered by Navy HQ, searching for enemy vessels to attack. We saw only merchant ships and small anti-submarine vessels, but none of them was suitable for a torpedo attack.

When the level of fuel became an issue, we had two options: to be interned in Sweden or to pass through the straits (Danish). The CO decided to take the second option. Although the odds against us were a hundred to one, and the whole crew was aware of it, the morale was excellent. The crew were at action stations in case we were attacked. We encountered two Kriegsmarine vessels, which we miraculously passed by, but that's an another story ...

I can honestly say that it was a pleasure to submerge in the Skagerrak ... After 22 days of silent hiding in the depths, we saw daylight again. We were off the coast of England.

**Polish Officer\* of ORP *Orzel*;** interviewed on 18 December 1939; from IWM Sound Archive 2360

*Orzel* went to sea on 1 September. After a patrol of 12 days, and with her captain sick and no communications with Gdynia, they headed for a neutral port.

---

\* According to the IWM catalogue, this is a BBC interview with Lieutenant-Commander Jan Grudzinski. However, the interviewer addresses the officer as Sub-Lieutenant, which implies it might have been the First Officer, Andrzej Piasecki.

We entered the port of Tallinn at night, on 14 September, thinking of repairing a charger and, what was the most important, to land a sick commander and send him to the hospital. We knew that, according to the international law, we had 24 hours of stop-over, and with the promise, we were assured by the Estonian officers, that we would be fully equipped and that they would fix defective parts.

Being tired after the long-night watch, conscious of security in a neutral port, I went to sleep. Awakening was more than painful. I was informed that in the meantime the submarine had been moored in the naval port, and not only had the captain been taken off, but also the breech-block of our gun. We were, against the international law, being subjected to mysterious pressure from unknown factors on the shore – interned. The crew was hastily destroying codes and documents. The submarine was moored at the jetty in the inner basin. An Estonian guard was at the hatch. At first, we thought of individual escape, because from this submarine's position, leaving the port was impossible. The following morning, the Estonians turned the submarine around in order to use the crane to unload the torpedoes.

In the evening of the same day, an event happened that raised the possibility of an escape with the submarine. When we sat in the mess, the light went off because of a short-circuit somewhere in the port. In those few minutes of darkness the idea came up of making a short-circuit in the submarine and escaping in the darkness. But on the other hand, this would cause an alarm in the entire port. We decided then to cut the cables of the lights illuminating the submarine. During the next day, we cut the hawsers under the deck and prepared them for a fast release. We cunningly managed to save a few torpedoes from being unloaded. We were aware that sailing without the maps would be enormously difficult, but we couldn't get them because the Estonian guards did not allow us even on the jetty.

Cutting the light cables was the signal for action. At 0200 hours an Estonian guard was invited on the deck for a cigarette. The rest was done in a minute. When the lights went off, both guards were silently put out of action, pre-cut hawsers dropped down to the water, the gangway came down with a crash and *Orzel* slowly moved towards the exit ...

We had not reached the pier before an Estonian Navy ship fired a shot [to raise the alarm]. The searchlights began to illuminate the port. We couldn't make a turn and we bumped into the rocks at the pier. In order to release ourselves from the rocks we had to turn on the noisy diesels. It took a few minutes and it was enough for the Estonians to open fire from the jetty. Fortunately, they couldn't open fire with the artillery or they would have hit their own ships moored at the port. Finally we slid back off the rocks and we approached the sea.

That's where the biggest danger was awaiting us. At once, the Estonian ships left the port and the searchlights began to light up the sea. From the port on the island the guns began to fire. When the sounder showed enough water under the keel we submerged at once. But even then, the Estonians didn't give up. We heard detonations of depth charges, one after the other. We felt then quite secure. We had enough water under and above us and we directed to exit from the Gulf of Finland.

The interviewer lastly asked if they had spent a long time in the Baltic.

All of three weeks. It would be difficult to describe in a few words our adventure during this period. Finally we reached England [Scotland] and we didn't have any drinking water. We were not far off dying under the water for lack of it.

The evasion had been made without charts, relying on the memory of the torpedo officer who managed to draw charts of an accuracy to amaze the British officers who examined them. Sub-Lieutenant Piasecki managed to send out a weak signal to the British which was picked up on 14 October. The arrival of the two Polish submarines was not publicised until December.

## Korvettenkapitän Günther Prien, Kriegsmarine, *U-47*;
from *U-boat Commander*

It was October the 13th and it was four o'clock in the morning.

I made my way to the forrard mess. The men were already there, and stood against the walls or crouched in the bunks. The glare of the unshaded lamps made their faces look chalky white, with deep black smudges for eyes.

'Tomorrow we shall enter Scapa Flow,' I said without any introduction.

There was a silence so profound that I could hear water dripping somewhere, clop ... clop ... clop ...

'Everyone except the watch will go to their bunks and sleep, the watch will wake the cook at 14.00 hours. At 16.00 hours we will have dinner. Then for the duration of the mission there will be no more hot food. Only cold sandwiches at all stations. And everyone will have a slab of chocolate. All superfluous light will be extinguished, we must economise on current; no one is to move unnecessarily, for we shall be lying aground for this evening and must be careful with the air. During the mission itself there must be absolute silence. No message is to be repeated, do you understand?'

'Yes sir,' they said as one man.

'Crew dismiss.'

Silence. They were crouching on their bunks and looking at me. Their faces were quite calm and nothing was to be read in them, neither astonishment, nor fear ...

At 14.00 hours I heard the watch wake the cook and saw him creep past through half-closed eyes.

He had wrapped his feet in rags to avoid making any noise, for the hearing apparatus of the enemy was very sensitive. In some circumstances it was possible to hear the tread of a boot on the iron floor plates in the next ship.

At 16.00 hours we were all awakened. The meal consisted of veal cutlets and green cabbage. It was a feast and the orderlies were kept on the run. I sat with Wessels and Barendorff. The latter kept us entertained. He was as lively as a cricket.

The tables were cleared. Three men went through the boat and fixed the charges with which to blow up the ship in case we should fall into the hands of the enemy.

Once more I went through all rooms and gave my final instructions. During the whole of the action no one was to smoke and even more important no one was to speak unnecessarily. The last preparations were made. Everyone inspected his lifejacket. I cast a last glance at the escape hatch. The navigator fixed his chart.

Those of us who were going on the bridge put on oil-skins.

19.00 hours. It would be night outside. Brief commands, 'Diving stations,' and then, 'Get in trim.' The bilge pumps began to work and Wessels, the chief engineer, reported: 'Boat rising ... 1 metre up, 2 metres up.'

The whine of the motors started up and the boat began to surface. I went to the control-room.

'Up periscope'; slowly and cautiously the tube rose and its glassy eye scanned the horizon. It was night.

I took a deep breath and ordered, 'Surface.'

Compressed air streamed into the tanks from which the water rushed gurgling. 'Down periscope', and the tube sank back into the boat. And then came the noise when the boat breaks surface, rocking as if half drunk from the immersion. With a dull thud the hatch opened. A current of fresh air streamed in and we climbed out as fast as we could, the two officers, the Bo'sun and myself.

Straining my ears I listened in the darkness. There was nothing to hear and nothing to see. The wind had dropped and there was a slight swell. I looked around and the others reported half aloud and yet quite clearly. 'Starboard clear!' ... 'Port clear!'... 'Aft clear!'

'Ventilate the boat,' I commanded and the two fans began to spin.

'Both diesels?' and from below, 'Both diesels are ready.'

'Stop electric motors! Both diesels slow ahead.'

The familiar hum of the engines began and with a spreading bow wave the boat moved forward.

By now our eyes had become accustomed to the night and we could see everything clearly – almost too clearly. The boat, the approaching waves and behind them – the coastline.

'It's curiously light tonight,' I said.

'I can't imagine why, sir,' answered Endrass.

There was a strange brightness which came neither from the moon nor from a searchlight. Its source was hidden. It seemed as if in the north, behind the horizon, bonfires were illuminating the cloud bank. Like a blow it struck me. The Northern Lights! No one had thought of that! We had selected the night of the new moon for the enterprise and now it was becoming lighter every moment, for the north wind was slowly pushing the cloud bank aside.

I asked myself whether I should submerge once more and wait for the following night, for in these latitudes the Northern Lights are rarely seen twice running. I turned round. With his glasses to his eyes Endrass was staring across the sea to port.

'Well, what is it?' I asked.

'Well, sir, it is a good light for shooting,' he said quietly, and at the same time I heard Barendorff whisper to the signaller:

'Man, it's going to be a sticky night, tonight.'

I wondered whether my lads would be in the same mood on the following day.

Then I ordered the new course. 'Both engines half-speed ahead.' The bow wave increased and threads of spume were flung across the deck.

We gazed into the night.

It's curious how responsibility sharpens one's faculties. A long way in front of us a shadow lay on the water, too dim to be properly seen through the glasses. Perhaps it was a fishing smack, perhaps a neutral steamer passing in the distance. But in our situation every encounter threatened danger. 'Alarm: Diving stations.'

We scuttled through the hatch into the boat. 'Flood tanks', and water poured into the tanks. 'Up periscope.' I rushed to the periscope and searched for the vessels. From below came Number One's voice giving orders to the planesman, and then came Spahr's deep and calm voice, 'To the commander, time to alter course, 20 degrees to starboard.'

'Starboard 15,' I called back.

After a short pause the planesman answered, 'Steady on new course.' Up above the shadow had disappeared. On the other hand the north wind had pushed the compact bank of clouds over to the south, only a thin veil of mist was trailing behind them across the sky. But in this veil the Northern Lights showed brighter than ever, shooting orange and blue rays to the zenith of the heavens. A magic light as on the Day of Judgment.

We had approached closer to the land. The hills had become more solid and their silhouettes showed black and sombre against the bright sky. Their shadows fell dark and hard over the pale and gleaming water.

'Sir, have you seen the Northern Lights?' said a calm and rather oily voice behind me. 'I have never seeen anything like it.'

I turned round. ' Man …' I started to curse, but immediately I became silent again when I saw Samann. There he stood, his eyes wide open like a child's listening to a fairy tale. And yet he knew as well as I what was at stake. Wordlessly I turned back again. The shadows of the hills right and left merged together and the water darkened. For the glow in the sky had vanished.

And then suddenly it was light again. A bay opened out in front of us far into the horizon, in which the burning sky was mirrored. It was as if the sea was illuminated from below.

'We are inside,' I said.

There was no reply, but it seemed to me as if the whole boat was holding its breath, and as if the hearts of the motors were beating quieter and faster.

It was a wide bay. Although the hills which surrounded it were very high, from the boat they looked like a low chain of dunes. Cautiously peering in all directions we moved forward into the still water.

A few lights over the water flared up like shooting stars. I felt the blood hammer in my temples. But they were only tankers, sleeping at anchor.

At last over there … close to the shore appeared the mighty silhouette of a battleship. Hard and clear, as if painted into the sky with black ink. The bridge, the mighty funnel and aft, like filigree, the tall mast. Slowly we edged closer. At such a moment all feeling stopped. One became part of the boat, the brain of this steel annimal which was creeping up towards its enormous prey. At such a time you must think in iron and steel – or perish.

We crept closer still. Now we could clearly see the bulge of the gun turrets, out of which the guns jutted threateningly into the sky. The ship lay there like a sleeping giant.

'I believe she belongs to the *Royal Oak* class,' I whispered, and Endrass nodded silently.

We crept closer still and suddenly behind the first silhouette loomed up the outlines of a second battleship as large and as powerful as the first. We could recognise her superstructures behind the stern of the *Royal Oak*; the bridge and the forrard gun turret.

It was the *Repulse*.

We had to attack her first, for the *Royal Oak*, right in front of us, was a certainty, anyhow.

'All tubes ready.'

The command echoed below in the boat. Then silence, but for the gurgling sound when water ran into the tubes; a sharp hiss of compressed air followed and then a hard metallic click when the lever snapped into position.

Then came back the report, 'Tube one ready.' 'Tube fire,' commanded Endrass.

A thud trembled through the boat; the torpedo was on its way. If only it would hit – it had to hit – for the silhouette had been right in the ccntre of the sights

And now Spahr's dark voice was counting, 5, 10, 15. Time became eternity. There wasn't a sound in the boat, only Spahr's voice dropping heavily into the stillness. 20. Our eyes were fixed on the target but still the steel fortress remained unmoved. Suddenly at the bows of the *Repulse* a column of water spouted into the air and immediately after it the dull detonation reached us. It sounded rather like blasting in a distant quarry.

'He's got his,' said Endrass.

I had no reply but, 'Second tube ready?'

I manoeuvred the boat towards the *Royal Oak*. We had to be quick about it otherwise they would be in our hair before we let go the second torpedo.

'Port 5', the boat turned slowly to port.

'Midships. Wheel's amidships.' We were pointing straight at the *Royal Oak*. She grew mightier than ever. Her shadow seemed to come to reach out at us. Schmidt was steering as though he could see the target himself The thread of the sights cut directly amidships.

Now was the moment. 'Tube, fire,' commanded Endrass.

Again the recoil shuddered and again Spahr's voice began to count. '5 ... 10 ...'

But now something occurred that no one had anticipated and no one who had seen it would ever forget. A wall of water shot up toward the sky. It was as if the sea suddenly stood up on end. Loud explosions came one after the other like drumfire in a battle and coalesced into one mighty ear-splitting crash.

Flames shot skyward, blue ... yellow ... red.

Behind this hellish firework display the sky disappeared entirely. Like huge birds, black shadows soared through the flames, fell hissing and splashing into the water. Fountains yards high sprang up where they had fallen, huge fragments of the mast and the funnels.

We must have hit the [am]munition magazine and the deadly cargo had torn the body of its own ship apart.

I could not take my eyes from the glass. It was as if the gates of hell had suddenly been torn open and I was looking into the flaming furnace. I glanced down into my boat.

Down there it was dark and still I could hear the hum of the motors, Spahr's even voice and the answers of the planesman. I felt as never before my kinship with these men below who did their duty silently and blindly, who could neither see the day nor the target and who died in the dark if it had to be.

I called down, 'He's finished.'

For a moment there was silence. Then a mighty roar went through the ship, an almost bestial roar in which the pent-up tension of the past twenty-four hours found release.

'Silence!' I shouted ... and the ship became quiet. Only Spahr's voice was heard. 'Three points to port', and the planesman's answering, 'Three points to port.'

Over the *Royal Oak* the fireworks died down, revived for a short while by an occasional belated explosion. The bay awoke to feverish authority. Searchlights flashed and probed with their long white fingers over the water and died.

Lights were flitting here and there ... small swift lights low over the water, the lights of destroyers and U-boat chasers. Like dragonflies they zigzagged over the dark surface. If they caught us we were done for.

I took a last look round. The stricken ship was dying. I could see no other worthwhile target, only pursuers.

'Hard aport,' I ordered. 'Both engines full speed ahead.' There was only one thing to attempt now. Get out of this witches' cauldron and take the boat and the crew safely home.

The hills closed in again; the current, which here had the force of a raging torrent, took us in its grip and shook us from side to side. The engines were running flat out.

We seemed to advance at a snail's pace and at times even to be motionless like a trout in a mountain stream. Behind us the headlight of a destroyer detached itself from the welter of light and came streaming towards us. But we could not, we could not get ahead. The boat being tossed from side to side while the enemy was steadily gaining on us. Already we could make out its narrow silhouette against the sky.

'Wonder whether he'll get us?' said Endrass in a husky voice.

'Extreme speed ahead,' I called out.

'Engines are running at extreme speed,' came the reply.

'Couple up electric motors. Give us everything we've got.'

It was a nightmare. There we lay, held fast by visible power, while death came closer, ever closer.

A spot of light flashed dot-dash-dot.

'He is signalling,' whispered Endrass.

The boat shuddered as it strained against the current.

We must get out ... we must get out. This single thought throbbed in my brain to the rhythm of the engines. We must get out ...

Then – wonder of wonders – the pursuer turned aside. The light slid away over the water and then 'weeyummm' of the first depth charges.

Laboriously, painfully, the boat wriggled through the narrows. It was dark again. From the distance came ever more faintly the thuds of the depth charges.

Before us lay the sea, broad and free, vast under the limitless sky.

There appears to be no record of any damage to the *Repulse*.

## Leading Seaman 2nd Class René Mazères, Marine Nationale, *Amphitrite*

CASABLANCA, NOVEMBER 1939.

It's the seventh or eighth day of our patrol. It's easy to believe we are the only ones in this sector and our only job is to defend ourselves against the elements. After a pretty stormy night at sea, we have been proceeding all morning more often at periscope depth than at 30m.

Where are we? I haven't the foggiest. Authority isn't used to keeping us informed – it's probably a tradition – as if those of us below only have a single use: keeping the engines going.

It's 1100: lunchtime for the midday watch. But the central tanks have just been blown, enough so the bridge breaks surface and the deck is level with the sea. None of us has noticed any mechanical or steering problem, and everyone is left speculating, because there's got to be a very good reason for surfacing unexpectedly in broad daylight. Arrocéna (nicknamed Zoso) has been summoned to the bridge. The motors have stopped. The boat, which has had to make a running moor, is rolling strongly. Then there's a lot of activity midships where some crates are being sent down.

A blast on the klaxon, dive, and here we are back at 12 metres.

On his return, Arrocéna tells me that we just surfaced next to a Spanish trawler and swapped some fish and shellfish for a few litres of engine oil. They needed him because he spoke a bit of Spanish. We proceed in silence, the air permeated with a delicious scent of fresh fish.

This evening, and perhaps tomorrow, there will be a fine bouillabaisse and gloriously fresh prawns. Tordo, our cook, comes from Marseilles. We can put up with tinned bread, but for a short while we can forget about the *carissan* in the form of choucroute, casserole or else pork chops in tomato sauce which all end up having the same sharp, metallic taste.

This evening we savour it, we enjoy it. We even go looking for seconds, and we talk about it.

'The Old Man's got a nerve [Lieutenant de Vaisseau Saglio].'

'Fancy running the risk of getting a kipper [a torpedo] to go with his grub.'

'The Spanish will be keen to give away our presence in the sector.'

But our job is to keep patrolling. In a few days we'll be heading back to port. Probably empty-handed as the enemy seems to have sent out more submarines than surface ships. There will be no firing of torpedoes, no boardings to carry out with the help of our 75mm gun, nor depth charges to endure.

The men are exhausted and the boat herself is weary.

We look back on yesterday's incident which we don't think of as an exploit but which we appreciate as an amusing diversion. We're just at the start of the war.

### Lieutenant-Commander Edward Bickford, DSO, Royal Navy, HMS *Salmon*; from Patrol Report, ADM199/1839

Nothing of interest occurred until December 4th, when I was on patrol in my area and at 1330 a U-boat [*U-36*] was sighted in position 57° North 5°10' East by my First Lieutenant. Its conning tower appeared like a box floating in the water, but he had noticed that it did not go up and down with the waves and had come to a shallow depth for further investigation. Simultaneously the Asdic office reported a hydrophone effect on the same bearing.

On going to the periscope I found the U-boat to be steering approximately 350 degrees, evidently on passage outward bound. I was a long way off track and closed her at full speed and eventually fired at 5,000 yards on 110 degrees track, the salvo being spread at seven-second intervals, torpedoes being set at eight feet.

At least one torpedo broke surface and much disturbance was visible on the surface on firing. I lost trim temporarily but regained it in time to be at periscope depth before my shot could have taken effect. I saw her through the periscope blown to small fragments which rose at least 200 feet into the air.

I surfaced to pick up survivors but found nothing but oil, wreckage, one dead body and a lifebelt. Bubbles continued to come up from the bottom for some time. Many volunteered to swim out through the oil to retrieve the life belt as a memento. I considered this unnecessary and, fearing aircraft and the possible presence of another U-boat, I dived once clear of the oil patch. The U-boat had one gun and was therefore of the sea-going or ocean-going class. It is impossible to tell the difference between these types except at close range ...

December 12th. *Salmon* was on the surface at 0745 in position 57 degrees 2' North 5 degrees 52' East, when forced to dive by a Heinkel 70. At the time it was thought curious that enemy aircraft should be so far from home at the break of dawn. *Salmon*, who was regaining patrol position, decided to proceed deep at speed before starting a normal periscope watch.

At 0930 Asdic office reported hydrophone effect 200 revolutions. *Salmon* came to periscope depth to investigate and found *Bremen* [passenger liner owned by Norddeutscher Lloyd] crossing her stern at high speed, range 2,000 yards. The submarine turned to a firing course at full speed while I searched *Bremen* through high-power [magnification] for signs of offensive armament. None could be seen and she looked much the same, except for funnels which had been painted light grey, as when I had crossed to America and back on her in 1933. I decided to surface on a firing course and stop her with my gun with the intention of firing torpedoes if she opened fire on me, or gunning her only if she refused to stop but did not open fire.

0940. Surfaced and made 'K International' by Aldis Lamp five times over the space of a minute. There was no reply and I ordered a round to be fired ahead of her. Just as the gun layer was about to fire, a Dornier Do 18 appeared and I was forced to dive.

By now *Bremen* was nearing the limit of effective torpedo range, being on a 140 degree track, steaming at high speed, range 5,000 yards. Went deep as I still considered I was unjustified in firing torpedoes at her ... Shortly afterwards I intercepted signal from Admiralty telling [HMS] *Ursula* that *Bremen* was not a target and felt much relieved ... I decided that this area would most likely become unhealthy in the near future and so decided to go beyond my patrol line to the Great Fisher bank in the hopes of stalking a U-boat whose periscope had been reported the previous day by aircraft ... from 2100 to 2100 I investigated three merchant ships ...

0945. My First Lieutenant called me to the periscope and I observed enemy forces to the northward, steering to westward at a range of about 12,000 yards. At ten o'clock, by coming up to 28 feet on the gauge, I was able to identify the enemy as two or possibly three heavy ships from the following: *Scharnhorst*, *Gneisenau*, *Admiral Scheer*, *Graf Von Spee* and four cruisers who were two *Hipper* class, the *Leipzig* and a *Konigsberg* class.

1030. *Blücher*, *Leipzig* and *Hipper*, in that order, turned to the south in line ahead. *Salmon* turned to the westward to attack.

1036. Fired spread salvo at eleven-second firing intervals. At this moment *Leipzig* was on a 90 degrees track, range 5,000 yards and *Hipper* appeared slightly out of station on the starboard quarter of *Leipzig*. I gave their speed as twenty knots, but on further consideration I now think that that was an under-estimation.

I fired a spread salvo with point of aim just ahead of *Leipzig's* bow with the object of winging [damaging] two ships rather than sinking one, hoping thus to provoke a fleet action. Went deep and altered course to 90 degrees from firing course at full speed.

1040. Heard a loud explosion and said, 'That's the *Leipzig*.'

1041. Heard two loud explosions which were either hits on the third ship or the commencement of depth charging.

Until this moment I had been attempting to regain trim for a periscope observation, being very heavy forward after firing (I had flooded 'A' to keep her down). Now, however, I considered it unwise to return to periscope depth as I was still not under slow speed control. I continued at full speed.

1046. Heard three explosions which were considered to be remainder of the salvo hitting the bottom...

1050. Took evading action ... *Salmon* was subsequently depth charged until noon ...

The German warships proved to be the three light cruisers *Leipzig*, *Nürnberg* and *Köln* which were providing cover for destroyers returning to Germany after laying mines in the North Sea off Newcastle upon Tyne. *Leipzig* and *Nürnberg* were both hit but managed to return home. *Leipzig's* damage was so great that she was subsequently used only as a training ship.

## FAR EAST

**Commander P. Bartlett, OBE, Royal Navy, HMS *Perseus***; from the Papers of Commander Bartlett, Imperial War Museum

Hong Kong time is eight hours ahead of London. At 7 p.m. Sunday 3 September I was in the Club having a drink when my first lieutenant telephoned to say that the signal 'TOTAL GERMANY' had been received, which meant that war was declared. I came back into the bar and told everyone present, but there did not seem to be much else to do but to go to a Chinese restaurant and have a good meal. The following morning the Commodore obviously felt that, with the Commander-in-Chief maintaining wireless silence, it was up to him to do something, so we were all told to establish a patrol line east of Formosa, to try and intercept one of the German liners which had left Manila for Yokohama. It was unlikely that this vessel would use her usual route through the Formosa Channel and take some other way, so it was anybody's guess that she would go where we were going, but it was better than doing nothing, and it was arranged that we should leave at dusk. All our stores were on board and we just had to top up with fresh provisions, so my Gunnery Officer decided to overhaul the recoil mechanism of our 4-inch gun. This is done by training the gun as far off as possible and securing a wire to a special ringbolt provided on the barrel of the gun and then bringing the wire to the capstan on the forward casing of the submarine. The capstan is then started up, and the wire hauls the gun barrel against the action of the recoil spring, which is secured to the gun sleeve. When full recoil point is reached there is a mark on the sleeve to show this, the wire is suddenly released, allowing the gun to return to its normal position, but cushioned by a hydraulic braking cylinder. The test is carried out to ensure that the braking system and the recoil spring are working correctly, but on this occasion there was an indescribable clatter and a bang, which had me springing on to the bridge from my cabin in the conning tower like a jack-in-the box to see what had happened. To my horror our precious gun had slid almost completely through its sleeve backwards onto the saddle tanks, just clear of the water, so that just three inches remaining in the sleeve jammed further movement; otherwise it would have been lying on the bottom of the harbour. The barrel and breech block of a 4-inch gun is a hefty affair, but luckily no serious damage had been done, just a dent here and there, and we were only delayed sailing half an hour or so whilst a dockyard crane was able to sling and coax the barrel back into its sleeve and the vitally important nut screwed back into place, for this had been removed in error!

The four submarines made a surface passage of about 600 miles, passing through the string of islands that lie between the Philippines and Formosa through the Balingtan Channel, and into a corner of the Pacific where I personally felt that no ship had ever been. We were strung along a patrol line about 30 miles apart in the most perfect weather, the trade wind clouds passing endlessly across the sky, and so clear was the air and so extreme the visibility that the horizon was a series of tiny clouds mounting the rim of the sea, and at night the moon rose crescent-shaped out of the dense black of the ocean into a sky brilliant with stars – very exceptional conditions I had never met with before or since. But nothing else to be seen, and certainly no splendid German liner to be captured.

At that stage of the war we were not allowed to attack, so in fact all she had to do, if we had sighted her, was to turn tail and run for it. After four days of steaming first to the east for 20 miles and then to the west for another 20, the Commander-in-Chief, arriving back in Hong Kong to find no submarines, recalled us and we arrived back after an absence of eight days during which everyone had settled down nicely to a patrol routine, though one with strictly no enemy to bother us.

*Perseus'* next patrol was to blockade the easterly Sea of Japan, informing the cruiser HMS *Dorsetshire* of any suspicious vessels.

I did indeed sight one such vessel, let it go by and then surfaced to report her, but never managed to raise the cruiser on my wireless. After being on patrol for about 5 days we received a typhoon warning. The storm was a thousand or more miles away, but we were theoretically in the path it would take that month of the year, and day by day we plotted its inevitable advance, and it arrived as we left an area on being recalled to Hong Kong, punctual and on the proper tram-lines. I knew the correct thing to do was to get across its path, so we were waiting on the extreme southerly border of our patrol area at midnight on our last day, as no authority had suggested that we should take earlier avoiding action, and off we set as fast as we could go in rough weather which was getting rougher all the time with torrential rain.

For the next eighteen hours the wind was steady and the barometer falling steadily, indicating we were in its path, and we made slower and slower progress as the swell, at right angles to the wind and most of the waves, increased, but during the second night we began to think the wind was veering and I suppose the centre of the storm passed astern of us; and apart from not having too clear an idea of where we had got to, as our speed was guesswork and so was our leeway, we came through it with only superficial damage, and we had had plenty of time to prepare for a dusting so that everything that could possibly be moved was lashed and double lashed. The 12-foot-long refrigerators, which run along the seaman's mess deck, wedged into the curve of the hull, were not as immovable as they looked, and the mess tables and some bedding had to be used to prevent them from leaving the starboard side for the port! The weather started to clear on the second day and we sighted and identified a group of islands, amongst which was Okinawa, virtually unknown to the world in 1939!

Arrived back in Hong Kong after 20 days at sea, and felt rather outraged to hear that our supporting cruiser had avoided the typhoon by leaving the area a day before it arrived and dodged around to the Yellow Sea on the other side of Japan.

**Lieutenant Ian Anderson, Royal Navy, HMS *Odin*;** from the Papers of Lieutenant Anderson, Imperial War Museum

Lieutenant Anderson was at Hong Kong when war was declared. HMS *Odin* was ordered to Colombo.

FRIDAY 22 DECEMBER.
With a small army of little folk busily engaged inside my head with hammers and chisels, and an army of red ants apparently determined to saw their way

out of my stomach, I staggered on deck at 0530 to pull the anchor up and we set off for Colombo again …

MONDAY 25 DECEMBER.

Christmas day in the workhouse would have been equally interesting. This was the first Christmas I've ever spent at sea and it was hardly a festive occasion. Even with the prospect of getting in during the afternoon, I could raise little enthusiasm – Colombo is such a poor spot. However we did arrive eventually, at about 5.30pm with a bunch of coconut palm leaves waving from the mast – the best we could do in the way of a Christmas tree – and secured alongside the [depot ship] Lucia which by now is nearly habitable, though hardly a happy substitute after *Medway*.

There was little thrill about arriving back here – nothing to look forward to, not even a relief. A dismal outlook made bleaker by the fact that there was no letter from Myrtle. I expect she's got fed up waiting and married someone else; at least I don't really, but in the present pervading gloom I could believe anything. Come on – snap out of it.

# 1940

If the tonnage sunk by Dönitz's handful of Atlantic U-boats in the first weeks of 1940 was not alarming in total, it still represented significant achievements for individual boats. However, in the spring the focus of the submarine war temporarily shifted to Norwegian waters. As part of Hitler's preparations for Operation 'Weser', the invasion of Norway, all Atlantic-based U-boats were recalled to support the April offensive. Troopships began leaving for Norwegian and Danish ports.

One such, the *Rio de Janeiro*, was heading for Bergen when she was sunk by the ORP *Orzel* on 8 April, but the significance of the uniformed men she carried was to be discounted in London. On 9 April, totally unaware that this was the precise day of the planned German invasion of both Norway and Denmark, Churchill ordered minelaying in the waters of neutral Norway as a prelude to British plans to provoke Germany into aggressive action against Norway which the Allies could then counter. Although it met resistance from British and Norwegian forces, the German operation was successful. German submarines involved in the attack were badly hampered by their ongoing torpedo problems; the Allied boats enjoyed success, but only when the enemy ships were on their return run.

Norway's small and ageing navy sailed for Britain. It included just one submarine, too old for anything but training. The Royal Norwegian Navy's active submarine contribution would come later, when three British boats were loaned.

The invasion of Norway was followed exactly a month later by that of France and the evacuation of Allied troops from Dunkirk. On 10 June Mussolini declared war on Britain and France. At this time, almost all the French submarines which had been operating out of Harwich were back in France, and, as the Germans closed in, boats that could be got away left for English ports; the rest were scuttled. On 22 June the Vichy French Government signed an armistice. Germany now had control of French ports and bases along the English Channel and the Atlantic, and demanded that the French fleet be disarmed in its various home bases. Afraid of the fleet falling into German hands, Churchill had asked the French to send it to Britain, but that was never a viable proposition for the French. A diplomatic nightmare ended in tragedy when Force H of the Royal Navy reluctantly destroyed France's Atlantic fleet in the Algerian port of Mers el Kebir, causing more than 1,000 deaths. Operation 'Catapult' remained a scar on Anglo-French relations long after the end of the war.

French submarines in Britain were immediately taken over by force. The exception was the *Rubis*, still operating out of Dundee, to which Vice Admiral Max Horton sent a personal letter expressing his confidence in the crew. The British response to the French armistice withered enthusiasm for General de Gaulle's call for a Free French force, and only a handful of submarines remained to fly the FNFL flag.

The heterogeneous Allies had already been joined by Dutch elements after German attacks beginning on 10 May saw Dutch submarines crossing the North Sea. Following an agreement with the Dutch Government in Exile, those boats also came under Royal Navy operational command. Dutch colonial boats operating in the East Indies were able to continue independently until the Japanese declared war.

For the moment, the multinational force, operating out of Scottish bases, most famously as part of the 9th Flotilla at Dundee, would be deployed on patrols around the Norwegian coast to warn of any signs of the predicted invasion of Britain.

With Italy's entry into the war, the Mediterranean became a significant theatre. Within days of the declaration, British army units seized the Italian fort of Capuzzo in Libya, the first move in the North Africa campaign. For the British, the Mediterranean was the gateway to their empire via the Suez Canal, and also the 'underbelly' of occupied Europe. For Italy, the dominant power in the region, it was their 'private lake' and it provided their supply routes to North Africa. Moreover, Italy possessed the second largest submarine fleet in the world – 115 boats, 84 of which were operational. They were, however, comparatively noisy, slow to dive, subject to breakdown, very visible on the surface thanks to their large conning towers, lacking Asdic and, like the rest of the Regia Marina, handicapped by an overly cautious high command. Italy lost ten of her own submarines in that first month. Indeed the Mediterranean proved a graveyard for submarines: it was a congested area, soon to be heavily mined, vulnerable to short-range air attack from British carriers and Italian land bases, and with shallow, clear waters that gave little protection to submarines at periscope depth. The large, ocean-going boats such as HMS *Odin* which had been brought back from the Far East were particularly ill-placed.

The British maintained three bases: Gibraltar, Alexandria and the highly strategic island of Malta, the last two of which were already home to submarine flotillas, now strengthened by the redeployment of some of the submarines that had been kicking their heels in the Far East and Indian Ocean to oppose a Japanese threat that had not yet materialised. Almost immediately after Mussolini's declaration of war Malta experienced the start of a sustained bombing campaign by the Axis powers that would last for more than two years.

By around August and with the Norway invasion over, Dönitz was able to step up the campaign of unrestricted warfare against Allied merchant shipping and neutrals carrying supplies to Britain. The U-boats no longer had to return to their German bases after patrols; following the armistice with France they were able to use the strategic French ports of Lorient and Brest.

Dönitz despatched his U-boats out into the shipping lanes, and the Battle of the Atlantic had begun. Information on convoys was sent out from U-boat headquarters, and the first submarine subsequently to sight the convoy was able to report back and shadow the target while other boats in the area converged ready for a night attack, on the surface. On 16 October 1940, *U-48* sighted Convoy SC.7 from Sydney and over the next three days the German boats sank 20 ships, totalling just under 80,000 tons.

The U-boat commanders called it the 'Happy Time'. Safe from Asdic, which could not detect them on the surface, and from aircraft, which lacked sufficient range, knowing that convoys were insufficiently protected and that their own communications were secure thanks to the 'Enigma' code, they exploited their advantage to the full. Commanders exceeding 100,000 tons of sunk merchant tonnage received the Knight's Cross, and several rapidly became celebrities. They included Kapitänleutnant Joachim Schepke in *U-100* who managed to sink seven ships in just two days; Prien, who augmented the reputation he had won for himself at Scapa Flow, and Kapitänleutnant Otto Kretschmer, *U-99*, who was well on his way to becoming the top-scoring submarine commander of the war. He had worked out that the way to maximise success, in addition to the standard wolf-pack tactics, was not to attack from outside the convoy but to get in among it.

Based at Bordeaux, having run the gauntlet of the Straits of Gibraltar, the first of some 30 Italian submarines were now collaborating with the Germans in the Atlantic, although, with a couple of exceptions, they did not achieve the effectiveness of the Germans whose advantages included the better part of a year's experience at a time when the Allies had not fully organised their convoy defences.

By the end of 1940, U-boats and aircraft had accounted for almost four million tons of Allied shipping, an unsustainable figure for the Allies. The shortage of escorts to defend convoys was increased by the need to defend Britain from the threatened invasion and by the fact that the Germans had broken the British code; it was not changed until August 1940. The figure might have been higher, but as the year waned the weather in the North Atlantic turned ferocious.

The likelihood of a war in the Pacific had increased when Japan signed a pact with Italy and Germany in September. It was a direct warning to the USA not to enter the conflict on the Allied side.

## NORTH SEA, BALTIC AND ARCTIC

**Eryk Sopocko, Polish journalist and writer**; from *Orzel's Patrol*

On 8 April 1940, off Lillesand, ORP *Orzel* encountered and eventually twice torpedoed the German troopship *Rio de Janeiro*

'The torpedo got her almost at the same place on the other side, and she broke in two straight away,' is the news which greets me from the Torpedo Officer. 'Come inside the conning-tower; I'm sure the Captain will let you see.'

I don't need asking twice.

'You're making for the periscopes, I suppose?' the Captain asks me a moment later.

'Yes please, sir, if I may.'

'Carry on. Oh, by the way, are you any good at taking photographs?'

'Well, sir, I've been taking photographs for about eight years,' I answer.

'Good! You might take some with my camera. I'm afraid I'm not much good at it myself.'

I take the Captain's camera and look through the periscope at the outside world. What a picture! *Rio de Janeiro* is broken in two pieces. Already the bow portion is sinking ... gone ... It has vanished beneath the surface, and only the stern stands out high above the water. There you can see the propellers, rudder ... I put the camera to the eye-piece of the periscope and try to take some pictures with various apertures, exposures and distances. But I don't somehow think they will turn out well, as it is the first time in my life I have used a camera in such circumstances. For this kind of thing I have had no practice at all. But still, perhaps I may be lucky. Who knows?

Once again I look outside. The Norwegian trawlers have given up any further rescue work and are hurrying to the coast at full speed. Apparently they have no wish to endanger themselves any longer.

This happening was a cause for rejoicing, but unfortunately I must finish my observation because all this time more and more have been queueing up for the periscope.

Meanwhile the ship has sunk, and there is nothing more to look at, so we disperse to various parts of the boat. The chief cook announces that dinner is ready; it is already late owing to the morning's happenings.

During the meal the spirits of the crew run high. I have never seen anything like it. Lively quips and funny stories are bandied about the table. Petty Officer Sz. feels like having recourse to a glass of whisky. This pleasure, alas, cannot possibly be arranged before the end of the patrol. I relieve my opposite number on watch so that he can have time for his meal. I take a look at our course plotted on the chart in the conning-tower. We are still hovering obstinately round the sunken victim.

'Is there any help arriving for the Germans?' I ask the First Lieutenant.

'No, the aircraft was over again a few minutes ago, but hasn't sent any assistance.'

'Have they any chance themselves of making the coast?' I ask again.

'Absolutely none. It would have been different if they had hoisted out their boats, but as they didn't, I can see only one way, and that is to swim for it. It's true, they've got life-saving jackets, but at this time of year it is quite impossible to keep going in the water longer than an hour, at the very most, two ... Just look at the snow-covered coast-line; those fiords. It's not England, you know, with the full bloom of spring.'

I have to admit the truth of this. A trifle subdued, I volunteer no further remarks, and spend the rest of the time in silence, waiting for the proper watch to finish their dinner.

It was four o'clock in the afternoon, or perhaps a little later, when the news received from the conning-tower begins once more to arouse us by its sensational tone.

There appear floating on the surface above the submarine a number of bodies from the *Rio de Janeiro*.

Accurate observation by periscope assures us, on examination of their uniforms, that without doubt we are dealing with some invading troops. At the same time, however, they lack any characteristic mark which would make it possible to identify them with certainty as German soldiers.

Intrigued by these events I state that I am going to the conning-tower to collect more accurate news. In the wardroom I meet the Torpedo Officer who is writing something in the log, and seems a little excited. It is clear that his mind, too, is engaged on the problems connected with this mysterious affair. In the control-room are more officers. I stop here as the subject of their conversation interests me greatly.

'It would be senseless,' says the Captain to the First Lieutenant. 'In any case those men have been in the water over three hours already, there isn't the slightest chance of any of them being alive.'

'I doubt it too, sir, but as far as I can see it is the only way of clearing up this matter,' insists the First Lieutenant.

'What's up now?' I ask the Boatswain in a low voice.

'The First Lieutenant wants to surface and bring one of these soldiers inside the submarine. Good idea, I think, What do you say, sir?'

'Yes, good; but I'm afraid there's nothing doing. I don't think the Captain will allow it; it's too late now.' I finish this sentence on my way to the conning-tower where the Navigating Officer is keeping watch.

'A lot of pigs' snouts, sir,' is Petty Officer Sz.'s greeting as he busies himself with the steering-wheel.

'Where?' I ask confusedly, not yet following his meaning.

'There! Up top!' the helmsman explains with a slight sweep.

'Humour of this kind is rather out of place, Sz. How can you say that? There are only corpses left now,' admonishes the Sub-Lieutenant.

'Once a snout always a snout. Alive or dead makes no difference,' repeats Sz., full of venom. 'I know those *** too well.'

'Stand by, I'm about to raise periscope,' says the Officer of the Watch to the men on the hydroplanes.

A warning of this kind is necessary as, at the moment of carrying out the operation, the submarine gains additional displacement, and a moment's inattention, especially in rough weather, is sufficient to bring the boat inadvertently to the surface.

The periscope is ready. The Officer of the Watch grasps the handles and puts his eyes to the lenses. Such a picture will be familiar to many from films or magazine pictures of submarine life.

'Ah, they're close to us again,' he says. 'Look!'

At what distance it would be difficult to say, but sufficiently near to be able to determine their features, are three human shapes, drifting farther out to sea on the ebbing tide. Their life-saving jackets keep them on the surface, but only hold them up by their armpits. The heads, drooping from exhaustion, are plunged in the water.

They keep together with folds of uniform clutched tightly in a last spasmodic grasp. The one on the right is face downwards in the water. It is better so. In spite of the fact that they are our mortal enemies, the faces of the two others, livid red and screwed up in a contortion of dread and fatigue, leave a pitiful impression. Those two I shall never forget. They were both boys; capless, with yellowish hair.

Enough sentimentality.

*Orzel* returned safely, but on 11 June, after she failed to return from her next patrol she was pronounced overdue, presumed lost. Journalist Eryk Sopocko, who spent just that one patrol on *Orzel* – allegedly the first journalist to go on a submarine patrol – was killed in 1943 when *U-378* sank the Polish destroyer *Orkan*.

**Chief ERA William Pook, Royal Navy, HMS *Truant*;**
from IWM Sound Archive 9167/1

I only remember the second captain ... Lieutenant Commander Hutchinson, and he very soon became known affectionately by the crew as 'Jockey', due to his habit of wearing riding breeches at sea. Now with him we had three very exciting patrols. On the first one we came across the *Altmark*, which had been grounded in a fjord, and our task was to keep an eye on her and sink her if she came out. We patrolled outside the fjord and eventually went in to have a look and see if she was still there. This was a tricky manoeuvre, but we managed it, confirmed she was still there, and returned to our patrol position. After some days we were sent away from that position because the *Altmark* apparently was not coming out and we had trouble then with fishing nets.

On the next patrol we sank – made our first kill, put it that way – a German collier. She was ordered to stop. She didn't do, so shots were fired by the 4-inch gun, she was hit, and eventually we picked up the captain and took him as a prisoner of war, and left the crew to pull for shore. She was *Edgar Hugo Steins IV* [*Edmund Hugo Stinnes IV*].

One problem with being crew in a submarine is that you don't see anything. The captain is really the only man who sees what's going on and knows what's going on. Unless it's a gun action of course and the gun action crew do see what's happening. But the normal crew inside the boat, you have to judge by remarks passed as to what is happening.

The captain who came aboard, we had him down below with us. He was a very pleasant chap. He'd been a prisoner of war in the First War and we got on very well with him. He was quite happy to be a prisoner of war. We spoke to him and he could speak English. He joined with us and talked to us. So it was no problem with him at all. As far as I know it was off the Danish coast; I don't know the exact spot.

The next patrol was in April 1940 and before leaving harbour the captain cleared lower deck and told us that the Germans were expecting to invade Norway. Now our billet was inside the Skaggarat, just south of Oslo, which we duly arrived having negotiated the minefields at the entrance, and things were quiet until the evening of the 9th April. This I remember well because it was the birthday of one of the artificers: Bill King. I've never forgotten that date, 9th April 1940, and we were called to diving stations, had about half an hour at diving stations, fell out and the captain came on the Tannoy and gave every-body a blast for being slow to get to diving stations as he's missed an attack on a flotilla of destroyers. The crew, of course, were quite pleased about this – they didn't want to attack a flotilla of destroyers. However, a little later, diving stations again, and an attack was successfully made on the German cruiser *Karlsruhe*, a 6,000-ton cruiser.

Ten torpedoes were fired in that attack, in a spread, and the cruiser sank. The destroyers attacked us; we were so close that the first destroyer coming down, throwing charges over the side, was so close that the captain couldn't see the bridge, so we did a crash dive and the first charges split our after trim tank. As I was ... Chief Artificer ... I saw the water coming in through the tanks. The after tank was full up, the bulkheads started to leak and we were very heavy aft, so we were at an angle and the after end, eventually, we were down to 420 feet which was way over our diving depth. We were like that for some hours. Every time we tried to come up we were depth charged again, and it went on until very nearly morning when we did eventually get up and the enemy had gone and we were lucky enough to be able to get out the Skaggarat and back to harbour ...

Stern glands were leaking and I had to tighten those up. We had to hammer up the bulkhead of the trim tank which had been damaged. We were jamming off valves which had blown open with the charges. Apart from that, if there was nothing to do we laid in bunks and waited. It was terrifying, there's no doubt about it. I don't care who it is that's been on these jobs, you must be frightened. It's not that charges that are frightening, it's the waiting for them, particularly in a submarine where you hear the destroyers coming towards you. And you know that the next thing you are going to hear is a depth charge. When they're dropping, it's gone: you get used to it. You hear the propellers through the water, the thrum hum of the propellers. Gradually it gets louder and louder, almost like a train going over the top ... you would hear noises in the ship if they dropped a spanner or something, same as they could hear you and you always went to quiet routine if you're being attacked so that you didn't move about too much. You made sure you didn't drop anything, you spoke in whispers, you didn't use the Tannoy or anything like that. Because water does conduct sound over a great distance.

I wouldn't say that people showed their fear. You're all together, you're all on the same boat, and I think it's a matter of disciplining yourself. A submarine is obviously a disciplined service. You don't show it. You're probably churning over inside but you don't show it,

The atmosphere was getting a bit thick. We'd been down some time, we'd been dived all day, the day before. We hadn't been able to get charging up, so our battery was getting low, the air was getting thick – and in those days you had no means of refreshing the air like you have in the modern submarines ...You start to pant, your senses start to go a little bit, you don't think so quickly and, of course, that's always a danger.

**Captain George Hunt, DSO\*, DSC\*, Royal Navy, then a sub-lieutenant in HMS *Unity***

From August 1939 we had been patrolling regularly in the North Sea, leaving from Blyth, which is halfway up the English east coast. On this occasion (April

1940) we were to go up the swept channel to St Abbs Head (we were unescorted) and then go straight across the North Sea to our position off Heligoland in Germany. It was evening – getting dark anyway – and it was thick fog [29 April]. And this Norwegian merchant ship loomed out of the fog. Now, due to an unfortunate mix-up in the signal department in Blyth, we hadn't been told that there was a convoy coming down the coast. We thought we would just be going up the coast and we wouldn't meet anybody, but there was a convoy coming down and we could hear the sirens of people making fog signals. One ship sounded pretty close, and she suddenly loomed out of the fog. We were going north, she was going south.

The chief officer of the Norwegian ship (the *Atle Jarl*, a neutral at the time) said to the captain: 'That's a U-boat!' And the captain said: "Hell's teeth!' or whatever they said in Norwegian, and they went hard over to ram us; at the last minute, however, they saw the White Ensign and went full speed astern but it was too late; otherwise, if they'd just kept going, we would just have passed. I know all this for a fact because I was talking to him after we had been rescued.

And so our captain, Lieutenant F. J. Brooks, who was on the bridge at the time, because it was thick fog and we could hear all these sirens, ordered 'Collision stations' before we were actually hit, and then 'Prepare to abandon ship', because there was only one way in which to abandon ship, and that was to come up the conning tower.

I was told by my captain: 'As each chap comes up on the bridge just tell him: "Go to the back of the bridge and blow up your life-ring."' But, of course, by that time we'd been hit, and so water was really pouring into the submarine. Fortunately, we were hit fairly far for'ard and so nearly everybody got out and then went down on to the after casing, except for two people who stayed down below to stop the engines, which were still going – to stop them and also to get people out. These two were the First Lieutenant, Lieutenant J. N. A. Low, and Able Seaman Henry Miller, and for their gallantry and calmness in doing their duty to the end they were both awarded, posthumously, the George Cross.

In those days we had no lifebelts worthy of the name, except we were issued with an inflatable rubber tube, and of all the colours to choose from, it was covered in a blue sort of denim stuff!! It also had a tube so that it could be inflated by mouth. Now, if you blew it up before you got out of the submarine, it made you so big it was difficult to get through the conning tower hatch, so the theory was, you tied it round your body while deflated, came up to the bridge, and then got into the water and blew up your life ring – unless you had been able to do it on the bridge. It was ridiculous really, but that was the beginning of the war and we were learning. My God, we were learning. You can do exercises in peacetime till you're blue in the face, but when real war starts you learn fast. So we did lose a couple of chaps in the water, I'm afraid, but otherwise we swam about and were rescued. One or two had got DSEA sets, but there really wasn't enough time.

My captain and I, and Lieutenant J. F. Trickey, who was in the South African naval forces, and who was also the officer of the watch at the time, all got sucked down quite a long way as we were on the bridge, and I burst an eardrum.

As soon as we got back to the surface we tried to rally the chaps, and we all tried to keep together as much as possible. They started a singsong in the water, so as they went around I advised them to 'keep your breath for staying afloat'.

But they all more or less stayed together. A couple drifted apart and were drowned. There was a fair tide sluicing along, of course.

Eventually the ship that hit us came back, which was lucky – because at the last moment the Norwegian captain had said, 'That was a White Ensign.' But by then they had disappeared in the fog, and so he did came back as near as he could to the position where he had hit us. From the lifeboat which they launched they managed to pick us up. The Norwegian ship, I may say, was very good to us. We went down to the engine room and dried our clothes. They lent us trousers and shirts and all sorts of things. But the ship had no wireless (not compulsory then!) and so we had to wait until morning when we saw a destroyer and she was able to report the tragedy to our base in Blyth.

About six o'clock in the morning we were landed at North Shields but there were a lot of people hanging around at the time, and they saw us bedraggled-looking, and they started booing because word had got around that we were a captured U-boat's crew. And then they got quite a lot of Old English from the sailors and a few Anglo-Saxon swearwords with it, so they then started cheering!

In retrospect we should have been escorted in a busy swept channel in Home Waters and the blue rubber 'life ring' was a farce.

After the inquiry, we were sent on a few days' 'survivors' leave', but I was recalled after 24 hours because Holland had just been invaded and their submarines were coming over to Portsmouth, UK, and I was required as one of the Liaison Officers.

### Luitenant ter Zee 1 Peter de Jong, Koninklijke Marine, O.24

Then a Luitenant 2, Peter de Jong was at Rotterdam supervising the completion of O.24 when on 10 May Germany attacked the Netherlands. The submarine had only been launched in March.

*O.23* and *O.24* were at the Rotterdam Dry Dock. *O.23* had done her trials; we hadn't done a thing yet. I was in my rooms in Rotterdam and I got a phone call that the Germans had attacked and the war had started. I went to the ship in the dockyard, and in the ship there was a letter to be opened in case of war. I opened that letter and it was a very short and clear one: 'As soon as the war breaks out, go across to Britain. Finish the ship, and come back and take part in the war'. That last sentence took me six years. But it was quite clear.

There was one captain for *O.23* and *O.24*. I was looking after *O.24*. He had the supervision, but I did it, and I had a very small crew. There was a very small aerodrome about one, two miles away from the ship. We had no weapon whatsoever, and we saw to our surprise that German parachutists came down. We thought: 'Good lord, in a minute they'll come here, and I had got nothing to shoot with or do anything with. We must go away.' That was the captain of *O.23*. So I had my men quickly bring as much of the spare parts that still had to be built in on board and we went away and crossed the river and berthed the other side in a harbour on the north side of the river. And then we rang The Hague, the headquarters, and we said: 'We're *23* and *24* – we're going out to Britain; tonight, we leave.' And they said: 'No, you can't, because the Germans have dropped mines in the river, and you can't get out. We've got to clear these mines first. So you must wait.'

So we waited, and in the meantime I tried to get some food on board from the shops, and we thought – I had an engineer officer; he and I were the only officers at that time – we were far too light to submerge. And there was a big building there, one of those commercial stores with copper stocks. We started to figure which things we needed, and we thought we needed quite a bit. So we asked the crew to go and bring a lot of these copper ingots and put them down in the boat.

Next day we rang again and said, 'Are the mines clear?' and they said, 'No, unfortunately there are more mines.' Then we said, 'Well, we'll go.' At that last minute, practically, in the afternoon – we'd said we'd go tonight – there came a captain of submarines, Luitenant ter Zee 1st Class Koudijs. He'd come from the Hague and he'd been on the staff, and he said 'It's going to end; can I come with you?' And then Captain Van Erkel said: 'Alright, you take *O.23*, she's farthest along, she's had her trials. I myself take *O.24*.'

So we had a captain.

The engines were pretty well brand new. They'd had a quarter of an hour without any load, that's all they had done. And the gyros, just that moment finished. Funnily enough, that was a German gyro – Anschütz Kompass.

We had a compass and we had engines, but we had never been submerged. Anyway, that night we sailed, very close to the north wall. There were troops there, and they thought: well, what is this in the darkness? We had put every-body on deck in case we hit a mine, and they started shooting. There were a lot of bullet holes, but they didn't hit anybody. And we came out to some sort of net near Hook of Holland but we put the engines at full speed and cut the net, and out we went. It became clear that later we must submerge, try it out at least ... The boat had never been submerged yet. There's one way to do this, and that is to take in a high pressure of air inside. We figured that if the air can't get out the water can't come in. So we took compressed air in the boat. And it held, so we pulled the plug and submerged. We hit the ground at 30 metres. We had made a mistake with our figures and we were far, far too heavy!

We were all a bit tired and so we thought: let's have a few hours' sleep. The engineer was going to have one watch and I'd take the second half. I'd hardly touched my cushion when he came and woke me up and said: 'We'll have to surface again. It's the pumps.' Quite a lot of water had poured in here and there through little holes and things. He had tried to pump it away but there was all sorts of stuff in the boat so the pumps stopped and the air leaked away in the meantime ... We had to do something, and the only thing to do is blow. So I went to the captain and said: 'We've got to surface quickly.' We called all hands, and then we started blowing and there was terrific over-pressure in the boat. I thought: I'm going to the conning tower hatch myself, because if you open it too hastily you will get blown out yourself and the hatch is damaged: you must ventilate first. I was carefully ventilating that hatch and then I opened it and all I saw was a Messerschmitt coming straight down on us. But these things are funny because he was diving straight at us and I could see he had no bombs. He had only machine guns, so he was rattling away, and in the mean-time the captain had come up and we jumped behind the conning tower. The pilot gave it up as a bad job and disappeared.

We went to Dover and on to Portsmouth. We weren't quite finished so we were sent to Southampton to the yard there. They were really geared up for destroyers, they were not used to submarine building. But the major part was the pressure hull, and all the important parts were in place There was an over-seer at the yard, a Mr West. He came to me one day and said 'Mr de Jong, I have a beautiful chart from the man who built the ship – he was in England, too. He has given me lovely drawings. It is steel 51 and steel 54. All I have got is gun metal and mild steel!' So I thought, well it can't go wrong, all the important parts to submerge are in place. I said: 'Do you know what we'll do Mr West? On even days we'll take the gunmetal and on odd days the mild steel.'

He said: 'A perfect solution, sir.'

We did our trials in Scotland and we started doing business.

## CHANNEL AND ATLANTIC

**Capitaine de Vaisseau Etienne Schlumberger, FNFL;**
from *L'Honneur et Les Rebelles de la Marine Française, 1940–1944*

French Naval Engineer Etienne Schlumberger had been supervising construction of a quartet of submarines at Cherbourg in June 1940, and in anticipation of events had ignored orders to make changes to the battery mountings. On 19 June 1940, the Germans entered the town, which surrendered at 1700, and then the shipyard. Starting from the previous evening, the submarines had already left under tow.

Those people who wanted to leave gathered on the quay. In front of a dock gate which had been mined and was about to explode was a large and elegant launch belonging to the Direction des Constructions Navales, but she was hard to handle. Usually she needed two men: a coxwain and a mechanic. I tried to get her going on my own. The engine started, I cast off the ropes, went full speed astern, threw myself at the wheel and got away just before the gate went up.

Others have described Cherbourg at that moment as apocalyptic: exploding bombs, huge blazes and hell-fire ...

I ran a taxi service between the DCAN quay and the boats on their way to England. I took on board, five or six at a time, those who wanted to go, about 30 all told, and ferried them out to the small vessels ... A naval lieutenant tried to argue he was senior to a naval engineer and told me to take him to another part of the Arsenal. I told *him* where to go.

In the afternoon, my launch and I caught up with one of the submarines for which I was responsible. Like the others, she was being towed by a tug which also took us in tow for I didn't know how much fuel I had ...

I was proud of myself. If I had not disobeyed orders, the battery supports of the four submarines would have been modified, but the boats themselves would have been unable to put to sea. I could not know, then, that the departure was only the prelude to an exciting and passionate love affair with one of them: the *Junon*.

We reached England in the course of the night, and the following morning it was Portsmouth for the *Orion* and the *Ondine* and my launch. The *Minerve* and the *Junon* went to Plymouth. I came ashore into a different world

Etienne Schlumberger became one of the staunchest advocates of the Forces Navales Françaises Libres (FNFL), and the *Junon* and the *Minerve* joined the *Rubis* as FNFL submarines. Schlumberger's other pair, *Orion* and *Ondine*, were used for spare parts for their two sisters.

**Ship's Doctor 1st Class L. N. [Louis Nistour]**; Report dated 8 December 1940 at Toulon, to the Chief of the Medical Branch of the Third Naval Region. Source: Francis Louis, printed in *Plongée*

REPORT ON THE EVACUATION OF BREST AND TIME SPENT IN ENGLAND.

On the morning of 18 June, the order to evacuate Brest made no difference to the courage or the confidence of the crew who reaped the rewards of the last weeks of uninterrupted work on final adjustments at the dockyard. In emergency, the *Surcouf* could sail and we all wanted to carry on the fight. Morale was high; health was excellent. The previous days had allowed us to load all the medical supplies essential for a long patrol. Putting to sea on the evening of the 18th was difficult for us against a background of fires which began to spring up at the end of the Brest roads.

Major faults led to a change of destination from our original choice, which was Casablanca. We could only proceed, surfaced, at four knots, towards the English coast; no enemy aircraft appeared. Off the Longship, a Sunderland, not yet our enemy, identified us and gave a friendly greeting.

We sighted land at Penzance late afternoon on the 19th. The aft hydroplane problem was repaired. After some hesitation, marked by turning two full circles, we decided to proceed to Plymouth, which we reached during the night. We anchored in the outer channel: our arrival appeared to rouse the considerable interest of two English launches, which continually circled us. We all felt a degree of foreboding. Were we already prisoners? Wouldn't it be better to leave at once? We would soon find out.

We sailed into Devonport on the 20th. During the voyage bathers and holidaymakers waved joyfully at us, the last display of 'good old England'. Having arrived at the end of the mousetrap, opposite the Devonport construction yards, *Surcouf* moored alongside the *Paris*. There we endured 15 days of anxiety and uncertainty, which was finally ended on 3 July.

On 2 July, towards 2230, while I was on medical duty, I was called by the *Paris* to examine a sick crew member aboard the destroyer *Ouragon* that was moored on the other side of the river. Drizzle, all quiet on the dockside, and on the English vessels there was complete blackout. When I got back on board at around 0015 on the 3rd, I asked the captain who was still sitting at his desk if he had any news regarding our concerns. He said he had just had all the reassurance he needed on the Paris.

3 July. I was woken with a start at about 0430 by the Lieutenant de Vaisseau C [Crescent]. shouting: 'The English are here!' I got out of bed and dressed; the engineer, D [Lieutenant Daniel], was pulling on his overalls. Lieutenant de Vaisseau Bouillaut opened the pistol rack, which was next to our quarters. With self-defence in mind, we got out the ammunition we had secretly distributed

the day before. I put a box of rounds as well as my pistol on our washstand. When I entered the wardroom all the officers were present except for Bouillaut who was on guard at the top of the ladder which came down into the wardroom. The [British] commander, S [Commander D. V. Sprague], was leaning by the bunk, a form in his hand. On either side of him were Lieutenant-Commander G [Lieutenant Patrick Griffiths], a sub-lieutenant and two or three sailors, all armed. Commander S, who looked pale, continually mopped his brow; 'I'm sorry, I have my orders.' We were often to hear this particular refrain, which in the eyes of an Englishman excuses everything.

After a momentary hesitation, our captain abruptly decided to go aboard the *Paris* and put the Admiral in the picture. As he went up the ladder, he said to the exec: 'P, over to you.'

Gradually the wardroom emptied of English. Eventually there was only Lieutenant Commander G standing by the entrance to my quarters. I suggested to D that he should take advantage of the brief respite and load his pistol. As an extra precaution, I went out and exchanged a few words with the English officer to distract his attention. Returning to my quarters I found D who had just finished changing. Voices were being raised in the wardroom, which was filling with the English. I leaned back against the bulkhead of the gangway leading to our compartment. At this moment, Commander S was in the entrance to the captain's cabin; Lieutenant-Commander G by the ladder; next to me, a sergeant wearing a helmet and dressed in khaki, bayonet in his rifle; next to him, an English sailor carrying a revolver. Of the French officers I saw only Lieutenant de Vaisseau C, standing up and leaning against the edge of the wardroom table, opposite Commander S.

Lieutenant-Commander S appeared nervous now. Sharply he ordered us to get off. Taking a very brave stand, C told him in no uncertain terms that we were not leaving without our captain's order. S seemed to lose patience and asked for assistance. In French he repeated his order to C, saying, 'If you don't chose to leave I will kill you.' Not without risk, for we knew the English, C answered: 'Shoot if you like; I'm not going.'

I rushed into my cabin saying to D who was busy tearing up plans: 'There's going to be trouble' and picked up my pistol. I had hardly time to turn round when I heard shots, just as the English sergeant hurled himself at us, bayonet advanced. I emptied the barrel into him. Under the force of his own momentum, he fell dead at our feet in front of the washbasin, having just had the time, alas, to fire his own weapon. Engineer D, hit in the right side, collapsed with a cry. I stepped over the body of the sergeant and leapt at the English sailor who was following him and who seemed to be having a problem with his pistol. I managed to disarm him and with a blow sent him staggering into the curtain door of the Engineer. I advanced on him and with a more accurate punch, which dislocated my thumb, I sent him tumbling to the foot of the wardroom ladder where he played dead.

As the English had now opened fire on those of us in the control room, after having passed in front of my comrades who were now all holding pistols, I went into the cabin of the Exec, who was loading his pistol. I asked him if he had another one; he answered 'No.' All the English in the wardroom were *hors de combat*.

We retreated to the end of the wardroom. The firing had finished. Bouillaut told me he was wounded. I gave him reassurance. Bouillaut explained to C that he fired to defend him because the English were going to shoot him down. That's my opinion, too. Only the speed and accuracy of Bouillaut's shot saved him from death.

The Exec felt there was no point in prolonging the fight. Bouillaut protested. However, it was clear we couldn't achieve any more with our pistols. And so Commander P advised the English that the affair was over and they could come down. Wisely, they preferred to see us come up, which we did, one by one. I was the last one in the wardroom; I went to see D who was unconscious and dying, mortally wounded. I then went to S whom I found with his back against the screen by the captain's office. He was able to tell me clearly that he was wounded in the right shoulder. He had also been hit in the abdomen. His lips were beginning to turn pale.

One of Bouillaut's bullets must have passed through his shoulder and cut one of the larger blood vessels, causing a haemorrhage which had to be fatal. Lieutenant G looked dead to me. The English ordered me to come up. I could not tell the full extent of the damage.

In the control room the blood-soaked sailor whom I'd hit pointed me out to his comrades, but nothing happened. Anyhow, I took Bouillaut to the sickbay and gave him preliminary treatment under the watchful eyes of the English sailors who, pistols in hand, observed our every movement. All the time some English sailors were repeatedly asking me to see to their wounded officers. I told them to wait.

I left Bouillaut lying bandaged-up on one of the bunks in the sickbay and went to the control room. There, stretched out on the floor, Lieutenant Commander G was surrounded by frantic medical orderlies. He had been hit in the liver, the thigh and in one arm (he may have been hit elsewhere, too). His condition gave no cause for hope. I advised the orderlies to get him to hospital as a matter of urgency. I was about to go down to the wardroom where I could see the English gathered round commander S when an English sub-lieutenant strictly forbade me to proceed and sent me off the boat. Commander S and Lieutenant Commander G would not have survived their injuries.

At no moment during those events did I find any trace of medical organisation. Although they later acknowledged that they were prepared for bloodshed, it seemed that the fight had taken them completely by surprise. The ambulances had not arrived before I left for the Paris, in other words roughly half an hour after the battle.

After having been taken to the naval barracks, at about 1130 we were allowed back on board, one at a time. A sub-lieutenant told me to take only what was essential and gave me his word of honour that the rest of our baggage would be boxed up and sent to us. Another broken promise. That evening, having refused us permission to attend the funeral of our dear comrade, D assembled us and locked us up in a train bound for Liverpool. A new life, that of the prison camps, was about to begin.

Eventually, and under a different crew, the *Surcouf* also became an FNFL submarine.

## MEDITERRANEAN

**Sub-Lieutenant Robert Lagane, Vichy Marine, *Iris*;**
from *Cinq Ans dans le Brouillard*

On 4 July the French Navy's 15th Submarine Flotilla, which included Robert Lagane's *Iris*, was ordered to protect any French surface ships escaping the carnage at Mers el Kebir.

There was an air of unreality about the situation. The 44 of us going along at 10 knots, alone, in a little steel tube, lost in the fog somewhere between the two greatest battle fleets ever assembled at sea – which were heading our way at 26 knots with 40,000 crew and half a million tonnes of guns and scrap iron in the same fog that you could cut with a knife.

I took comfort from the fact that in this sort of weather we were safe from surprise attacks by the *Ark Royal's* planes.

0800. I handed over to Dégé while, over a snack, I carried on with the task of absorbing the differences in outline between French and English ships so I could tell at first glance a *Marseillaise* from an *Arethusa* (easy) and also a *Tramontane* from a *Faulknor*, which didn't seem obvious.

I was back on duty from 1000 until 1200. The fog had lifted occasionally. At 1150 the coxwain, Quilliou, came to take my place on the bridge.

'I'm relieving you early, sir, because the captain is waiting for you to have lunch with the 2nd and 3rd below.'

I had hardly sat down at the wardroom table when I heard shouting from the voice pipe.

'Sir! French destroyer dead ahead, 400 metres. No, two destroyers line abreast, right ahead of us! Fire recognition shells!'

When I got up onto the bridge behind the captain, we were just passing into the gap between the two destroyers which were steering an opposite course sometimes less than 100 metres apart and at 35 knots. Their entire armament was trained on us. The muzzles of a dozen 130mm guns followed us as we went through and we could see into their open mouths right down to the end of the barrel. Thank God they were not English ones!

As they passed, the captains waved and exchanged good wishes by semaphore.

From the *Tigre*: 'Thank you and good luck.'

From the *Iris*: 'Bravo and safe journey."

The destroyers faded into the fog. I reckoned that they had been in sight a little over 45 seconds.

Hearty congratulations went out to the coxwain.

'Hats off to you for spotting it. That's no mean feat, identifying a ship by its stem as it looms out of the fog at 400 metres.'

'Rubbish,' he replied with a smile. 'There'd have to be something wrong, to have spent four years knocking around in one of those tubs and not be able to recognise it!'

But suppose the destroyer had emerged a few minutes earlier, in front of a midshipman and a signalman, neither of whom had served in one of those tubs? A chill went down my spine when I thought of it afterwards.

**Lieutenant Ian Anderson, Royal Navy, HMS *Odin*;**
from the Papers of Lieutenant Anderson, Imperial War Museum

WEDNESDAY 10 JANUARY [1940].

It is some time since I did anything about writing this journal, up for little enough has happened recently. Also, I've been feeling so bored, fed up and generally depressed of late that I couldn't give my mind to a diary. Colombo is pretty vile, all things considered, though it improves slowly. Also the climate was getting us down, hot and sticky and conducive to lassitude and as we went into dock on the 5th and there was plenty to be done, that didn't help much. But today we came to Diyatalawa Camp, 6,000 feet up in the hills where the air is pure and powerful and already I feel a new man. Now to start reducing my stomach which is beginning to assume balloon-like proportions for lack of exercise of late.

MADAGASCAR PATROL, 5 FEBRUARY TO 31 MARCH 1940.

Monday 5th.

We sailed at 0800 this morning and spent the day exercising off Colombo. It is going to be very different from the days of Mousie and Paul; I'm not sure how I shall like it without them, though there is no doubt that our new captain will make the boat a far more efficient concern than it was before, as Mousie, delightful fellow and all that, was much too lazy and bored with life to bother much about anything. Woods is young and keen and, judging from the way he attacked today for the first time, extremely capable! He is also very pleasant, so there shouldn't be any difficulty. I would like to have Paul here still, though, but Lee seems reasonable enough. Wingfield, well, I'm not sure yet; I think I've had about enough of him.

For a change I've taken on navigation; there should be plenty of opportunity to become a rival to Vasco de Gama on this trip. Our first stop in Sundiva – then Peros again, and then across to Diego Suarez.

9 February, Friday.

Once more at Peros Bahars, a feat which causes no little excitement. We made Sundiva (with extreme accuracy of course) on Wednesday and spent the night there. This time the natives had got over their initial panic and were happy to barter flying fish and turtle eggs, for stale bread and cigarettes, out of which bargain the advantages seemed to lie with us, although the turtle eggs were not appreciated.

12 February, Monday.

There has been little rest for us this weekend. On Saturday and Sunday we were over to Salonas to try and get this wireless in working order and teach their operator, who spoke little English, a rather complicated code, a task almost beyond the scope of my French. However, it was a good excuse for going ashore the first day and we were most hospitably entertained by M. Caboche, the Manager, his daughter and another female who plied us with rum and turtle steaks. They also put a live pig in the boat which brought us back, unknown to me, but it was returned with thanks as we decided killing a pig in a submarine would be too much. Unfortunately, the wireless side of the show was not successful and early next morning we returned meaning to do the test ourselves; the PO Tel and I set forth in the skiff to try and land on the beach, as it was low tide and we couldn't cross the reef. It looked calm enough from the ship but landing proved quite impossible as there was a heavy surf and long jagged tongues of coral projected some way out. After three or four attempts to land, the last of which was very nearly disastrous and we escaped being swamped by a hair's breadth, I decided that discretion in this case undoubtedly came before valour and that our four lives together were of more value than a wireless organisation, so we returned unsuccessful but not disgraced as the skiff's antics had been watched with interest from the submarine.

We then received instructions from the C-in-C to proceed to Diego Garcia and collar 100 bags of rice for [illegible] and Peros where they are very short, owing to the disappearance of the island's schooner, and the late arrival of the schooner from Mauritius. Accordingly we sailed last night and arrived at Diego this morning in absolutely bloodstained weather – rain poured down from 4 a.m. till 1 p.m. and we very nearly missed the place altogether as we did last time; however, we got in about 10 this morning which wasn't so bad and we didn't have to spend all day searching this time; on the last occasion one of our stokers was heard to say to his chum, both fed up at having to keep an extra watch – 'Cor, if Columbus 'ad bin in this ruddy ship America would never have been discovered!'

We sailed again at 4.30 p.m. for Peros, the whole of the torpedo room piled high with sacks of rice. No longer HMS we are now the 'SS *Odin*, freighter, regular and fast steamer service between the islands with space for a few passengers'.

HMS *Odin* was transferred to Malta in anticipation of Italy's entry into the war.

Tuesday 4 June.
The balloon is going up, or someone thinks it is. At any rate tonight we sail, just in case – that we shall be all set to do our worst at the earliest opportunity. I don't think I shall take this diary with me; it would be a pity for it, as well as myself, to be fish food if the worst occurred. Personally I still feel optimistic and believe that Musso is merely putting up a gigantic bluff and that it won't be long before the excitement of the moment will have died down and be a thing of the past. And then perhaps I'll get home. There is no time for more now as there is much to be done, and so, for the time being, I bid farewell to myself, and, incidentally, to anyone who has waded through the monotonous mono-logue of these pages.

On 19 May 1940 Anderson wrote a letter to be sent to his family in the event of his death:

Things being in a state of acute tension here in Malta just now with no one quite knowing when we shall hear the drone of Italian bombers overhead, it seems necessary to write this letter – just in case. I sincerely hope you will never receive it, but I should hate to die without making a farewell of some kind to you all ...

And now it is late and I must end.

I hate this finish to everything as much as you do, especially as there has been no chance of seeing you first. It is a little hard after three years to be robbed of the leave I had so much looked forward to. But I do hope you won't be sad – any of you – because really the world is so unsatisfactory just now that one can hardly grumble at being forcibly removed from it. In any case I shall watch with interest your doings on earth from my next port of call and if I can be of any assistance to you there I shall do my best to render it. And in a few years time no doubt we shall all meet again and the things which have seemed so important on this earth, which have made us sad or glad or happy or angry or bored or excited or disappointed will all have been forgotten in the context of that new place. And so good-bye and remember

No Tears!

With all my love to you all

Ian

On 14 June the submarine was sunk with all hands by the Italian destroyers *Strale* and *Baleno*.

### Stoker Sydney Hart, Royal Navy, HMS *Triad*; from *Discharged Dead*

July of 1940 found HM Submarine *Triad*, in company with Submarine *Truant*, outward-bound for the Middle Sea, *Mare Nostrum* as Mussolini vaingloriously called that interesting stretch of water. Not that we knew we were bound in that direction. All sorts of rumours flooded the mess deck – we were heading for Africa's West Coast to deal with the U-boats gathered there to wreak havoc with our southbound trade, now that Italy's entry into the war had practically sealed the Mediterranean to our commerce, which was switched to round the Cape, and waste valuable time in so doing. Or, so the buzz (rumour) went. We'd base on Gibraltar and work up towards Biscay, to deal with possible enemy U-boats that might dog our outward convoys. All we knew exactly was that we were outward-bound from Dundee, and that we were proceeding down the west coast somewhere – a voyage into the Unknown. As far as Land's End we had the escort vessel, *White Bear*, in company, and then *Triad* and *Truant* parted company prior to making rendezvous off the Rock.

With a last farewell look at England's 'high, grey western land', our course was laid for Gibraltar. Only myself, and, I believe, two others, ever saw that blessed land again. Such was the fortune of war. Our voyage out was uneventful, but *Truant* had different luck. The story ran that HM Submarine *Truant* would find an enemy ship in the middle of the Sahara ...

We now had a new Captain in Lieutenant-Commander Salt, a very competent and experienced officer, and we were all anxious to know how the luck would run. In Gibraltar we tied up alongside the jetty and also alongside *Truant*. As little repair work was necessary we spent the lazy days sunbathing or fishing; an hour or so's work sufficing to keep the ship in spick and span order. Most of the nights found us in the Universal or Trocadero Bars, drinking that lukewarm Spanish *cerveja* – a beer that didn't get you far, but did quench the human thirst.

On our last night at Gib, prior to sailing for Malta, the majority of both *Triad's* and *Truant's* crews stayed aboard, the shore failing to attract. It was a night out of a dream; calm and still, warm and happy. Those southern stars glowed in the purple sky like nothing ever seen in sterner northern climes. The soft lap of water on the submarines' sides spelt peace; and to add to the illusion, Seaman Jones brought up his guitar to produce haunting music. In this peaceful and happy state I little thought that this would be the last night I should spend with *Triad's* crew in port. I'm never likely to forget that wonderful night, for Jones's music – very soft and languishing – floated across the harbour until pretty late. He was lost not long afterwards. The combined crews sat lazily around, listening, and occasionally joining in a chorus. I saw two tired Rock Scorpions [naval slang for the local people] get up from their prone position and squat lazily on their haunches, as Jones played on.

Next day found us Malta-bound with only haunting memories of a wonderful night. I was by now a Leading Stoker, but still shared Thomas's watch. We were due to arrive in Malta three weeks after sailing from Gib, as we were billed to carry out a short patrol en route. On this patrol we attacked one convoy, but before any results could be ascertained the convoy's escorts drove us well below the surface, so that, on arrival at Grand Harbour, we were unable to lay a claim to any successes.

By doctor's orders, on that first day of arrival, I was ordered to hospital. I begged to be allowed to stay in *Triad*, as I felt I'd be quite fit in a couple of days, by the time *Triad* was due to sail again. He thought for a moment and then said:

'No. You'd better miss a trip. You can rejoin when she comes back.' A fateful decision for me. Had the doctor accepted my point of view I should not now be writing this story. That clean, white hospital bed in which they installed me was unspeakable luxury after sleeping for so long in a hard submarine bunk.

The afternoon before *Triad* sailed, on what proved her last patrol, Thomas and Thompson paid me a visit, making me realise the sort of shipmates I'd sailed with, men who'd spend their last few hours ashore in visiting a man in worse case than themselves. And they had a whole month's busy patrol in front of them – they deserved something gayer. I admit my eyes were a bit hot and damp as I wished them luck, and gave a solemn promise to be back in their company in time for their next patrol. Half an hour later I had another visitor: Stoker Taff Evans. As I wished him luck and good hunting, he forced a pound note into my hand with the words, 'You can find more use for that than I can.' I resolved then and there that I would be back on board the old *Triad* when next she reached port.

And then, a week before I left hospital, I heard that *Triad* was overdue – 'Missing, presumed lost.' Poor old *Triad*! Grand old shipmates. I walked from the ward with tears in my eyes, and slumped on the veranda, with bitter feelings in my heart and with an acute desire to avenge these gallant lads. My brain was numbed, but through the numbness flashed the memories of these men and the runs ashore we'd shared together. How, for instance, we had placed about forty beer bottles in the train compartment where the Chief Stoker was the only occupant – sound asleep – when we knew his wife would be meeting him at the station, hoping she'd see the empties and believe he had drunk the lot! How, too, just a few weeks ago, ERA Hayward had said, 'My father was lost in a submarine in the second year of the First World War. I wonder if the same fate awaits me!' And now all were gone, and by some odd twist of Fate, I was left. What did it all mean? 'To-day to me, to-morrow to thee?'

Repinings got no man anywhere. A week later I walked into the ship's office at the submarine base at Lazzeretto. I was there for duty and glad of it. The officer-in-charge asked me my rank and name, looked through the books and said: 'I can't find anything about you. Where did you come from?'

'Hospital, sir,' I replied.

'I know that. But where before that?' '*Triad*,' I replied.

'Good God man, you're supposed to be dead!' he said.

I looked at the wall, where I saw the names of four T-Class submarine crews. *Triad* was still there, and my name was still amongst the muster. The officer-in-charge then informed me that, first thing next morning, I was to go over to St Angelo and get my pay sorted out, but I knew that there were other things to be sorted out as well. No one could be blamed for thinking me still on board *Triad*, as when we arrived the Base had not been formed, and my ship had come out more or less as a lone wolf.

On arrival at St Angelo the next day I went into the Pay Office, and down came *Triad's* pay ledgers. My name, of course, was there with *Triad's* crew, and for some minutes, whilst my pay account was being made up, I looked at those significant names, the last time I'd ever see them together in a pay ledger. All of them, my own included, had the bold red ink line through them, and DD again was against each name. I asked the writer, in my ignorance: 'What does DD stand for?'

'Discharged Dead,' was his reply ... My feelings may better be imagined than described! On my way back to the Base I sent off a cablegram to report myself OK to my home. Safe, yes – but for how long? I pinched myself to make certain that I was still alive. I confess it is an odd emotion to be a hale and hearty ghost!

At Base I was drafted to the submarine *Perseus*, which I found was docking for a prolonged period I knew quite well that, by hook or by crook, I must get clear of *Perseus* and on to an operational submarine, as the feeling of action would lessen these morbid thoughts. From now on I had a private war on my hands – a war in which to wreak vengeance on the enemy on my shipmates' behalf.

That same evening I crossed the little bridge that connects the submarine base with the mainland on the Sliema side of Malta. As I stepped off the bridge it was dusk, and there I saw George Spendlove from the submarine *Tetrarch*. His jaw dropped low, and his eyes bulged. He was like a man transfixed, unable to believe the evidence of his own eyes. It was with something of a gasp that he asked: 'Are you Syd Hart?'

I assured him that I was, and went into an explanation of why I wasn't aboard *Triad* on her final, fateful patrol. Spendlove had spent a lot of his spare time with *Triad's* crew. He reacted in approved Navy style:

'This,' he said firmly, 'calls for a celebration.'

Into the Great War Bar we went and George ordered three drinks. The girl behind the bar looked oddly at us as George paid for three honest swigs with just the two of us present. It was still too early for mistakes!

'Here's to the crew of the *Triad*!' toasted George as we lifted our glasses; and then he tossed the third noggin down the drain. Three more drinks were ordered, and we drank a toast to Cullingford: once again the third drink was thrown away. The barmaid looked hard at us, but made no comment. We were paying 'the shot' [the bill] ; it was no affair of hers and it went on that way all night, a toast to Thomas, Evans, Howels and the rest. Each time we threw the third measure away – a libation to good men dead.

Next morning, on my way down to *Perseus*, with a dust-dry throat, and a head like the capstan, through hazy eyes I spotted *Truant* tying up to a buoy in the Creek, with two more bars on her Jolly Roger, as indication that she had sunk two fresh ships on her latest patrol. I had an instinct then that my destiny was coupled with *Truant's*. I must at the slightest opportunity get aboard her, as here was the famous *Truant*, the ship you could trust to make history; someone might leave her before her next voyage, and I, I knew, was the man to fill any such vacancy.

**Naval Engineer Lieutenant Elios Toschi, Regia Marina;**
from *Nine Times Lucky*, and
**Sub-Lieutenant Luigi Durand de la Penne**; from his Official Report,
published in *I Mezzi D'Assalto*, Volume XIV of *La Marina Italiana Nella
Seconda Guerra Mondiale*

The British naval base of Alexandria became a prime objective for the Italian Navy, and August 1940 saw the first of three attempts to attack it using human torpedoes. Toschi was one of the two men who perfected the earlier prototype. The converted submarine *Iride*, Captain Francesco Brunetti, arrived in the Gulf of Bomba on 22 August 1940 to pick up the torpedoes and their crews. While practising submersion she, together with the surface support vessels, was attacked by three British Swordfish from 202 Squadron. Some of those on the *Iride's* bridge, including the commander, were pulled from the water, but the *Iride* went down in 20 metres of water with men trapped. For the frogmen, who had seen the disaster and who, like Toschi, had been submariners, there was a new challenge.

TOSCHI: We immediately stripped and, though lacking all diving equipment, plunged into the water, diving again and again to lower and lower depths, till we reached the clearly visible hull and fastened a rope with a floating buoy to the sunken vessel.

The submarine was lying almost completely on its side at the bottom. It had been split in two at the level of the gun position. The central port was open, showing that the officers' quarters, at any rate, had been completely flooded, causing the death of all who had been there at the time. The other two ports were closed. But could the interior watertight fittings have resisted the force of the explosion?

There was no sign of life anywhere. Only the flag, still in position, stirred sluggishly in the water. We returned to the trawler ...

We now made hasty preparations to begin diving, and shortly afterwards the launch from the base arrived with the first underwater breathing sets, oxygen cylinders and other material. We numbered five officers and a few men, all thoroughly experienced in the use of breathing sets even at considerable depths.

When we started diving this time, the hull was still distinctly visible and the water clear. Maximum depth was about sixty-five feet. It was not long before Tesei came to the surface with the most exciting news. From the interior of the compartment aft voices had replied to his signals when he tapped with iron tools on the plating of the hull. There were living men to be saved!

Three of us went down at once to get more information. Reaching the hull we struck a few blows against the plates and waited anxiously for a reply. It came immediately, in the form of loud answering taps. Directly afterwards, to our astonishment, we distinctly heard several voices coming very clearly from the interior. They were talking among themselves, discussing what was to be done. Their words came to our ears, as if no intervening obstacle existed, up to a short distance from the hull, as clearly as though we were in their compartment, although we were separated from them by twenty millimetres of the hardest steel. On an impulse, I made an attempt to establish reciprocity. Detaching from my mouth, inside the mask, the rubber tube used for breathing in oxygen, I left it floating close to my lips, so as to be able to continue to breathe, while I called a petty officer by name, steadily approaching the hull meanwhile. The reply came from the interior at once. We were able to talk in this way, with perfect safety and intelligibility, for the whole time the salvage work lasted.

'What's it like in there? How many are there of you?' we asked. 'Why don't you try the direct method of escape, through the hatch controlled from the interior?'

The replies were far from reassuring. Nine men in all, including two petty officers, they were in utter darkness, the compartment being partially flooded and the air slightly contaminated with chlorine. They had already tried the escape but were obliged to give up the attempt, the exterior port being jammed tight, probably owing to distortion by the explosion. We suggested certain steps they could take to improve conditions and assured them that we should start at once to remove the port that was preventing their escape.

A tense underwater struggle against steel accordingly began. For a whole day and night we fought that obstinate port with the aid of a diver, using standard apparatus, who had meanwhile arrrived from Tobruk. With the aid of his pump we managed to supply the survivors with fresh air, gradually increasing its pressure so as to prevent water from entering the compartment in increasing quantities. Towards evening the imprisoned men began to give signs of restlessness, amounting in certain cases to mental instability. We did our best to console them, in order to stop them doing anything foolish. Our advice, however, was not unanimously accepted.

DE LA PENNE: The work was very tiring because of the cold, especially during the night, either because we were diving naked or because we kept having to come back up to change the respirators which only lasted for twenty minutes.

TOSCHI: During the night the two petty officers disobeyed us by trying to force the hatch. As soon as we realised what they were doing we tried to persuade them to desist. But we were evidently too late, for shortly after having entered and flooded the manhole they ceased to answer. Carried away by a despair amounting to madness they had attempted the impossible and met a most dreadful death, suffocated in the icy water that filled the narrow steel cylinder. At last, on the following morning, after we had removed all the fittings of the port that attached it to the hull and fastened strong steel cables to it, we made a final effort to tear it away by force, using a small windlass driven by the trawler's engine. As the trawler backed away the cables stretched, creaked and seemed about to break. In the end we heard a sudden metallic crack underwater. The port had yielded to our efforts and trawler and cables could move freely again.

We had no sooner dived once more than we were confronted by a gruesome vision in the manhole. The corpses of the two petty officers who had tried to force the hatch during the night had stiffened to the consistency of iron in the convulsive attitudes in which they had clung to the metal rungs as they made prodigious efforts not to succumb. We had to pull their bodies out by the hair, by sheer force.

Then came the last and most difficult stage of the rescue. Owing to the angle at which the submarine lay and the complete exhaustion of the oxygen in the breathing sets inside the vessel by the nine imprisoned men, all the survivors could do was to flood the compartment by direct action and try to regain the surface by swimming. But it was doubtful whether these untrained men could swim so far under water. Would they have the strength and confidence necessary to open the barrier that still separated them from the sea and stand up to the tremendous avalanche of water that would then pour in, without losing heart? We ourselves had calculated the chances with great care during pauses in the work. We were sure that the proposed action, however risky and unprecedented it might be, would be successful. We dived again in order to explain exactly what had to be done, what positions were to be taken up and all other details, trying to choose the words which would give them most confidence.

The imprisoned men listened in silence.

'You understand, don't you? You must act very quickly,' we told them.

After some seconds, which seemed hours, of utter silence, a single voice answered:

'Yes, sir.'

Were they convinced? Or was it only a reply dictated by the force of discipline? We continued to wait. At last what we had foreseen happened. 'We are not going to open the door,' a voice said. 'Better die here in peace than be drowned in that rush of water.'

A short silence ensued. Then a violent argument broke out among the seven half-crazed survivors, who had lost all power of reasoning and common sense. It sounded like a quarrel among madmen, and we listened to it with anguish. Only one of the men seemed to be retaining a cool head, trying to persuade the rest, with every argument he could think of, to open the water-tight door. At last clear thinking and determination on the part of this one man began to make headway against the frenzy and irresolution of the others. The time had come to intervene on his behalf. We did so brusquely and decisively, giving orders for the door to be opened within the next half hour. 'If you don't obey,' we told them, 'we shall at once take our departure and leave you to your fate.' As an indication that this was no empty threat, we did in fact return to the surface.

From the little ship on which we had now been living for two days we stared fixedly at the expanse of blue waters, vainly trying to avert our eyes from the spot where we hoped to see the eddy indicating that the hatch had been opened.

For a long time nothing happened. The minutes passed slowly, till the agreed time of half an hour was almost up.

Suddenly a column of water and turbid air spouted from the sea, and after a few moments dropped back with a heavy splash. They had opened the door! We got ready to dive again so as to give assistance directly if needed, while the surface of the sea gradually grew calm.

A shrill cry and the sight of a man waist-deep in the water abruptly disturbed the tranquillity of the elements almost as soon as it had been restored. It was the first of the shipwrecked men to save himself. After forty-eight hours in his steel tomb of darkness and poison-laden air, on the verge of insanity, he was uttering the wail of a new-born infant magnified a hundred times by the strength of his twenty years.

The rest followed at short intervals, while the eyes of some of us were still shining in the reaction of our excitement.

DE LA PENNE: I went into the compartment, taking a respirator to one man who remained inside the submarine unable to reach the exit. Having reached him in the chamber, where the air was very depleted, I attempted to convince the seaman to get out using the breathing apparatus I had brought specially for him. He tried, but the respirator ran out because he was in a state of despair. I then gave him my respirator and helped him towards the exit to regain the surface. The place was in darkness and, after an attempt to get to the watertight door, the seaman turned back, telling me he would never reach the exit. After I had convinced him, I went with him, underwater, to the watertight door, helping him to slip into the airlock … Having returned to the chamber to regain my breath, and after a short wait to ensure that the airlock would be empty, I succeeded in swimming underwater to the watertight door, and, getting through the airlock with some difficulty, I finally returned to the surface.

TOSCHI: Unfortunately, pulmonary lesions and hæmorrhages mainly due to inexperience in resisting medium pressures caused the deaths of two of the rescued men, despite the efforts of the doctors and our own vigorous measures of artificial respiration.

At last, after two days of struggle, when we had recovered our machines and the flag and taken leave of our fallen comrades in a sad underwater ceremony, during which we could clearly make out their bodies in the submarine's interior, the unhappy trawler, with its cargo of death and bitterness, began her return voyage.

# 1941

Not until the weather moderated in the spring could Admiral Dönitz resume the wolf-pack attacks on Allied convoys, which had maintained their Atlantic crossings despite the storms. The torpedo problems were being addressed, production of new U-boats had risen to some 20 per month and tonnage was being sunk at an unsustainable rate as far as Britain was concerned. In a single patrol in the South Atlantic starting at the end of March, Kapitänleutnant Günther Hessler and *U-107* sank 14 ships, a record patrol tonnage of 86,699.

None the less, Dönitz still lacked the numbers of boats he needed to launch the decisive onslaught required to starve Britain into surrender, and just as in 1940 he had been forced to divert boats into Norwegian waters, in 1941 he would have to divert some into the Mediterranean. He was already disappointed by the Italian submarines, he faced stronger Allied resistance in the Atlantic, and in April several of his finest commanders had been killed or captured by destroyer escorts. The capture of *U-110* and her 'Enigma' code machine was a major coup for the Allies, a secret they guarded for 20 years.

With the Royal Air Force victorious in the Battle of Britain the previous year, additional Allied destroyers had been released from coastal protection work into convoy duty. Their numbers would be swelled by a batch of elderly US destroyers which were being refitted, by the increasing role of the Royal Canadian Navy, and the arrival of the Flower-Class corvettes. From July, homeward bound convoys were fully escorted. In addition, the US government had extended the Pan-American Security Zone 40° farther west towards Iceland.

Trials of radar took place in 1941, not only on Allied surface ships – it had been instrumental in sinking in the sinking of *U-100* and *U-99* – but also in submarines. Together with Asdic, it offered the submarine hunters a more complete picture of U-boat activity in their area – whether the submarines were surfaced or submerged. Allied escorts also began testing out High Frequency Direction Finding equipment (usually abbreviated to HF/DF but popularly called 'Huff-Duff') which allowed two ships to use triangulation to pinpoint the position of a third vessel – i.e., an enemy submarine – while it was transmitting. These developments sowed many of the seeds of eventual Allied victory in the Battle of the Atlantic.

On 22 June, Germany declared war on its ideological enemy, the USSR, and Soviet submarines would be active in northern waters and the Black Sea. The Soviets possessed a fleet of more than 200 submarines, some obsolete and most designed for coastal defence work. Driven out of their main Baltic base at Liepçja within days, the First Flotilla withdrew to Riga and then Tallinn where they were joined by the Second Flotilla, which had had to leave Hanko, Finland. They were then forced back to Leningrad and Kronstadt. They achieved very limited success in the war, beset by bad weather, German minefields and air power and the logistical difficulties of operating out of besieged bases. Greater impact was achieved by the boats of the Northern Fleet based at Murmansk.

Allied submarines continued to patrol in the North Sea and around the Bay of Biscay, looking to intercept German warships and protect coastal convoys.

In the Mediterranean, three campaigns were in progress. At the end of 1940, Italy had declared war on Greece and unsuccessfully invaded; the Allies had retaliated by establishing themselves on Crete. Early in 1941 German aircraft were sent to Sicily for a few months to support the Italians in the ongoing campaign to crush Malta, by attacking the Allied convoys attempting to supply it with food and fuel, and shortly afterwards German forces under Rommel arrived in North Africa to prop up the collapsing Italian army. Allied submarines in the Mediterranean had the tasks of supporting the Malta convoys by deterring the Italian surface warships, and disrupting Axis supply lines. While some Italian submarines were being used offensively against the British fleet, others were acting as cargo carriers. Neither side's submarines were initially very successful, but despite the conditions at their base, and the slow surface speed of the new little U-Class submarines, the Malta boats began to achieve results against the odds. During the course of the war, the 10th Flotilla, as it was designated later in 1941, produced aces such as Lieutenant-Commander Wanklyn, Lieutenant Tomkinson and Captain George Hunt. The Allied flotillas at Malta, Alexandria and now Gibraltar gradually became as multi-national as the 9th Flotilla at Dundee, with Polish, Free French, Dutch and Greek boats flying their flags alongside the Royal Navy's White Ensign. The Greeks had even brought their own depot ship, *Corinthia*, to Alexandria, which was at the disposal of other Allied submariners when *Medway* was overcrowded.

On 27 March, Yugoslav armed forces overthrew the pro-Axis government, prompting a German-led Axis invasion. Most of the country's navy was seized by the Germans, a few vessels managed to scuttle themselves, and a tiny minority, including one submarine, decided to attempt to join the Allies. Yugoslav resistance ended on 17 April. The same day saw the beginning of the German invasion of Greece.

In June, the Italian naval code was finally cracked, giving Admiral Cunningham, C-in-C Mediterranean Fleet, vital intelligence on Italian movements, but, despite success in sinking Axis convoys, the good luck was not all on the Allied side: during the summer the first of some 20 German U-boats were seconded to Mediterranean operations and promptly sank HMS *Ark Royal* and HMS *Barham*. The Italian human torpedo teams of the Decima Flottiglia MAS achieved their first success at Gibraltar in September and followed it with a devastating attack on Alexandria in December.

The Axis powers failed to capitalise on their sudden position of dominance in the Mediterranean, and December 1941 would always be remembered for the Japanese attack on Pearl Harbor and the official entry of the USA into the war. A step towards that theatre of war had been taken in April with the Russo-Japanese Non-Aggression Pact and, more significantly, the oil embargoes imposed on Japan by the Dutch in the East Indies and the US. Now the Japanese moved swiftly with the intention of seizing the oilfields owned by the Dutch. Before the year was out, their swift two-pronged advance on Java had secured gains in Borneo, Guam (Marianas), and islands in the British Gilberts. Dutch submarines sent to oppose the landings in Malaya were badly mauled: four were lost before Christmas. In the middle of the year the British Government had agreed to take operational control of the Dutch colonial boats if hostilities broke out with Japan. Some of those boats scuttled themselves rather than be captured; the rest sailed hastily for the British base at Colombo or to the Australian port of Fremantle.

In December 1941 the Japanese submarine fleet comprised some 64 submarines, only 43 of which were sufficiently modern to be of value. This was far too few for such a vast theatre of war and, unfortunately for the Imperial Japanese Navy, their finest characteristics – their powerful deck guns, high surface speed and long range – came at the expense of swift diving capability and manoeuvrability while submerged. The USA had also built large, ocean-going boats with high surface speed, but their inherent deficiencies would not be exposed in the kind of war that was to be fought – though their disastrous torpedo defects quickly became apparent.

## ATLANTIC

### Midshipman Volkmar König, Kriegsmarine, *U-99*

The Germans had lost 24 boats in 1940 before the savage weather interrupted their activities. König joined *U-99* in January 1941 as the submarine completed her refit. She was scheduled to sail on 20 February.

At Lorient I was sent to the headquarters of Dönitz one day to get to get some documents, or something. And I came into the hall. There was a big map on the wall, a map of the Atlantic. There were two* little flags showing where submarines were. I said, 'Where are all the others?' and the petty officer in charge said, 'What do you mean by others?'

* In Terence Robertson's *The Golden Horseshoe*, a biography of *U-99*'s commander, Otto Kretschmer, König is reported as claiming to see four flags rather than two.

'Yes, but there must be more submarines.'

'No, there are only two in the Atlantic.'

I thought there were many more submarines in the Atlantic.

Although 'Huff Duff' was a year away from being fitted in Allied anti-submarine vessels, the technology had never been a secret. Even in early 1941, Kretschmer was uneasy about the security of boats when transmitting messages.

The German submarine captains had a certain self-assurance and this was fostered. I remember Kretschmer told me that every time he had to report at Dönitz's headquarters after a patrol, he was bawled out by Dönitz that he didn't give wireless messages as asked for. As he had been in England as a student before joining the navy he had acquired a book on deciphering of wireless messages during the world war, and he always had in his mind: 'If ever I come into a situation when I have to put out a wireless message, I always have to consider that the code may be cracked.' So when he was asked to give his position he didn't. He went off and then he sent a message: 'At that time I was there.' And this was not correct according to Dönitz who bawled him out, and Kretschmer said,

'Did you read the book so-and-so, Admiral?'

'Oh, go away with your funny book.'

Every time he got bawled out because he didn't act as ordered he replied:

'But I am responsible for the boat and I take into consideration that the code can be cracked and they can pinpoint us by direction finding. So why should I send wireless messages?' He objected to this terrible use of wireless messages for every kind of purpose: how's your weather, how many torpedoes you have left, and Petty Officer so-and-so is father of a little girl, or twins born to the wife of petty officer so-and-so: all this was done by wireless, and Kretschmer hated this because you never knew what the enemy was doing with all these messages, whether they can control them, whether they can decipher them whether they can pinpoint them by huff-duff and so on.

On 15 March, Kretschmer and Schepke (*U-100*) both received signals from Lemp in *U-110* stating that he had sighted a convoy. *U-99* found the target and, operating inside it, accounted for five ships, three of them tankers. However, the convoy was in the hands of a destroyer escort led by Commander Donald Macintyre in HMS *Walker*. On 17 March 'Silent' Otto's luck changed.

We had this wonderful experience of torpedoing six ships in the convoy. We were the only ones there. We said: 'Where are the other subs?' Schepke was supposed to be there, I think two other subs. But we were the only sub in this convoy. And we were on the surface. We sank these tankers and freighters. And one time we dived, we had an alarm. We dived because we were between a burning tanker and a destroyer. So we dived. But most of the time we were on the surface. We were cruising inside the convoy and were looking for the target.

So then, when all torpedoes were gone, we moved out of the convoy, direction north. The general course of the convoy had been south-east. We intended to go home because our torpedoes had been used usefully and there was discussion in the control room between the captain and his comrade, the trainee captain – Hasselbarth was his name. The crew was not happy that he was probably going to be their captain on their next patrol.

Well, the discussion was: shall we go on the west course now, into the open Atlantic or shall we go on a little bit farther to the north because there is this Rockall rock and we didn't have an exact position so we didn't know whether we would already be clear of the Rockall rock if we would go on a course west.

'No, let's go a little bit to the north.' Then they said:

'No, it's good enough; let's go on the west course.'

But then we crossed the old course of the convoy and exactly at this spot two destroyers had been chasing *U-100* for hours, and on our conning tower there was a hilarious attitude because of the success we had had with the convoy. And they were not as cautious as they should be and the officer of the watch on the conning tower had a look into the sector of his opposite number on the other side of the boat, and he suddenly discovered a destroyer which was quite near. The other one hadn't seen it because he was thinking of something else at home or something like that. Nevertheless there was a wrong reaction because he gave 'Alarm!' And we dived against standing orders, because standing orders were: if you have contact with a destroyer on the surface at night, show them a small silhouette and drive away. He will normally not have seen you. But in the case that you were under water he would probably catch you on the Asdic.

So old Petersen was watch officer and Kretschmer bawled him out and said: 'Why did you put out Alarm?' but Petersen couldn't give an answer. In the meantime the destroyer was quite near and we could hear the swishing of his propellers when he crossed over us on the surface while we were just underwater. And when he came back he dropped six depth charges, and they were so close that Kretschmer said later on he didn't experience any depth charges so close [until that moment]. So we went down and the instruments' glass was broken, we only had one depth gauge in the bow room, and the first officer was in the bow room and he cried out the metres the gauge was showing: 100 ... 110 ... 120 ... so we were diving quickly down under the water to a depth that nobody would ever reach.

When we were at 250 metres Kretschmer gave orders to blow out the water from the diving tanks and this makes an enormous noise of compressed air pushing out the water. But the boat still went deeper ... 265 ... 275 ... and the petty officer in charge of these valves for the air pressure turned around with a pale face and said to the captain 'The boat doesn't come, sir.' And Kretschmer answered. 'Go on: blow, give her air.' And then, as far as I remember, about 280 metres, the boat didn't go deeper. So it stayed there. Everyone took a deep breath, and the gauge read 275, and everyone said 'Aahh!' So we came up to 90 metres and Kretschmer ordered: 'Stop blowing' – and we dropped down again, so with the last air we came to the surface directly next to a destroyer.

Later on the British sailors from the HMS *Walker* told us how surprised they were that such a big boat was directly at their side coming up. And they manned their guns and tried to shoot it out, but we were so close they couldn't train their guns and so all their ammunition went over our conning tower. And then Kretschmer ordered our 8cm gun to be manned. I remember when our wireless operator, who was one of the men to operate this gun, said 'Now we're going to die the hero's death.'

But the gun didn't work because it was damaged by the depth charge as well. So Kretschmer gave orders: put on your life vests, and he asked for a Morse lamp to be handed over to him, and letter by letter he gave a signal to the destroyer. As far as I remember the first signal was CAPTAIN TO CAPTAIN. MY BOAT IS SUNKING – he didn't say sinking – PLEASE SAVE MY MEN. MY MEN DRIFTING TO YOU IN THE WATER. And then came a signal from the destroyer: DON'T SCUTTLE THE BOAT. And the question came from *U-99*, WHAT IS SCUTTLE? And the answer was: DON'T SINK THE BOAT. So in the meantime some of us jumped into the water.

I had a pistol in my pocket, a Polish pistol. I had discovered once in the autumn of 1940 in Boulogne in France. We cleaned up quarters where we were supposed to sleep – it was dirty and we cleaned the room – and I discovered this pistol. I put it in my pockets and had it with me all the time from then on. And when we were ordered to jump into the water I went back down into the submarine to my little locker and took out the pistol and put it in my pocket. I don't know what I wanted to do – fight a war on the surface of the water! I don't know what kind of reaction this was.

I saw Lieutenant-Commander Hasselbarth and the petty officer of the control room, Popp, jump into the water. I thought: 'They're experienced sailors, they know what they're doing: jump into the water as well.'

This decision was not so good. I should have stayed on the deck with the others: they later on dived into the water and held each other by the hand in a kind of chain, but I was swimming on my own. And the first thing you do when you are swimming in the lake or some kind of water is to try and see if I can touch the ground with my feet. I did this and what a silly idea: there were hundreds of metres of water under your feet! So I already got tired. I had my arms on the life vest and had my eyes already closed, but then I was wide-awake because there was a searchlight in my face. I was quite near the destroyer, I swam to the scrambling net and the British sailors fished me out of the water. I don't think I climbed up the nets because I was too numb to do this. I think they came down the scramble nets and helped me to climb up to the railing. They dragged me along the deck and I remember that I more or less woke up in an officer's chamber – lying on blankets on the floor shivering and sleeping and it took some time until the shivering was gone. I don't know if they took off my clothes – they must have because I don't think they put me on the floor on the blanket in my wet clothes. But later on I had all my things: they were dried in the meantime, so it must have been some time when I became conscious, more or less, again. I wouldn't say I was unconscious but this must have been some kind of unconsciousness, thinking of the shivering, and thinking: 'My goodness, you have survived something others die in.' This is what I remember …

Before U-99 sank, Kretschmer and the Chief engineer – Schroeder – were on the conning tower. We were on the upper deck or in the water already and there was no one else present. Kretschmer told us later on when we asked him:

'What happened? Where is the leading engineer?' (because the leading engineer went down with the boat.) Kretschmer said:

'I told the leading engineer: "Schroeder, the boat does not sink." And he said: "Yes, sir", and he went down, and went down with the sub.'

So if you imagine you were standing there, on the conning tower, and looked down into that dark hole, the hatch; and perhaps Kretschmer shouted for him, and there was no answer. That would haunt you for the rest of your life. And you would have said, 'Why didn't I go down there? Why didn't I go down with the boat as the famous Kretschmer? As the captain.' So this must have haunted him. Only these two were on the bridge … The boat was nearly sinking. Sometimes the water came over the conning tower into the hatch, but it didn't sink. It was swimming and floating on the last air. The remaining air was gone the minute the leading engineer touched the lever. The boat went down like a stone.

Kretschmer was greeted by the Royal Navy Captain Macintyre. He saw their horseshoe and said:

'Oh, so you have a horseshoe for good luck. We also have a horsehoe as a talisman, but yours is upside down.' Macintyre said:

'No, no, ours is in the right position because the luck stays in. But you have it upside down and the luck runs out. So we sank you, and you didn't sink us.' Macintyre asked Kretschmer if he could play bridge, and Kretschmer said yes, to which Macintyre replied, 'Good, now we have a fourth.'

In the officer's wardroom, together with merchant marine offers whose ships were sunk by German submarines – by our submarines, I don't know – the attitude was a little bit frosty to say the least. But we were sleeping, sitting on a chair having our heads on the table on the night from 17 to 18 March and when we got up in the morning we discovered that some medals and some badges of the uniforms had been taken away for souvenirs. This was a once and for all opportunity for one of those merchant seamen, but he had to give all this back.

The Royal Navy radio man asked, 'Who's your wireless operator.'

'It's me,' said Joseph Kassel.

'Come on.' So he took him to his wireless room. The 'Jimmy' came along and said:

'What are you doing?'

'I'm showing him my wireless room.'

'Are you crazy? Get out of here!'

And then we came to Liverpool. I remember what nice weather it was. We came into the Minches, the water between Scotland and the Hebrides. And the hills of Scotland blue and yellow and lilac was a wonderful sight. Then they put us ashore in Liverpool, the other ranks had to walk and officers were put on a lorry …

*U-100* had been sunk just before – her captain, Schepke, died on the bridge of his submarine when she was hit amidships by HMS *Vanoc*. Prien was killed when *U-47* was lost with all hands on 7 or 8 March, traditionally sunk by HMS *Wolverine*, but possibly by a rogue torpedo. Lemp's *U-110* returned home, but on her next patrol, off Iceland, she was spotted by the escorts.

**Chief Quartermaster Otto Hackbarth, Kriegsmarine, *U-110*;**
from his diary written after capture, ADM186/806

8 MAY 1941.
At 1810. Vessel reported with high upper works. As it is difficult to make out what she is, we assume she is a battleship, but this later proves to be wrong. We follow astern of her and keep in touch. The wind is increasing and the sea becomes heavier. After an hour we have made out her course and speed, 270°, seven knots. Nothing is to be seen of the convoy, only destroyers. We seem to be to the north of the convoy and somewhat ahead of it. We proceed at slow speed until the destroyer comes in sight, then we increase to 3/5 speed and keep away. Visibility is poor.

9 MAY 1941.

At 0000 on 9 May 1941, we proceed on opposite course 90°, as we have seen nothing more of the convoy since 2200. Nothing is to be seen, the convoy has disappeared. There are two possibilities. Either the convoy has altered course to the North or to the South, it is extremely improbable that she has gone northwards, so we decide to proceed to the south. At 0100 our course is 200° and we are proceeding at 4/5 speed. In the meantime it has become dark, but there is some moonlight and visibility seems to be improving.

At 0300 there is nothing to be seen, we submerge and listen on our listening apparatus. The convoy can be heard 40° to port at a distance of about three miles. We surface in order to follow her. Tanks are blown but the bow wave of a destroyer can be clearly seen in the moonlight, so we submerge again. There is great tension and we wonder if we have been sighted. But she turns away and we blow tanks again. Then we continue to keep in touch. But in spite of every endeavour we only sight destroyers, not a single merchant ship. This is most unfortunate since, as a rule, we always sight the shadows of merchant ships before we sight the destroyers. At last, at 0430, we have crept up so close that we can recognise the merchant vessels, about 40 or 50 of them.

After a short discussion, an attack for this night is abandoned. A surface attack cannot be carried out on account of the strong escort, and for an attack submerged the light is too bad. We prefer to wait until the following night, hoping that the convoy may then be without any escort. The course of the convoy is 240°, speed eight knots. We continue to keep in touch.

At 0900 I turn in.

At 1230 I am awakened. The order comes 'Action Stations', so the game is beginning. The morale among the trained ratings is not too good. They are convinced that we shall be caught.

At 1237 we submerge and we intend to creep inside the convoy.

At 1245 the convoy is sighted, we are at periscope depth and the Captain is at the periscope. There is considerable excitement among the crew. Everyone prepares himself in his thoughts to abandon ship. I don't notice anything of the attack, as I am not in the control position. All of a sudden at about 1310 comes the order to submerge.

At 1312 the first depth charges explode, but they cause no damage; nevertheless there is a feeling of depression in the boat. From our listening apparatus we establish the fact that we are being hunted by three destroyers. And then at 1325 comes the end. We are enveloped in a whole series of accurately placed depth charges. The boat is terribly shaken, and it seems as though, all the instruments are out of action. Chlorine gas is escaping and then the Captain gives the order to blow the tanks. But the blower has been smashed, the batteries are out of action and there seems scarcely any possibility of reaching the surface. A very bitter end. We are slowly sinking, and then suddenly the boat begins to roll. For some inexplicable reason the boat reaches the surface, the Captain opens the conning tower hatch and gives the order 'Abandon Ship.'

*U-110* failed to sink. Sensing an opportunity to capture the submarine, Lieutenant-Commander A. J. B. Cresswell, RN, commanding HMS *Bulldog*, had the prisoners on HMS *Aubretia* quickly shepherded below decks while his men boarded the U-boat and seized papers and the 'Enigma' code machine. Lemp was killed, probably shot while attempting to return to the boat and sink her.

**Kapitän zur See Klaus Korth, Kriegsmarine, then Kapitänleutnant commanding** *U-93*; from *Ritterkreutztraeger Erzahlen*, extract published in *U-Boat Archive* No. 3, November 1999

A real seaman is always a little superstitious. For some the number '13' represents bad luck, for others it is a fortuitous number. I was christened on a 13th and had already had so much good luck that the number didn't present me with any great concerns when we commenced our 13th operational mission. We sailed north, into the far reaches of the Atlantic, where night time has no significance during the summer because it doesn't get dark. Up there I succeeded in tracking a convoy, but found it exceedingly difficult to get within shooting distance. We tried and tried again, circling right round the merchant ships, but every time we approached we found a destroyer bearing down on us. It was infuriating. In the end we managed to see the group on the horizon, as if it was one long uninterrupted chain of overlapping ships. An ideal target of several hundred metres in length. We couldn't miss. Aiming at a large tanker we waited patiently while the torpedoes shot towards the unsuspecting opponents. It was a long run and the torpedoes had almost come to the end of their range when there was a massive detonation. A huge fireball rolled high into the sky.

Shortly after this, a storm with bad visibility helped the convoy in slipping away. We were all sitting comfortably, enjoying afternoon coffee, dreaming away with our duties in the far reaches of our minds when some whispering called the II WO, who was responsible for the radio room, away from the table. Then the LI was called away by the radio operator. I noticed that there was something in the air and wondered what these chaps were trying to hide from me. I was getting rather annoyed because I don't like secrets in the boat. Then the loudspeakers, which could broadcast to every compartment, sprang to life. 'We have just received a signal ...'

This was the most outrageous impertinence. How dare the radio room announce the contents of a signal without letting me see it first!

'... from headquarters that the Knight's Cross of the Iron Cross has been awarded to ...'

Am I going mad?

It can't be me. My sinking figures have reached only 80,000 (grt). Still spinning with surprise I find men around me with filled glasses, offering their heartiest congratulations. None of us had expected anything like this. It had come completely out of the blue as a complete surprise.

The best thing about this was the joyous reaction from my men. Without them nothing like this could ever have happened. The boat only works because every man is always there to do his duty and a commander can only be successful if he has an efficient crew to back him up. A few days later Claasen, the most senior officer on board, handed me a boat-made Knight's Cross, which Obermaschinist Recknagel had made out of aluminium. It was difficult to distinguish it from the real thing. Petty Officer Kaiser, who was responsible for running the central control room and Obermaschinist Klein had provided their own personal Iron Cross 2nd Class Ribbons, which were sewn together to complete the new Knight's Cross. So, I did have the right feelings when we set sail for our 13th operational voyage. That the number was lucky for us.

Korth was certainly lucky: he was one of a handful of survivors from the sail training ship, *Niobe*; after he left *U-93* she was sunk in January 1942 by HMS *Hesperus*; and he survived the war.

## Oberleutnant zur See Herbert A. Werner, Kriegsmarine; from *Iron Coffins*

Several of that first generation of aces were either dead or prisoners, but at that time there was no shortage of young officers anxious to emulate them. Herbert Werner reported to *U-557* at 0800 on 22 April 1941. Six hours later she sailed from Königsberg for Kiel, and the young Ensign was given a bewildering tour of his very first U-boat.

I was at the navigator's small plotting table when the Captain called from the bridge: 'Prepare for diving manoeuvre. Alarm for exercise!'

Moments later, the man on watch came tumbling down the aluminium ladder, hitting the deck plates with violent jolts. Then the alarm bell shrieked throughout the boat. To open up the ballast tanks to the sea, machinists grabbed the handles of leverage valves and hung from them, using the full weight of their bodies to speed the opening action. Others turned handwheels frantically. With a loud uproar, air escaped the tanks and water rushed in. *U-557* dipped so swiftly that I had to grab something to stop myself from falling to the metal deck plates. Again I was reminded that I had to remain constantly alert.

Suddenly there was a cry, urgent and piercing, 'Outboard air induction valve doesn't close!'

*U-557* sank fast, bow first, at an angle of thirty-five degrees.

A machinist appeared in the round opening of the rear bulkhead, yelling, 'We can't stop the leak! Head valve must be jammed!'

Paulssen shouted, 'Blow all tanks – both planes up – surface, Chief!'

Within seconds, the depth-gauge needle gyrated to 60 metres, 70, 85, 110 metres. Then the boat briefly balanced out on even keel – and began to tilt down at the stern. I slid aft until I grabbed an overhead pipe. Now the boat tumbled rapidly towards the bottom of the Baltic, stern first. Her descent was so steep that everything not fastened – suitcases, boxes, food cans, personal belongings – rolled dangerously down the centre aisle. The two men who operated the hydroplanes slid from their seats into the valve station. One man, flying through the round hatch in the forward bulkhead, clung to it in desperation.

The Chief yelled, 'Stop blowing, boat is out of control!'

As *U-557* neared the ocean floor, a terrifying roar came from the diesel compartment. Tons of water rushed through a leak. Then the boat hit with a shuddering jolt. The lights went out. I lost my grip and landed on top of the navigator, who himself had fallen over somebody else. Then there was silence.

A hollow voice drifted up from the stern: 'Inboard air induction valve is closed and secured.'

The leak was stopped. But the boat, her stern buried in the mud, hung at a fifty-degree angle, swinging back and forth gently like a pendulum.

'By auxiliary lighting, all men to the bow room!' This was the Captain's encouraging voice. At once, some lights came on, and shadowy figures began the climb uphill. Taking stock hastily, I noted that the depth gauge read 142 metres; *U-557* seemed to be stuck solidly in the mud beyond reach of rescuers from above. Her electrical circuits were out of order. The batteries had lost much of their acid, and poisonous chlorine fumes were escaping. There was also the possibility of an explosion.

My appraisal was interrupted by someone shouting through the voice tube: 'This is the diesel room. Mechanic Eckstein is dead!'

It flashed through my mind that Eckstein might have got the best of a bad bargain. If the deadly gases did not burn away our lungs, we would die of suffocation as our oxygen supply was used up.

We continued struggling uphill on hands and knees, bracing our feet against a pump, a valve, a convenient pipe. As I dragged myself along the deck plates,

I looked into the faces of men I hardly knew. Soaking wet, smeared with oil and grease, dirty and sweating, they followed Paulssen's order without showing emotion. We had all become important ballast, putting our weight on the scale of our fate. It was indeed ironic that the Captain had called me surplus ballast when I reported aboard.

Eventually, the men reached the forward torpedo room. But the bow of the boat lowered only slightly. She seemed to be locked in her position, the tremendous weight in the aft bilges acting as an anchor. I heard the Captain conferring with the Chief in the control room. I could see the two through the round opening of the hatch in the sparsely lighted section. It was as if I were standing atop the stairwell of a ten-storey building, looking down into the lobby.

Paulssen ordered twenty-five men to form a bucket line to transport the water from the flooded engine rooms into the bilge of the bow compartment, thus equalising the weight and putting the boat on even keel. I joined the group and descended the steep grade, sliding on my seat along the floor plates through the aisle. Arriving in the diesel room, I saw dark, oily water covering most of the rear torpedo room. Out of reach, caught in the mechanism of the aft torpedo tube, hung the dead mechanic. His head was split open at the right temple; blood streaked his yellow face.

The pool of black liquid seemed too wide and deep to move with buckets and cans. I calculated that our efforts to bale the water to the bow would serve only to use up our oxygen at a much faster rate. Nevertheless we baled. We worked in near silence, passing the full buckets from man to man up the elongated tomb, spilling the oily, salty substance over ourselves. Unable to hold any position for long, we skidded over the plates while trying to hand the full buckets uphill. Sometimes an empty can came flying past our heads like a projectile. Some men groaned under the load. Others uttered curses when the ugly water was spilled into their faces.

Three hours passed. We counted the buckets and cans in agony and in hopelessness: 'Four hundred and twenty, four hundred and twenty-one, twenty-two ...'

Four hours passed. With enormous effort we fought against fatigue and resignation. The water level in the stern had fallen only a little. But the containers passed from hand to hand in an unbroken chain, 'Five hundred and eighty-two, eighty-three ...'

After we had put in six hours of hard labour, the second half of the crew took their turn. The air had become thick; it stank of oil, sweat, chlorine, and urine. Our breath grew short, our movements weak. And still we continued to pass the containers in agonising sluggishness. Now everyone was half suffocated, half drowned.

Nothing changed until we had been submerged for over fourteen hours. By then the first brigade had long since commenced its second shift, and *U-557* still had not lowered her bow appreciably. But then Paulssen made a new attempt for survival. He ordered the bucket line to quit work and all men to return to the bow compartment.

Gasping for air, we struggled uphill towards the tip of the boat. As I forced myself in between the torpedo tubes, the impossible occurred. Very slowly and gently, the hull began to sway. Air bubbles suddenly escaped the forward buoyancy tanks with a guttural sound. Then the bow descended and hit bottom with a thud.

Somehow the men drove themselves into action. The dead mechanic was carried to the Captain's nook and covered with a canvas; the Captain closed the green curtain and separated his corner from the traffic. The bilge pumps were out of order, but the excess water in the after bilges was distributed with buckets to balance the boat. The water damage in the electrical compartment – damage that could not be repaired at sea – had disrupted our cooking facilities, but the cook handed out cans of peaches, pears and strawberries. Spirits rose as hunger and thirst were assuaged. But the fact remained that we were trapped. Some forty tons of water kept the boat pressed to the bottom.

The Chief went to work to free us. At his command, compressed air shot into the buoyancy tanks with a hissing sound. The boat remained glued to the bottom. More air rushed into the tanks. Still no sign of a lift. Then the stream of air diminished, stopped. We had exhausted our compressed-air supply. We were still doomed.

But the Chief did not give up. Spinning around, he yelled, 'All men to the bow!'

Everybody pushed and stumbled forward. As we crowded into the forward compartment, the Chief ordered us to turn around and run aft. We tumbled and tripped in the opposite direction, ducking through the hatches in the bulkheads, slipping and sliding along the wet deck plates. Arriving in the aft Compartment, we heard the Chief calling us back, and again we turned around and started forward blindly, like mad steers in a stampede. We gasped and coughed and ran and ran. Almost imperceptibly, the boat began stirring. Then, as we poured into the bow torpedo room, the stern suddenly lifted. *U-557* had worked herself free.

The men ran to their stations. Then, unbelievably, the bow lifted and the boat floated gently upwards in complete freedom. As I stepped into the control room, the needle of the depth gauge had already reached 140 metres. It swung to 130 metres and moved steadily along the dial. Excitedly the Chief shouted the figures to the Captain in the conning tower: 'Eighty metres. Forty metres. Twenty metres. Tower comes free. Boat has surfaced!'

Paulssen flipped open the lid of the bridge hatch, ending twenty hours in our underwater tomb. Fresh, crystal-clear air streamed through the hull, reviving every man but one.

**Quartermaster 2nd Class (Steuermannsmaat) Carl Becker, Kriegsmarine,** *U-76*; letter written by the 28-year-old to his family; ADM178/221

*U-76* had been forced to the surface by depth charging on 5 April 1941 south of Iceland, in position 58°35′ N, 20°20′ W.

I am now a prisoner of war on board a British U-boat patrol vessel [HMS *Wolverine* or *Scarborough*]. I will tell you what has happened. We were proceeding in the Atlantic, searching for merchant ships, the weather was bad, strength of the wind 6–7. Shortly after 12 noon on Friday, we sighted a merchant ship and proceeded at utmost speed through the mountainous sea in order to overhaul her. Towards evening we got into a favourable position and sank the ship with one torpedo. Thereupon, we proceeded away submerged, because we calculated that this ship had summoned a destroyer. As soon as it was dark we surfaced, but hardly had we achieved this when we saw a destroyer quite close to us. We immediately submerged. She had not noticed us. After a few hours we surfaced again because we required air and our batteries were almost exhausted. We proceeded for about one minute on the surface, when a destroyer came up again. You can imagine what we felt like. So again we had to submerge.

In a short time it would become daylight and we should be very fortunate to escape. Had our batteries been fully charged, it would perhaps have been possible. Astern of us the whole time was the sound of the destroyer's searching apparatus – 'tsst' – so it continued for quite a long time and then she was above us and dropped three depth charges, which caused comparatively little damage. Then she proceeded away and we breathed again, but after about 40 minutes we heard the noise of the propellers of two destroyers and again this 'tsst tsst' which went through us and through us. And it is quite definite that they would find us. Then things began to happen.

Three depth charges on us. The boat shook all over. Ten minutes later there was a hailstorm of depth charges. Everything in the boat was shattered, the depth gauge moved like blazes. The boat assumed a vertical position and all was over. I had my escape apparatus and crawled up the ladder to the conning tower hatch. With the greatest difficulty and using all the remaining air we managed to bring the boat to the surface. Then came the order 'Abandon ship'. I was on deck at once. So was the Captain. Two destroyers and one patrol vessel were lying a few hundred metres from us. As we came up on deck, the destroyer opened fire with her machine-gun. However, no one was hit and they immediately ceased fire when we jumped into the water. They probably thought that we intended to man our gun. Most of the crew were swimming about behind the Captain. I made for the patrol vessel, which tried to fish me out of the water, but on account of the heavy seas this did not succeed, nor did a second attempt. In the meantime, I had been swimming in the icy-cold water for half an hour and I noticed that our boat was still afloat. So I turned round and after much struggling succeeded in getting on board again.

In order to put up some defence,* I tried to reach the gun, but they immediately opened fire on me with their machine-gun, but only a few rounds. The Captain of the patrol vessel told me that they had at first thought that I intended to open fire with our gun. Then suddenly I was washed overboard again. Then the patrol vessel came alongside again, so close that I could jump across. Very good seamanship on the part of the Captain!

I was immediately taken down below into the engine room, where it was pleasantly warm. Someone helped me off with my wet clothes and rubbed me down with a towel. I was almost stiff with cold. Then someone brought me a thick overcoat and one of the officers took me into his cabin, gave me a good drink of rum and a blanket. Then I had to hand over my personal belongings, and I was given something to eat. They are all very friendly here and ready to help. The Lieutenant gave me some of his gear and a pair of slippers.

Shortly before dinner, the ship stopped, and I was told that they had sighted two boats with shipwrecked sailors. When they came on board I discovered that they were from our ship. Now we sat together in peace. I am feeding with the officers and sleeping on a sofa in the mess. The food is excellent. I was given cigarettes and the wound in my hand was dressed. After the midday meal I slept for two hours, then I was given coffee and cake. In the evening again there was something warm to eat. After that, I felt so poorly that I was sick – all the salt water that I had swallowed was the cause of this. Then I sat up with the officers until 10 p.m. Three of them are from the merchant navy ...

Early this morning we got ham and eggs to eat, and before that porridge and milk. After breakfast they gave a Gillette razor so that I could make myself respectable. I can move around quite freely, except that I am not allowed on the bridge. Just now I am sitting beside an officer in the wardroom.

I do not know what has happened to the rest of our crew; some may have been picked up by a destroyer, also the Captain. I have barely escaped with my life, and all my possessions are at the bottom of the Atlantic. I had hoped to have gone on leave in four to five weeks, but now that is all changed. Perhaps

* Given the context, this may be a slight mistranslation of the now-lost original – he may mean 'to protect himself against the waves'.

it is all for the best and who knows whether I should have been saved on the next occasion.

Yours,

Carl

**Boatswain's Mate 2nd Class Kurt Guennel, Kriegsmarine**;
*U-95's* departure for her seventh cruise on 16 November 1941; ADM186/807

It was just such another day as so many we had experienced. The evening before there had been the usual goodbye parties, which usually end in the majority of the men becoming helplessly drunk. Anyone who knows the life of a U-boat man in a French harbour will certainly understand this. Although we always have time on our hands while our boat is in dock, everything is inevitably left to the last day. Suitcases have to be given up, quarters cleaned, fresh provisions taken on board, letters written, medical examinations undergone, and so on. In the meantime everyone brings their personal possessions on board. Everybody knows how cramped space is aboard a U-boat, but nevertheless many people would be astonished at the amount of 'private treasure' smuggled into the ship – photos of every sort and size, all kinds of French scent, souvenirs, necklets, rings etc. Each man has a talisman. When everything is finished the crew fall in to be numbered off and are dismissed. All must be on board one hour before sailing. The short interval is generally filled with saying goodbye to friends. The over-thirsty ones stop for a 'quick one' on their way to the ship.

For some days we had been noticing much that seemed strange to us. What it actually was, no one knew, but something was different, the rumours which went the rounds of the ship hinted at something mysterious. We did not remain long in suspense; as soon as we cast off the Commander made something known to us. It was wretched weather. Thick mist and drizzling rain, which naturally did little to raise our spirits. A band was playing farewell tunes. All the dockers who had been on board during our stay in port were standing on the jetty together with many of our comrades. Naturally the fair sex was well represented. We received flowers as a parting gift. The chief of the flotilla spoke a few heartening words and our Commander then went to say 'Goodbye'. Two boats were leaving at the same time. As we had the outside berth we had to cast off first. We waited for the other boat to cast off and then increased speed in line ahead, passing the crowds assembled on the pier. The noise of our diesels nearly drowned the 'Hurrahs' from the pier, but we answered with three cheers, upon which the band played 'We're sailing against England.' Almost immediately we were swallowed up in the mist.

Scarcely were we away when the fun started. The escort which should have accompanied us out was naturally not there; she had gone to meet an incoming boat. After half an hour the U-boat hove in sight, of course without the escort. We lay with stopped engines.

'Haven't you seen the escort?' our Commander sang out.

'Yes! She'll be here soon.'

Slowly the dusk deepened and and the Commander wanted to drop anchor for the night, if the escort did not arrive shortly.

'Vessel off the starboard bow,' shouted the lookout. The escort came in sight. Our diesels started up again and we were off. After two hours we dropped the escort. The signalman reported a message from the escort to our Commander: 'My escort finished. Wish you and your crew good voyage, much success.' We replied: 'Many thanks.'

Those who were not on watch were grouped on the bridge. The weather had slightly improved, it was now pitch black. 'Escort out of sight,' cried the lookout. As soon as we dropped the escort we increased to full speed, in order to get well clear of the coast and through the minefield. For a while we stayed on the bridge finishing our cigarettes, then we, too, climbed down into the boat. My duties from now on were merely to be the watch on deck. An officer and a petty officer forward and two ratings aft. I had just gone down to the petty officers' mess when a voice came over the loudspeaker: 'From today we belong to the 2- [sic] U-boat Flotilla: Operational Area, Western Mediterranean: Base, Spezia, in Italy.' There was a sudden hush. Then there was a hubbub. 'Why?' 'What's it all about?' 'What's the idea?' And so on. It gradually dawned on me what it meant. We must pass through the Straits of Gibraltar.

'Well, it looks as if we're going to have a little swimming to do,' said the 2nd Petty Officer Telegraphist. He was off watch, as I was. My watch was at 0400.

'If other boats have got through, we shall manage it too,' I said.

'Hm, I should feel a good deal better, if we were already there.'

With this last remark he swung himself into his bunk and drew the curtain.

It was some time before I fell properly asleep, a good deal of talking was still going on. Thoughts kept racing through my mind; for some time I allowed them full rein. Then I pulled myself together sharply: at 0400 the night would be over and it was already 2300. The happy days in port were over and we were again out on a war cruise, and keen wits were required. One small mistake, something left undone and disaster might follow.

### Signalman Louis Corolleur, Vichy Marine, *La Sultane*

Following the Franco-German Armistice and the internment of the main French fleet at Toulon, the Vichy government was allowed to operate its North-Africa based warships for the protection of its colonies. The bases included Casablanca and Dakar, Senegal, on the Atlantic coast.

On 9 December we sailed from Toulon for Casablanca to relieve the 16th Flotilla which had been there for several months. A 72-hour stop-over at Oran gave us the opportunity to go in small groups to the cemetery at Mers-el-Kebir to pay our last respects to those comrades killed in the course of that dreadful tragedy …

At Dakar, where we arrived on 5 January 1941, the flotilla comprised eight submarines. Patrols were organised on a rota basis so that there were always three or four submarines at sea at any one time. The boats submerged before daybreak and surfaced as night fell. All night, with engines stopped and all lights out, diesels ran only to recharge the batteries so the boat could proceed submerged on electric motors. As smoking while submerged was forbidden, the smokers on board went up to the bridge to smoke and get a break of fresh air. They only had about ten mins because their mates were at the bottom of the ladder awaiting their turn. They had to sit down in a small corner of the bridge because no flame or light must be seen from outside.

As a signalman I was on duty on the bridge, unlike the seamen whose work was limited to the boat's interior. With the bridge open to the elements, in bad weather you kept getting a faceful of water, but as a compensation, a sailor who was on duty on the bridge at night had the job of going below to make tea laced with a good measure of rum, not forgetting the submariner's speciality: the double.

In the course of March '41, after we had left to patrol off Dakar, the air valve of No. 2 after ballast tank did not open as we dived. The boat became unbalanced and went bow-down at an angle of minus 30 to minus 40 degrees. Our position was desperate; the battery acid was beginning to spill. After the control panel short-circuited, the batteries cut out and we were in a catastrophic situation.

The important thing was not to panic. Some stripes of luminous paint on the plates, on the principal pressure gauges and the main controls allowed us to locate them.

But the boat was still nose-diving.

Without waiting for orders, Engineering Petty Officer Arnault leapt at the compressed-air valves to blow ballast forward. Gently the boat began to regain her normal trim. The electricians were working on the switchboard to restore power; several bulbs had cracked.

Meanwhile, Leading Torpedoman Arnis delivered a sharp blow to free the air valve of No. 2 after ballast tank.

All these measures were taken quickly and without panic, with everyone at his post. A few seconds later and the boat would have been vertical, it would have been impossible to correct her – and the crew would have suffered a dreadful death, asphyxiated by the acids and gas given off by the batteries.

Thank God; it was a miracle we escaped with our lives.

After that accident we broke off our patrol and changed course for Dakar. As soon as we reached the quay towards 1600 one half of the crew, wearing sports kit, went off to the sports ground for an hour of physical exercise to clear the chlorine out of their lungs. Then the other team took their turn.

We stayed in port forty eight hours before going back out, after having had a good clean. The whole crew went back to sea, glad to be going, just as if nothing had happened.

Louis Corolleur took the opportunity to leave the Navy in 1942 to study for his Master's ticket. His studies were interrupted after some of the students stole a fishing vessel to get to Britain and join the Free French. As a reprisal, the Germans temporarily closed down the school.

## NORTH SEA, BALTIC AND ARCTIC

**Commander M. B. St-John, DSC, Royal Navy, HMS *Tuna*;**
from *All Round Look*

I was moved to command an operational boat, the *Tuna*, based on HMS *Forth* in the Holy Loch. Finding to my joy the job of Engineer Officer vacant, I forthwith applied, successfully, for Digger [see page 119] to join me.

*Tuna*, unbelievably in retrospect, had been fitted with German MAN main engines, delivered to the UK between Munich and the outbreak of war, so there were virtually no spare parts and, as time passed, it became clear that the enemy had understandably tinkered with the more sensitive tolerances. Their hollow pistons were cooled with oil pumped into an internal chamber through copper walking pipes, hinged like a human limb to follow the piston's vertical movements. The top of this chamber was sealed by the piston-head doubly-bolted to the main body.

At the end of one of our North Sea war patrols, when nobody was due to take over our area, I, as usual, deliberately compromised our position by breaking wireless silence before withdrawing, to con the enemy into thinking we were still around, and set off on the surface after dark for Lerwick, our advance base in the Shetland Islands. Almost immediately, there was a violent thump that felt as if someone had swung a 7lb sledge hammer up under my feet on the bridge, and silence fell. One of the nuts holding down a piston head on the port engine had worked loose and, being cocked on edge, had slammed against the cylinder-head on the next upstroke, shattering the skirt of the piston, the pieces of which were propelled like shrapnel through the sump casings all over the Engine Room. It was more than lucky no one was hurt, but the piston and its walking pipes were destroyed and our retreat from our compromised position almost brought to a halt. The best we could do was to hobble through the usual rough North Sea till dawn at no more than steerage way with the starboard engine on a 'running charge', necessitated by the need to re-charge our batteries after the previous day's dive. We wallowed through the wild, dark Northern night with agonising slowness while Digger and his merry men made ready to remove the damaged piston and sling a spare in its place which would enable the engine to run on seven cylinders at very low revs. Better than nothing, but still not enough for us to feel safe from the Luftwaffe, who we expected to react to our compromise ploy.

At dawn we dived to 120 feet to ensure complete calm for this tricky operation and I duly retired to my cabin to contemplate an uncomfortable retreat, on vastly reduced power, with the alerted Luftwaffe after us in force. The difficult work was soon in progress and at lunchtime I turned out and walked for'ard to the wardroom. As I did so I was horrified to see what appeared to be lambent flames reflected on the circular interior of the hull ahead of me.

Any fire is dangerous. In a submerged battery-driven submarine it is lethal, so that not even a spark was allowed from an auxiliary motor, let alone a naked flame, due to the hydrogen given off by the batteries. You may imagine how Fear lent speed to my dash to the scene.

I discovered that the flames were in the machinery space below the deck on which I was standing and, jumping down the circular hatch with an extinguisher and acute terror, I found Digger with a blow-lamp going full-bore armed only with a hammer and his bare hands creating, out of spare copper tubing, a replacement set of the very intricate walking-pipes. As I appeared, he extinguished the blow-lamp and grinned at me with the happiness born of a difficult obstacle overcome.

'That should fix the bastard,' he remarked in a matter-of-fact way. 'I didn't ask your permission, Skipper, because I knew you'd refuse.' If there had been anything constructive to say at that moment, it was patently too late. I suppose I must have reacted from sheer fright but I don't remember anything beyond 'God, Digger ...' thus invoking the two agencies responsible for (a) our escape from a terminal hydrogen gas explosion and (b) as it subsequently proved, Digger's hand-trade gear being good enough to enable us to use all eight cylinders of the port engine and escape safely home from what might well have been a more than fraught situation of our own making.

## Torpedoman Nickolay Leontievich Tolokonnikov, USSR Navy, Baltic Fleet, *P-3*

The Soviets distinguish between the Second World War in general and their struggle against Nazi Germany in particular by referring to the latter as the Great Patriotic War.

I joined the Soviet navy in 1937 after graduating from the Submariners School as a torpedoman in the *P-3 Iskra* submarine of the *Pravda*-Class. It was not a very good design. There were only three submarines of the type: *P-1*, *P-2* and ours *P-3*.. They were designed to support capital ships at sea, which was something new for the Soviet navy. The subs had some unusual construction features which gave them a serious tactical disadvantage. It had such such a great reserve of buoyancy that it was slow to dive, and that reduced the main advantage of a submarine: to stay stealthy. Later this disadvantage would be the reason why our submarines were restricted to the role of training boats.

The beginning of the Great Patriotic War found our submarine in the Orienbaum naval base near Kronstadt. On one occasion we were anchored on the Orienbaum and saw a boat on fire. Our submarine and our sistership, *P-2*, went to help the boat and the hurry led to collision. *P-2* hit our starboard and we sustained serious damage. So we had to be docked in Kronstadt. On 23 Sept Kronstadt naval base was attacked from the air. It was an awful attack and we got another hit. A 250 kilogram bomb ran through our hull and exploded under our keel. I was not on the submarine at this moment, but I remember this attack very clearly. Me and my friend had been sent to the town and were on our back way to the dock when the attack began. We were near one of Kronstadt's lighthouses and a German aircraft saw us and started to hunt us. When the aircraft made a run at us we hid ourselves on the opposite side of the lighthouse. So we played the game with the German pilot for some time, and it seemed an eternity to me.

When the attack ended we got back to our sub and found her in a bad condition. The outer hull was blown away within a radius of several metres from the centre of the explosion. So we had to stay in the dock for even longer and had no chance to take part in the war then. Maybe this saved our lives. The only two cases of *Pravda*-Class in combat operations led to the loss of *P-1* and serious damage of *P-2*. *P-1* was assigned to deliver supplies to Hanko naval base which was under siege by the Finnish army. The sub arrived at Hanko but then was lost without trace on her back way to Kronstadt. Some believe that she struck a mine in the Gulf of Finland. *P-2* was assigned to attack enemy shore targets with gunfire in Narva Bay, but because she was carrying extra shells, she was incorrectly trimmed while on deployment and dived at an excessive angle of of 25–28 degrees. As a result, battery acid leaked and chlorine gas was given off. She had to surface and was attacked by German aircraft with two bombs which exploded near the sub and wounded one seaman. After those failures of P-Class subs it was decided not to use the remaining two *Pravda*-Class subs in active combat operations and use them for training only.

After being repaired we were assigned to Leningrad. By that time the enemy was besieging the city and the 900 days of hunger began. The autumn of 1941 and winter of 1942 was a very difficult time for Leningrad. The famine became very serious, especially for civilians. We were prepared for street fighting. Our sub was included in the plans of the city's defence as we had quite powerful artillery. There were some events I cannot forget. One of them shows that although it was an extremely hard time for the city and its citizens because of famine and cold in winter, some of the people managed to live well. Once, we were on patrol during curfew looking for enemy saboteurs. We were asked to help the NKVD (People's Commissariat of Internal Affairs – the future KGB) men to arrest someone. We came to a block of apartments and were met by a dog in the doorway. It was unusual to have a dog then as there was not enough food for people, not to mention dogs. Children died of starvation; people received 150 grams of bread per day and nothing more. So it was abnormal. The apartments were filled with such a strong smell of roast meat that one of our sailors collapsed in a faint, although we had better rations than the ordinary civilians.

The city was often under fire from German heavy guns. Once when we were moored in the Neva River near the site where the cruiser *Aurora* was now anchored we got a direct hit from a heavy shell. We had a small barge near us and were taking oil from her when the firing began. Then we heard a great din. When we climbed up the conning tower we saw that one of our two 130mm guns was now on the barge as if it had been moved there deliberately [not simply blown off the deck]. The barge master (a woman) stood up on the barge deck too, saw the gun and began to protest, asking who allowed us to move our gun on to her deck. Then I replied that she should ask Hitler.

**Lieutenant-Commander Ben Bryant, Royal Navy, HMS *Sealion*;**
from an undated note to Captain 5th Submarine Flotilla; ADM157/192114

Operation 'Foremost' took place on 16 September 1941.

This was one of several operations done at this period whilst *Scharnhorst* and *Gneisenau* were in Brest. From memory this was the fourth and last.

*Sealion* had a liaison officer called 'Daniel' who used to be delivered in a plain van by DNI [Director of Naval Intelligence] just before sailing and removed similarly on return. His real name I have forgotten (Lechaboc or something like it). We originally had picked him out of a fishing vessel when he was on the run from the Gestapo. Later in his career he joined the RNVR and carried on the Channel ferry in more suitable vessels than a tunny [tuna] boat with high speed engines and so forth. On one of these trips he had difficulty with his captain who wanted to surrender – because they had broken down at daybreak close in by Ushant – and was rumoured to have bumped [off?]* his captain and brought his boat back under sail. He got a DSC (or two) on these runs and later came into S/Ms. He was an excellent bloke, though at the time we had him in *Sealion* spoke virtually no English. His people were tunny canners in Brittany, and were under arrest as hostages by the Gestapo.

The object of these exercises was to take petrol and money to the resistance movement. The petrol was used to run the W/T sets they used for reporting S & G, and the money (French franc notes by the suitcase) to pay any agents. We were given a rendezvous off the French coast and there were to meet a fishing vessel, whose description we would have, and it was to [show?] a masthead light, and a man was to swan up the mast at zero time as a method of identification. This would have worked better if the fishing vessel had been the one described, and its navigation more accurate – as the place was always full of fishing vessels. From memory on this occasion they had had difficulty and had to use an open boat, and we had cruised around, Daniel engaging the fishing vessels that looked likely in conversation (Breton) until we found the right one. In fact [we/he] always connected. We would give our franc notes and petrol (not to mention rum, coffee, tobacco and diesel oil off the ration) and received suitcases of spy reports, often [?] escaped from the Gestapo, and fresh fish (off the ration). We used to get fresh fish from other fishing boats (not reported in patrol reports!) also to relieve the diet.

The chaps we collected varied, and on one trip, not this, I had seven, including a Polish airman who had been in most of the countries and prisons of Europe en route, the Inspector of Brothels of Brest (who had been done out of his job by the Gestapo) [illegible word] spies, airmen, etc.

Sorry I cannot give you more details. It was really very easy and no danger but it used to worry FO S/M [Flag Officer, Submarines] and staff …

**Lieutenant Zarmair Arvanov, USSR Navy, Northern Fleet**;
from his memoir *The Front Beneath the Sea*

The submarines of the Northern Fleet, patrolling and minelaying in the Arctic and particularly round the northern coast of Norway, were arguably the most effective

* The document is not in perfect condition.

of the Soviet boats. Between mid-April and late August, however, operations on the surface in those latitudes were hindered by Polar day, when the sun never goes below the horizon.

Most submarines had their own way of advertising 'kills', ranging from the Jolly Roger (embellished with different symbols for different kinds of actions) which was popular with certain Royal Navy commanders, to the pennants hung on some German U-boats. The inexperienced crew of K-2 were keen to find a way of marking their first success – when it arrived.

At the beginning of the Great Patriotic War, I was the Weapons Officer and first mate (3rd in command) of *K-2* of the Northern fleet. We sailed on our first patrol on 7 August and returned on 31 August,1941. It was a quite difficult patrol. It was Polar day so we were unable to recharge our batteries in the normal way. As soon as we surfaced to recharge batteries we had to dive again because of enemy aircraft. However, it helped us to become highly proficient in the crash dive procedure, and by the end of the patrol we could crash dive from running ahead at flank speed on the surface to periscope depth in just 37 seconds. We spotted and attacked enemy merchantmen eight times, [each time] firing a single torpedo, but we missed every time. Twice we attacked enemy cargo ships with our guns but all in vain as we were too cautious. We didn't have enough experience yet. Although we hadn't sunk a ship then we were warmly welcomed home by the Commander-in-Chief of the Fleet, Rear Admiral A. Golovko. He congratulated the crew and said that we were doing a great job, as our presence and attacks forced the enemy to withdraw part of its own forces from our waters in order to escort its cargo ships. The Germans realized that their 'happy time' had passed and they had to form convoys ...

Three days after our return, the British submarine *Tigris* returned from her patrol, too. Entering Ekaterininskaya harbour where Polyarnoe naval base is situated she raised two flags bearing the Nazi swastika, which we detested. The English liaison officer explained to us that it meant that the sub had sunk two enemy ships. It was extremely strange and offensive to us to see such a custom in our home base. This came at the time when we were suffering defeats on all fronts, our army was retreating, our cities and towns were being occupied by the enemy. And I said to myself that we would celebrate our victory another way. I went to our submarine division commander (a submarine division usually consisted of several submarines of the same class) Captain 2nd Rank Mahomet I. Gadzhiev and shared my thoughts with him. However, he replied that we needed to gain the victory before we could celebrate it and proclaim it to the base.

The second patrol was preceded by an event that got me into trouble. I was the senior officer aboard when the air-raid alarm sounded over the base.

Our gun crew quickly went to their stations and reported that they were ready. I climbed up to the bridge and spotted a Junkers 88 flying north, far off the harbour. We did the calculation and in a few seconds the gunlayer reported that the target had been picked up. I gave the order to fire. Both of our 100mm guns opened fire. Being intent on tracking the aircraft, I hadn't noticed that we were the only ship that was firing. None of the other ships nor the AA guns on shore opened up. Of course, we didn't bring down the plane although our shells were exploding quite close to it. It turned out that a special order regarding AA engagements had been issued while we were at sea. It said that ships were not to open fire against distant aircraft. That firing put us right in the spotlight. The news reached even Golovko and he reprimanded me for 'unnecessary firing in the harbour'. The submarine commander Captain 3rd Rank Vasiliy Utkin and the division commander Captain 2nd Rank M. Gadzhiev tore me off a strip, too, so I was in a pretty foul mood.

On 7 September we went out on the second patrol. We approached Vardø naval base and laid mines at the entrance to the port. Then we embarked on our second task, to find and destroy enemy ships in the area of sea close to Vardø. On 11 September* I spotted through the periscope an enemy cargo ship steaming close inshore. I sounded the alarm for torpedo attack and began to issue the orders that would get the submarine in a position to fire. When the Captain reached the conning tower I hurried to my station in the first compartment. I was expecting to hear the order to fire torpedoes, but it wasn't given. Then I was called to the conning tower. I thought that I might have done something wrong and was very anxious. I met the flotilla commander Gadzhiev and Captain Utkin there. Gadzhiev asked me if I could sink the ship with gunfire. I felt considerable relief and replied, 'Yes, comrade', and then added that we needed to close the ship and asked his permission to take a look through the periscope to gauge the range more accurately. Fifty seconds after surfacing we opened fire. After the third shot we hit them. Every following shot hit the enemy freighter. The enemy ship started to fire his machine-gun, but he was too far away to get us.

The engagement took place quite close to Vardø and our signalman reported: 'They're pulling out a seaplane from its hangar'; then 'the seaplane is afloat'; then 'the plane is taking off'. All those reports made us nervous. We were keen to sink the ship first. At last the machine-gun fire stopped and the freighter caught fire. She started to list to starboard, settling by the stern. Gadzhiev, who stood behind me, put his hand on my

* According to Russian sources, the attack – which actually took place on the 12th – was on the Norwegian freighter *Lofoten* which was damaged but failed to sink; some other sources suggest the ship was not hit at all.

shoulder and said: 'Finish him off!' Meanwhile the enemy plane was still heading toward us and it was too dangerous to stay on the surface. Captain ordered, 'Everybody down! Crash dive!' I threw a last glance at the sinking freighter and dived into the boat. We got the impression that the submarine wasn't going to dive. At last, after several seconds she started to dive. Then we went down fast. A few minutes later, when we dived to 95 metres (the maximum official depth was 100 metres), we heard two bombs that had been dropped astern at our recent position. However, we didn't get hit. After that engagement, I mentioned to Gadzhiev my idea of celebrating the victory when we came into our base. I suggested we should fire a gun for each ship that we sank. He replied, 'Listen, haven't you already had one reprimand for firing in the base? Do you want any more? Look, we'll discuss it later, when we go home.'

We had no contact with enemy ships during the remaining days, and on 19 September we were recalled. At the approach to the base we were met by a motor-boat with the submarine brigade (flotilla) commander aboard. As the boat approached, Gadzhiev looked at me and said: 'Sorry, Lieutenant, there's no way of doing what you want.' I was a little upset. My idea couldn't be put into practice while that boat was running alongside and all our preparations could be seen from it. Fortunately, before too long the motor-boat accelerated, overtook us and made for the base. Then Gadzhiev smiled at me and said. 'Well, now's your chance! Go ahead!' So I ordered the forward gun's crew on deck. They hurried to their stations and loaded the gun with a blank round. On entering the harbour I gave the order: 'For the greater glory of our arms, fire!' and the burst of fire echoed over the base. Everybody on the shore who was meeting us ducked down: they thought it was an air attack. AA crews ran to their guns. However they soon realized that we had been the ones doing the firing. When the submarine moored at the pier our Captain disembarked and reported to the Northern Fleet commander, Admiral Golovko: 'Comrade Admiral! Submarine *K-2* has returned from patrol and successfully carried out all missions. One enemy ship was sunk by gunfire!' Golovko glanced at our forward gun, the barrel of which was black with powder, its paint peeled off, and he smiled. He asked why had we fired as we entered the harbour and our Captain replied that it was a shot to celebrate our victory. After that, it became a custom for all Northern Fleet submarines returning home to base to fire a round for each ship sunk.

Arvanov later joined *K-21*, a posting which saved his life: *K-2* left for her last patrol on 26 August 1942 and failed to return. She probably struck a mine off the Tanafjord.

## MEDITERRANEAN

**Wireless Officer and Meteorologist John de Majnik, Yugoslav Navy,**
*Nebjosa*; from *Diary of A Submariner*

As it became clear that Yugoslavia would have to capitulate to Axis forces, John de Majnik and four other crew members decided they would fight as partisans on land rather than surrender the submarine. As they were planning this, three of the *Nebjosa*'s officers, led by the First Lieutenant, Dkojo Djordjevic, proposed escaping with the boat, certain that the Captain was on the verge of receiving an order to surrender her.

Standing on the jetty [at Kotor] waiting for us was our ex-captain Lieutenant Commander Mitrovic, now in charge of the mine and torpedo arsenal and of the barricade at Kumbor. As soon as we were secured and the gangway placed he came aboard. The way he was greeted by all showed how immense was his popularity as a submariner. After a brief discussion with the First Officer he asked the crew to be assembled on the after deck. His address to the crew was short and to the point.

He said, 'The Italian motorised units are expected to arrive in Herecegnovi late today. The town's population is preparing to receive them with open arms. The Italian Navy is, supposedly, waiting outside the Bay with instructions to destroy any ship or ships that may try to escape. They have laid new minefields and ours have been tampered with. Within a few hours you will receive the order to surrender yourself and the submarine to the enemy. If your captain follows these orders will you accept me as your Captain? We will try to take the submarine out of the country and join the Allies. I am now going back to Kumbor to prepare the barricades to be open for our escape. The rest of the journey will have to rest in God's hands. Those in favour of escape step forward, those against may go and fetch their belongings, if any, and are free to go wherever they want.'

The next moment will stay with me for as long as I live as thirteen out of fifty-two men stepped out, looked quickly up and down the line, then at each other's faces to see with whom they had formed the pact of 'death or freedom'. At this moment great respect and sense of brotherhood was felt as they instinctively knew that from this moment they would totally rely on each other to survive.

Six of the men were already in the submarine, each guarding the allotted compartment against any act of sabotage. My place was on the bridge: the heavy machine-gun ready to be used.

When the boat's current captain came out by MTB the situation was explained. He chose to obey orders, so the submarine returned to Kotor that night to disembark him and those who were staying behind, and to look for replacement crew.

Some of the crew we had left behind in Kostajnica must already have arrived at Kotor. The news about our escape out of the country was all around us. There was a gathering of people on the quay, asking questions, some just pointing at the submarine – wondering whether we were heroes attempting to cross the minefields and pass through the blockade or just plain mad. Some of our crewmen went aboard the depot ship to persuade the reserve crews of the four submarines to join us. They were lucky to persuade some, but not as lucky as the First Lieutenant was. He was inundated with students, generals, ministers, naval officers, air force captains and civilians, all desperate to die with us. Some were offering a great deal of money for the privilege of being blown up on mines, being gunned to death or gaining freedom ...

A sailor from the depot ship arrived with a verbal order for the First Officer to report to the Flotilla's captain immediately. He instead ordered the gangway to be removed. But when the request was made to the people standing and watching to remove the rope off the bollard an amazing thing happened – nobody would cast the rope off. Not even after several requests. They all knew of our attempt to cross the newly laid minefields and run the blockades. In their minds (and ours) it was suicide – and none of these people wanted to soil their hands with lifting the rope and sending us to a certain death.

A very young student girl arrived on the scene and it was she who, with great difficulty, lifted up and cast away the heavy rope. The last link with the mother country and life was now severed. There was no way back.

Soft rain started to fall. When we reached and safely passed through the Verige channel that narrows the passage to about 290 metres [sic]. Our first danger spot was eliminated. Even before we had arrived abreast with Kumbor a few challenge signals had to be answered. Holding the Aldis lamp at the ready my hands almost froze to it. That's how cold the rain was. When we approached the barricades with caution, we knew that now was the time for the shore batteries to open fire in spite of the fact that  Brigadier General Djukanovic, who was in charge of the shore defences, was now with us aboard the submarine. They must have obeyed his order as all was quiet. At Kumbor I flashed out the pre-arranged signal. It was answered immediately. Out of the sheet of rain a small boat appeared. In it were Lieutenant-Commander Mitrovic, our new captain, and three other persons ...

As we arrived at our minefields we had to take into consideration the talk of last night that the positions of the mines had been tampered with. As we were going through at a very slow speed, to us on the bridge every second became a lifetime and every next one even longer. We had arrived into the Bay of Hercegovni in one piece.

We were hugging the shoreline of Lustica when, on our starboard side and almost three kilometres away, fully lit, the town of Hercegnovi came into our view. Flashes and sounds of machine-gun fire came from out of town. We had no idea what sort of a battle or celebration was going on …

When I entered the Control Room the smiling expression on my face gave the answer to their unasked questions. Then came the barrage of questions to all of which I answered, 'We are clear of the shore and heading for Greece. All is well.'

They in turn came forward with their news. How all the newcomers were shown their duties at 'Diving Stations' and how to operate the toilet. Some were coached by the Engine Room Artificer, who required a staff of sixteen men to run the engines, as only two were available. How many problems arose soon after we came to the open sea! The sea sickness set in. Four army officers were affected by the confined space and suffered attacks of claustrophobia. Gripped with panic, and before anyone in the Control Room realised what had happened, a rather rotund army officer rushed into the conning tower in a frantic effort to get out. Soon there were cries of excruciating ear pain all through the submarine. The hungry-for-air diesels sucked all the remaining air causing a vacuum. The Engine Room Artificer knew the cause immediately, rushed into the control room and with the help of two other men released the stuck-in-the-hatch officer. They all admired the way Lieutenant Pazin cleverly employed the four officers suffering from claustrophobia in the engine room where the din of the engines and the constant oiling of the diesels seemed to take their minds off the problem …

On Thursday 24 May *Nebjosa* reached Suda Bay and tied up alongside the Greek submarine *Papanicoli* just in time for an air raid. From there she limped to Alexandria for repairs, and de Majnik was transferred for a time to HMS *Queen Elizabeth* for further wireless training. He subsequently served in the submarine minelayer HMS *Rorqual* and in 1942 joined a British rifle regiment.

**Commander P. Bartlett, OBE, Royal Navy, HMS *Perseus*;**
from the papers of Commander Bartlett, Imperial War Museum

18 MAY 1941.
To begin with, expecting a seaborne invasion of Crete and not having any information as to where this might be mounted from, I made up towards Piraeus and spent the day waiting for something to happen. Either the first or second

day the rumble of explosions to the south went on all day, and a great many aircraft were seen to be flying from the north towards Crete and returning, and that evening the 'news' told us that a tremendous airborne invasion of the island had taken place, but all parachutists had been mopped up by our troops positioned around the airports which had been the main targets. I recall after a very optimistic news signal – these were all transmitted in Morse code from the transmitting station Rugby – and received a signal informing me that I was the only Allied vessel in the Aegean, which certainly showed us that the battle for Crete was not going too well. Later I was told to investigate shipping in the harbour of Milos, where it was thought that German troops might be arriving in troopships and being trans-shipped to Crete in smaller vessels under cover of night. The following morning we fixed our position and set course to lie SE to cover the remaining two or three miles to the harbour entrance. Accurate navigation was important around these small islands and this was impossible at night time with no navigating lighthouses in use. It was about six o'clock as we approached Milos, and we should have passed a small precipitous island called Anti-Milos by about a mile, but just as we were coming up from 80 feet to periscope depth there was a bump and a rumble and we came up quicker than we meant to. We had run into Anti-Milos, fortunately at a speed of only about two knots, but the towering cliffs were in sight less than 100 yards as we went astern out of it, a rude awakening indeed for the two-thirds of the crew off watch. Diving astern is a dicey business and it was a little while before we got a steep angle off her and on to a safe course.

Our troubles were not yet over, as we cautiously reconnoitred the entrance to the harbour of Milos. This was about three miles long and tapered to less than half a mile wide, with the anchoring waters only partially in sight at the bottom of this funnel. The sea was flat calm and through the periscope I could see our bows ... through the water as clearly as if we were surfaced, every rivet and every scratch on the plates. But apart from a few small fishing boats there was nothing to be seen, certainly nothing to justify a torpedo. So before we were too far into the entrance to prevent us turning around, we reversed our course and headed out to sea again. The Torpedo Officer then asked if it would be convenient to give the two torpedoes in the stern tubes a routine overhaul. Normally the torpedoes in their tubes are flooded, ready for firing at short notice, so that it is advisable to drain the tubes and hank the torpedo back on to the compartment and check on air vessel pressures, etc., about every 10 days, so I told him to go ahead, one at a time. When reloading the port tube, the 'top stop', which prevents the torpedo sliding too far into the tube, could not have been fully 'down' and the torpedo must have come up against it with a bang, forced it up and allowed the torpedo to slide past it. At the time it could not be known that this had happened, but when the water was blown back into the tube from the special WRT tank, the torpedo was forced past the top stop, the firing cover triggered off and so started the torpedo engine (run on a mixture of fuel and air ignited by a cartridge – there is no stopping it). The tube vents were open and the exhaust fumes came into the after ends, two sailors becoming unconscious from breathing them. Two others put on Escape Apparatus and dragged them into the engine room, and vented the tubes into the sea. It was a few minutes before the cause of the vibration of the torpedo engine, which could be felt and heard in the Control Room, was reported and explained.

For an unpleasant five minutes it looked as if we might be forced to surface to ventilate the after torpedo compartment, but we were not at all anxious to do this so close to Milos, so we cruised along bubbling madly from the torpedo tube's vents for about 10 or 15 minutes, or until the engine stopped for lack of fuel in its air vessel. Large numbers of aircraft were almost always in sight, but we told ourselves that they were primarily troop carriers and not looking out for inoffensive – as far as they were concerned – submarines.

Later that day, sometime in the dog watches, I sighted a small vessel making for Milos and started to attack it. I was in a good position but the sea was very calm, so I was using very little periscope for very brief periods, and didn't get a good look at it until it was quite close, when it turned out to be a small corvette. These were very shallow draught, too shallow for a good chance of a torpedo hit, but we had also been warned not to attack them as they were very manoeuvrable anti-submarine vessels. So I stopped the attack and let it go past and then I saw the ship it was evidently escorting not too far stern, so I transferred my attack, though I wasn't quite so close to her track. She had a close escort of four small motor launches and E-boats, but I was able to let these go past and fired three torpedoes at what I hoped was a small troopship going into Milos. As usual, we altered course violently to get away from the gerfluffle made at the start of the torpedo tracks, which of course pinpoints where the S/M fired from to the A/S vessels.

Shortly afterwards the Torpedo Officer reported that only one of the three torpedoes had actually left the tubes – some fault in the firing system. This was something we had dreaded as we had had no chance after our refit to try out the torpedo firing drill – you will recall that we were ordered out on this patrol with no working-up period at all, after seven weeks in dockyard hands! This was just one of several infuriating defects that the normal 10-day work-up would have disclosed.

We were hunted very ineffectually, a few distant depth charges a long way off, but the single torpedo missed its target as far as I know ...

Around midnight, as I was sitting or sleeping in my armchair in my cabin in the conning tower, the diving hooters went, the bridge personnel came hurtling down the ladder just outside my cabin and Drummond, the officer of the watch, called out, 'Destroyer to starboard.' I followed them down to the control room and when we were down at 80 feet and cruising comfortably Drummond explained that he had sighted a darkened vessel which he thought was a destroyer, which we soon picked up on the hydrophones, so we went dead slow and picked up a dense layer at about 90 feet. The shallow water gauges (0–100 feet) were switched off and we watched the deep water (90–500 feet) gauges settling around 100 feet for some time until the engineer officer, I think, came into the control room and reached behind the deep diving gauges and altered the position of its cock on the hull. It whizzed round to 300 feet, slowed and continued to get deeper. Someone had switched the cock off at the same time as that of the shallow water gauge! The engine room gauge, of course, showed the true depth … At this moment, as we were speeding up to regain depth, a sailor from the crew space reported water coming out of the gun tower vent. The open-ended vent pipe is at the top of the gun tower, which told us why we had suddenly lost our trim and carried out an involuntary deep dive. We shut the gun tower vent, of course, pumped out the equivalent amount of water from a midship trimming tank and in time settled down at 80 feet. No sound of any surface vessel, so we blew main ballast and surfaced. On arriving on the dark and dripping bridge I was more than startled to hear a loud groaning sound, rather like a shore fog signal. It was the air in the gun tower, trapped by the water which had flooded through the joint that we had not been able to test properly at Port Said … It was this air, trapped at diving pressure, forcing its way past the rubber seating and making a huge raspberry.

I remember little about the remainder of that patrol … but I shall never forget the sight of the battered cruisers and destroyers of the Med. Fleet lying in Alexandria Harbour. Every vessel seemed to have sustained damage and close to the *Medway* lay the cruiser *Orion*, with its 'A' turret and the guns of 'B' turret obviously askew. A large number of soldiers, caught by a direct hit on the mess deck, were killed and had not yet been reached. The whole harbour was a mass of damaged ships and we knew by now that we had lost Crete in a week.

## Luitenant ter Zee 1 Peter de Jong, Koninklijke Marine, *O.24*

During 1941, the Dutch submarine *O.24* was based at Gibraltar with Peter de Jong as her Executive Officer.

Gibraltar was a crazy place. There was one time when a huge ship came with women and children from Eritrea. The men were all prisoners of war, but the women were put on a huge passenger ship to be brought back to Naples. They came to Gibraltar. Now Gibraltar was a peculiar place: there were thousands of men and about six women, nurses in the hospital. The youngest one was 45, I believe, and she became more and more beautiful by the week. There it was, a ship full of Italian women. The captain in Gibraltar had anchored the thing in the middle. Armed boats circling around it ... Chaps on shore looking at these Italian women. People by the anchor chain trying to get on board ...

### Prince Junio Valerio Borghese, Regia Marina, commanding the submarine *Scirè*; from *Sea Devils*

After the loss of first the *Gondar* and then the *Iride*, the *Scirè* was fitted with caissons to transport human torpedoes on their mission to attack shipping in Gibraltar. Commanded by Borghese, who had also been responsible for the planning, the submarine departed from her base at La Spezia and passed through the Strait of Gibraltar, surfacing in Cadiz on 17 September.

The telegram received from the Naval Staff at 2330 hours on the evening of the 19th, an hour before the pilots left the submarine, reads as follows:

'Situation of vessels in harbour at 1200 hours on the 19th: at Mole I, battleship; at anchorage No. 27, aircraft-carrier; at anchorage No. 5, cruiser; at anchorage No. II, a second cruiser; in addition, seven tankers and three destroyers in harbour. One destroyer in dock. Convoy of 17 steamers in roadstead.'

As a result of this information I assigned the pilots their targets as follows:

Lieutenants Catalano and Vesco both to attack the battleship of the *Nelson* class (35,000 tons) anchored at the South Mole; Lieutenant Visintini to attack the aircraft-carrier; if impracticable, the three crews to attack any other units, in decreasing order of importance; no clue to be left in the hands of the enemy, so that he may be left completely in the dark about the nature and origin of the explosions.

DESCRIPTIONS OF THE OPERATIONS OF THE THREE CREWS FOLLOW, COMPILED FROM THEIR REPORTS.

VESCO-ZOZZOLI: 'At about 0030 hours on 20 September 1941, in accordance with Commanding Officer Borghese's orders, I left the submarine, followed by my Number Two, PO/Diver Antonio Zozzoli. The target assigned to me was a battleship of the *Nelson* class, moored inside the harbour, halfway along the south breakwater. Surface approach was normal, though impeded by wind and high seas. I removed my mask at intervals, so as to see with the naked eye, but on each occasion only for a few seconds, because, even when I was stationary, the waves breaking over my face were a great nuisance, especially to my eyes.

After an emergency submersion to evade discovery by a patrol boat on duty I sighted the entrance to the harbour.

'I was about 300 metres from the defences and slowed down so as to prevent my being heard by hydrophones and in order to have time to find out about the manoeuvres of a boat which was shuttling, with her lights on, in front of the entrance ... I set a bee-line course and submerged to the greatest possible depth, proceeding at low speed to prevent the phosphorescence of my wake from being detected from the surface.

'At about 3.15 I got down to a depth of about 26 metres, just grazing the bottom, which was hard and smooth and did not interfere in any way with my progress. At about 3.30, at a depth of 15 metres, I heard and felt against the cask of the 'pig' and against my own body three consecutive underwater explosions. As everything continued to function normally I decided to go on. At 3.40 I was at a depth of 13 metres when I heard two further explosions, slightly more subdued than the previous ones, but of greater volume.'

The presence of a patrol boat and other considerations induced Vesco to renounce the attempt to force the entrance and accordingly, 'to my deep regret, while I was about 50 metres from the defences, I resolved to abandon the target assigned to me and turn my attention to a vessel in the roadstead'.

Vesco surfaced and reached the steamers in the roadstead.

'At four a.m. I started to look for the most important target. A boat with its lights dimmed was moving about among the steamers. At last I sighted a vessel with a long, slender outline, lying low in the water and therefore heavily laden; I guessed her to be about three or four thousand tons displacement. I made my approach and performed the manoeuvre of contacting: I submerged deeply beneath the ship, stopped and came up, exhausting the tanks, till I reached the hull. I managed to do this unseen and unheard, but owing to damage to my breathing set I could not avoid swallowing water containing soda-lime which caused painful burning to my mouth and throat.'

He surfaced hurriedly, got rid of his damaged breathing set and fitted the spare one. He then went back underwater and, with the aid of his second man, fastened the charge to the hull in line with the funnel position. Finally, after setting the fuses, he disengaged and made for the pre-arranged landing point. He sank the torpedo after setting the fuzes of the self-destructor charges every human torpedo had, and swam for the shore.

'We had a good deal of trouble owing to our bad physical condition and to the sea, which repeatedly broke over our heads. My second was very tired and feeling ill. We got ashore just before seven a.m., about 200 metres west of the prearranged point, where we were halted by two armed Spanish sentries. One of them instantly fired two rifle-shots into the air. We had just time to hide our two breathing sets in a secluded spot of the beach, as, for obvious reasons, I did not want the sentries to see them. I told the Spaniards we were ship-wrecked Italians ... We were taken to the coastguard station, where we were met by the agent P., who took steps to recover our breathing sets.'

Vesco and Zozzoli watched, from the station, the punctual explosion of the charge.

'The vessel split in two, slightly astern of the funnel. Her stern disappeared, the bows rising high out of the water.' (From the report of Lieutenant Amedeo Vesco.)

So sank the British tanker *Fiona Shell*, 2,444 tons.

The operators left the submarine without a hitch.

CATALANO-GIANNONI: 'The night was extremely dark. At 1.25 a.m. approach was begun. Rough sea and an east wind impeded our progress considerably; we could hardly breathe while surfaced. The lights of La Linea, Gibraltar and Algeciras were a perfect guide for us. At 2.35 we sighted a motor boat, moving at slow speed, 70 metres to starboard. I stopped and took careful note of its course and speed, then turned larboard to get away from her. I waited for another few minutes, then proceeded towards the north entrance at slow speed. In spite of the wide detours I had made I did not succeed in shaking off the patrol boat, which was moving slowly and almost in silence, in such a way as to be inaudible at a distance of 50 metres. I guessed it to be fitted with entirely silent electric engines and hydrophone detectors.

'I took a course between two steamers so as to cover up my tracks once and for all, but the patrol boat continued to follow me a short distance away. I decided to submerge and proceeded on a southerly course for about 15 minutes; I then surfaced, at about 3.30; I stopped: the patrol boat had lost track of me.

'As time was now running very short and I was still a long way from the entrance to the port, I thought it best to attack the steamers in the roadstead.

'I had seen three large steamers on my route. I made for them surfaced and in fourth gear.

'On arriving near them, I took careful note of the position of a large, empty tanker, and resolved to attack it astern. I approached it slowly, surfaced; but at some metres from the stern I discovered a launch moored to the tanker; I stopped, but was unable, despite the short distance and an intense observation of the launch, to discover whether there were guards aboard her; in order to run no possible risk of alarming the whole base I decided to attack another ship.'

The second man, Giannoni, had already attached the warhead to the propellers of the new target when Catalano managed to read the name on her stern: she was the *Pollenzo*, of Genoa. Though this was a captured vessel in the service of the enemy, Catalano did not wish to destroy an Italian ship. He therefore, with the help of that excellent fellow Giannoni, detached his warhead, found a large armed motor ship and attacked her.

'The work proceeded in first-rate style, owing to the splendid conduct, both in skill and in enterprise, of my second operator. At 5.16 I set the fuses of the warhead. We left at high speed and I sank the 'pig' in 51 metres of water, after setting the fuzes of her self-destructor charges: by that time it was 5.55. I surfaced with Giannoni; after removing our breathing sets and sinking them, we swam to the shore, landing at 7.15.

'At 8.55 I saw, at the place where I had sunk the 'pig', a characteristic white spouting and then a number of gulls flying over the spot; the self-destructor charges of my human torpedo had done their job.

'At 9.16 a violent explosion took place at the stern of the motor ship I had attacked; a column of water rose to about 30 metres. The motor ship settled slowly by the stern, the entire structure of her bows emerging from the water. Four powerful tugs came to her assistance and towed her ashore, with considerable trouble, at a point opposite the neutral zone.

'I afterwards found out her name; she was the armed British motor ship *Durham*, of 10,900 tons.' (From the report of Lieutenant Decio Catalano.)

After normal launching, they immediately began their approach.

Visintini-Magro: 'Magro and I removed our masks so as to obtain good visibility. But we had trouble from a high and persistent easterly sea which reduced our speed. However, we made good progress; by way of variety I noticed on two occasions the shock of a depth charge against the cask ...

'About 2.30 a.m. we sighted, almost starboard abeam, the dark outline of a patrol boat, not more than 100 metres away.'

Visintini took evasive action. He continues:

'... a little later I sighted the entrance to the port. At this stage I felt the shocks of two depth-charges, but did not worry as they seemed a long way off. I now saw that a patrol boat, coming from the south, had just arrived at the north gate; she was going very slowly, at a speed of not more than two knots an hour. I held on my course, but found at one point that the patrol boat was very close to me, patrolling the stretch of water between me and the defences and turning in my direction. I submerged at once ... and felt an explosion take place not far off; but its effects were not alarming.

'I surfaced ... a rapid survey enabled me to see that the patrol boat was now proceeding towards the south gate and I was almost inclined to fancy myself clear of her; but I had no time to feel relief at this discovery, for I instantly sighted a smaller boat coming straight at me, in silence, with her lights on. I was afraid I had been seen, but I submerged all the same, much preferring death as the result of an explosion to capture on the surface without being able to defend myself; then there was the question of the craft, which had to be sunk. But they had not seen me.

'I heard distinctly the hum of the propeller passing over me. From that moment, for a period of about 10 minutes, I played hide and seek with the enemy, now surfacing, now submerging, so as to avoid the effects of the depth-charges and reach waters where I should be less likely to be sighted.

'Finally, the patrol boat moved away southwards and I got into position to negotiate the defences: it was then 3.45. I set my course carefully and submerged, proceeding in third gear at a depth of 11 metres. I stuck to my three components (course, speed and depth) with the greatest precision and at the time foreseen I perceived three steel cables, undoubtedly forming part of the gate defence nets, which grazed my cask as I slipped between them. Having thus penetrated the harbour I surfaced and took off my mask to see better. I sighted a cruiser of about 7,000 tons ahead of me, and four large tankers at the Detached Mole.

'It was now five minutes past four and I calculated that I had no time left for operating at the south end of the harbour where the targets assigned by our commander were anchored.

'I also rejected the cruiser, for the following reasons:

'(1) because she was too near the depth-charges which were being almost systematically dropped at the gate (in the immediate neighbourhood);

'(2) because I hoped to be able to inflict greater damage by attacking the tanker (by setting the oil alight and so setting fire to the harbour).

'I resolved, accordingly, to attack one of the four tankers, choosing the second from the north end, because she was fully loaded; I guessed her to be of about 8,000 tons.

'As we were carrying out the attack at seven metres depth we were knocked against the hull of the tanker by a violent explosion, which did not, however, do us any damage.

'I proceeded with the work. At 4.40, after detaching the warhead, I set the fuzes.'

Visintini left the harbour, manoeuvring in the same way as he did to enter it, avoided the two patrol boats cruising about the entrance, set course for the

Spanish coast, sank his 'pig' and got safely ashore, with Magro, at 6.30 a.m., when he met the agent P., who was waiting for them.

'From the place where we were hiding we heard an explosion at 8.43, followed by four or five others a few minutes later.'

At 8.43 a.m. the naval tanker *Denby Dale*, 15,893 tons, blew up and sank inside Gibraltar harbour. A small tanker, moored alongside her, also went to the bottom as a result of the explosion. Though the fire which Visintini had hoped to start did not take place, the operation performed was an extremely brilliant one.

'At last, after so many disappointments, we had a positive result, though not of the importance we had desired. It was the first success of the piloted torpedoes; three vessels, including a large naval tanker and amounting in all to 30,000 tons, had been sunk.'

The operation had proved highly instructive.

**Boatswain's Mate Kurt Guennel, Kriegsmarine, *U-95*; from ADM186/807, and Seaman Jan Biesemaat, Koninklijke Marine, *O.21*; as told to his son, Ton**

Despite the misgivings of the crew, *U-95* had successfully run the gauntlet of the Strait of Gibraltar, and on 28 November she was south of the Spanish town of Almeria.

GUENNEL: When I came off watch I happened to meet the Commander [Kapitänleutnant Gerd Schreiber], I said: 'Shall we have a little celebration this evening?' He replied: 'I'll be along later.' He brought a glass of brandy and we sat down, there were four of us, and we played 'Skat'. When I go on watch at 0400 I usually turn in at ten or half-past – by that time, after the news, I am tired enough to fall asleep at 2300, and wake up at 0400. At 2300 we were just going to stop, after one more hand, when suddenly the order came through the speaking tube, spoken in a rather quiet voice: 'Lower deck, action stations.' We thought it was a joke. Then we heard that someone on deck had seen a shadow, and a rating in the conning tower, returning from a smoke, came in and said: 'There's something happening.' Then they all came along and nobody said a word; the control room was quite quiet. All of a sudden the loud-speaker said: 'Lower deck, action stations.'

BIESEMAAT: We returned from a patrol in the Mediterranean Sea, which wasn't a great success. We did manage to penetrate to just off the coast at the Lido di Roma, the Italian Scheveningen (a famous Dutch beach resort). We were so close to the shore that we could see the Italians sunbathing through the periscope.

On the afternoon of 27 November, we were ahead of our sailing schedule and, in order to stay within the territory, we needed to dive at around three o'clock. We surfaced again after dark and continued our course, zigzagging at a speed of 15 knots.

The watch was changed at midnight. We kept war watch, six hours on, six hours off. My division was sleeping when we surfaced. Sometimes, when you're sleeping, and you look at that thin layer of steel around you, you think to yourself, if they hit you, in such a small boat, you'll be blown to smithereens.

I was on the forward watch. This means that you search a sector of 180 degrees together with the officer from the watch who is also responsible for the two look-outs who keep an eye on the aft side. By the way, there are always four of you in the tower so that we can dive as quickly as possible in the event of danger. It was a clear moonlit night and the sea was as smooth as glass. There were a few wisps of clouds here and there; it looked as if the water were blending with the night air. Mr Kroeze, the Second Officer, had eagle eyes. He always saw everything; it was incredible.

Mr Kroeze suddenly says to me, 'Bies, three rings ...!' So I ring the bell in the tower hatch three times, which means alarm and that the commander must report to the bridge and the head of the engine room to the engine room. The Captain comes rushing in and asks Kroeze what's going on. 'I see a silhouette directly ahead,' he says. We look but no one can see what it was. You could only see a bow wave. I couldn't look because I was on the forward watch. We were close to the Spanish coast and lights were twinkling everywhere. It was possible that there were more enemy ships in the area. You never knew.

GUENNEL: No. 1 Boatswain's Mate was asleep at that moment; No. 3 was due to go on watch. He came out of his bunk and said: 'What's up?' I put on my leather jacket and quickly put my cigarette case into my pocket, folded back the seat, and went up into the conning tower. Then No. 1 said: 'Take your life-jacket, we're in for something.' At that time I had no idea where mine was: under my pillow, perhaps. Anyway, I said: 'Time to fetch that later', and as I went into the conning tower the order came from the control room: 'Port!' My God, I thought, what's happening now? The men forward opened the torpedo tube caps; you can imagine how they ran forward to open them. Then the show started. What sort of a boat was she? Italian? German? There had been three other boats with us. In the meantime we got the order: 'Close the caps', then again: 'Open the caps', and then another order to close them. The men forward were starting to curse. Then for the third time they wanted to fire. The order was given again: 'Open the caps.' As we were about to make our fourth approach they spotted us because we came too close. It was a beautiful moon-light night just three days before full moon. You could see your way about better than by day, when it was often a bit misty down there at this time of year. You could see the coast and the dark mountains better than by day. When we were seen we were in an unfavourable position with the moon behind us. They could see us in the moonlight better than we could see them. When we still held our fire, they drew away and showed their stern, so we challenged them two or three times in Morse.

BIESEMAAT: And then the commander says, 'Two engines slower.' We were moving quickly at the time. And naturally the bow wave was approaching quickly. 'I think it's a submarine,' says Kroeze. Suddenly a blue light flickers behind us. Someone was signalling with a covered light. The light flickers again as our English signalman/telegraphist Rees climbs the stairs. Rees doesn't recognise the code. We then know for sure that we're dealing with a German submarine. The commander ordered full speed ahead, because you shouldn't let such a boat get too close or it will fire. We had used up almost all our torpedoes during the patrol. We didn't have a single torpedo left at forward and not one shell left for the deck gun. Only two torpedoes left in the aft tubes, no more. The commander gives the order to 'reverse' and then 'stop the engines'. The submarine approaches us at high speed. Now it is simply a matter of which one of us is going to be the first to fire; after all, we're lined up opposite one another.

GUENNEL: The Captain ordered: 'Gun crew, clear away!' As a matter of fact we always had the guns ready, and the ammunition lay ready below in the control room; it always lies there. So the first thing was to get the gun loaded and sights on the target. For the time being, I was to stay in the conning tower in case we began to fire. I had my recorder with me in the conning tower as messenger. He was there to take notes, because I have to write down the data when we fire. He said we must hoist a few rounds to the upper deck when the order came to fire.

While they were getting the gun ready, we went ahead at slow speed. Then the Captain said: 'Now try some gunfire,' and we went full speed ahead. At that moment the Dutch fired their torpedoes and we couldn't see them easily on account of the moonlight. Luckily the Junior Officer saw it: he has good eyes trained in flying. He shouted: 'Torpedo track to port!'

BIESEMAAT: The commander is on the bridge casing because he doesn't have any more direction indicators, not a damn thing. The commander aims with his thumb over the bridge casing. 'Fire!' he cries. The torpedo is launched in the direction of the submarine. By the way, I only know this by word of mouth because naturally I had to keep an eye on the situation ahead. Because the weather was good and there was a full moon, the U-boat must have seen the torpedo coming because it turned to port. This probably deflected the torpedo, which didn't explode. As the U-boat turns away, we turn with it. The commander is still on the casing of the bridge and the chief officer, while looking over his thumb across the stern, cries, 'Fire!' Our second torpedo hits the U-boat precisely behind the tower. In its throes of death the U-boat sticks straight up into the air. And then disappears into the depths ... You could instantly smell cordite (torpedo explosive).

GUENNEL: The Quartermaster, who was standing forward at the port lookout, pushed him out of the way, leapt to the bridge rail, had a look over the side and put the helm hard over to starboard. Suddenly I heard a hissing noise – if that one had hit us amidships or forward I shouldn't have been able to get out. It was a very nasty feeling! I heard a bang aft and we supposed that the first torpedo had just grazed along our side. The second one came a bit further over to port, so we turned to starboard and turned, so to speak, right into the course of the torpedo. The torpedo must have exploded right on the screw. There was a loud report and I thought my head would split. I looked down and saw a red flame and a fearful cloud of smoke. I pulled myself up, and at that moment water began to come in. I was outside. I looked round and there were a few men aft and a few to our right. The Captain shouted: 'Keep together!' Then he began to count us all and call our names to see who was there. He asked me: 'Has anybody else come out?' And I said: 'No, I'm the last.' Then we began swimming. I had completely lost all sense of the enemy's position, I could only see the moon and the water and, faintly in the distance, the coast. All at once I saw the black bow of a ship in front of me. My greatest fear as I swam towards the ship was that they would open fire with machine-guns. Then the first of us got on board and I heard them speaking German. Three men pulled me up on the deck.

BIESEMAAT: We were nearby when we heard cries for help in three or four different languages ... We see the Germans swimming and holding on to each other. One of them is unconscious and is being held above water by the others. He's the helmsman who was blown off the bridge. Because I'm small, I'm able to sit on the braces of the protective cover of the hydroplanes. You're then sitting a little bit above the water. In that way I was able to grab a guy by the wrist and pull him up, after which he was handed over to someone sitting on the hydroplanes. Our engines were stopped at this time. Fuel oil was floating on the water everywhere and there was this awful cordite smell. A truly disgusting stench! So we pull up the Germans. They aren't even on deck and the German commander Gerd Schreiber starts mouthing off! He was a highly experienced submarine commander. He starts yelling at his men who had just been rescued, 'Maul halten, nichts sagen!' [Keep your mouths shut; say nothing]. Gerd Schreiber also wanted to congratulate our commander for the good shot! Van Dulm then screams at Schreiber, 'That's none of your business, keep your big mouth shut, you have no authority here, go down immediately.'

The Germans have all kinds of good equipment on them. Good quality binoculars in watertight cases with chamois cloths for cleaning them. Much better equipment than we had. The German sailors are relatively quiet, but the officers continue to mouth off. Because I was one of the youngest sailors I have to fetch coffee for the Germans. I only brought it to the sailors, not the officers. I had no interest in bringing them coffee. When the commander instructs me to do so, I tell him I need to go on watch again. The cook was then told do it but, because he's from Rotterdam (that had been bombed by the Germans a year earlier), he initially refuses. But the commander insists. Our telegraphist Joop van der Pijl, a big guy, keeps them covered with a gun. But you had to be careful. If one of the German officers goes to the head [toilet] you need to go with him because they leave the outboard valve open in an attempt to flood the boat. That's what those guys are like, not the sailors, but the officers. They tried that at least once.

There was a triumphant return to base for the Dutch boat.

BIESEMAAT: We formed into line proudly in our white sweaters with the Jolly Roger fluttering from the raised periscope. A brand-new red, white and blue flag had also been raised. The entire fleet is in a state of commotion as we enter the harbour of Gibraltar. Admiral Sir James Somerville is standing on the shore, an impressive sight. The crews of battleships are all lined up and forming a front. Sinking such a German submarine sure produces quite an effect. The commander is immediately given the DSO, which is pretty much the highest honour a foreigner can get from the English.

## Captain George Hunt, DSO*, DSC*, Royal Navy, HMS *Proteus*

After three brief appointments in a Dutch submarine, HNMS *O.10*, as a liaison officer, followed by a spell as 2 i/c of *H31*, I went again as liaison officer in a brand new British submarine given to the Poles and renamed ORP *Sokol*. From there I went as second in command to HMS *Proteus* which was sent to the Mediterranean, patrolling from Alexandria in Egypt, mainly in the Aegean Sea and the Adriatic. In *Proteus* we were the first British radar-fitted submarine. We had been given a RAF radar and they had to alter and 'marinise', as they called it, the aerial because it had to withstand diving depth and so required special treatment. At that time the PPI – Planned Position Indicators, as they were called – hadn't been invented, and the only thing you had was a rectangular screen about 8 inches × 6 inches. There was a row of green vertical 'uprights' across the bottom of the screen about an inch in height and looking like grass. When the radar detected an object, it got a return echo or pulse. This showed up on the screen as a 'spike' of 'grass' higher than its neighbours by, perhaps, another inch, depending upon the range and, therefore, the strength of the signal. In those early days the aerial was only geared up to show the bearing of the 'target' relative to the ship's head, so, of course, that had to be noted at the same time in order to obtain the true bearing. And that was about as far as we had got in a submarine with radar in those days.

However, on one occasion we did actually detect a small convoy of ships taking Germans to Crete, and the first detection that we had of this convoy was at night, was from the radar cabinet, so this was a plus for the radar. And because it was brand new and nobody knew very much about it we had two Dundee University students manning the radar set.

And I never forget when this radar was first installed. The chief ERA, who was lord of all he surveyed in the engine room, came along and poked his head into the radar cabinet to see what was going on, and Bendle, the senior of the two operators, said, 'I wouldna' stand there if I were you, Chief, it will render you sterile.' And he was off like a shot from a gun, as you can imagine. Anyway the radar on this occasion did produce this contact and sure enough there was a convoy. We couldn't see it, of course, but we shadowed the convoy all night by radar and got ahead of it and dived in position so that it would go across the path of the rising sun and we would be at periscope depth. So my captain did all that and torpedoed the ship, which was called the *Tampico*. That was really our first radar success.

The sinking took place on 3 November 1941 east of Andros Island, Greece, 37°53' N, 24°30' E.

### Ammiraglio Elio Sandroni, then Navigating Officer, Regia Marina, *Emo*

The *Emo* was taking supplies for the North Africa campaign.

Life beneath the waves passed slowly and monotonously. Admittedly it gave me long hours of sleep and I could eat my meals at the table in peace, but I preferred my hours of duty up on the bridge in the open air and no matter what the time was.

At 2150 on 24 December I had to plot our position using the Navy's radio station at Bardia. There were two hours to go before midnight and I found myself at the radio post with my Chief Telegraphist. We looked at one another, and found we were both a bit emotional. We were thinking of our distant families, getting ready to celebrate Christmas. We clasped hands and hugged one another: feelings ran very deep …

31 December 1941, New Year's Eve, at Suda Bay.

During the day both the *Emo* and another submarine, the *Veniero*, carried on loading cases of food supplies, together with the auxiliary cruiser, *Barletta*. We saw in the New Year in the wardroom. We didn't have any sweets or *pannetone*, much less any sparkling wine. We made up a good plate of spaghetti with garlic, oil and *peperoncino*. Our captain, followed by the rest of the officers, went round the various compartments to offer good wishes to all the crew. I was aware of lots of bottles of wine being passed round. The ratings were in a good mood. The petty officers, especially the senior ones, were a little sad. According to an agreement made with the *Veniero*, the latter would leave the base that night for Bardia, followed next day by the *Emo*.

## FAR EAST / INDIAN OCEAN

### Ammiraglio Elio Sandroni, Regia Marina, *Perla*

At Massawa [Eritrea] in January 1941, with the rank of midshipman, I embarked on the Royal Submarine *Perla* with barely one month of service as navigator.

Previously, from March 1940, also with the same duty, I was on the submarines *Macallé* and *Guglielmotti*. When we were not on wartime missions, the submarines of the flotilla remained moored in the small bay of Taulud close to the commercial port along with the CC.TT *Tiger*, *Lion*, *Panther* and various torpedo boats.

In case of daytime air raids the subs immersed themselves, remaining awash leaving one turret appearing on the surface, and with only security personnel on board, two machine-gunners and the watch officer.

The *Perla* was armed with a 100mm gun and two Breda 13mm single-barrel machine-guns. In case of aerial attack, the crews of the shore unit and those of the subs were authorised to open fire only if their shots were absolutely likely to be effective, that to economise on munitions.

One night I was on watch when the DICAT (Difesa Contraerea Territoriale) announced an air raid over the radio. We armed the two machine-guns and, together with two gunners, Gino Deluzia of Rome and Rolando Mantovani of Fano, exchanged our berets for helmets. After some time the unmistakably well-known rumble of approaching enemy planes was heard. The beams of DICAT searchlights began to stab the sky in search of the aircraft. One heard in the distance the crackle of anti-aircraft fire hoping to land one shot in the barrage. I looked to see if any planes had been hit. Suddenly one of the attacking planes headed down towards our bay. The searchlights were not able to reach it and the plane now came within range of our machine guns. The red tracers joined together as one. The noise was infernal – a terrible game –

seeming like the fireworks at Piedigrotta. The plane appeared to be hit as it descended still more rapidly, and I imagined that I might have to deal with a torpedo bomber. The gunner Deluzia at my orders opened fire and in good Roman style murmured, 'Go to Hell.' Mantovani was busy changing his magazine. I wanted a 'baptism by fire' and, taken by euphoria and youthful boldness, and I would say, anger, I grabbed the other machine gun and together with Deluzia directed fire towards the plane, by now no more than 500 metres away. We saw the damaged plane hit the water and soon after, out of the darkness, came a cry, 'Help, help, help!' The two sailors and I quickly made for our stern. We released the painter of our dinghy and started rowing in the direction of the cries for help. Floating on the water was the enormous white expanse of a parachute, and a man desperately groping. He was very agitated, flailing his arms, gurgling, and continuing to yell, but by now a bit more weakly – 'Help, help, help.' When we reached him we freed him from his harness and from a small life jacket around his neck, and pulled him aboard with great difficulty.

He was a young man in flying fatigues having the distinctive patch of the RAF (Royal Air Force). We laid him down on the bottom boards of our dinghy and made quickly for the wharf. Soon an ambulance from the infirmary at Marisupao (Comando Superiore Marina Africa Orientale) came to take away the pilot who was wounded and bleeding from splintered aircraft parts.

As soon as I was off duty I contacted the infirmary and found out that the young man was a junior flight officer in the RAF and that the other crew-member aboard had been killed since he was unable to deploy his parachute.

As I visited the 'victim' he extended his hand to me and said weakly, 'Thank you.' The next day around lunchtime I found the English junior officer by now a bit restored, but bound up in gauze bandages and with many plasters on his face. He was seated at a table with some noncom submariners. He had in his hand a glass of whisky. As soon as he saw me he struggled up and said, 'God bless you', and after a spell. 'And God save our country.'

### Torpedoman Billy Grieves, US Navy, USS *Thresher*

On October 21, 1941, the USS *Thresher* (SS 200) put out to sea from Pearl [Harbor] on what we thought was just another training mission. Our assignment was to conduct a 48-day simulated war patrol protecting the northern approaches to the island of Midway. The southern approaches as well as the islands of Wake and Guam were similarly patrolled. But it was our mysterious sailing orders that puzzled the crew.

We were to maintain radio silence and remain submerged throughout the daylight hours, surfacing only after dark to charge batteries. We were to keep two torpedo tubes ready for firing, fore and aft, at all times. And if any offensive action against the island of Midway was observed, we were to sink anything in sight. In October 1941, such action was unheard of.

Four days later we arrived on station and commenced all-day dives. As tedious days lapsed into monotonous weeks, fresh provisions ran out and dehydrated substitutes, bland and unappetizing at that stage of their development, took their place on the menu. Fresh water showers were terminated as primitive waste-heat evaporators struggled ineffectually to keep up with demand. Fresh water was for cooking and drinking only.

On December 4th after forty consecutive all-day dives with food, fuel and fresh water critically low, a wave of relief swept through the boat as our skipper, Commander William Anderson, announced that Trout was relieving us, and *Thresher* turned her bow eastward toward Oahu.

But an angry sea had been running for several days and submarines on the surface do not handle heavy winds and mountainous waves with the best of facility. As our bow plunged into the swell, green water climbed the conning tower and cascaded over the bridge and periscope shears. On one such immersion, Seaman Bill Grower, the port lookout, was washed from his perch high on the shears to the small deck on the after end of the conning tower known as the 'cigarette' deck.

On Captain's orders, Grower was carried below and laid in the Captain's bunk. In considerable pain from a broken femur, he could not be left alone and Doc Millis, the pharmacist mate, maintained an around the clock vigil at his side.

In his lucid moments Grower talked of home and shore leave and he made a strange prediction. He said he would never live to see dry land again. He seemed particularly sad that he would never go on liberty again, never be with a girl again. Doc Millis made light of the remark saying we don't shoot people for a broken leg any more, but when word reached the crew the reaction was that maybe Grower was just a little bit gutless.

No one knew it at the time, including Grower, but he had also sustained a fractured skull in the fall. Slowly his vital signs deteriorated as his brain began to swell and Doc Millis administered more and more morphine to ease his pain. The date was December 7th, the day we were to make port, but then word came of the Japanese attack.

As we approached Oahu, air and surface contacts increased, all of them menacing. We were never given time to establish recognition. All submarines were treated as enemy. The minefields around the channel had been activated and we were given a rendezvous point with the destroyer USS *Litchfield*. She was to escort us through the mines and the channel. At one point we sighted her but, responding to a mistaken identity, she ran off leaving us on our own.

Approaching the minefield submerged, we sighted another four-stack destroyer which we thought was the *Litchfield*. Captain Anderson ordered a recognition signal transmitted by sonar and we sent up a smoke flare from periscope depth. But the gunners aboard the destroyer took bearings on the flare and as we broke the surface machine-gun fire was heard and a five-inch shell whistled across our bow. A row of dents laced the conning tower. In our flooded condition, we dove to 287 feet in 37 seconds. But although a wave of irritation had been building among the crew over the many persistent attacks, all this was put aside that night. As Doc Millis sat helplessly by his side, Bill Grower died just as he had predicted.

We spent the night evading 'friendly' forces and the following day we successfully rendezvoused with the destroyer USS *Thornton*. As we entered Pearl Harbor, we were greeted with the first evidence of the attack, the USS *Nevada*, aground at the mouth of the channel and down by the bow. Rounding the bend, the USS *Oglala* appeared, capsized on her port side. But these did not prepare us for the shock of what came next.

Nearing the Navy Yard, a spreading cloud of heavy gray smoke, so dense it blotted out the Hawaiian sun, hung low over the harbor and the odor of burning oil was everywhere. Then the battleships came into view: the *Oklahoma*, capsized and keel up, the *Arizona*, on the bottom, the *California*, *West Virginia*, *Tennessee*, *Maryland*, all heavily damaged, some still smoking.

As we slowly sailed by Battleship Row, our bow sliced through a layer of black, viscous battleship oil that covered the water completely. Motor launches, working among the wrecks searching for bodies, wore the black coating almost to their gunwales.

On our deck, the men stood silently, staring at the water, each overwhelmed by an incinerating rage. Gone was the exhaustion, the frustration and the monotony of six weeks at sea. We forgot the oppressive heat, the monotonous meals and the acute shortage of water. The irritation of these discomforts was replaced by a bitter urge to take a short break and then get back to sea and exact terrible retribution. Standing there, side by side, there was little conversation because for many, like me, speaking would have erupted like a sob.

Today the world has largely forgiven the Japanese for what they did on December 7, 1941. Their industry and their business acumen are respected and their commitment to tradition is admired. The affront to America six decades ago is not recalled with the same intensity as the holocaust for example. We are not constantly hammered with reminders of the outrage of that attack.

But when one steps aboard the memorial erected over the hull of the USS *Arizona* and is reminded that the bodies of 1,100 young American sailors are still entombed beneath his feet, his peace of mind is shattered for days after and the rage rekindled. Forget Pearl Harbor? Never!

**Admiral Corwin Mendenhall, US Navy, USS *Sculpin*;**
from *Submarine Diary*

Although peacetime submarine procedures were obviously designed to prepare a submarine crew for wartime, the sudden change brought about some swift re-assessments in the interests of security and operational efficiency. Lieutenant Corwin Mendenhall, the most junior officer on the USS *Sculpin*, then at Manila, had been woken in the early hours of 8 December, 1941 with the news of Pearl Harbor.

We were to be submerged from one hour before sunrise until one hour after sunset, remaining undetected and maintaining radio silence in accordance with long-established peacetime submarine patrol doctrine. Once we got to our area it would be unrestricted warfare. No friendly ships would be in our patrol area, so we were cleared to attack any other ships that we saw.

9 December. Being so suddenly immersed in a war patrol routine – under radio silence, submerged all day and on the surface at night – was a very different world for us. *Sculpin's* air conditioning was not at all efficient, particularly in the humid tropical climate. Showers were closed to conserve water. We depended on the exhaust heat of the diesel engines to distill whatever fresh water was made, and the water was more important for the battery and for cooking than for cleaning people. The boat took on even more of that peculiar submarine smell of diesel fuel, cigarette smoke, cooking odors, paint, and human aroma.

After a few days the Captain ordered only limited smoking while submerged. We nonsmokers vigorously agreed with that order, although no smoking at all would have been much better. We were reminded of how thoughtful the limited no-smoking was when the boat abruptly filled with smoke after the smoking lamp was lit about fifteen minutes before surfacing each evening. It was a while before we became hardened to our living conditions; and my, did that fresh air smell sweet when *Sculpin* surfaced after a day underwater!

After a particularly oppressive day when we ran submerged, an air suction could be taken through the boat to clear the atmosphere. This was accomplished by opening the forward torpedo room escape hatches and all the compartment doors between the engine rooms and the forward torpedo room. Because our diesel engines required quantities of oxygen, starting one up sucked a hurricane of air through the boat, purging the foul air. Hatches and doors needed to be open for only a few seconds to do the job. Papers, trash, loose clothing, and odds and ends were caught up in the rush of air to the engine rooms.

One aspect of diving procedure that bit the dust early in the war had to do with the use of the main ballast tank flood (kingston) valves, large valves located at the bottom of the main ballast tanks. Cautious peacetime safety procedure was to run on the surface with kingstons closed. Standard diving procedure called for kingstons to be opened as the boat submerged. If the kingstons weren't opened, there was no way for seawater to fill the ballast tanks and allow the submarine to submerge. A submarine on war patrol, however, needed to be able to submerge with the least amount of delay. So right away *Sculpin* ran with the kingstons always open (termed 'riding the vents'). There was also the possibility that a malfunction would not allow the kingstons to open, or that they would open too slowly, impeding the dive ...

The fathometer (depth finder) quit working, and the electronics technicians concluded that the fathometer head, located on the ship's keel, was flooded. Repairs would have to wait until we got back to port.

The sonar watch kept reporting noises that were diagnosed as coming from the deck superstructure. On the surface after dark the captain stopped the boat, and Gunner Caserio and I went topside to investigate. The gangway gripes had worked loose, and the gangway was vibrating in our flow stream. It took only about fifteen minutes to secure the gripes. The captain was concerned that the boat might be forced to dive while we were on deck, so we carried survival gear – side-arms, knives, and watertight flashlights – and were prepared to stay afloat in our life jackets until our 'home' could come back and pick us up. If it did not, we might have to swim to a nearby island.

**Seaman Gerrit Tigchelaar, Koninklijke Marine, *K. XII*;**
© www.dutchsubmarines.com

The Japanese attack on the Dutch East Indies began on 14 December 1941 with aerial bombing of the Anambas Islands. Two weeks later they invaded the Tambelan Islands, approximately 200 miles from Singapore.

21 Dec 1941. We were lying on the inside of the *K. XIII*. Three men came back to move the *K. XIII* so that our boat could get out to go on patrol. When they opened the hatch they put on a light and there was a huge explosion. Chlorine gas from the batteries had built up inside the hull and exploded. The three sailors were all killed. I ran on board and found one in the front hatch; he had been cut in half across the torso. The other two had used the hatch amidships; one was half hanging out of the hatch; he had been cut from under the arm

through the stomach. The worst was yet to come. I heard a sound coming from the third man and tried to pull him through the hatch. He was burnt almost to a cinder. I grabbed him and his skin and flesh was all I held in my hands, it came off like a snake sheds its skin, he stared up at me with eyes that had been burnt to charcoal, and then he died. I shall never forget the look of those eyes.

When we were able to sail we went on patrol and headed for Surabaya … The Dutch East Indies fell to the Japanese three days after we arrived in Surabaya. We had to scuttle *K. XVIII*, which was heavily damaged, and prepared to blow up the whole Base. The commander of *K. XVIII* died when he blew himself up in the torpedo store.

We had orders to evacuate the Dutch High Command, and had to wait seven days for them to arrive. We spent the days sitting on the bottom of the harbour and surfaced at night. With the Base destroyed we had to go into the town for supplies; we just took what we needed as the town was empty; everyone had fled into the mountains.

On 6 March 1942 *K. XII* escaped from Surabaya before the Japanese arrived. Fourteen days later she arrived safely at Fremantle, Australia.

# 1942

The entry of the USA into the war initially provided an opportunity for the German U-boat campaign in the Atlantic, opening up a new source of soft targets along the US coast for the larger Type IX U-boats with their extended range. That range was increased and also extended to the smaller Type VIIs by the use of large supply submarines known as *Milchkühe* ['milking cows']. Lack of coordinated organisation between the US and the British contributed to a new 'Happy Time' for the Axis, with the Italians finding rich pickings around the Caribbean. HF/DF and radar were coming into use, but the Germans had brought in a four-rotor 'Enigma' code machine early in the year, negating the previous year's Allied gains, and it was autumn and the capture of *U-559* before the Cypher School at Bletchley Park managed once again to decode transmissions. Air cover remained incomplete, though aircraft were being equipped with searchlights to find U-boats at night on the surface, and while mass-produced Liberty ships were pouring out of US yards, Dönitz was acquiring increasing numbers of U-boats – though he could never deploy as many as he needed for the Atlantic campaign, which remained his priority. In reality, however, Allied ship production was increasing at a faster rate than the Axis submarines could sink them. Allied escorts were also being trained in the new tactics of coordinated hunts.

Although the Treaty of London, the terms of which forbade the sinking of merchant ships before the crew had been given the chance to abandon ship, was now comprehensively violated, the European submarine war was not conducted without an element of decency on both sides, contrary to propaganda. On a couple of occasions survivors *were* machine-gunned, but that was the exception, not the rule. Famously, *U-156* broke off hostilities to assist the survivors of the *Laconia* which, as well as British military personnel, women and children, carried 1,800 Italian POWs, only to be attacked during the rescue mission by the US Air Force. After this, Dönitz issued the ambiguous Laconia Order, pointing out that *Rescue contradicts the primary demands of war with respect to the destruction of enemy vessels and their crews*. The Laconia Incident was swiftly mirrored by the sinking by HMS *Sahib* of the Italian troopship, *Scillin*, which was transporting 800 British POWs. In both cases, survivors complained of terrible conditions and of being held below decks after the torpedoes struck.

Allied patrols, often harsh and fruitless, and minelaying continued in the North Sea particularly to contain the threat posed by the German battleship *Tirpitz*.

Submarines were also used to drop off agents for hazardous missions in occupied Norway. Meanwhile the Mediterranean was becoming an ever more dangerous place for submarines to operate in.

The 10th Flotilla at Malta suffered under a continual onslaught of Axis bombing intended to force the island to surrender. By day, the submarines were forced to submerge for their own safety. Out on patrol or passage, the losses included *Upholder* and *Urge*. At the end of April, the 10th had to leave Malta for Alexandria, and when Alexandria was also temporarily evacuated both the 10th and the 1st were obliged to find refuge at Haifa. This was an excellent outcome for the Axis powers, who could send their supply convoys from Italy to North Africa with less hindrance and keep a stranglehold on Malta, to which the 10th returned in late July. Allied submarines had played a part in running fuel and supplies to the island, but at the beginning of August submarines on both sides took part in the most famous Mediterranean convoy of all: Operation 'Pedestal'. Allied submarines were ordered to prevent the Italian Navy from reaching the massively escorted convoy; German and Italian submarines were deployed to attack the freighters and their powerful escorts. The convoy took heavy losses from submarine, E-boat and, primarily, air attack, but just enough of it struggled into Valletta to save the island from capitulation within days. Allied submarines in the Mediterranean continued to take losses, particularly from both mines and Italian anti-submarine vessels now equipped with Asdic, while their Italian counterparts had also suffered heavily.

One of the consequences of Operation 'Torch', the Allied invasion of North Africa which began overnight on 7–8 November, was the German decision to take control of Toulon, the Vichy base where much of the French navy had been lying idle since the armistice, disarmed and short of fuel. The Vichy Government ordered the fleet, including 19 submarines, to be scuttled rather than fall into German hands, but five submarines ran, one scuttling itself in deep water from where it could not be raised. The French fleet in North Africa was instructed to join the Allies, and the terms Vichy and Free French could be replaced by Marine Nationale.

In the Pacific the rapid Japanese advance continued; in January they established a major naval base at Rabaul and in March they took Java and were about to realise their ambitions. The Americans and their New Zealand and Australian allies moved to defend themselves with a line from the Hawaiian islands to Australia and New Zealand – and in April the US launched an opportunistic bombing raid (the Doolittle Raid) on the Japanese mainland. Japan attacked New Guinea, which was to be part of her own defensive perimeter and the launch-pad for any attack on Australia and began a bitter campaign among the Solomon Islands. It was a strategy that left her forces fatally over-extended.

The submarine contribution in the Pacific was limited during the first part of 1942 where surface fleets dominated. *I-6* inflicted considerable damage on the

USS *Saratoga* on 11 January, but not one of the submarines assembled at Midway played any active part in the pivotal battle on 4 June, apart from *I-68* which subsequently sank the heavily damaged USS *Yorktown*. Japanese submarines had formed a patrol line north-west of Hawaii to warn of any approaching US carrier fleet, but US Naval Intelligence had learned of the Japanese plans and so the carriers were despatched in advance of the arrival of the submarines. Neither side had yet developed the policy of coordinated assault on enemy supply routes in the way that Dönitz had prioritised the U-boats' Atlantic campaign. In any case, the US needed to place far less reliance on the disruption of supply routes as they had more or less all the natural resources they needed and, with their escort carrier-based air-power and superior anti-submarine warfare technology, were well able to protect their naval supply lines.

The Japanese fared better in the Indian Ocean, using their submarine-based reconnaissance aircraft to detect the British battleship HMS *Ramillies* and the tanker *British Loyalty* before launching a successful midget attack against them on 28 May.

Carrying out a policy of unrestricted submarine warfare, US boats operated alone, making reconnaissance, rescuing downed aircrew from the carriers and picking off targets around the Philippines and the Japanese islands, with an emphasis on sinking tankers. They were hamstrung by the failure rate of their torpedoes which, though at least now acknowledged, had not yet been addressed, but they were fortunate in that the Japanese had vastly underestimated the depths to which their enemy could dive and set their depth charges accordingly.

## ATLANTIC

**Kapitänleutnant, later Korvettenkapitän, Peter Cremer, Kriegsmarine, *U-333*; from *U-Boat Commander***

And so we sailed westwards in *U-333* under a low wintry blanket of cloud, rolling and pitching while the diesels puttered monotonously and everyone was busy with his job, in the conning tower, the control room, the engine room, at the electrically-controlled helm, at the radio and sound detectors, in the torpedo space, including the cook at the electric stove; he only cooked but he was so important for the morale of the crew, for, as Napoleon remarked, an army marches on its stomach.

Meanwhile the watch was changed every four hours and some of the men going off duty crept into the still-warm bunks of those relieving them, for a permanent sleeping space was not available for everyone. And from time to time the captain glanced thoughtfully at the course marked on the chart and kept watch for the enemy. Hardly were we in the Atlantic than I heard *U-701* reporting a convoy. The New Year, 1942, was starting well.

Night-time on 2 January, we surfaced again. I was standing on the bridge and could not believe my eyes when suddenly through my binoculars I saw a cloud of black smoke which quickly dispersed against the dark night sky. Visibility was good. I dried the wet lenses, looked again – and there she was again, my first opponent. (Had the vessel been neutral, her display of lights, and her national colours painted on her hull would have made this clear.) Slowly the outline of a tanker revealed itself still too far away to get in a shot. Behind me the sky was black and overcast, but the air was cold and clear, and by chance the moon came out of the clouds. I turned at maximum speed towards the tanker, offering her a slim silhouette – and then I had her about 400 metres in front of me.

A lot has been written about how a submarine commander feels when he sees his first opponent in the crosswires of his sights. He is compared to a hunter who has his first royal stag before his gun and trembles with excitement. With me it was nothing like that. I was neither excited nor ice-cold. For me it was part of a well-rehearsed routine, culminating in the deadly dialogue:

'Tubes 1 to 3, stand by for spreading salvo.'

Factually, coolly, position, speed and distance are fed into the fire-control apparatus for the torpedoes, as into a computer.

'Open bow caps.'

'Bow caps open.'

'Tubes 1, 2 and 3 ready.'

'Ready."

'Salvo – Fire!"

A shudder runs through the boat as all three 'eels' leave their tubes at two-second intervals. Suddenly the boat has become lighter by 4.5 tons and must be counter-trimmed forward at once. Everything goes like clockwork, just as it did on the attacking course in the Baltic. But what is this?

One of us is not playing the game, not sticking to the rules. The tanker has no intention of keeping still and allowing herself to be despatched. She has, to stay with huntsman's language, smelt powder. Despite the darkness her lookout probably spotted the tell-tale tracks and the captain has enough experience of war to turn towards them at once. All three torpedoes miss by a hair's breadth.

On top of that, the ship now comes towards me and I have no choice but to turn. From the new position I try to give her a stern shot and call: 'Tube 5 ready and fire!' Nothing doing – the second watch officer has 'stepped on the gas' too soon and the fourth 'eel' is already on its way. The heavy pitching and rolling of the boat prevents the tube being reloaded. Another miss.

The tanker meanwhile is so taken aback that she forgets to bring her gun to bear, but radioes continually for help, giving the signal 'SSS SSS SSS' and her position, calling down fire and brimstone on my neck. And so, to cap it all, an aircraft of RAF Coastal Command comes at us at low level and there is nothing more to be done but dive, and creep away from the scene.

The tanker was the *Algonquin*, an American ship of 10,800 loaded displacement tons. She survived the whole war intact.

### Korvettenkapitän Reinhard Hardegen, Kriegsmarine, *U-123*

Hardegen's greatest successes, which won him the Knight's Cross, were obtained off the US coast in 1942 as part of Operation 'Paukenschlag' [Drumbeat], when the U-boats were sent to attack 'soft' targets off the US Atlantic coast. He was popularly believed to have penetrated close enough to New York to have seen the Statue of Liberty.

No, that's all nonsense. The Americans wrote that rubbish at some time. I was supposed to have seen the dancing on the Waldorf-Astoria Hotel's roof garden, but I was never in the Upper or Lower Bay – I was outside, near the Ambrose light-ship and on the horizon I could see only the bright glow of the lights of New York. Off Sandy Hook I just saw what was along the beach, the big ferris wheel, but nothing in the foreground. Later, after the war, I went with my wife to the top of the Waldorf-Astoria Hotel and stood in the roof garden, and made certain that you could not see any water from up there. Therefore, from the sea you can't look up to the roof garden. So it wouldn't have been possible, but the Americans kept writing this idiotic stuff and there are always people who believe it, but it's all nonsense. I had seen New York earlier for the first time, while on a foreign visit aboard the cruiser *Karlsruhe*, and afterwards I have been repeatedly with my wife, most recently last July on the *Queen Mary 2*.

### Sub-Lieutenant Dr Wolfgang Pohl, Kriegsmarine, *U-581*

*U-581* left St Nazaire on 1 December, 1941; she was sunk on 2 February 1942.

I was Oberfähnrich zur See, and, our Obersteuermann [CPO navigator] was very ill, I had to do his duty as a third officer of the watch. I was stationed in St Nazaire in the 7th Flotilla.

First of all, it was always looking, looking, looking. It was very boring, looking at the horizon. Looking for some masts or some smoke, and then, when you detect a ship the first question is: is it an enemy ship; is it one of our ships; is it a neutral ship? We also have passed ships of Sweden and of Switzerland. And of course we didn't shoot them, we passed them, greeted them, and went away. But of course if it was an enemy ship we dived – we attacked at night on the surface; during the daylight time we attacked from a position below the water, of course. When we were in action, you had no other chance to think.

We were sent to the American coast, a little bit after Operation 'Paukenschlag', but when we left we hit a British convoy, and the convoy consisted of a very well protected troop transport ship. We were about two or three submarines who attacked this convoy. The *Llangibby Castle* – about 12,000 tons – had, I was told a long time after the war, more than 1,000 military personnel, most of them, it was said, commando troops for the African front to be sent to Montgomery (Eighth Army).* So we attacked this boat. It was torpedoed but didn't sink. The stern was blown off, and the British had a very good idea. They filled the open space with fast-binding concrete, and so they cut off the stern but you can see pictures in the submarine museum at Gosport of this *Llangibby Castle* in the port of Horta, in the Azores. They are hanging out, arms and legs of the killed British soldiers. About 26 were killed by the torpedo.

The escort destroyers and corvettes chased us off and we lost the convoy, so we thought we must find the *Llangibby Castle*. Well we looked for the *Llangibby Castle* and searched, but we couldn't find her at first so we went to the Bay of Gibraltar to wait till she came in. But on the way to Gibraltar just at dusk we hit a British warship. To me it's not clear if it was a corvette or it was a minesweeper.** She was zigzagging, so we lost her, couldn't find her. And then we said: general course is Gibraltar. We went with full power to find her again, and one of our lookouts – there were only four on the conning tower – saw a very tiny light: a British seaman had lit a cigarette! And that's it: we were in a very good position. Two torpedoes. She exploded; a high column of water splashed down. Afterwards the sea was bubbling and bubbling, and our skipper decided: let's go there. Then the depth charges [on board the British vessel] exploded one after the other because the depth charges were set to a certain depth. When we approached we found nobody. Not a single survivor. Nothing left, just rubbish. We would have picked up the sailors, if there had not been too many of them.

Then we got notification from the German agents on the Azores islands who reported to Dönitz in France that the *Llangibby Castle* was at the island of Fayal. So we drove to the Azores, went round the island of Fayal. Couldn't find any ship there. In no bay, in no harbour: nothing. No ship. So our commander, Lieutenant Commander Werner Pfeifer, decided she must be in

---

* She was bound for Singapore when torpedoed by *U-402*. In November she took part in Operation 'Torch'.
** The warship was probably the anti-submarine trawler HMS *Rosemonde*, which was believed to have been sunk on 22 January.

the harbour of Horta. But the harbour of Horta was neutral, was Portuguese. And so he decided we should go into the harbour. In submerged condition we crept into the harbour, on one of the last nights in January, and we looked at what was going on there. So when we came round a long, long quay, we came in, submerged just with the periscope up, he said, 'Look at this: there she is lying.'

Suddenly he had to decide what he should do. Torpedo? The aim would have been good, but … first of all, she was full of ammunition – it was clear. Troops and ammunition. She would explode in a way that all the houses [facing seawards] in the bay of Horta would be torn out. And second, it was Portuguese, it was Neutral. And he decided in a very wise and responsible manner: *If I torpedo the ship in a Portuguese harbour, Portugal will declare war*. So he decided not to shoot the torpedo but to go back and wait until she came out. And she did. We were informed by agents that the ship was preparing to leave. We waited for about two days after entering the harbour, and there was another submarine which joined us, and they had been attacking the same convoy: it was *U-402*. The skippers met outside, very far away from the island, and they made a common plan. There is a strait between Horta and Pico – and a very strong current there. If she leaves to the north, going to Gibraltar, then *U-402* attacks her. If she leaves south, we attack her.

She left south, but before she left south there came a whole flotilla: three destroyers [HMS *Westcott*, HMS *Croome* and HMS *Exmoor*] and – I don't know – maybe some corvettes. So they chased us all the night with their sonar – [we were] dived – and they threw some depth charges but not very many. But one was enough. We got a leak.

We had water in the boat. The water was filling up the aft section of the boat and our chief engineer tried to stabilise the boat. And by this operation she dived down, bow first, deeper than we were meant to dive. You know, perhaps, our boats were allowed to dive up to 200 metres; we dived to 270 metres, and then we heard the 'tk, tk' and a bristling: 'hsh-hsh-hsh', by the pressure. It was deforming the hull, and it gave a bristling sound like 'hsh-hsh-hsh'. Then I myself and others, I think we said: 'Oh, my Lord, you are in heaven. Father God, help us.'

The boat came up again. However, the batteries were nearly used up and we had only a very small amount of air pressure. But finally we could rise up to the surface. And when we came up, the three destroyers charged straight at us with their guns and tried to ram us. They came twice, one after the other and passed our boat at the distance of approximately 10 yards. They couldn't shoot with their large guns because they couldn't lower the large guns, but they used the quadruple pom-poms* – there were, together, eight pom-poms. We hid behind the conning tower but there was much iron flying around. Then the destroyer approached us – it was HMS *Croome* – to ram us at the end.

Afterwards, 40 years after the end of the war, one of the lookouts of the British destroyer asked me: 'Didn't you send a torpedo against us at the last very moment?' I said, 'Yes, we had one last torpedo in the rear tube. And we shot this torpedo.'

He had observed it, and therefore the destroyer turned away in a hurry. She didn't ram us but she drove off. He stated that he saw the torpedo running. If he had not seen the torpedo I am sure that they would have blown up.

I had no life jacket because I was standing in the navigator's position at the table in front of the map. My life jacket was in my bunk and I couldn't go there because all hands were streaming to the conning tower, so I took what you would call the DSEA, but you couldn't blow this up inside the boat because you couldn't get through the conning tower. I waited until I got up to the deck, and I turned the screw in the bottle, and air pressure came in, but when I jumped into the water I felt that the air pressure didn't hold; there must have been one of these splinters from the gunnery that cut it. So the only thing to do was to throw it away. I pulled off my long boots because they were very heavy, and then I swam.

A very odd thing I remember. When we were about 30 metres away from the boat – it was standing up vertically – it sank soon and some of our swimming shipmates shouted: 'Three cheers for our beloved sub: hurrah, hurrah, hurrah!' Even in this position!

We lost four of our men but I am not sure how they died. We had two destroyers who picked us up. One of them was HMS *Westcott*, the other was HMS *Croome*. I was on HMS *Croome*. There were only five [of us on *Croome*]. We were saved at the last. The others were saved first by the *Westcott*. When we were swimming in the water – the boat had sunk already – the *Westcott* threw two depth charges. And they exploded between us. And maybe there were some killed by the depth charges or by the destroyers which drove very, very fast, zigzagging through that region. And therefore it may be that one or two of them were trapped by the propellers; I don't know. One depth charge blew up in front of me. If you are in the water you cannot guess how far away is this column of water. I suppose it must have been 200 yards. But my lungs were partly blown up so I bled from the mouth. I went on swimming, weakened by the loss of blood. The only thing you think about in this situation is your mother. My mother was the first person who was in my mind.

* Colloquial name for the Royal Navy's multi-barrel automatic QF 2-pounder, normally used against aircraft.

I was getting weaker and weaker, and suddenly a cutter approached from the destroyer HMS *Croome*, jumping up and down, and one of the able seamen, Richard F. Coulson from Leyland, Lancs, dragged me out of the water and put me in the boat. I was so weak that I fell into the bottom and couldn't stand up again.

Forty-nine years later Richard asked me: 'What did you get from one of our friends? As the first present?' And I said, 'As I was lying in the boat, there came a seaman and he gave me his cigarette, put it into my mouth. It was such a symbol of friendship, of comradeship at sea.'

Richard said: 'I am the one who saved you; I am the one who gave you the cigarette. But could you imagine that my skipper told me off in the bloodiest way: "You stupid so-and-so".'

'Why is that?' [I asked] 'Was he against the fraternisation?'

He said: 'No, it wasn't the fraternisation. It became daylight and he [the captain] looked through his binoculars and he saw that you were bleeding from the mouth. He said to me: "You are a stupid man. You cannot give cigarettes to such a man because his lungs are damaged." And he was right. And I said to him, "Oh, I didn't know."'

I said: 'Your captain must have been a very human-feeling man.' He said: 'Yes, we had a very good skipper, and much respected by us.'

More than 50 years later our British friends of the Croome have met – during the common reunions of our crews – also our captain. Do you know what they have said? 'You had a very human feeling skipper, too, and, we believe, much respected ...' Together we stood at his grave, when he died in 1993, the British and the Germans: HMS *Croome* and *U-581*. What a story, but it's reality. I still have contact with a member of the *Croome* and also to the children of the ship's doctor who treated me on board for my lung lesion. They have visited me two years ago.

Wolfgang Pohl found himself in the same Canadian POW camp as Otto Kretschmer and Volkmar König from *U-99*. Kretschmer was the camp leader in 1942/3 for all the prisoners in the officers' camp, and the two young men became adjutants to Kretschmer's Flaggleutnant. Leutnant Walter Sitek, however, avoided capture by swimming to shore; eventually he returned to Germany where he became a U-boat commander. The *Llangibby Castle* continued to ride her luck through the war and also survived.

### Kapitänleutnant Erich Topp, Kriegsmarine, commanding *U-552*; from *Fackeln Über Dem Atlantik*

*U-552* left her base at St Nazaire on 9 June 1942. On the same day, Convoy HG.84 left Gibraltar led by Commander F. J. Walker, leader of the escort in HMS *Stork*.

Each side knew of the other's activity: the French barmaids of St Nazaire and Baule collected information from their German customers and passed it to the Resistance; German intelligence operated from Spain, just across the border with Gibraltar.

*U-552* was operating with other submarines, all belonging to the Endrass group, against the convoy coming from Gibraltar. The convoy had the entire Atlantic at its disposal and could pick and choose its route to England. The view from the bridge of a submarine is limited, as is the chance of meeting the convoy.

Then the 1st squadron of the [Luftwaffe's] KG 40 based at Bordeaux came to our aid and flew air-reconnaissance missions. A plane located the convoy on 13 June, reported and sent a radio signal which we were able to pick up. We now knew the direction of the convoy but not how far away it was. Assuming that the convoy was steering a northerly course and making around 10–12 knots, we fixed our 'collision course'.

Late the following afternoon we spotted an aircraft on the horizon, flying low and definitely not one of the Focke Wulf 200s of the KG 40. Careful, then. Is there an aircraft carrier with this convoy?

The aircraft turned and did not return. (We learned later that one of the vessels in the convoy had a catapult from which a Hurricane had been launched to carry out reconnaissance and engage the Fokke Wulf 200.) Shortly afterwards traces of smoke: the convoy.

We made contact, sent a signal to the other U-boats, were driven off by escorts, regained contact. That lasted until nightfall. We had familiarised ourselves with our adversary. Now we knew that it was a comparatively small but well protected convoy of some 20 merchant ships.

The days are long in June. We did not attack before midnight. The weather was hardly favourable for an attack, by which I mean that even after nightfall the escorts had good visibility. Where the bows and propellers of the ships and submarines churned up the sea, the water shone in gilded silvery curls and streaks, marine phosphorescence.

From 3,000 metres away we could barely discern the outlines of the ships but, conversely, we could see the traces of their wake. Our boat was also creating a shining trail that would intrigue anyone out at sea and hamper our attack, which had to be invisible if it were to succeed, with additional unwanted risks.

So it became an exceptionally delicate business to launch an attack while dangerously close to two corvette escorts and on a bright night with a comparatively calm sea, in a way that would offer a good chance of success without taking unacceptable risks.

Four torpedoes from the four bow tubes, and four targets. Turn the boat 180° to fire the fifth torpedo from the stern tube.

Three minutes running time is an eternity when you are waiting for the possible hits and when you are being hunted by a corvette. Just after we attacked with our bow torpedoes, and when we were forced to show our broadside silhouette in order to turn around for the stern shot, it had turned towards us at full speed.

There was just time to observe the gleaming bow-wave, throwing up spray as it came ever closer, growing ever bigger. We were going at 3×AK using our electric motors as well. The boat shook under this extreme power which a surfaced submarine can produce. I had already sent the lookouts down; the boat was clear to crash dive. It was clear to me that if I was forced to crash dive now, the boat would be in for a heavy depth-charging with the possibility of being destroyed or sustaining irreparable damage.

It sounds rather unbelievable. The pursuer was slowly but relentlessly getting closer. I could make out details of her bridge superstructure. Suddenly a huge mountain of shining pearls rose up behind her; almost simultaneously came a massive explosion that rocked our boat. What was going on?

Our hunter had dropped depth-charges on the spot where our boat had supposedly dived – our boat which was still racing away at breakneck speed, throwing out a shroud of smoke and steam from her exhaust which made her invisible to the enemy just as if she was camouflaged. In addition, the corvette – it was HMS *Stork* – had picked us up on her radar screen. When contact was broken at about 500 metres the operator believed that the quarry had dived. We had never before gone through a depth-charge attack at such a safe distance. When the torpedoes exploded, an unearthly pyrotechnic display beyond the escort illuminated the ships, revealing them as figures on a chess-board. Three of them were sinking. Leaking oil, torpedoed tanker began to burn. The fluctuating glow, reflecting russet on the swelling sea, reached us in startling bursts ...

Shortly before 0600 we had loaded our last·two torpedoes.

All attempts at a third attack were prevented by the extreme alertness of the escort and the coming of dawn. The inner conflict between the desire to attack and the responsibility for the safety of the boat and the crew came down in favour of that third and fourth attempt, until daybreak left us with a submerged attack as the only option.

Now a long way off, the submarine tried to use her speed to get a position ahead of the convoy in order to dive.

Now we had a fine tussle with the leading escorts who had picked us up on their hydrophones. A heavy counterattack with depth charges caused a tear in diving tank number 4 which contained fuel. The oilslick drew the hunters to us just like Valerian [catnip] attracts cats. Yet another series of depth-charges until, shortly afterwards, we were able to surface in order to pump the oil into one of the torpedo tubes, so there would be no further trace.

Nine days later we were back in St Nazaire.

The girls at the Bar Royal were able to pass on the information that we had sunk the convoy commodore's flagship, the Pelayo, the Etrib (both Liverpool-registered), the Norwegian tanker Slemdal, the Thurso (Hull) and the City of Oxford (Liverpool).

**Kapitänleutnant Horst Degen, Kriegsmarine, commanding *U-701*;** translation of statement prepared while held as POW at Camp Devens, Mass., 16 July 1942; ADM186/807

*U-701* was on her third patrol off Cape Hatteras, laying mines, when she was sunk by a Hudson belonging to US Army Bomb Squadron 396 piloted by Harry Kane. Seven out of her crew of 46 survived.

7 July 1942. At 2015 hours (DZS) two bullseyes – air bombs. All instruments out of order. Tanks blown. Within one to two minutes control room and conning tower filled with water. Ship had list to starboard of approximately 20 degrees. Conning tower hatch opened easily. Ship is at a depth of about 15–20 metres and no longer able to surface. Depth of water about 80–100 metres.

The following saved themselves (all through the conning tower hatch):

Commander
Boatsman Hänsel
Faehnrich (Ing) Lange
Bootsmaat Etweiler
Maschinenmaat Damrow
Gefreiter Schmidtmeyer
Obermaat Gründler
Oberleutnant (Ing) Bahr
Maschinenmaat Schuller
Maschinenmaat Bosse
Maschinenmaat Fischer
Matrose Leu
Matrose Michalek
Obersteuermann Kunert
Maschinenmaat Vaupel
Funksmaat Grootheer
Obergefreiter Weiland.

We had three escape lungs and one life preserver, and in addition two small life preservers which had been thrown to us by the airplane (landplane). Force of sea – 1. The plane circled about several times, threw smoke floats into the sea and then departed. Later we sighted the plane again, apparently in search of us, but it was unable to find us again because of the rough sea, even though we had remained close together.

Despite warning, Hänsel and Lange left us. They definitely decided to swim to shore [30 sea miles distant].

Around 2100 hours Etweiler drowned. He did not know how to swim and was unable to keep himself above the water any longer.

We were in good spirits as we could look forward to being saved at an early hour.

8 July 0300. As darkness descended we consoled ourselves with hope in the morrow. A few of us were ready to give up, but these we cheered up, so that we were all together when it became light again.

Around 1200 a Coast Guard ship passed within 200 metres of us at slow speed. Despite our cries and waving we remained unnoticed. The ship passed out of sight. Although we all hoped it would return, some of the men now gave up. Damrow and Schmidtmeyer were delirious as though in a fever.

8 July. Around 1400 the following drowned, one after another: Damrow, Schmidtmeyer, Gründler, Bahr, Weiland, Schuller.

We saw many airplanes – apparently we were still being sought.

About 2300 the following drowned: Bosse, Fischer.

Later we came across the Matrose (apprentice seaman) Laskowski, who wore two escape lungs and who was still very fresh. He reported that several more of the crew had escaped, among others the first and second watch officers.

9 July 0300. With the oncoming darkness we huddled close together in order to survive in this way also the second night. Fortunately, the sea subsided. We found a lemon and a coconut. Each man received a swallow of coconut milk, a piece of the meat and everyone had the opportunity to suck the lemon. Tremendous refreshment! Our thirst was awful, and the large quantities of salt water burned mouth, nose and stomach. (The coconut was opened by Vaupel after the greatest exertion with the help of the oxygen flask from the escape lung.)

0800. In the course of the night the following drowned: Leu, Michalek, Laskowski. All three were delirious and yelled terribly.

1100. At dawn my strength began to leave me too. I seem to recollect vaguely that I talked nonsense and that Kunert kept quieting me. As the sea was still like a pond I kept up the practice of discarding my life preserver, saying that I would swim to shore. I assumed that with a few strokes I would feel bottom under my feet and would be able to stand up, but every time I tried this I went under. That would bring me to again and I would swim back to my life preserver. This occurrence must have happened many times. Then I lost consciousness. I awakened as though I had been asleep when I suddenly heard myself called. About 30 metres away sat Kunert, Vaupel and Grootheer making for me in a white rubber boat. I was taken into the boat as Kunert was about to open a can of pineapple with a knife. Out of a can already open, Grootheer gave me tomatoes to eat, and all the while a Zeppelin [sic] airship circled above us. The situation was as follows: the airship had sighted us and thrown the rubber boat into the sea. Shortly thereafter a large rubber sack was also thrown down. In this we found: one small first aid kit, two loaves of white bread, one sack of water. All this happened in the late afternoon.

2100. As the coastal waters are thoroughly oily, we were covered completely with a thick black layer of oil. Now, while in the boat, the sun shone down upon us, and this resulted in terrible sunburn.

Around 2300 a large flying boat arrived and took us on board. We were given water and hot coffee. All four of us were completely finished. We shall probably never forget this 49-hour endurance swim. Thus we have escaped the reaper to whom we have already given our hand. The U-boat heaven lay open before us, and Kunert said that he was already looking forward to the first half-litre they would serve him there. We were delivered to the Navy Hospital at Norfolk [Virginia] where we were treated with the greatest care and attention and made into humans once more. There we found three other survivors:

Gefreiter Seldt

Matrose Faust

Gefreiter Schwendel.

I could not ascertain how they were saved. It is doubtful that there were any others who were saved. We were told that we were picked up 90 sea miles north of the place where the ship sank. (Gulf Stream!)

We are all well. On 11 July the air officer who bombed us paid me a visit, and inquired after our well being.

On 12 July we were transferred by rail to the military encampment 'Fort Devens' (in the vicinity of Boston, Mass.) where we shall now pass the days of our detention as prisoners of war. We are being correctly handled and receive good treatment. There is plenty of good food to eat.

### Comandante Mario Rossetto, Regia Marina, 1st Officer of the *Enrico Tazzoli*, based at Betasom (Bordeaux)

6 August 1942. Dawn was more than an hour away when the *Tazzoli*, which was operating east of Trinidad under the command of Capitano di Corvetto

Carlo Fecia di Cossato, spotted the silhouette of a tanker – faint in the darkness – proceeding on a zigzag course.

As the crew were being called to action stations, the approach was begun. I was the boat's Tenente and had come off duty a couple of hours earlier, but I woke up with a start and rushed to my post on the bridge to follow the operation at the Commander's side.

Once we had got ourselves into a favourable position, and put the bows towards the target, the commander ordered two torpedoes angled 10° starboard. I had been watching the shape of the tanker, which was no longer so dark against the background of the starry sky, and I ventured to observe that the target looked to be stationary.

'That's not possible!' replied di Cossato. 'We've been chasing her for more than half an hour!'

Anyway, he reduced the firing angle to 5° and fired. The two torpedoes raced forwards, missing the target. The Commander then took account of the fact that the tanker was effectively stopped, came about (we were getting too close) and presented the stern, allowing me the fun of firing. This time, the two torpedoes, which were fired with zero angulation, hit the target spot on.

For a long time we waited to see the tanker go down, while the sky was starting to lighten; the Commander then decided to fire a few shots to encourage her to sink more expeditiously, but while the gun was being loaded the ship suddenly raised her bows to the sky and went down by the stern. Shortly afterwards she was back again with her bows pointing up. It seemed as if she had no intention of foundering, but, finally, she vanished beneath the waves.

By now it was daylight: we surveyed the sea in all directions to see whether there were any survivors to save, but we spotted nothing but wreckage and one small life-raft with no one on board. We went closer and discovered that there was a survivor: a little tom-cat, soaked and frightened. There was no trace of the crew anywhere around; yet this would have been the time to be rescued!

So what was the mystery? Was this perhaps the case of the phantom tanker, an updated version of the Flying Dutchman? She was sailing without a crew, but it had taken a pretty good chase to catch and sink her. And the cat? Maybe he had been able to steer her on his own before the sinking. Was he perhaps a deep-sea cat?

The mystery was solved the following evening. A radio broadcast announced that an Argentinian ship had picked up the crew of the Norwegian tanker, Havsten, sunk by an Axis submarine. Evidently the crew, having spotted the submarine in good time and knowing just what to expect, had thought it wise to cut and run before it was too late.

But not everyone had abandoned ship. In the best maritime tradition, the deep-sea cat, having allowed the whole crew to save themselves, remained on board to go down with the ship. But as in many other cases, Providence decreed otherwise, ensuring that it would be found clinging to the raft which, when the ship sank, had been released and remained afloat.

Back at Betasom at the end of our patrol, nothing more was seen of the cat. Just as it had turned up in the middle of the Atlantic, so it suddenly vanished on the dock at the base. Yet the sailors on the *Tazzoli* had made such a fuss of it.

Most likely, feeling itself to be a prisoner of war and afraid of ending up in a POW camp, it had chosen freedom, slinking away on land. It wanted nothing more to do with a sea-going career and, instead, had set off on its own long journey, determined to put the greatest distance in the shortest possible time between itself and the sea which had not been kind to it.

The Norwegian tanker, Havsten, was part of Convoy OS.29, bound from Freetown to Trinidad in ballast. On 3 August 1942 she was torpedoed by *U-160*. The captain and radio operator were captured, one man was killed, and the rest were picked up from their lifeboats by another tanker, the Juncal. The Havsten was believed to be in a sinking condition but in fact remained afloat until that second salvo from the *Enrico Tazzoli*.

### Fregattenkapitän Reinhard 'Teddy' Suhren, Kriegsmarine, *U-564*; from *Teddy Suhren, Ace of Aces*

In August 1942, Suhren, now a Kapitänleutnant commanding *U-564* and on his way to the Caribbean, rendezvoused with a *'Milchkuh'* supply U-boat to refuel, but having expended four torpedoes was anxious to acquire more. He was told that he could get some from a returning U-boat – but they had no crane ...

We met the captain of the homeward-bound boat at a prearranged time and place, and the first thing he did was ask me the same question. By a quirk of fate he turned out to have previously been my divisional officer at the Naval Academy at Murwik, where they had taken such pains to prepare me for the officers' exam. He was the one who had given me the hardest time despite my being one of the best. On that day, though, he gazed stupidly at me as I stood there with decorations up to my chin. It was quite a reunion! When I asked him why he was intending to go home with all his torpedoes still on board, he replied that it was because he was ill: he had a liver problem and needed to get to a doctor. 'Oh, I see, belly-ache; spare me the details. Now, let's get the things over here.'

So I and some of my crew swam across to his boat and tied lifejackets all along the torpedo. Yes, lifejackets! One jacket can support 10 kilos, and with more lifejackets we provided enough support for a torpedo to stay afloat under our watchful eyes. Then, with *U-564* alongside, we pulled the torpedoes across with blocks and lines one after the other. On our foredeck was fitted a cradle, which we had used in harbour for letting the torpedoes slide into the boat. So the order was given, 'LI, let the bows dip, so that the foredeck is under water.' After we'd pulled the floating torpedo across and over the cradle with the lines, the order was given to surface, so that the cradle came up to grip the torpedo. The next bit all had to be done very fast. 'Torpedo hatch open', and the eel slipped down the sloping cradle on its own into the boat. Tackle away, torpedo hatch closed again. Next please. Pulling lines and blocks. Dip the bows, get it over the cradle, up again; one by one we get the eels in. I stand by with a boathook to help if there's a hitch.

All went brilliantly right up to the last one. We'd forgotten one small detail: namely that lifejackets always lose a bit of air, and hence lift. We should have kept blowing them up again in between times. Suddenly the fourth torpedo stood on its head, and we had to literally let it drop. Away it went, down to 5,000 metres. Well, they say there's no such thing as the perfect crime. As I've said, a good deal was said about the exploit afterwards. But one thing we never let on: that we'd already spent a day practising the whole thing down to the last detail, moving one of our torpedoes from the stern to the bows and back again. In the event, the whole thing went like clockwork!

We had passed the island of Tobago, and sailed west into the Caribbean, a setting for pirates, sunken treasure galleons and Spanish colonialism, of tropical magic and island romance. But most of this was history, and the only romance was now well and truly in the past. War – and after all, this was what we were living through – is always grim and bloody. An unbearable heat came off the boat during the day, though the breeze from astern brought a bit of cool relief. One day I sat with the LI in the wardroom making plans, and sniffed. 'Tell me, Gabler, can you smell anything? Isn't that freighter smoke? Let's go up on deck and see what's happening.' Over us, the blue-black night, silver moonlight on the sea, and good visibility. I couldn't believe my eyes. On the starboard quarter, about 5,000–6,000 metres off, and clearly visible without the glasses, was the shadow of a big freighter. The night was definitely too bright for a surface attack; we would have been spotted as we approached.

'Action stations, both engines half-ahead.' Cautiously we follow the zigzag course of the other ship, which allows us to overtake it comfortably and finally watch it from ahead. We dive carefully. I hang on to the periscope, and report the course and the timings of the turns so as to work out our shot. The freighter stands there big and black before my eyes. The listening-room takes a bearing on it too. 'Now, Nav. Officer, how's that, shouldn't we turn towards it?' 'No, Boss, not yet.' But a few minutes later, 'Now!' We swing on to the target. 'Prepare torpedo for firing, enemy ship bearing 060 degrees, speed 12 knots. Ready to fire, tube 3: stand by, tube 3 – fire!' 'Stürkorl' stares at the stopwatch and counts. Soon, it all happens. The bow of the freighter moves across my field of view, and crosses into the torpedo's path. A few heartbeats more, and then a boom – detonation! Exactly amidships. The cargo burns brightly. We surface and through the smoke we land a few 8.8cm shells on him. Behind her two more ships must have thought they were for it.

*U-564* is cruising in one of the most beautiful areas of the Caribbean, in a little corner of the Little Antilles, between the Windward Islands and Leeward Islands. The North East tradewind blows reliably all year and is at its strongest in the evening, when it takes away the heat of the day before dropping at night. The names of the islands could have been taken from exotic novels or a tourist brochure. They fire the imagination: Antigua, Guadeloupe, Dominica, Martinique, St Lucia. We cross from Margarita, the island of pearls, to Cuba, the assembly point of the Spanish silver fleet. We make a detour to Curaçao, where oil is shipped from Venezuela, and from where we suspect the big tankers come. But though there is a lot of bright light, there is also a lot of shadow, and the serene summer picture is marred by oil, blood and the wrecks of steel ships. Well, I didn't start the war. There's not a lot of point in worrying about it. If you do that, you've had it – you won't be much longer for this life. My philosophising in this evening hour is quickly terminated by the warning cry, 'Plane!'

That was Suhren's last patrol: he was brought ashore and ended the war as Führer der Unterseeboote in Norway.

## NORTH SEA, BALTIC AND ARCTIC

**Lieutenant Ian Nethercott, Royal Navy, HMS *Tactician*;**
from *All Round Look*

As a Seaman Killick LTQ [Leading Seaman on a Lieutenant Qualifying Course] I took over the Motor Room and Torpedoes aboard *H.43* (circa 1918) when she was based on Londonderry. We had a crew of 22. One bunk (the skipper's) while we slept in the Motor Room, on the lockers, while the other unfortunates kipped in the Fore-ends. In Derry itself we had an ancient shed near the Bridge called Transatlantic Shed, where the emigrants to the United States were collected in the troubles.

We had an old coal range for cooking, and coming up the River Foyle and awaiting the Irish Free State Pilot to bring us up the river, the fishing boats from

Moville would come alongside and exchange cartons of new laid eggs, hams and bacon for Navy 'Tickler' tobacco. Kelly's Bar open from 10 am until 10 pm was across the road from Transatlantic Shed, and we could go over there when we liked. In fact when the coxswain couldn't find the crew he mustered us over there.

All good things come to an end, and I was drafted to a brand new 'T' boat building at Barrow in Furness. Here I went into L and RA with a crabby old land-lady who practically starved us until the boat actually commissioned in October 1942.

We had the Pennant Number P14 allotted to us and our skipper was the famous 'Teddy' Woodward from the 10th Flotilla in Malta.

The first boat of this new breed was P311, which went to sea and was sunk under that number, only afterwards being named the *Tutankhamen*. She was sunk on her first patrol off the Italian Coast, I misremember which boat was allotted P312, which followed, but think she survived the war. The next one on the stocks was P313 which became HMS *Taurus*. There was so much trouble from her crew at the number 13, that the Admiralty changed her Pennant No. to P339, However, my boat had the number P314. She was given the name Tenacious and a ship's badge of an aggressive looking bulldog.

As the T-Class destroyers were just being built and commissioned, the Admi-ralty pinched our name and gave it to a destroyer. We were given the name Tactician and a badge of a bloody Chess Board.

**Capitaine de Vaisseau Etienne Schlumberger, then Exec, FNFL, *Junon*;** from *L'Honneur et Les Rebelles de la Marine Française, 1940–1944*

Having escaped to Britain, Etienne Schlumberger was one of those who actively assisted in recruiting his compatriots for the Free French Navy, and the Vichy government condemned him in absentia to hard labour for life for treason and desertion. After serving in surface ships until the very end of 1941 he was appointed second-in-command of one of the submarines he had seen off from Cherbourg – the *Junon*, which had been serving with the 9th Flotilla at Dundee.

At the end of August 1942 we returned to patrolling towards the entrance to the Sognefjord and 'made land' (fixed our position from a landmark) at Alten.

We were passing very close to the lighthouse on the Utvaer and, through the periscope, we spotted the figure of a pretty blonde girl swimming in the nude. We decided she had to be the lighthouse keeper's daughter.

We were recalled to Lerwick to replace the submarine *Minèrve*, which could not undertake a mission due to technical problems.

An important hydroelectric station, situated to the South of Bodö, northern

Norway, powered a large aluminium factory and an electrolysis plant that could make heavy water. At the end of 1942 it was in the process of expansion, supervised and supplied by the Swiss company Brown-Boweri.

The British considered this power station extremely important for the German war effort and thought it essential to knock it out.

And so, rather than a very risky attack by sheer force, the British commanders opted to try a special operation. A dummy run for putting the men ashore was carried out on 9 September 1942 at Boatsroom Voë, a fjord north of Lerwick. We spent the day sitting on the sea bed – the sea was not very deep – and were able to raise the periscopic aerial and pick up the music of peacetime, which seemed so far away, such as *I'm dreaming of a White Christmas*, or *The Bells are Ringing for Me and my Gal*. Did those men have any idea that, out of the twelve of them, eight would not be returning?

The real mission began on the 11th. We set course for Bjoeranfjord with a commando team composed of two officers, eight British SAS men and three Norwegians including Lieutenant Munthe Kaas …

But where were we going to disembark the team? Initially it was to be the northern side of Tenholmfjord, but Munthe Kaas, our Norwegian guide, advised against it because of the length of journey on foot (20 miles) for a heavily loaded commando and the presence of numerous German garrisons. Finally, Captain Querville decided on the north side of the Bjoerangfjord despite all the navigation problems because the commandos would have a much shorter walk (7 miles).

On September 14 we identified the summits of the Seven Sisters on Alten Island.

On the 15th while we were in the Lyngvaerfjord, a strong surface current forced us to go down to 60 metres to find better conditions. This was a delicate business because the sailing instructions advised that the fjord should not be entered without a pilot with local knowledge.

We identified two tankers and some other interesting ships, which we were not allowed to torpedo until we had completed our mission.

We entered the Bjoerangfjord. The sea was flat calm and we found ourselves nose-to-nose with a Norwegian fisherman whose eyes were popping out of his head as he stared at the periscope and its tell-tale wake.

In the afternoon we lay 30 metres down and not very far from the end of the fjord. All motors were shut off; in the silence we heard the worrying and mysterious sound of a propeller.

At 2115 we surfaced to disembark the commando team, but encountered a few problems blowing up the two inflatables, for it was cold out there and the compressed air lost pressure. Some buckets of hot water sorted that out.

There was calm all around us and the silence was broken by the barking of dogs, the familiar sounds of the countryside and even the ringing of bicycle bells. The wind brought the scent of the pine forests to us: it was so serene. And within that magical scene our likeable, anonymous men (one of them worked for a bank) left in their camouflage, faces blackened, loaded up with their equipment and explosives.

At 2200 our part of the operation was over; we left using our motors. The lighthouses and light-buoys of the Melöfjord were burning; that's how little the enemy knew of the danger arising from our presence.

But we weren't out of the woods yet. All sorts of problems lay ahead. A launch seemed to be following us. In a cloud of smoke resulting from water in the system, we started the diesels, which were faster than the motors. The danger receded. Surfaced, in the pitch black, working by dead reckoning, surrounded by the reefs and shoals of Gjesöflesa, we looked for the way out, running on our electric motors because they are silent and more manoeuvrable. We worked our way out from the centre in all directions, using the sounder to measure the depths. Daylight was approaching: dawn would break at 0300. Phew, we emerged into the open sea just in time. It's worth saying here that the work of the glaciers that carved out the fjords left them much deeper inland than at the outlets to the sea.

We returned to Lerwick then, escorted by our guardian angel of a trawler [HMS *Breda*], to Dundee.

The commandos partially succeeded in damaging the power station, having first given the Norwegian workers time to get out. However, the alarm was raised before they could put the plant beyond repair, and they themselves had to escape as best they could. One Norwegian was taken prisoner and died in hospital; five were captured and sent to Germany where, despite their uniforms, they were shot; three British and one Norwegian eventually reached neutral Sweden.

But that wasn't quite the end of the story because, in a later patrol, the *Junon* disembarked wireless equipment and weapons for the Norwegian resistance in a fjord on the Island of Senya – the Mejfjord – in the north of the Lofoten Islands, not far from Tromsö. With bad weather setting in during the operation, two of our own men who were taking the equipment ashore had to be left behind. Via the Norwegian Resistance we knew later that they were safe and had found shelter. So it was decided to go and find them, and the Norwegian submarine Uredd, attached to the 9th Submarine Flotilla, was given the task. They had on board Sverne Granlund, the Norwegian who had escaped from Glomfjord. But the Uredd disappeared.

Long after the end of the war she was discovered, disembowelled by a mine, not far from the mouth of the Glomfjord. Now a national monument, the wreck remains as the tomb of those brave Norwegians. A small monument on land keeps the memory alive. I have made several emotional pilgrimages to it.

## Sub-Lieutenant Ruari McLean, DSC, British Naval Liaison Officer, FNFL *Rubis*; from *Half Seas Under*

*Rubis's* 13th Minelaying Patrol, 12–26 March 1942, was complicated by problems of identifying the designated area, Jutland Bank.

For all he knew it might now be a matter of great urgency if something big was coming south. They should have told him about the plan, and put him in the general picture, but they hadn't, and so he decided to proceed from our fix that afternoon and run out all night, and if he could not find the bank, he would lay in an approximate position, which should not be more than five miles away; and if the Admiralty didn't like it, he said, he would tell them to go and shift the mines themselves …

The next morning we were somewhere near the bank; we began a slow, precise search for it with our echo-sounder, like a bat looking for a mouse in a cathedral.

The Captain had his navigational chart in his cabin; and as the day wore on, he became more and more restless. Out to the echo-sounder, to gaze reproachfully at its face; into the wardroom for a cup of coffee; back to his cabin to pore over the chart again, as if to learn every sounding on it by heart, and then to detect our position by will-power. Had he allowed enough, or too much, for the set of the current? Was the bank still where the chart said it was, or might it have shifted? Was the echo-sounder working properly? Where was the bank?

The day wore on, and up and down we went, quartering the sea-bed. The echo-sounder ticked away and scratched its trace on the gridded reel of paper; the men at the 'planes chewed their quods of tobacco and spat accurately into their bucket; those off watch slept or played dominoes; and the Captain almost swallowed the chart in his efforts to absorb it. Still we could not find the bank.

At last the Captain decided to surface and take a sun-sight. We were at that time within a stone's throw – or at least a gun-shot – of the enemy coast, so this decision, although popular with the French officers, was not applauded by me. Luckily, however, there was no sun. As a last effort, he turned ninety degrees to port – and found the bank. It was a great relief.

Once we had found the bank, it took us some time to run to our correct laying position, and it was dusk when we began to lay.

Everything appeared to me to go well, until the sixteenth mine was laid. Then to my alarm and despondency I heard the order to surface. I sat still, but my eyebrows must have been raised to their fullest extent. Hémar, coming into the wardroom, explained that it was feared that the eighth mine had not left us. It was thought that the dashpot had gone; that was to say, the weight anchoring the mine to the bottom had gone, but the mine itself was still in its chamber. If that was so, then in fifteen minutes or so the mine would become live, and if, in joggling about, one of the horns had broken, it would blow us up.

So we surfaced, and everyone was ordered up on deck. It was now dark, and fortunately it was also utterly calm, after eight days of storm. If we blew up, with sixteen mines still on board, it might be quite a bang; but on the surface, there just might be some survivors; while submerged, there couldn't be. So forty-nine men and a dog huddled on deck and looked at the cloudy sky and their watches.

Being the only person on board (except Casey and Whitbread) who had been taught how to use Davis Escape Apparatus, I asked the Captain if I might put it on and go down beneath the submarine to try to free the mine, if it were stuck. The Captain thought, probably wisely, that he was safer without me fiddling with his mines beneath him, and politely declined my offer.

It was a really pleasant evening, and good to be in the fresh air again. Eventually it was decided that the eighth mine had probably left after all, although it had not given the proper signs. We finished our lay on the surface, and when all our mines were laid, the boat itself gave a sigh of relief, and we headed north again for Norway.

### Lieutenant Konstantin Sergeev, USSR Navy, *K-21*

In the middle of 1942, after the loss of several submarines, the flotilla officers were given only limited opportunities to go to sea in submarines as they were very valuable specialists. However, Lieutenant-Commander Michail Galkovskiy, the intelligence officer on the Flotilla staff requested and obtained permission to take part in the eighth mission of the *K-21*, as one of the submarine's tasks was the landing of a reconnaissance group on the enemy shore. The landing of the party was very successful, but as is generally known, the appetite comes with eating. This success seemed little to Galkovskiy. Another part of intelligence work was the photographing of enemy objects and even the hostile shores.

So Michail started begging at first the submarine navigators – Michail Leoshko and Dmitriy Kamkin, then the executive officer, Arvanov, and finally, by personal request, Captain Lunin – for permission to take some pictures through the periscope of the Norwegian coastline when it was sighted. Of course, there was a point to that request.

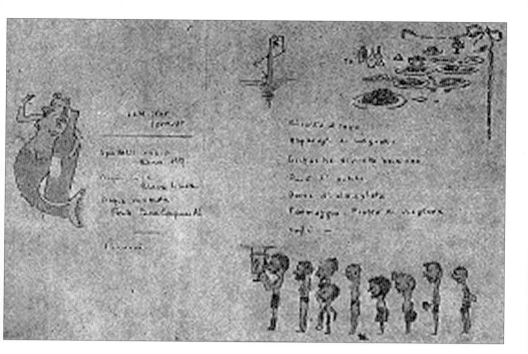

**Above:** The menu of the virtual 'Pranzo di Ferragosto' on the *Giuseppe Finzi*, showing the officers queuing to peer through the periscope at their imaginary feast. Mario Rossetto is second in line. Even the periscope has grown a beard during the long patrol. (Mario Rossetto)

**Right:** Oberfähnrich Zur See Volkmar König leans out of the starboard side of *U-99*'s conning tower. (Volkmar König)

**Above:** Survivors of *U-95* leave the Royal Netherlands Navy submarine *O.21* at Gibraltar in 1941. (Imperial War Museum)

**Left:** Jan Biesemaat (at left), the Dutch seaman who sat on the hydroplane guard pulling those German survivors out of the water, on *O.21*. (Ton Biesemaat)

**Opposite page, bottom:** An official photograph commemorating the comradeship of the Baltic Fleet submariners. Nickolay Tolonnikov can be seen second from left, top row. (Nickolay Tolonnikov)

**Above:** Five of *U-99*'s crew pose for a photograph in 1944 at the Bowmanville POW camp in Canada. *From left to right*: Oberfähnrich Zur See Volkmar König; Leutnant Zur See Heinrich Petersen, the first NCO to win the Knight's Cross in the Second World War and whose commission came through while he was in captivity; Korvettenkapitän Otto Kretschmer; Oberleutnant Zur See Hans Jochen Knebel Doeberitz, formerly Flagg-Leutnant to Admiral Dönitz; and Oberfähnrich zur See Gunter Ruhbahn. (Volkmar König)

**Above left:** Rescued from the sea after the sinking of *U-581* in 1942, Wolfgang Pohl poses with Seaman Geordie Brown on HMS *Croome*. (Wolfgang Pohl)

**Above right:** Lieutenant de Vaisseau Etienne Schlumberger, seen here with Coco in 1943 aboard the French submarine *Morse*. (Etienne Schlumberger)

**Below:** The crew of the Free French submarine *Rubis* demonstrate the 'V-for-Victory' sign. Identifiable by his Royal Navy uniform, Ruari McLean stands in the centre, down towards the front. (Royal Navy Submarine Museum)

**Right:** Luitenant ter Zee Aart Hopman and Seaman 1st Class D. de Jong, both serving on the Royal Netherlands Navy submarine *K-XV.* (Aart Hopman)

**Below:** During a patrol of almost 10,000 miles in 1943, Comandante Mario Rossetto had two and half months to cultivate 'the most beautiful beard on the Atlantic'. (Mario Rossetto)

**Left:** Lieutenant James Roxburgh, DSO, DSC, makes a triumphant return to Malta after the sinking of the Italian submarine, *Remo*. As well as her Jolly Roger, HMS *United* famously flies a flag depicting a stork to mark the birth of her commander's baby boy. (Royal Navy Submarine Museum)

**Below:** Roxburgh can be seen on the right, in conference with Lieutenant J. M. C. Fenton and Sub-Lieutenant P. G. Evatt, the navigator, in the wardroom of HMS *United* at Plymouth in October 1943 (Imperial War Museum)

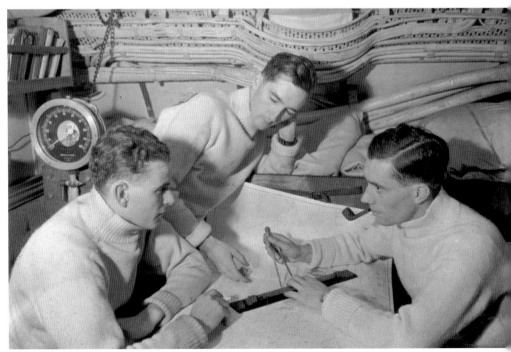

**Right:** The grim reality of winter in the North Atlantic for the US Navy's Bob Haughney and the training boat *O3* (SS-64) in 1943 before he was posted to the brand new USS *Threadfin*. Unable to dive, they radioed for a destroyer to escort them home. The destroyer can just be made out in the top left. (Bob Haughney)

**Below:** Lieutenant-Commander Jerzy ('George') Koziolkowski shows off the latest in headgear at the periscope of the ORP *Sokol*. (Royal Navy Submarine Museum)

**Above left:** Patrol report in hand, Lieutenant George Hunt leaves HMS *Ultor* at Maddelena. (George Hunt)

**Above right:** Immaculate in white, the 21-year-old US Navy Torpedoman Billy Grieves at the start of his naval service. (Billy Grieves)

**Below:** The photograph quality may be poor, but Billy Fong can be seen, far right, with three of his USS *Tautog* shipmates, sitting in the ruins of a Japanese shack on Saipan, New Year's day, 1945. Although the other three man are shadowed, the skull they took back to the boat is clearly visible. (Billy Fong)

First he tried to persuade the navigators roughly like this: 'Misha, Dima, let's take some pictures of the shore; it will help you and others in future to fix a sub's position from distinctive headlands and rocks!' It did not enthuse the navigators; they answered that, generally speaking, they could fix their position without any headlands. And, of course, they could not permit photography.

Then he started on the executive officer: 'Zarik, dear friend, let's take pictures of the shoreline, then we could fulfill one more reconnaissance task!' The Executive officer answered reasonably that this task had not been assigned to the submarine, but on the other hand there was a real danger that from those 'headlands' the enemy look-out stations could spot the periscope wake, and the submarine would betray itself. 'So, go to the captain!' he said.

Lunin heard Galkovskiy's request attentively, grinned and said: 'I think some pictures may be taken, but it's no good doing it at this moment – the waves are quite big up there.' Lunin decided not to explain to Galkovskiy that, because of the waves, there was little danger of the submarine's giving herself away, – unless those waves forced her up to the surface.

The boatswain operated the hydroplanes, the sub was trimmed a little in accordance with the conditions, and the photography started. Ten pictures were taken through the periscope. Galkovskiy positively bloomed and thanked everybody.

But all's well only that ends well. When, after the arrival at the base, the navigators had given the films to the staff photographer Nikolay Sibilev, and he had printed the pictures, it turned out that on five of the photographs there was only the nearest wave, and on the other five, the sky. The shoreline did not get into the photographs at all because of the rolling.

Our mischievous navigators Leoshko and Kamkin put the photographs carefully into two envelopes and wrote on these envelopes respectively: 'Enemy's waves' and 'Enemy's sky', and then sent them with a special courier to the Flotilla staff for 'Intelligence Officer Galkovskiy'...

## MEDITERRANEAN

**Ammiraglio Elio Sandroni, Regia Marina, then Navigating Officer of the *Emo***

2 January 1942, and the *Emo* surfaced outside the Libyan port of Bardia ready to enter and unload her cargo.

The narrow little channel looked no different to what it had on our previous visit. Only when the *Emo* was already inside the line of the two outermost buoys did we notice that the obstruction corks inside had all been taken away from their positions and attached to the last buoy. We tried to make contact with the shore by DONATH signals and then, while the captain started the manoeuvre that would bring the boat out of the port, with two blasts of the siren as well. At the same time, the mooring cables came snaking out the deck to tie up the lighters into which we would be unloading the cans of supplies. The manoeuvre was still in progress when gunfire was opened from the north, gunfire which quickly intensified from all sides of the bay.

Comandante Roselli was clearly taken aback by this unexpected greeting and yelled through the megaphone: 'We're from the submarine *Emo!*'

At the same time, as the fire was becoming extremely brisk, he ordered the few men who had come on deck to go back down into the boat, recover the mooring cables and close the hatches. As the manoeuvre to turn the submarine was completed, either by the captain or the gunner and myself as navigating officer, we realised we were under small-arms fire, none of which could penetrate our hull.

Given that fact, and the unlikely possibility that enemy artillery had been deployed along the coast ... Roselli was confident that the submarine could be withdrawn. He tried in vain to locate the position from which the heaviest fire was coming in order to counter it.

The clear moonlight and the greyish colour of the coast made it impossible to make out either the flames or smoke from the guns. The gunner, a brave Sottotente di Vascello by the name of Fioretini, wanted to load the two machine-guns and return fire, but our commander wouldn't authorise this because the tracer would have told the enemy the direction from which the firing was coming and so pinpointed the submarine.

Because the bridge had taken quite a few hits, all the lookouts were ordered into the conning tower and officers who were next in rank were told to move to the sail ready to take over if the commander and navigating officer should be hit.

The helmsman, Campisi, remained on the bridge. In such a complex situation I decided to get the two iron boxes, containing the codes, ready for destruction, and, via the speaking tube I reassured the crew below and reminded the captain to lower the periscope.

While Comandante Roselli was preoccupied with manoeuvring the submarine to retreat, the helmsman, Campisi, from Syracusa, collapsed, hit in the leg, and, with blood running from the wound shouted:

'Captain, I'm dead.'

Unmoved and calm, Roselli responded:

'Get below.'

At this point, after having handed over to the coxwain in the control room, I dragged poor Campisi to the conning tower hatch where the second-in command and the master at arms helped me to take his weight and get him inside. Splinters hit our commander in the left cheek and he temporarily lost the sight in that eye. I saw that the Captain's face was bleeding and shouted:

'Sir, there's a bit of blood on your face.' Roselli wiped the back of his hand across his cheekbone and replied:

'No, it's nothing.'

Control room told us that the ultrasonic sounding gear was no longer registering in the shallow water. Roselli decreased the port engine from full ahead to slow ahead, increased the starboard engine to full ahead and so the boat reversed towards the middle of the bay to avoid grounding on the bottom and to miss a sunken hull which lay pretty well dead ahead. The manoeuvre was extremely difficult, but Comandante Roselli managed it with the delicacy of embroidery, while the enemy fire continued, and outside the submarine a hail of bullets crashed against the superstructure and hammered the hull. It was nothing short of a miracle that Roselli was not mortally wounded and that I escaped without a scratch. Now that the bow was free, Roselli asked me for the safe route.

'70 degrees, sir,' I answered.

'Steady at 70 degrees!' called Roselli.

And thus we escaped from the bay, pushing the engines to maximum speed. Shortly afterwards, when the *Emo* was safe, the senior wireless operator asked me to come and decipher a message which had just arrived. 'DO NOT APPROACH BARDIA. OCCUPIED BY ENEMY FORCES. GO NORTH PUNTO VELA.'

Roselli and I looked at one another aghast ...

The capture of Bardia from a joint Italian-German force by the British at New Year 1941/2 was a single action within the Libyan campaign. Following the Italian Armistice in September 1943, Roselli, now commanding the *Cagni*, was ordered to put into Durban to hand the submarine over to the Allies on the understanding that the Italian flag would not be lowered.

At Durban, a South African colonel paid a visit to Roselli aboard the *Cagni* and did not attempt to hide his admiration for Italian submarines. He talked about a couple of episodes in the war and then asserted that one day at Bardia he had sunk an Italian submarine which had unexpectedly entered Bardia harbour, a deed which had genuinely grieved him.

'When was that?' asked Roselli with sudden attention.

'I remember it precisely,' said the colonel. 'It was the evening of 2 January 1942: we had just occupied Bardia when the submarine entered port. She obviously had something to offload in a hurry because she was trying to get as close as possible to the shore and we opened fire with machine-guns, light machine-guns and rifles.

'Yes, the submarine succeeded in extricating herself under enemy fire and, manoeuvring very carefully in shallow water, managed to reach the exit of the little bay and escaped at speed.

'Excellent seamanship, but we hit her repeatedly,' continued the colonel.

'There was a full moon that night, mild, and a little overcast,' observed Roselli.

'We sank her,' concluded the South African colonel, 'and she must have gone down just beyond the entrance to the port.'

'Did you find the wreck?' asked Roselli, a trace of irony in his voice. The other man grew a little thoughtful, then admitted that, no, they had not found it, but in truth they didn't have the time to go looking because they had only remained for a short time at Bardia in January 1942.

'Then let me tell you,' went on Roselli with a smile, 'that the submarine wasn't sunk at all because the *Emo* was my command.'

The *Emo* was eventually sunk on 10 November 1942 by HMS *Lord Nuffield*.

**Vice Admiral Sir Hugh MacKenzie, KCB, DSO\*, DSC, Royal Navy, then lieutenant commanding HMS *Thrasher*;** from IWM Sound Archive 011745, and **Leading Stoker Sydney Hart, Royal Navy;** from *Discharged Dead*

The first two Victoria Crosses to be awarded to submariners for personal courage were won by a lieutenant and a petty officer on the same submarine on 16 February 1942.

MACKENZIE: We had one other exciting episode when we were attacking a heavily escorted ship in flat calm conditions – bright sunlight – north of Crete. This was in February 1942 and we got hit by two bombs dropped from an aircraft which fortunately (or I wouldn't be here now) failed to go off. Flat calm conditions and brilliant sunshine: the worst sort of conditions for a submarine to do an attack in the clear waters of the Mediterranean. I knew perfectly well that at periscope depth any aircraft flying over us could see us as clearly as if we were on the surface. And sure enough, just as I fired my torpedoes at this ship, which was escorted by five or six escorts, and three aircraft flying round it – as I put the periscope down having aimed and fired, I heard what were undoubtedly machine gun bullets hitting the water and followed by a fairly large explosion close to; so I reckoned we'd been spotted by an aircraft. Anyway, I'd fired my torpedoes so we went deep to avoid the inevitable counterattack from the surface escorts, which followed in due course.

HART: We knew the enemy escort ships would be listening intently on their echo-sounding gear, ears strained to the utmost in the effort to detect any suspicious sound from below. They couldn't be listening more tensely than we were. That 200-foot cushion of water above us might be our safeguard; it might also be our grave.

'Half ahead, both motors!' came the signal.

Obviously the enemy were coming in for the kill. Science had obviously betrayed us. Thrasher's screws seemed to be only just turning; would they rotate fast enough to get us away from the position where the escorts were about to drop those destructive depth charges? Strained faces and bulging eyes amongst our crew indicated the tension, but the bonds of discipline held stoutly, and the will-power that discipline had ingrained in us kept us outwardly calm during the ordeal.

The escort ships roared as they approached our position. When the inevitable 'Clang-clash-clang …' came it was for all the world like a frantic giant striking on an outsize anvil, except that the din was magnified a thousand times. We were the unfortunate 'so-and-so's' inside that anvil! Thrasher plunged up as if a volcano had erupted beneath her, she bucked savagely and plunged down again: our state of suspense is better left to the imagination since words fail to do it justice. The third attack concluded, leaving the submarine trembling like a whipped dog.

After several more attacks, each one seeming farther away than the one before, we realised that Thrasher had eluded the hunters.

MacKENZIE: I was asleep in my bunk about midnight, and I was woken up by something going 'bonk, bonk, bonk' overhead, clearly something rolling about in the casing. Well, this was anathema to any submariner: something making a noise like that, which could give your position away to anyone listening for you, so I told the Officer of the Watch on the bridge to send somebody down to see if he could find out what it was and secure it to stop it rolling around. I got a rather startled report back that there was what appeared to be a bomb lying on the fore-casing just under the gun, and there was a hole in the casing which seemed to indicate that something had gone into the casing and which might be causing this noise. I went up on the bridge myself and went down to investigate, and there, sure enough, there was a bomb lying on the casing – about two feet long it was. I reckoned about a 50lb–100lb bomb, and there was a hole in the side of the gun casing that looked as though it had been made by another bomb, from its size; and on further investigation, sure enough there was another bomb inside the casing.

HART: At the time of this discovery I was on watch in the engine-room. Turning round from the fuel tanks I spotted Leading Stoker Rembrance making urgent signs to me. Going to his side, I heard him bawl in my ear above the roar of the engines, 'Heard the latest? There's two unexploded bombs in the casing!'

It was necessary to put on an act, I being the tried old-timer. 'That's all right, Nippy, leave them there,' I said, feeling a lot less cheerful than I pretended to be. Live bombs in such a position might mean anything. About the least they could mean was that our number, if not actually up, was being put in the frame. There is no need to exaggerate the situation, but on the best showing it was, as Mr Chucks* would have said, 'Precarious and not at all permanent!' The ship's people rose to the emergency with true Service coolness and practical action.

MACKENZIE: So I sent for the first lieutenant [Peter Roberts] and the 2nd coxswain [Petty Officer Thomas Gould] who were the people normally concerned with the housekeeping and husbandry of the casing anyway and told them to drag the first bomb lying on the casing up to the bows and get a sack and lower it over the side, and when they were ready I would go full speed astern and they could drop it – let go – which they duly did. I was fairly confident that the bombs in themselves were not likely to go off because we'd taken them to a depth of 200 feet anyway in evading the counterattack after we'd been depth charged, so I thought they were probably safe alright.

But the bomb in the casing was a much more difficult problem. The two men concerned had to get into the casing by the forward hatch and then crawl aft on their stomachs to get to the bomb underneath the gun and then drag it back with them to the opening where they could get it out, which was by the forward hatch, a matter of 30 feet or so, on their stomachs or on their hands and knees, dragging the damned thing.

HART: Inside the ship there was an eerie silence, as if all hands were waiting for the usual depth-charge attack, to which we had grown more or less accustomed. But this occasion told a very different story. Above our heads two daring men were working in a confined space, a space slimy and slippery with stagnant sea-water, handling two slithery, live bombs dragging them inch by inch out of that narrow casing, where there was little enough room for manoeuvring the deadly things. I doubt if any one, even the most expert bomb disposal squads, ever handled bombs under such dangerous conditions. It seemed like eternity before the welcome news wafted through the ship that Roberts and Gould had the two missiles out of the casing, and were ready to drop them overboard. They had worked as coolly as if on a formal parade.

The order to 'Stop both motors: Slow astern both motors!' came like the sudden snapping of a cord to break the breathless tension. The bombs were

* Mr Chucks was the boatswain in Captain Frederick Marryat's novel *Peter Simple and the Three Cutters*.

lowered gently over Thrasher's bows with all the respect and reverence shown by a funeral party and they were committed to the deep with a prayer of thankfulness, not of pity. Is it any wonder that both these heroes received the Victoria Cross in reward for their bravery? Never were those bits of bronze more rightly awarded.

MACKENZIE: And of course, the whole time they were there, if we happened to be surprised by an enemy patrol, we'd have had to dive and they'd have been drowned, which was not an easy thing for me to contemplate standing on the bridge. However, all went well, and eventually they got it out and dropped it over the front end. We went on our way rejoicing ...

We'd been blitzed out of Alexandria in a hurry as a result of, probably, an 'Ultra' message, to go and patrol north of Crete and to intercept a certain ship, and we'd sailed 48 hours in advance of what we'd been prepared to do – and it happened to be we'd sailed on Friday 13th. Sailors never like sailing on a Friday anyway – traditionally it was supposed to be unlucky – and to sail on Friday 13th was doubly unlucky. However it was lucky for some, anyway.

The official report, ADM1/11887, clearly states that Lieutenant Roberts volunteered. Initially the pair were put forward for the George Cross because the VC was for courage in the face of the enemy, and the enemy had gone. Admiral Cunningham, however, insisted on the VC because at any moment the submarine might have had to dive, drowning both men.

### Torpedoman Alfred Fraedrich, Kriegsmarine, *U-372*

And on the last trip we were sunk.* We left from Salamis in Greece, and we put an Arabian on board. He was an agent, a spy, and we were supposed to put him ashore in Haifa, in Palestine, and he was to take over the underground movement there against the British. This guy was, I would guess, around forty. He spoke perfect English and perfect German, and this was the first time I knew about karate: he showed us, and he was terrific. After we left harbour our Captain announced over the radio who he was, because he was brought aboard very secretly – everybody had to go inside, and nobody was on the shore to see it. And the Captain told us that if it ever should happen that we were sunk and caught, the story was to be that we rammed a Palestinian fishing boat and picked up one of the people. He must have gotten away with it because we never saw him. We were sunk just off Haifa and put ashore and there was an interrogation camp, and we never saw him again. A couple of years later when I was in the POW camp in Phoenix, Arizona, another captain

---

* By depth charges dropped by British destroyers *Zulu*, *Sikh*, *Croome* and *Tetcott* and a 221 Squadron Wellington. There were no casualties.

came there as a prisoner and told our captain (we were sunk on 4 August) that on 5 August in Rome they knew everything that had happened to us. The only person who could have told them was this guy.

**Tenente di Vascello Renato Ferrini**, Regia Marina, commanding *Axum*; from his Patrol Report

As the Malta-bound 'Pedestal' convoy approached the Straits, *Axum* was one of five Italian submarines lying in wait off Skerki Banks.

Sailed from Cagliari on 11 August. Reached billet on 12th, approximately 25 miles north-west off Cape Blanc.

12 August 1942

0600 On station – submerged – the ambush set up.

1400 Because the signal from reconnaissance made me think that the convoy might attempt to pass much farther south near the coast while the escort force was sailing to the north, I proceeded submerged on a heading of 230° towards Cap Blanc.

1821 In position 37°37′ Lat, 10°21′ Long, submarine bearing 229°, I spotted 11° to starboard a dark shape in the far distance which, after careful observation, I took to be a large merchant vessel or an aircraft carrier. I immediately decided to approach submerged in order to get a better idea of what it might be, given that even with greater magnification it was not possible to distinguish it clearly.

1840 As I continued my approach (the bearing of the shape remained constant) I observed two traces of smoke 295° to starboard; immediately afterwards I observed in the sky the classic traces of anti-aircraft fire directed against two aircraft which flew off to the east; I deduced from this that the convoy had to be in that direction.

1841 I approached from the north to get closer.

1850 Observing that the smoke had shifted to 300° I submerged to 20 metres and proceeded at full speed on a bearing of 30°.

1927 Came to periscope depth. Position 37°37′ Lat, 10°19′ Long bearing 30°. I saw a formation with the following details: $\alpha$ [enemy polar bearing] = 290°, $\beta$ [torpedo angle for the launch] 10° to port; distance 8,000m, enemy course 110°.

1928 I closed at once following the same route as the enemy in order to study it.

1933 I set new course, submarine bearing 111°, $\alpha$ = 170° $\beta$ = 40° to port. Enemy bearing 140°. In other words in the intervening time the enemy had changed course 30° to starboard. I changed course to 180°.

I had the opportunity to establish that the convoy consisted of some 15 merchant ships, two cruisers and many destroyers. It was proceeding in three columns in delta formation, with the merchant ships divided between the three columns, the two cruisers at the centre and the destroyers spread throughout the outer columns. I further observed – not very clearly because she was screened by the other vessels – a ship with two tall lattice masts like those of the US battleships. Given the flat-calm sea, I preferred to have a quick look at the situation so that my periscope would not be spotted, as its wake, notwithstanding we were sailing at the lowest possible speed, could be sighted.

1937 Changed course at a distance of about 4,000 metres. Enemy course steady at 140°, speed 13 knots. Turned 220° to starboard to gain a position ready to fire.

1942 After a very quick glance at periscope depth, went to 15 metres and ahead half full speed to reduce the range.

1948 Returned to periscope depth. I was close to the angle of attack 28°, target the cruiser in the second column, whose whole length was clear to view; in the column closest to me, ahead and astern of the cruiser were, respectively, a destroyer and a large freighter.

1955 Fired all bow torpedoes in the order 1, 4, 3 and 2. 1 and 2 with zero angulation, 3 and 4 angled 5° to starboard and 5° to port respectively. Immediately after firing I disengaged. Range from the first column 1,300 metres, to the cruiser, 1,800 metres

63 seconds after firing we heard the first bang; after 90 seconds two more explosions, very close together. That led me to believe we had hit one vessel in the first column followed by another in the second one.

According to the speed of the torpedo the firing distances proved to be less than appreciated and precisely around 1,000 metres from the first column and 1,400 from the second.

Four and half minutes after firing, with the boat at 65 metres, the hunt began with a well-targeted cascade of depth charges. I went to 100 metres and went to silent routine. The hunt continued for about two hours with studied care and generally accurate attacks. I noted that every time the boat came up to about 80 or 90 metres we could hear the pinging of the Asdic, which was immediately followed by depth charging. I therefore decided to stay at between 100 and 120 metres; moreover, at 2135 a destroyer started up, and while it was passing over our entire length we heard – as well as the noise from its propellers – a noise like a cable slithering which made me think they were using a towed torpedo.*

After 2215 noted the presence of another vessel farther away while the destroyer hunting for us seemed to be moving away.

---

* A short torpedo, without an engine, towed by an anti-submarine vessel and designed to explode on contact with a submarine, this first A/S weapon dated from 1914.

2250 Surfaced. Bearing 330° and observed about 3,000 metres astern a large vessel in flames; 45° to starboard another one in flames and giving off a lot of smoke; 70° off the stern quarter a third ship already burnt which was again giving off the typical dense black and grey smoke. The fire from the first vessel was clearly illuminating me and immediately I observed that not far away two sailing destroyers which were signalling each other. Because I needed first to replenish air and power I submerged to evade another potential hunt and left the area.

In fact, all four torpedoes had been successful. *Axum* sank the old cruiser and now Anti-Aircraft Ship HMS *Cairo*, badly damaged the cruiser HMS *Nigeria* and also hit the tanker *Ohio* which, further damaged by ferocious air attack, would eventually be helped into the Grand Harbour, *Valletta*, by two destroyers, HMS *Penn* and HMS *Ledbury*.

Meanwhile, Lieutenant Alastair Mars, commanding the British submarine HMS *Unbroken*, formed part of the screen sent out to protect the beleaguered convoy from the Italian Fleet. Detected in his original billet, Mars had moved to a position 15 miles north-west of the volcanic island of Stromboli, only to receive a signal from Malta in the early hours of Thursday 13 August informing him that enemy cruisers were proceeding into the very area he had left. However, reasoning that the Italian Fleet would know that an Allied submarine had been sighted in that area, Mars calculated that the Italians would change course and in fact turn up exactly where he now lurked – as they did, around 0730, putting an end to breakfast.

### Lieutenant-Commander Alastair Mars, DSO, DSC*, Royal Navy, HMS *Unbroken*; from *Unbroken*

They were now well over the horizon. 'Two ... Three ... Four! Yes, four cruisers in line ahead, coming straight towards ... Range?'

Chief ERA Manuel read off from the range scale above my head. 'Range, twelve thousand, sir.'

'Down periscope. Port twenty-five. Group up ... Up after periscope.'

As the smaller periscope cut the surface I had a quick look round for aircraft close to. There were none; but two anti-submarine Cants hovered over the cruisers.

'Down after periscope. Fifty feet.'

Fifty feet would have to do. I wanted to keep my eye on this magnificent array of ships, and it would take too long to get down to eighty feet and back.

As the needles passed thirty-five feet I ordered: 'Full ahead together.' I turned to Haddow. 'Two 8-inch cruisers and, I think, two 6-inch. Anyhow, four cruisers for certain.'

Haddow raised an eyebrow. I nodded. He passed the glad tidings over the broadcaster in a commendably calm quiet voice.

Archdale was manipulating the fruit machine, knowing it was my intention to get into a position whereby, as the cruisers passed, I would have the entire lengths of their sides at which to aim. 'Course for a ninety-degree track, sir, one-four-oh.'

'Steer one-four-oh.'

The helmsman eased his wheel. The planesman levelled up.

'Course, sir, one-four-oh.'

From Sizer: 'Depth, sir, fifty feet.'

We shuddered as the propellers lashed the water and the submarine leapt across the enemy's bows at her top speed. Assuming the cruisers kept to their course we would have to get some eight hundred yards off their path, turn around and fire. I had fifteen minutes in which to do this, just time enough.

I then announced an item of information I had kept to myself. 'There are eight modern destroyers and two seaplanes escorting. Shut off for depth-charging.'

As Haddow relayed the information to the rest of the boat, I felt a moment of queasiness. It was a feeling I knew of old – a boyhood memory of a twelve-stone brute flashing down the touchline of a rugger field, the full back at the other side of the field, and only myself to bring him down ...

This time, however, I was not alone. I looked at the faces around me.

Haddow, an enigmatic smile on his lips, watched the depth gauges like a lynx. On him depended whether I would be able to see or not when the moment of firing came. Thirsk was crouched low over his chart, oblivious to everything save the job in hand. Archdale gazed oddly at the fruit machine as though it was about to give birth. On him depended the director angle. Cryer, humped over the now repaired Asdic, had a grin on his face I can only describe as fiendish. ERA Lewis hovered by the telemotor and blowing panels, watching the pressure indicators with deep concentration. Manuel stood behind me ready to read off the periscope and keep me clamped to the director angle at the time of firing. The planesmen, communicating numbers, and helmsmen sat with their backs to me, working their controls with prac-tised ease ...

'Bring all tubes to the ready,' I ordered. 'Torpedo depth settings fourteen and sixteen feet.'

After a run of three minutes we crept back to periscope depth. I lifted my finger and the attack periscope was raised until the eyepiece was just clear of the deck. I curled into a squatting position and looked. Still underwater. Lewis raised the periscope, slowly dragging my body up with it. As soon as the top glass cut the surface I whisked around to see if anything was too close to us. Then on to the target.

'Down after, up for'ard periscope.'

The line of cruisers had altered course to starboard away from the direction in which we were heading – and had taken up a form of quarter-line. This meant the nearest would be one of the 8-inch cruisers. She would be my target. Although the range was rather more than one could wish, the disadvantage was cancelled by the fact that the new formation presented an excellent multiple target – one of the more distant 6-inch cruisers might be hit by a torpedo that missed the 8-inch job. I congratulated myself on this stroke of luck, and turned to study the eight evil-looking destroyers and their accompanying aircraft, the boys who could well wreck my chances.

Fortunately five of the destroyers were well out of it on the far side of the cruisers. Obligingly, the aircraft had gone that way, too. The aircraft might come back, but I reckoned I was safe at periscope depth for the time being. The other three destroyers were still in line ahead, and if they did not alter course I would be able to sneak across their bows and fire from inside the 'screen' – from between them and the cruisers.

'Down periscope.'

Archdale looked round. 'New enemy course, oh-seven-oh. What speed shall I allow, sir?'

Thirsk said: 'Speed from plot twenty-two knots.'

Cryer reported: 'Two hundred revs, sir. That gives twenty-five knots according to the table for Italian 8-inch cruisers.'

'Give them twenty-five knots,' I said. Archdale manipulated the fruit machine.

'Director angle, green three-six-and-a-half.'

Thirty-six-and-a-half degrees. That was the amount I would have to 'lay off' from the direction in which our bows were pointing. A big angle. It would need care.

'All tubes ready, sir. Torpedoes set at fourteen and sixteen feet.'

'Very good.' Torpedoes set at that depth, hitting a ship doing twenty-five knots, would make as big a mess as anyone could wish for. I glanced at my watch. Exactly eight o'clock. They'll be having breakfast now, or getting ready for a run ashore at Messina. They'll be lucky!

I felt good. In my pint-sized submarine I was going to tackle twelve enemy warships all at one time. A story for my grandchildren – if the destroyers and aircraft let me live to tell it!

'Slow together ... Stop starboard. Up periscope.'

The tip of the attack periscope nosed out of the water. I grasped hard the handles as though to stop it protruding too far, and raised my little finger when six inches were exposed. Lewis stopped it dead. I swept round quickly to fix the covering aircraft. They were still over on the other side of the 'screen'. From Archdale: 'Target bearing green five-oh.' 'How much longer to go?'

'Three-and-a-half minutes, sir.'

The three destroyers in line ahead were still tearing towards me, although I was just a fraction inside them. With luck I would have a clear view of my target. They could not have picked us up on their Asdics or they would be circling ready to drop depth charges, but they were going to pass us too damn near for comfort. I could go deep and fire by Asdic, but I was reluctant to do this as firing at a noise is obviously less accurate than firing at a seen object. None the less, we set the Asdic firing angle, just in case.

All this flashed through my mind in less than a second, and a moment later I uttered a loud curse as I saw the nearest destroyer alter course straight towards us. She was no more than fifteen hundred yards off. I did some quick thinking.

'How much do *Navigatori*-Class destroyers draw?' 'Fifteen to eighteen feet, sir.'

It meant she would pass over our hull but not over the conning-tower. Unless she missed us by the narrowest of margins, her keel would snap off the periscope and slice our conning-tower with the ease of a tin-opener. It was a risk we would have to take. I had no intention of losing my target.

Our target ... I swung the periscope. There she was, still on the same course. To my joy I saw that overlapping her was one of the 6-inch cruisers. I had a double length at which to aim.

I winced as I swung back to the destroyers. The crashing bow-wave of the nearest was less than a thousand yards off. A little voice nagged at the back of my brain: Remember your command course training. A fast destroyer, head on at under a thousand yards. Go deep! Go deep, you bloody fool! You haven't a hope ... 'Down periscope.'

Archdale said: 'Just under a minute now, sir.'

'Stand by all tubes ... Lewis, if my periscope is knocked off as the destroyer passes over, put up the for'ard periscope without further orders. Understand?'

'Very good, sir.'

'Director angle green three-six-and-a-half,' Archdale reported.

'Asdic bearing of target green four-two.'

'Eighty feet! Group up!' 'Fire Four!'

'Hard a-starboard. Full ahead together.' 'Fourth torpedo running, sir.' We spiralled downwards ...

On a south-westerly course eighty feet deep we hurried from the firing posi-tion at a rattling nine knots. I was very aware that the passing destroyer had caused me to fire late and I hoped the speed of my target had been over-estimated. The seconds crawled past.

The scene in the control-room might have been transplanted from a militant Madame Tussaud's – the tense, still figures, some standing, some sitting, others crouching, all rigidly silent, unblinking and tight-lipped, straining to catch the sound of a torpedo striking home. For two minutes and fifteen seconds we were like that, until a great clattering explosion brought a back-slapping roar of triumph to shatter the illusion.

We've done it! We've hit the cruiser!

Then, fifteen seconds later, a second explosion.

'Tell the boys it's two hits for certain!'

What a moment that was! Fused into one mighty brain and body, the 600-ton *Unbroken* had tackled four cruisers, a couple of aircraft, and eight submarine-killing destroyers. Had tackled them and beaten them.

### Comandante Sergio Parodi, Regia Marina, then (October 1942) Exec of the *Delfino*

The Mediterranean was not always as flat as a millpond. Bad weather could strike, even in high summer.

During the last war I have been on submarines in the Mediterranean Sea and, on many occasions, I have avoided to lose my life in very lucky circumstances. I remember a fact that convinced me that I would arrive alive at the end of the war.

When I was the tenente [Exec] on the submarine *Delfino*, the 'battello' (as are commonly called the submarines by submariners) was coming back home to Taranto from Buerat-el-Hsum at the bottom of Sirte Gulf, where the crew had unloaded several tons of gasoline, ammunition for tanks and other explosives for the Italian and German Army in retreat from El Alamein. The *Delfino*, at about 40 miles south of Santa Maria di Leuca cape, was running zigzagging, in order to avoid torpedoes possibly launched by some English submarine, always present in this sea.

The sea was rough because since three or four days strong winds had been blowing from north-east; frequently the waves covered the submarine deck and violently broke against the bridge that surrounded the conning tower.

The place I preferred on the bridge, every time I was substituting for the Captain, was between the binnacle and the breastwork of the bridge; the space was narrow but enough to introduce my body and sustain it during my watch.

I think two hours had already passed when the lookout on the astern right side called for my attention, having sighted something. I left swiftly my place approaching the lookout, and looking with my binoculars in the direction shown I saw some dolphins playing on the waves.

During the time elapsed (less than one minute) I perceived, without paying much attention to the noise, that another wave had broken with great violence against the bridge. I paid much more attention to this fact when I saw that my watch post was no more available, because the breastwork had been so bent as to touch the binnacle.

Perhaps I lost an imposing funeral at Taranto, but surely the dolphins became very lovable animals for me.

**Lieutenant Commander Ian Fraser, VC, Royal Navy**; from *Frogman VC*

In October 1942, Ian Fraser, then a sub-lieutenant in HMS *Sahib*, was sent to Malta.

The siege went on. The fortress took a daily hammering. Food became scarce, and then scarcer, and then scarcer still. At one time some of the troops were rationed to two slices of bread a day – and there were 'sleep parades' so that, with their heads down, the men might try to forget the distress that empty stomachs bring. At the height of the siege the only way in which petrol and munitions and essential supplies could be got to the island was by submarine. Hence the voyage of the *Sahib* 'with stores'. While the stores were unloading, we went ashore and were billeted in one of those rock-hewn shelters; and there we heard and saw the bombs come down as the Italian and German bombers droned in, and the few fighters on the island soared again and again into the blue skies to do what they could in the battle to keep Malta out of the hands of the enemy.

Then, for the *Sahib*, it was off on patrol again – a wide-ranging patrol covering a considerable part of the Mediterranean, submerged by day, surfaced by night. It was on a night patrol that there occurred one of those war tragedies that are best told unemotionally: otherwise anger at the futility of man could get in the way of a plain tale.

We had been on patrol off the West Coast of Greece, had moved eastwards along the Mediterranean to the north coast of Sicily, and thus down to the coast of Tunisia and the Gulf of Sirte. We were surfaced on the night of a full moon that spread radiance over the calmest of seas. And there, ahead of us, picked out by the moon, we could see a 2,000-ton Italian freighter. She was a sitting target. We fired twenty rounds of HE and only one torpedo. Nothing more was needed. The freighter – for the record, she was an Italian steamship named *Saillin* [*Scillin*] – went down with a rush. We moved in to pick up survivors. In all, we picked up sixty-one men, all unharmed. And then we found that twenty-six of them were British, the rest

Italian servicemen. What were British soldiers doing on an Italian freighter? It did not take long to establish the shocking truth. We had indeed sunk an Italian ship which certainly carried 200 Italian troops but, and here lay the tragedy for us, she was transporting 800 British POWs from the desert campaign.

And now, of those 800 British prisoners of war, only twenty-six were alive. The rest were dead – dead as the result of the unwitting action of a British submarine whose job it was to try to cripple enemy shipping so that, in the end, there would be no more prisoners of war and no more war ...

We took the twenty-six to Malta. We arrived there with the *Sahib* shining and spotless below decks: the British survivors had seen to that. Their NCOs had put the thirty-five Italian prisoners to work scrubbing the boat out as we made our way to the fortress that other Italians were trying to reduce to helpless and hopeless subjection.

**Capitain de Vaisseau Jean L'Herminier, Vichy Marine, *Casabianca*; from *Casabianca*; and Enseigne Robert Lagane, Vichy Marine, *Iris*; from *Cinq Ans Dans le Brouillard***

The Franco-German Armistice Commission had been making moves to render French submarines at Toulon operational; the Vichy Government was about to give orders to the French fleet to scuttle itself. The 19 submarines included *Casabianca* and *Iris*, whose officers had other ideas.

L'HERMINIER: As we were to make exhaustive tests of our diesels we had been allowed a good deal of fuel oil, and when the oil tanker came alongside we were naturally anxious to take as many tons of the precious liquid on board as possible. Trials at full speed consume a lot of fuel oil! And then, we were also anxious to take advantage of the opportunity to test the efficiency of our ballast and external fuel-oil tanks.

With such good reasons to support our demands we were allowed to have our way, and my Engineer Officer was able to fill up our interior and exterior storage tanks with no less than eighty-five cubic metres of fuel oil – enough for a very nice little cruise! Quite enough to cross the Mediterranean in fact, or to get out of it at full speed!

We were informed sternly that on our return to port we should be required to deliver up whatever surplus remained. 'Of course!' we agreed, but by this time we were sliding joyfully down the dangerous incline of temptation ...

Every time the question of fuel oil was raised we looked either astonished or blank, and we had already made our preparations to deceive the inspectors of the Armistice Commission if they took it into their heads to make inquiries.

The members of the Commission were not submariners and it was, there-fore, an easy matter to lead them up the garden [path] with a number of simple tricks such as stopping up the pipes leading to the check taps of the fuel-oil tanks. After their departure it was an equally simple matter to remove the obstruction.

Although we did not yet admit it even to ourselves, preparations had entered on a new stage and now different objective. What we were preparing for was no longer just to take the *Casabianca* out to sea in order to scuttle her in deep water. For that we need not have the whole crew on board. All we needed were enough to get her under way and open the sea cocks when we got beyond the Roads. The fewer the better, because they would have to be taken off in dinghies before she disappeared for the last time under water. No, this time we were preparing to make our escape and join the Allies ...

Every night after a long chat we would stretch ourselves out in our bunks but it was not always easy to get to sleep. Our nerves were too keyed-up. And when we slept we usually had bad dreams. The look-out watches relieved each other during the night. On 27 November, at five o'clock in the morning, Torpedo Gunner's Mate Lyonnais relieved Engine Room Artificer Heichette.

'Nothing doing tonight by the look of it,' said Heichette as he went below.

But he had hardly got to his bunk when Lyonnais pressed the button of the klaxon.

Machine-gun fire sounded from the arsenal, about two blocks away in the direction of Porte Bazeilles.

The crew of the *Casabianca* leaped from their bunks and rushed to casting-off stations. When I got up to the bridge I was told that the Germans were attacking. My officers were on deck hurriedly making a last-minute check to see that everything was ready ...

LAGANE: 0405 – The klaxon gave the General Alarm. The watch-keeper on the bridge shouted down the voice pipe:

'Action stations, boys! Fritz is in the Arsenal. Action stations! The bastards have come. They're everywhere! They're shooting everything. Action stations. My God, they're blowing up the base. That one just missed *Vénus's* stern! Action stations!'

They were Waffen SS troops from the Das Reich armoured division who were attacking the place ... Dégé leapt on to the bridge.

'Action stations. Ehrardt, get on the machine gun. Euzen, get on the aft casing. Slacken off the ropes ... Control room, send up three helmets and life jackets. Start the Gyro. Lagane, prepare to sail on motors.'

'Understood, bridge. Grenade and magazine are ready for the fireworks. Ship ready to sail handsomely.'

Commander Barry burst on to the dockside at a run. He just had time to shout to everyone before he was stopped.

'Submarines, get under weigh! Get under weigh, but await my orders to scuttle!'

'Harbour stations! Let go aft! Starboard motor, forward, two! Let go forward! Port ten!' And the *Iris* left in the direction of the small channel.

Just as the boat crossed the entrance to the North basin, the signalman spotted the fourth officer, Midshipman Cheney, who was running along the quay shouting:

'*Iris*, *Iris*, wait for me!'

The *Diamant* and the *Vénus* were manoeuvring nose to tail ahead of us; the *Marsouin* was waiting astern. Junkers 88 aircraft circled, dive-bombing, dropping flares and depth charges ... Too late. We left Cheney to his fate.

L'HERMINIER: I don't know whether the order to scuttle was actually given, but the time had passed for orders. In any case, the red lamps whose extinction was to be the signal for scuttling, had never been lit in the first place. Our command had been completely overwhelmed by the German coup, and we were on our own now. Only instant action could save the day.

At least their lightning blow should not succeed entirely. For days now we had been preparing for just such an eventuality, and we were not caught napping. I gave the order to cast off. The hawsers clattered away readily alongside; they had been weighted with kentledge to that very end. The evening before my first lieutenant had drawn an old lighter into position between us and the quay to prevent us from scraping against the pier and perhaps damaging our starboard propeller.

I ordered speed 4 ahead in order to break through the boom, which lay about a hundred yards ahead of our bows. The lighter creaked and we began to make way forward. At the same moment the *Vénus*, a submarine of 600 tons, which had been tied up on the other side of the jetty, also began to move. Thanks to her lighter tonnage, she picked up speed rapidly and quickly overhauled us.

'Let me pass,' shouted her commander from the bridge. 'I can go ahead.'

I let the *Vénus* pass in accordance with our agreement that the first submarine out should break the boom, and we followed closely on her stern, passing her on the port side at the boom where she had caught her starboard hydroplanes in some steel wire.

I very much feared that the two exterior jetties of Port Mourillon would be occupied by the Germans and that we should get a hail of anti-tank shells which would tear through both outer hull and pressure hull and make it impossible for us to dive. We had to pass within fifteen yards of the jetties and from there our bridge could be raked with machine-gun fire. Bellet, my First Lieutenant, obviously had the same idea, for he ordered the distribution of steel helmets to the officers and men of the deck watch and to the gun-crew.

However, the delicate manoeuvring necessary to get us through the boom took our minds off personal considerations, and, in fact, the Germans had rather foolishly omitted to station any of their men on the jetties ...

We passed through the boom and swung our helm to port to cross the Toulon Roads and make for the sea. I offered to take the *Vénus* in tow, but she succeeded in breaking the steel wire by manoeuvring backwards and forwards at full speed until finally she broke loose.

We then raced off towards the anti-submarine net which closed the Roads, hoping to have it opened for us and those of our comrade ships that managed to follow us.

We crossed the Roads at twelve knots. There were no signs of life on the surface ships anchored there. A score or two of aeroplanes were flying around with navigation lights on as though nothing were amiss. Now and again the searchlights of our own anti-aircraft batteries would light up a plane, but there was no firing. Apparently no warning had been given in the West Arsenal, and our men were misled by the fact that the planes were flying with their navigation lights on.

Then some of the planes began to drop flares. The moon was already shining brightly and now with the flares it soon became as light as day. We were speeding along as though on the surface of a mirror, and from above we must have stood out sharply against it. A plane appeared from the direction of Les Sablettes and flew towards us.

We came up with the tug which was stationed at the anti-submarine net and shouted to the tugmaster to open up, but he replied that he had no orders to do so. Bellet ran along the fore deck flourishing his revolver whilst I manoeuvred to bring the nose of the *Casabianca* alongside the low deck of the tug. Bellet sprang on board her to persuade the good skipper to open up, but the fellow refused to budge: only his superior orders mattered.

The plane now dived towards us and released a bomb which exploded between our stern and the destroyer *Mars* which was moored with damped fires against the Lazaret jetty. A fountain of water rose before the astonished eyes of the tug master, who realised at last that we were in deadly earnest and he now began to manoeuvre his boat to open the net. Bellet rejoined us successfully.

Unfortunately in his haste the tug master fouled his own propeller and the net opened only partly.

We got through, scraping against the buoy.

Hardly had the searchlights come on than they went out again. In all probability they too had been captured by a surprise coup, for although the dropping of the bomb had dissipated all doubt about the situation the guns did not open up.

Things were getting hot. It was dangerous to remain surfaced, and yet there was very little depth on either side of the entrance to the Roads and we had to bear round to negotiate the last barrier, the anti-speedboat boom, before we could reach the open sea.

Three planes were now coming down rapidly towards us. Three objects dropped from them and three white parachutes opened. The objects were magnetic mines intended to bar the way out of the Roads. Columns of water rose on the port bow.

That was that. I ordered Speed 6, full speed ahead, and pressed the button of the klaxon, which meant 'Dive!' The air vents whistled and the *Casabianca* submerged.

I steered as near as possible to the right-hand jetty to keep as far away as I could from the centre of the boom where the magnetic mines were now dropping like rain.

Lowering myself hurriedly into the conning-tower, I saw the end of the jetty right ahead where the boom ended.

'Five left. Fifteen metres. Trim zero,' I ordered.

I gave the helm a slight turn to port in order not to run smack into the jetty, but at the same time not to go too near the mines on the port bow. We were perhaps fifty feet below the surface now. The water is quite shallow near the Saint-Mandrier jetty, and it grows deeper only after the outer jetties have been passed.

I had ordered full speed ahead in the hope of passing the mines before they became active. We cleared the jetty without scraping the hull, and I put the helm to zero and went forward parallel with the exit channel until I had more water under the keel. After that I intended to bear to starboard round Cape Cepet, hugging the promontory as close as possible and navigating by soundings.

The manoeuvre stood us in good stead. The mines went off in our wake instead of athwart the conning-tower, which might have knocked us out. The *Casabianca* shuddered violently to her beam ends …

A tragi-comic incident occurred on board the *Casabianca*. Having negotiated the right-hand jetty – we almost touched it and the margin of safety must have been measured in inches – I looked through the periscope to see if I could fix our position more exactly by the familiar silhouettes of the Colle Noire and Cape Cepet, which would be visible thanks both to the moonlight and to the flares which the German planes were dropping.

I raised the after periscope and looked into the eyepiece, but could see nothing at all. I drew it down into the water to clean the headpiece. But that old trick of the submariner made no difference at all; I could still see nothing. Suddenly I understood, and so did the signalman in charge of the periscopes. He turned pale – not on account of the danger but because he fully expected to be torn into strips.

When a submarine is in harbour the periscopes are, of course, lowered into their wells, and for still greater safety the periscope heads with their delicate prisms, which jut out a few inches above the wells, are covered with metal guards to prevent damage by men working on deck.

The white-faced signalman had just remembered that in the general excitement he had forgotten to remove the guards when we cast loose.

I looked at him with feelings far too deep to be put into words. It was too bad even to get furious about.

We did our best to get rid of the guards by going at full speed ahead, but without success. Towards six o'clock, after various unsuccessful attempts to get our eyes open, we risked surfacing and my Fourth Hand, Sub-Lieutenant Lasserre, hurriedly clambered on deck and removed the guards so that we could see again.

At 1850, with no orders received, the officers of the *Iris* had to make some decisions.

LAGANE: First of all, the legal position. To whom did we belong? That is a life-or-death matter for an armed ship in wartime. Sailing while armed and without a proper commission issued by a recognised government – as we were – classes as piracy under international law and left us liable to death before any established court of justice. There was indeed a commission in the document chest, but it was in the name of Commander Collomb who had not handed over power to anyone, whether in writing, verbally or by death. That was why, after consideration and just to be on the safe side, I ingenuously entered the following into the boat's patrol report.

'27th November 1942. Assuming command ... In carrying out the order to get under weigh immediately, given to all the submarines by the commander of the submarine base, and in the absence of Commander Collomb who remained ashore, Lieutenant de Vaisseau Dégé assumed command of the submarine *Iris* ...'

By the morning of 30 November, *Casabianca* was close to the Bay of Algiers, hoping to join the Allies, but with no operational radio she was unable to transmit her identity or intentions.

L'HERMINIER: On approaching the Bay of Algiers we switched on our supersonic detector to pick up the Asdic waves of Allied submarine chasers, and at seven o'clock, when day was just breaking, we rose from about 130 feet to periscope depth in order to scan the horizon.

To my dismay I realised that we had travelled faster than I had estimated. The Matifou light was already visible quite close. At the same time our detector apparatus was registering Asdic waves. Looking round I observed half-a-dozen British vessels circling slowly round between Matifou and Caxine, the points east and west of the Bay of Algiers. They were obviously the anti-submarine curtain protecting the Allied armada moored in the bay.

We were right in the thick of it! As soon as one of the British corvettes picked us up by Asdic we should be chased, depth-charged and sent to the bottom.

At 0715 hours I had not yet been able to make my decision to surface. From the control-room the minutes were announced pitilessly.

'All ready for surfacing,' came to me through the voice pipe.

I explained the position to Bellet and told him to be ready to hoist the lookout mast and get two men on deck as quickly as possible after we surfaced in order to display our largest French flag from a position before our gun. Speed was the essence of our problem.

We went down to about 125 feet, ready to blow the ballast tanks so vigorously that we should break surface at a steep angle and thus reveal our superstructure as completely as possible, and give our friends the best possible opportunity of recognising the characteristic silhouette of a French submarine of the 1,500-tons class.

At 0718 hours we broke surface. The British corvette nearest to us spotted us at once, turned her helm over and raced towards us at full speed, making the challenge and demanding the reply. But we didn't know it!

The forward gun crew of the corvette were at action stations with their weapon trained on us.

At last our signal projector was ready and we flashed feverishly: '*Casabianca*! *Casabianca*! French submarine!'

By this time the corvette was about three hundred yards away and our two men holding the French ensign had been spotted. But apparently the corvette commander feared some sort of ruse, and his ship circled round us, ready to fire instantly.

In the meantime the signal lamps were busy.

'Why don't you answer our challenge?'

'Because we can't.'

'What's your liaison officer up to?'

'We haven't got one.'

'Why not?'

'Because we've just escaped from Toulon.'

On the bridge of the corvette the British commander threw his hat into the air enthusiastically and his crew began to cheer.

Dégé and Lagane decided to make for Spain where they hoped for some breathing space. With no practical help forthcoming from the French or British to help her reach Algiers or Gibraltar, the *Iris* was forced to accept internment at Cartagena. As the war progressed, Lagane and Dégé pondered the question faced by so many of their countrymen: where did their honour lie? Should they leave the boat and take up the fight in some other way, or stay with her? They chose the latter, and, forced to reduce their crew, picked the best of the volunteers.

LAGANE: From that moment on, the story of the *Iris* will wither as the months pass into the uninteresting narrative of 11 men and an immobilised boat, until hostilities end or, possibly, Spain enters the war.

Seen from the inside, it is an interminable wait on the part of a tiny band of bloody-minded men, forced to live from hand to mouth from one day to the next, abandoned by everyone in a magnificent piece of equipment which was now worthless because it was temporarily useless.

Two years without orders, without any communication from the Vichy French, from London or from Algiers to which accounts, requests and reports would be sent regularly. Without any wages during that time. Condemned to live by their wits, on the private charity of some French people and the kindness of Franco's navy – which had an ulterior motive behind it.

In fact, the Spanish authorities didn't miss an opportunity to remind us that they were always ready to facilitate voluntary repatriation to Paris, Algiers, Lisbon, Bern or Montevideo – and to take care of the submarine that they were lusting after.

In the course of those days in Spain, this marooned little crew racked up more than 20,000 hours of continuous guard duty on board, spent 8,000 hours painting and cleaning the boat, 30,000 hours on maintenance …

It filled its free time with physical activities on and around the boat … reading, learning Spanish, getting to grips with navigation and naval mathematics, tarot, dominoes, fishing, rat catching, cooking and coming up with cheap, tasty dishes, including the preparation of three hundred cats accompanied by every sauce imaginable.

3 December 1945

Thirty six months after her arrival in Spain, seven months after Germany threw in the towel and four months after the surrender of Japan, *Iris* regained her freedom after protracted inter-governmental negotiations. She sailed immediately with her stubborn skeleton crew who, next day and after a fifteen hour voyage without relief, were particularly proud to hand her over in pristine condition to the French authorities at Oran.

Fifteen submarines were scuttled at Toulon; the *Vénus* scuttled herself at the entrance to the harbour; *Marsouin* joined *Casabianca* at Algiers and *La Gloireux* reached Oran.

## INDIAN OCEAN AND PACIFIC

**Rear Admiral Corwin Mendenhall, US Navy, Retd**; from *Submarine Diary*

With Lieutenant Mendenhall in command, USS *Sculpin's* first patrol had taken her to Surabaya to be refitted by the Dutch; her second, beginning on 30 January 1942, took her into the Molucca Sea for a dramatic period among the Japanese transports and warships.

With all quiet and torpedo tubes reloaded, we surfaced just after midnight to find that we were right in the middle of a formation of destroyers.

By this time Jack Turner had relieved me as OOD, and we pulled clear on the surface, taking advantage of the rainstorms and the frequent lightning flashes that illuminated the enemy. We were still apparently undetected.

At 0100 we sent an urgent message to CSAF concerning the ships we had seen. A primary mission of this patrol was to inform CSAF promptly of any significant ship movements. The captain believed that this took priority over attacking the destroyers, because the Allied high command needed information on Japanese fleet movements to direct the actions on Java.

The night was far from over. At 0215 Jack sighted another formation, and *Sculpin* went to battle stations to begin a surface approach. This time one of the six destroyers saw us and forced us to dive.

He closed in as we were going down, and a string of eight depth charges exploded around us as we passed 225 feet, shaking the boat severely, breaking light bulbs, and causing numerous leaks and much other damage.

*Sculpin* plunged alarmingly down to a depth of 345 feet. The control room crew was dead silent, and all eyes were glued on the depth gauge. The rudder and the stern planes were jammed, making depth control very difficult. Sweating profusely, Jack managed to stabilize at 345 feet, far below the test depth of 250 feet, by holding a ten-degree up angle on the boat at two-thirds speed. Too much noise would be created if he pumped ballast to adjust the trim.

Painfully Jack worked *Sculpin* upward. When we finally reached test depth the rudder and planes worked normally. The sea pressure at 345 feet must have bound the shafts, causing the rudder and planes to be difficult to operate.

Jack was pleased to have the two-thirds speed to keep *Sculpin* from going any deeper and help move up to a safer depth, but he knew that at that speed we were making much too much noise. The commotion might draw the enemy to us with disastrous results, so it was imperative that *Sculpin* slow down as soon as possible. Some discreet pumping was done to adjust ballast.

While Jack was fighting to control the boat, an electrical fire broke out in the control room behind the interior communications (IC) switchboard, filling the control room with harsh black smoke that burned the eyes and made breathing difficult. The fire was quickly snuffed out with a $CO_2$ fire extinguisher, but the charred-rubber odor permeated the air. Investigation established that the fire was due to seawater coming down the multiple conductor cable to the port annunciator from a ruptured box on the bridge, allowing water to flow inside the cable to the IC board. That leak was quickly stopped.

The after engine room reported that their hatch had momentarily lifted and a small amount of water had come in there. Reports were coming in from throughout the boat of grounded circuits, broken gauges, and other damage. Charlie kept a list of the items as they were reported. I was at the TDC, ready to go where I might be needed.

Once ballast and trim were adjusted, Jack signaled the maneuvering room to slow to one-third speed. Maneuvering telephoned that they were unable to answer his order – the electrical controllers were jammed at two thirds and couldn't be shifted to any other position. Tension mounted. Everyone in the control room realized that the propellers had to be slowed in order to cut down noise and permit *Sculpin* to escape.

The Captain, Exec, Jack, and 'plank-owner' Chief Electrician's Mate John Pepersack conferred over the dilemma; then John ran aft to the maneuvering room to assess the situation. After a few minutes he returned to report that someone would have to enter the main electrical cubicle, a locked cage with DANGER signs posted all around it. Inside it were the bus bars that carried the ship's electric power, and through which power was transmitted to the main motors. No one was allowed to go inside without the captain's permission, and then only when the electric circuits were not energized.

After more discussion, Pepersack, insisting that he could safely remedy the controller problem, was given permission to go into the cubicle. The Exec relieved Jack as diving officer, and Jack went with Pepersack to the maneuvering room.

They unlocked the cage door and, with Jack aiming a battle lantern and ready to assist as best he could, Pepersack entered. He found that the depth charging had loosened a nut, which had fallen into the controller linkage and was jamming the controllers in the two-thirds speed position. His primary concern was to get to the dislodged nut without being electrocuted. With extreme caution he gingerly wriggled into position, removed the guilty nut, and restored the ability to vary the ship's speed.

A faint cheer and deep sighs of relief broke the tension in the control room when Jack telephoned to say that maneuvering could answer all bells. Smiles erased the distressed frowns, and eyes quickly turned from the depth gauges where they had been glued for an eternity. Jack returned to the control room and resumed his duty as diving officer.

During Jack's struggle with depth, speed, and damage control, the soundmen were busy following what they estimated to be at least eight destroyers, which were industriously charging around, pinging furiously, as *Sculpin* crept away. Through the noise, the soundmen could distinguish many heavy ships going south. Forty ships were counted moving out of Staring Bay. A major operation was in progress. The presence of that large force, with the water noise they generated, was of major assistance to *Sculpin*'s getaway. After things settled down, an inventory was made of damages. Not only were there broken light bulbs, shattered gauge glasses, and grounded circuits, but the entire torpedo firing system and the battle order transmitter were out of commission, and would be until we reached port. The transmitter cable had been pushed through the hull stuffing box, allowing water to enter the conning tower until the hole was plugged.

At sunrise all was quiet.

Pepersack was subsequently promoted to chief warrant electrician for that display of courage.

### Luitenant ter Zee 1 Aart Hopman, Koninklijke Marine, then Luitenant ter Zee 3, *K. XV*

Within a few weeks of my coming aboard the *K. XV* was used against the Japanese war machine, and between 7/8 December 1941 and the Xmas days the Dutch lost four submarines.

The *O-20*, cornered, tried to fight it out on the surface with a Jap destroyer. Later on we met two of the officers, who had escaped from the Japanese Prison camp in Hong Kong and with help from the Chinese moved to Chung King and so on to Colombo. The *O-16* and the *K. XVII* were lost on Japanese mines, laid in that area near Singapore, just before or on the day of 8 December 1941. The *K. XVI* belonged to our division operating near Kuching, North Borneo. The *K. XVI* torpedoed the first Japanese warship in the Pacific area, the *Sagiri*, but was torpedoed on the same day [Christmas 1941] by a Japanese submarine.

That was the situation in those days, but we were mostly unaware of what happened. Most news was gossip. Submarine service did not look a healthy occupation, but so what? Nothing could happen to us, and life in the Merchant Navy was just as dangerous, even if we heard the news by general word of mouth. We just accepted the situation.

We heard about the loss of these boats, four out of the fifteen available and of these fifteen, seven were older than the *K. XV* and three were never used against the Japanese Enemy. One of these was lost by a bomb anyway.

I would like to give an idea of how little we knew of what happened around us.

We were in February 1942 on patrol in the South China Sea, near Natuna Islands, north of Singapore – Singapore fell on 13 February 1942. We were called back to the Java area and arrived in the Sunda Straits area north of Bantam Bay, where we were under water in the morning of 28 February. We were discovered by the sonar of HMAS *Yarra* and her convoy. We exchanged recognition signals – *Yarra* was one day behind, but the answer was in my mind and worked. *Yarra* wished us 'Good hunting' and we submerged again. Shortly thereafter we were directed to Tandjung Priok to fuel and arrange food and water. We arrived in the early afternoon of this last day of February.

Perth and Houston were also in harbour, but left soon afterwards, unbeknown to me. *K. XV* was moored alongside the top between the first and second harbour to fuel and take water. I went – was sent – by taxi to the Navy Barracks in [now] Jakarta to arrange the food. It was a Saturday and a Chief PO was on duty. He could not help me and there was no one else available who could. I asked for the home address of the Commander and arrived there some time later. I was dressed in 'short whites' and had a light gun strapped.

A Commander in those days was to a subbie [sub-lieutenant] a rather odd person. They did not exist aboard the submarines and in general, a subbie kept 'out from under' that type of goldbraid [avoided such senior officers].

I reported that we were in Tandjung Priok and would like to be supplied with food. The Commander said that he was very busy and that I should return on Monday.

Well, that was enough. I could not argue with a man so high in rank and returned to my taxi back to Priok, but on Gunung Sahari Road near the bridge of Pasar Baru the taxi driver stopped and would not go any further. I paid the man and hailed another taxi, but the moment I said I wanted to go to Priok, that driver also refused. There I was stuck.

I was lucky. Whilst standing there in my short whites, and the evening was falling, a European stopped his car and asked me if he could help me.

Well, I was sitting next to him before he knew it, and said: 'Yes, I have to go to Priok.'

He said: 'Oh No,' but I said: 'Either you go, or I'll take the car.'

Anyway we travelled to Priok and all the time he asked me if I did not think I was far enough. In the neighbourhood of the station of Priok, I got out of his car and said, 'Thank you very much'. But he was gone so quick, that I am still amazed if I think about it.

Of course I still did not have an inkling of the reason of my transport troubles.

From the station I walked in the falling tropical darkness of a deserted harbour, not a soul around. I walked through the open gates of the 'Harbour Authority', the gates swinging and squeaking in the evening wind. I walked on to the second harbour and towards the head of the harbour, where I expected the *K. XV* to be fastened to the jetty and hoped to feel safe again amongst my fellow mates.

I came to the head of the harbour and there was no submarine. My heart dropped somewhere down into my shoes.

Loneliness in distress is real loneliness.

I looked around in the darkness and saw a bollard with the ropes around.

The *K. XV* had submerged alongside the jetty, and I sat on the bollard and waited and waited and thought and thought. The proverb says 'shared pleasure is double pleasure and shared pain is only half the pain'. About two hours later the submarine surfaced and I reported back aboard.

The Captain asked me: 'Where is the food?', and I said the Commander said that I should come back on Monday.

The Captain did not comment and told me to go and sleep to be ready for the Morning Watch on the first of March, the day that the Japs landed in Bantam Bay. A day that *Houston*, *Perth* and *Evertsen* were lost against the Japs, and we got a memorable hammering for attacking that landing force.

### Torpedoman Bill Grieves, US Navy, USS *Thresher*

The sea was calm off Tokyo Bay that morning. Through the periscope, the skipper sighted a freighter with one destroyer escort coming out the channel. The date was April 10, 1942 and the skipper was Commander Bill Anderson.

It was *Thresher's* (SS 200) third war patrol. We conducted the approach and in due course fired one fish with the torpedo depth set to pass beneath the keel. When the magnetic exploder detonated the warhead, the 3,039-ton *Sado Maru* was blown into two sections. She sank in two minutes. But the destroyer, following the torpedo wakes, was right on top of us. The first depth charges were close aboard our stern and drove us down to 410 feet. This was well below *Thresher's* test depth. Hanging, as if suspended, down by the stern, the planesmen fought to regain our lost trim. Slowly we struggled back up to 350 feet and as sea pressure decreased, the hull cracked loudly as if being struck by shell fire as the pressure hull regained its configuration.

---

Then a more ominous problem became evident. The severe concussion had knocked the port propeller shaft out of alignment, causing the boat to fish-tail wildly. This set up loud vibrations throughout the boat. In the torpedo room, cans of food, stowed in the frame spaces behind the reload torpedoes, sprang loose and crashed against the reload racks. In the engine room, a heavy wrench suspended on the side of a locker set up a loud drum-like thumping. In every compartment men pounced on the sources to eliminate the noise, but we couldn't find them all. When power was placed on the port shaft the noise was intolerable. But without the port screw, depth control was impossible. Then two more destroyers joined the hunt.

In the hours that followed, the destroyers trailed tenaciously. Whenever we came up above 300 feet, depth charges drove us back down. At 11:30 that night, after 14 hours under attack and 18 hours submerged, the oxygen content in the boat was perilously low. Normal breathing was in deep, rapid gasps and our depleted batteries were running critical. An air of hopeless resignation settled over the crew.

It was then Captain Anderson made a precarious decision. He ordered a 180 degree course change back toward Tokyo. This was closely followed by, 'All ahead full – surface!' As we came up past 300, depth charges rained down close aboard on all sides violently rocking the boat. But, miraculously, we came up through them. We broke the surface 500 yards astern of the closest destroyer which was playing the water with powerful search lights. But a submarine in a low, flooded down condition upon surfacing and one that is going away has a very narrow silhouette. And the sea was so filled with depth charge echoes, the sound of our screws went unnoticed. When we were clear, four engines were placed on the line and from the horizon we could see the sweeping search-lights and hear the probing pings of their sonars as they echo-ranged on an empty ocean.

*Thresher* was severely damaged. Another attack was out of the question and we should be heading for the barn, but we had another mission. Just at that time Lieutenant-Colonel James Doolittle with a force of sixteen B-25 bombers aboard two aircraft carriers and escorted by a fleet of four cruisers and eight destroyers known as 'Doolittle's Raiders' was heading for Tokyo. Sea and weather reports were needed constantly. On April 18 and about 550 miles off the coast the bombers took to the air. They arrived over Tokyo about noon. We were submerged at the horizon.

That night we came to the surface and three men at a time were allowed to come up to the 'cigarette deck' and view the scene before us. I stood there amazed and immeasurably accelerated. The entire city appeared to be ablaze from one end to the other with flames shooting high into the heavens. For those of us who had witnessed Pearl Harbor it was the most moving and exciting scene we had ever seen in our lives.

The crew was worn out from the long attack at Tokyo harbor but now the exhaustion was forgotten and a jubilant up-beat spirit took over for several days. When we limped into Pearl we were immediately placed into dry dock. Both sides of the hull were dented in and rippled like a wash board. A strip 100 feet long and 6 feet wide was replaced on the starboard side and a strip 60 feet long and 6 feet wide was replaced on the port side. The propeller shaft was replaced.

Many of our boats had exciting stories to tell of patrols in WW II. But the *Thresher's* (SS-200) story was unique. No submarine in history ever went through an attack like *Thresher's* fourth war patrol. [26 June to 15 August, commanded by Lieutenant-Commander W. J. Millican.]

On the day of departure from Pearl, we picked up our escort, the old 'four-pipe' destroyer, *Litchfield*, in the harbour and following closely in her wake we transited the channel and the minefield and turned west toward the Marshall Islands. In due course we passed Midway Island and the International Date Line and approached the Marshalls at the island of Maloelap. The first day on station the skipper, Commander Bill Millican, sighted a four ship convoy coming through the channel. But the last ship in line was a tanker and, in compliance with orders by COMSUBPAC to sink the tankers first, we let the first three go by and fired two fish at the tanker ... one hit. She burst into flames and sank in two minutes. The escort attacked and dropped nineteen charges during the next couple hours but we surfaced after sundown and escaped in the darkness.

The next day we approached the Island of Kwajalein submerged through a pass called Gea Pass. Gea Pass is good submarine water. The pass is deep and wide enough to maneuver in and we had learned that Kwajalein was now the eastwardmost naval base of the Japanese navy. We could just picture a nice big aircraft carrier or a big, fat battleship. To hell with these tankers, we wanted a man-o-war. Throughout the day the skipper sighted several ships through the periscope including three 'I-boats' (Japanese submarines) but none came within torpedo range. At sundown, we surfaced but remained in the pass.

As dawn approached, the batteries were charged and the cooks had finished their baking in time for the ovens to cool down. We dove just before sunrise. It was about 0800 hours and the skipper raised the periscope for his regular sweep when he was momentarily blinded by a flash of white light through the scope. When his eyes became accustomed to the light he could see it was the sun gleaming off the side of a brand new ship. Her decks were lined with

Japanese sailors in white uniforms. Great! A navy ship! She was the 4,836-ton Motor Torpedo Boat Tender, *Shinsho Maru*. She was steering a straight course without escorts! The sky above was dotted with aircraft, but a ship, holding her course and speed and without escorts, which comes within a submarine's torpedo range is dead meat! The set-up was perfect.

The skipper took his first bearings: 'Range, 7000 yards ... angle on the bow, 5 degrees starboard ... estimated speed, 12 knots. Down scope!' Now, this was the way a torpedo approach was made: the periscope was raised for only a few seconds because it left a white 'feather' on the surface which could give our position away. And we knew there were lookouts on the flying bridge of that target, sweeping the water with binoculars, looking for periscopes. So a torpedo approach consisted of a series maybe 12 or 15 ... sometimes more depending on the chase ... very brief bearings until the skipper could determine the exact course, range and speed of the target. These factors were then fed into the torpedo data computer in the conning tower together with our own course and speed and the torpedo speed. The computer then transmitted the proper angles to the gyro regulator between the tubes and from there to the gyros of the torpedoes in the tubes. As the target drew near, these angles gradually reduced to zero. The torpedo could be fired as much as 160 degrees to port or starboard, but the ideal shot, to avoid error, was a straight bow shot at zero degrees. In the torpedo room we knew exactly when we would fire.

As the target came within range we were ordered to make tubes three and four ready for firing. I had the starboard bank and went to work on number three while my buddy, Charlie Fry, made ready number four. In short order we raised the ready-to-fire levers giving them the light in the conning tower. As the target angle approached zero the skipper ordered, 'Final bearing and shoot! Up scope!' He zeroed the periscope on the target, checked the azimuth overhead, and said, 'Stand by three!' Then: 'Fire three' and five seconds later by the skipper's wrist watch: 'Fire Four!' The boat shuddered with the recoil. In the torpedo room we listened in dead silence as the fish sped down the track.

But the torpedoes were not set to strike the target. They were set to pass beneath the target. Because the exploder on the Mark XIV torpedo contained a magnetic feature which, when the torpedo passed within the magnetic proximity of the hull, detonated the warhead at the ship's most vulnerable point, her keel. Salt water is incompressible and an underwater explosion can only go one way, STRAIGHT UP!

The wait was short because the range was under a thousand yards and then BLOOM! And five seconds later BLOOM! Two hits! The first fish passed directly beneath the bridge and when 600 pounds of Torpex exploded, it blew the entire bow off the ship. The second fish passed beneath her quarter and blew the stern off. Within two or three minutes the three sections sank beneath the surface in a huge cloud of steam. Breaking up noises were clearly audible for some time as *Shinsho Maru's* watertight compartments ruptured. Where the ship had been the water came alive with white uniforms of survivors.

The skipper knew that somebody would be coming out to rescue those sailors and when they did, we would be here to meet them.

We were cruising slowly at periscope depth, the scope was down, the boat was silent when suddenly the loudest, most violent explosion we had ever heard went off right beneath our bow! We were rudely reminded of a basic fact of modern warfare ... aircraft carry depth charges too, but we were lucky.

Where the charge went off right beneath the bow, the configuration of the hull is very narrow. Most of the charge passed us and went to the surface. Had the charge exploded five seconds later beneath the for'd battery or control room *Thresher* would have been history.

The bow erupted with such violence that men sitting on the bunks were lifted clear of the bunks. Men standing back aft were thrown to the deck and Charlie and I grabbed on to our tubes and hung on. The order came out almost immediately: 'All ahead full! Depth, 300! All compartments check for damages!'

I checked my starboard bank and the bilge, Charlie checked the port bank, other guys checked the Pitometer Log well and the sound heads ... no damage. The man on the phones: 'For'd room to control, no damage in the for'd room.' The report, or so we thought then.

What we didn't know was this: the Mark XIV torpedo weighs 3,421 pounds and leaves the tube at 47 knots. It receives this impetus from 400 pounds of air stored in impulse bottles located in the superstructure above the tubes. And when the charge went off, the seal to No. 1 impulse bottle was cracked. *Thresher* was laying a brilliant stream of bubbles on the surface of Gea Pass and we didn't know it. We were at 300 feet, well out of visual range of the aircraft but the depth charges followed. Then sonar picked up the sound of three sets of screws coming off the beach.

Unerringly the destroyers homed in on our wake. As the captain gave orders to evade and try to get us out of the channel and into the ocean, the depth charges followed relentlessly. But then, amazingly, all depth charging ceased. We knew they had a dead fix on our position and our depth and yet the sea was dead quiet. The ominous silence continued for some time.

We were at 300 feet, running silent, when suddenly the silence was broken by a loud 'clanking' noise moving aft down the starboard side of the hull: 'CLANK ... CLANK ... CLUNK, CLUNK ... CLANK!' The man on the phones: 'For'd room to control, we are experiencing a loud clanking noise moving aft down the starboard side!' The message was repeated by each compartment, and then it was gone. What now?

It was the planesmen who discovered we were not out of trouble. The stern was rising appreciably and they were losing their bubble and there was nothing they could do to stop it. Then came the realization: we were hooked by a large grapnel into the starboard stern plane guard and we were being brought up, stern first.

The boat displaced 1,500 tons on the surface, but submerged it had a neutral buoyancy, neither heavy nor light. A relatively small ship can bring a submarine to the surface.

The Captain's first order was to pour more power to the screws. He ordered: 'Rudder amidships! Full dive on the planes! All ahead full!' The power hit the screws and the boat began to vibrate ... and vibrate ... and vibrate. No change ... the grapnel held fast. Then: 'All stop!' With such extravagant expenditure of amperage the batteries could not last long. The next order was to add more weight to the stern. In the series of orders that followed, After Trim tank was flooded from the sea, then After WRT tank was flooded from the sea, then the after torpedo room bilges were flooded to the deck plates. We took on tons of ballast with no slowing in the rise. Then we passed 250 feet.

As time slowly passed the Captain tried every maneuver he could think of to get us off the grapnel, but *Thresher* continued to rise inexorably. When we passed 100 feet it became apparent we were going to lose our boat. The Captain gave the order for the radiomen to demolish all decoding equipment. They went to work with sledge hammers and the pounding could be heard all over the boat. Then he ordered the gunner's mates to the torpedo rooms to position the demolition charges for scuttling.

Each torpedo room carried a 55lb charge of TNT which, when placed between the warheads of the re-load torpedoes and detonated would obliterate both these compartments and, hopefully, that SOB who was pulling us up. But as we placed the charges it was recognized that for our *Thresher* crew, there would be no survivors. But there was no objection to this. Some of the men bowed their heads in prayer. Wes Headington stood up and came over to me and as I stood up we shook hands, eye-to-eye, no words, but the silence was eloquent ... 'It was good sailing with you.' No one spoke, only quiet resignation.

I don't know how deep we were then, our periscopes must have been very close to the surface, then the Captain tried one last desperate manoeuvre. He ordered Forward Trim flooded from After Trim. The down angle, already steep, now became steeper. Then he ordered: 'Left full rudder! All ahead emergency! 'The power hit the screws with a shudder! The boat heaved slightly into a port list, and then, incredibly, we were off the hook! But why? Did the grapnel cable part? Did the manoeuvre cause the stem plane guard to lift off the hook? Nobody knows the answer, but with the extra ballast and steep down angle, we headed for the bottom. 'Blow Bow Buoyancy!' came the order, and as 3,000lb. of air hit the forward tank, the bow heaved upward and we were saved from striking the bottom. For the next several minutes all concern for silent running was disregarded as tons of ballast were pumped and blown overboard to regain our lost trim and the depth charges rained down.

We remained at 300 feet maneuvering evasively until the sun went down and they could no longer see the bubbles ... or possibly they ran out, and sometime after dark we surfaced, chased by the destroyers. But we eluded them in the darkness. We had taken 41 depth charges.

We continued the patrol past Truk Atoll, then Yap and Palau then turned south across the Equator, through the Dutch East Indies to the Indian Ocean and we made port in Fremantle, Western Australia. We had made two more attacks but with no success: shallow waters, torpedo trouble.

Captain Millican made four more runs with us, earning two Navy Crosses for the tonnage we sank and the first submarine mine plant of the war. Then he was relieved and transferred back to the States to take command of the new *Escolar*. He took several *Thresher* officers and key enlisted men with him.

In time, *Escolar* went into commission and joined the Pacific fleet at Pearl Harbor. Their first war patrol was to the Yellow Sea off the coast of China. We know she arrived on station but then nothing was heard from *Escolar* again. She was lost with all hands on her first run. Our crew was deeply saddened when we learned this.

But that's the way it was then. Some of us made a lot of war patrols, I made thirteen, and when we came into port from many of these, the message was the same, overdue and presumed lost. One or more of our boats failed to return, some on their very first run.

### Yoshio Uchikado, Imperial Japanese Navy

*RO-61* was sunken by an American boat [31 August 1942] and most of the crew died because of the icy water. I was one of the five survivors picked up by American. I still remember that icy water. I became unconscious because I thought my heart stopped. I spent four years in US prisons as a prisoner of the war. I think I did my part in serving my country. I did it more for my family's honor than the love for my country. However, it still gives me a lot of pain when I think of many comrades who died so young.

# 1943

During 1943, German shipyards were turning out significant numbers of U-boats for the Atlantic campaign. More than 300,000 tons of shipping were lost in February alone. The tally for March was over half a million tons. But the April figure was half that, as Allied tactics improved, and in May the Battle of the Atlantic turned in favour of the Allies. A major weakness of the convoy system had been the 'Atlantic Gap', the area to the south of Greenland that lacked air cover. After the heavy losses of March the Americans deployed very long-range Liberators to bases such as Newfoundland. 'Huff-Duff' now allowed Allied escorts to pinpoint a transmitting U-boat; the new centimetric radar could pick up enemy submarines on the surface (and without the target being able to detect it), just as Asdic found them underwater, and aircraft – either launched from merchant ships converted to aircraft carriers or flown from British or US bases – could spot them with search-lights and radar. The British had developed a new A/S weapon – the Hedgehog – that proved far more effective than the depth charge. It threw a cluster of 24 contact-fuzed projectiles, each containing 30 or 35lb of explosive, well ahead of the destroyer on which the launcher was mounted. They landed in a roughly oval shape, covering a sufficiently wide area to enable at least one to hit the quarry, and because they went off on contact rather than at a predetermined depth, going deep was no defence against them. Escorts, too, hunted in packs, and powerful Admiralty tugs could bring home damaged merchantmen that might otherwise have been sunk. In consequence, 242 German submarines were lost in all theatres, almost three times as many as the previous year and seven times the figure for 1941. Such losses could not be replaced quickly enough, and even if they could, submariners were also being killed – over 10,000 in 1943 alone – leaving new, inexperienced crews conscripted to take their place. Nevertheless, the U-boats fought back tenaciously and making use of new technology such as the Federapparat or FAT torpedo. It was, however, becoming a vain campaign: the critical ratio of Allied tonnage sunk to Allied tonnage launched was running against the Axis.

Although the Allies had largely contained the threat posed by the German battleship *Tirpitz* by confining her to Norwegian bases, her presence and occasional sorties constituted a constant drain on resources, and in September 1943 the first secret operation to destroy her, codenamed 'Source', was carried out by British midget submarines. The operation was partially successful, putting the ship *hors de combat* for several months.

Allied landings in Sicily, commencing in July and codenamed Operation 'Husky', led to an Allied armistice with Italy in September. Allied submarines were active in supporting the landings and helping to round up individual units of the Italian fleet. German forces seized what warships they could before the Italian commanders put to sea to surrender to the Allies. A handful of crews declared loyalty to the Germans and/or to the fascist Repubblica Sociale Italiana when that was subsequently proclaimed.

Allied submarines in the Mediterranean subsequently found themselves carrying on spirited operations in the Aegean as the emphasis shifted towards disrupting the German presence in Greece and the islands. For one French submarine came the chance to play a leading part in liberating the first part of France: the island of Corsica. Increasingly, however, a number of the larger British T- and S-Class were redeployed together with Dutch submarines to the Indian Ocean to oppose the Japanese and German submarines who were successfully raiding merchant shipping. The Dutch in particular became heavily involved in the landing, supplying and retrieving of agents.

At a conference in Casablanca in January the Allies had thrashed out a coherent policy aimed at attacking the Solomons and pushing on, eventually, to the Philippines. The Japanese failure to defeat the US Navy in the Pacific during surface fleet engagements had now concentrated the Far East conflict into a series of struggles for individual islands, particularly in the Solomons, with both sides having to maintain their supply lines across thousands of miles of ocean. In February the codebook was captured from *I-1*, soon allowing the US to decrypt Japanese transmissions, and Japan was also forced to evacuate her forces from the strategic Solomon island of Guadacanal. Rather than trying to retake some of the most heavily defended Japanese-controlled islands such as Rabaul, the Allies – primarily the US – leapfrogged them, the strategy being neutralisation through the stopping of supplies rather than bloody fighting.

To the list of dead submarine aces that included Wanklyn and Prien was added that of the US Navy's Lieutenant-Commander Dudley Morton, whose first patrol as commander of the USS *Wahoo* resulted in eight sinkings at the start of the year but who was lost in October. It was Morton's experience with torpedoes that finally led to the deactivation – at least for the boats based at Pearl Harbor – of the faulty magnetic exploders that had plagued US submarines. This merely exposed problems with the contact exploders, but in the autumn the trouble was over, and, in addition, electric torpedoes were now being issued.

By the end of the year aircraft, surface ships and submarines had sunk more merchant shipping than Japan could hope to replace, forcing the Japanese high command to admit to their emperor what had been evident after their failure at Midway the previous year: the war was unwinnable. Given that their strategy required long supply lines, their slowness to build escort carriers in the run up to the war implies that they had no conception that merchant ships would become prime targets in unrestricted submarine warfare.

## ATLANTIC

### Comandante Mario Rossetto, Regia Marina, *Giuseppe Finzi*

Like their German counterparts, Italian submarines were also operating much farther afield in the Atlantic, and required re-supplying. The *Giuseppe Finzi* was despatched with orders to proceed at a moderate speed to ensure she had sufficient fuel not just for her own patrol but in order to transfer a quantity to the *Leonardo Da Vinci*. At 28, Rossetto was the youngest Italian commander to serve in the Atlantic.

While commanding the *Giuseppe Finzi* I received the order to transport a full load (fuel, torpedoes, food, etc.) to re-supply the submarine *Leonardo Da Vinci*, Capitano Gazzana-Priaroggia, off the Cape of Good Hope. She was bound for the Indian Ocean. Early on the night of 18 March 1943, while I was proceeding to the rendezvous, which was fixed at 0800 the following day, I observed a ship steering directly toward my boat. To avoid compromising my mission, I was under orders 'not to attack', but the occasion was too inviting and I decided to disobey.

I manoeuvred, ready to fire when the ship came in range. Unfortunately the attack failed because she sighted my boat and, above all, because faults caused two of our torpedoes to go astray. The ship fired back several times without hitting, and I was obliged to submerge, regretting my disobedience. Even while we were submerged she tried to attack us, dropping several depth-charges, without success, before taking flight.

I changed my mind once again and, surfacing after a few minutes, went in pursuit of the ship, which was going at full speed. My maximum speed was perhaps a little lower, but my target was zigzagging and I could slowly approach. The ship's direction was exactly opposite to the course I was supposed to be following to reach the supplying point, and to which Da Vinci was committed to follow for the same reason.

So happened that, at 10.30 p.m., I saw *Da Vinci* at a short distance to starboard (what a piece of luck!), and proceeding in the opposite direction. I wanted us to be recognised, but without making the kind of signals that would have been too obvious to the ship to port. *Da Vinci* answered my signal with a big searchlight, which I attempted to make her put out. Holding my course, I attempted to explain the situation to Gazzana, but the signalmen (of both submarines!) did not understand anything. Only after 10 minutes Gazzana and I could communicate, when *Da Vinci* was able to come alongside *Finzi* because both her engines gave up simultaneously (I had asked too much of them).

Gazzana told me that he had not been able to decide whether the submarine he had seen racing at high speed in the opposite direction, away from the rendezvous point, really was the *Finzi*. Because of his doubts he had ordered the gun to be prepared, loaded and aimed. If I had done anything that might have been interpreted as hostile, he was ready to open fire on me. Then, when he saw me stop he was able to approach and ask me what was going on. I gave him all the information he needed to close down the ship I had been chasing and in a few hours he had caught and sunk it.

Next day, during the transfer of supplies, Gazzana told me the steamer's name: *Lulworth Hill*.

After the war, I found out the name of the British corvette which had sunk our submarine, *Pietro Calvi*. The captain of the *Calvi*, who went down with the boat, was Capitano di Fregatto Primo Longobardo, who, the year before, had been the Director of the Scuola Sommergibili at the time when I had been there. I'd always had a lot of respect for him, and kept a grateful memory. When I found out that the name of the corvette was *Lulworth* I confess to having felt satisfaction at having made a vital contribution towards the sinking of a ship which had – almost – the same name.

On 20 March 1943, after we had finished re-supplying the *Da Vinci* and just before we resumed our course for Betasom, Commander Gazzana transferred to the *Finzi* a survivor from the *Lulworth Hill*. His name was Leslie James Hull, born 1910 at Newcastle upon Tyne.

Three days later, we received a telegram from Betasom for one of our crew: 'For Secondo Capo Monzo: I am pleased to inform you that your wife has launched a little submarine with a periscope. Mother and baby are well. Many congratulations'.

On the early afternoon of 28 March, having spotted the smoke of a steamer, I set about pursuing it, and the upshot was the torpedoing and sinking of the Greek steamer *Granikos* in the early night.

Throughout the long operation the shipwrecked prisoner had been sitting on a bench in the electric motor room where he remained quietly the whole time. He could not understand the orders that were being passed down from the bridge but he soon worked out the gist of them, and above all the result, when he saw that another survivor had been brought on board: this was a Portuguese chap called Joaquim Rodriguez.

The following day, again in the early afternoon, there was a new sighting. And so at night, 29 March, and after ten hours and more of exhausting chase off the Liberian coast, I sank British steamship *Celtic Star*. The crew escaped in three lifeboats, and I approached the nearest, to get information about the ship's name and nationality. Then I asked whether they had on board either the captain or some officer (to be taken prisoner): obviously the answer was 'No.' Then I said I had to take somebody prisoner. At once a young sailor stood up saying, 'I'll come.'

I again asked the survivors on the boat if they needed something. They replied that they were in good physical condition and they requested only cigarettes. I did not smoke, but I had my personal allowance and I gave it to the survivors. I think that was the only time English people asked (and got) cigarettes from Italians!

When he was on board I asked the prisoner (a Canadian sailor, George Pattinson born 25.12.1920) why he volunteered himself. He replied: 'This is the third (or fourth) time I've had to take to the lifeboats; every time, I've been rescued, taken back, put on another ship, torpedoed again, put into the lifeboats again, rescued again and taken back again. I am tired of being a survivor!'

Since the beginning of the action, my other two prisoners had been sitting on that bench in the electric motor room. They couldn't talk to one another because each of them only spoke his own language. But even if he couldn't understand the orders coming from the bridge the Englishman could tell what was happening, and at the moment of the attack he knew how it would end. And so, without saying anything, he dug the Portuguese man in the ribs, inviting him to move up and make another place. He realised that a new 'companion' was about to arrive.

Also transferred to the *Giuseppe Finzi* was S.T. Physician Vittorio Del Vecchio, an Italian doctor and Italian POW, saved after the *Leonardo Da Vinci* torpedoed and sank the British liner, *Empress of Canada*, on 14 March. The ship had been carrying 3,000 British soldiers and 500 POWs. In all there were some 390 casualties. Of the *Lulworth Hill's* fourteen other survivors only two were picked up alive from their raft. Two died when the *Celtic Star* was torpedoed. *Finzi* returned to Bordeaux on 18 April with enough fuel for a mere 70 further miles.

**Oberleutnant zur See Hartwig Looks, Kriegsmarine, commanding *U-264*;** from *The World At War*, Thames Television, 1972

*U-264* was one of 28 U-boats making up the Fink group, which launched an attack on the 42 ships of convoy ONS.5. One ship, a straggler, was sunk on 29 April; the main attack began on 4 May.

As far as I can remember, I was under way with Submarine *264* since 8 April 1943 and at the beginning of May I was positioned in line of reconnaissance to find one of your convoys coming over from the States to Great Britain, but this group was not successful in finding this [expected] convoy. Instead of this I got contact with one British … destroyer proceeding with high speed in a south-westerly direction … I was on the surface at that time and this destroyer didn't notice me or did not get contact with me, and after this destroyer disappeared I tried to find any sound bearing. I submerged and I was successful in having one bearing of a noise which couldn't belong to the destroyer …

So I surfaced again and proceeded in the direction of this bearing, and just before dusk I was successful in finding a convoy proceeding in a south-west-erly direction, too. And it was not really the convoy which we expected, but another convoy going over to the States, and the weather was not very conve-nient – we had rather rough sea – but we tried to close in to the convoy and fight off the heavy sea. And we could do it: we could come closer and when it was night, during the dark time, we closed up to 5,000 metres and we could see the whole convoy proceeding in three or four columns (I don't exactly know). And on the portside, where I was proceeding at the time, we sighted two escort vessels, smaller destroyers also, and I tried to find a good position … for attacking the convoy. And it was a bit difficult due to the bad weather because our binoculars were absolutely wet from the overcoming sea and from the over-coming waves, and so we had to give the binoculars into the conning tower (you see, the watch of the submarine was standing on top of the conning tower and we gave the binoculars down and they were cleaned there and they gave them back to us, and so we could see for two or three other minutes, and then we have to do the same because the binoculars were wet again). But after a while I had a good position for attacking and I had the chance to slip through a gap just through two escort vessels and I could close into the portside column, and I had the chance to fire four torpedoes …

I torpedoed two ships, each with two torpedoes, and one of the ships, well, it didn't explode, but after the explosion of the torpedoes another big explo-sion happened on board of the ship. Perhaps the boiler also exploded, and in our glasses during the dark night we could observe that this ship was sinking very quickly … then I turned around with the submarine to fire the stern torpedo, but this torpedo had a malfunction and it ran straight on the surface with a big, white, shining [track] against the target ship but as it didn't run with exact speed – much slower than expected – this torpedo passed the target ship behind the stern and came into the second column of the convoy and hit there another steamer. But I couldn't observe any result, just the explosion of the torpedo, because at that time one of the escort vessels certainly picked me up and got contact with me, and so I was forced to submerge and get out of the way. This escort vessel depth charged me for some minutes and then joined the convoy, and I had the chance to recharge two of the torpedo tubes in the bow of the boat. After about one hour I submerged again and proceeded into the last bearing of the convoy where the convoy disappeared and I was once more successful to get contact with the convoy ...

I proceeded on the portside of the convoy to a position where I had the chance to attack the convoy, and once more I was lucky by slipping through a gap between two of the escort vessels and closing into the port column of the convoy, and I fired two torpedoes and both torpedoes hit the target ship. And then the escort vessel was alerted and closed in about 1,000 metres distance. I had to disappear. I got once more depth charges for about one hour without hitting me, but this happened just before dawn, so I had no chance to find the convoy once more during the dark time ...

Looks regained contact with the convoy, but his second approach was thwarted by dense fog and the likelihood of being run down by the escorts. Wisely, he returned to base. Although 13 merchant ships were sunk, two of them by Looks, the pack lost six boats to the determined escorts. The battle for the 43 merchantmen of Convoy ONS.5 (Outward North Atlantic Slow Convoy Five) – and it was a battle of epic proportions against several wolfpacks – became a triumph for the eight ships of Escort Group B7 under Commander Peter Gretton, RN, and a catastrophe for the U-boats. A seventh U-boat foundered trying to get home; a number of others were badly damaged.

### Oberleutnant zur See Herbert Werner, Executive Officer, Kriegsmarine, U-230; from Iron Coffins

U-230 left Brest on 24 April bound for a central Atlantic sector. During the early days of May, she intercepted a number of alarming distress signals from damaged and sinking U-boats that had attacked Convoy ONS.5. On the 11th it was her own turn to experience at first hand that the world was changing.

I was in the conning tower as the alarm bell sounded the call to action. Five, minutes later the boat was properly trimmed and floated just below the surface. The Captain, seated at the scope, informed the crew over our intercom system,

'We have sighted an extremely large convoy, probably over one hundred vessels. We shall attack submerged. I need not remind you that this is no holiday cruise. I expect your utmost effort to make this attack a success.' Then he activated the motor of the scope.

07.05: No visible contact yet. Siegmann ordered all tubes prepared for firing.

07.10: I reported U-230 combat-ready as the convoy's thumping roar spread through the depths.

07.16: The soundman conveyed news that ruined our plan for a submerged assault: 'Convoy apparently has changed course. Sound band changed to three-one-oh.'

The Captain, visibly annoyed over the unexpected change, raised the scope farther into the air to catch a view of the parading fleet. The high-pitched spinning of escorts' propellers echoed through the water, and the grinding noise of the huge armada hit our hull like the beating of countless jungle drums.

'Damn dirty trick,' muttered Siegmann. 'The convoy zigzags to the north-east. There are at least a dozen corvettes spread over its starboard side.'

The convoy steamed away at eleven knots while *U-230* floated undetected by the outer defence, unwilling to attack till she had passed through the cordon of destroyers. The rhythmical thrashing of a hundred propellers pene-trated the heavy steel of our hull and bounced forth and back inside the boat. The Captain relinquished his seat at the scope, snarling, 'Come over here, Exec, take a look. If I only had a faster boat I could roll up the convoy like a carpet.'

I swung into the seat. Seven miles on port I saw an amazing panorama. The entire horizon, as far and wide as I could see, was covered with vessels, their funnels and masts as thick as a forest. At least a dozen fast destroyers cut the choppy green sea with elegance. As many as two dozen corvettes flitted around the edges of the convoy. I said in awe, 'Quite a display of power, sir. It's probably the largest convoy ever.'

'You might be right. Once we are close to that wall of ships our torpedoes can't miss.'

Before we could risk surfacing to race into a new attack position, we had to put distance between us and the convoy. The swishing of propellers, the pounding of piston engines, the singing of turbines, and the chirping of Asdic pings accompanied us on our clandestine run. For almost two hours we trav-elled diagonally away from the giants of steel.

09.15: *U-230* surfaced. Mounting the bridge while the deck was still awash, I took a hurried look in a circle. Far to the north-east, mastheads and funnels moved along the sharp line which divided the ocean from the sky. *U-230* forged through the sea, parallel to the convoy's track, in an attempt to reach a forward position before dusk. Riedel flashed the message of our contact to Headquar-ters and the other wolves in ambush: CONVOY BD 92 COURSE NORTH-EAST ELEVEN KNOTS. STRONG DEFENCE. REMAIN SURFACED FOR ATTACK. *U-230*.

09.55: A startled cry at my back, 'Flugzeug!'

I saw a twin-engined plane dropping out of the sun. The moment of surprise was total.

'Alarrrmmm!' We plunged head over heels into the conning tower. The boat reacted at once and shot below the surface. At this moment of our maximum danger and minimum ability to act, our lives depended upon a miracle, an accident, or the good luck that had so far saved us from extinction.

Four short, ferocious explosions shattered the water above and around us. The boat trembled and fell at a sixty-degree angle. Water splashed, steel shrieked, ribs moaned, valves blew, deck plates jumped, and the boat was thrown into darkness. As the lights flickered on, I saw astonishment in the round eyes of the men. They had every right to be astounded: the attack out of the sun was a complete mystery. Where had the small plane come from? It did not have the range to fly a round trip between the nearest point of land and the middle of the Atlantic. The conclusion was inescapable that the convoy launched its own aeroplanes. It seemed highly likely, though we did not want to believe it, that the planes returned to the convoy and landed on an aircraft carrier. The idea of a convoy with its own air defence smashed our basic concept of U-boat warfare. No longer could we mount a surprise attack or escape without meeting savage counterattacks.

10.35: *U-230* came up to periscope depth. A careful check with our 'sky scope', an instrument similar to the periscope, revealed no aircraft. We surfaced at high speed.

The hunt went on. We pressed forward obstinately, with that terrible constriction in the stomach. The diesels hammered hard and pushed the boat swiftly ahead. I glanced only occasionally at the dense picket fence along the horizon and concentrated on the sky. Thickening white clouds scudded along at medium height under a stiff breeze from the west. The wind pitched the water up on deck and once in a while blew a sheet of spray across the bridge.

11.10: I detected a glint of metal between the clouds. It was a small aircraft, and it was diving into the attack.

'Alarrrmmm!'

Fifty seconds later, four explosions nearby taught us that the pilot was a well-trained bombardier. Shock waves rocked boat and crew. Friedrich, struggling to prevent the boat from sinking, caught her at 180 metres, balanced her out, and brought her up to periscope depth.

11.25: *U-230* surfaced. We drove forward and clung to the fringes of the convoy with grim determination. Instinct forced us ahead, kept us moving despite the constant threat from above, made us numb to the repetitious detonations. We raced in defiance of fear and sudden destruction – always forward, towards the head of the convoy.

11.42: 'Aircraft – alarrrmmm!'

*U-230* plunged into the depths. Four booms twisted the hull, but the boat survived the savage blows. We waited for the plane to disappear with our hearts beating under our tongues.

12.04: We surfaced in an increasingly choppy sea and surged ahead, the boat jolting and shaking. The convoy had slipped into a north-westerly position, and despite our constant harassment we had gained considerable headway on it. I spotted the escorts on the horizon but the real danger lurked above. The clouds had lowered and thickened, covering the last patches of blue sky.

12.08: A call from below reached us on the bridge. 'Message for Captain, signal just received: ATTACKED BY AIRCRAFT. SINKING. *U-89*.' Again we were stunned. With a shudder, I pictured what would happen to us, once our own hull was cracked.

12.17: 'Aircraft dead astern, alarrrmmm!'

*U-230* dived once more and descended rapidly. I bit my lip and waited for the final blast. At forty-five seconds, four booms ripped the boat with violent force. Every second we were able to snatch from the pursuing aircraft brought us closer to the convoy and success. But if we dived a second too late, bombs would end our hunt with sudden death.

12.30: We surfaced again. This time only three men went to the bridge, the Captain, the first seaman's mate, and I. We raced ahead stubbornly, plagued by the thoughts of being annihilated within the hour.

13.13: A twin-engined plane dropped suddenly out of a low cloud, only 800 metres astern. It was too late to dive. After freezing for a horrifying instant, Siegmann yelled, 'Right full rudder.' I jumped to the rear of the bridge to shoot while the mate manned the second gun. The small aircraft grew enormous fast. It dived upon us, machine-gunning the open rear of the bridge as the boat turned to starboard. Neither the mate nor I were able to fire a single bullet; our guns were jammed. The aircraft dropped four bombs which I saw falling towards me, then roared over the bridge so close that I could feel its engines' hot exhaust brush my face. Four bombs in a row erupted alongside our starboard saddle tanks. Four high fountains collapsed over the two of us at the guns. *U-230* was still afloat, still racing through the rising green sea. The aircraft, having used up its bombs, turned and disappeared in the direction of the convoy.

13.23: Our radio-mate delivered an urgent message to the Captain: ATTACKED BY AIRCRAFT. UNABLE TO DIVE. SINKING. 45N 25W. HELP. *U-456*.

'Have Prager check position,' Siegmann shouted back. 'Maybe we can save the crew.'

The Captain's impulse to rescue our comrades might well result in suicide. We were closer to death than to life ourselves. But help was imperative – we would have expected the same. Moments later, Prager reported that *U-456* was only twelve miles ahead, fifteen degrees to starboard. Immediately, the Captain changed course.

13.50: We spotted a plane circling four miles ahead. Then my glasses picked up the bow of *U-456* poking out of the rough sea. The men clung to the slippery deck and to the steel cable strung from bow to bridge. Most of them stood in the water up to their chests. The aircraft kept circling above the sinking boat, making it foolhardy for us to approach. Another danger prevented rescue: astern, a corvette crept over the horizon, evidently summoned by the plane. Now our own lives were in jeopardy. We turned away from the aircraft, the escort, and *U-456*, and fled in the direction of the convoy.

14.22: 'Aircraft astern!'

Again it was too late to dive. The single-engined plane came in low in a straight line exactly over our wake. I fingered the trigger of my gun. Again the gun was jammed. I kicked its magazine, clearing the jam. Then I emptied the gun at the menace. The mate's automatic bellowed. Our boat veered to starboard, spoiling the plane's bomb run. The pilot revved up his engine, circled, then roared towards us from dead ahead. As the plane dived very low, its engine sputtered, then stopped. Wing first, the plane crashed into the surging ocean, smashing its other wing on our superstructure as we raced by. The pilot, thrown out of his cockpit, lifted his arm and waved for help, but then I saw him disintegrate in the explosion of the four bombs which were meant to destroy us. Four violent shocks kicked into our starboard side astern, but we left the horrible scene unharmed.

The downing of the aircraft must have upset the enemy's flight schedule. Minute after minute passed without a repetition of the attacks. Running at highest speed, *U-230* gained bearing ahead of the convoy. In about an hour, we approached the calculated intersection with the convoy's track.

15.45: A report from the radio room put our small victory into proper perspective: DEPTH CHARGED BY THREE DESTROYERS. SINKING. *U-186*. This new loss was the eleventh we had heard of since our patrol began. A naval disaster seemed to be in the making. But we could not afford a moment of sorrow for all the men who died that one death that every submariner pictures a thousand times.

16.00: *U-230* cut into the projected path of the convoy. I saw four columns of ships creep over the sharp horizon in the southwest, headed in our direction. We had to halt them, had to spread fire in their midst and blow gaps in the mass of steel and iron.

16.03: 'Aircraft, bearing three-two-oh.'

We plummeted into depth. Four detonations, sounding like one, drove the boat deeper and caused rudder and hydroplanes to block in extreme positions.

Minutes later, more explosions occurred in the vicinity, but in defiance of our attackers, Siegmann ordered his boat to periscope depth. He raised the scope but downed it instantly, cursing angrily, 'Verdammt! The fellow has dropped a smoke bomb and has dyed the water yellow.'

Despite the dye marking the spot of our submergence, the Captain ordered an attack on the convoy before the escorts could attack us. Chirping Asdic pings, bellowing detonations, and the grinding roar of a hundred engines provided grim background music for our assault.

16.38: Up periscope. Then: 'Tubes one to five stand ready.' 'Tubes one to five are ready,' I answered quickly, then held my breath.

Siegmann swivelled around to check the opposite side. Suddenly he cried, 'Down with the boat, Chief, take her down for God's sake, destroyer in ramming position! Down to two hundred metres!'

I fully expected the bow of a destroyer to cut into the conning tower momentarily. As the boat swiftly descended, the harrowing sound of the destroyer's engines and propellers hit the steel of our hull. It grew so fast, and echoed so deafeningly, that we were all unable to move. Only our boat was moving, and she went downwards much too slowly to escape the blow.

An ear-shattering boom ruptured the sea. A spread of six depth charges lifted the boat, tossed her out of the water, and left her on the surface at the mercy of four British destroyers. The screws of *U-230* rotated in highest revolutions, driving us ahead. For seconds there was silence. For seconds the British were baffled and stunned. After a whole eternity, our bow dipped and the boat sank – and sank.

A new series of exploding charges lifted our stern with a mighty force. Our boat, entirely out of control, was catapulted towards the bottom five miles below. Tilted at an angle of sixty degrees, *U-230* tumbled to 250 metres before Friedrich was able to reverse her fall. Floating level at a depth of 230 metres, we thought we were well below the range of the enemy's depth charges. *U-230* was specially rigged to withstand pursuit. Once again we were condemned to sit it out in crushing depths.

16.57: Distinct splashes on surface heralded the next spread. A series of twenty-four charges detonated in quick succession. The bellowing roar slammed against our boat. The explosions again pushed her into a sharp down tilt while the echo of the detonations rolled endlessly through the depths.

17.16: A new spread deafened us and took our breath away. The boat listed sharply under the shattering blow. The steel knocked and shrieked and valves were thrown into open position. The shaft packings leaked, and a constant stream of water soon filled the aft bilge. Pumps spouted, the periscope packings loosened, and water trickled into the cylinders. Water everywhere. Its weight forced the boat deeper into the depths. In the meantime, the convoy crawled in a thunderous procession over our boat.

17.40: The uproar was at its peak. A sudden splash told us that we had ten or fifteen seconds to brace against another barrage. The charges went off just beyond lethal range. While the ocean reverberated under the blasts, the bulk of the convoy slowly passed the spot of our slow execution. I pictured the freighters making a detour around the escorts massed above to end our existence. Perhaps we should risk going deeper. I did not know where our limit was, where the hull would finally crack. No one knew. Those who had found out took their knowledge into the depths. For hours we suffered the punishment and sank gradually deeper. In a constant pattern, spreads of twenty-four charges battered our boat every twenty minutes. At one time we thought we had won. That was when the escorts departed and rushed to take their positions in the convoy. But our hope was short-lived. The hunters had only left the coup de grâce to the killer group following in the wake of the armada.

20.00: The new group launched its first attack, then another, and another. We sat helpless 265 metres below. Our nerves trembled. Our bodies were stiff from cold, stress, and fear. The mind-searing agony of waiting made us lose any sense of time and any desire for food. The bilges were flooded with water, oil, and urine. Our washrooms were under lock and key; to use them then could have meant instant death, for the tremendous outside pressure would have acted in reverse of the expected flow. Cans were circulated for the men to use to relieve themselves. Added to the stench of waste, sweat, and oil was the stink of the battery gases. The increasing humidity condensed on the cold steel, dropped into the bilges, dripped from pipes, and soaked our clothes. By midnight, the Captain realized that the British would not let up in their bombardment, and he ordered the distribution of potash cartridges to supplement breathing. Soon every man was equipped with a large metal box attached to his chest, a rubber hose leading to his mouth, and a clamp on his nose. And still we waited.

May 13th. Over 200 canisters had detonated above and around us by 01.00. Several times we had used a ruse in an effort to escape. Through an outboard valve, we repeatedly expelled a great mass of air bubbles. These screens of air floated away on the current, reflecting the Asdic impulses like a large solid body. But our attackers were fooled into chasing the decoys only twice, and both times they left at least one vessel behind, directly over our heads. Unable to sneak away, we gave up the game and concentrated on conserving our power, our compressed air, and our dwindling supply of oxygen.

04.00: The boat had fallen to 275 metres. We had been under assault for twelve hours and there was no sign of relief. This day was my birthday and I wondered whether it would be my last. How many chances could one ask for?

08.00: No lessening of the attacks. The water in the bilges rose above the deck plates and splashed around my feet. The bilge pumps were useless at this depth. Whenever a charge erupted, the Chief released some compressed air into the tanks to assure the boat's buoyancy.

12.00: The boat's down angle had sharply increased. Our compressed-air supply was dangerously low, and the boat slipped ever farther away.

20.00: The air was thick, and even more so as we breathed it through the hot cartridges. The Devil seemed to be knocking on our steel hull as it creaked and contracted under the enormous pressure.

22.00: The barrage increased in violence as dusk closed in on the surface. Wild attacks at shorter intervals indicated that the enemy had lost his patience.

May 14th. By midnight, we had approached the limit for boat and crew. We had reached a depth of 280 metres and the boat was still sinking. I dragged myself through the aisle, pushing and tossing men around, forcing them to stay awake. Whoever fell asleep might never be awakened.

03.10: A thunderous spread rattled down, but without effect. We were closer to being crushed by the mounting pressure than by the exploding canisters. As the echo of the last blast slowly subsided, something else attracted our attention. It was the thrashing of retreating propellers. For a long time we listened to the fading sound, unable to believe that the Tommies had given up the hunt.

04.30: For over an hour there was silence. We spent all that time doubting our luck. We had to make sure, so we turned on our fresh-water producer, went high with the motors. No reaction from above. Using the last of our compressed air and battery power, the Chief managed to lift the overloaded boat, metre by metre. Then, unable to slow her upward movement, Friedrich let her rise freely and yelled, 'Boat rises fast ... fifty metres ... boat has surfaced!'

*U-230* broke through to air and life. We pushed ourselves up to the bridge. Around us spread the infinite beauty of night, sky, and ocean. Stars glittered brilliantly and the sea breathed gently. The moment of rebirth was overwhelming. A minute ago, we could not believe that we were alive; now we could not believe that death had kept his finger on us for thirty-five gruesome hours.

*U-230's* ordeal was far from over. Savagely attacked by escorts and aircraft, demoralised by the increasing number of messages from sinking U-boats and now alive to the fact that her Metox had been outsmarted by the centimetric radar, the boat and her shattered crew crawled home to Brest.

## Comandante Mario Rossetto, Regia Marina, *S.6*

Only when the war was over did I realise – just like those who went through the same experience and many others – the vast evils perpetrated by the Nazi regime. As far as the war fought alongside the Germans, our allies until 8/9/43, I have to say that I don't have a bad memory of it.

I'll begin on the evening of 8 September 1943 – an unhappy day if ever there was one. I was at Danzig, commanding the submarine *S.6*, one of nine boats which the Kriegsmarine had allocated to the Regia Marina in exchange for some submarines attached to Betasom, the Atlantic base at Bordeaux, which after extensive Atlantic operations had become too worn out to carry on the campaign effectively. They had been converted into transports for the exchange of weapons and specialised German equipment for essential raw materials which could not be sourced in Europe but which were available in Japanese occupied territory.

The nine S-Class submarines were built at the naval shipyard in Danzig and were handed over to the Regia Marina between the end of June and the end of August 1943.

After going to sea for training, the boats were moored in the Vistula canals and the crews quartered on the liner Deutschland; only a guard was left on the submarines.

During late afternoon on 8 September, on our return to the Deutschland for dinner, I and the other oficers were informed that Italy 'had signed the Armistice'. Not one of us, nor our Flotilla commander, had had any orders nor any information about it; but, although incredulous, we had to change our minds when we heard it on the radio, on the 8-o'clock evening news. It was impossible to contact our Admiralty (the Government had fled to Brindisi) nor with our fleet commander who was sailing for Allied bases. The only head-quarters we could contact was Betasom where Comandante Grossi had already signalled his availability to continue the war on the German side.

The crews at Danzig (only *S.1*'s crew was on leave in Italy having completed their training period) were given the freedom to decide their own futures. Of course, there were only two options available in Danzig: either stay with the Germans or go to a concentration camp as prisoners. The third choice, that of going home, was simply not possible. The result was that only about 10% of the men opted for surrender.

In the meantime, the Italian sentry on each boat had been replaced with a German: he raised the Italian flag in the morning and lowered it at sunset. The nine S-Class boats were only handed back to the Kriegsmarine on 19 September, after the high command of the Italian navy remaining in the North (this was before the creation of the Repubblica Sociale Italiana), which had decided to continue the war on the German side, made an agreement with the Kriegsmarine. The transfer from the Italian to German command was formalised in a signed regular report between the giving (Italian) and the receiving (German) commander. I won't speculate on the reasons why they wouldn't let us keep the boat and which we did try to find out.

All the Danzig personnel were transferred to Bordeaux where a large number of disbanded soldiers were gathering, having been left without orders in many areas of France.

In March 1944, together with a crew assembled from the submarine personnel at Betasom, I was ordered back to Italy to take command of the submarine Beilul. After having been scuttled at Monfalcone on 8 September, she had been raised by the Germans who brought her back into service, and she should have been ready in June. Together with another two or three boats, likewise raised after having been scuttled in other north Italian ports, she was to be handed over to the RSI Navy. That wasn't to be for the Beilul because on May 10 an Allied aerial bombing raid scored direct hits on the Monfalcone shipyard, sinking her and every other vessel at the yard. The Beilul had not been raised.

My crew then dispersed to various destinations. After a short stint at the Admiralty in Vicenza I was called by Comandante Borghese to the Decima Flottiglia MAS and appointed as Operational Commander of the Spezia Naval Base which was then immediately behind the front line that had shifted to Garfagnana.

Here I stayed a few days after 25 April 1945, and when the German division (under General Fretter Pico) and the Italian division (under General Carloni) pulled back to the Po Valley I too withdrew my units towards Parma. When the two divisions surrendered to the Brazilian troops* that were moving up towards Milan, I disbanded my units (but did not surrender myself) and when it was possible I went home to Imperia.

I have absolutely no regrets about that period of the war after 8 September on the German side. I should rather reflect on so many painful events which took place in the civil war, that caused the loss of so many brothers. But I had no opportunity to be directly involved in it.

## NORTH SEA, BALTIC AND ARCTIC

**Lieutenants Konstantin Sergeev** and **Zarmair Arvanov, USSR Navy, Northern Fleet, _K-21_**\***

---

\* 1st Brazilian Expeditionary Division.
\*\* Lieutenant Sergeev compiled this piece from his own memory but also incorporated material from Arzanov's memoir.

In February 1943 *K-21* went for her 8th patrol. Our priority tasks were to land a reconnaissance group in one of the Norwegian fjords and to lay mines in enemy waters. The additional task was an unlimited hunt for enemy ships. It turned out to be quite a difficult patrol for the submarine and her crew. The first challenge we faced was the onboard fire during the mission. The fire occurred because of some design failure. Part of the induction outer casing surrounding the induction system pipes that came into Compartment 5 (The engine room) of the K-Class was not watertight. That could cause serious problems during heavy weather. The sea often broke over this intake, and water came into the engine room.

That's exactly what occurred on *K-21* while she was running three nautical miles off the enemy shore. Water flowed into the diesel compartment through the leaking casing and poured on to the electric switchboard. That caused a short-circuit and a fire in the engine room. Despite all measures to extinguish the fire, it was growing stronger and everything was blazing: the paint on the bulkheads, the cork lining to the hull, the rubber insulation of the wires and cables, oil, old rubbish and so on. There was a real risk of explosion because the compartment contained fuel tanks with around a ton of diesel fuel in them. If the fire became more intense, an explosion would be inevitable. So, as a last resort, we had to take passive action. All we could do was to lock the diesel compartment and hope that the fire would burn out all the oxygen and extinguish itself ... or ...

Meanwhile, in all the other compartments we were preparing for anything else that might happen. The submarine was under way on electric motors and the rudder was controlled from the aft compartment (Compartment 7). If the submarine were to be attacked, it was decided that we would fight to the bitter end and then blow up the submarine. Small charges were put in the compartment nearest the torpedoes. The commander ordered the preparation of three coded radio messages: 'SUBMARINE ON FIRE', 'ENGAGED IN GUN ACTION WITH ENEMY', 'DYING BUT NOT GIVING UP'. However we didn't go into panic. Everyone was doing his job. Cook Assistant Sailor Eligulashvilli (a Georgian) peeled potatoes near the bulkhead of the fifth compartment which heated to 150 degrees C, and he sang Georgian songs at the top of his voice. Gun crew were on duty near their guns under the piercing wind and waves, ready to open fire. Meanwhile the fire was slowly put out. After 70 minutes it became clear that the fire had extinguished itself. Senior Mechanic Officer Braman, Midshipman Sboev and four sailors donned breathing apparatus, took fire extinguishers with them and went into the fifth compartment. They extinguished the smouldering remnants and took away debris. After that, mechanics and electricians inspected the results of the fire. All the fore part of the compartment was burned out. Most of the wires and cables and electric switchboard were destroyed. The switchboard supplied power to the oil and water pumps of the submarine's diesel engines and some other important equipment. So without repairs the submarine was unable to complete her operation. In other circumstances the submarine would have to be returned to base. However, Captain Lunin gathered the officers together and after their reports said: 'I'm delighted that none of you is claiming that the damage obliges us to return into base. I can see that I can rely on you in a tight fix.'

So it was decided to repair the submarine at sea. The Commander asked Braman how long he needed to make all the repairs and start both diesels. Braman replied that he needed about 20 hours. The Commander asked him to shorten the time as much as possible. First of all we started the auxiliary engine and supplied power to the aft hydroplanes and rudder. Then we started repairing the cable lines and wires. We insulated the cables with rubber mats and other materials but the wires gave us serious problems. We could not insulate small wires. And now the thriftiness of our electrician man Nickolay Suslov helped us. After every repair at the base he had collected any left-over wires, spare parts and so on. He had often been reproached for cluttering up the submarine with them, but he always stuck to his guns. And his finest hour arrived. When the other electricians saw the burned wires they became gloomy. But Suslov was optimistic. He knew that they were able to do it with his stores. So he led the repairs and they managed to do it. Consequently his prestige increased dramatically. Other electricians rose to the challenge, too, offering ingenious suggestions and procedures. Finally after 18 hours the repairs were finished. The submarine was ready to dive.

Lunin called his officers together. They had to decide where to go from here. While the submarine was under repairs she had drifted well off course and the navigators had lost her position. There was no opportunity of fixing the position because of a snowstorm and fog. For now, the submarine's task was to lay mines. On top of that, she had to pass through two enemy minefields to reach the position to be mined. We decided to proceed submerged, fixing our position by sounding. But that was not the right decision as that part of the Loppa Sea, a rocky part of the Norwegian coast was bounded by reefs. So while we were running at a depth of 70 metres we hit a reef in a place where the chart showed 200 metres depth. As a result, we had to go back out to sea and wait for better weather to fix our position. At night our navigators fixed the submarine's position by the stars and we went through the minefields on the surface using the high tide. In the morning we laid the mines and went to the enemy coastline to carry out our next task. We proceeded parallel to the shore while the commander looked for a good landing place. When night fell, we half-surfaced (we blew out just the central ballast tanks having fore and aft tanks filled) in the very lair of the enemy in a small bay – ready to submerge immediately. While the landing was in full swing we had an enemy destroyer pass close to us. We heard the sound of her ventilators and saw her navigation light clearly. It wasn't strange, because the fjord was well protected from the sea with minefields, so even all the lighthouses and buoys were working there. Our rubber cockboat made 17 trips for one and a half hours to land the reconnaissance group and their equipment. After that Lunin decided to continue the patrol and carry out the additional objective. So he planned a daring attack on Vågen naval base. The plan was based on the tactic of surprise. We had to go 10 miles southward down the enemy fjord to reach the base. Then we had to double a high rocky cape and enter the harbour from the south. So we surfaced and switched on the navigation lights and ran full ahead.

We soon came to the enemy's first coast observation post. The post started to ask us with a light for our call-sign. Lunin gave the order to reply with three letters: OCS, which meant 'Our Character is Strong'. The German post cheerfully replied something or other and we kept on going. So we went through the next posts in the same way. It sounds unbelievable: a large Soviet submarine (the K-Class had a displacement of about 1,500 tons, 2,100 tons submerged, and about 98 metres in length) ran full ahead down the enemy's fjord replying to all challenges with some nonsense that acted like 'Open Sesame'. So we reached the entrance to the Vågen base and saw a number of torpedo boats and their mother-ship moored alongside the moles. Our torpedo tubes were ready by that time and we fired four torpedoes at once against the moles. After 15 seconds (so close we came up to the moles) four explosions rumbled and several moments later the Germans started AA fire, in the belief that it was an air attack. Meanwhile we switched off the lights and were running away from the harbour. Suddenly we saw a small submarine without navigation lights and we tried to ram her, but at the last moment she managed to submerge and we ran above her. Using the high tide again, we passed through the minefields which were now six to eight meters below us. Thus we escaped northwards at 22 knots, slicing through the waves to the accompaniment of the roar of both diesels. And, more than that, the Northern Lights silently blazed dead ahead.

After we passed through the minefields we submerged to reload torpedo tubes and soon we heard the explosions of depth charges. It seems the Germans had came to their senses and started to search for us. We heard the explosions till the morning, and they died away. We lay on the seabed all the night round and then surfaced and went to our home base. On the way we were attacked by a Junkers 88 but managed to submerge while the bomber

SUBMARINE

made a turn to dive at us. The plane dropped two bombs which, however, caused only minor damage to the gyrocompass and several safety-fuses. And that's what our eighth patrol was like.

## Lieutenant-Commander Max Shean, DSO*, RANVR; from *Corvette and Submarine*

In September 1943 the German battleship *Tirpitz*, the destruction of which was a priority for Churchill, lay secure at her base in Norway's Kaa Fjord while the crews of six Royal Navy midget submarines put the finishing touches to the plan to sink her. Each submarine had a passage crew for the long tow to Norway and an operational crew for the attack itself.

As the date for departure drew near, many interesting things were happening. Officers came aboard to brief commanding officers for the attack. They had intelligence relating to many aspects of the operation. I was included in all of these, but not in subsequent discussions between skippers …

Finally, the six submarines arrived. Then, in the last practice of net cutting, the diver in *X9* lost confidence and pulled out, leaving a place into which I was appointed. A last minute draft is known, in the Navy, as a 'pierhead jump', and this was one certainly. So, I rejoined Lt Terry Martin, S/Lt Joe Brooks, and joined ERA Vernon Coles who had also been recently appointed. S/Lt Paddy Kearon was passage crew CO with Leading Torpedo Operator A. H. Harte and Stoker G. H. Hollett. Our towing was to be by *Syrtis*, Lt Jupp, RN.

A few days before sailing, it was decided to photograph each crew, all crews together, and then all CO's together. It was like family grouping after a wedding. In the CO's picture, Digger McFarlane can be seen making a rude sign, with a smile, while Henty can't be seen at all. He had expressed displeasure at all this photographing, claiming that it showed lack of confidence in the operation on the part of the senior officers, and departed to his cabin …

The night before we sailed, the operational crew ERAs went ashore to the bar that they had rigged in a cow-shed, for a last drink together. Ralph Mortiboys, of *X5*, declined to go. He wanted to remain aboard Bonaventure to write to his widowed mother, because he had a premonition that he would not return from Alten Fjord.

On 11 September 1943, six submarines were berthed alongside HMS *Alecto* and six X-craft were ready, with side charges fitted, alongside HMS *Bonaventure* in Loch Cairnbawn. Admiral Sir Claude Barry, Flag Officer Submarines, had come from 'Northways', the S/M headquarters in London, to see the flotilla leave and to wish everyone well. He was a genial, thick-set man, with a fringe of hair above the neck, but none on top. He fulfilled my mental picture of Friar

Tuck, and inspired all of us with his enthusiastic support. In the prevailing fine weather, the pairs of submarines and several ship's boats moving towards the sea created a scene reminiscent of a regatta.

As each pair of submarines approached the entrance to the loch, the Admiral's barge, with Captains Banks and Fell also on board, drew close alongside while words of encouragement were exchanged. I was on the conning tower of *Syrtis* when our turn came. The submarine captains each had some symbol of the chase. Lt Jupp had a forage cap and a bulb horn, as used long ago on automobiles. He was keen on using this when the Admiral came alongside, if he could do so without impertinence. The Admiral called out 'Good luck, Jupp and Martin, and a safe return.'

'Thank you, Sir. If we have any trouble, we'll take a taxi.' Honk, honk, honk. This went down well with Sir Claude, and everyone else.

Soon we were on our own, *X9*, manned by S/Lt Paddy Kearon, Leading Torpedo Operator 'Darkie' Hart, and Stoker 'Ginger' Hollett, dived and speed was increased to ten knots for the thousand mile journey. Security precautions were extraordinary.

According to the Prime Minister's definition, the hunt was for the most important target in the war at sea. It must not fail, and the enemy must not get the slightest hint that anything was afoot. The six pairs were routed separately on parallel tracks, ten miles apart. X-craft would be dived all day, except for a ten minute ventilating period at 0600, 1200 and 1800. After dark, they would surface to charge batteries and air for an hour or two. Within two hundred miles of Alten Fjord, the towing submarines also would dive by day. The most any aircraft would be likely to see would be a submarine apparently on patrol.

To guard against the possible compromising of radio signals, each submarine had a different re-coding book, and would not send signals except for matters of first importance and then only from a position far from the target area, north of the Arctic Circle, in the later stages. Targets had been allocated among the six X-craft. *X5*, *X6* and *X7* were to attack Tirpitz, and *X8*, *X9* and *X10* other capital ships which might include battlecruisers *Scharnhorst* and *Lützow*.

Aerial reconnaissance was made as frequently as possible, but was difficult because of the weather and the extreme range from Britain. Some flights were staged via Russia, but this required lengthy and delicate diplomatic negotiation. A good deal of information was radioed, at great risk to themselves and their families, by Norwegians. It was possible that changes would be made to the allocation of targets according to the disposition of German ships and the X-craft. This was the first time such an operation had been mounted, so flexibility was essential.

Towing routine had become standardised following trials ... Telephones were not expected to last long, so a timetable for ventilating and charging was prearranged. SUE signals were available for emergencies. Passage crews undoubtedly had the more onerous task, as I well knew. My sympathies were with Paddy and his two crewmen.

We of the operational crew were comfortable during the passage. We did stand watch as lookouts to keep active and to provide another pair of eyes, but still had plenty of leisure time ...

Our telegraphist intercepted a signal to the Admiralty from one of our fleet. We were unable to decode it, but estimated from the strength of the signal, that it was transmitted from a position nearby. All we had was about twenty groups of five numbers. The telegraphist and submarine officers off-duty pondered at length. It had to be important, so it would not be just a weather report: at the same time, weather would be reported if radio silence were to be broken for any important reason. What were the possibilities? It could not be an enemy sighting report or this information would have been passed on to all by Admiralty. It could be difficulty with an X-craft. Had one been lost on tow?

After much thought and discussion, it was agreed that something was amiss with an X-craft, and so it was. *X8* had broken her tow and Seanymph, Lt J. P. H. Oakley, RN, was searching for her, but we did not know that. In fact, we all knew nothing of the progress of the rest of the fleet until after the operation, by which time we had received several undecipherable signals, and were of the opinion that separate recoding tables were not a good idea. If six submarines had the one exclusive set, the risk of compromise before the attack was negligible, and the benefit to the participants considerable.

What was happening was that the four boats with manilla tow lines all had breakages. Nylon rope was a new material, developed for glider towing, and only two of these lines were available in time. These were used by *X5* and *X6*, and performed well. *X8* joined company with another submarine who directed her to her own. The passage CO, Jack Smart, was exhausted after days of continuous watchkeeping and was promptly relieved by McFarlane and his operational crew. Her side charges were starting to leak, and eventually had to be dumped. Although set not to detonate, they did so, and severely damaged *X8*, which had to be scuttled.

*X7*, with Peter Philip in command, had several towline breakages, but succeeded in passing another towline each time, and got to the slipping position on time, a splendid effort of seamanship and endurance by a man who, in his youth, had been crippled by polio.

The worst setback was our own, on the morning of 16 September, two hundred and forty miles from the slipping position. At 0900, according to the now well established routine, *Syrtis* reduced speed for *X9* to surface for ventilation. There was no *X9*: only a slack towline streaming astern. *Syrtis* stopped, hands went aft along the casing to pull the line aboard. In the long swell, her stern was rising and plunging, making it difficult to stand, let along to pull in six hundred feet of heavy line. It was cold as well, for we were near the Arctic Circle. Part way in, the rope snagged under the submarine's stern and could not be freed. It had most likely fouled the port propeller. Lt Jupp ordered the X-craft diver to clear it. That was me. My diving suits were aboard X9. All that *Syrtis* had were the standard DSEA escape sets which provided breathing only; no protection from the cold water, neither had they any weights to compensate for their positive buoyancy.

I dressed in a pair of overalls and the DSEA set with some steel weights from the engine room, and went aft along the casing, where a rope had been rigged for support. Lt Jupp urged me to be quick. If we were surprised by enemy aircraft he would have to dive immediately. I climbed, with a lifeline attached, on to the after hydroplanes, switched to oxygen, and launched myself into the North Atlantic Ocean. It was cold. When my face went under, it took my breath away. I was floating. The weights were not only too light, but loose as well. They were long pieces of metal which swung about with my every movement. It was impossible to get down.

The water was absolutely clear. In the few moments that I could remain submerged, I noted the shafts of sunlight descending into the depths. It made me feel giddy. I tried to see the propellers, but, as *Syrtis* pitched in the heavy swell, the hydroplanes smacked the surface with an almighty splash, which forced me to the surface again. I was cold all over, and more frightened than I have ever been. This was not Loch Striven diving. It was beyond my ability to get down to the propellers. In a proper suit, correctly weighted, insulated from the cold, I could have swum down, but, floating as I was, and being pumped to the surface with every swell, it was more than I could do. But there was no giving up. The rope had to be cleared, otherwise we were limited to the use of the starboard propeller only.

I swam along the surface to get clear of the hydroplanes, and looked down. There were the infinite light beams converging toward the great deep, and there was the port propeller, with the rope around it, not tight, but in a big loop. That was fortunate so long as the propeller was not rotated. I looked up to the First Lieut on deck and removed my mouthpiece, 'Do not turn the port propeller. Let out some slack on the tow, and carry it as far aft as you can.' This they did. I saw, to my enormous relief, that the bight of rope was now lying aft of the propeller.

'Right. Heave in now.'

The rope straightened above the propeller and slid across the top of the big shaft as the casing party heaved it aboard. Eventually the end came up, frayed from the break and having been towed for some time afterwards.

The casing party hauled me back to the hydroplanes and up on deck. The crew were complimentary as we hurried forward and up into the conning tower. *Syrtis* was already underway on diesels, and heading back along the way she had come. 'Well done Shean,' from Jupp, and down I went to change. The rush of engine air down the conning tower, as I stiffly clambered down the ladder, was hardly felt. I was numb.

That crisis over, we had time to consider the situation. *X9* must have broken her tow soon after diving at 0120 according to the engineer officer, who came up with hourly fuel consumption figures. If we retraced our track for the same time, at the same speed, we should meet up with her. This we did, without success. All that was seen was an oil slick running in the direction of the Norwegian coast. This may or may not have meant that *X9* headed that way. The logical course for Paddy to steer would be the one we were on, prior to the tow parting, which he would know. We turned, and covered the distance again, still without sighting anything. *X9* was lost, for the time being, or forever, we did not know. The situation must be radioed to Admiralty, and to do this, we had to travel north to the Arctic Circle. We turned north.

Of the operational crew members, I believe that Joe was most affected, although we all felt the absence of Paddy and his two shipmates, and also what looked like the end of our chance to attack the German fleet. So far as we knew, the other five were still OK, though in fact it was only four. I thought of Paddy. He was a cheerful Irishman, short, slightly on the heavy side of average, fair, with a broad countenance and a smile to go with it. He had a third officer WRNS acquaintance at HMS *Ambrose*, the submarine base for Allied boats, at Dundee, where my Mary was now a Wren herself. On his last leave, Paddy had gone to Dundee to see 'Touche' as he called her, and carried a letter from me to Mary. Paddy's friend was probably French; I think her name was La Touche. I had not got to know his other crew members very well because of my pier-head jump only a matter of days earlier.

Leading Torpedo Operator 'Darkie' Hart, was a quiet, industrious Londoner. Stoker 'Ginger' Hollett was a ball of fire, always cheerful, always doing something in the boat of his own initiative; a very good submariner.

A signal to all submarines struck a note of resolution, if not desperation: 'All X-craft attack *Tirpitz*.'

We were out of it, except that any submarine could attack any major warship, but nothing less. This proved frustrating for Jupp because, as we approached the slipping position submerged, he sighted a U-boat on the surface, and had to hold fire. As if that were not enough, the U-boat altered course and came within range a second time. We X-craft hands were not too popular for the rest of that day.

Our orders were to continue to patrol off the entrance to Alten Fjord for several days after the attack day, 22 September, to torpedo any major ships flushed out, and to tow any X-craft needing one. There was an emergency rendezvous in a bay north of the entrance. We entered this bay one still night while I was keeping lookout on the periscope standard. There was no moon. It was black and calm as we crept through the narrow waterway, and cold. After an hour on lookout duty, fingers would be numb. Suddenly, the sky lit up with a vivid display of the Aurora Borealis. It was as if a giant were shaking an enormous fluorescent silk scarf above us. We could have read by its light, and a lookout ashore could have seen us clearly. *Syrtis* quietly headed for the open sea, counting the minutes and awaiting gunfire. But the rendezvous had been well chosen, and there was nobody there to see us. All the same, it was an anxious few minutes. Eventually, we turned sadly from the recovery area empty handed, and headed for the Shetland Islands.

*X10*, with Ken Hudspeth, was being towed in the same direction, as it happened, having been defeated by defects in the last stage of approach to *Tirpitz*. He too, thought that five other craft were attacking. In fact, three were – *X6* and *X7* successfully, and *X5* nobody knows. All three sank in Kaa Fjord. *X6* attacked and then scuttled alongside *Tirpitz*, and all four crew were taken prisoner. *X7*, after attacking, was damaged by the resulting explosion, surfaced, and was sunk by gunfire, the skipper and diver escaping. They were taken to prison camp in Germany with *X6's* crew. *X5* was sunk by gunfire seven hundred yards from *Tirpitz*: there were no survivors, so little more was ever known.

*X10* was scuttled on her tow home, following several tow breakages and a deterioration in the weather. So, the tally was six X-craft and nine men lost in the process of crippling one battleship. *Tirpitz* did not sink, but she never fulfilled a battleship's role again ...

The disappointment of the last days was weighing heavily on all crew members. We knew only of our losses. Bill Whittam, in particular, I missed. To this day, whenever a period of silence is observed for departed comrades, he comes to mind. I think of his ravishing Ruth, their love, his remains recovered from the wreck of *X7* and buried on the shore of Kaa Fjord, and of her lonely sorrow.

There were the other eight whom, apart from Henty and Paddy, I did not know as well, all missed by someone. And our entire flotilla wiped out. This was my immediate view of things. The overall fact was that it was a splendid achievement. Compare it with the sinking of the sister ship, *Bismarck*, which took a large fleet of the Royal Navy and the loss of the battlecruiser *Hood* with all but three of her crew.

Lieutenant Donald Cameron, RNR, (*X8*) and Lieutenant Basil Charles Godfrey Place, RN, (*X6*) were both awarded the VC. Lieutenant Henry Henty-Creer was mentioned in dispatches, but, in the absence of proof that he had actually attacked the *Tirpitz* before *X5* was sunk, denied any higher recognition.

## MEDITERRANEAN

### Secondo Capo Mechanista Carlo Pracchi, Regia Marina, *Velella*

We were sailing due north through the Tyrrhenian Sea towards La Spezia to start an overhaul when, crossing the Gulf of Naples and passing Capo Miseno, the starboard engine unexpectedly developed a fault. We were forced to shut it down. We informed the bridge because the port engine was working normally and they would have to be ready to compensate for the undesired change of course that would be caused by the greater thrust of the port screw.

However, because the order was not executed immediately, the boat slowed down and veered a little to starboard.

At that very moment the bridge gave the alarm: 'Spread of torpedoes at nine-o-clock!' Each of the three ran at an angle across our bow.

Whoever had launched them had done his homework! But as we had suddenly lost power from our starboard engine and reduced speed, it was our good luck that our enemy's calculations ended in unexpected failure.

Thanks to that fortuitous breakdown and our loss of speed, which nobody had wanted, the crew and the boat came home in one piece on that occasion.

Definitely a lucky break-down.

Carlo Pracchi had a second escape when, during the two days of uncertainly leading up to the general announcement of the Allied-Italian Armistice on 8 September, he was arrested by the Germans at Milan railway station while waiting for a train back to Naples to rejoin *Velella* after a period of leave. He escaped through a toilet window, but reached Naples the day after the boat had sailed. Torpedoed by HMS *Shakespeare* on 7 September, *Velella* went down with all hands.

### Lieutenant-Commander Jerzy ('George') Koziolkowski, Polish Navy, ORP *Sokol*; from Patrol Report, ADM199/1854.

Two new U-Class submarines had been given to the Poles as replacements for their own submarines which had been lost or badly damaged. Known affectionately as 'the terrible twins', *Dzik* and *Sokol* were both eventually sent to the Mediterranean where they were attached for a time to the 10th Flotilla. On 11 June 1943 Koziolowski was bringing *Sokol* home to her base at Malta.

A barrage balloon was sighted afloat 10 miles north of the end of the eastern search channel. It was picked up, being practically undamaged, and fixed to the submarine's bow, producing quite an unusual sight. When meeting the escort she must have been pretty puzzled by our appearance as, after exchanging recognitions, she flashed, 'Are you a submarine?'

## Lieutenant-Commander Boleslaw Romanowski, Polish Navy, ORP *Dzik*; Adm 199/1853

ORP *Dzik*, attached to the 10th Flotilla, left for patrol in the Gulf of Taranto on 2 July 1943. During the Allied invasion of Sicily, codenamed Operation 'Husky', *Dzik* was one of several submarines employed on patrol or as navigation markers for the surface ships carrying troops and equipment. The waters around the island were infested with both friendly and hostile submarines and the difficulty, as always, was knowing which was which. On 11 July, *Dzik's* CO sighted a submarine but was unable to decide whether or not it was HMS *Unbroken*. He refrained from an attack. A week later, he had less of a problem with a sighting.

19 July
0020 – When proceeding on course 270 degrees zigzagging 25 degs either side and in company with *Unshaken* about 3,000 yards on starboard bow spotted periscope 40 degs to port, distance 1,000 yards. I altered course towards, gave full speed ahead together and ordered torpedoes set to 24 feet. Periscope disappeared, then reappeared moving in course NW which would cross our bow and I am convinced he was attacking *Unshaken* and had not yet seen us as we were on his beam. I altered course slightly to starboard and fired four torpedoes aimed independently. They all missed. I attempted to ram with no result and conclude, as periscope had disappeared after second torpedo left the tube, that he had seen us and dived deep. Thus unwillingly I taught her Commanding Officer to have an all-round look when attacking …

The submarine seen 11 July could have been *Unbroken*. Having had no sights on night of 10th, imagine I had encroached on Area 5. However, periscope seen on 12th, in our area, could have been friend or foe.

The reason why Commanding Officers of submarines go bald is not because they are not recalled but because the submarines are invited to share the same area.

Romanowski's report drew the following observations from his Commander (S), Captain George Phillips, at Malta.

This prompt action may well have prevented the U-boat from carrying out an attack on *Unshaken*.

In his remarks, the Commanding Officer indicates that patrolling in close proximity to friendly submarines has its worries. Unfortunately, to sail five submarines to reach an area 50 miles in width and to maintain patrols there for eight days will almost certainly mean that friendly submarines will be sighted but such a situation has got to be accepted under the special circumstances, namely Operation 'Husky'.

### Comandante Sergio Puccini, Regia Marina, *Alagi*; from *Aria Alla Rapida*

In July 1943, after an uneventful mission east of Sicily, where the Allies had already landed, we were on our way back to Naples. A few days earlier we had met a destroyer and, without any harm to either of us, exchanged our visiting-cards – depth charges and torpedoes. We had just crossed the Strait of Messina: it was stiflingly hot and we were tired and disillusioned by the way things were going.

But Heaven was to give us a sign of hope that day.

Concerned about the exhaust valve which had its own ideas of when to shut off completely (thus forcing us to cross the Tyrrhenian Sea without the assurance that, in the event of an emergency, we would be able to dive), we held a council of war and decided to attempt a repair with what we had on board.

We surfaced between Stromboli and Strombolicchio, a few dozen metres from land, and with those on the conning tower keeping their eyes peeled, we set to work on the valve.

A short while later we saw two little rowing boats put out from the shore approach us. When the boats came somewhat closer we were more than a little surprised to discover that an enterprising teacher had decided to bring out her class to greet us. They had brought a gift of fruit, cheese and other things from the countryside. They came on board; the youngsters were crazy, all talking and shouting at the same time. It was like finding yourself in the middle of a fireworks display. It was quite a celebration.

Towards dusk, when work on the valve was complete, we said an emotional farewell to the charming teacher and her lovely children and, feeling much more content, we went on our way.

It was clear: our pessimism belonged to the past. The future lay in the happy cries of those children.

**Flag Officer Submarines Sir John Roxburgh, KCB, CBE, DSO, DSC,**
**HMS *United*; from Patrol Report, ADM199/1820**

With Lieutenant Roxburgh in command, *United* sailed from Malta on 7 July to patrol in the Gulf of Taranto. At 1809 on 15 July she sighted a small object some four miles off, which Roxburgh identified as a submarine. It was, in fact, the Regia Marina's *Remo*.

I was fine on her port bow on a course of 160 degrees. The sun was shining brightly just abaft the U-boat's starboard beam, so I altered course to starboard and ran across the U-boat's bow in order to get up sun of her. She was not zigzagging and her speed was 280 revs according to the Asdics, so I gave her 10 knots.

1825 Did an advancing turn and came round to starboard on to an 80-degree track. I now had a much better view of the U-boat and identified her as an Italian U-boat (the Italian flag was clearly visible) probably of the *Pisani-*Class. She was painted a greenish colour in various shades giving her a camouflaged effect.

1831 In position 39°19 N  17°30 E fired four torpedoes spread over 1½ lengths, at a range of 500 yards. Torpedoes were fired individually. Two torpedoes hit 32 and 41 seconds after firing the first torpedo. The first torpedo was seen to pass ahead of the U-boat and the second seen to hit it under the forehatch, which made the running time 19 seconds, giving a running range of 500 yards. The third torpedo was heard to hit 10 seconds later, fitting in with the firing interval.

Almost immediately after the second explosion I saw the stern of the U-boat rise high out of the water at an angle of 60 degrees and she then sank within about four seconds. Asdics heard loud and very pronounced breaking up noises which went on for about six minutes, also a regular tapping which was timed at 120 taps to the minute. Between 9 minutes 21 seconds and 9 minutes 44 seconds after firing there were loud and distinctive explosions at irregular intervals. At first I thought I was being bombed by aircraft, but there was nothing in sight, so it must have been some of the U-boat's tanks bursting – especially as the Asdics reported no further breaking up noises after the explosions ...

1836 sighted four survivors swimming in the water.

1849 surfaced and picked up the four survivors – the only ones visible. They were together in a bunch and were the Commanding Officer, a midshipman who was the navigating officer and two seamen. Apart from superficial cuts and bruises, none was injured – though they were all well soaked in fuel oil.

1852 dived.

The commanding officer, whose 29th birthday it later turned out to be, stated he had seen our periscope at a range of 300 metres after we had fired. He attempted to comb the tracks, but their ship's head had only altered 10 degs when the second and third torpedoes hit. He saw the track of the first one pass ahead. I refrained from asking him why he wasn't zigzagging. He also stated he had heard the three loud explosions some nine minutes after I had fired and that he thought it was the U-boat's tanks bursting.

1935 Went deep to reload ...

2230 Received S10's 151145B recalling *United* on 20th July, and also announcing the safe arrival of a 'grommet' for the Commanding Officer. A happy day taken all in all ...

Had the baby been a girl, the signal would have been 'toggle'. Later in the report Roxburgh wrote at length about his four prisoners, in particular about the captain of the *Remo*, Salvatore Vassallo, with whom he evidently established something of a friendly rapport.

Age 29 (birthday the day he lost his submarine). Married with two sons aged 3 and 1½ years and a third due in October. Comes from Imperia where his wife is living at the moment. Speaks French and a very little English. Been in the navy 10 years, the last seven being in submarines.

His first words on being picked up were, 'Are there any more survivors?' followed by, 'Are you American or English?' He later stated he had seen *United's* periscope 300 metres away after she had fired but it was too late to take effective action. He said he had been hit by two torpedoes and seen the track of a third rise ahead. Apparently there were seven people altogether on the bridge only three of whom survived – the fourth survivor having the amazing luck to escape from the control room after the U-boat was hit.

He was very keen to find out how many torpedoes we had fired at him and whether they had magnetic heads (he was under the impression they had) and also from what range we had fired. I only told him the range we had fired from. Neither he nor the other three would divulge the name or class of their submarine, but Vassallo informed me his crew consisted of seven officers and 45 ratings; apparently extra junior officers were being carried for training, which would account for the large number of officers onboard.

After recovering from the initial shock, he cheered up considerably and during the nine days we had him proved a pleasant enough individual. Conversation on the whole was kept off service matters and anything he might later be interrogated on, and kept general.

His morale seemed reasonable in so far he never openly admitted considering the war was finished as far as Italy was concerned – though it was not hard to see that this was what he thought. On being asked what he thought of Germany and Hitler, he shrugged his shoulders and said he 'was a fighting man and was paid to fight not to think' and ever afterwards would not commit himself on this point – though here again it was not hard to see that his real feelings towards the Germans were not exactly friendly. He said, however, quite openly, that he thought the Japanese were mere animals. The Russians and Communism appeared to be his 'bête noir' and he also seemed to dislike the Americans intensely.

On being asked point-blank why he especially disliked the Americans he said that unlike the English when they bombed places they often as not dropped booby traps (explosive pens was what he mentioned) which the children picked up and so blew themselves to pieces. The English bombs which exploded right away or were delayed action he reckoned were fair enough. He was most insistent on the genuineness of the explosive pens, which he said he had seen himself as well as many photos of their effect in the Italian newspapers ... His general impression of the Americans were that they were nearly all gangsters! I told him he had been seeing too many American movies.

His main concern was for his wife and he was most anxious she should be informed of his safety as soon as possible before his reported loss affected her condition ...

He took an interest in the BBC news, asking that it be translated to him in French each evening. He seemed to take the events in Sicily fairly philosophically and said that he did not think the Italians would surrender but that we should have to invade and conquer Italy before the war with Italy was over ... when he heard of the first air raid on Rome he smiled and said, 'That will make the people of Rome sit up. They don't know what war is yet ...'

He found out without being told that we were bound for Malta, and when, on the last morning before making the island we were unable to get sights due to cloud, he seemed genuinely anxious because of all the mines he said were all round the island. '

## Midshipman (Guardiamarina) Marino La Nasa, Regia Marina, *Alagi*; from *Aria Alla Rapida*

On 7 September 1943, in the run-up to the Armistice, we sailed from our base at Pozzuoli, with orders from Mariscom to put into action the plan drawn up to oppose the Allied landings in the Gulf of Salerno. With us went every submarine that was operational at that time, around twenty in all, some directed to the Golfo di Gaeta, others, like the *Alagi*, to the Golfo di Policastro and some to Jonio.

We left Pozzuoli after a night spent on board in a state of readiness and, at 1145, following the swept route, we set course for the point of ambush which lay roughly south of Capo Palinuro. Towards 1600 we passed the mouth of the Golfo di Salerno, the exact spot where, an hour earlier, the submarine *Velella* had sunk – hit, as we found out afterwards, by a salvo of torpedoes from a British submarine. During the evening of that same day we reached the ambush zone and began to sweep the area. We received a coded radio message via a German aircraft informing us of two large Allied convoys which were sailing north up the Tyrrhenian Sea. There was no signal from Supermarina.

At dawn we prepared to dive in the area to set up the ambush. The control room alerted the bridge to a malfunction in the exhaust valves of the diesels. In other words, we couldn't submerge. Commander Puccini then decided to leave the area and make for Naples and get the repairs done. Supermarina was duly informed of all this.

At 1600 on 8 September we were nearly at Naples Harbour. Suddenly a navy-manned motor-launch came out to meet us, signalling that we should stop. An officer on board the launch told us that because of the rapidly changing situation in the area our destination had been changed. Our new orders were to go to La Spezia. At the same time he gave us a package containing a plan of the safe route and – heaven knows why – four sextants from the magazine of the Comando Marinia di Napoli. I remember those Salmoiraghi sextants extremely well because they were to remain on board for about two years before they were delivered!

Having altered our course, around 1900–2000 when we were off the island of Ischia, we saw flashes of light and identified bursts of flak in the Golfo di Salerno. We kept in the swept channel and half way across the Golfo di Gaeta, during the night, we heard a loud explosion in the sea. It had all the hallmarks of a ship being torpedoed or striking mines …

Finally, Supermarina informed us of the Armistice and of the end, from that moment on, of all radio transmissions from Rome. On 9 September, coming up to 0700 we arrived outside the harbour of Civitavecchia, where we intended to put in and repair the fault in the exhaust valves before going on to La Spezia. In vain we made signals in semaphore, giving our name and saying we had permission to enter the port. Nobody responded to our signals; the city seemed completely deserted. In front of the harbour mouth some fishing vessels approached, with the fishermen making signs to us as if they wanted us to go away. We assumed that they were concerned about the nets that they had set out in the sea and feared we might damage them as we crossed them.

And so we steered for the harbour entrance, but just as we reached the mouth, three German motor launches came out at full speed. We quickly noticed that their torpedo tubes were open and that the machine-guns on the deck were quite clearly trained on us. They came alongside and astern and directed us to enter the harbour. The commander obeyed, and once in port we moored at the mole below the fort. Two launches remained alongside us and the other moored astern.

In vain we tried to call up Supermarina by radio to ask for instructions. At the request of a German officer, our commander was invited to go ashore, which he did despite the misgivings of many of us on board. The German officer ashore did not return the commander's salute and asked him to get into the launch moored astern. We awaited our commander's return to the *Alagi* with a great deal of anxiety, having noted the open hostility on the part of the Germans during the encounter.

When he came back we were told the following: the Germans believed we were responsible for last night sinking one of their destroyers in the Golfo di Gaeta – a former French ship – and when he denied it they demanded to check the torpedoes on board; they also told him about the situation created in Italy following the armistice which had been called by Badoglio's government, and indicated we could either leave the submarine at Civitavecchia or wait until the afternoon for one of their convoys and follow it to La Spezia, having first deactivated the torpedoes and the guns. All this talking had taken place in an atmosphere of open hostility and mistrust on the German side which, for the moment, gave our commander no choice but to go along with the second proposal. While trying to repair the fault in the exhaust valve, we deactivated the torpedoes by removing the pistols, and the deck guns by removing the breech-blocks. During the first hour of the afternoon, we were warned to cast off and move to the exit. At the mouth of the harbour we actually found a German convoy waiting: two destroyers and a merchant ship, the nationality of which escapes me. They signalled to us what place to take up in the convoy and asked us what speed we could make.

So we began steering north with the convoy in the following formation: German destroyer at the head of the convoy, the merchant ship, the *Alagi* and, bringing up the rear, the other German destroyer. I was on duty on the bridge with Comandante Puccini and the three lookouts. Shortly afterwards, unexpectedly, the commander gave orders to alter course by 10 degrees to port. The order was carried out – not without some surprise on my part and that of everyone else. A few minutes went by, and then the convoy captain ordered us to return to the correct course. Puccini replied that he had a steering problem, and at the same time gave orders to prepare to dive. He then had the course altered a further 10 degrees to port and, while the Convoy Captain was commanding him to return to the proper course immediately, he gave the 'crash dive' order. We submerged and, reaching a depth of 30 metres set a westerly course. Shortly afterwards, the hydrophones picked up the sound of propellers. It was one of the Germans coming to look for us. Then we heard a few depth charges explode, not very close to us. Until sunset we continued our route submerged. When we tried to come up, the sight of an aeroplane forced us to submerge again. At long last, late in the evening, we received by radio from Rome a long message – signed, if I remember rightly, by Admiral de Courten – which, after a patriotic opening, instructed us to make for the port of Bône in Algeria. We followed the instructions contained in the message, painting a black circle on the bows and hoisting a triangular black flag, the recognition signal agreed with the Allies.

On the morning of 11 September 1943, in sight of the port of Bône, an English patrol boat came to meet us: after recognition and then at the stiffly spoken words of the English officer, 'follow my tracks', we entered the harbour and moored at the mole, side-by-side with other Italian submarines.

The *Alagi* returned to Italy, to Taranto, on 2 November 1944 after having served with the Allies at Alexandria, Egypt and Haifa. It was then that we delivered to Submarine Command at Taranto the four sextants which had been consigned by Naval Command in the afternoon of 8 September 1943.

### Lieutenant-Commander Jerzy ('George') Koziolkowski, Polish Navy, ORP *Sokol*, from Patrol Report, ADM 199/1854

Two days before the Allied-Italian Armistice was signed on 6 September 1943, *Sokol*, still attached to the 10th Submarine Flotilla, had left Malta to patrol off the Italian port of Brindisi. Informed of the new situation, *Sokol* approached Brindisi on 10 September, where her captain and liaison officer were to find themselves cast in the alternating roles of diplomats and traffic police.

10 September
0910 Dived and approached Brindisi submerged. During the day observed one *Regolo*-Class cruiser with one torpedo boat in company entering Brindisi, also one 6,000-ton tanker and a number of small coasters, tugs and schooners. All were wearing big Italian colours.

2012 Surfaced and transmitted my [signal number] 102001 reporting presence of cruiser in Brindisi.

2300 Received S10's 102124 [flotilla commander's signal number], with orders to communicate with authorities in Brindisi, concerning merchant vessels leaving the harbour for Allied ports.

11 September
0200 Closed entrance to harbour to three miles and tried to pass by V/S a signal to NOIC [Naval Officer In Charge] Brindisi. Signal station appeared to be

completely helpless with international system of signalling, and before signal could be passed in Italian the moon set, and Asdic heard HE of two MTBs leaving harbour. Withdrew seawards, breaking communication. MTBs were heard in vicinity for one hour.

0415 Dived for stopped MTB sighted 300 yards ahead.

0630 Surfaced and found dense fog all round.

0830 Passed two-masted schooner under Italian ensign and with naval personnel on board. After altering course to avoid collision, contact was lost in dense fog.

1000 Fog cleared – approached harbour to three miles off entrance. Called signal station by V/S (6-inch lamp) for half an hour without anybody on the signal station or shore batteries paying any attention to a submarine off harbour.

Cruiser was seen in inner harbour, inside the boom; harbour crowded with merchant vessels.

1050 Withdrew from entrance to harbour and dived, waiting for any patrol vessel to come outside.

1220 RD minesweeper left harbour. Surfaced and commenced V/S communication, keeping her outside 5,000 yards range, as her gun was manned and trained on submarine. After a tiresome half hour of signalling, assured her of our friendliness and closed for conversation as she had no means for flashing. They must have been still afraid however, for when submarine approached to some 300 yards, minesweeper went full speed to harbour.

1300 Followed minesweeper and closed to two miles off harbour, calling signal station again by six-inch lamp, without any success.

1315 Sighted a big hospital ship approaching Brindisi. Met her on the way.

1400 Stopped and requested a boat. Signals passed quickly and a few minutes later boat came alongside bringing an Italian Capitano di Fregatta onboard. Hospital ship *Saturnia* was coming from Venice with some thousands of troops onboard including naval cadets. Minesweeper closed *Saturnia* and disclosed there were no Germans in Brindisi.

1435 Directed *Saturnia* to Taranto and sent Liaison Officer Lieutenant G. C. Taylor, RNVR, with two ratings onboard a minesweeper in order to find out the situation in Brindisi and to contact Italian NOIC concerning evacuation of merchant vessels.

1515 Transmitted my 111405 reporting situation.

1530 Sighted conning tower of a submarine below horizon about 12 miles off shore on course 130°. Gave full chase but could not close to more than 8,000 yards, calling her by V/S all the time. As she was making some 14 knots and range was opening, fired one round from gun, aiming 20° ahead of her bow. Submarine answered immediately by firing one round too, and altered course towards, replying now by V/S. Stopped her at 4,000 yards and interrogated, then closed and came alongside.

She appeared to be the *Vittore Pisani*, escaping from Pola. Her captain was not pleased at all and gave rather ambiguous answers about his destination. This was caused most probably by professional jealousy, the captain being an elderly Capitano di Fregatto. Informed him to keep company, until receiving orders, and after putting Sub-Lieutenant Fritz with two ratings aboard *Pisani* – set course for Taranto by coastal route (two miles off shore), anticipating that coming orders would approve sending *Pisani* to Taranto.

2030 Passed Otranto one mile off coast

2200 Received S.10's 111905 concurring with sending *Pisani* to Taranto.

2220 parted company with *Pisani* off St Maria di Leuca and returned off Brindisi by coastal route …

2340 When approaching Otranto, submarine was sighted close to the shore. Closed to 1,000 yards and then challenged. She appeared to be panic-stricken, turning away, smoke-screening herself and calling all hands on deck. It was obvious *Sokol* was not sighted before Aldis lamp was switched on. She declared herself to be the *Otaria* coming from Pola (?) without any knowledge of recent situation. Having no more officers and men to spare for boarding party, as well as no more small arms – left her to go alone, directing her to Taranto.

12 September

0015 Transmitted my 112330 reporting interception of *Otaria*.

0350 10 miles south of Brindisi met convoy of six merchant vessels going south. Recognised 6,000 ton tanker which was observed to enter Brindisi two days ago. Assumed this was the result of action taken by an officer sent ashore and did not challenge merchant vessels.

In the morning Lieutenant Taylor RNVR, came back from Brindisi. He contacted Italian NOIC, who appeared to be very willing to do what he was told to do. He immediately gave orders for seven available merchant vessels to prepare to leave Brindisi for Taranto and six of them left at midnight unescorted, by coastal route.

Taranto was chosen as nearest port in Allied hands, Italians being very unlikely to be persuaded to leave Brindisi for Malta unescorted. The harbour at Brindisi was packed with shipping and the intention was to clear it as soon as possible.

There were one *Regolo*-Class cruiser *Scipione Africano*, two destroyers and about eight corvettes in the harbour, for which the Italians insisted to be granted permission to stay in the harbour. One submarine found shelter in Brindisi, but she appeared now to be refitting and unseaworthy.

I consider Lieutenant Taylor has done very well with his mission, especially as he must first have convinced Italian Admiral of his identity, all the talking going through an interpreter who was the ship's cook. Italians appeared to be very formal, asking on whose behalf he was acting, etc – but were quite satisfied when Lieutenant Taylor gave them written 'Sailing Orders' for the convoy, assuring them he had orders from the Commander in Chief, concerning realisation of Armistice terms.

13 September

This day I went personally to see the Italian Admiral. He appeared to be in trouble, which I believe was quite true – having the harbour overcrowded with shipping and more ships were expected to come, including Vulcania and two naval [sail] training ships – *Cr. Colombo* and *Am. Vespucci*. I was shown the daily report of ships in the harbour and out of 18 in number only three were not marked 'damaged' or 'unseaworthy'. I remarked to have watched them in the previous days to come in under their own power, all being new, modern ships, which remark quite embarrassed the Admiral. I believe the masters claimed their ships damaged because they did not like the prospect of being sent far away from home, and especially to proceed without minesweepers like the first convoy, sent to Taranto on the 12th, from which one vessel sank, striking a mine on the given 'safe' side. This route was the Italian coastal route.

Besides, sending ships to Taranto was not a solution, and the Admiral agreed to prepare next convoy in two to three days time which might go to Malta. The reason for this delay was that all ships were bringing hundreds of evacuees and as there was no possible accommodation for them, they were kept for the time being on board.

Concerning the warships – the Admiral insisted they were here on a 'Special Mission' – and bearing in mind the presence of the King and Marshal Badoglio and the entire government in Brindisi, I understood the cruiser was there to take them away in emergency.

Both Italian authorities and submarine *Pisani* were unbelievably astonished to find a submarine under Polish colours in the Adriatic. The Admiral was full of hospitality, offering *Sokol* berth on the cruiser. As the recall signal was received with orders to leave the area that night, I did not enter the harbour.

The reception of the shore party in the town was extremely enthusiastic, including hugging and kissing by women, offering champagne, expressing welcome to the Allies and hate of Fascism – it appeared that there was never any single Fascist in Brindisi!!!

## Capitaine de Frégate Jean L'Herminier, Marine Nationale; from *Casabianca*

The Allied-Italian Armistice led to an immediate rising in Corsica against both the Italians and the Germans. The Corsicans begged for French reinforcements, and while the French al Algiers had the troops they were short of transports. However, the crew of the *Casabianca* had been secretly spending their shore leave practising how to load commandos, and L'Herminier maintained it would take only a couple of hours to embark 105 commandos and their kit.

Wet and glistening, the *Casabianca* started up her diesels and two clouds of black smoke spurted out towards Algiers behind us. When our escort turned round and went back we set our speed at 15 knots in order to land our cargo – this time our parcels had legs! – in Lava Bay in the night from 13 to 14 September as arranged. After that a short march of about nine miles ought to see the men in Ajaccio, where – if the arrangement with the cruisers worked well – they would find the bulk of the battalion already landed.

Since the capitulation of Italy … submarines were allowed to remain on the surface during the day … Even apart from this relaxation I should have chanced surface cruising in order to gain time because the PBI battened down below had no desire to prolong their acquaintance with the inside of a submarine. It must have reminded them of the Paris Metro in the rush hour – only worse. These fellows had all the guts in the world and there was nothing they weren't ready for, but, despite Jules Verne, a submarine is not a convenient conveyance for the man in the street and I realized very well that men in their position would not be feeling very comfortable. They didn't know the rules of the game and they knew that if anything went wrong they would be both useless and helpless.

As soon as the diesels were running smoothly and everything was in order I made a tour of inspection of my passenger boat. I felt something like a ticket inspector in the rush hour myself. It was then that I discovered that we had three 'stowaways' bringing the total number of passengers up to 109 and the total number of men on board to no less than 170 – a record if ever there was one for a submarine of 1,500 tons! …

Our warriors cooped up below the hatches took their discomfort in good part, but they were very much annoyed to think that the rest of the battalion, voyaging in comfort like millionaire yachtsmen on board the *Fantasque* and the *Terrible*, would get there before them. We comforted them with the fable of the hare and the tortoise. When we left Algiers the two cruisers had not yet returned from Salerno. If they happened to be a few hours late we might well be in Corsica before them, particularly as after a closer scrutiny of our charts I had increased speed to seventeen knots and decided to make direct for the entrance to Ajaccio Bay, which would permit us to arrive in the night from the 12th to the 13th.

If the two cruisers were a little delayed we should be in first, and I had no doubt that in that case we should be given orders to land our contingent in the port itself to hearten the population of Ajaccio and take the first measures against the return of the Germans until reinforcements arrived.

Although we were cruising along the coast of Sardinia, whose airfields were still occupied by the Luftwaffe, we were hoping that no enemy air patrol would appear on the scene and force us to submerge, which would mean losing precious time.

At 11.34 on 13 September we received a message informing us that the *Fantasque* and the *Terrible* had arrived in Algiers and would leave at once doing thirty knots. We were also told that if the cruisers wished to communicate with us en route they would do so via Algiers using the British naval code for surface vessels. It rather looked as though we were going to lose the race.

At 13.16 hours the wireless operator came out of his hutch waving another violet form. Excitement mounted and we hurriedly cleared the table to make room for the code books. The message read:

'*FANTASQUE* AND *TERRIBLE* DELAYED STOP TRY TO LAND AT AJACCIO STOP PILOT WILL EXPECT YOU AFTER 23.00 HOURS ON THE 22ND HALF WAY BETWEEN THE ISLES SANGUINAIRES AND CAPE MURO STOP PILOT WILL GIVE RECOGNITION SIGNAL P FOR PERCY STOP YOU WILL REPLY F FOR FREDDY STOP.'

The glad news that we were going to be in first after all swept through the submarine like lightning, a remarkable phenomenon of spontaneous transmission, and there was a roar of cheering. Fate had given us the victory. Our passengers were now bubbling with optimism and so was our crew: we had been waiting for this moment for months.

Our ambition was to be realized. We were to be rewarded for all our labours. After having been the first to leave Toulon we were now to be the first to return to a French port to begin the battle to drive the enemy out of our country! Bernard, my batman, produced the last bottles of wine on board and there was great rejoicing.

Our diesels were working satisfactorily but running rather hot. My Engineer Officer Kerneur and his right hand man, Chief Engine-Room Artificer Tagland, looked after them like nursemaids and the diesels stood up to it magnificently, though since our escape from Toulon on 27 November 1942, we had never spared them. In order to be at our rendezvous on time and recharge our batteries en bloc for long periods of submersion in enemy-patrolled waters, we had often driven them very hard. Apart from our electrical auxiliaries which had blighted the lives of our mechanics and electricians, our mechanical equipment was first class, but nevertheless it was due above all to the skill and devotion of the men in charge of the diesels that they successfully survived the gruelling time we gave them.

At 2300 hours, Chailley with his cat's eyes spotted the Isles Sanguinaires. We turned to starboard on the look-out for the pilot boat awaiting us in Ajaccio Bay, and it was not long before we spotted it and the agreed light signals were exchanged. Examining the craft through our night-glasses we observed with astonishment that the flag of the Italian Royal Navy was flying at the peak. The armistice was only a few days old and our ex-enemies were still running the port services.

By megaphone we asked the pilot to come on board, but he refused, telling us to follow him in. Apparently he didn't trust us and we had no cause to trust him. However, I was disinclined to waste time in argument, so we followed in his wake, using our soundings apparatus to make quite sure that the fellow wasn't treacherously leading us into a field of magnetic mines, which would have been quite harmless to his wooden boat. Incidentally, we were following the axis of the bay, on a course of 045, where the sea bed was precipitous and there was little danger of minefields.

The Bay of Ajaccio is one of the most beautiful in the world. High mountains arise almost out of the sea all round, and on that night great fires were burning on all their peaks, creating a fairylike and impressive picture. Were they the work of the Patriots or had the Germans set light to the maquis? A pale yellow moon added a magnificent touch to the general decor.

When we came in sight of the beacon, which was about 200 yards from the entrance we stopped. A boat came up and a Corsican pilot from Ajaccio clambered on board. He informed me that we were to berth at the Quai de la République to the north of the first dock. I steered the *Casabianca* to come alongside starboard beam to the quay.

Suddenly a heavy fusillade sounded and I immediately ordered full speed astern, but the pilot reassured me.

'The quays are crowded with people,' he said. 'They have come to welcome you in. The Patriots are firing into the air out of sheer joy.'

'As far as I'm concerned they're wasting the ammunition we sweated blood to get here,' I said.

'You'll just have to excuse them this evening, Captain.'

'All right,' I said, 'but they put the wind up me.'

The *Casabianca* went forward again and after a while we could see the crowds waiting on the quays.

'Full astern port 25. Stop!'

We manoeuvred the *Casabianca* into the quayside and all the while the crowds set up a tremendous patriotic roar that we are not likely to forget for a long time.

'Vive la France! Vive la *Casabianca*! Vive de Gaulle!'

The darkness was there to hide our tears of joy.

To be perfectly frank, I think our arrival caused a certain disappointment because the crowds were expecting the two cruisers Fantasque and Terrible with strong landing forces.

This was the end of L'Herminier's war. He suffered from chronic arthritis and upon his return from the mission both legs were amputated. To the delight of the crew, Bellet succeeded him.

## Lieutenant-Commander Jerzy ('George') Koziolowski, Polish Navy, ORP *Sokol*; from Patrol Report, ADM199/1854

Attached to the 1st Submarine Flotilla at Beirut, and operating around the Dodecanese Islands in the Aegean, *Sokol* left on her sixth Mediterranean war patrol on 4 November. On the day of 11 November, this being Poland's Independence Day, *Sokol* was travelling submerged between the islands of Amorgos and Anydro.

At 1215, while seven miles north of Anedro [Anydro], two-masted schooner was sighted on bearing 315°, at a distance of nine miles. Schooner was proceeding on her motor on course 100° towards Amorgos, at a speed of about eight Knots. Course north was set to approach schooner at close range.

At 1250 schooner passed at 200 yards, beam on. She was about 140 tons, fully rigged with topmasts, flying German flag. The crew of more than a dozen were seen wearing naval uniforms. Her bulwarks were suspiciously high, with canvas covering amidships, and high superstructures beside both masts. Something like DC rails were seen under the stern. Two boats were on tow. Observation was difficult due to haze low above the surface and the sunlight played tricks with the shadows on the superstructures – they appeared to have no fore and after bulkheads, thus looking like only side coverings.

Went to action stations at 1313, surfaced four miles off SW point of Amorgos Island. Schooner was 140° on the starboard bow at a distance of 4,000 yards, steering 110° parallel to the coast. Opened fire with 3-inch gun at a range of 4,000 yards firing on rel. bear. Red 020° and closing on course 090° at full speed.

First three rounds were scattered about 500 yards – the following ones straddled the target within 50–80 yards.

Schooner turned towards the coast, showing 140° on the port bow and opened fire with two heavy MGs. The 11th round hit the foremast and brought it down. Enemy ceased fire for a while and slowed down. After 24 rounds the gun jammed beyond quick repair, due to defective ammunition. Enemy immediately reopened fire, apparently stopping – the range closing to 2,000 yards. Fired 400 rounds from 2 Vickers MGs and at 1230 dived hurriedly, for enemy's fire was becoming unpleasantly hot. Examined target through periscope – she was stopped and adrift, two small rowing boats leaving towards shore, but with only a few men; the others were still on board ...

Manoeuvred to obtain firing position, and at 1347 fired one torpedo set to two feet at 500 yards, on 100° track. Torpedo slightly turned to the port and either it deviated from its track or schooner was on the drift – torpedo passed under stern and missed. It caused, however, considerable panic on board, and remaining crew left schooner in a hurry in a motor boat, steering to the coast. Closed to 200 yards and confirmed schooner was really abandoned ...

Surfaced at 1406 and put S/Lieutenant Fritz in charge of boarding party of four on board. As soon as boarding party landed, lookout was much impressed by mountainous islands all round the horizon, and in the same moment aircraft, E-boat, merchant vessel and caique were reported approaching from different bearings. A/C was possible, for intensive A/C patrolling was carried out during the forenoon, and CO without confirming the sighting blew the whistle for the boarding party to come back. Two demolition charges were fired with 10-minute fuze, and boarding party hurried on board. At this moment, securing line broke, schooner started to drift away and the last two of the boarding party, including S/Lieutenant Fritz carrying charts, books and signals, had to jump overboard and swim a few yards. Of course, none of the panicky-sighted targets materialised, but now the fuze was set and the chance of a considerable prize was lost.

Schooner was 120 feet long, estimated at 140 tons, and carefully equipped. Captain's cabin was fully loaded with charts, books etc. – a pair of earphones was seen but whether these belonged to the wireless or listening device could not be confirmed. She was carrying some stores: bunches of naval clothing, rifles, ammunition belts, bayonets, boots – all brand new and stored in the focs'le. There was a loading hold amidships, but locked tightly. Two 0.5-inch MGs were counted on each side, and rifles were dropped on the deck, apparently freshly used. Possibly four depth charges were astern, covered by canvas, with movable doors on the bulwarks.

At 1435 schooner blew up magnificently and sank. When jumping overboard, S/Lieutenant Fritz could only save charts. Schooner's course led from Nio to Stampalia.

SINKING OF A 20-TON CAIQUE OFF SANTORINI

On 18 November, *Sokol* was patrolling submerged four miles North of Santorini Is. When at 0820 a caique of 20 tons was sighted on bearing 025° at a distance of six miles, 24° on her starboard bow, steering south. Course 090° was set to close her, preparing for gun action.

At 0840, when caique was only 2,000 yards away, thus five miles off Santorini, she turned back and steered 340°, showing 140° of her port bow. Surfaced and opened fire on rel. bear. Green 020°, 3,000 yards range, firing across her bow. The fourth round was nearly a hit astern, and caique turned towards waving white flags.

Ceased fire and closed. There was no cargo on board. The crew consisted of two half-naked incredibly dirty Greeks and two Germans in uniform, armed with MG rifles, automatics and hand-grenades. They were taken on board – Greeks weeping with joy and blessing everybody, Germans disbelieving their luck at not being shot on the spot – and the caique was sunk by gunfire. She was *Taxiabari No. 370-S1*, based on Nio Island and used for patrolling round Nio Island and used for patrolling and requisition of every kind of Greek caique and boat and probably robbing them of their fishing. Germans' uniforms were worn out years ago and they were not given any food for day's patrolling except dog-biscuits and a little rotten black bread, and were living on fish they could kill by hand grenades.

Towards the end of the report, Koziolowski added the following information about his prisoners.

They were Army men, 23 and 27 years of age; a Sergeant and Private of Alpine section of 'Waffen SS'. After fighting in Yugoslavia in 1942 they were sent to Greece. Being stationed in Nio Is., they were used to patrol surrounding waters in a small caique manned by Greeks in order to catch and requisition all possible craft and probably to rob fishermen of their catch. Their uniform and boots were pretty worn out and they were visibly undernourished; they used to be sent to sea with only dog biscuits and had to rely on what they could catch or steal. After two days of full normal feeding they developed stomach troubles and were unable to retain their food.

They were quite talkative, and although not in any way arrogant or fanatical were definitely imbued with a spirit of Nazism. They were subjected to re-educational propaganda, i.e., listening to BBC German broadcast, shown illustrated magazines with situation in Russia and bombing of Germany vividly portrayed. They were surprised by good treatment on board; when captured they could not believe their lives would be spared ...

MASSACRE OF ABOUT 200 HUNS OFF MIRABELLA BAY
After patrolling for 12 days in rather fruitless area between Amorgos and Santorini, *Sokol* was ordered to examine Sitia before leaving Aegean. *Sokol* left Santorini I. on the evening of 18 November and arrived off NE coast of Crete next morning. Sitia Bay was approached from N Westward, when at 0730, big

two-masted schooner under foresail was sighted on bearing 105°, distance six miles, proceeding from [Gianysada] Is towards Cretan coast, steering S. West. She was right against the sun and difficult to be examined. Closed her slowly – she was 200 feet long, of about 200 tons, fully rigged with topmasts, proceeding under German flag, crowded with troops which were estimated to amount to over 100. Proceeding at about five knots, she passed Paneromano [Phaneromani] Cape, rounding next cape, hauled down sail and increased speed to eight knots, closing the coast. *Sokol* surfaces at 0903, 4,000 yards astern of schooner, opening fore on rel. bear. Red 050° at 4,000 yards range, closing at full speed. After 20 rounds the gun jammed again beyond quick repair. Schooner was hit eight times and caught fire astern, hauled down Nazi flag and hoisted Greek colours; fired red-star grenade and headed towards the shore of the bay. Two AA batteries opened fire on *Sokol*, from their post high on the mountains, using time fuze: shrapnel was spreading all around.

*Sokol* dived, embittered; schooner then turned westward and came alongside steep rock on the coast, anchored and started to unload the troops, exposing her beam to seawards. The turn of luck seemed incredible, and *Sokol* prepared for torpedo attack.

Small motor caique of under 10 tons came from the bay and approached the schooner, placing herself between her bow and shore as a sort of gangway. The place must have been used for mooring for some lines were hung from the top of the rocks and about 10 half stripped men were climbing up.

At 0950, one torpedo was fired from 1,100 yards, set to run on surface and aimed amidships. Unfortunately, after leaving the tube it deviated slightly to port and missed schooner astern, hitting the rock. All the climbing party disappeared as well as considerable numbers of men just landing. Schooner was damaged, listed about 20° towards the rock and touching it with her masts. There were still a lot of troops on her. They saw the periscope and waved white flags. It was pretty hard on one's feelings but German uniforms and caps unmistakably reminded one of Lord Vansittart's slogan and at 0955 a second torpedo was fired from 900 yards, set to run on the surface and it struck the schooner at the foremast. She blew up, showing her big Nazi flag painted on the roof of the fo'c'sle. When the explosion subsided there remained about 15 men high on the rock and about 10 in the caique, which moved away in time ...

When surfacing for gun action, another schooner was sighted inside a small bay off S. Nikolo Islet. After sinking her first victim, *Sokol* hurried westward. Schooner of similar size was moored to a buoy close to the sandy beach in the middle of the bay, heading west, beam on to seaward. She was difficult to examine closely, being against the sun she was heavily laden and very low in the water, with something long and bulky amidships, covered with canvas – and crowded with half-stripped men, apparently sea-bathing. They amounted again to over 100.

The sea was glassy calm in the bay and the periscope was sighted on the schooner. For one hour and a half, while *Sokol* manoeuvred to place herself on the target's beam, schooner was swinging on motor, keeping submarine right ahead Finally at 1115 mooring lines broke and the schooner drifted to the westward. Foresail was hoisted, but her motor was apparently too weak, and she was turning very slowly. It seemed at the beginning she was leaving for Mirabella Bay and *Sokol* prepared for chase, but at 1140 she was approached by 3 small caiques of under 10 tons, which towed her in the SW corner of the bay, where she secured to the mooring buoy, half screened by S. Nikolo rock. One caique brought survivors from the sunken schooner, while two others came from the village in the bay, and they all laid behind the schooner, alongside the rocky coast.

When being towed the schooner offered a convenient target on 90° track at 600 yards, but as she was moving and turning, and having no confidence in the torpedoes, fire was withheld, waiting for a 'sure' shot.

While she was being secured and *Sokol* approached to attack, HE of a fast motor-boat was heard at 1200 on bearing 270° and soon an E-boat was sighted coming from Mirabella Bay under German flag. Attack was broken off, shut off for depth charging and started to withdraw to seaward. E-Boat, however, went straight towards schooner, secured alongside and was seen to use her engines to keep her bow facing the bay, thus exposing the smallest target. Having two targets alongside it was a gift and *Sokol* hurried to the attack.

Schooner was lying inside a deep inlet, heading East and screened from north by S Nikolo Islet. Attack was possible only on 50° track, allowing torpedoes 50–80 yards clearance off S Nikolo rock. To fire at some 1,000 yards S. Nikolo must have been approached pretty close – depths around her were safe, being 9 fathoms 1 cable East of S. Eastern point, decreasing to 5 fathoms when 1 cable East of S. Eastern point. The chart available was inconveniently small and it was estimated to fire torpedoes from outside S. Nikolo rock. The enlarged plan was made only later.

*Sokol* set course 217° to fire on 50° track and before reaching firing position, her periscope was sighted from the schooner, causing alarm on the E-boat. At 1247 one torpedo was fired at 1,100 yards range, while the periscope was fired at by two 20mm guns from E-boat and some MGs ashore. E-boat was seen to drop securing lines and part company with schooner. Unfortunately torpedo altered course slightly to port and missed the schooner ahead, hitting the coast and blowing up one of three caiques.

One precious minute elapsed until torpedo exploded – echo-sounding reported only four fathoms under the keel. But on the other hand, E-boat was nearly on the move, delayed only by the crowd of panic-stricken men jumping overboard, through which she could not move. This was the only chance to have the final strike, or be struck in the next moment. The chance was seized without delay; second torpedo was brought to 'stand by', but as always happens in such cases, trim was lost, and another precious minute elapsed.

Finally, at 1279, second torpedo was fired at 900 yards, this being the last available one, and the helm was put hard to port; the bottom was struck while still at 30 feet, bumping slightly, and in the next moment a submerged rock was struck right ahead. Two depth charges exploded nearby. These must have been fired from a depth charge thrower. *Sokol* then went full ahead GU for half a minute, then put the periscope up just in time to see torpedo missing the target again and hitting the coast some 20 yards behind. Second caique blew up and splash from the explosion deluged the E-boat, which was still among the swimming crowd. Although the crowd vanished after explosion, E-boat herself seemed immobilised and ceased fire.

Being afraid of damaging propellers in the move astern, blew Nos. one and six and went full ahead GU with helm hard to port. E-boat did not move, but shore battery opened fire with 88mm or 4-inch gun, as well as with at least three MGs. When swinging through 090° echo-sounding still recorded five fathoms, then increased to 11. Dived after being for nearly two minutes on the surface (10 feet) and withdrew at full speed to seaward, apparently with no damage. After 'cooling down' torpedoes were reloaded and as schooner was still unmoved 'the thief came again on the scene of his crime'.

The luck seemed incredibly favourable this day, for schooner with E-boat alongside was apparently abandoned, heading 150°, thus exposing full beam. Closed to attack on course 259°. When steadying for firing, a heavy stream of two or three M.G.s bullets were seen across submarine's course. One torpedo was fired at 1508 at 1,500 yards, set to run on surface – this went dead straight, with no air bubbles (as all previous ones) and hit schooner amidships. Schooner disintegrated, E-boat was lifted by the explosion and got 30° bow up angle and then collapsed gently; small caique, the last one of three, was stranded on the rock and turned over, broken in half. *Sokol* turned to port grouping up and passing well clear of 10 fathom line. E-boat was still afloat for about four minutes and while the whole crew enjoyed her agony she capsized slowly, showing big Nazi flag painted on the deck, and sank.

## FAR EAST

### Captain Zenji Orita, Imperial Japanese Navy, *I-165*; from *I-Boat Captain*

Captain Orita's new boat completed her trials at the end of 1942, just as both the US and his own side were engaged in an increasingly desperate battle for Guadalcanal in the Solomon Islands, 1,000 miles from Australia and more than 3,000 from Japan itself.

Historians all state that the first six months of 1943 were a combat 'lull'. I and other Japanese submariners can tell them quite differently.

On Jan. 14 I took *RO-101* out through Tokyo Bay on her way to Rabaul. I arrived at Rabaul on Jan. 27, hoping to accomplish great things. I made none of the Guadalcanal runs, as it turned out, being assigned to patrol missions instead. But 16 other submarines were assigned to that type of work. Torpedoes were loaded into their tubes, but all spare parts were put ashore, together with most of the topside armaments. Rations for each submarine's crew were reduced to the minimum, so boats would have more room for rations for the 20,000 starving soldiers. One large-size submarine could carry enough food to last the Guadalcanal garrison for two days, and Rear Adm. Mito made a run himself in *I-8* to see how the operation worked. By February of 1943 a total of 28 successful runs, delivering about 1,500 tons of supplies and ammunition, were made. Our submarines were attacked on seven different occasions and two were sunk. One, *I-3*, I have already told about. The other was *I-1*.

Lt. Cdr. Eichi Sakamoto took *I-1* out of Rabaul on Jan. 24, and put into Buin to pick up supplies. Then he moved down to Guadalcanal, arriving off Kaminpo point on Jan. 29, having traveled most of the way submerged. This grandfather of our modern submarines was nearly 16 years old when she surfaced that night about 9 p.m. and prepared to off-load cargo. Unknown to Sakamoto, his boat had already been picked up on radar by the Australian corvette, HMAS *Kiwi*. *I-1*'s after gun had been removed to make room for a landing craft to move cargo to shore. So, on finding herself under fire she could only man her forward deck gun. Its crew was wiped out instantly. Sakamoto himself was mortally wounded by fire from this small but deadly enemy, which kept pouring out shells from her deck and machine guns. Even rifle fire was exchanged during the battle and, during one of the three times I-1 was rammed by HMAS *Kiwi*, her navigator tried to board the Australian ship and fight it out hand-to-hand with his sword. A sister ship of *Kiwi*, the HMAS *Moa*, joined the battle after a while, and also rammed *I-1*. With 30 men dead, the executive officer, Lt. Sadayoshi Koreeda, tried to beach the submarine. He ran his submarine up on the beach and with the remnant of his crew (50 men) joined our forces in Guadalcanal's jungle.

The US Navy claimed that it captured many secret documents from the beached *I-1*, but this is open to question because Lt. Koreeda told me he burned them on shore.

My first patrol in *RO-101* was made on orders from Rear Adm. Kaku Harada. Harada sent three submarines out to stations east of Port Moresby, with orders to stop any enemy attempt to interfere with the planned withdrawal from Guadalcanal. *RO-100* and *RO-103* went out when I did. *I-18*, already in the Coral Sea for this purpose, was lost carrying out her mission.

In the first week of February, Japanese destroyers made 60 runs to Guadalcanal, bringing off an evacuation which for daring and success compares favorably with the English at Dunkirk and the Americans at Hungnam, Korea. It had one more thing in common with the American evacuation during the Korean War, too, because when American marines in 1950 said 'Retreat, hell! We're advancing in another direction!' they were copying a phrase from their former enemies, the Japanese; who had coined it seven years earlier. Altogether 13,030 of our men were taken off Guadalcanal, 832 of them Navy men, without a bit of opposition, in what our high command called a tenshin (turned advance) …

*RO-100* was almost sunk. She was 30 miles south of Port Moresby on Feb. 14, when Lt. Kanemi Sakamoto sighted an enemy transport. He began maneuvering to attack and became so engrossed in trying to make a kill that he neglected to observe the submariner's routine precaution, frequent sweeps of the entire seascape with his periscope. As a result, an American destroyer escort was able to approach him almost unnoticed. Sakamoto saw this onrushing ship at the last moment and dived. The DE dropped over a dozen depth charges. They smashed *RO-100's* periscope, and caused other damage. Sakamoto, unable to continue on patrol, had to make for Rabaul.

I was almost trapped, too. I got word on Feb. 16 of what happened to *RO-100*, and arbitrarily maintained radio silence for four days to avoid detection. On Feb. 22 my navigator, Lt. Shigeshi Kondo, sighted a single-stack ship of about 4,000 tons displacement. She was obviously an old ship and appeared to be an easy victim. Still, something about her bothered me when I took over the periscope from Kondo. Her Plimsoll line was well above the ocean's surface and I could clearly make out the difference between her above-water and below-water paints.

'That ship is very nearly empty,' I told Kondo, 'and if she is empty it is because she's returning from a supply trip to Port Moresby. In that case, she would be heading east. But – she is heading west! I don't like it. Let us wait a while before attacking.'

So we waited. The enemy ship continued on her eastward course for some time, then turned to the north. I waited some more. After a while she changed course again – to the west!

'Aha!' I cried out. 'A Q-ship!'

During the First World War the British, whom the Japanese helped in escorting ships through the Mediterranean (in exchange for which Britain backed her demand for a mandate to the German islands north of the Equator) had disguised and equipped old merchant ships with masked gun batteries and depth charge racks. These vessels proved to be deadly lures for the German U-boats, many of whose captains paid with their lives for taking the bait. I decided that I would not join those dead German submarine captains. I kept *RO-101* submerged (instead of surfacing to close in rapidly) and used my periscope sparingly. We had sighted the enemy ship about three PM I decided I would stay down until well after dark, surface very late at night to recharge batteries, then submerge to prep for a dawn attack.

My plan didn't work. At sunset the enemy vessel suddenly picked up speed, and ran away in the direction of Port Moresby. I searched for it the next two days without success and returned to Rabaul on Feb. 28. *RO-103* came in two days later. Her skipper, Lt. Hidenori Fujita, had had no luck either.

When our submarines began their transport work to Guadalcanal Gen. MacArthur's offensive in New Guinea intensified. It became very difficult for Japanese surface ships to get in past MacArthur's air umbrella, so submarines were ordered to lend a hand there. Before I came on the scene, nine submarines had made a total of 20 trips from Rabaul to New Guinea. After my *RO-101* joined the operation, 75 more trips were made, through September of 1943. Total supplies put ashore on New Guinea by submarines from December 1942 to September 1943, was about 3,500 tons. These operations, strangely enough, cost us only one submarine, *I-4* (although, *I-176* did suffer heavy damage during an attack).

In replenishing New Guinea, Japanese submarines employed two ingenious devices. They were called *unkato* (stores carrier tube) and *unpoto* (cannon carrier). The *unpoto* was introduced first. It consisted of two hollow cylinders, placed side-by-side with a platform built over the top of them. Overall length of this device was 71 feet, overall width 13 feet. On top of the platform an artillery piece was lashed into place and tied down securely, along with cases of shells for the gun. Slung under the platform were the after parts (the power plants) and fuel flasks of two torpedoes. An *unpoto* weighed 20 tons and displaced 37 tons after cargo was loaded.

One of our submarines would strap a loaded *unpoto* to its after deck at Rabaul, after loading its other cargo, then head for a New Guinea rendezvous. There the submarine would rise to just below the surface, its deck just a bit awash. Crewmen would climb out, unlash the *unpoto*, then return to the submarine's hull leaving only the cannon carrier's operator above the water. The submarine would then lower itself only enough to let the *unpoto* float free, after which the operator would start the torpedoes' power plants, which could drive the mechanized raft about two miles at six knots. The operator would run it right up on the shore at a selected spot, then let down a special ramp at the *unpoto*'s bow. Soldiers would hasten on board, carry away the ammunition, and roll the artillery piece into the jungle.

The *unpoto* was already working successfully when the *unkato* was introduced. This was truly a remarkable experiment. The *unkato* was a cylinder 136 feet long, with cone-shaped ends. It was 16 feet in diameter. Both of the cones were ballast tanks, and there was a third ballast tank in the *unkato*'s center. These three compartments were separate from the long cargo space, which had a capacity of 377 tons of food, ammunition and medicines. With a strong hull structure that permitted submerging to a depth of 400 feet, the *unkato* was adjusted after loading so that it had slightly negative buoyancy, then it would be towed out into the middle of Simpson harbor and secured by a long tow line to the stern of a submarine. Once the submarine cleared Rabaul, it would cruise along the northern coast of New Britain to the point where its submerged run was to begin. When the submarine dived, the *unkato* would submerge with it. On arrival off New Guinea, the submarine would surface and release the *unkato*, which was then towed to the beach by men from the shore.

### Rear Admiral Richard O'Kane, US Navy;
from *Wahoo – the Patrols of America's Most Famous WW2 Submarine*

USS *Wahoo* left Brisbane on her third patrol, her first with Lieutenant-Commander Dudley Morton in command and with Richard O'Kane combining the duties of Exec and Navigating Officer. Her patrol area was to be the shipping lanes around the Palaus Islands and Wewak harbour, New Guinea. On 26 January a convoy was sighted near the island of Wewak. On 24 January she sank a destroyer, then went after the rest of the convoy. On 26 January she caught up with it.

Volunteers were in line for a turn at the scopes, and Fireman Whipp reported smoke from the fleeing ships at 1530. The single puff was on our port bow, and we changed course to intercept. In minutes we had mastheads indicating their course of north. We had intercepted the enemy the long but sure way and had ample daylight hours to gain an attack position.

Morton conned his submarine parallel to the enemy's track on courses I provided from the mooring board plotting sheet. My information came from Chan on the search scope and we would alter positions. Backing us up was George Misch, perched like King Kong atop the shears. The courses would keep us just beyond the enemy's horizon – unless George should stand up – giving *Wahoo* a tremendous advantage. Roger and the fire control party were not idle, and had the enemy zigging along a base course of 350 and still at 10 knots. George Grider, with Lenox and Keeter, had all mains carrying their maximum load, even the one with the twisted vertical shaft, and at 1721, *Wahoo* was dead ahead of the fleeing ships. After my final look, confirming that the masts were in line, the captain pulled the plug for our submerged approach and attack.

Wild zigs by the enemy ships, sometimes in unison (which is usual), but at other times in column movements (ships turning in the same water), taxed our fire control party and our battery. At times, our log showed speeds up to 10 knots, but by 1830, the captain had *Wahoo* in a good position on the tanker's, or engine aft freighter's, port beam. We would attack this undamaged ship first.

'Constant bearing – Mark.' Hunter read 016.

'Set,' came from Roger; her stern was coming on.

'Fire!' Morton hit the plunger; the shudder, zing, and momentary pressure told that all was well. The second and third torpedoes went to her midships and bow, but our own screws drowned out the torpedoes' propeller noise. The captain was swinging *Wahoo* with full speed and rudder to bring our stern tubes to bear on the freighter. I was passing bearings to him when a great flash enveloped the tanker, followed almost instantly by the whack of one torpedo's detonation. The freighter turned away before reaching our firing bearing. But we still had those torpedoes. Three blasts sent *Wahoo* up and after her. To our surprise, the tanker was still going, now close on the freighter's port quarter. Instead of four torpedoes aft for the freighter, they must now sink both ships.

Staying with the tanker, our first approach to another good firing position went well. Turning to bring our stern tubes to bear put us broadside to the enemy for a moment. That was all the tanker needed in order to spot us, and she was turning away before we could bring our stern tubes to bear. We tried from various positions, but now alerted, the tanker was even faster in her evasion. Perhaps she had all extra hands on lookout, or had better binoculars than ours. But our captain was not at a loss: he simply turned *Wahoo* around, and ordering all back full, we chased the tanker down going backwards. All did not go exactly as planned, for as we neared full speed late in the approach, the force of the sea against our rudder was greater than that of the hydraulic steering rams. The rudder swung right, looking aft, taking us into a sharp turn. That served to confuse the enemy more than it did us. We barged ahead at full speed on the convoy's next zig and were in fair position when the ships zigged back.

Accepting a range of 1,850 yards, the Captain's 'Any time, Dick,' came over the TBT's [target bearing transmitter's] speaker. I checked my binoculars again to be sure that the hinge pin was firmly wedged in the 'V' – shaped receptacle, and then called, 'Constant bearing – Mark.' The wire was amidships, and now her engine spaces aft were coming on.

'Fire!' The second torpedo was marked on her bow and fired to hit under her bridge structure forward. The tanker was apparently waiting for us to make our move, but two curving phosphorescent wakes were doing that for us. Morton came to the bridge in time to see the wakes disappearing into the night, but with lead angles that appeared correct. We had not long to wait, for the torpedo run would take only 72 seconds according to the word over the speaker. A flash aft of amidships and the instantaneous whack below our feet made the time academic, and the captain called, 'All ahead full,' as we went after the remaining freighter. The course took us by the sinking tanker, but only in time to see her after section canted at about 30 degrees. The details in silhouette checked with Lindhe's party, the *Manzyu Maru* of 6,515 tons.

We had spent an hour and a half putting this last ship down, and would have to do better on the freighter or we would be attacking in partial moonlight. It would give enough light for her to spot us, but not sufficient for our scopes. The time was 2036, just 11 minutes after firing on the tanker, and we commenced an approach on the last ship of the convoy. Our plan was simple – present only our sharpest silhouette when within her sighting range – and that meant an abbreviated end-around [manoeuvre to pass a ship and gain a position ahead]. Her zigs were frantic, but far from bothersome, for they slowed her progress along the base course. Her gunfire, however, was something to behold. A dim, reddish flash, no more than from a flashlight, would be followed by thunder and the thump of a shell splash. It was the same flashless powder that we had observed in Argonaut off Midway on the night of December 7, 1942. But here, we, not the island, were the potential target.

The gunfire was obviously at random, but became a bit disconcerting when a nearby splash was the first indication that we had been spotted. They weren't supposed to be able to see us at this range. The 'convincer' was a shell splashing dead ahead that ricocheted over our shears. The gun had our range and the captain pulled our plug [gave the order to dive].

In the security at 90 feet, we thought this one over as the 'wumps' of shell splashes resounded through our hull. It was dangerous up there, and a dawn attack at periscope depth seemed the answer. We were, after all, a submarine. But the captain decided to size up the situation on the surface before making his decision. The intensity of the 'wumps' had now diminished, and three blasts sent us up.

The surfacing procedure was normal; lookouts manned their stations, the engines were firing, and the turbos would screech for about five minutes. Above it all was Seaman Wach, our port forward lookout, pointing and shouting, 'Searchlight broad on our port bow!'

Richie hopped up with Wach; the beam was just coming over the horizon, and with full power, *Wahoo* would be able to intercept the freighter should she close it. Morton had already presumed that she would, and that this was a destroyer sent to rescue this remaining ship. Chan had plotted the freighter's position with a radar range and my bearing from the forward TBT, and now we did the same with the destroyer. The captain directed plotting the destroyer at 20 knots to go with the known 10-knot freighter's speed, so Chan solved graphically the algebraic problem of their meeting point. Morton picked a point on the freighter's track five miles before the junction, and then a firing position 3,000 yards off the track. Chiefs Lenox, Keeter, and Pruett got us there with minutes to spare, and after reversing course with full rudder, we slowed to steerageway.

I commenced almost continuous bearings on the freighter's stack from the after TBT, not calling angles, for on a known course TDC's would be better than mine. The captain kept our stern pointed directly at the freighter, which was now steering a steady course. A reassuring, 'Checks with TDC,' or 'Checks with plot,' followed my bearings and the one angle I had just called, 'Port ninety!'

Perhaps grasping my impatience, 'Any time, Dick' came immediately.

'Constant bearing – Mark!'

'Set,' came over the speaker. Her stack was coming on the wire. 'Fire!'

The second and last torpedo followed 15 seconds later to hit in exactly the same spot, for the captain wanted no cripples. The shudder and zing, followed by Buckley's report, were normal for each torpedo, and I reported their phosphorescent wakes on course. The range was longer than had been our custom, but everything else looked good, and after all, our torpedoes could hold a course within one-half of a degree. All of this gave me confidence as Hunter called the seconds over the IMC [announcing system] for the troops. There was more than a freighter involved, for if these torpedoes hit, a return to Pearl and a ticket to the Royal would be assured. Morton came to the bridge and then aft to watch the freighter from beside the TBT. Two minutes had passed and there was less than a minute to go. In the speaker's background, we could hear George exclaiming over the torpedo run. He must have moved over to the chart desk, next to the IMC, and seen Chan's plot, for in his measured, southern voice, the following words came over loud and clear: 'Paine,' he said. 'If those torpedoes hit, I'll kiss your butt.'

About 15 seconds later came the first of two detonations that shook *Wahoo* a mile and a half away. A quarter hour after the detonations, the destroyer was sweeping a clear sea with her searchlight. The freighter, long since identified as of the *Arizona Maru*-Class, had sunk. The time was 2128, still Tuesday,

January 26, and we set course 358 for Fais Island with its phosphorite works, and just off the route to Pearl.

Except for George and Jack with their customary watch, and the captain, we were gathered in the wardroom. After a word and friendly smile through the doorway, Morton started forward to seek out every hand and personally thank and congratulate them. As far as he was concerned, this was their day, but I believe they felt just the opposite. For sure, our captain had lived up to his statement to all hands after taking command, and he had the wholehearted respect of every one of us. Naturally, there was only one subject in our discussion: none of us had heard of any other submarine sinking her first ship before reaching her patrol area, to say nothing of a convoy of four more ships. These were the things submariners daydreamed about but never expected to happen. Like some other boats, we had long possessed the capability, but it had taken Morton to cast aside unproven prewar concepts and bugaboos. Dead serious during battle, he still commanded with a flair that captured the support of all hands.

The fighting was over, but not the flair. Returning to the wardroom, the captain called for a pad of lined paper and started composing a message for ComSubPac. Crossing out words and adding others, the final version read:

SANK DESTROYER IN WEWAK SUNDAY AND IN FOURTEEN HOUR RUNNING GUN AND TORPEDO BATTLE TODAY SANK CONVOY OF ONE TANKER TWO FREIGHTERS AND ONE TRANSPORT DESTROYING HER BOATS TORPEDOES EXPENDED PROCEEDING PEARL HARBOR VIA FAIS ISLAND

Handing it to Chan for encoding by the board and transmission, he reached for the cribbage board. While I was dealing, Morton raised his forearm diagonally in front of his chest, and with his finger pointed for emphasis, like a preacher, he said with a smile of satisfaction, 'Tenacity, Dick. Stay with 'em till they're on the bottom!'

The success of this patrol, of any patrol, was in that statement. The captain had made his own luck by starting already 400 miles en route, and with some well-planned daring. His luck didn't hold for cribbage, however, and after the rubber game, I joined Krause for midnight stars. While on the cigarette deck, he related the captain's having assured him that taking over the firing panel had nothing to do with Krause's lucky torpedo; he had just realized when in that position he could hold up a firing at the last second should it be advisable. Then the captain had added, 'It's fun too!'

Our midnight stars had shown us in the ball park, and dawn stars on the money. *Waboo* would make a dawn landfall on Fais Island, 24 hours hence, and have the day for a submerged reconnaissance. All was going well, so I changed the Plan of the Day, making it a ropeyarn Sunday. No action would be required;

the duty chief would simply run the schedule accordingly. But the call, 'Smoke over the horizon!' took precedence.

The time was 0720, January 27, and John Campbell had made, perhaps, his first wartime sighting in submarines. He had called an initial TBT bearing, the required first action. Standing watch with Chan, they had already brought *Wahoo* to an intercepting course. This would provide a good drill for our tracking party; they were called, and I told the captain what we were doing. At 0801, the topmasts of three ships poked over the horizon. Plot had a mean course for the enemy of 146, and we pulled the plug for a truly realistic drill.

A half hour into the approach, upon reporting the masts of three more ships, the captain could stand it no longer and took the conn. With 10 feet of scope exposed, I gave him the picture: four large freighters in column, followed by a large tanker, and then trailing by about two ship lengths, a small freighter. For one of the few times, the captain took a look for himself, sweeping past the major ships and then concentrating on the small freighter before lowering the scope.

'Dick,' he said. 'We're the only ones who know we don't have any torpedoes; the enemy doesn't know that. Supposing we were to battle surface and make a run at them. Wouldn't they likely run off leaving the small freighter behind for our deck gun?'

Having seen big guns on the leading ships and none on the trailer, I was all for it, but with one slight modification – that while the gun crew got ready, we move out to about 9,000 yards from our present 7,000, to put us outside their guns' expected range.

Chief Carr had jumped the gun and had his crew ready before we were. The battle surface went smoothly, but this time only Carr with his pointer and trainer went out to cast the gun loose and then returned through the conning tower's after door. The captain headed *Wahoo* diagonally towards the convoy to see what would happen, and all engines went on the line. It had taken the enemy a couple of minutes to assess the situation, but now black smoke belched from their stacks, and flag hoists were being run up to their yardarms, and the signals executed (hauled down). Zigs and column maneuvers ensued, giving the impression of general confusion. Perhaps they had been warned of a mad-dog submarine on the loose. Quite suddenly, however, a column reformed and laid down quite respectable gunfire.

The splashes of the shells remained short, and we headed for the trailing ship as planned. When the smoke, pouring down the length of the convoy, cleared, we found that our small freighter had been replaced by a tanker. That did not change the captain's plan; she might be carrying gasoline, and our deck gun could blow her up, or at least set her on fire. All looked good as we raced towards an initial firing range of 6,000 yards. Buckley on the SJ called 7,500, then 7,000.

'What's that?' said Morton. 'Right beyond the middle ship!'

In seconds, two thin masts slightly canted to the right came into the clear between ships. Their relative movement, opposite that of the convoy, gave the impression of high speed. They had to belong to the convoy's escort, which had been off on a morning search somewhere on the convoy's port bow. As her hull came in view on rounding the tanker's stern, our captain reluctantly put her astern using full rudder. Already at four-engine speed, we handily left her behind as she shoveled on more coal, leaving a black cloud of trailing smoke.

'Why, that antiquated coal-burning corvette!' chided Morton. 'What a hell of a thing to have escorting a six-ship convoy. Why, the Emperor deserves to lose every ship he's got.'

Within 20 minutes, *Wahoo* had opened the range to 14,000 yards. The 'antiquated coal-burning corvette' by now had stopped her profuse smoking; all of that smoke could have come from lighting off more boilers. Exhorting our engineers, we continued to gain another 3,000 yards. Motormacs can always find an extra knot or so at a time like this. But now, looking aft with our 7×50s, we tried to convince ourselves that the escort was not gaining. The SJ had taken this delightful time to act up, but it doesn't take much of a seaman's eye to recognize the tips of a bow wake's 'V.' They appeared to be even with her deck, and very slowly the 'V' filled in as her bow came over the horizon. She would know that coming much closer would put her within torpedo range, and it was with some relief that I observed her turning slowly to the right.

The captain had different thoughts, saying, 'Hot dog, she's giving up. Why, we've dragged her a good thirty miles from her convoy, counting its run. She can't afford to leave it unprotected.'

We were both wrong. As the escort continued to turn, her appearance changed to that of a full-fledged destroyer, at least the equivalent of the Asashio or Fubuki in Wewak. When broadside, she seemed to lay over to starboard as she let fly with a salvo that gave the impression of a battleship shooting at us.

'Watch for the splashes,' said Morton, still undaunted and keeping his binoculars towards the destroyer.

Now I had spotted shellfire in gunnery practices – from the firing ship, not from the target. But if the captain thought this was the only salvo or that it was going to fall way short, then I would spot the splashes with him. About 3 seconds later a mighty clap of thunder to port and starboard sent me towards the hatch with ringing ears. I saw the shell splashes a half ship's length ahead;

she had straddled our shears horizontally. In the excitement, the captain sounded five blasts instead of two, and I had to drag him down the hatch when he stopped to check on his lookouts. Hell, they had dived for the hatch on the flash of gunfire. It was *Wahoo*'s fastest dive, and well so; the next salvo whacked overhead as our shears went under.

The speed log still showed 15 knots, with *Wahoo* at a 15-degree down angle as she passed 250 feet.

'What depth, captain?' called George, who had already blown negative.

'Just keep her going down,' was the reply. It was obvious that *Wahoo* was going to exceed test depth, so George used his best judgment and caught her somewhere below the last numeral on the depth gauge.

Morton's luck continued, and *Wahoo* sank a total of eight ships before returning to Pearl Harbor.

## Commodore Brian Cleary, Royal Australian Navy, Retd, then a midshipman, RANVR, HMAS *K9*

When the Japanese attacked and then occupied the Netherlands East Indies the Royal Netherlands Navy (RNN) moved their remaining surface ships and submarines to Australia and to Ceylon (now Sri Lanka). Three submarines, *K. VIII*, *K. IX* and *K. XII*, arrived in Fremantle, Western Australia. As the 'K' (Kolonien) designation indicates, these were built for service in the Dutch colonies. *K. VIII* and *K. IX* were sister boats built in the early 1920s. *K. XII* was a slightly later class.

On their arrival in Australia in April 1942 the Dutch Admiral offered to place them under Australian operational command. He stated 'Submarines *K. VIII* and *K. IX* are almost obsolete and have little value as warships. I think these boats can best be used for Asdic training.' Accordingly the *K. IX* arrived in Sydney about 19 May 1942 with the expectation that she and her crew would be available for A/S training at the end of August 1942 following refit. This plan was aborted on 31 May 1942 by the Japanese midget submarine attack on Sydney Harbour when a torpedo intended for the USS *Chicago* exploded on the sea wall under the *K. IX*. The damage caused coupled with her already poor mechanical state meant so much time out of service that it caused the RAN to withdraw her from service and to post her crew away to other submarine service.

The Commanding Officer of the RAN's A/S School made a strong plea to the Australian Naval Board to acquire the *K. IX*. The Naval Staff agreed with the need and steps were taken to acquire the submarine on loan and to obtain a crew from the Royal Navy. The RNN and Admiralty agreed so that the submarine was placed in refit in Sydney and 12 trained submariners were despatched from the UK. Local recruiting produced 5 submarine-trained sailors from the Fleet Reserve and 19 untrained sailors.

The *K. IX* commissioned as HMA Submarine *K9* under the command of Lieutenant F. M. Piggot, RNR, on 22 June 1943. However she was still in refit as more and more defects came to notice.

In late July 1943 the wardroom of the HMAS Kybra, an A/S training ship, in which I was serving, gave a welcoming party to the officers of the *K9*. As a Midshipman RANVR I was left to look after Sub-Lieutenant Peter Fickling, RN. Most of our conversation covered his submarine service and passage from UK to Australia via the USA. Towards the end of the evening he told me that his Captain, Lieutenant F. M. Piggott, RNR, was looking for a fourth officer. I was brash enough to say that I was prepared to be considered. Next day there was a signal from Naval Headquarters ordering me to undergo a medical examination to determine if I was fit for submarine service. The examining doctor determined that I would need to have my tonsils removed. I was admitted promptly to the Naval Hospital for the tonsillectomy which was not quite as simple as I thought. When I eventually surfaced I was told by a motherly Naval Matron that I was haemorrhaging badly and was going straight back into the theatre. After a couple of weeks I was declared fit. I joined the *K9* on 31 August 1943.

There being no depot ship the crew was billeted ashore at HMAS *Rushcutter*, the home of the Anti-Submarine School. The officers were fortunate to be allowed to live in a mansion which had been lent to the Navy as a headquarters staff mess. It was located adjacent to the Naval Dockyard then being expanded on reclaimed land between Garden Island and the mainland. This enabled us to walk to *K9's* berth.

Our first trip under way was for a trim dive at Rose Bay within the harbour. For safety a grass rope joined the *K9* to HMAS *Kybra* which was standing by at anchor. Hatches were shut, tanks flooded but she would not go down. The Captain tried to drive her down with main motors and with the crew mustered in the forward torpedo space. She still would not budge so we returned to the dockyard. The Captain reasoned that the cause was insufficient ballast.

*K9*, like others of her class, was fitted with a drop-keel which was meant to be released as a safety measure if the submarine was unable to surface for any reason. K9 was dry-docked and it was found that the drop-keel and some other lead ballast had not been replaced at an earlier docking. After remedial work in the dock we returned to Rose Bay. This time our dive was successful but we novices on our first dive were alarmed by the jets of water entering around the conning tower hatch. The first lieutenant restored morale by raising an umbrella. The hatch had been distorted in the Japanese torpedo explosion and became watertight once we were below periscope depth.

We were now able to begin A/S training exercises at sea. Our first cruise was to Jervis Bay with HMAS *Kybra* in company. She anchored in the bay and we berthed alongside. This enabled us to have access to showers and meals. The next day we returned to Sydney to complete our shakedown cruise of some 150 nautical miles. At last we were able to meet our training commitments. The allocated submarine exercise area was established off Broken Bay some 20 nautical miles north of Sydney Harbour. On one of our early visits to the area we dived at the western end of the area. After adjusting trim at periscope depth we went to exercise depth. We soon had difficulty in holding depth as the boat tended to head towards the bottom. The Captain realised that we were encountering fresh water pockets as we were in the estuary of the Hawkesbury River. We altered course and speed to the east and soon had more stable conditions. As far as I recall this was the only exciting moment at sea during training. We did experience some trouble with the starboard motor but our exercise commitments were met by using the port motor alone when dived.

Fortunately most exciting incidents occurred in harbour. The starboard motor suffered from poor internal insulation resulting from the habits of rats which had chosen to nest there whilst *K. IX* was immobilized in dock yard hands. The high pressure (HP) air system included large steel air bottles fitted in banks along the hull in the battery compartments. The air bottles were connected by manganese-bronze pipes. The after battery compartment contained the officers' accommodation on the port side. Fickling and I were sitting there one morning doing paperwork when a pipe behind us fractured. It flew out like a whiplash nearly beheading us. Fickling was able to shut the valve on the air bottle supplying the pipe. The pipe was replaced by a steel one. A few weeks later a similar incident occurred but the offending pipe was a few feet away from us.

The incident which finished the *K9's* submarine life occurred on 22 January 1944. During a simple harbour movement to change berth the after battery exploded. Fortunately only the duty watch and the officer of the day, Fickling, were on board and no one was in the compartment. These old Dutch submarines were fitted with single-cell ventilation, a system long abandoned in British submarines. The danger from such a system was the possibility that small pockets of hydrogen would be left in the complicated single-cell ventilation pipe system. The risk of explosion was increased by the aged state of the battery and a poorly performing battery exhaust fan suffering from its own insulation problems. The Board of Inquiry investigating the matter concluded that no blame was attached to the Dockyard or to Ship's Officers.

In a minute to the Naval Board dated 14 February 1944 the Flag Officer in Charge reported, 'I have given serious consideration to the question of employing *K9* in her capacity as a training S/M and I have reluctantly come to the conclusion that an unjustifiable risk is being taken every time that she carries out a diving operation. I do not think that her officers and ship's company should any longer be asked to take such grave risks ...'

The *K9* was paid off on 31 March 1944 having spent only 31 days at sea in her eight months of service. The three officers and eight men on loan from the RN were sent to Trincomalee to join HMS *Adamant* and her flotilla, the Australian sailors went back to RAN service and I was lucky enough to be sent to UK for submarine service.

## Commander Donald 'Pete' Sencenbaugh, US Navy, communications officer, USS *Raton*

Submarine stories always start with 'We were pooping along, with two engines on the line, and the dinky on a zero float ...' That means that the auxiliary engine is supplying the auxiliary electrical load. Thus, the main batteries are just sitting there, fully charged, and under no load.

I reported to USS *Raton* (SS270) in May 1943, and it was commissioned into the US Navy on 13 July 1943. We made our first dive in Lake Michigan, in Fresh Water, a bit less dense than sea water, which had to be compensated for.

Since I was Communications Officer, I had to go to the Great Lakes Naval Station (I think it was) to pick up our classified library. So off we went, armed to the teeth. Everyone had a .45 and we also had a Thompson submachine-gun. As we drove down there, we hoped that some Patrolman would stop us for some reason. We didn't speed, however. Anyway, we wanted to be stopped so we could poke that machine gun out the window, and say pleasantly, 'Yes officer, what can we do for you?' But it didn't happen.

Not long thereafter, we headed for the war. Down the Chicago Drainage Canal to Cairo, Ill. as I recall. Then, we were loaded aboard a floating dry dock, and headed down the Mississippi. We had to take the shears down to pass under the bridges across the Mississippi, so when we got to New Orleans, we put them back, shipped the periscopes, and were ready to go. I must digress, at this point, and tell you the story of the potatoes.

I was commissary officer (that is the lowest job available for officers). We went down the Mississippi, and it turned out that the cooks (who were supposed to know what they were doing) had neglected to order adequate potatoes for the trip. The skipper (Jim Davis) was mad, and I got the heat. I went back to the tug that was pushing us down river, and traded a couple of canned hams (we had plenty of them) for potatoes. That didn't help much. Jim

Davis and I were not very friendly from them on. He used to threaten me with, 'if you don't shape up, I'm going to send you to high octane tankers.'

Anyway, from New Orleans, we headed for Brisbane. Through the Panama Canal, a few days exercising at Coco Solo, and then West. North of New Zealand. When Jim Grant was OOD, he observed a Japanese long lance torpedo pass up the starboard side, just a few feet off. The Lord has his hand on us. We arrived in Brisbane 19 Oct. 1943.

In Brisbane, we had to wait a month while a couple of main engine crankshafts were shipped out from the States. General Motors Winton Diesels. Terrible submarine engines. It was impossible to run them 80/90. (If memory serves me right, that means 90% of the speed with 80% of the power). It was impossible to get rated horse power out of them. (Give me Fairbanks Morse any time.)

Our first war patrol was in the Bismarck Archipelago, Solomons, New Guinea area. We had good luck. We managed to sink three ships. Our first attack was west of Massau, when we sighted a couple of cargo ships, with two escorts and a floatplane. We trailed the convoy and made a night torpedo attack, sinking one ship. We liked night attacks on the surface; you don't get depth charged. The escorts kept us from sinking any of the other ships in this convoy. Later that month, we sighted another convoy of S ships, and sank a couple of them in a submerged attack. Then we really got pounded The depth charges went click-boom, which means they are too close. The 'click' is the detonator going off. The air induction to the forward engine room was smashed flat. With torpedoes about gone, we were trailing the last convoy, (sending position reports) on the surface, with night scope up so we wouldn't be sighted, when we saw a premature explosion of a torpedo off the side of one of the ships. *Gato* had made an attack. We ran up closer to the convoy, and sort of 'waved our periscope' saying, 'Here we are!' The escorts turned and headed our way. Praise the Lord they were not destroyers, and couldn't catch us.

For that little escapade, Admr Bull Halsey sent us a dispatch, commending us as 'STARRING IN THREE ACTS OF THIS MIGHTY DRAMA AS HUNTER KILLER AND ESCORT ENTICER!' Not a bad accolade.

Our second patrol was in the Mindanao–Celebes–Halmahara area (South China Sea along the French Indo-China coast) where we sank a couple of ships, and damaged an auxiliary aircraft carrier. Our first attack was on 24 December, where we sank a merchantman and damaged an auxiliary aircraft carrier. Since this was Christmas Eve, we asked the skipper if we could 'splice the main brace.' And, he said NO. Heck of an attitude. That particular ship had drums of gasoline on deck, and as it burned it was quite an event, pyrotechnics a batch.

## Lieutenant William Ruhe, Gunnery Officer, USS *Crevalle*;
from *War in the Boats*

After his experiences in the *S-37*, and after a short period in the *Seadragon*, William Ruhe was appointed as Gunnery Officer to the new fleet submarine USS *Crevalle*, whose first patrol commenced on 20 October 1943. Her captain was the successful and experienced Lieutenant-Commander Henry G. Munson.

On the morning bridge watch on November 1, I dove the boat on a fast-closing radar contact that seemed to be a plane but that was never sighted by anyone on the bridge, even though the skies were clear and the last range to the contact was 'five miles,' as the *Crevalle* went under. The captain, when I came down from the bridge, was waiting at the foot of the ladder in the control room with a disgusted look on his face. With an ugly, grimacing smile showing lots of teeth, he then cackled at me like a chicken and flapped his arms as though he was a bird. He was insinuating that I was 'acting chicken' and had dived away from a bird. But throughout his condemnation of my actions as an officer of the deck, I kept reciting to myself one of my many litanies to stay alert and alive. 'He who spots a plane and dives away will live to see another day.'

The captain had done this flapping of his arms and cackling business on Jerry Gromer, who took the *Crevalle* down on a contact he never saw on the previous day. Then, later after my incident, the OOD, Luke Bowdler, received the same treatment when he dove the *Crevalle*, having seen no sign of a plane but with the radarman claiming that the contact was 'at five miles and closing'...

... On the second, the *Crevalle* was on the surface crossing the Sulu Sea, when Luke, the OOD, dove the boat on an unsighted contact 'six miles.' The captain sneered at Luke as he dropped into the control room. 'Another bird?' the captain asked, contemptuously. But as the *Crevalle* passed seventy feet, going 'down express' to one hundred feet, there was a teeth rattling 'Wham-mmmm' as a bomb exploded close overhead. Light bulbs were shattered and cork flew off the overhead. Luke looked very pleased, while the captain turned on his heel and went silently to his stateroom, where he pulled his curtain closed.

By the time the *Crevalle* reached Fremantle on 28 February 1944 at the end of her second patrol, Lieutenant-Commander Munson had completed eight war patrols. During that last and very successful patrol his behaviour had become erratic, swinging from the decisive and the aggressive in surface actions to the lethargic while submerged; one moment he had declared he would courtmartial two of his officers, including Ruhe, for mutiny; the next he had praised them for making the patrol a success.

It was a six-day trip to Fremantle and all seemed peaceful until the third day when the captain started brooding. He took his meals on his desk in his state-room, claiming that he had to concentrate on writing the patrol report. He kept the curtain to his room drawn. He also failed to show up for the field days he had instituted for the boat, 'to clean up all the dirt.'

On the fourth day, the captain called me into his bunkroom and with the same wild-eyed approach, he told me he was going to see that I was court-martialed when we got in for my insubordination during the patrol. 'You think I've forgotten about how you and Frank tried to take over my command. That's mutiny, you know!' he snarled.

When I protested that he'd praised Frank and me for making the patrol a great success, it just made him angrier.

'You'll never go back to sea on my submarine and I'll see that you're bounced out of the Navy,' he emphasized. There was much more invective as my legs got weaker and weaker.

I saw that things were bad right now, but he should soon snap out of this dark mood and return to his mercurial but rational personality. With no more stress and after he had gotten a Navy Cross for his exceptional patrol, he'd probably forget about pressing charges against me. At least I hoped so.

When I related this session with the captain to Frank he said we'd just have to go to Admiral Christie when we got in and lay our cards on the table. And pray …

When the *Crevalle* tied up at 0800 after two months of steaming Admiral Christie was on the dock and pinned a Navy Cross on Captain Munson when he went ashore to greet the admiral. In his remarks, the admiral said that four ships sunk and three more damaged made this an outstanding patrol. The admiral then came aboard for only a few seconds, nodded to the men standing on the main deck, looked them over approvingly and then turned around and went back across the gangway. Frank intercepted him on the dock as he was about to get into his car and said, 'Lt. Ruhe and I have to talk with you about this patrol.' Scarcely showing that he'd heard Frank's request, the admiral said, 'You two be in my office at nine.' Then his staff driver whisked him away …

At 0900, Frank and I entered the admiral's office in his headquarters in Perth. He greeted us warmly and said he had expected that we would want to see him, and he guessed that it should be before Captain Munson had paid a call on him. 'I've known there was something wrong going on aboard your submarine,' he said, 'from the messages I received as well as a few things I heard about Selby's encounter with your sub in Makassar Strait, your yeoman's version of what happened when you shot at a Japanese sub and the way

Munson acted when he was in Darwin.' Then he added, 'What's the story?'

When Frank told about the periods during which the captain was irrational and how he'd zeroed in on us as troublemakers, the admiral merely nodded and quietly said, 'Don't worry about this. Just stand easy. I'm seeing your captain in a few minutes and he'll probably tell me the whole story of what went on.'

I had to add, 'He's threatening to court martial us for mutiny, Admiral.' The admiral looked amused by Captain Munson's threat. Then an aide entered and told the admiral that Commander Munson was waiting outside to call on him. At this, Admiral Christie slipped us out through a side door and we went back to our rest home, Lucknow.

Within an hour the captain drove up and asked to see both Frank and me privately in the reception room. We waited for the axe to fall. But the captain, all smiles, said, 'I told Christie about how I had periods during the patrol when I wasn't putting it all together, and even blanked out at times. Then I told him about how you two, taking a big risk, carried me through those periods, and did a superior job despite my problems.'

This made me feel like the lowest of heels for not being totally loyal to this high-strung man who had suffered from the terrible strain of a very trying submarine patrol. The captain's eight combat patrols as a skipper had taken a severe toll, psychologically.

'I also told the admiral,' Captain Munson explained, 'that I needed a rest to recoup and wanted to spend a couple of months in a relief crew in Fremantle before I'd be ready to get another submarine command.' Expansively he mentioned that he'd recommended that Lt. Comdr. Frank Walker relieve him and take the *Crevalle* back out to sea. And that he was recommending Silver Stars for Frank, Luke, and me. At that, both Frank and I sagged down into our chairs. It was all too unexpected. Luckily for us, we'd managed to hit one of those really good days for the captain.

Shortly, Commander Hank Munson was relieved of the *Crevalle's* command by Lt. Comdr. Frank Walker. Munson then remained ashore as head of the Refit Detail, working on submarines between their patrols. In July, Admiral Christie sent Munson back to sea as Commanding Officer of the USS *Rasher*. Munson soon ran into a very large convoy of ships off the west coast of Luzon. In a night surface action, much the same as the one on the *Crevalle's* last patrol, he sank five ships totaling 52,600 tons, one of which was a 28,000 ton aircraft carrier, and damaged four more ships totaling 22,000 tons, for a total patrol tonnage of 74,600 tons of ships sunk and damaged. It was the most sunk and damaged tonnage on a single patrol for any US submarine in World War II.

**Engineering Officer Ludovico Simone, Regia Marina, *Comandante Cappellini*; from *Aria Alla Rapida*, originally published in *L'Alcione Si Ritrova***

*Cappellini* was one of the large Italian submarines converted into a transport for the Germans. None of them had completed a return voyage to the Far East before the Allied-Italian Armistice was signed.

August 1943. 8 September hadn't happened yet. For us, the crew of the Cappellini, in that scorching summer, that was just a date, a day in the future like so many others and of which nobody was thinking.

We were tied up at a wharf in Singapore harbour, getting on with the job of loading tungsten and rubber which we were to take to Bordeaux – a trip that was to end the operation that had begun on 1 May at the port on the Gironde and which had seen our safe arrival 59 days later at the little island of Sabang, loaded with various German supplies for the Japanese allies. That voyage is described, at least in the official accounts, as a model and with solemn words like 'historic' …

The return cargo for Bordeaux consisted primarily of tungsten and pure rubber; the tungsten was stacked inside without any problems. When it came to the rubber, some of it was stowed outside, between the hull and the casing, and in the sail given that its specific gravity of approximately 'one' made it possible to correct the resulting positive buoyancy when dived by taking on sufficient quantities of water as ballast.

But one portion had to be accommodated in the large ballast tanks. I remember that when we began packing in the first tank designated for this purpose it was on a sweltering tropical summer afternoon. I lowered myself down from the only access, the manhole, followed by three locals whom I was to supervise and help with the stowage.

The rubber came in prismatic-shaped bales, covered with some sort of talcum and weighing around 30 kilograms. The signal that the first bale was to be dropped into the tank came when everything was plunged into blackness as the bale was put into the manhole. The return to illumination coincided with the arrival of the projectile which bounced almost as high as it had fallen, and I dodged the ensuing ricochets through the quick reflexes of youth. I stowed the now motionless bale and, with my new expertise, awaited the fall of the next one – this time as if I were under starter's orders on the blocks! And so it went on for several hours while those above, who had got the hang of it, were saving time by letting the next projectile drop before the previous one had been tamed, so that, when the latter was hit, it took on unexpected new life. Our gymnastics turned into a kind of grotesque game of piggy-in-the-middle, while the space in the tank, which was steadily being reduced, filled with a stifling dust mixed with the smell of sweat: bitter, in the case of yours truly and pungent in the case of the Malaysian workers. Falling over had ceased being a problem since we were completely surrounded by rubber.

At last we could reach the weather deck: the heat and the frenzied running and jumping made me much more agile when it came to getting up out of the manhole.

It was then Simone's task to calculate the weight of cargo, fuel, stores and crew and, taking into account its stowage, trim the boat.

Calculations made and double-checked by hand, with the welcome assistance of a slide rule, it was on the basis of the results that I distributed the water to trim the submarine.

I reported to the captain that the submarine was ready for her trim dive. The depth of water was around 50 metres, and we plummeted down (the seabed was fortunately muddy) at a somewhat unexpected speed, but, to my partial satisfaction, with perfect longitudinal trim. I remember the captain's withering, but never less than gentlemanly, criticism of the 'excessive impetuosity of youth'.

All the water from the trim tank was expelled … No use. The *Cappellini* had no mind to part company with the seabed. We had to blow all ballast and float miserably to the surface. I say 'miserably' because the subsequent inquisition resulted in an order to get rid of the many kilograms of pepper which everyone, or almost everyone, had planned to take home.

Well, it was a cargo submarine, and that commodity was worth a thousand lire per kilogram in Italy! I set a good example and ditched my bag. The others followed suit.

The subsequent trim dive was perfect: we just had to lighten her by a few kilograms forward, probably because of some hidden bags.

Then 8 September ceased to be just another day in the future.

After the announcement of the Armistice, the boat was seized by the Germans and renamed *U-IT24*. Following the surrender of Germany she was in turn taken by the Japanese and renamed *I-505*.

**Luitenant ter Zee 2 Henri Reitsma, Koninklijke Marine, *O.24*;**
from IWM Sound Archive 9312/3

*O.24* was sent to the Far East, to be attached to the 4th Submarine Flotilla based at Colombo for a spell of duty which, in Lieutenant Henri Reitsma's opinion made the Mediterranean seem like 'a submariner's paradise'. The incident to which he refers occurred on 28 September 1943 during a patrol lasting from 12 September to 3 October.

Funnily enough, you thought it was another theatre of less importance, and anybody will tell you the Fourteenth Army is also complaining about that still today. So was Lord Louis Mountbatten. The adventures being nightly attacks on enemy shipping, dropping agents ashore, having skirmishes. We were run over once by an enormous Japanese submarine, which was just as surprised as we were. Both sides were hanging over the conning tower with big eyes, looking at each other. We were looking at an enormous Japanese flag which was flashing past at tremendous speed, and we happened to be at tremendous speed, too. We just missed each other. It was pitch dark, mind you, with a phosphorescent sea so once you got close to some other ship you could read the papers, but in reality only a short distance of it. Good visibility for 500–1,000 yards, but anything farther you really couldn't see a damned thing. But once you get close to each other we really looked into each other's eyes. I'm amazed we didn't wave at each other. And then we both crash dived of course, and were listening in the water, where he was, in order to possibly fire a torpedo at him. No one did.

According to the Flotilla captain, ADM199/1879:

Had not O.24's radar not been defective, it is possible that an attack could have been made on the Japanese submarine … though in the visibility obtaining at the time it would have been very lucky had this been possible.

# 1944

German submarine sinkings continued to rise, even as increasing numbers of Allied convoys completed their voyages either unscathed or with minor losses. As the summer approached, the U-boats active in the Atlantic and northern waters were ordered to oppose at all costs the anticipated Allied landings on the European mainland – wherever they might take place. Two groups were set up for this, one based in Norway, the other at Brest and St Nazaire.

Unsurprisingly the Allied forces provided massive defences for the D-Day invasion force; the U-boats sent out into in the Bay of Biscay and the Channel had no chance; even those with the schnorkel proved vulnerable. The Type VIIs and IXs which had been the backbone of the Kriegsmarine's U-boat arm had been neutralised by advances in anti-submarine warfare; the new Type XXIs with their fast underwater speed and endurance were not yet operational. All told, 8,000 German submariners were killed in 1944.

The submarine campaign in the Mediterranean drew to a close. The Royal Navy's 10th Flotilla had moved to Maddelena, Sardinia, leaving Malta to the 1st Flotilla, and was disbanded in September. Nevertheless, the Germans were still active around the Greek islands and provided targets for the remaining boats. The last Mediterranean sinking occurred on 3 October.

By the end of 1943, with the Allied invasions of Bougainville and the defeat of the surface fleet in the Battle of Empress Augusta Bay, Japanese submarines were increasingly used as transports, and they had sunk very few ships for the loss of 27 of their own boats. Their successes had come in the Indian Ocean; the losses were greater in the Pacific. 1944 was to be a desperate year for them as US and Australian forces attacked one Japanese conquest after another, island-hopping and keeping the Japanese Navy guessing as to where their main assaults would come. Whether as transports or part of scouting screens the Japanese submarines increasingly fell victim to radar and 'hedgehogs'. In just twelve days during May, the USS *England*, a *Buckley*-Class destroyer escort, set a record by sinking six submarines in the waters off Bougainville.

In June, as US troops invaded Saipan, the two surface navies met in the Battle of the Philippine Sea, a serious defeat for the Japanese. None of their submarines was able to play a part: all had been held back behind the 145th East Meridian. The Japanese response was to revive a 1943 proposal to build their own, single-man, version of human torpedoes: kaiten. They were not initially intended as suicide weapons, but, following another naval disaster, at Leyte Gulf, the situation was so serious that they became such.

By contrast, US submarine operations had become far better organised. Towards the latter part of 1943 the first wolf packs had been formed, much smaller than their German models, and in January 1944 *Haddock*, *Halibut* and *Tullibee* sank almost 300,000 tons of merchant shipping, an unsustainable rate of loss for the Japanese who were dependent on imported oil. American submarines also operated singly, scouting, screening and still rescuing carrier-based airmen who had been shot down.

In the Indian Ocean, Force 136, the Far Eastern division of the British Special Operations Executive, continued to use British and Dutch submarines to land and recover agents on Japanese-occupied islands.

## ATLANTIC

### Oberleutnant zur See Herbert Werner, Kriegsmarine, *U-415*; from *Iron Coffins*

Kapitän Roesing patted his silvery hair, which seemed to interfere with his thinking. Not until he had caressed it into submission was he ready to speak. 'Gentlemen, as you know, the Allied invasion is expected imminently. You must be in the position to sail at any hour. Because our Intelligence has been unable to discover the exact date and location of the landing, I have only general instructions for you. We shall be prepared to counter the blow wherever it falls. In Norway we have twenty-two boats on alert. The Biscay ports of Lorient, Saint Nazaire, La Pallice, and Bordeaux are staffed with another twenty-one boats. Most likely, however, the invasion fleet will simply cross the Channel and try to land some twenty to fifty miles from England. This is where you gentlemen step in. Headquarters' directive is short and precise: 'ATTACK AND SINK INVASION FLEET WITH THE FINAL OBJECTIVE OF DESTROYING ENEMY SHIPS BY RAMMING.'

Deadly silence gripped the room. Fifteen Captains, all experienced U-boat men, could not believe what they had heard. This was sheer madness. We had battled ferociously to preserve our lives and our boats through months of defeats and mounting losses. Now, with only a few of each left, Headquarters had ordered the sacrifice of all survivors without a thought for continuing the war. It was ludicrous to use a U-boat to accomplish what a torpedo should do. Was suicide the purpose for which we had been trained so long? Was this futile gesture the greatest glory and satisfaction we were permitted to take down with us into our wet graves? ...

At 14.40 we fifteen Captains were told to report in Winter's office. There was silence all around as Winter gave each Commander sealed orders. I opened my blue envelope and unfolded the red paper which contained the Lion's [Dönitz] long-delayed instructions. As I peered at the teletype I froze. The bold letters fused into one another. But I managed to read: *U-415* TO SAIL AT MIDNIGHT AND PROCEED ON SURFACE AT TOP SPEED TO ENGLISH COAST BETWEEN LIZARD HEAD AND HARTLAND POINT. ATTACK AND DESTROY ALLIED SHIPPING.

The message was even more insane than our present standing order from Headquarters. It required me and seven of my friends, all of us without the schnorkel, to remain on surface and race unprotected towards the southern English coast at a time when the sky was black with thousands of aircraft and the sea swarmed with hundreds of destroyers and corvettes.

Clearly we would not survive long enough to commit suicide by ramming cargo ships in the English ports ...

22.30: The Coast Guard vessels began to float towards the harbour mouth. As they sailed into navigable waters, our diesels coughed to life and the black silhouettes of the eight U-boats swerved into single file astern of the leading minesweeper. First came *U-441* under Captain Hartmann; as the senior among us, he assumed the lead. *U-413* with Sachse followed closely. Teddy Lehsten sailed his *U-373* into the line. Then came *U-740*, Stark; *U-629*, Bugs; *U-821*, Knackfuss; *U-415*, myself at the helm. *U-256* with Boddenberg closed the long chain. The moon had risen fully above the horizon in the southeast. Standing like a giant lantern in the sky, it illuminated the long row of U-boats and was sharply reflected in the calm sea. Contrary to common procedure, all the men had put on their yellow lifejackets. The bridge had been stacked with piles of' ammunition, the conning tower turned into an arsenal. The gunners hung at their automatics in tense expectation of the first enemy plane. I stood in my nook trying to keep my boat directly in the wake of *U-821*, and to hold the distance to a prearranged 300 metres ...

7 June. At 00.15, our long chain of boats was racing at top speed towards the Atlantic. The diesels hacked, the exhausts fumed, impulses haunted us all the way. I found myself glancing repeatedly at my watch as if it could tell me when the fatal blow would fall.

00.30: Radar impulses chirped all around the horizon, their volumes shifting rapidly from feeble moans to high-pitched sreams. The Tommies were obviously flying at various distances around our absurd procession. They must have thought we had lost our minds. Sometimes I could hear aircraft engines at fairly close range, but could not spot a plane. The hands of my watch crept slowly ahead while the British waited for reinforcement; our eyes sharpened and our hearts beat heavy under our breasts.

01.12: The battle began. Our leading boats were suddenly attacked. Tracers spurted in various directions, then the sound of gunfire hit our ears. Fountains reached into the sky.

01.17: One of the enemy aeroplanes caught fire. It flashed comet-like towards the head of our file, crossed over one of the boats, dropped four bombs, then plunged into the ocean. The bombs knocked out Sachse's *U-413*. With helm jammed hard-aport, the boat swerved out of the column. She lost speed rapidly and sank below surface.

01.25: The aircraft launched a new attack, again directed at the boats in the front. Three boats, brightly lighted by flares, concentrated their gunfire and held the planes at bay. A spectacular fireworks erupted, engulfing U-boats and aircraft. Suddenly the Tommies retreated. Radar impulses indicated that they were circling our stubborn parade, regrouping for a fresh attack. I raised myself over the rim of the bridge, straining to see and sound out the roaming planes.

01.45: The boat at our stern, the last one in the column, became the target of a new British tactic. Trying to roll out the carpet of fire from the rear, a four-engined Liberator came roaring down on starboard, diving for the bow of *U-256*. Boddenberg's men opened fire. But the aircraft veered off in front of the boat, where her guns became ineffective. That was our chance.

'Open fire!' I screamed.

Five barrels, all that we had available, blazed away at the Liberator as it dropped four depth charges ahead of *U-256* and roared past us. Four giant water columns leaped skywards behind the riddled aircraft as it tried to escape our fire. But some shells from our 37mm gun hit the plane broadside. It exploded in mid-air, then plunged into the sea.

*U-256*, beaten and mutilated by the depth charges, lay stopped and helpless in our wake, slowly falling out of line. That was the last we saw of her. Realizing that her demise left us the first target in any new attack from the rear, I called for more ammunition. Radar impulses increased rapidly. For a while, however, the British held back.

02.20: Impulses now from starboard. I presumed several planes were approaching. Suddenly a Sunderland shot out of that night from starboard ahead. I yelled, 'Aircraft – starboard forty – fire!'

Short bursts from our two twin 20mm guns followed the sweep of the plane. It cleverly flew in from dead ahead, making our guns ineffective, and dropped four barrels in front of our bow. Simultaneously, a Liberator attacked from starboard bearing ninety, firing from all its muzzles. An instant later, four detonations amidships. Four savage eruptions heaved *U-415* out of the water and threw our men flat on the deck plates. Then she fell back, and the four collapsing geysers showered us with tons of water and sent cascades through the hatch. This was the end. Both diesels stopped, the rudder jammed hard-astarboard. *U-415* swerved in an arc, gradually losing speed. Above on starboard floated a flare, its treacherous glare enveloping our dying boat. *U-415* lay crippled, bleeding oil from a ruptured tank, slowly coming to a full stop – a target to be finished off with ease.

Bewildered, I peered down through the tower hatch into the blackness of the hull. All life below seemed to have ceased. I feared the boat might sink at any moment and ordered, 'All hands on deck! Make ready dinghies and lifebuoy.'

Not a sound came from below. The men must have been knocked out by the blows. Interminable seconds passed. From the distance came the drone of planes regrouping for a new assault. It had to be fatal. Suddenly, some men came struggling up the ladder, shaken, mauled, groggy, reaching for air, tossing inflatable rubber floats to the bridge. As they jumped on deck and prepared the dinghies, the gunners raised their barrel towards the invisible aeroplanes circling their disabled prey. The speed of the attack and the resultant damages prevented us from sending a distress signal. This, I thought grimly, was the way many of my friends had died – the silent way, leaving no word.

*U-415*, hopelessly damaged, lay waiting for the coup de grâce: since the boat did not seem to be sinking, I told my men to take cover behind the tower instead of lowering the dinghies into the water. I was determined to remain on board as long as the boat would float and to shoot as long as there was ammunition and men to handle the guns. It turned out, however, that we would not die unreported: the radio mate managed to patch up our emergency transmitter and sent Headquarters news of our destruction.

02.28: Increasing engine noise heralded a new attack, a fresh approach by Sunderland from starboard ahead, guns blazing. Zooming over our bridge, it dropped four canisters. Four deafening booms tossed the boat aloft. At that moment a Liberator attacked at low altitude from port ahead. Our men on two 20mm guns started firing at once and emptied their magazines into the plane's cockpit. The black monster swept across our bridge, dropped four charges, then zoomed away, blowing hot exhaust fumes into our faces. As the boat made four violent jumps to port and as four white mushrooms soared high alongside our starboard saddle tanks, the gunner at the 37mm automatic sent a full charge of explosive shells into the bomber's fuselage. The flaming aircraft plunged into the sea. Somewhere, the sound of the Sunderland's engines faded in the distance.

Then all was very quiet. The flare still flickered on surface next to our boat. *U-415* was near death, but still afloat. The Fly and the Bug had been shot away; we were without a warning device. The bridge was punctured by many projectiles. A gunner lay scalped by a shell. Other men had been hit by steel fragments. The Exec moaned in pain, his back badly lacerated by countless splinters. In the aftermath of battle, I felt hot. Assuming I was sweating, I wiped my burning eyes. But my hand came away red, and I realized that blood was streaming down my face. My white cap was punctured like a sieve, and the tiny fragments had torn my scalp.

Then I heard the Chief's voice from below: 'Boat is taking heavy water through galley and bow hatches. Strong leak in radio room. I'll try to keep her afloat, if you keep the bees away.'

'Can you get her repaired for diving?' I shouted back.

'Can't promise. We have no power, no light. We'll do our best.'

I lowered myself to the slippery deck. It was split in several places by the impact of depth charges which had hit the planks before falling into the water where they had exploded. One barrel had bounced off the starboard saddle tank and had left a deep dent. Far more serious, the starboard aft ballast tanks were split wide open. Diesel oil escaped in a thick stream, spreading rapidly over the surface …

Miraculously *U-415* limped back to Brest. Of the eight U-boats that had sailed out together, only two others returned. Werner's assertion that Dönitz's order specifically ordered ramming as a last resort is highly controversial, and no documentary evidence supports it. Peter Cremer remembered that the order to oppose the landings even at serious risk to the boats was interpreted by some as an exhortation to self-sacrifice, though his own view was that it was precisely the kind of rhetoric expected at such a time.

## NORTH SEA, BALTIC AND ARCTIC

### CPO Radio Operator Finn-Christian Stumoen, Kongelige Norske Marine, *Utsira*

His minelayer sunk, Norwegian radio operator Finn-Christian Stumoen was sent to a new construction, a V-Class submarine launched as HMS *Variance* but handed over to the small band of Norwegian submariners and renamed *Utsira*. She joined the other Norwegian submarine, *Ula* (another V-Class, previously HMS *Varne*) as part of the 9th Submarine Flotilla based at Dundee. *Utsira* went into service late in 1944.

I had never been in a submarine and I thought it was so claustrophobic. When I first came on *Utsira* she wasn't completed: she was lying at Barrow in Furness, in the dock, and we were working on her all this time. We had a very good time there, and of course we did all the training with her, and tested her torpedo firing, with the yacht HMS *Philante*. We fired torpedoes at her, to see if we could aim properly, and the torpedoes went right underneath her. They were ordinary torpedoes with a propeller. And today that *Philante* is the Norwegian Royal Yacht. An English lord built it in 1943, and that cost £500,000, and the Norwegian people bought it and gave it to the King as a birthday present.* Yes, it was a good thing we didn't hit it.

The first time we dived on our trials at Barrow, it didn't affect me very much. We had so much to do: I was Radio and Radar operator. We didn't think of being fifty feet, a hundred feet, under the surface, but it was very interesting. Then we had to go down to 200 metres. That was the maximum we could do in *Utsira*. And then you could see along the periscope ... small trickles of water came out through the washer ... And we couldn't use the telegraph for information for the whole submarine had shrunk more or less. It must have been a terrific force, and when we were down at 300 feet we heard a very big bang: the voice pipe from the bridge to the control room had been pressed flat by the pressure from the sea.

On board it was pleasant for us. Three of us had a little cabin together: the engineer, the coxswain and me, a chief petty officer, amidships. The crew had to lay down on deck, forward, in between the torpedoes. It was not good at all. My job was to get all the news every day, and we could lay 30 feet below the surface and hear the radio. I found that very interesting. We had a loop antenna that went all the way around the boat, and when you put that on to the radio you could pick up thirty feet down.

You had to be careful of the water you used, but we had excellent food on board – we had a marvellous cook. The comradeship was very good, a good working team. And having a commander like Lieutenant Valvatne makes you feel safe. What he couldn't do, no one else could do. He was cool as a cucumber. Once on the Norwegian coast, a German convoy formed up. Valvatne was quick to pick out the biggest ship.** He fired his torpedoes and hit the German admidships. As *Utsira* was very close to the German escort, the depth-charges started to come down. By a technical error *Utsira* came to the surface and was a very good target for the Germans.

Now he ordered all the crew right forward, and then she started to come down. Valvatne knew about the German minefield and went for it. He went underneath it, and they could hear the wires from the mines scraping on the ship's side. Valvatne brought *Utsira* out in safe waters. That was after I left her.

* *Philante* was built in 1937 by Camper & Nicolson for Sir Thomas Sopwith. During the war she was used by the Royal Navy as an Atlantic convoy escort; shortly afterwards, and by public subscription, she was bought by the Norwegian people, refitted and renamed *Norge* as a 75th birthday present for King Haakon.
** *Utsira*'s victim was the 1,500-ton *Torridal*, a Norwegian ship under German control. She was sunk with the loss of most of her crew on 5 April 1945 close to Folla while on a voyage to Trondheim in ballast.

One day she was next to the depot ship, and one of the officers, Sub-Lieutenant Weisser, was on the conning tower, holding his hand on the railing there and the ship rolled and he caught his hand between the ship and the railing. It cut his finger off. I bet that hurt.

I went out on my last patrol on *Utsira* in the North Sea, from Lerwick. It lasted 28 days and it was boring. Absolutely nothing happened at all. But that's why we are alive today. I left her in November 1944, because I took ill with stomach trouble, and I guess that was the nerves. I went to Edinburgh as an instructor.

## Jean Grill, Kriegsmarine, *U-1054*; from *J'ai Porté des Rubans, Plongée*

Jean Grill was one of a large number of young Frenchmen who, following the German annexation of Alsace and Lorraine and when old enough for military service, were conscripted into the German forces. They were known as the *Malgré Nous* – literally 'in spite of ourselves'.

After three months of training we had to pass another medical examination, and from there we were screened: surface fleet, or naval artillery. For me it was to be the submarine school, once again at Gotenhafen [Gdynia] where we were given a first-class course in engineering. We were pushed to the limit, and they would even wake us up in the middle of the night to ask what should be done in the event of a fault occurring. Every day we had engineering duties to perform, too, and we weren't allowed out if they hadn't been done. On the other hand, we didn't get any lessons in politics, just geography and submarines ...

After three weeks at the school we were sent to a camp close to Husum awaiting transfer to the dockyard where 'our submarine' was building. I didn't enjoy that camp; we had to play at being soldiers and we were given lectures in politics and how the party operated (the only things that we had scant interest in).

At the end of June 43, we were on board the submarine which became ours, and we were working with the real specialists from the dockyard, who promised us that we had an indestructible boat. We did all the trials with these men who raised our confidence. They knew all too well what was in store for us and were like fathers to us.

In February 44 we put our Type VIIC submarine, *U-1054*, into commission with three months of training in the Baltic. We left on our first mission which was to observe and 'sink' all the ships we could find in the Bay of Finland; but after two months we were recalled to the yard to have a 'Snorkel' fitted, which we did. Unfortunately, while we were passing the Baltic states (Lithuania, Estonia and Latvia) we collided with the steamer Stuttgart which was bringing home wounded men from the Russian front. There was a terrific snowstorm and we had to surface for ventilation. During that manoeuvre in the pitch darkness the Stuttgart hit us forward, and we had to put into Swinemünde with a few men (a skeleton crew of 15). The rest were taken on board the Stuttgart. As *U-1054* was no longer operational, she was sent back to the dockyard. We immediately got another boat, the Type VIIC *U-637* which had already completed her trials and been fitted with a Snorkel. At the end of November, after several weeks of exercises with the famous Snorkel which still wasn't perfect and which gave us a lot of trouble until it just about worked, we were ordered to Leningrad [St Petersburg] Bay for a special operation.

The details were in a sealed envelope which the captain alone was permitted to open after three weeks. That was a few days before Christmas 1944.

The special operation consisted of entering Leningrad Bay unseen and to photograph all the ships at anchor in the port; every time the German aircraft had been sent, the Russians smothered the whole area in artificial smoke, and they were unable to see anything. After several days of observations, the two coastguard vessels operating between the nets were relieved. During that change-over, we followed the two vessels and thus we managed to enter the port. During the manoeuvre and mooring we were able to turn our submarine round. In the morning we had the opportunity to photograph the ships but we did not leave yet. The hardest thing was to wait 24 hours before following the exit route behind the patrol boat. During those 24 hours we were under orders to maintain absolute silence, and there was only fruit to eat.

When it was time, we followed the two coastguard vessels, the way we had come in. Everything went well until the two nets, which we unfortunately hit – something which the pair of Russian ships obviously spotted, for they went after us, bombarding us with depth charges which didn't damage our instruments. We managed to escape.

It was 24 December 1944 and we settled on the bottom and celebrated Christmas.

Three weeks later we entered Danzig and after basic repairs we went back to Kiel. There, those who had already been discharged were entitled to go on leave, but I still wasn't.

After five weeks the submarine was ready to sail again. For me, it was the end. The captain summoned an Austrian, a Czech and myself as a Frenchman ... He told us that he thought we knew what we had to do. We then went off on our own, into the countryside and spent three weeks among the peasants because the English were 30kms off.

On their arrival I presented myself. I was then sent to a camp close to

Lübeck to await repatriation on a train for POWs (all from Alsace-Lorraine) and survivors from the concentration camp near Hamburg.

## MEDITERRANEAN

**Lieutenant-Commander A. Rallis, Royal Hellenic Navy,** *Pipinos*;
from his Patrol Report, ADM199/1850

Launched in 1943 as HMS *Veldt*, *Pipinos* had immediately been loaned to the Royal Hellenic Navy, which had lost four of its own submarines. In the spring of 1944 she was based at Malta as part of the 1st Submarine Flotilla, operating in what for her and her compatriots were home waters at a time when German forces were trying to secure their hold on Greece and the Aegean islands. She left Malta on 23 May on her third war patrol, one which demonstrated the value of extreme vigilance and efficient diving as well as audacity. On 27 May 1944 she recorded her position as 36°56.8′ N 23°58.7′ E.

1714 Action stations. Altering course towards 270°. An MV of a medium tonnage was sighted at a range of about 4,600 metres with inclination 50° to Port proceeding towards South. The ship is silhouetted against the sun and cannot be identified, also visibility was hindered due to the rough sea. 1742 We altered course towards 250° (track angle 110°) in order to delay for a short time the attack, hoping to be able to identify her outside the reflection of the sun. But in vain.

1745 I could not wait longer. If the ship was an enemy one she would have passed undisturbed. With rather uncertain speed and course elements, I fired four torpedoes against her from a range of about 3,500 metres.

1750 The ship can be seen now. She was a Red Cross relief ship. Having seen our torpedoes she dropped a few depth charges.

1756 Fortunately the hindrance in aiming the torpedoes correctly and the incorrect attack elements, due to the rough sea, as the target was sighted just a little before firing our torpedoes, was in favour to us and the ship was not hit ...

On 1 June *Pipinos* received a report of a convoy comprising three merchant ships and 14 escorts south of Makronisi.

1420 At a range of about two miles from our starboard beam the British submarine HMS *Vox* (P73) surfaced, and she ought to have set off at utmost speed for her new area since day-break.

1440 With the Aldis lamp I asked: 'Have you received orders to proceed south of my patrol area'. Reply: 'No, I am receiving them now.'

1448 From *Pipinos* to P73: 'Decipher first Nos. 741, 745 and 580 messages.'

1500: From P73 to Pipinos: 'I failed to receive Nos. 741 and 745.' From *Pipinos* to P73: 'Request repeat my recognition signals.'

1510 After replying correctly to my recognition signal I passed these immediate messages by aiming with the Aldis lamp to the seaward and then P73 set off at full speed towards her destination.

1550 With his 01 160- FOLEM [Flag Officer Levant and Eastern Mediterranean] gave us the position of the convoy at 1530 to be in position 36°11 N, 25°03 E and that the convoy was proceeding towards Heraklion.

1742 S/ONE with his 01 1458 gave permission to both S/Ms to take action as they wished and attack any ships of the convoy which have fallen back after the air bombardment.

1755 Sighted two aircraft to the Westward at a range of five miles proceeding from North to South.

1810 Asdics reported explosions coming from far away.

1812 Many aircraft were reported by radar at a range of over 25 miles (it is about the over [more than] 70 planes attacking the convoy).

1854 A violent explosion was heard coming from the direction of the attacked convoy.

1917 smoke was sighted at bearing 118°.

1918 Proceeding at full speed towards the smoke.

1929 Sun set.

1931 Another violent explosion heard.

1955 AA firings were sighted towards the direction of the sighted smoke.

2000 As we were approaching we could see more clearly that the smoke was coming out from a stopped ship which was ablaze, at a range of about 10 miles.

2010 Sighted aircraft at a range of about five miles setting off towards NW.

2011 Sighted recognition signals from a friendly aircraft towards the ship on fire.

2015 From the same direction two aircraft were sighted to set off, while a third aircraft was approaching us. Crash dive.

2035 Surfaced in position 35°52 N 24°58 E and at full speed we are proceeding towards the bombed area shown by the blazes of the burning ship.

2036 Due to the presence of two aircraft approaching us from short range we were compelled to Crash Dive again.

2100 With the radar, diving, we could see continuous movements of aircraft. For a third time we attempted to surface and approach the burning ship, but due to the moonlight and patrolling aircraft we were compelled to dive again.

2130 Surfaced. A violent explosion was heard towards our bow. The radar located this direction and at a range of about 12,000 metres the burning ship and the blazes shortly afterwards stopped to show. I think, this ship must be considered sunk after the last explosion taking place.

2132 Towards bearing 100° two surface craft were sighted faintly, while in the meantime these were reported also by the radar, at a range of about 10,000 yards, proceeding in a single line ahead towards North. Probably these were corvettes.

2135 Due to approaching aircraft compelled to dive for fourth time so the watching of these surface craft was cut off. Asdic searching reported nothing ...

Just after midnight on 4 June, *Pipinos* was proceeding towards the Gulf of Nauplion.

Windless. Sea calm. Clear night, moonlight, moonset at 0342.

0053 Aircraft flying from North to South approaching us from short range. Crash dive.

0013 Surfaced.

0015 Aircraft flying from north to south approaching us from short range. Crash dive.

0034 Surfaced.

0040: Aircraft approaching from short range from our port beam. Crash dive.

0132 Surfaced.

0402 Dived in position 37°14.5 N 23°0.5 E and advanced to the innermost position of the Gulf of Nauplion carrying out a sweep.

0900 Nothing sighted. We reversed course proceeding towards Spetsai Channel.

1400 Towards bearing 100° a caique was sighted projected from Trikeri Island. Manoeuvring to approach her.

1500 Action Stations.

1525 The caique was seen to carry Red Cross markings. Action stations cancelled. Passing through Spetsai Channel altering course to south.

2050 Surfaced in position 37°0.7 N, 23°08.3 E proceeding towards Kyparisi Bay on the Peleponnese coast.

2345 Entered Kyparisi Bay [on the Peloponnese coast N. of Monemvasia]. There was nothing in the Bay. We asked a dinghy from the inhabitants of the picturesque village after having previously ascertained that there were no Germans around the place. The customs officers and two other compatriots approached us full of suspicions. When they perceived that the S/M was Greek the word was passed around, and the whole village came up to their feet and many boats surrounded us. Men and women were kissing the deck of the submarine and ourselves. With great difficulty I kept the head of the village to restrain the ringing of the church bells for celebrating our visit. We distributed provisions to the inhabitants, and under the quietness of the moonlit night, with a great emotion, we heard enthusiastic local patriotic songs sung by men and women.

5/6/44

Windless, Sea calm, clear night, moonlight.

0045 After hearty farewells and cheers from the inhabitants, we left the Bay, proceeding towards Monemvasia. I took on board the 26 years-old MN seaman Adamantios Tsarouchas, feeling sorry to refuse his wish to render his services for the cause of liberating our country.

The apparent dropping of depth charges by the Red Cross ship *Boreland* caused some consternation to Lieutenant-Commander Rallis's superiors; his submarine's visit to Kyparisi was another source of concern:

No doubt this visit had good propaganda value and a beneficial effect on the partisans following so closely on the recent mutiny in the Greek Navy; nevertheless, to enter what may be an enemy-defended port must constitute a risk to the submarine and is to be discouraged.

Lieutenant-Commander Rallis had been due to leave *Pipinos* after that patrol. He was succeeded by Lieutenant-Commander Loundras, RHN, who was also in command during her fifth war patrol.

0605 Smoke observed in Karlovasi harbour. [Samos, off the coast of Turkey.]

0800 Inside Karlovasi harbour observed one destroyer of *Palestro-Class*, berthed alongside the Western breakwater, and the S/S *Orion* berthed alongside the eastern breakwater. From bearing 030 degs ⅓ of the *Orion* appeared exposed through the mouth of the harbour. Being uncertain of securing a straight torpedo run, from this position, decided to stand by at a short distance from the mouth of the harbour to drive home the attack when the ships would come out of the harbour, which I expected them to do in the evening.

1210 Two MVs of about 200 tons each were also observed inside the harbour.

1211 A Dornier flying boat was observed flying overhead at a short range. Increased depth.

1220 I rose to periscope depth. Patrolled at a range of about 2,500 from the entrance of the harbour.

1658 The destroyer cleared the harbour, transmitting by Asdic. Action Stations.

1705 Four torpedoes were fired at a range of 2,500 yards against the German destroyer of *Curtazone*-Class, in position 1.6 miles 050° from lighthouse on external breakwater of Karlovasi harbour. One minute and 45 seconds after the torpedoes were fired the second torpedo hit the destroyer amidships under her forward funnel and exploded. The destroyer turned round to starboard and attempted to run aground. Her engines are stopped.

The destroyer is filling gradually.

1715 I ordered immediate reloading of torpedo tubes.

1730 The destroyer listed to stbd, broke in two; both ends rose vertically upward and sank rapidly within sight of Karlovasi. I noted that the deck of her forecastle was painted with red and yellow diagonal stripes ...

Inferring that the ships inside the harbour were not likely to sail before another escort craft arrived, I decided to attack them where they lay. I did not attack them by gunfire, although the harbour was undefended and I was master of the situation, in order to avoid killing Greek inhabitants and destroy their homes.

1805 The MV which was berthed on the western breakwater manoeuvred and berthed alongside the one that was berthed alongside the eastern breakwater.

1914 I fired the torpedo of No. 1 tube from a range of about 1,000 yards on a course 210 degrees, towards the entrance of the harbour. The torpedo struck the end of the east breakwater. Columns of water, smoke and stones covered the harbour, rising up to 100 metres. A short time before the explosion of the torpedo I saw the crews of the German ships in a hurry and in panic diving overboard or running on the breakwater.

1918 I fired the torpedo in No. 2 tube from a range of about 800 metres and course 210 degrees; this torpedo did not function.

1920 Reversed course and returned to the axis of the entrance to the harbour.

1926 Fired the torpedo in No. 3 tube which struck slightly to the North of the end of the East breakwater, and probably exploded against the bottom in shallow waters, with some spectacular results.

1928 Fired torpedo in No. 4 tube. The torpedo went through the mouth of the harbour, just along the axis thereof, and exploded against the stern of *Orion* or close by. The ship was covered with water and smoke. When the smoke cleared, S/S *Orion* was still on an even keel with her superstructure damaged. Due to the oncoming darkness more details could not be obtained.

*Pipinos* withdrew and returned safely to Malta. She survived the war.

### Outside ERA's Mate Cyril Bowden, Royal Navy, HMS *Virtue*

I did most of my time in the Aegean Sea. The Germans hád landed on Crete by parachute first, and then the trouble was they'd got nothing to come off with, so they came off in what they call caiques. We went to gun action with quite a few of them. Some of them were a lot bigger than us because we're only 200 feet long and 500 tons. Well, when you take the average fishing boat, it was bigger than that.

We finished up right at the northern end of the Aegean, Chios, and the Germans were still there when we arrived there. This was '44. We had a couple of Germans with us. The naval orders were, when you sank anything, and if there were any survivors, always get the commanding officer and the engineer officer. Just imagine, trying to sort that out. And on top of that, in the Aegean at the time some boats had a yellow disc painted on them and some had a blue disc. I can't remember which colour meant they were friendly, or otherwise, but you had to know the difference. Just imagine trying to do that through the periscope. I can remember the Old Man [commander] doing his nut. We sank quite a few of them, by gun action mainly because they weren't worth wasting torpedoes on. And of course they used to hit back. We were depth charged off Crete by the Germans: that was naughty. And we got caught in a minefield.

That was off Crete [15 September]. They'd had a minefield laid there some time at a certain depth. We used to go under with no problem, and apparently we were going along underneath and all of a sudden we heard this scraping down the side. Next thing, the port screw stopped.

Of course, we don't know what this is, whether it's a mine or what. We tried to get out, to wriggle ourselves free. Nothing would happen. Nobody seemed to know what was going to happen. You don't ask the skipper – I mean, I don't. I'm not supposed to talk to him. I remember I went to the engine room and got my head down behind the engine and went to sleep. There's nothing you can do. You'd been told by the powers that be: don't worry about dying on a submarine, just go to sleep. Next thing I knew my mate was shaking me. 'Wake up, Cyril, wake up. We're going up.' I heard the diving stations being called and I went to diving stations and we blew every tank we'd got. We had a chance to look now. We were just off Turkey. I don't think there was a special name for this place we went into but it was in Turkish waters [Casteloriso]. There were some British people came out that were resident there and they told us that if we didn't go within 48 hours …

The wire was stuck to the motor. We could get down to it, but we hadn't got the tools or the equipment to get all the stuff off, and down behind was a whacking great buoy. Now the mines had been attached to this buoy but they had gone, broken free. The cable was wrapped right round. So they sent out a diver from Malta who went down underneath the stern and cut it off with underwater acetylene gear. That got us away, only just in time, and we carried on. And that's when we went to Chios [on the next patrol, reaching Chios on 16 October].

Now, when we went to Chios they were starving. Little kids with their bellies out … I always remember one thing we did. We used to have big tins of hard-boiled sweets which we used to use on board as you didn't have to drink as much water. Somebody came up on the conning tower and they started throwing handfuls of these sweets at the crowds. Oh dear, there was knives out: the lot. Terrible! And of course we had to maintain order then. The marines who were on shore came along and helped and got some kind of order and then we gave them all the food we'd got. I'll always remember that because we had to go all the way from there back to Malta – that would take a week – and, believe you me, all we'd got to eat was hardboiled eggs. That's all we'd got left.

## Captain George Hunt, DSO*, DSC*, Royal Navy, HMS *Ultor*

George Hunt was credited with sinking 20 ships by torpedo and eight by gunfire in addition to damaging four other vessels, a record for British submarine COs. His aggregate tonnage, however, fell short of that achieved by David Wanklyn, VC, in HMS *Upholder*. Nevertheless, he achieved his success at a time when important targets were in short supply and heavily guarded. The 28-year-old lieutenant had commanded *Ultor* since launch.

It was 15 June 1944, and the next day *Ultor* was due to sail for her 15th Med patrol. I was in the Staff office getting briefed on recent intelligence in the area off Nice where we would patrol. My old friend Lieutenant 'Paddy' Gowan came into the office and said, 'Barry Rowe has gone sick and is being operated on tomorrow!' But he went on, 'Not to worry. I'll come as your first lieutenant instead.' Lieutenant Gowan and I had been together in HMS *Conway* as officer cadets aged 14 to 17 and now here he was: CO of the spare crew and dying to get to sea. It could not have been better, although I went and saw poor Lieutenant Rowe and commiserated.

So we sailed on 16 June and established patrol in our area, only to find very considerable anti-submarine activity for some reason. On 20 June we attacked and sank with two torpedoes an 'F' lighter escorted by an 'R' boat. We watched the 'R' boat apparently picking up survivors, but it wasn't long before a U J Boat, a specialised anti-submarine hunter, appeared from behind Is. St. Marguerite, so we went deep and retired to seaward to reload torpedoes. Some days later, on 27 June, at 0415, after we had decided to spend the final day off Nice, we picked up Asdic impulses to the west and eventually we dived because we would have a background of dawn light. However, through the periscope we detected a shape through the periscope, though it was still too dark to identify it. By 0445 I knew we were dealing with a convoy, and five minutes later distinguished a large vessel escorted by three destroyers and a corvette. The target, an old 'three-island' merchant ship, about 3,000 tons, with straight stem and counter, was painted black with white upper works and was going quite slowly – timing her past the graticules of the periscope gave an estimate of six knots – so the escorts were weaving. They were only three miles south of Villefranche and were obviously marking time until it got light. I crossed ahead and inside of the starboard beam destroyer, despite the fact that she, like the others, was weaving, and managed to get into 1,000 yards' range. At 0504, in position 43°38 N 07°19 E we fired four torpedoes spread over two lengths, point of aim, half a length ahead. I had ordered the submarine swung to port against the target to reduce the firing interval.

Forty seconds later two hit and there was an almighty explosion followed by a continuous stream of rumbling and breaking up noises which persisted for several minutes. The noise was quite incredible and I thought it very possible that she was carrying munitions. I had little doubt that she had sunk.

We immediately went deep, in position 43.37° N, 07.20° E, and made our way south to clear the area. However, the vessels hunting us were persistent, and while we were being hunted we could not start reloading our two remaining torpedoes without making some noise.

As we had already picked up more HE and Asdic impulses, we concluded that the four escorts had been reinforced, and so we remained deep and at 'silent routine'. I was very aware of the fact that we must try and reload as soon as possible, but not while being hunted. The vessels looking for us were really very persistent (it transpired that the original four vessels had been reinforced by four more) and were dropping depth charges singly and in patterns. After all, they knew there was a submarine thereabouts and were no doubt keen to destroy it.

We had fired our torpedoes and gone deep at 0504 and it was now 0610 and it did seem that we really must assess the situation, so we came to periscope depth. We saw aircraft circling overhead, but our own late antagonists were some distance away. So immediately we started to strip the fore ends, ready to start reloading the torpedoes.

At 0655, to our astonishment, we sighted a tanker to the South West, just off Cape Antibes, together with the masts and upper works of several other vessels. They were evidently heading for Nice, so we began a crash reload of our remaining two torpedoes. By 0725 the first torpedo had been reloaded. It was broad daylight now, but I was puzzled by the slowness of the tanker – she was about 7,000 tons – as continuous ranging gave a speed of only four knots. Then I saw that she was being towed by two tugs. She had five escorts: one destroyer, one corvette, one large U J boat and two 'R' boats, and there were four aircraft circling overhead. I was less than pleased to see that the escorts of our previous victim were proceeding to the SW to join the tanker escorts, making nine escorts, and up to five aircraft at one time.

The tanker's speed was so slow that the escorting vessels had to weave in a very exaggerated fashion, sometimes turning a complete circle, to kill time.

With only two torpedoes left, I simply had to penetrate the screen and get in close. One thing in my favour was that the escorts were churning up the water, making it difficult for their Asdics which would be 'masked' by a confusion of disturbed water; my difficulty was to avoid being rammed by the escorts whose movements were so unpredictable. I had to stay at periscope depth so that I could actually see, because if I went deep my Asdics could not give me a clear picture of the whereabouts of each escort and I would not know if it was clear to come up.

Eventually, however, I passed between the two leading escorts and the starboard bow destroyer. The destroyers, with lots of time to spare, frequently turned complete circles, which did nothing for my peace of mind. The tanker was a large vessel of 7,000 tons, painted grey and not more than half-laden. By now, 0815, the second torpedo was loaded. I ordered the torpedoes set to 16 feet to go off on the keel, or under it if she was drawing less than estimated. The destroyer on the starboard quarter gave me several qualms as he surged up nearly on the beam and I was quite unable to forecast the next move of any of the escorts. The sooner I fired, the better!

I had got in to a range of 1,500 yards and at 0831 fired, aiming for the break of the forecastle and the poop. Sixty-nine seconds later, both torpedoes hit.

We went down to 200 feet, shut off for depth charging, went to silent routine, and tiptoed away – bearing in mind that we were completely surrounded by angry escort vessels. In a few minutes, the first depth charges arrived, which certainly shook the submarine, but only did very minor damage.

For the benefit of my crew I had already given a word picture of the situation up top, and it certainly kept everyone on their toes. Now of course we were all well aware that the hunt for us would be on in earnest! We certainly received over 100 depth charges during almost an hour, but eventually things quietened down and we returned to periscope depth where we saw the tanker stopped and with a broken back – the bow and stern were cocked up out of the water.

We took some periscope photos and several of the crew were also able to see the results of their handiwork. I was able to get PO Trewhela along – the Torpedo Gunner's Mate who (with his team) had, up to that point, lovingly cared for the 66 torpedoes that we had fired. We fired two more on our next and last patrol.

Eventually the shore batteries had some practice, shooting at the part of the tanker still afloat. By 1000 our victim had sunk. The escorts, however, were still hunting, and it was not until noon that we finally shook them off and, having made a signal to our base that we had expended all torpedoes, we set course for 'home'! My old friend Paddy Gowan had done a splendid job reverting to that of 1st Lieutenant and had shown all his old expertise in trimming *Ultor*; I completed my patrol report with the remark that, 'It was noted with satisfaction that Lieutenant Gowan had not forgotten a) any of a First Lieutenant's "patter" and b) how to play "ukkers"[ludo].'

When we arrived back at La Maddelena the following morning we were delighted to see Barry Rowe waiting for us on the jetty, and the intelligence was so good that we were actually told the names of the ships we had just sunk.

They were the requisitioned French cargo ship *Cap Blanc*, 3,315 tons and the *Pallas*, 5,260 tons. The double success brought forth an encomium from the flotilla commander:

The attack on the 3,000 ton merchant ship was brilliantly carried out, but I have no hesitation in saying that in my considerable experience of submarining the attack on the tanker only three hours later is the most superlative exhibition of which I have ever heard. That Lieutenant Hunt should achieve an unseen, undetected position at 1,500 yards inside such a massive and violently zig-zagging screen argues consummate technical skill but shows, moreover, determination and courage of the highest order ... Lieutenant Hunt very seriously described the screen and their manoeuvres to me on his return as 'very off-putting', a rather attractive understatement ... A performance that will be difficult for herself or any other submarine to rival.

(signed) P. Q. Roberts, Captain, 10th Submarine Flotilla
[ADM199/1821]

From Admiral Claude Barry, Flag Officer Submarines, came a personal letter:

I want to tell you that I consider the record of you and your company in *Ultor* is one of the most outstanding I have ever heard of ... and I doubt if anyone has caused more destruction and discomfiture to the enemy in so short a time as you have ... I hope you have a jolly fine leave.

### Sub-Lieutenant Stephen Dearnley, Royal Navy, HMS *Sportsman*

Sub-Lieutenant Dearnley joined the submarine in early 1944 as fourth hand.

*Sportsman* had been due to move east to join the rest of *Maidstone's* flotilla at Trincomalee in Ceylon but her voyage was aborted when it was discovered that those waters were unsuitable for S-boats that had not been modified for the tropical conditions of the Indian Ocean. Instead, she was being sent on patrol in the Aegean and to return to base at Malta ...

My two operational patrols in *Sportsman* were quite eventful. Following a tip-off from the Greek underground in Athens, we waylaid a 5,000-ton German troopship just off the Cretan port of Candia (Heraklion). It was important enough to be escorted by a dozen surface vessels and a large number of aircraft so it was not an easy target. After we fired our torpedoes we immediately went deep to avoid the inevitable counter-attack, and with all the noise and confusion it was not possible to hear if any of the torpedoes hit their mark. It was not until several hours later when we were game enough to surface and charge batteries that we learned from Malta that our attack had been successful. Apparently members of the Cretan resistance had seen the whole affair from land and managed to get a signal back to our intelligence with all the details.

By this stage of the war there were not many targets as big as that, though. Most of the supplies to the German garrisons were brought in by caiques or vessels too small to warrant an expensive torpedo so we would try and sink these with the three-inch gun mounted just forward of the conning tower. We relied on the element of surprise, surfacing suddenly at almost point-blank range and getting a round or two away before the crew realised what was happening. In most cases they would then take to their boats and row like mad for the shore while we would wait until they were clear before finishing the job with a couple of incendiary shells.

We achieved a moment of fame when one of our exploits was the subject of a graphic double-page sketch by a famous war artist in the *Illustrated London News*. Monemvasia is a little port towards the southern tip of Greece, and through the periscope we could see that it held a ship of reasonable size in its inner harbour. This was protected by a boom net with a small gap for shipping to enter, and while it was probable that the place was well fortified, we didn't know how well. We waited until it got dark before surfacing then, trimmed down to minimise our silhouette, we moved slowly up to the boom, stuck our bow in the gap and fired two torpedoes. We didn't wait to see if we had hit the target but backed off as fast as we could and, in all the confusion of bangs and lights that followed, managed to get out to sea safely. The attack was successful, though, which is why we got our picture in the magazine.

At the end of May our time was up at Malta and we were sent west in convoy to go back to the Clyde. We stopped for ten days or so in Gibraltar to acquire some good sherry and work with the air force on Leigh light exercises. The theory behind these was that an aircraft, having picked up a submarine on the surface at night with its radar, could fly low over its victim and, at a certain moment, switch on a very bright light under its wings. This would dazzle the crew of the submarine long enough for the plane to drop depth charges before the target could dive. In practice the aircraft would fly either too high or too low, or switch its light on at the wrong place and time, causing amusement for ourselves and anguish for the RAF guests we would take out on these exercises.

It took nearly two weeks to travel in convoy back to home waters and the base at Holy Loch before going home on leave with a bunch of bananas brought all the way from Gibraltar for my young sister, Ruth, who was then just nine years old. With the restrictions of wartime rationing she had missed out on a lot of the treats little girls would normally have enjoyed at that age, so the bananas, though quite overripe by then, were very welcome.

## INDIAN OCEAN

**Commander Edward Young, DSO, DSC, RNV(S)R, Royal Navy;**
from *One of Our Submarines*

Having served in the North sea, the Arctic and the Mediterranean, it was almost inevitable that Edward Young, now commanding HMS *Storm*, should find himself out east based at Trincomalee with the 4th Submarine Flotilla.

The remaining days were uneventful. We were now getting used to the conditions of tropical submarine life. While dived we wore nothing but a towel or sarong wrapped round the waist, and sandals to give ventilation to the feet. In our bunks we lay on rush mats, for they were cooler and less irritating than sheets or blankets. The air-cooling fans were a godsend. Glimpses of what a whole patrol would have been like without them were given us on the occasions when we were so close to the enemy that we had to switch them off – at the very time we most wanted to keep cool. For within five minutes the heat began creeping about us like a deliberate evil and the sweat welled up from every pore, glistening on our naked backs, trickling down our ribs and dripping over our eyebrows. If you were looking through the periscope the perspiration steamed the glass of the eyepiece so that you had to keep wiping it clear with tissue paper. When the air-conditioning fans were running, louvres in the ventilation shaft directed currents of chilled air into various corners of every compartment. Even then the humidity was such that we were never free from perspiration. Towards the end of the day the air grew heavy and foul from the sweating and breathing of fifty men. Tiny, untraceable leaks in the compressed-air pipes (under the enormous pressure of 4,000 pounds to the square inch) seeped into the atmosphere and gradually increased the pressure inside the boat. By teatime we would be feeling lethargic, suffering from headaches and breathing shorter and faster. Then, taking a tip from Lumby's practice in the Mediterranean, if no enemy was in sight through the periscope I would give the order to run the air-compressors for about ten minutes. This would take the excess pressure out of the atmosphere and put it back into the air-cylinders, not only making life pleasanter but obviating the dangerous sudden escape of pressure when the time came to open the hatch on surfacing.

Water being precious, we could not wash as often as we should have liked. I used to wash face and hands once a day, and all over every second or third day. Some of the men did not shave at all during the whole patrol, but I personally felt horribly scruffy with a three- or four-day beard and found a clean shave every other day was a good tonic for one's morale.

Our amusements were much the same as in northern waters: the usual uckers, cribbage and liar dice. We read a good deal. My own reading was very miscellaneous: the short stories of Somerset Maugham, *The Oxford Book of English Verse*, Balzac's *Droll Tales*, any light novel that was going the rounds, Macdonell's *England, Their England*, and of course dips into Shakespeare. We had now acquired a gramophone, though few records; Bing Crosby we ran to death, and we had a tune called *Beyond the Blue Horizon* which is still sometimes played and always has an absurdly nostalgic effect on me. In later patrols, when we were closer to land, it amused me to be looking through the periscope at an enemy harbour to the accompaniment of music from the wardroom.

### Lieutenant J. A. R. Troup, Royal Navy, HMS *Strongbow*; from IWM Sound Archive 12336/2

Actually, the Japs were not that bad. They had what we call good Asdic – Sonar, now. They were really quite good at it. Contrary to general feelings we thought they would be fairly primitive and they would only be using hydrophones, but they used both, and they used sonar quite effectively, certainly, because eventually I got badly caught at night at the top of the Narrows in the Malacca Strait – what's known as the 1 fathom bank channel. I got caught by five anti-submarine vessels: a couple of frigates and three anti-submarine trawlers. They gave me a very bad time and I was considerably dusted up, as they say, and had to eventually make the harbour, which was 1,000 miles away, so it took a time. We had irreparable damage done which was infuriating. We had the pressure hull pushed in. In those days the submarines were riveted, at least mine was, and the force of the explosion sort of pushed the double buckstrap in so the water ran down between the joint, as it were, and we also had the main engines moved on their beds, and that made things very difficult. A lot of vibration, and we couldn't get the tailclutches in, and we had the torpedoes jammed in the tubes. You name it. The air compressors smashed, and everything else. So we were in a bad way, but not so bad we couldn't get home. But it was really the end of our time because the assessment was that we really shouldn't go below 150 feet and that really wasn't any good to anybody, so eventually I came home.

I think everybody disliked the Japanese intensely. I mean they were bestial towards their prisoners. We knew – Intelligence told us – they did shocking things to people, and, indeed, my cousin, Pat Pelly, was in charge of a submarine called the Stratagem in the same Flotilla, and he was sunk in the Malacca Strait just about a couple of months beforehand … and they had a hell of a time. And we all knew this and so we didn't go much on them, whereas the Germans – oh, we didn't like the Germans but we respected them. Their navy in particular, I think, were good clean fighting people, better than the Italians, really. But not so the Japanese.

We relieved some people who were lying on an island off Padang on the west coast of Sumatra. There was an American, a black man, and a native. Anyway, we took them off and replenished them with stores and things and put them back again, and they were there for a while reporting all the shipping movements. They may have been there for ages. Amazing people. And we had a lot of difficulty in doing that, but we did it.

We were due to rendezvous and we see these people in an outrigger canoe and we had to make contact. That was the broad gist of it. We did meet them, and see them paddling around – and they saw the periscope in the broad daylight but we couldn't come up because we were too exposed with aeroplanes overhead on patrol, but we waited until after dark – but not before they had almost exhausted themselves paddling after the periscope trying to catch us up all the time. There was nothing we could do, but eventually I decided that what I would do was to send them a message in a bottle. We wrote out a message and put it in a Zachary and Speed sherry bottle, saying – well, I thought I had better be careful with what I say because if they don't pick it up, someone else may – 'Anchor and wait 'til dusk'.

Then we had to decide how to get it to them.

Well, in submarines in those days we had an underwater gun (we still have one) for firing out smoke candles and whatever, so we put this inside the gun and the idea was – and it actually worked – we would not let them see our periscope at all for about 20 mins so they stayed still, and then I would go underneath them – they were only in a little dugout canoe – and then I would let this thing pop out (I wouldn't blow it out). And it worked: it came up right alongside them, but unfortunately, as it came up, I put the periscope up and saw it come up. The coloured chap saw the periscope, and they were both so

380

excited as it was so close, they started paddling after me again. So I realised they were not going to [spot it]; I found out later they did not get the message. So I then withdrew, knowing where they were, and waited until it was nearly dark and then came back – and fine: we got them all on board, and we replenished them with every blinking thing they wanted. But then the weather blew up and I said, 'Okay, I will tow you back to the island,' because we'd drifted miles off. So we tied them on astern and we towed them – and then, of course, it was so rough we towed them under. And it was five or so by that time: it was beginning to get light, and we then had to rig a derrick – we had a torpedo derrick. We had to get that rigged, we had to hoist their thing out of the water, we had to do it all over again, and by the time we had finished it was broad daylight, and I was getting hellish worried. However, it was alright: the wind eased and they paddled off and I shot off on the surface to get as fast as possible away from them so's not to compromise them. And I subsequently found out they survived.

It was fun ... but it wasn't the same as attacking enemy shipping. It was not something one welcomes ...You were putting the submarine at risk to a certain extent by going in the places you really wouldn't want to go.

### Sub-Lieutenant Tony Eldridge, DSC, RNVR; from IWM Sound Archive 11259

The idea of the human torpedo as used by the Decima Flottiglia MAS had been taken up by the British following the Alexandria raid in 1941, and developed with the help of some of the Italian team following the Italian Armistice. It had been used several times, with mixed success, before Eldridge was sent out to Trincomalee.

I'd just been promoted from ordinary seaman in the RNVR to midshipman down at *King Alfred* in Hove. This was in fact on Christmas Eve in 1942 and while still at the training course a Commander [Captain W. R.] Fell came along and we were all mustered in the hall there and he asked for volunteers for a special and hazardous service. He couldn't really explain anything at all about what it was. All he could say was that it would be a good idea if we could swim and also that it was to do with small craft. I suppose 15 midshipmen and sub-lieutenants volunteered, and in no time at all we found ourselves along at HMS *Dolphin* at Gosport ... Here we were pushed through the DSEA tank ... And even this experience managed to reduce our numbers by a few and we were then introduced to helmet diving. The suit was the same as everyone thinks of when the word diver comes into their mind, with their big spherical brass hat on, with the circular glass window in the front, 25lb weights on the chest and on the back, big weighted boots on your feet – and you could hardly stagger across the diving cutter and over the side down the ladder and into the water. The air was pumped from the diving cutter through a pipe down into the brass hat, and the exhaust air was exhausted through a valve on the hat. Of course the first thing we found out was that the bottom of Portsmouth harbour is extraordinarily muddy and they got us down there doing half hour dives, then gave us work to do. They gave us a piece of chain, hammer and a chisel and told us to stop down there until we had two pieces of chain. Another exercise we did was to go down the bottom, walk away from the shot rope and instead of coming up hand over hand up the shot rope we stopped the air coming out of the diving helmet and the air was continually pumped into the suit until you had enough buoyancy to be sucked out of the mud and you ended up on the surface like the veritable Michelin man ...

Well, quite soon we were graduated to a lighter diving suit with no metal helmet or anything like that the carbon dioxide was absorbed by what we called a protosorb canister which was within the breathing bag. We used these diving suits in a torpedo testing run further up Portsmouth harbour and once again endurance was extended: we were told to stop down for half an hour, then a bit longer for an hour and of course the whole idea was to get us to breathe underneath the same as on top. We were given work to do on the bottom. We had a steel bench down at the bottom and had a vice on it and we had to cut pieces of metal in two and we were breathing oxygen the whole time. We were cold and wet and numb up to the knees because it was January time. We had a small wooden buoy attached to our harness so that a skiff up on top could keep count of the divers underneath and what they were doing and where they were going, and I can remember some enterprising gentleman who crawled away surreptitiously, got himself up to about 9-inches water on the bank and lay there until the skiff suddenly noticed there was one buoy missing and there was a big panic on to try to find him ...

This diving was in depth only about 25 feet deep and didn't offer any hazards at all in breathing the oxygen. But we were told that at greater depths in fact anything over 30 feet everybody can suffer oxygen poisoning. This comes on in various times and in various depths. However to try and find out if we were particularly susceptible to this we took the diving cutter out to a position off Southsea where we anchored and in 45–50 feet of water we did our dives there and waited until we got the symptoms of oxygen poisoning, which were tingling in the fingers and tingling in the toes and probably a bit of tingling in the lips and you were unable to hold the mouthpiece in your mouth properly, and this can progress to complete unconsciousness. In fact one guy, he showed symptoms of this and he came up, took his suit off and he laid down in the bottom of the cutter, hugging the fender as if it was his girlfriend.

And all along a few guys gradually fell away and numbers dwindled to about 12. Latterly we were told what it was all about. And we were given a brief description of a human torpedo. In fact it wasn't called a human torpedo at that time. That only came later as a result of the media putting a name to it.* We called it a chariot or a jeep. And this was a cylinder about 20 feet long. It had an electric motor inside, had a pump, main motor for driving the single propeller at the back and had controls to enable us to dive and rise, and it had some wooden superstructure on it to give some protection to the two personnel, one driving, one to help manoeuvre through nets, etc., and also to store any equipment that we had to carry. We were only introduced to the real thing when we got up north to the depot ship which was HMS *Titania*. We did daylight dives on the chariot; we went and looked at submarine nets and anti-torpedo nets; we put warheads on the bottom of the target, the depot ship and it was all very great fun.

And then along came the night dives, as all chariot operations were to be carried out at night. And it's a completely different proposition. One can't talk to any degree underneath and everything has to be done by touch. When we hit the nets we got a big shower of phosphorescence and if you think it's dark on a moonless night in the sea you want to go underneath a ship on a moonless night. It's *really* dark.

Once again our endurance was extended on the machines ... It took quite a lot of stickability ...

In the first quarter of '44 we were introduced to the Mk 2 Terry Chariot, which was a much bigger and better machine with a bigger battery – we could go up to 30 miles on a machine. Because we had to go farther we had to carry extra oxygen and we had oxygen on board. This was a very nice machine to control. We had the honour of going up and being inspected by the King just before D-Day ... While D-Day was going on we were on embarkation leave awaiting to go out to the Far East. We proceeded out to the Far East on HMS *Wolf* which was the depot ship to the 2nd Submarine Flotilla and we went out to Trincomalee in Ceylon.

Now diving out here was a totally different proposition. It was pure pleasure to dive in the warm water. However, there was an additional risk, we thought, because the phosphorescence in the water was so much greater. However, it was very pleasant indeed. We had lots of working up exercises in Trinco harbour putting warheads on unsuspecting boats including the Unicorn and I remember we put a 'head' under there one night and went to collect the 'head' next morning much to the consternation of the boat commander and stupidly

* Admiral Cunningham had used the term as early as December 1941 when warning the fleet at Alexandria to be on the alert against Italian special forces.

he went as far as putting the sentry on a charge. Poor guy, there just wasn't anything to see. You see, there was complete ignorance of what we could do in a harbour by all and sundry right up to the top. They really didn't understand the way in which we could penetrate a harbour and put an 1,100lb charge on a ship's bottom without being detected.

Eventually we learned with great glee that an operation was being planned and fortunately I was one of the team of four divers chosen to go and attack Phuket harbour. There was myself and Petty Officer S. Woolcott, and Petty Officer [W. S.] Smith, the other No. 1, and his No. 2, Able Seaman Brown. We did working-up exercises, launching from a submarine, regaining the submarine at night, attacking the harbour from seawards and eventually we left in HMS *Trenchant* on 20 October. In a pretty crowded *Trenchant* there were 4 crew, two dressers and the Flotilla Asdic Officer extra to the normal crew, and we hot-bunked for the whole trip. It all got rather sticky after a while.

On passage we were completely spare numbers and had no job to do in the running of the boat. And it was an odd life, not seeing the sun for a whole week. As we approached Phuket on 28 October we realised that everyone was a bit tensed up in the boat as the CO, who was Lieutenant Commander 'Baldy' Hezlet, picked his way through a minefield and then from four and a half miles off the harbour all chariot crews were able to make a visual periscope reconnaissance of the targets and landmarks behind the harbour to enable us to identify our course later on.

I was to attack the recently salvaged *Sumatra* and [Petty Officer W. S.] Bill Smith the *Volpi* which was still being worked on and this reconnaissance was of enormous assistance to us later on that night. The sea was absolutely dead flat and the captain decided he wouldn't be able to drop us off as close as he wanted. Anyway, Trenchant surfaced at about 1900 on a perfect night with a brilliant moon, and this was super for finding the targets and eventually homing the submarine, but we were a bit concerned about being sighted in the vicinity of the targets. After a good supper we started dressing about 9 o'clock. It was so hot down there in the boat being dressed in the suit and we were soon dripping perspiration. We'd stowed away on our person our escape and evasion kit, which comprised a 38 revolver, various denominations of currency, a small bag of 25 gold sovereigns, silk maps of Malaya and Siam [Thailand], a small commando dagger, needle and thread, heliograph, prismatic compass, a tiny little telescope, hacksaw blades, emergency rations and a capsule of cyanide, of all things, if things got rough. We also carried a Siamese blood chit, which was a smallish square of white silk with the Union Jack in the middle surrounded by the following message in several oriental languages:

384

I'M A BRITISH NAVAL OFFICER WHO HAS BEEN ENGAGED IN OPERATIONS AGAINST THE
JAPANESE. IF I AM CAPTURED I CANNOT CONTINUE TO FIGHT AGAINST THE JAPANESE SO I
APPEAL TO YOU TO HIDE ME AND PROVIDE ME WITH FOOD UNTIL I CAN REJOIN OUR FORCES.
IF YOU WILL HELP ME BY GIVING ME FOOD AND HIDING ME IN A SAFE PLACE UNTIL OUR ARMIES
ARRIVE IN MALAYA YOU WILL EARN THE GRATITUDE OF MY GOVERNMENT WHO WILL GIVE YOU
A BIG REWARD AND I AM AUTHORISED TO GIVE YOU A CHIT TO THIS EFFECT.

Fortunately, we never had to use it.

The submarine crew saw how we were getting distressed by the heat and, fortunately, some enterprising guy rigged up a rubber pipe from a ventilation louvre into our face-pieces.

Zero hour came at 2210 and the command from the conning tower: open fore hatch, out divers. We were already on oxygen and groped our way up the ladder and along the casing to the machines already unstopped on the chocks. By the time we were seated and ready to go it seemed as if we were breathing superheated steam. And submariners, they don't like having the fore hatch open when on patrol ... Finally the navigation officer came down and on to the saddletanks and gave us our course: North 65° W for 6.5 miles going in, and South 75° E for seven miles coming out.

At last the main vents on the submarine were opened and she sank, leaving us on top, and we were on our own. This is quite an experience, in fact, this opening of the vents because there is an enormous rush of air leaving the saddletanks of the boat – and at any rate we were very pleased to have this welcome cooling off of our breathing bags. After a few minutes Butch told me he was getting no oxygen from the machine so after a short run back to Trenchant it was decided to do the long run in on air. He would be in big trouble if I had had to dive in a hurry. Fortunately things sorted themselves out and I did a perfect trim and tried to proceed at full speed to make up for lost time. Full speed in this Terry machine was about four knots, and if you've ever hung onto the painter of a dinghy going at about four knots ... you'll find that it gives you quite a buffeting about. But a following sea lifted the stern out with quite a lot of threshing of the propeller so I reverted to third speed and kept it at that the whole way in. We probably went through a few freshwater patches on the way because I kept on finding myself dropping from 18 feet to 30 feet with no apparent reason. I dived for a final time on a compass course when 500 yards from the target and after what seemed a very long time we finally passed under the narrow beam of the bows. We'd made it.

I turned round and came in again at about 22 feet went under the shallow of the hull again and I stopped, blew main ballast and came up again hard on the bottom. The time was half past midnight so we'd been away two hours.

The jackstay protected us as we came up and Number 2 got out and went forward to fix the head. Finding the head not near enough to the bilge keel he signalled me to come forward a bit and as soon as I did the jackstay, held in the enormous barnacles on the bottom, folded over backwards leaving me cramped over to one side bearing off the ship's bottom with my shoulder and one arm. I could breathe so I suppose I was alright. To bring up the head to help Butch fix it I moved the battery aft a bit and he tied the head by two boiler clamps to the bilge keel and set the clock for six hours. He returned to the machine and shook hands over the cockpit, and the time was a quarter to one. Just 15 minutes. And it was a very satisfying feeling I can assure you that we'd actually done the job the first time.

Then we had to do our withdrawal back to the submarine and on the way we shone a shaded red torch seawards at a given interval so that the submarine could put themselves in our way. And thus we were recovered without us having to look around for them. And as we were approaching the sub we got a terrible flashing of Morse which I don't understand too well and what happened: they thought they were being attacked by a motor torpedo boat. In fact it was our overzealous Asdic officer who had heard us coming back. Anyway we got back and they told us to ditch the machines and come inboard and we were unceremoniously dragged out of the sea and back down into the boat.

At 0600 the *Sumatra* blew up, followed by the *Volpi*.

**Lieutenant D. C. Douglas, Royal Navy;**
Official Report on the loss of HM Submarine *Stratagem*

The report was compiled in 1945 after his release from POW camp.

HM Submarine *Stratagem* sailed from Trincomalee on 10 November 1944 for patrol off the port of Malacca. Passage, until well down into the entrance of the Strait of Malacca, was uneventful, the enemy not being sighted in any form. On 16th November, whilst proceeding on the surface, a junk was sighted. This was investigated and found to be of no importance. However, further passage by daylight was carried out submerged. Many junks of varying sizes were sighted in the vicinity of Malacca. Our presence was possibly suspected, as indicated by the activities of a Japanese Zero floatplane carrying out search patrols in the area.

The 17th and 18th November were spent off the port, with little of interest happening. A thorough search was carried out for the pier, which was reported by Intelligence to be in existence and which was thought to be in use by the enemy as a loading pier for bauxite ore. No traces of this pier could be found.

During the night 18th/19th the submarine proceeded south and daylight found us in a position about 30 miles south of the port.

At approximately 15.00 on 19th November, smoke was sighted to the southward. This soon proved to be coming from a convoy of five Japanese ships. The convoy, escorted by three small destroyers, all appeared to be in ballast and were steaming in line ahead on a steady course. The escorts were disposed one ahead and one on either side of the convoy.

At about 15.30 torpedoes were fired with 'impact only' pistols, from Nos. 1, 2 and 3 tubes. The range at the time of firing was 2,500 yards. The Commanding Officer – Lieutenant G. R. Pelly, Royal Navy – had chosen the second ship in the line for his target and stated that it was a cargo vessel of about 2,000 tons. This, as I later learned from the Japanese at Singapore, was probably incorrect. The ship was stated to be a tanker. [The ship was not a tanker; she was the 1,945-ton cargo vessel *Nichinan Maru*; Pelly was right and his estimate of tonnage was accurate.] One hit was observed well forward on the target. The destroyers then commenced a wild and ineffective counter-attack, dropping about 20 charges. The submarine was taken deep and turned through 180°. While charges were still being dropped, the submarine was brought to periscope depth. The captain reported that the target was still afloat, although stopped and very much down by the bow. The external (stern) tube was then fired at a range of 1,000 yards. This torpedo was observed to hit the target which immediately split in two and sank. The counter-attack continued but was still ineffective and we were able to get clear of the area.

During the hours of darkness the submarine was taken to a position north of Malacca. The captain, changing his mind about going north to the junk area, returned to the port of Malacca on 21st November. Daylight on the 22nd found us in a position four miles off the shore. When I was relieved of the watch at 08.30, the submarine was in a position as ordered by Lieutenant Pelly, approximately three miles south-west of the port.

The report of activities during the forenoon on the 22nd is compiled from information received from Leading Seaman Gibbs. This rating was on watch in the control room during the forenoon.

The aforementioned reconnaissance plane appears to have been very active in our area during the four hours preceding our depth-charging and the captain, who spent the greater part of the watch on the periscope, reported the presence of a Japanese destroyer patrolling up and down the coast close inshore.

At approximately 12.10 I was awakened by the order, 'Diving Stations'. As soon as I arrived in the tube space the order, 'Shut off for depth-charging,' was passed. This was carried out and a report sent to the control room. About four minutes elapsed without any further orders coming through – no one in the fore ends knowing what was taking place – then the thrash of the Japanese destroyer could be heard very loud as she passed overhead. Almost immediately a depth-charge exploded somewhere extremely close under us, lifting the stern and causing us to hit bottom hard. This charge extinguished the greater part of the lighting although one or two of the emergency lights held. About five seconds later a second charge exploded, as far as I could calculate, right amidships, extinguishing the remaining lights. By this time I had a torch in operation and could see water flooding through the door at the after end of the torpedo stowage compartment. Immediately I gave the order, 'Shut watertight doors' and turned to make sure that the three ratings in the tube space were brought out of that compartment before the door was shut. By the time this door was shut, the water was flooding very much faster and had risen above the deck boards in the torpedo stowage compartment. It was now above our knees. It was flooding through the after door so fast that the ratings were unable to shut this door. The position of the stop (retaining door in 'open' position) on this water-tight door was such that to remove it one had to stand in the doorway as the port side of the door was blocked by stores. Hence, due to the furious rate of flooding, this stop could not be removed.

According to Able Seaman Westwood, who came forward from the control room, the captain gave the order for main ballast to be blown as soon as he found that the ship was being flooded. The valves on the panel were opened without effect.

In what appeared to be an incredibly short time, I was keeping above water by clinging on to a hammock which was slung from the deckhead. The crew in my compartment began to sing but I ordered this to stop and told the crew to get out and put on DSEA sets. The first I managed to reach had a defective valve on the oxygen bottle and I could not move it. The second was in working order and I put this over the head of one of the older ratings who was panicking and in tears due to the pressure effect on his eyes. The pressure in the boat at the time was immense and the chlorine content in the air considerable. The water all round us must have been full of oil fuel as we were all drenched with it, although I did not notice it at the time. The air could be heard to be escaping through the hull forward and the water was still rising fast. At this time Leading Seaman Gibbs was in the escape hatch trying to slack back the clips. He shouted to me that he could not move the third clip. Speaking was nearly impossible due to the pressure. I swung up into the trunk alongside Gibbs and tried to remove the clip. After what seemed like an hour, and what I suppose was really a minute, I managed to move the clip by hammering it with my fist. By this time there was no hope of using the escape

---

trunk as the water was already up to the metal combing which houses the twill trunking. I took off the last clip and as I did so, the hatch commenced to open. Immediately this clip was free the hatch was blown open and Leading Seaman Gibbs was shot out so suddenly that I cannot remember him going. The hatch slammed shut again and hit me on the top of my head but immediately blew open again and I was shot out in a bubble of air.

Ten of the men in the compartment, which contained 14 at the time, are known to have left the submarine alive although only eight were picked up. The ship's cook was later seen to be floating, face downwards, on the surface but was obviously drowned. Another rating was seen, while in the submarine, to have on a DSEA set and apparently working it correctly; although he was observed to leave the boat he was not seen on the surface. The Japanese destroyer had dropped two more charges after we were hit but these were not so close and did not seem to harm us although they probably accelerated the flooding.

Throughout the above experiences the behaviour of the crew in my compartment was magnificent. I should especially like to mention the ship's cook (Leading Cook Weatherhead) who kept up a cheerful narrative about the wonderful fruit cake which he had recently cooked and who showed great bravery and coolness throughout the dreadful experiences in the flooded submarine. This rating was responsible for the singing and by his behaviour greatly assisted in preventing panic. It is with deepest regret that I have to report that this extremely brave rating failed to survive the ascent to the surface.

The following is a report of experiences after escaping from the submarine. The destroyer circled us for about three-quarters of an hour, dropping a lifebelt and some baulks of timber. All of us were suffering from 'bends' and I do not know about the ratings, but I myself was scared 'pea green' at the sight of the Japanese ensign flying from their masthead. This was more or less justi-fied as we later found out. However, I managed to overcome this somewhat by swimming around and seeing to the ratings. Able Seaman Westwood was just on the verge of sinking. His eyes were full of oil and he could hardly keep himself afloat. I fixed him into the lifebelt and then went to the assistance of AB Phillips. He was in a similar plight but a puff of air into his DSEA set kept his head above water and he was all right, although he was almost delirious with shock.

The Japanese eventually lowered a cutter and picked us up, clubbing us as they hauled us into the boat. Then we were each compelled to pull an oar. This was practically impossible due to 'bends' but we reached the destroyer assisted by their clouts and unpleasantness. By this time another destroyer of a similar type had arrived on the scene. The Japanese were certain there was another submarine in the vicinity and got furious with us when we denied this. On being hauled on board we were bound, blindfolded and beaten. We were not given food at any time whilst on board the destroyer and spent the night on the top of the hatch which was about three feet square, all bound together. We were not clothed and the night was extremely cold. The pain from the 'bends' was now at its worst and every time someone murmured, the guards would come and hit us over the head with their clubs. We were being taken to Singapore where we arrived at about 21.00 on 23rd November. No food was given us and we were locked in separate cells, still bound and blindfolded. We remained in this condition for 28 days although I was allowed to remove my bonds after about ten days.

Our first meal arrived on the evening of the 24th and consisted of a small rice ball. When I stated that I did not like rice, I was informed that I should soon learn to like it. Little did I know at the time how true this statement was to prove. However, I eagerly devoured my first rice ball after returning from six hours' extensive interrogation by a Japanese captain. My first interrogation had taken place at about midnight on the night of my arriving in the base. At this I was in very bad shape and refused to give them any information except that permitted by international law. However, I was informed by the interpreter that I had better give some sort of answer otherwise I would be shot. I later brought to mind a lecture which I had attended in England on the subject of being taken prisoners, where the lecturer had told us that the Japanese would never recognise international law and that they would probably use all manner of torture for extracting information.

Daily interrogation, varying from two to six hours at a time, continued, all manner of Japanese individuals being employed for the purpose. The ratings were also being taken away for interrogation although not for such long periods. I was greatly assisted in misinforming my captors by the Japanese interpreter. This individual had no pro-Japanese tendencies whatsoever. He was born, educated and had lived in England all his life prior to his coming to Japan in 1940. He had been educated at Kingston Grammar School and was born of an English mother. He had been brought to Japan by his father, against his mother's will, in 1940, had been unable to return before the Pearl Harbor episode and had been conscripted into the Japanese Navy. Being employed on short wave radio, he was able to bring me the BBC news each night and in this manner I was able to keep up with world affairs. He also took messages to my shipmates, brought me cigarettes and sweets etc and kept me well informed as to how the others were being interrogated. Later on I always knew what to expect before I went in front of my questioners and also if they had any idea of the answers to their questions ...

**Vice Admiral Sir Hugh Stirling Mackenzie, KCB, DSO\*, DSC, Royal Navy, then lieutenant-commander, HMS *Tantalus*; from IWM Sound Archive 11745/4**

We sank one small ship by gunfire and picked up the crew, who were largely Malays or East Indonesians, and subsequently transferred them to the first junk we came across because we couldn't carry them all on board, but we also pulled out of the sea a Japanese soldier who'd been the armed guard on board this ship we'd sunk. We had great difficulty in catching him because he kept on trying to swim away from us, and to try and manoeuvre a submarine to catch a swimmer who is determined to try and swim away from you is not easy. But we got him on board in the end and we kept him as a prisoner – and he became a mascot almost.

We gave him a daily task to do so he wouldn't get too bored, which was to polish a ration of valve wheelhandles. Well, there are hundreds, if not thousands, of valves in a submarine with wheelhandles and, by the time we got back into harbour in December, he had practically every valve handwheel in *Tantalus* burnished gleaming.

The day we arrived in harbour was the day when the Commander-in-Chief of the British Pacific Fleet which was then forming – Admiral Sir Bruce Fraser – flew into Perth, and of course he came on board the only British ship in harbour then, the depot ship. And he was asked if he would like to come on board *Tantalus* – we'd just come in that morning from patrol. I think our Captain of Submarines must have thought we'd be in a pretty filthy state, and warned the Commander in Chief not to expect too much. In actual fact, when he came on board and walked through the ship, there we were gleaming and almost ready for an admiral's inspection thanks to our Japanese prisoner.

## PACIFIC

**Lieutenant-Commander Zenji Orita; from *I-Boat Captain***

On Dec. 30, 1943, I made the report on my Sio mission to Rear Adm. Noboru Owada, who had relieved Admiral Harada as ComSubRon 7. Owada wanted me to take supplies into Buin, Bougainville, where none had been sent since *RO-100* hit 2 mines and sank (five weeks before). 'You know I am not exaggerating, Orita,' he told me, 'when I say that the lives of men there depend on successful completion of this mission.'

I did not doubt that. We had more than 20,000 men on Bougainville. They had been using up their supplies rapidly in the two months since the enemy had landed there. Unless they received some assistance, they would suffer the same fate as so many on Guadalcanal: malnutrition followed by death. I began preparations the following day, knowing it would not be an easy mission. Both straits leading into Buin had been heavily sown with American mines and PT boats kept a close watch. I doubted that even a mouse could slip into Buin but I was determined to try. My work was interrupted for Distant Emperor Worship on New Year's Day (and that ceremony itself was interrupted by an air raid) but I got *I-177* to the harbor's bottom and out of danger swiftly.

On the night of Jan. 2, 1 was summoned to SubRon 7 headquarters. From there I accompanied Admiral Owada to the operations room in the headquarters of Vice Adm. Jinichi Kusaka, commander-in-chief of the southeast area fleet. His chief of staff, Rear Adm. Ryonosuke Kusaka, told me that my mission had been changed. 'Our forces at Sio are surrounded, Orita,' he said. 'The enemy landed troops at Saidor today. Road communication between Sio and Madang is cut off.'

The enemy had been steadily pushing our troops westward, out of Buna, Lae, Salamaua and Finschafen, and were pressing against Sio. Our next strong point was Madang, about 110 miles farther west. But the enemy had made a landing between those two places, at Saidor. This movement trapped the headquarters of the 18th Army and the 18th Naval Base Force at Saidor, where Lt. Gen. Hatazo Adachi and Rear Adm. Kunizo Mori were based.

'General Adachi has ordered a general withdrawal toward Madang,' the chief of staff told me, 'but estimates that it will take as much as two months to circle around through the jungle past the enemy. During that time he would be out of touch and could not direct land operations. So we have decided to use a submarine to move the General quickly from Sio to Madang.'

This seemed to me like a good idea. If the enemy could leapfrog, so could we. I left Rabaul the following day.

Traveling most of the way submerged, I did not reach Sio until sunset of Jan. 8. Again I held a flashlight against my periscope's eyepiece so it could be seen from the shore; and my men were very swift in transferring cargo to the daihatsu that soon came out to us. Then a boat started from the shore, carrying General Adachi and Admiral Mori. It was less than halfway to us when a lookout shouted 'PT boats!' My signals petty officer quickly blinked a message to the shore that I would return the following night. Crewmen secured what cargo was still on board. I dived *I-177*.

I came back the next night at sunset, as promised, but found PT boats hovering near my rendezvous point. I kept the boat submerged, but ran up the radio antenna and sent a message. 'We will return tomorrow night,' I messaged, 'but before sunset. We will then try to take passengers aboard. Please stand by to repel enemy torpedo boats if they try to interfere.' Then I moved out to sea.

On the following night (Jan. 10) I brought *I-177* off Sio while it was still light. If the PT boats followed their usual custom of coming in after sunset, I hoped to be gone before they arrived. I also went in much closer to the shore than before. As soon as my periscope showed above the surface, three daihatsu took stations around me, machine guns mounted and manned. Then, when I was sure that my passengers had left the shore, I surfaced the boat and crewmen ran to our 25mm machine gun. Two PT boats showed up right after that, but ran into a barrage from my machine gunners and the daihatsu men. They returned the fire, but it made them cautious and they hove to more than a half-mile away.

Gunfire rattled as I took aboard General Adachi, Admiral Mori, 10 of their staff members, and 25 bags of headquarters equipment and records. The daihatsu and PT boats were still exchanging fire as I backed *I-177* off, put her about, and dived. The next day I put my passengers ashore at Madang safely, and returned to Rabaul without further incident.

When I left for Sio, two other submarines left Truk, heading for Rabaul to help us in the transport effort. Lt. Cdr. Mitsuma Itakura (with whom I was later to work closely in the *kaiten* effort) had *I-41*. An Etajima classmate of mine, Lt. Cdr. Takeo Shimada, had *I-171*. Itakura made a successful run to some of our troops in western New Guinea who were trapped and needed supplies, then left Rabaul on Jan. 31 to do what I had been scheduled to do a month earlier. He headed for Buin. Displaying great skill, Itakura took I-41 through mine fields and enemy patrols to land his cargo. Then he made his way out again, returning to Rabaul on Feb. 7.

Shimada did not have such luck. He was heading for Buka (at the other end of Bougainville from Buin) when he ran into a force of enemy destroyers on Feb. 1. These had on board a party of raiders who were heading for Green Island (not far from Cape St. George). Their mission was to determine whether that island was suitable for building an airstrip before the enemy would decide to take it. *I-171* was picked up by the electronic fingers of USS *Fullam*, and pointed out to the destroyers *Guest* and *Hudson*. They sank Shimada's ship.

Two other submarines were lost in 1944 before Shimada's boat went down, The first was I-181, commanded by Lt. Cdr. Kiyoshi Taoka. He left Rabaul on Jan. 13, heading for Gali, New Guinea (about 40 miles west of Sio), to land supplies there for the troops retreating toward Madang to rendezvous with General Adachi. *I-181* was scheduled to meet the troops on Jan. 16, but never arrived. A radio message from New Guinea said that PT boats or destroyers must have sunk the submarine in Vitiaz Passage, the strip of water off northern New Guinea.

The other submarine lost was *RO-37*, commanded by Lt. Cdr. Sakuma Sato. It had left Truk on Jan. 3 for a patrol off the New Hebrides. Sato met the American fleet tanker, USS *Cache*, on Jan. 23, and put a torpedo into her. She got off a distress call. Sato continued on his way, unaware that a nearby US destroyer, *Buchanan*, had intercepted the call and was rushing to aid the stricken ship. Their paths crossed before *RO-37* had traveled another 30 miles, and Buchanan's radar picked her up. *RO-37* was sunk by a depth charge barrage.

I was relieved of transport duty on Jan. 13, 1944. *I-177* by then had been operating almost continually for six months. Her crew, hull, weapons and engines were all about ready to collapse. My own health had been going steadily downhill, too, like all my men, although I had been fortunate in not contracting malaria. The sub needed overhaul badly, but enemy air raids on Rabaul had destroyed most of the shops, tools and equipment needed. So I left Rabaul for Truk on Jan. 14.

When I first arrived in Simpson Harbor (a year before) it had been filled with ships, nearly 200 of them, and I had difficulty maneuvering through them to moor. On the day I left there were no vessels present other than the scorched hulks of three transports that had burned after being beached. There were still 100,000 men on New Britain. I felt sorry for these orphans of the South Pacific, surrounded and cut off. There was little hope for them.

The situation for our 6th Fleet was not much better at Truk. The Gilberts operation had cost six submarines, and captains of the three surviving ones had complained bitterly. 'I am positive,' Lt. Cdr. Nobukiyo Nambu reported, 'that all the submarines lost went down without even getting a chance to attack the enemy.' He claimed that radar had picked up all of them (including his own *I-174*) before they got within striking range. Nambu also pointed out that *I-169* and *I-175* should never have been sent at all, because their crews had already been out for some time and were tired. 'As for *RO-38*,' he said, 'she was fresh from home waters, with an inexperienced crew that still needed lots of training.' Lt. Cdr. Tabata, who had sunk *Liscome Bay*, and Lt. Cdr. Toyama, of *I-169*, agreed with Nambu.

'The enemy had his interceptors spread and waiting for us,' they said, 'and we made his task easy by putting so many boats into one small area. He had no trouble finding us. Wherever he looked, we were underfoot. And 6th Fleet headquarters required reports from us too often, again making for easy discovery through radio detection. And the orders to cruise on the surface, or wait on the surface, were ridiculous!'

I was in just as bad a temper when, dressed in my whites, I boarded flagship Katori. Vice Adm. Takagi, chief of staff Rear Adm. Hisao Mito, and operations staff chief Capt. Chosaburo Takahashi wanted to hear about our transport operations. I minced no words:

'As all here know,' I began, 'using submarines for transport is throwing away the reason for their construction. Presently, however, it appears that we have no choice. Still, the work is not as easy as headquarters planners seem to think. It takes too much out of the crews, both physically and mentally.' Then I went on to give detailed reports on the 14 missions I had carried out, adding that my men wanted to fight, not pass boxes of cargo.

'I understand the problems very well, Orita,' said Admiral Takagi, 'and you may rest assured that I shall have attack submarines attacking as soon as the special transport submarines now under construction begin coming off the ways. Thank you for your efforts. I hope you and your men will get a good rest while here at Truk refitting.' With that he started to rise from his chair, closing the meeting.

But I was not passing up the only chance to say what I felt. I had an obligation to speak for all my friends who had given their lives in submarines.

'Admiral,' I said, 'I have other things I would like to add.'

Takagi, a polite man, begged my pardon, resumed his seat, and bade me continue. I did.

'My year down here has taught me many things.' I said, 'For one thing, submarines are of no use for counterattacks against enemy beachheads. Those places are too well screened. We do not have the underwater speed for getting in past them, or for escaping after detection. Submarines should be interposed between the enemy's beachhead and his supply sources, thus giving indirect support to our troops on land by reducing the amount of men and equipment that can be used against them.

'Then there is the matter of sentry lines. The wolf pack system makes it easier for the enemy to detect us. And where he detects one, he can detect the others even more easily. Thus, all are endangered by one. We must face the fact that submarines are designed not to give the enemy one great blow, but a number of small ones. Submarines should be deployed widely and independently. Their achievements cannot be measured over short periods but over great lengths of time.

'Third, our chief weapon for detecting the enemy at present is 120mm binoculars. Top priority must be given to equipping I [Class] submarines with radar and electronic countermeasure devices.

'Lastly, there is the matter of surface mobility. Planning officers have too much faith in our high surface speed. This advantage is now gone because of radar. Nor is poor weather an advantage for us. In *RO-101* I realized that even darkness is no longer our friend. I charged batteries twice a day, using the dim twilight, in *RO-101* and also in *I-177*. The fact that they both survived many missions is proof that it is a good tactic.'

Capt. Takahashi thanked me for my report, saying that his assistants would certainly take my ideas into consideration. Then Rear Adm. Mito spoke up. 'What Lieutenant Commander Orita says may be correct when weighed against new principles and developments in antisubmarine warfare,' he said, 'but operational control cannot always be tethered to principles. Sometimes we have to send our submarines out when there is not even a fifty-fifty chance of their returning.'

Mito's bland disregard of all I had said angered me, and I lost my temper. 'All submariners are willing to give their lives at sea!' I said, pounding the table. 'What we expect of you and your staff is that you keep that fifty percent chance in mind! Otherwise, we will lose all of our boats! It will be mass suicide for submarine captains!'

Mito didn't like this tone in a junior's voice. 'Are you dissatisfied with the way the staff does things, Orita?' he asked, angrily. 'Are you criticizing us?'

'It is not a matter of dissatisfaction, or of criticism!' I shouted back at him. 'I am merely expressing my honest and ardent hopes, based on my experience in the combat areas!'

Vice Adm. Takagi broke in then. 'Orita speaks from experience,' he said, 'and his views are valuable. There is no doubt of that. But, in my opinion, they reflect a negative attitude. No matter what the difference may be between our capability and that of the enemy, we still must carry out our orders, mustn't we? This has always been the battle spirit of Japanese submarine men, has it not?'

I wanted to say more, I wanted to tell Takagi that his words were immediate evidence of his own underestimating the enemy. The man with the longer sword usually wins a duel, no matter how great the 'battle spirit' of his opponent. But I held my tongue. The admiral had his problems. Even though he was as worried about the proper use of submarines as I, he had to display confidence and optimism at all times. As the top man in our submarine command, he had to radiate calm and never doubt. I felt sorry for him.

The conference ended and a luncheon was served, but the situation was awkward. No one at the table said very much. And (an unusual thing for Japanese officers gathered around any kind of table) no one laughed.

## Commander Donald 'Pete' Sencenbaugh, US Navy, then Lieutenant, USS *Raton*

The third patrol was in the Java Sea, Karimata Strait and South China Sea. We sank nothing, a complete dud.

Our Fourth Patrol was in the southern part of the South China Sea and eastern end of the Java Sea. We did better on this patrol. We sank half a dozen ships, a couple of them rather small. However, we did damage a 10,000 ton freighter. Three ships sunk with torpedoes, a couple of small ones with gunfire, and scuttled a very small sampan. The last small freighter we sank provided us with 11 prisoners: the Japanese engineering officer and 10 Celebes Island natives. This patrol, we also sank a small sampan, picking up eight Chinese nationals. We made mess cooks out of the Chinese. So we had quite a batch of extras. En route on return to Freemantle, we put them all to work, and we had the cleanest, polished submarine that ever landed in Australia. When we arrived, Admr. Christie asked if we had picked up any prisoners for him to interrogate, as he had asked the Skipper before we departed. And, did we ever! Jim Davis replied in the strong affirmative, and up they came. Admr. Christie pointed out that he really had not wanted so many.

This particular patrol had another very interesting incident. We were advised by an 'Ultra' message (we called them 'burn before reading') regarding a Japanese *RO-51*-Class in the area, coming out of Singapore. The *Lapon* patrol area was in the same vicinity and was also hunting the Japanese Sub. Around midnight 27 May 1944, we had radar interference. 10 cm interference. It clearly was from another SJ Radar, the kind of radar installed on US submarines. We had a key on our radar transmitter, and I tried to contact him with Morse Code. But the radar operator on the submarine (USS *Lapon*) wasn't very bright, and we never made contact.

I came on watch at 0345 and we still had interference. However, not long before dawn, the radar interference vanished, so I assumed that he had made his morning trim dive. However, just before dawn (0615) we were hit, or hit something. Eight seconds later the same thing happened again. We were in 1,000 fathoms of water, so it didn't appear probable that we had hit a shallow spot. My JOOD was in the conning tower taking a look around through the night scope. He saw an oil slick on port side.

When we got back to Fremantle, we observed two big dents in safety tank (¾ inch rather than ¼ inch ballast tanks) and that *Lapon* had been ahead of us. As we came by they fired, thinking we were the Japanese *RO-51*. This was a 'trigger happy' event by the XO of *Lapon* who mistook us for the Japanese submarine. This was an impossible assumption, the Jap sub could make maximum 10 knots. We were doing 17 knots. The Jap sub was half the size of *Raton*. We were 1,800 tons surface displacement.

As an aside, I might note that when I got command of a submarine in New London, who would show up as my Division Commander, but XO of *Lapon* who had ordered FIRE! We were what is called a target of opportunity, and the boat never went to battle stations. Needless to say we didn't get along very well. This was probably the end of my naval career.

There was no question in my mind that a couple of angels had their hands on the exploder mechanisms of those two torpedoes. A lot of mothers had been praying fervently.

### Admiral I. J. Galantin, US Navy, Retd; from *Take Her Deep*

In May 1944, USS *Halibut*, Lieutenant Galantin in command, was homeward bound for refit, and her crew could relax a little more.

After forty-eight hours in Pearl we were under way once more, heading north-east into brisk trade winds on the final 2,100-mile leg of our trans-Pacific dash. By this time the Japanese Navy was too badly mauled to be a threat in the eastern Pacific. Even their submarines were no longer a major concern … Still, recurring attacks on our boats by our own air and surface forces showed that the danger from mistaken identity was real. To minimize this danger we were routed to be always at least thirty miles south of the shipping lane from California, and we kept strictly to the prescribed fifteen-knot speed of advance.

The weather was good; we were clean and well fed; we were going home. For three months we would sleep in beds that didn't roll or bounce, and there would be no depth charges to count. There was reason for the high spirits and hilarity on board. We had off loaded our unspent torpedoes at Pearl, and the torpedo rooms seemed cavernous. Routine ship's work was quickly attended to so that the card games, cribbage, and acey-deucey tournaments could resume. Mack and I had our nightly chess match without fear of interruption. I knew I would have to detach him for his own command when we reached port, and I needed to win two games to be sure of a draw. We never played chess for money, but in cribbage Mack was a few dollars up on me.

Alex was in especially good humour. In time I would find out why. He was Jack Hinchey's assistant engineer and electrical officer, and the two men had a running battle of wits, with Jack generally in the lead. He had assigned Alex the keeping of the battery record book. This required daily, cumulative entries. If a mistake was made one day it carried forward and all later entries would be in error.

Early in our patrol Jack saw an error, and told Chief Electrician's Mate Allan Braun, 'Alex made a mistake in the record book, but I won't tell him until we reach Frisco. It will take him three days on board to correct.'

Chief Braun had taken a liking to the unconventional, good-humoured young officer and privately tipped off Alex. Thereupon, Alex hatched a plot of his own. He kept a double set of books – one with the error, and a second, hidden book all corrected.

Sure enough, shortly after we reached San Francisco Jack said, 'Alex, I have bad news for you. You made an error in the battery book a couple of months ago and now all entries have to be corrected. Don't go ashore until that's done.'

Alex pretended consternation and confusion, protested, pleaded for more time, but Jack was adamant. Grabbing the book, Alex stormed out and pretended to get on with the corrections. Fifteen minutes later he broke out the secret second set of books and presented it to Jack. 'Here you are, Jack, all corrected.'

This was incredible; Jack couldn't believe it, so he spent hours checking the figures while Alex gloated. It was in such playful mood that we passed under the Golden Gate Bridge on May 24 and threaded our way through the shipping in the busy harbour.

While USS *Halibut* was undergoing repairs at San Francisco in 1944, young Ensign William Kidwell, Assistant Torpedo and Gunnery Officer, took the opportunity to impress his new girlfriend and her mother by giving them a tour of the boat.

Bill escorted the two ladies across the brow and was greeted by the deck watch, Seaman 1c Richard Schoenlaub. 'Good evening, Mr. Kidwell.' Schoenlaub was surprised by the unexpected night-time visitors, but was not about to impede the progress of an imposing, self-assured ensign.

'I'm taking my guests below for a quick tour. We'll be going back ashore in a few minutes,' said Bill.

By this time our boat was tolerably neat and clean, and the proud young officer led the ladies on their exciting tour. As they passed my room I heard the female voices and Bill's explanation of the officers' living quarters. The heavy, green drape was drawn across the entrance to my sacrosanct stateroom, and I sat out of sight at my desk, wearing only underwear and sandals.

When Bill assisted his guests in their awkward passage through the door to the forward torpedo room, he found torpedoman 2c Bertheau stripped to the waist, tattoos showing from shoulders to wrists, and torpedoman 3c Tudor Davis doing some work on the tubes. Eager to assist the new young officer who had not yet mastered the intricacies of torpedo firing, Bertheau volunteered, 'Mr. Kidwell, do you want me to fire an inboard slug?'

Without really knowing what was involved, Bill impressed his ladies with a confident, nonchalant, 'Yes. Carry on.'

An inboard slug was an exciting exercise at any time; in the night-time stillness of the boat, it was a spectacular event.

Bertheau charged one of the impulse air tanks, had Davis open a breech door, manipulated various valves, said, 'Standby! Fire!' and tripped the firing valve.

The resounding blast of air from the open torpedo tube into the torpedo room had hardly abated when there appeared at the door from the forward battery compartment an astonished sub skipper dressed only in underwear and sandals. I was intent only on apprehending the idiot who seemed bent on wrecking the boat.

Ensign Kidwell quickly recovered from his momentarily stunned surprise. 'Captain, may I introduce Mrs. Johnson and her daughter, Louise?'

'How do you do? Mr. Kidwell, I'll see you in my cabin at nine in the morning. Good night.'

Years later Bill confided that my coolness under the fire of such unexpected events, and in such informal costume, convinced him that I would be safe to go with on war patrol.

**Rear Admiral Corwin Mendenhall, US Navy, USS *Pintado*;**
from *Submarine Diary*

The Germans were not the only ones to use the wolf pack technique: the US Navy later adopted it for their Pacific operations. Lieutenant Corwin Mendenhall had left the *Sculpin* and been appointed to the *Pintado* as Exec while she was a new construction. Together with the newly commissioned *Shark* and *Pilotfish*, *Pintado* became part of a wolf pack known as Blair's Blasters, from the name of their commodore. On 16 May 1944 they left Pearl Harbor with the task of preventing the Japanese reinforcing the island of Saipan, which the Americans were to invade early the following month.

9 May. At 0500 the Blasters submerged for the day only thirty-seven miles from the patrol area. Our hope was to enter it undetected. In midmorning we sighted another Betty [Japanese bomber] through the periscope. The Japs were looking for us. At dusk we surfaced, and two hours later we were in our area west of Saipan.

Patrolling submerged during the day and on the surface at night, all three boats were exposing their vertical radio antenna for the first five minutes of each hour to maintain group contact and control by radio. The distance between boats was fifteen miles.

30–31 May The thirtieth was a quiet day with no contacts. But at 0758 on 31 May the Blasters surfaced to check a contact report from Silversides of a convoy located to the southwest of Saipan, headed for that island. The message came to us as a rebroadcast by ComSubPac. The Blasters moved to the southwest on a scouting line, fifteen miles apart, to intercept the convoy. After searching all day on the surface, near sunset *Shark* reported seeing smoke to her south about twenty-five miles from *Pintado*. The commodore instructed *Shark* to take a position on the port side of the convoy, *Pintado* the starboard side, and *Pilotfish* to take a trailing position. The moon was bright, with good visibility.

Ten minutes after *Shark's* report we sighted three columns of smoke to the southwest about twenty miles away, drawing right, so we changed course and increased speed to intercept.

In the fast approaching darkness, after closing for ten minutes, we could see the dim outlines of ships on the horizon but couldn't identify or count them. Continuing to close, a few minutes later we made radar contact with an escort at 8,500 yards on the starboard bow of the convoy. We couldn't see him until coached on by radar. *Pintado* went to full speed and turned to put the escort astern and open the range, track the convoy, and gain a better attack position.

The convoy was tracked as it headed due north at a speed of eight knots during the next two hours of stalking. Then we sighted *Shark* 6,500 yards to our west, exchanged SJ recognition signals, and with visual signals by shielded search-light compared notes on the composition of the convoy and its course and speed. *Shark* had counted three cargo ships and three escorts. At that time their base course was still north; the zigzag leg was course 310, still at eight knots.

Both subs continued to stalk the convoy. By then we believed that at least one of the ships had radar because our radar was picking up persistent inter-ference from the direction of the convoy. We were being very careful with our radar, using it only intermittently in order to reduce the chance that they would detect it.

1 June Continuing our maneuvers to gain position ahead, right at midnight *Pintado* submerged 24,000 yards ahead of the projected track of the convoy and waited, tracking the smoke that was plainly visible in the bright moonlight.

At 0122 the bearing of the smoke began to change radically, drifting to the east, indicating that our convoy had made a major course change. The zig caused *Pintado* to lose contact, so we surfaced and ran at full speed to the northeast to reestablish it. At 0223 we picked up SJ radar interference to our port that was evaluated as being one of the Blasters near the convoy, so we headed that way. The moon set at 0256. The night became quite dark, making conditions excellent for a surface attack.

Thirty-five minutes later we reestablished radar contact with the convoy at 18,000 yards. They tracked as back on course 310, still at speed eight knots. As we closed to 10,000 yards, the outlines of ships were visible even in the inky darkness, and *Pintado* continued toward a position to attack.

At 0342 we heard three explosions that we believed to be *Shark* hitting a ship in the convoy. The convoy made another course change, which placed *Pintado* in a favorable position on the port side of the formation.

We promptly went to battle stations, commenced our approach, and prepared for a surface torpedo attack. There were then two 5,000–6,000 ton freighters in column on the starboard side of the convoy, and one identified as a big *Tarayasu*-type freighter (10,254 tons), alone and heavily loaded, in the port column, with the columns about 800 yards apart. Escorts were on the bow and quarter of the *Tarayasu*.

At 0415 the range to the *Tarayasu* was 4,700 yards, torpedo run about 3,900 yards. Then a lookout reported gunfire from the convoy, so the skipper rashly turned *Pintado*, at flank speed, to open the range, thinking we had been detected. That was a mistake; no one else saw any gunfire. I told him that I thought we should have more evidence than what the lookout 'thought' was gunfire. The movements of the convoy and the escorts gave no evidence that they had sniffed us out, but by turning away and going to flank speed we lost our attack position.

Again *Pintado* maneuvered at full speed to regain position for attack. At 0430 we made our second move in, on the port side of target *Tarayasu*. Ships in the starboard column were in the line of fire beyond our target. Slipping undetected between the two escorts just before daybreak, the skipper fired a spread of six fish from the bow tubes, set to run at six foot depth and explode on impact. The setup was near perfect: a 1,200-yard torpedo run, near zero gyro angle, ninety-five-degree port track.

Five torpedoes hit the *Tarayasu*. He disintegrated and sank. Other explosions were heard as *Pintado* turned to bring the stern tubes to bear on the remaining freighters, passing only 700 yards from one of the escorts. Both escorts turned toward us, so we went to emergency flank speed, running directly away from them, reaching a speed of twenty-one knots. (The order of speeds, from low to high, was: one-third, two-thirds, standard, full, and flank. 'Emergency' flank meant for the engineers to 'pour on everything including the galley range,' but that speed could not be maintained for very long and could damage the engineering plant.) Surprisingly the escorts didn't press a counterattack, and we pulled clear to regroup and attack the remaining ships.

Several unidentified explosions were heard during the excitement of evading the escorts. Ed Frese, operating the TDC, predicted that our sixth fish should have hit the leading unidentified freighter in the starboard column. That ship turned on two green lights in a vertical line on the port wing of his bridge, and we wondered what the significance of the lights could be.

That first torpedo attack impressed me as solid proof of the value of having the TDC with the fire control team in the conning tower, where all aspects of the problem were easily watched and controlled. Further, with the fish set to run at a depth of six feet and to explode on impact, we had a real winner. Everyone was elated.

With daylight near, *Pintado* pulled clear on the surface, reloaded torpedo tubes, and prepared to attack the remainder of the convoy. At 0500, in daylight, there were several more explosions, and we saw a second ship in trouble. From our bridge the flashes of the blasts were vivid. The ship broke in two, and the bow and stern sank separately. The tops of one remaining ship were visible at the scene, with escorts milling around, apparently picking up survivors …

Near sundown a radio report from *Pilotfish* advised that she was in contact with another convoy of at least five ships on a northerly course. The commodore directed her to follow her contact, report positions, course, and speed, and wait for *Shark* and *Pintado* to join her before attacking.

During mid evening *Shark* reported that she had lost contact with the one remaining ship of the first convoy, so *Pintado* and *Shark* turned south to look for Pilotfish and convoy number two …

Blair's Blasters were ordered out of the area on 9 June to guard against their being mistaken for enemy submarines during the Allied landings, and *Pintado* was set course for Majuro in the Marshall Islands with the satisfaction of knowing that each of her 16 torpedoes had hit.

## Chief Electrician Yoshio Nakano, Imperial Japanese Navy, *I-165*

This incident happened at Biak, in the Schouten Islands and some 350 miles north of New Guinea, on 18 August 1944. *I-165* was then seriously damaged by US PT boats, whose sustained depth charging pushed her more than 100 metres down and at a steep angle.

*I-165* was almost sunken when we went to deliver rice to the starving Japanese soldiers at Biak. Five American cruisers were waiting and hundreds of explosives were dropped for 2 consecutive hours. As I worked in the engine room, the things I still remember by my body is that heat, 50 to 60 degrees, in the battery room. One time a rod of a motor was burned and we had to replace it. The burned rod was so hot that everybody fainted after an hour's work. We took turns and worked for 24 hours straight to finish the replacing work. That is my still haunting memory. *I-165* barely survived and came back to Japan after repeating repairs in Singapore, Hong Kong. Then the totally new crew including the captain left Japan and never came back. They were sunk [in 1945] by an American strike from the air.

# 1945

As the Allies closed in on Berlin, and the European naval war was all but over, German submarines still went to sea to engage the attention of Allied air power in British and Norwegian waters and so restrict the number of aircraft able to launch raids on German cities. Dönitz was trying to buy time until the first of the new Type XXI U-boats became operational, but the time had already run out. On 4 May the U-boats were recalled to surrender.

The two-pronged attack by US and Australian troops on Japanese conquests was pushing forwards relentlessly through the occupied territories, and in anticipation of a US invasion of Japan itself the kaiten were pulled back to Japanese bases. British, Dutch and US submarines were now mopping up in the Pacific and Indian Oceans. Singly and, in the case of the US Navy, also in packs, they decimated Japanese merchant shipping, tightening the noose on a nation that had all but run out of fuel and food. Using guns and small arms they sank the smaller craft which Japan was now using in a last attempt to supply her starving soldiers on the scattered islands. A US submarine sighted the pride of the Japanese fleet, the *Yamato* – the most powerfully armed battleship to put to sea in the Second World War – and, without even firing a torpedo, ensured she would not trouble the Okinawa landings.

However, before the atomic bombs dropped on 6 and 9 August led to the Japanese surrender, the war had come to a welcome end for many crews. Those in boats unsuitable for the Pacific conditions, or due for refit, had been sent home, grateful for their survival. The final submarine to be lost in the war was *I-373*, sunk by USS *Spikefish* on 14 August.

## ATLANTIC

**Korvettenkapitän Aadelbert Schnee, Kriegsmarine, commanding *U-2511*;** from *Plongée*

Following losses during 1942, Dönitz had summoned German naval architects to design a new breed of U-boat. The result was the Type XXI, with vastly more powerful batteries, giving a submerged speed of 18 knots, an immensely strong and streamlined double hull, an electric motor for silent running at slow speed, a very long range without the need to be resupplied, and a fast crash dive. The first of a huge programme emerged from the shipyards in the autumn of 1944, beset by the problems that usually accompany a radical new design and too late to change the outcome of the war. Recalled from active service to join Dönitz's staff and work with the programme, Schnee was subsequently given command of one of the first two Type XXIs to be sent out.

But we were not immune to teething troubles … and by the time we were ready and the first Type XXI put to sea at Bergen in Norway, it was already 30 April 1945, just a few days before hostilities ceased.

Two years had passed since the start of the new submarine project and its entry into service. Given the situation at that time, that was not very long, but for us, the submariners, it obviously seemed like an eternity. The great adventure we had been looking forward to was about to begin. Although the imminent end of the war was hanging over us, that faded when we thought that the goal for which we had been striving for two years had been achieved: we were going into action with a new boat that was powerfully equipped for both combat and submergence.

We left Bergen Fjord at night and dived once we were at sea, not far from the Marstein lighthouse. We would reach this precise point at the end of the war and see daylight once again: the whole of our Atlantic patrol was to take place submerged. The batteries were rechargeable while submerged and the radio equipment that kept it in touch with headquarters was designed to work underwater.

The following day we made our first contact with our adversaries in the North Sea. There wasn't much reaction, apart from a slight rise in the pulse rate. The voice of our Asdic operator (might add: listening on the hydrophones for clarity) who had just picked up a group of submarine chasers did not fail to reflect the inherent dread which was felt in all earlier submarines of seeing a string of depth-charges descending upon us.

Well, that was the job of the submarine chasers which rarely let a submarine escape once they had picked it up. Four Asdic transmissions by the chasers were clearly perceptible throughout the boat and left no room for any doubt that they had found us. The vessels were closing and it was decision time. I increased speed from five to 16 knots and altered course by about 30° before proceeeding submerged the exact opposite course to that of the surface vessels. In a little while we had shaken off our pursuers. We heard them searching for us for quite a while after; the reason we had escaped must have been beyond them. Those sorts of situations must have cropped up several times once we reached the Atlantic. No vessel succeeded in depth-charging us, even if in close proximity …

It was while we were in the Atlantic that, on 4 May 1945, we received the order to cease hostilities. We set course for Norway, saying to ourselves: 'too late'. Nevertheless, our return voyage was to provide a touch of adventure as theoretical compensation for our efforts over the past years.

On 4 May, a few hours after the order to cease fighting, the hydrophones picked up the unmistakable sound of a propeller, coming from the north. After coming up to a suitable depth, I was able to spot a British cruiser of the *Suffolk*-Class escorted by several destroyers. I'd never had such a sitting duck in my sights during the whole war, and now it had come just as hostilities had ended! However, I was closing on the British cruiser. Our submarine dived, regaining periscope depth when between the escort and the cruiser. I summoned my engineer-officer and the officer of the watch so they could enjoy a periscope view of something remarkable: an enemy cruiser barely 600 metres away, in other words at a range from which we could hit the bull's-eye every time ... We just had to dive again, pass beneath the cruiser and resume our homeward course.

Our approach to the cruiser had been made with absolute care, some unusual bursts of top speed allowing us to get close to the target. No zigzag manoeuvring would have been any help at all to our opponent; submerged, our submarine could follow the least change of course. An attack would have been child's play in comparison to what preceding submarines had faced.

We surfaced off Bergen on 5 May and entered port. Much to our surprise we met up with the British cruiser who could count herself lucky to have encountered *U-2511* a few hours after hostilities ended, rather than a few hours earlier. They took a great interest in our new submarine.

I was taken on board the British cruiser and introduced to the senior officers. As can be imagined, I was very tight-lipped during this first meeting with the enemy to whom, as they say, I gave nothing away. However, when the admiral questioned me about my last contacts with the enemy I realised that those concerned the very same cruiser we were now on board.

Then things deteriorated. They called my assertions into doubt. The captain of the cruiser and the destroyer captains were questioned, which finally established the truth of what I had told them.

Schnee's account of the contact between *U-2511* and HMS *Norfolk* remains controversial. Discrepancies between the logs of the two vessels have led some historians to claim the encounter could not have happened, others to conclude that it is impossible to state that it did not.

## NORTH SEA, BALTIC AND ARCTIC

**Leutnant zur See Alwin Hullman, Kriegsmarine, commander of a *Seehund*-Class two-man submarine**

In the fall of 1943 the German high command of the navy tried to make a group of special forces, small units with submersible boats and surface boats. The name given to them, and their motto, was 'Commando der Kleinkampfverbände' ('The Band of Brothers'). I was one of the first people who came there, from E-boats, and they tried to develop various different vessels: small submersible craft, converted torpedoes, etc. They were given animal names as codewords. None of this was very successful, and later my main interest was the two-man submarine.

The first type that came out was the *Hecht*. I got a flotilla to go to the east coast of North Denmark, to the fishing port of Saeby, because there they expected the landing operation of British and American forces. I was there for a couple of months, but nothing happened, and so I asked to be relieved to go back [to Germany] because I heard that the new type was ready. This type they called the *Seehund* – Seal. We had the Type 27 and it was a construction by the German Navy's drawing office, just as all other German submarines. It was a little boat but it was a real submarine with a diesel engine, an electric motor and torpedoes. She could do about seven knots on the water and, on batteries, just for a short time of course, let's say about five knots.

Anyway, the training was such that in the Baltic we had to try to use torpedoes and so on. I belonged to the first group of 18 boats that came to Ijmuiden, the seaport of Amsterdam (Netherlands) transported on the road, and on 1 January 1945 18 boats left the port to go on the convoy route from London to Antwerp. We had our own meteorological people and they said the weather would be good for the operation, but they had been very, very wrong. The weather was very bad. There's no doubt that a lot of the boats that didn't return were unable to find their way back because of this change in the weather development. But nobody knows exactly how many boats were lost and why each of them was lost.

Of these 18 boats the first one went out of Ijmuiden port and hit a mine and exploded. Of the 17 remaining, only 10 boats arrived in the operation region, and of these 10 boats mine was the only boat that came home. All the other boats had been lost, and there were several reasons why they had all been lost (we are now talking about 16 of them) – one: probably, navigation mistakes; two: probably, technical breakdowns; three: probably, operating mistakes; four: probably, attacks by the British Navy and Air Force.

Very little navigation was possible on a *Seehund*. We had only one magnetic compass and the height over the surface was very small, so it was affected by the steel hull. We did not have any wireless on board, and there was no method of communication with the outside world.

We spent a lot of time on the sea bed because when you have very harsh winds outside it is very dangerous for this sort of boat to break the surface. It does not behave like a full-size submarine. The other thing, of course, was that the aeroplanes could find you and fight against you. Moreover, if you want to hit somebody with your torpedoes you have to steer with the boat. (The normal torpedo receives its information regarding course, speed and depth at the moment of firing.) Also, our torpedoes were very slow, so it was difficult to estimate the torpedo shooting angle. Very difficult.

In those hours and days we had exact information about convoys sailing to the continent. I counted the number of ships crossing by listening to their underwater screw noises, and that was for me the moment when I thought: this war is definitely lost. Every ship passing over you is carrying ammunition, soldiers, equipment: all they needed. And we are probably not in the smallest way able to stop that.

The reason why I came home – the eastern Channel depths are about 30 metres; in some areas there are holes of 60 metres. Where I was, my chart showed there were three. I chose one of them near the convoy route as a point to set course to come home. You see, we could go home only during the night time because in daytime we had no plane protection.

On 6 January 1945, when I came up to the surface I went up to my control room and I saw the big chimneys of the Ijmuiden steelworks.

And then I made one big mistake. I was standing up, holding on to the periscope, and the sea was running – not because of the sea, but there was a big swell from the days before – and I didn't spot one of the waves until it broke over the boat. So the after part of the boat was very submerged. Then, of course, I wanted to get into the boat again and had to close the hatch, and probably I was too nervous and I couldn't close it very fast so a lot of water came in, but in the end I got it shut. The boat went down by the stern and the depth was 18 metres there. And then both of us were sitting in the water up to our waist. Then we had to pump.

One thing was good: we were trained to test the air. We had a small glass phial. There was a liquid in it, and when the colour was red – that meant danger. And we were trained that in such a case we had to do something. We were trained to get out. We had one little life-raft for every man, and diving escape apparatus that fitted over the nose and in the mouth. And that would have been possible, but we – the engineer and myself – decided to pump out the water and it was not so very difficult. Eighteen metres is 1.8 kilos of pressure. So we were very glad when the boat came up from the sea bed. We were also trained for the next problem: the boat was in this situation and the batteries were leaking dangerous fumes into it. So I told my engineer: 'We have two solutions to the problem. We try to start the diesel or we go out with our little life-rafts and someone will probably see us and pick us up.' And more or less we came to the same decision and said, 'OK, we will try it with the diesel.'

This man was very competent. Sitting behind me, he did something, and next moment the diesel was running.

There were two seats on this little boat, and you never can stand up: it's too narrow. If you eat or drink something, you have to answer the call of nature somewhere. And it was very difficult because we had very warm clothing and leather clothing on top of it, and trying to undo clothes while sitting down is very difficult. And it was cold: it was January, and if the diesel motor wasn't running it really was very cold. If you wanted to urinate you just did it – nothing open. Wonderfully warm. Smell no problem – the diesel masked everything. This does not bother you.

And, of course, I could never, or very seldom, see in the face of my engineer, and he looked only at my back. He was just sitting there. You think sometimes: five days – nobody can stay awake all the time. You say: 'You sleep now and I sleep then. One of us has to listen to what is going on.' This went quite well but nobody knows how many hours he slept in those five days. When you came home after an operation like that you'd lost between four and five kilos.

I was coming into port. I was the only boat, there was nobody to see or to get the ropes. We just had to do it ourselves. I went up to the lock-keeper and I said, 'I am here again,' and he said, 'Oh, you are reported lost with all the others.' And then we got in a sauna – I had never done that in my life before. And in the sauna I passed out. They got me out and then I was asleep, probably for a long time.

**Captain First Rank Viktor Korzh, USSR Baltic Fleet, _L-21_;**
from _Red Star under the Baltic_

Late in 1944, after Finland had pulled out of the war, the Soviets were able to operate their submarines from Turku. Having spent a year ashore, Viktor Korzh had asked to go back on patrol in order to avenge the death of his father who had been shot in Kiev. In March 1945 he left Turku as Chief Engineer on the submarine minelayer, _L-21_. After minelaying around the Gulf of Danzig, they moved farther out to attack German convoys, but the bow hydroplanes had been irreparably damaged in heavy weather. Although Germany was close to capitulation, A/S activity in the Baltic was still intense.

There was little opportunity for sleep. At 10.00 hours the hydrophone operator reported that 'the sea is noisy all around': there were freighters on the move. A lot of them. Apparently, the Germans had rushed in a mass exodus out of the ports towards which our troops were advancing. We rose to periscope depth. The sea was calm. The boat was holding up well. And it was hard to believe that the bow hydroplanes were out of action.

'Chief Engineer to the conning tower!' I heard. I went up. Oryol beckoned me to the periscope and let me look through the eyepiece. I took a look and actually recoiled. Brought close by the optics, a huge ship seemed to be absolutely on top of us. Yes, a steamer with a displacement of 5,000 tons was going along right in the periscope-sight, so that it was not even necessary to manoeuvre. 'Should we risk it?' asked the Divisional Commander.

I realized what he was talking about. We had carried out all earlier attacks from a surfaced position. We had not risked firing from periscope depth: we were afraid that, without the bow hydroplanes, the loss of weight from the torpedoes would thrust the boat's bow out onto the surface.

'Let's risk it!' I gave my assent, although I knew that after even a two-torpedo salvo, the turbo pump would not be able to suppress the positive buoyancy. I shared my misgivings with the Divisional Commander and the Captain. Mogilievsky found a way out: 'Put the men in the control room. All the off-watch men in there! We'll do it the way they did on Snow Leopard in the First World War.'

A sizeable group assembled, some fifteen men. Hurriedly I gave the sailors their instructions. 'Torpedo attack!' the signal clanged. Events unfolded swiftly, like in a film. Here was the Captain already giving a long drawn-out word of command: 'Fire!'

'At the double!' I urged the sailors on. They ran on winged feet to the bulk-head door. 'Start the pump! Fill the rapid-diving tank!' ordered Dolgopolov. 'Torpedoes away,' Petty Officer Shevchenko reported in a sing-song voice.

It was the third day that his torpedomen were in action, and each time they had coped successfully with the task.

The Bosun was struggling with all his might to hold the lighter boat steady with the stern hydroplanes. But her bow was beginning to ride up. And confusion was affecting our runners. There were many people, and the hatchways are narrow, and they were all trying to elbow their way through them. It took them too long to reach the torpedo tubes. And all that time the depth-gauge needle was creeping inexorably to the left.

I worked it out mentally: at a depth of eight metres – the periscope standard appears on the surface; at five metres – the peak of the bridge shield becomes exposed; at three metres – the anti-aircraft semi-automatic is completely on the surface. Fortunately, by that time, all fifteen runners had turned up in the bow, at the very torpedo tubes. That meant a ton of additional ballast. The ship's bow froze in position, and then began to go downwards.

The Divisional Commander and Mogilievsky were following the run of the torpedoes through the periscopes. There was the crash of an explosion.

'They're hit in the mainmast area!' shouted Mogilievsky. The boat, gathering speed and trim, went below the water. Not a single depth charge. Even the propeller noise ceased.

'The direct-listening system is not working,' Buzulukov reported to the First Lieutenant. 'Can Kovaliov, the senior radio operator, be called here? He will quickly get it sorted out.'

Five minutes passed by: silence.

Eight minutes passed by: silence.

Oryol was getting fretful and pressed the Captain to go up to periscope depth.

Ten minutes passed by: silence.

'Captain, surface. We need to know the outcome of the attack,' said the Divisional Commander, going up into the conning tower. We rose to the surface. We raised the periscopes. From the remarks that Oryol and Mogilievsky were exchanging, we could clearly picture for ourselves what was happening on the surface. The torpedoed freighter was sinking by the stern. Her stern flag was, by then, sticking up out of the water. Right up close to the sinking ship, a second one was standing by. People were climbing over from the stricken steamer; they were throwing some kind of crates over from one ship to the other. 'If only we could slam a torpedo into the second freighter, too,' said the Divisional Commander. But Mogilievsky was not about to attack. He shouted below: 'Emergency dive! Dive!'

The *L-21* survived an intense and carefully coordinated hunt by the Germans, who dropped 250 depth charges, returning safely on 29 March.

For the USSR the war officially ended on 9 May 1945, and news reached the submarine base.

I flung open the cabin window. From the deck a din burst in. Ratings, leading seamen and officers were hugging one another, talking loudly and joyfully.

One after another the submarines began to return to base. The officers of the 1st Division assembled in the base officers' mess. Captain First Rank A. Y. Oryol congratulated everyone on the victory and thanked them for their selflessness and their devotion to duty. We stood silent and uplifted. I looked closely into the faces of my friends. Few remained of those with whom I had begun the war. Many comrades, many ships had been lost in the Baltic submariners' battles. And those who had survived had suffered so much that they would remember it to the end of their days. Yes, it was hard for us. But we held out. Our people have a huge reserve of strength.

Yet to look at, they were totally ordinary lads. Thinner and weary after the patrols, but this was only their outward look. In fact, these were men of steel, not knowing fear, doubt or fatigue.

Amazing people!

### Commander Brian Cleary, Royal Australian Navy, Retd, HMS *Varne*

After his experiences in the old HMAS *K9*, Brian Cleary passed through the submarine training school at Blyth (HMS *Elfin*) and joined HMS/M *Varne* in the 3rd Submarine Flotilla at Holy Loch as a sub-lieutenant.

On one occasion around Christmas 1944 the *Varne* sailed to Fishguard to conduct secret trials with RAF flying boats based near Milford Haven. There being no naval accommodation in Fishguard we were billeted in the Great Western Hotel there. At the end of a day's work 2/3rds of the crew would go ashore and the others would be the duty watch. One evening when I was on duty a fierce storm hit the small port. A trawler anchored nearby dragged its anchor and was blown down upon us. We were secured to a buoy by our one anchor cable. The trawler forced our cable across our stem and the cable parted. I was on the bridge and started manoeuvring away from the trawler. Once clear of the trawler I was left trying to keep clear of the breakwater which made the harbour very confined. In the darkness I decided that we would be safer at sea so out through the entrance we went. We stayed out until dawn when we returned to harbour to be boarded by a very anxious Captain and crew. The storm had largely blown itself out by then. It was quite an experience for a Sub-Lieutenant to take command of a submarine at sea.

On escorted surface passage from the Clyde to Fishguard we ran into another mighty storm at night. I had the middle watch. We were at the northern end of the Irish Sea abreast the Isle of Man. We were rolling badly between 25 and 30 degrees. One huge swell pushed us beyond 30 degrees to port. I had to hold on grimly as we went past 40 degrees. She hung there for a moment and then righted herself. The weather slowly improved and we reached Fishguard without further stress.

Later we found that battery acid had spilled into the battery tank. When our Fishguard duties were completed we went into dry dock at Ardrossan in Ayrshire. The batteries were removed and it was found that the existing Rosbonite protective covering in the tanks was defective and had allowed acid to attack the steel. The covering was removed, affected steel repaired and new covering applied. This must have been done in February 1945, as the hotel where we were staying was preparing for a St David's Day dinner. I recall this because leeks were hanging on the walls of the dining room. We left just before the day.

Before going on patrol in Norwegian waters in April 1945. it was apparently decided that the *Varne* should be painted in a camouflage pattern of white and sky-blue. Our patrol area was off Stavanger during a full moon period. This meant that when we surfaced at night to recharge batteries a sailor and I, as forecastle officer, had to clamber down to the casing with bucket and stirrup

---

pump to spray the conning tower with a brown glutinous substance which would come off when we dived. The captain [Lieutenant I. G. Raikes, DSC] promised to come back for us if he had to crash dive!

## Tenente di Vascello Ezio Cozzaglio, Regia Marina, Exec, *Tito Speri*

Throughout the war, anti-submarine warfare training was ongoing, which led to a demand for submarines to play the part of the enemy. Since the Italian Armistice, a number of submarines of the Regia Marina had been used in that capacity by the Americans.

From time to time on a submarine unusual and dramatic things can happen that are really funny. And this one occurred in the *Tito Speri* in February 1945 when we were off Bermuda and taking part in a US Navy anti-submarine exercise.

On this particular occasion a pilot from the airforce was sent on board as an Observer, with the task of assessing the conduct of pilots during approaches to, and simulated attacks on, a submarine.

Bud (as I'll call him) was not happy to find himself on board because he suffered from seasickness, and being very tall (1m 95) he was not well suited to the boat's confined spaces. To cap it all he loathed having to be on the bridge for any length of time waiting for simulated attacks by the planes of the task force. Bud suspected that he had been posted to the *Speri* as a cruel joke and he was doing his utmost to find out just who was responsible.

Everything was fine for a couple of days: a Force 3 sea, a couple of simulated daytime attacks and one at night, followed by crash dives on our part, and Bud was getting used to the boat. There was just one fly in the ointment: the opening in the watertight bulkhead between the wardroom and the control room was partially blocked by a large bronze repeater, part of the magnetic compass, on which he more often than not cracked his head. I myself had been on the *Speri* for about two years and I remember hitting my head a good twenty times, and I can picture poor Bud, newly arrived and easy prey for such deadly traps. There were times, after such concussions, when his eloquence reached levels of profanity utterly beyond the ability of normal mortals.

Early on the morning of the fourth day I asked the captain for permission to blow the cess-tank of the officers' toilet, and permission was granted seeing as all was quiet and the Force 4 sea would disperse all traces. The operation is – or should be – straightforward. All you have to do it to close the top, open the bottom and give a blast of compressed air which empties the whole thing. However, if an absent-minded burly sailor uses a bit too much force and operates the levers inversely, the result is a jet of slimy, stinking black liquid, and the tank empties not into the sea but into the wardroom.

My job then was a) inform the captain and b) organise the cleaning and emptying of the wardroom using a human chain to pass the malodorous buckets up the conning tower to be emptied into the sea. While this was in progress, the aerial attack alarm was given and we had to crash dive.

Maybe because we had a following sea, or maybe because we were light forward, the *Speri* made one of her fastest and most elegant crash dives: we reached periscope depth in 30 seconds with a bow angle of 15 degrees. The only problem was the filthy sewage that had now also invaded the forward compartment.

Where was Bud in all this? Suffering from seasickness, he was huddled in an upper bunk in the wardroom, one which had a cupboard down the side, which contained the officers' mess kit: glasses, cutlery, plates etc. The cupboard door came open as the bow went down and the contents cascaded down. Bud woke up with a start, hit his head on the upper part of the bunk, hurled himself to the floor and found himself ankle-deep in a foul liquid. Seeking refuge, he catapulted into the control room, naturally getting a terrific blow on the head from the infamous repeater, while everyone present, instead of showing sympathy and decency, doubled up with laughter.

Bud's powers of oratory assumed Ciceronian heights. He managed to curse every head of state, living and dead, from Roosevelt to Stalin and Churchill, along with Mussolini, de Gaulle and Chiang Kai-shek; all were consigned to hell or do something less than polite – literally or metaphorically. When he calmed down, I fixed up his scalp and suggested that I could request he be classed as 'Wounded In Action'. He repaid me with a look of such loathing that I trembled.

Luckily for him the exercise was suspended because the sea was making it impossible for the aircraft to land on their little Task Force carrier and we returned to base the following morning. Bud kept to his bunk for the whole time and once we were moored he was one of the first to go ashore, barely offering the captain a salute. He vanished into the base, probably looking for whoever had assigned him to the Speri. That was the last we ever heard of him.

### Premier Maître Mécanicien (Petty Officer Engineer) Charles Bernard, Marine Nationale, *Casabianca*

Bernard had served on *Casabianca* from her break-out until the end of the war. By the middle of 1944 her time in the Mediterranean was drawing to a close as German targets were thinly spread.

20 June, arrive Algiers with one success: a submarine chaser sunk by gunfire. It was our last Mediterranean patrol, and since [escaping from] Toulon we had spent 2,500 hours submerged. The Admiralty decided to send us to the USA for

refit, with eight days rest at Sidi Ferruch before our departure. 11 July at 1900 depart for Casablanca. Arrived Casablanca July 19 at 0900. August 02 sailed for Philadelphia with a US escort. Every morning at 0800 dived to check weight and trim and carry out exercises with the escort. While crossing the Sargasso Sea we admired the turtles and flying fish. 15 August came up the Delaware River, arrived Philadelphia 1500 and were quartered at the Submarine Barracks. Several months of American life while the *Casabianca* was refitting for a new destination, the Pacific. Things happened so quickly in the Pacific with the dropping of the atomic bomb that we were able to go back to France.

Initially, *Casabianca* went to England for trials and then on exercises with British and US aircraft off the Azores before sailing for Casablanca.

30 March [1945], arrived at Casablanca 1530. Alas, the crew is beginning to disperse. On 2 April Commander Bellot said goodbye to his crew. It was a very emotional farewell; he had taken us into action and to victory … A fine commander for a crew to have, and we would miss him. I still remember him. In dribs and drabs, one part of the crew returned to France. A new commander took over. After several calls at Moroccan ports the submarine *Casabianca* returned to Toulon on 29 September 1945 where her odyssey ended. In between her tragic departure on 28 November 1942 and her return, she had written some of the finest pages in the history of the war. Every tribute was paid to her. A few days later I went on leave to visit my mother and my two sisters, whom I hadn't seen since January 1940 at Gravelines. On 4 February 1946 I left *Casabianca* on the *Commandant Duboc*. I left her with a heavy heart, but proud to have been under the orders of commanders L'Herminier and Bellet and my Chief Engineer, Kermeur. In the good times and bad I can look back to the past through the honour and glory of having done my duty as a Frenchman. The memory cannot be forgotten.

## INDIAN OCEAN AND PACIFIC

**Radio Technician Billy Fong, US Navy, USS *Tautog*;**
*Tautog*'s 13th War Patrol, 17 December 1944 to 1 February 1945

We left San Francisco for Pearl and Midway and then made a stop at the recent captured Saipan Island. The ship had an allowance of a short period (Dec 30th to Jan 2nd) before leaving for patrol up North to the west coast of Honshu Island of Japan in the Sea of Japan.

Naturally, with time on our hands, a few (five) of us decided on our own – to go ashore up the mountainside to look for souvenirs! Of course, we armed ourselves with a few hand guns and knives. So, up the hill we five 20-year-olds went. As an old saying goes, 'It's a jungle out there!' We were into the enjoyment of noticing the traces of disguised Japanese fox holes, or rounding a narrow trail turn and finding a machine gun nest with its soldier skeleton left in place. In fact, one of us sailor sub boys picked up a leg bone and had it rattling in the owner's boot! That was part of our trip. Then we sighted a rusted disabled Japanese tank. Of course, we all took turn climbing on and had pictures taken with our finds.

On our return to the shore, the Marine guys sure told us what a dumb bunch of swabbies we were to go up the hills looking for booby-trapped prizes!

Once aboard our boat, the rumours set off an officers' clean sweep search of the boat. Lo and behold, the officers found a skeleton head with hair attached to it in someone's small locker! A quick disposal was made over the side of our new uninvited guest. Of course, no guilty souvenir hunter was named nor made his name on the patrol report. I think being that it was the New Years day 1945 and the midnight fireworks all night long in the harbour could have given us Dumb swabbies a big, big break. To check on the facts, I have a few pictures of myself and my buddies on the tank. My face and white sailor hat is in clear sun light, but my buddies are all in the darkened shade. Oh, the skeleton head shows up brightly! [See images.]

## Commander Donald 'Pete' Sencenbaugh, US Navy, lieutenant, USS *Raton*

The 5th War Patrol was not too successful. We only sank one ship, SW of Dasol Bay, just north of Manila. But that was when Sam Dealy, skipper of *Harder*, made his last attack. Sam was fond of the 'down the throat shots' against the escorts. He had already sunk five escorts that way. But, unfortunately, he missed the 6th.

To get back to the next Patrol, we made our 6th Patrol south west of Manila, except, we had trouble getting to our Patrol Area. As we were coming out of Mindoro Strait, SW of Manila we spotted a convoy right in front of us, heading SW. We followed them until it got dark, and then made an attack. There were six ships in two columns of three each, and four escorts. We got inside the escorts, on the surface (dark and stormy night) and at 600 yards, fired six bow tubes, then turned around and found stern tubes were within arming range, so we steamed slowly into position to fire them. By this time, the skipper (Mike Shea) was shouting for us to get going, as he had two escorts with a 'bone in their teeth', i.e., coming straight at us. So we fired the four stern tubes and got out of their way, and reloaded the tubes for another attack.

I claim 11 hits out of the 10 fish we fired. I guess someone's boiler exploded at just the right time. We worried that No. 10 tube had not fired, so fired a water slug, and timed to the distance to the convoy the boiler exploded. But weather getting very bad. A typhoon was building on the other side of Philippine Group of Islands.

Our next attack sank another ship, but torpedo performance was terrible. On the last attack, our torpedo ran under the target, but on the far side one torpedo hit one of the escorts. He was just in the wrong place at the right time. Since the weather is so bad, cleared the area. Later that day, we were ordered to Mios Woendi to refuel and reload. At this point, we had not even reached our assigned patrol area.

After refueling and reloading, we went back to our patrol area off Luzon. There we damaged a heavy cruiser, and later sank another freighter. When were down to only six torpedoes remaining, we were ordered to head for Mare Island, and overhaul. And, so back to Vallejo.

*Raton*'s seventh patrol (the last one for me) was in the Yellow Sea, off Korea. We only sank three small ships. The Japanese didn't have too many ships in May of 1945. On one attack, we sank a ship with no escorts, and as it was sinking, I called all hands to the periscope to watch the enemy drown. It was all good fun until an aeroplane dropped a bomb on our scope wake. I was detached when we returned to Guam, and was ordered to Post Graduate School at Annapolis, Md.

### Electrician 1st Class Bob Haughney, US Navy, USS *Threadfin*

*Threadfin* started her operational life on Christmas Day in 1944; her second war patrol began on 14 March 1945.

We were in a wolf pack and the Japanese fleet was in inland waterways. They have only three entrances between the islands and the Japanese fleet was in there. The Allies started invading Okinawa so we didn't want the Japanese navy to come out, or if they did come out we had to warn the navy and the army that they were out. We were up there one day and the captain announced about noon time: 'We're going to get picked up soon, so expect to take quite a beating.' So about an hour later they picked us up and then we sank a destroyer. Then some more destroyers came out and they beat the hell out of us. One of the other submarines, *Trigger* was the name, well, the Japanese navy picked *Trigger* up and sank her.

We knew that *Trigger* had gone. We could hear the depth charging going on ... and all of a sudden there was rapid gunfire. So they must have forced the *Trigger* to the surface and then the guns of the destroyer probably sank it.

We were damaged and we were out to sea and we notified the third submarine that was with us to move in a little closer – that was the *Hackleback* [Sea

Dog]. And about 2 a.m. we'd made the repairs and we ran into a Japanese convoy and we sank five of their ships. They were shooting back, and after a while we thought: we've had enough for one day.

On 31 March, as the US prepared to invade Okinawa, *Threadfin* was ordered to join *Hackleback* and *Silversides* to patrol around Bungo Suido in case the last of the Japanese fleet came out.

Now two weeks later the Japanese fleet came out about 10 p.m. No moon, no stars, very, very dark and we could hear the Japanese navy passing over us through the noise of their screws. We surfaced among the Japanese fleet and started running with the Japanese fleet recording their speed, their direction, their location. We had a couple of hours but then the Japanese fleet was faster and we didn't want to be spotted. Then we sank, and the next morning the US Navy knew exactly where they were coming from and what speed they were making and they sent four American aircraft carriers up to meet the Japanese fleet. The *Yamato* was the kingpin of the Japanese fleet. Bigger than the *Hood*, bigger than any of our battleships [bigger in terms of firepower rather than dimensions]. They could fire over the horizon, their guns were so big. But that could be a disadvantage – we knew about that later on – because when the planes from the carriers flew over, they flew very high, and the Japanese gun crews, to get that range, could only raise their guns 45 degrees and were not able to hit the planes. And we were the ones who passed the message!

### Commander Edward L. Beach, US Navy; from *Submarine!*

USS *Trigger* had been the first submarine in which the future Commander Beach served. In June 1944, as a lieutenant, Beach was posted to the Tirante, then fitting out at Portsmouth, NH. Commissioning complete, she sailed for Pearl Harbor and operations against the Japanese in the Yellow and East China Seas. At the end of March 1945 she found and sank a target up the coast from Kagoshima Bay which lies at the tip of Kyushu. Elation was soon to turn to deep sadness.

The date was March 28, and we made a special note in our log for that day that the torpedo which had wrought such devastating effect was torpedo number 58009, donated to the navy as a contribution to the war effort by the employees of the Westinghouse torpedo factory at Sharon, Pennsylvania. It still bore its special paint job as it streaked through the water on its final errand. Sharon received pictorial proof of its special contribution about four months after the Navy had accepted it.

   That night, well offshore, I spread out the charts for the Captain as we debated where next to carry our hunt. However, a message on the submarine Fox radio intercept schedule brought a change to our plans. *Trigger*, which had completed two unproductive patrols since I left her, and was currently on her third, had been ordered to join *Tirante* in co-ordinated patrol in the East China Sea. On her present patrol – on which she had sunk two ships – she had a new skipper, David Connole, whom I had known slightly when he was a junior officer in the old Pompano before she was lost.

*Trigger* was due to rendezvous with us that very night. We should raise her by radio in a few hours. I became rather excited at the prospect of seeing my old home again. Since there would be some coordination to accomplish, someone would have to go aboard for a conference. This was too good a chance to miss, and there were plenty of volunteers from men who had once served in *Trigger* to help man our tiny rubber boat.

Several times that night we called *Trigger* by radio, but there was no answer. Silence. As morning drew near we dashed for the coast, submerged in a likely-looking spot, and waited impatiently for darkness again. Then we moved offshore once more to call my old ship. TRIGGER FROM *TIRANTE*. TRIGGER FROM *TIRANTE* ... S237 FROM S420 ... S237 FROM S420 ...

All night long the call went out. Carefully we peaked our transmitter to the exact frequency; gently we turned our receivers up and down the band to pick up the answer in case *Trigger* were a bit off key. All during that long and sleepless night we heard nothing.

The third night was a repetition of the second, except that I spent nearly the whole time in the radio room. At irregular intervals Ed Secard tapped out the unrequited call. His face was inscrutable, his manner natural and precise. But Secard had made many patrols in *Trigger*, and when the time came for him to be relieved, he waved the man away. Fine beads of sweat broke out on his forehead and a spot of colour burned on his youthful cheekbones, but his right hand steadily and precisely pounded the coded call letters over and over again: S237 V S420 ... K ... S237 V S420 ... K S237 V S420 ... K ... *TRIGGER* FROM *TIRANTE* ... I HAVE A MESSAGE FOR YOU ... *TRIGGER* FROM *TIRANTE* I HAVE A MESSAGE FOR YOU ... *TRIGGER* FROM *TIRANTE* ... COME IN PLEASE ...

A spare set of earphones on my head, I watched the silent instruments as if by sheer concentration I might drag a response from them. Every time I glanced up to the open door of the radio room, there were intent faces staring at me – worried faces, belonging to men I knew well, who said nothing, and did not need to. Once someone handed in two cups of coffee.

There never was any answer, and deep in our hearts, after three nights, that was answer enough. With your surface ships there are always survivors, messages, maybe a bit of wreckage. They always operate together, so there is always someone who can later tell what happened. With submarines there is just the deep, unfathomable silence.

We could visualise the sudden, unexpected catastrophe. Maybe a Kamikaze plane. Maybe a depth-charge – a bull's-eye, after more than four hundred misses. Maybe a torpedo, or a mine, or even – inconceivably – an operational casualty.

In some compartment they may have had a split second to realise that *Trigger's* stout size has been breached. The siren screech of the collision alarm. Instantly the angry water takes possession. The shock has startled everyone in other compartments, and the worst is instantly obvious.

Almost immediately she up-ends. The air pressure increases unbearably. Everything loose or not tightly secured cascades down to the bottom, against what used to be a vertical bulkhead. Some men have hung on where they were, but most are struggling around in indescribable confusion at the bottom of the compartment. Instinctively all eyes turn to the depth gauges and watch as the needles begin their crazy spin. Slowly at first, then faster and faster, they race around the dials. The shallow-depth gauges soon travel past their limits; finally jam against their stops on the second go-around. The deep-depth gauges and sea-pressure gauges soon afterward reach the limits of their travel. Nothing can be heard except the rush of water, the groaning and creaking of *Trigger's* dying body, and the trapped, pounding pulses of the men.

Down, down, down she goes, to who knows what depth, until finally the brave ribs give way, the steel shell collapses, and *Trigger's* gallant spirit ascends to the Valhalla of ships, bearing with her the souls of eighty-nine loyal sailors.

I could almost feel it happening, as the morning drew closer. We had decided to dive off Bono Misaki this morning, and finally I had to leave the radio room to plot our position. My heart felt like lead as I stalked out of the tiny hot compartment; a backward glance showed me Secard's head drooping into shaking hands.

That morning we sank a lugger by gunfire. It had refused to surrender when we fired a shot across his bow. We tried to pick up the survivors, but they dived into the water and paddled away, clinging to bits of wreckage. It was only about six miles to the mainland of Kyushu, so we let them be and unceremoniously departed.

**Petty Officer and *kaiten* pilot Yukata Yokata, Imperial Japanese Navy**; from *The Kaiten Weapon*

The first *kaiten* attack, launched from Orita's boat *I-47*, had taken place in November 1944. In May 1945, Yokata also found himself on *I-47*, dreaming of fulfilling his destiny. Having taken his leave of the crew, he got into his *kaiten* and waited for the signal to leave and attack a US convoy near Okinawa.

'Number Three is on board!' I called back in a firm, clear voice. I had reacted just as I did during the manning drills. But this was no drill. I reached into my pocket, took out my dead mother's picture, and placed it beside my compass. That dear woman, whom I had never really known, would be the last sight my living eyes would see before my soul joined hers in death.

I could hear sea water gushing into my access tube now. It was filled in a few seconds. I was all ready, only two things necessary to fire me away – releasing two tie-down cables, and starting my engine.

Every motion, every action, every requirement of concentration came to me automatically. It was just like one of the perfect drills I had experienced back at Hikari. 'Come on! Come on!' I silently urged the voice at the other end of my telephone line. I had only been inside my *kaiten* about seven or eight seconds, but I was already impatient to go.

'Control! Number Three is ready to go!' I called into the telephone, hoping I might prompt the conning tower to send me off at once.

The voice answering me was condescending. He sounded as though he had been expecting me to say something like that. 'All *kaiten* are ready to go, Yokota,' he said, speaking as to a small child. I realized his opinion of me might be lowered if I appeared too anxious. After all, Kakizaki was supposed to go first. I would be considered a very rude person if I asked to precede him. So I took several deep breaths, sucking strength into my stomach, and tried to calm down. I checked my instruments and stop watch again and fussed with my *hachimaki*, setting it more firmly down on my forehead. My hands kept moving automatically over the controls. I readjusted my depth gauge, setting pressure so I would not suddenly leap out of the water when fired off. Soon all was ready. I needed only to push my starting lever to get going.

Then, in much slower tones, to assure the conning tower that I knew my place, I asked, 'What is the enemy?'

'There are two ships. One is a large-sized transport. The other is a destroyer.'

'Only two?' This information upset me. I had hoped and prayed we would catch another large convoy, so that all six of us could go off in one general volley, dying together in a single, six-pronged onslaught.

The voice in my phone gave me further information.

'Angle is right, 60 degrees. Range, two miles. Enemy speed is 14 knots. Enemy course, 270 degrees.'

I repeated this back, according to our procedure, to show I had it correct, and noted it on my chart. My compass had been aligned with the submarine's fore-and-aft axis. That line would be my reference point when launched.

A new voice came through the telephone. It had cut into the general circuit, addressing all six of us together.

'Number One and Number Four will be fired. All others, remain ready.'

That meant Lieutenant Kakizaki and Petty Officer Yamaguchi would go. What would happen to me?

'Is Number Three going?' I asked, forgetting how calm I had intended to remain.

'Wait!' said the conning tower voice abruptly. 'There are only two enemy ships right now!'

I was ashamed of myself for being so presumptuous. Naturally Yamaguchi, very senior to myself in service, should go ahead of me. I sat still, holding my breath until it nearly choked me.

'Number One, get ready!' No voice was on the general circuit now. What I heard was another voice in the conning tower, coming dimly through the mouthpiece of the man who was in touch with me. I could not hear Kakizaki's voice. I bent forward and peered through my periscope. The water was a lovely blue, and at this level there was light enough for me to make out the stern of Kakizaki's *kaiten*, about thirty-five feet ahead of me on *I-47's* after deck. He had started his engine, and the noise was smooth, assuring me everything was going well for him. The image before my eyes jolted suddenly. Kakizaki's fourth tie-down had been released.

I had not heard the order 'Go!', but it had been given. In a second or two, Kakizaki started moving away. I spoke his name softly as a great mass of white bubbles floated back over around my weapon. These were from the high pressure air used to turn his torpedo's engine over for its first few revolutions. When they dissipated, and I could again see clearly, he was gone, his *kaiten* rack empty.

A short time later I heard the drumming, humming sound of a second engine. Yamaguchi was going, his bubbles also obscuring his departure. Two persons, two friends who had laughed and joked with me on the deck of a torpedo boat at Hikari, who had shared their cigarettes so often with me, were gone. I closed my eyes, conjuring up their faces for a final look at them.

A long wait came after that, followed by an explosion that rocked *I-47* and those *kaiten* still on her deck. 'A hit!' I shouted, not caring whether it went over my telephone line or not. Shortly after that I yelled, 'Another hit!' as a second explosion jarred me in my seat.

My two friends were now dead. Their lives were over. At that moment their souls were flying, side by side, to the great shrine at Yasukuni, there to be eternally revered like gods. I ached to join them, my voice shaking with sobs as I called the conning tower and asked, 'Are there any more targets?'

'Lieutenant Kakizaki and Petty Officer Yamaguchi have both scored direct hits,' was the answer I received.

This enraged me. I lost all control. 'I didn't ask you that, stupid' I screamed into the transmitter. 'Don't you think I have ears? I asked you whether there were any more enemy ships out there. Answer me!'

The conning tower must have been bedlam by then. I could hear shouting sounds on my line. Furukawa, Shinkai and Maeda were also calling into their transmitters and being answered. The conning tower watch let us shout all we wanted for a little while, then interrupted with, 'No more echoes have been detected by our sound operators. All *kaiten* are to stand by.' ...

Some more time passed, and then I could hear another dim voice in my receiver. 'Number Two,' it asked, 'are you ready?'

Furukawa had been alerted

'Angle is left, seventy degrees. Target is a destroyer. Range, three miles.'

I wanted to call out a protest again, but Furukawa was getting final instructions. If I began shouting, it might confuse him. I kept silent. Furukawa was my senior. I had to show him full respect.

Furukawa's telephone talker must have moved close to mine. His voice suddenly came through my receiver, loud and clear.

'The angle is not too good, but you can still be successful. Run at full speed for ten minutes. That will put you ahead of the enemy. When you put up your periscope, look to the left!'

I calculated rapidly on my chart. Captain Orita was making a good move. The target and Furukawa would both be well away from us. The enemy, if he survived, would be unable to locate the source of this attack.

'Ready? ... Go! '

Again, bubbles clouded my periscope. Mine was now the only *kaiten* remaining on *I-47's* after deck. When the bubbles cleared away I could now make out three empty *kaiten* racks ahead of me. The sight filled me with a deep loneliness, which must have been reflected in my voice a little later when I softly asked, 'Are there any more of the enemy?'

My question was the first of many pouring into the conning tower. All reason had left my two remaining comrades. All we wanted to do now was fight! I clamored as loudly as the others to be next *kaiten* off. We kept it up for about twenty minutes, when we were all cut off by a voice from the tower.

'No more enemy sounds can be detected by our equipment,' the conning tower telephone operator reported. 'The remaining *kaiten* pilots will return to the submarine. We are now clearing your access tubes.'

I cursed my luck. All that hope, and all that expectation, and now we could not go off. When the hissing sound of air ceased, I opened my lower hatch. Below, I saw the face of my maintenance man. 'Please come out,' he said, sliding up through the hatch and cramping himself into the small space behind my seat. 'I will take care of everything for you.'

Several crewmen were waiting as I re-entered *I-47*. 'Welcome back!' they said, which shocked me at first. Then it made me feel good, because I realized they were actually happy that I had not been launched. A few faces showed the same kind of disappointment I felt, but the older crewmen, for the most part, were glad that one so much younger than they had not ended his life.

I strode past them and went to the wardroom. Maeda and Shinkai were already there, peering at their watches. 'It should have been time by now,' said Maeda. 'How long has it been, Sir?' I asked.

'Thirty-eight minutes,' Maeda said. 'And there is no sound from the enemy, any more. He is out of range of our detection equipment.'

'Ak, so desuka?' I said. 'Is that so?' I became worried. Furukawa's course required a long run to get into position. Then he had to set his own intercept course from there. If he had any trouble controlling his depth, the destroyer might have seen him. It might now be running for its life, with him after it. Only a destroyer could approach a *kaiten*'s speed, but with a good lead, it might get away.

Furukawa would blow himself up if he could not catch the enemy. I was sure of it. There was no way we could ever find him if he ran out of fuel. *Kaiten* sat too low in the water when surfaced to be seen from a submarine if there were any kind of waves at all. And Orita did not dare surface, anyway, in daylight, to look for him, especially when there were enemy ships around.

Suddenly we heard the sound operator call out. 'I have an echo! Very faint! Degree of intensity is only one. It might be the *kaiten*, though.' Our watches had ticked past forty minutes, then forty-five. Maeda's face had darkened. Our watches now showed that forty-seven minutes had elapsed. In thirteen more minutes the last of Furukawa's fuel would be gone. I prayed that the sound was that of his final rush at top speed into the enemy.

Then, before the sound operator could even announce it, we heard an explosion! It was not as big as the first two – they had been closer. But it was the sound of a *kaiten*. There was no doubt of it. No American destroyer could make that big a sound with a depth charge.

'Banzai, Furukawa!' I yelled. Tears ran down our cheeks.

'Petty Officer Furukawa has scored a direct hit!' the loudspeaker announced. No more cheers sounded through *I-47* though. All suddenly became silent. I have never been able to explain why. The three ships credited to Orita's submarine for this mission, plus two credited to his torpedoes earlier, put *I-47* ahead thirteen-nine in the competition with *I-36*. Crewmen should have been cheering hysterically and pounding one another on the back. Through my mind, in this intense silence, passed the words I had heard so often since joining the Imperial Navy. 'In this crisis, you must stand ready to give your life, to save Japan!' Furukawa had given his, but the long wait during his attack seemed to take the steel out of all on board *I-47*. There was no feeling left in us to summon up more cheers. It had washed away during that forty-nine-minute wait.

Some time later, I don't know how much later, I returned to the crew's compartment. There, on two bunks, lay the small, carefully-stacked piles of belongings Yamaguchi and Furukawa had left beside their pillows. I fell into my own berth, sobbing endlessly. Death would be easier to take than this unendurable grief I felt at the loss of those two dear friends. Would Yamaguchi be able to get any beer in his new world? Would Furukawa, the true, staunch friend, be with him there, sitting quietly, and talking about his experiences in the Navy? I prayed for them between outbursts of weeping and sobbing, and for Lieutenant Kakizaki. 'I will follow you, my dear friends,' I said into my pillow, and asked them to welcome me with smiles when I came to the gate of Yasukuni.

Yokato never had the opportunity he craved; it was more than 18 months after the end of the war that he came to terms with all that had happened and enrolled at university.

### Electrician 1st Class Bob Haughney, US Navy, USS *Threadfin*

Rescuing airmen whose planes, launched from carriers, had been shot down or forced to ditch, was a task allotted to submarines.

Well, when we'd fired all our torpedoes they used to put us on what was called 'plane guard'. We kept good contact with the Air Force and if they were going to ditch they contacted us, and we made a rendezous – that was vital saving time. And we would be there when they came down.

We were up off Japan [at the end of *Threadfin*'s third and final war patrol which took place in the Yellow Sea and East China Sea and concluded at Guam on 27 July 1945] and we picked up some flyers that were shot down, and we took them on board and they were pretty badly damaged – they'd come down at about 150mph and when they hit the water it was like a brick wall, so we radioed that we needed a doctor aboard. On the way down to meet this destroyer with a doctor on board we picked up a radar of another ship coming towards us which was not an American. As it turned out, it was a British destroyer coming out towards us, and they thought we were a Japanese submarine, but we were able to identify each other. They turned around and we carried on and met the American destroyer. And the doctor said, 'Bring the injured on board,' and we told him we couldn't: they were too badly hurt. Well, at that he came aboard. We had fired all our torpedoes and the torpedo room was bigger than the operating room. He said: 'I'm making a recommendation that from now on if submarines have injured people on board the doctor is to come on board them.'

We were down about 50 feet and it's like sitting in a kitchen down there, so when the doctor had a sew, we weren't bouncing around. He could stand up. If he'd been on the surface, in the destroyer, he'd have been rocking back and forth.

We kept them with us for a couple of weeks until we headed back to port. He was able to sew them back together and take care of them for a while. They were lucky: most of the time, the planes sink fast.

One other group we picked up – well, we didn't pick them up, we went up to get them – were in the northern part of Japan, in the winter time. And you know how long we looked for them? Five minutes because nobody could live in that cold water more than five minutes. We had to try and get them even before they hit the water. We did save some men when they came down on the parachutes, we were there waiting for them and we were able to save them.

*Threadfin's* unexpected guests also included prisoners.

We took some Japanese prisoners after we sank their ships and contrary to what stories you hear we never ever tortured them or anything like that. In fact we had six, and the captain said 'That's too many', so we stopped one of those sampans and we put three of them on board. They kept three: the captain, the engineer and the wireless man. The Chinese didn't want them on board, but we didn't either. We sank a troopship earlier and naturally we could not save any of them, not one. They drowned themselves, but these ones were from merchant ships and they looked at things a little differently, and the war was going wrong for them, so that was probably the reason … And we treated them like human beings, only we kept them separated. When we brought them up to the compartment where the kitchen was, we made sure they didn't speak to one another, and when they finished we taught them to say 'Bum Chow' [bad food].

### Lieutenant Commander Ian Fraser VC, Royal Navy; from *Frogman VC*

The closing days of the war saw another extraordinary special operation. The British four-man midget submarine, *XE-3*, commanded by Lieutenant Ian Fraser, RNR, and with Leading Seaman James Magennis as the diver, had the task of blowing up the Japanese heavy cruiser *Takao* at Singapore in advance of a British invasion of Malaya which would lead to the liberation of the island. Following serious damage at the Battle of Leyte Gulf, she had been taken to Singapore and patched up to act as a shore battery.

At that part of the Strait where the *Takao* lay the water is shallow, with depths shown on Admiralty charts of from eleven to seventeen feet; but there is a depression in the sea-bed, which amounts to a hole, five hundred feet across, fifteen hundred feet long, and some five feet deeper than the water around. The *Takao* lay across this depression so that the first hundred feet of her length, beginning at her bow, lay in water which dropped to less than three feet at low tide; and the same conditions occurred at her stern. It was proposed that I should pass over this shallow patch and down into the hole where I was expected to manoeuvre my boat under the ship. As I have already said, I had made it clear that I thought this feat impossible.

'Stand by for a bearing, ship's head, now,' I ordered. Then I translated the bearing into a true bearing and laid it on the chart. The attack had started.

From that moment, until I was back on board the Stygian, all fear left me.

I felt only that nervous tautness that comes so often in moments of stress. I let each of the others have a quick look at the *Takao* through the periscope, and then we were ready ...

It was eight minutes to two when I finally decided that the position of *XE-3* was right enough for us to start the actual run in. By this time the sun was high in the heavens, the sea was as placid as a Scottish loch early on a summer's day, and visibility, both above and under the water, was excellent ...

When, during a spell on the run in, I glanced through the night periscope, I was disturbed to find that I could see both ends of *XE-3* quite distinctly, showing that the underwater visibility was ten feet or more. I reconciled myself to this disadvantage by thinking that I would at least be able to keep an eye on Magennis as he attached the limpet mines.

Later on, at eight minutes past two, the range was 2,000 yards, one mile away, about 30 degrees on our port bow.

'Four hundred and fifty revolutions, steer 218 degrees, stand by to start the attack.'

'Course 218 degrees. All ready to start the attack,' came the reply.

'Start the attack,' I ordered.

Magennis started the stop-watch, and we prepared ourselves. 'Up periscope.'

Magennis pressed the switch, the motor whirred. 'Whoa!'

The motor stopped.

'Bearing right ahead, range two degrees on her funnel, down periscope.'

Magennis changed the degrees into yards by means of the slide rule.

'Length 1,600 yards, sir,' he called.

I did not answer; there was no need to. Each of us was sweating profusely, and energy and air had to be reserved. In any case, we were only doing now the thing that we had practised time and time again when stationed in the Scottish lochs and when lying off the coast of Australia.

The only sounds in the boat were the whirr of the main motor, the hiss of escaping oxygen from the cylinder in the engine-room, and an occasional scraping sound of steel on steel in the well-greased bearings when the hydroplane wheel was turned. Ten feet, forty feet. 'Up periscope', range, 'Down periscope'. So it went on until the range had narrowed to 400 yards.

'Up periscope, stand by for a last look round.'

Click! Down went the handles: I fixed my eye to the eyepiece for the hundredth time, slowly swinging to port.

'Ah, there she is, range eight degrees.'

Slowly I swung the periscope round to starboard.

'Flood "Q", down periscope, quick, thirty feet. Bloody hell! There's a boat full of Japs going ashore; she's only about forty or fifty feet away on the starboard bow. God, I hope they didn't see us.'

So close had they been that I could make out their faces quite distinctly, and even had time to notice that one of them was trailing his hand in the water. The boat, painted white, stood out clearly against the camouflaged background of the cruiser. Similar to the cutters used in the Royal Navy for taking liberty men ashore, she was packed with sailors. The helmsman stood aft, his sailor's collar and ribbon gently lifting in the breeze caused by the boat's headway. She was so close that it seemed that her bow waves almost broke over our periscope. I could see the lips of men moving as they chatted away on the journey ashore. They should have seen us. I do not know why they did not.

'Thirty feet, sir.'

My mind re-focused.

'All right, Magennis, the range is 200 yards, we should touch bottom in a moment.'

To [Sub-Lieutenant 'Kiwi'] Smith, RNVR: 'Keep her as slow as you can.'

Followed anxious silence, then a jar and the noise of gravel scraping along the keel as we touched bottom. [ERA] Reid had to fight hard to keep her on course as we scraped and dragged our way across the bank at depths of only fifteen feet, which meant our upper deck was only ten feet below the surface.

Watching through the night periscope, I could see the surface of the water like a wrinkled window-pane above our heads, until it gradually darkened as we came into the shadow of the great ship. Something scraped down our starboard side, and then, with a reverberating crash, we hit the *Takao* a glancing blow which stopped us. I thought we had made enough noise to awaken the dead, and I was worried in case someone above might have felt the jar.

'Stop the motor! I wonder where the hell we are?' I said. I could see nothing through the periscope to give me a clear indication of our position in relation to the enemy ship, only her dark shadow on our starboard side. Obviously I was not underneath it, as the depth on the gauge was only thirteen feet.

I began to fear that we might be much too far forward, that the ominous-sounding scraping along our side had been made by an anchor-cable at the target's bows.

'We seem to be too far for'ard,' I reported. 'We'll alter course to 190 degrees and try to run down her side. Port 30, half ahead, group down.'

The motor hummed into life again, but we did not budge.

'Group up half ahead,' I called, and we tried many other movements. The motor hummed even faster, the propeller threshed, but still no sign of movement. We were jammed, and, looking back on this afterwards, I am inclined to think that as the *Takao* veered in the tideway, the slacking cable came to rest on us. Then it lifted as she veered away again, or else we were jammed for the same reason under the curve of her hull at this point. It was only after some really powerful motor movements in both directions, and ten minutes of severe strain, that we finally broke loose and dragged our way out across the shingly bottom to the deeper channel.

I had attacked from too fine an angle on the bow, and after running out again I altered course and steered for a position more on the Takao's beam, which would mean a longer run over the shallow bank, but I decided the risk was worth it, if I were to hit the ship amidships.

At three minutes past three we were ready again, a thousand yards away. Once more we started the run-in for the attack. This time we were successful. We slid easily across the bank with the gauge at one time registering only thirteen feet, and then blackness, as we slid into the hole and under the keel of the Takao. It was just as I had practised it so many times before, and I was surprised how easy it was.

The depth gauge began to indicate deeper water, 15 feet, 18 feet, 20 feet, and then a greying of the night-periscope and upper viewing window.

'Stop the motor.'

Then blackness in the night-periscope and upper viewing window.

'Full astern.'

The bottom of the *Takao* showed dimly, and then suddenly it was distinct, encrusted with thick heavy layers of weed as it fell sharply to her keel.

'Stop the motor!'

The hull stopped sliding overhead. We were under her.

We were resting on the bottom with the hull of the *Takao* only a foot above our heads. I wondered if we would be able to go straight through …

Magennis was ready: he must have been stewing in his rubber suit, and I thought, momentarily forgetting the dangers, how pleasant it would be for him to get out into the cool water. He strapped on his breathing apparatus. The only instruction I could give him was to place all six limpets in the container as quickly as possible and not to make a noise. I fitted in the Perspex window, patted him on the shoulder, and into the escape compartment he went. Reid closed the door on him; the valves were opened and shut, and the pumps started. Looking through the observation window into the wet-and-dry compartment, I could see Magennis breathing steadily into the bag as the water rose around him …

He shut the lid and disappeared over the side, and we settled down nervously to await his return.

We counted the limpets as he bumped them out of the containers and moved them one by one along the starboard side, and occasionally I caught a glimpse of him as he worked away under the hull above. Six limpets he took – three towards the for'ard end and three towards the after end. In all, the total time taken was somewhere round about thirty minutes. To me it seemed like thirty days …

The tide was still falling. Although the rise and fall in the Johore Strait is only eight feet, this was more than sufficient to allow the cruiser to sit on us in the shallow hole beneath her hull. High water had been at 1200, zero hour for the attack, and it was now nearly four hours later. I was very anxious to get away. Magennis still seemed to be an age, and just when I could hardly contain myself a moment longer, he appeared on the hatch. He gave the 'thumbs up' sign again and in he jumped. I saw the lid shut and the clip go home. He was back, and now at last we could go.

Quickly, we started to release the side cargoes. The fuses on the port charge, four tons of Amytol, had, like the 200lb limpets, already been set to detonate in six hours' time, so that it was only necessary for us to unscrew the small wheel which started the mechanism, and then to unscrew the larger wheel which released the charge. The first ten turns of this wheel opened a kingston in the charge to allow water to enter the compartment, previously filled by air, and rendered the charge negatively buoyant. The last turn released the charge itself, which should have fallen away and rested on the bottom. In order to relish the full pleasure of placing four tons of high explosive under a Japanese ship, the three of us took it in turns to operate the wheels as Magennis was draining down his compartment. The port charge fell away – we heard it bump down our side, but we hung on for Magennis to re-enter the craft before finally letting the starboard limpet-carrier go. As a result of this delay, it became too heavy and would not release or slide away. Such an emergency had already been thought of by the designers of XE-craft, and an additional wheel had been provided. This operated a pusher to push the side cargo off, and between us we wound the wheel out to its limit, but with no effect. The bottom of the cargo swung out from the ship's side, but the top was still held fast. By now I felt sure that the pins at the top were holding, but I thought to myself that the movement of the craft might shake it loose. We certainly couldn't make headway very far with two tons of dead weight fast to our side.

In the meantime Magennis reported that he had found it very difficult getting the limpets into position; the work of attaching them successfully had exhausted him … The limpets themselves, clumsily designed (they were big awkward jobs to drag through the water, all angles and projections, and they caught and tangled in the weeds), had to be attached. Unfortunately, owing to the positive buoyancy of the charge itself and the angular bottom of the *Takao*, there was a tendency for the charges to break loose from the magnetic hold-fasts, which, for reasons unknown, had become very feeble, and to run up towards the surface, with Magennis chasing after them to bring them back into position in two groups of three charges. In each group he had secured the limpets some 45–60 feet apart – three away along the cavern to our starboard side, and three along the cavern on either side of the keel, so that they could not dislodge and slide off on to the bottom. He had set the firing mechanism working, but in his exhausted state had become unable to remove three of the counter-mining pins, which ensure that should one limpet blow up the rest will follow immediately, even if the clocks have been wound for the set delay. The counter-mining device, which was lethal after twenty minutes, also ensured that any diver sent down by the Japanese to render the mines safe, or to remove them, would blow himself to eternity should he give the charges the slightest blow …

'Group up, half ahead – let's get to hell out of this hole!' I gave the order with a feeling of relief.

'Main motor, half ahead, sir,' from Smith. 'May I start the fan, sir? '

'Yes, start the fan.'

Magennis began to take off his breathing set and hood. 'What is the course, sir?' asked good, calm, cheerful Reid.

'Two hundred degrees,' I answered. 'Let me know if you have any trouble keeping her on.'

I moved over to the sounding machine and switched it on, and then back to the night-periscope to watch as we moved out under the vast hull which was slowly settling down upon us with the fall of the tide, and through which we hoped our charges would blow a hole big enough to sink her for good.

But although the motor had been running for several seconds, there was no sign of movement.

'Full ahead,' I ordered.

Still no movement!

'Stop, full astern, group up.'

Glancing at Smith, I sincerely hoped I was not becoming hysterical. I felt certain that the *Takao* must have settled down on us, thus preventing any movement whatsoever. We couldn't go astern as the Takao's keel was lower than the rear periscope standard. We must go ahead if we could go anywhere at all.

'Stop, full ahead, group up, lift the red, stop.'

This gave us maximum power, the motors whirred and we could hear the propeller thrusting hard against the water, but it was useless. We seemed to be well and truly stuck, and for a moment I thought of hanging on until half an hour before the charge was due to go off and then abandoning the ship. After all, I consoled myself, it was only 200 yards or so from the shore, and we might be able to hide in the swamps and forests until Singapore fell into British hands again ...

We tried pumping the water aft and then for'ard, out and then in, and finally, we even partially blew No. 2 main ballast tank to try to shake loose from what looked like being *XE-3's* watery grave. I was in despair. Sweat poured into my eyes. But still that black menacing shape stood overhead. Then suddenly, with a final effort, she began to move.

'Ship's head swinging to starboard, can't control her.'

Once again Reid's quiet voice calmed my turmoil. We began to move slowly ahead, the flooded charge dragging like a broken wing on our starboard side. The black roof slid astern, and fresh pure welcome sunlight streamed through the water into my upturned eyes.

We had a bow angle of some five degrees, and slowly the needle of my depth gauge moved in an anti-clockwise direction until it steadied at seventeen feet. The weight on our right swung the ship's head round until we were parallel to the side of the *Takao*, and I reckoned some thirty feet away on her port side.

'Stop the motor, we'll have to try to release the cargo. It'll have to be very carefully done as we're only a few yards away,' I explained.

Magennis was still sweating away in his suit, and I felt he had done enough to make the operation a success. As Reid had little or no experience of underwater swimming in the frogmen gear, and Smith wasn't particularly good at this either, I considered that it was justifiable for me to take the risk of leaving the boat for a few moments, even if I was the commanding officer. Should anything happen, I had enough confidence in Smith to know that he could get her out to rejoin the Stygian.

'Come out of the way, Magennis, I'll go out and release it myself. Get me the spare set from the battery compartment.'

'I'll be all right in a minute, sir,' said Magennis, 'just let me get my wind.'

What a wonderful lad he was! He said this with a most hurt expression on his face, quite obviously meaning that since he was the diver it was up to him to do the diving. And so we sat quietly for five minutes, and when he was ready

I replaced his hood and Perspex face. 'Thanks,' he said, and into the wet-and-dry compartment he went for the second time.

The wheels spun, the pumps started and the water began to rise. Reid had equipped Magennis with an elephant-size spanner, and as the lid of the hatch opened, I saw this come through the opening immediately behind a mass of air bubbles, followed by Magennis. Once again I wondered what he was thinking about only thirty feet away from a Japanese cruiser in seventeen feet of clear water, his only weapon being a spanner. The bubbles released from opening the hatch were quite enough to cause me a great deal of worry. Had anybody been looking over the side of the *Takao* – perhaps a seaman gazing idly into the water with his thoughts away at home in Yokohama, Nagasaki, or somewhere like that – he must have seen us. The water was as clear as glass, and Magennis in his green diving suit was sending out a steady stream of bubbles from the reducing valve of his set.

Inside the boat it was as quiet as death: none of us spoke. I could hear the ship's chronometer ticking away, the anxious seconds interrupted by an occasional clank as Magennis used his spanner. It took some five minutes to release the cargo; five of the most anxious minutes of my life. Watching through the periscope, I could see the position of both securing pins at which he should have been working, but for some reason or other he was out of sight. I bit my fingers, swore and cursed at him, swore and cursed at the captain and all the staff on board Bonaventure who had planned this operation, at the British Admiralty, and finally, at myself for ever having been so stupid as to volunteer for this life, and, having volunteered, for being so stupid as to work hard enough to get myself this particular operation. I wished myself anywhere except lying on the bottom of Singapore harbour.

I don't know what Reid or Smith thought of this little display, but as far as I know they never mentioned my temporary lapse.

I had told Magennis to make no noise, but his hammering and bashing, in what I thought to be really the wrong place, was loud enough to alarm the whole Japanese Navy.

'What the bloody hell is that bloody fool doing?' I asked no one in particular. 'Why the hell doesn't he come on top of the charge. Why didn't I go out myself?' Then I saw Magennis for a moment, and at the same time the cargo came away and we were free. He gave me the 'thumbs up' sign for the third and last time and slid feet first into the wet-and-dry compartment and closed the lid. Wheels turned, pumps started and down came the water.

Right, I thought. Then: 'Starboard twenty, steer 090 degrees, half ahead, group up,' I ordered all in one breath.

'Aye, aye, sir.'

'Twelve hundred revolutions.'

'Aye, aye, sir.'

'O.K.,' I said. "Home, James, and don't spare the horses.' I think we all managed a smile at that moment.

XE-3 achieved the difficult task of returning to her rendezvous with HMS Stygian, the submarine that had towed her from Borneo, and an explosion suggested the attack had been a brilliant success. It turned out, however, that the Takao had not been sunk: the explosion was, by strange coincidence, that of a crashing aircraft. The order to make a second attempt was nullifed by the dropping of the atomic bombs. Both Magennis and Fraser were awarded the VC.

### Outside ERA's Mate Cyril Bowden, Royal Navy, HMS *Virtue*

Some bright spark had told me once 'Well you won't go any farther than the Med in them [V-Class submarines] because you won't stand the warm water out East.' So the next thing I know we were in Colombo and, I always remember, we found a canoe on our way out to Colombo – a real pukka carved-out-of-a-trunk-canoe. We lashed it on to the casing and carried it with us, and when we were in Colombo I used to use that to go round the harbour in. A lot of them wouldn't go in it but I used to love it. It was smashing. From there we went to Fremantle, which was a long way for us because we were just about washing at the bottom, there was that little fuel left.

The US Navy was there, they used Fremantle a lot, and the bigger submarines, the T boats.

We went round to Sydney and got victualled up, and then we were off to the Islands. We got up to Manus. I always remember that. It was a huge harbour. The Japs were still on the islands there so the Yanks used to go out at night and bring back the ears. I thought it was a joke, but it wasn't … They'd sit there and they'd say 'I think I'm gonna get me a Jap …'

The next thing was, we'd set sail and I hadn't got a clue where we were going at the time but we finished up back in Sydney with a damn lot of the American fleet which had never been known before – they never had the two fleets in at the same time because of fights. I can't say we didn't get on, but there was rivalry. It all turned out [afterwards] that the atomic bomb was going to be dropped and they were expecting tidal waves in Sydney. Nobody knew what an atomic bomb was. The powers that be knew it was going to be dropped, that's why they took all the ships back. They didn't know what the repercussions of that bomb would actually be. Of course, when it did go off the devastation was terrible, but it was in that area. And the next thing was, the war was over. That was it. I was coming home.

# EPILOGUE

Looking back at a period of war I experienced as a duty, I can only review it serenely – although along with the calm memory of my survival comes the sad and sorrowful memory of so many friends and comrades who never went home. – Mario Rossetto

All warfare nowadays is impersonal …When the big guns start opening up, it gets impersonal. One battleship wants to sink another battleship and you don't think about the 2,000 guys who are about that ship, and what happens to every single one of these sailors: you want to sink this ship. When a U-boat sinks a tanker you don't think of the poor people who have to dive into the burning oil. It's impersonal. The memorial at Tower Hill … I've been there many times. I get a lump in my throat every time at Moltenort near Kiel, and at Tower Hill, the respective sites of memorials to the U-boat dead and the dead of British and Commonwealth merchant seamen. – Volkmar König

More than 50,000 men lost their lives serving in submarines during the Second World War, over half of them in German U-boats alone. The British (including Commonwealth submariners), Americans, Italians and Soviets all had casualty figures in the 3,000–3,600 range. Japan lost some 10,000 men. When set against the lives lost in the sinking of a single battleship such as HMS *Hood* or the *Bismarck*, these numbers may seem less dramatic, and they pale into insignificance against the staggering army casualties on the Russian Front, which are counted in millions. But numbers are cold and impersonal. The submarines were divided into flotillas, with bases to which, if their luck held, they returned after each patrol: those bases were intimate communities in which the crew of one boat knew the crews of the others. Boats transferred between flotillas; men transferred between boats: the sinking of one boat could mean the loss of forty or fifty comrades with whom many months had been spent on passage, patrol and shore leave. Even the sinking of an enemy submarine was subconsciously overlaid with that inevitable sense of 'there but for grace' … a knowledge that the dead and dying were also submariners who knew, far better than anyone on a surface ship, what life was like in a boat that, in a split second, could be transformed from a sardine tin into an iron coffin.

## REMEMBRANCE

I shall remember, long after this madness has passed away,
The sudden blare of klaxons by night and day,
The engines' incessant clamour borne on the midnight blast –
These things I shall remember, long after war has passed.

I shall remember the scramble, in the hours of early dawn,
Of the boat's sudden submerging, as the Winter day is born.
I shall remember sharp orders – the watch we had to keep
As we dipped beneath the surface, down to silence, and the deep.

I shall remember the laughter, the merry song and jest,
That comrade spirit born of war which gives the game its zest.
The thrill of our first attack – the Captain's 'Stand by ... Fire!'
These things I shall remember, when sweeter memories tire.

I shall remember the tasks, and times when all was still,
The muscles strained, the concerted action of a few men with a will.
But the heartache that knows no balm, the gnawing and the fret,
The sorrow of leaving loved ones – these things, by God, I'll forget.

Anonymous crew member, HMS *Thrasher*

# Bibliography

It is hard to find a submarine autobiography that is not worth reading, and this author has a personal affection for *Cinq Ans Dans le Brouillard*, *Half Seas Under* and *War in the Boats*. Anyone trying to track down long-out-of-print books will find www.addall.com a very useful search engine.

*All Round Look:* Yearbook of the Friends of The Royal Navy Submarine Museum

*Aria Alla Rapida*, the submariners' journal of the Associazione Nazionale Marinai d'Italia

Beach, E., *Submarine!* Blue Jacket Books, Annapolis, 2003

Borghese: J. V., *Sea Devils*, Naval Institute Press, Annapolis, 1995; Italian edition *Decima Flottiglia MAS*, Editore Albertelli, Parma, 2005

Cremer, P. and Brustat-Naval, F., *U-333*, Bodley Head, London 1984; published Annapolis, USA, 1984 by Naval Institute Press as *U-Boat Commander*, and 1984 in German by Verlag Ullstein GmbH, Berlin, as *Ali Cremer, U-333*

Fraser, I., *Frogman VC*, Angus & Robertson, London, 1957.

Galantin, I., *Take Her Deep*, Algonquin, New York, 1987

Hart, S., *Discharged Dead*, Odhams Press, London, 1956

*In Depth*: Journal of the Friends of the Royal Navy Submarine Museum

Korzh, V., *Red Star Under The Baltic*, Pen & Sword Maritime, Barnsley, 2004

L'Herminier, J., *Casabianca*, France Empire, Paris, 1992

Lagane, R., *Cinq Ans Dans Le Brouillard*, Editions du Houblot, Larmor-Plage, France, 2000

Majnik, John de, *Diary of a Submariner*, Asgard Press, Inglewood, Western Australia, 1996

Mars, A. *Unbroken,* Leo Cooper, Barnsley, 2006

McLean, R., *Half Seas Under*, Thomas Reed Publications, Branford Leigh, UK, 2001

Mendenhall, C., *Submarine Diary*, Naval Institute Press, Annapolis 2001

O'Kane, R., *Wahoo*, Presidio Press, Novato, USA, 1987

Orita Z & Harrington, J., *I-Boat Commander*, Major Books, Canoga Park, USA, 1976

*Plongée*, the Journal of L'Association des Amicales d'Anciens des Sous-Marins

Prien, G., *U-Boat Commander*, Tempus Publishing Ltd, Stroud, UK; first published as *Mein Weg nach Scapa Flow*, Deutscher Verlag, Berlin, 1940

Ruhe, W., *War in the Boats*, Potomac Books, Dulles, USA, 2005

Schlumberger, E., *L'Honneur et les Rebelles de la Marine Français 1940–1944*, Maisonneuve & Larose, Paris, 2004

Shean, M., *Corvette and Submarine*, privately published, Claremont, Western Australia, 1992

Sopoko, E., *Orzel's Patrol*, Methuen, London, 1940

Suhren, R., and Brustat-Naval, F., *Teddy Suhren, Ace of Aces,* Chatham Publishing, London 2006; originally published in Germany as *Nasses Eichenlaub*, Koehlers Verlagsgesellschaft, Hamburg, 1998

Topp, E., *Fakeln über dem Atlantik* Verlag
E. S. Mittler & Sohn GMBH, Hamburg,
1992
Toschi, E., *Nine Times Lucky*, William
Kimber, London 1948; first published as
*In Fuga Oltre l'Himalaya,* Edizioni
Europee, 1948, and Il Borghese,
Milano, 1968
*U-Boat Archive*, Journal published by the
U-Boot Archiv, Cuxhaven (now renamed
Deutsches U-Boot Museum Archive)
Various: *Even More Submarine Memories,*
Gatwick Submarine Archive, 2005
Werner, H., *Iron Coffins,* Cassell Military
Paperbacks, London 2006
Yokota, Y., *The Kaiten Weapon*,
Ballantyne Books, New York, 1962
Young, E., *One of our Submarines,* Pen
and Sword Military Classics, Barnsley,
2004

**Selected reference books
and good websites**
Antier, Jean Jacques, *L'Aventure Heroique
des Sous-Marins Français 1939–1945*,
Editions Maritimes et
d' Outre-Mer, France, 1984
Antier, Jean Jacques, *Les Sous-Mariniers*,
Editions Ouest-France, Rennes, 1994
Atkinson, John, *Royal Navy Submarine
Service – Losses in WWII*, Galago,
Bromley, 2004
Bagnasco, Erminio, *Submarines of World
War Two*, Arms & Armour Press,
London, 1977
Bagansco, Erminio, and Rastelli, Achille,
*Sommergibili in Guerra*, Ermanno
Albertelli, Parma, 1989
Bradshaw, *English and French Naval
Terms*, Williams & Northgate
Chalmers, Rear Admiral W. S., *Max
Horton and the Western Approaches*,
Hodder & Stoughton, London, 1954
Di Risio, Carlo, *I Mezzi D'Assalto* (Vol. XIV
of *La Marina Italiana Nella Seconda
Guerra Mondiale*), Ufficio Storico della
Marina Militare, Rome, 1964
Fioravanzo, Admiral Giuseppe,

*Sommergibili in Guerra*, Rivista
Marittima, Rome, 1956
Gannon, Michael J., *Black May*, Aurum
Press, London, 1998
Macintyre, Donald, *U-boat Killer*, Rigel,
2004
Mallmann-Showell, Jak, *The U-Boat
Century*, Chatham Publishing, London,
2006
Mattes, Klaus, *Die Seehunde*, E. S. Mittler
& Sohn, Hamburg, 1995; also available
from the author on DVD: email
klaus.mattes@uboot-typ127.de
Mattesini, Francesco: Betasom – *La
Guerra Negli Oceani*, Ufficio Storico
Della Marina Militare, Rome, 2003
McCartney, Innes, *British Submarines
1939–1945*, Osprey Publishing, Oxford,
2006
Milner, Mark, *Battle of the Atlantic*,
Tempus, London, 2003
Padfield, Peter, *War Beneath The Sea –
Submarine Conflict 1939–1945*, John
Murray, London, 1995
Preston, Anthony, *Navies of WW2*,
Hamlyn, London, 1976
Rossetto, Mario, *Missione Non Attacare!*
Vittorelli Edizione, Gorizia, 2002
Shankland, P., and Hunter, A., *Malta
Convoy*, 1961; also published in *Three
Sea Stories*, Collins, no date
Showell. Jak P. Mallmann, *U-Boats Under
the Swastik*a, Naval Institute Press,
1987
— *U-Boat Warfare*, Ian Allan, Hersham,
2002
Stern, Robert C., *Type VII U-boats*, Arms
& Armour Press, London, 1991
Trenowden, Ian, *Operations Most Secret*,
William Kimber, London, 1978
Tute, Warren, *The Deadly Stroke*, Collins,
London, 1973
Whinney, Bob, *The U-Boat Peril*, Cassell
Military Paperbacks, London 1986
Wilmot, Chester, *The Struggle For Europe*,
Wordsworth Publishing, London, 1977
Wilson, Michael, *A Submariner's War –
The Indian Ocean 1939–1945*, Tempus

Publishing, Stroud, 2000

Wingate, J. The Fighting 10th, Leo Cooper, London, 1991

www.naval-history.net, a wide-ranging and useful site

www.uboat.net, best website for information on the Kriegsmarine's submarines

www.dutchsubmarines.com, a comprehensive site on the submarines of the Netherlands

http://ussvi.org/home.asp, United States Submarine Veterans, Inc.

## CREDITS

Extracts from *Teddy Suhren, Ace of Aces* used by kind permission of Chatham Publishing Ltd (English language edition) and Köhlers Verlagsgesellschaft. Extracts from *Cinq Ans dans Le Brouillard* used by kind permission of the author and Editions Du Houblot. Extracts from *Casabianca* used by kind permission of Editions France Empire. Extracts from *Wahoo: the Patrols of America's Most Famous World War II Submarine* by Richard O'Kane, copyright © 1987 Richard O'Kane, used by permission of Presidio Press, an imprint of The Ballantine Publishing Group, a division of Random House, Inc. Extracts from *U-333: The Story of a U-Boat Ace* by Peter Cremer, published by The Bodley Head. Reprinted by permission of The Random House Group Ltd. (English language edition); and Bonnier Media Deutschland GmbH. Extracts from *Half Seas Under* used by kind permission of David McLean, Andrew McLean and Catriona Waterhouse. Extracts from *Iron Coffins* used by kind permission of Henry Holt and Company Inc. Extracts from *Fackeln Uber Dem Atlantik* used by kind permission of Verlag E.S. Mitler & Sohn GmbH. Extracts from *L'Honneur et Les Rebelles De La Marine Française 1940–1944* used by kind permission of the author and Maisonneuve & Larose. Extracts from *Frogman VC* used by kind permission of the author. Extracts from *Unbroken* reprinted by kind permission of The Random House Group Ltd. Extracts from *Red Star Under the Baltic* used by kind permission of Pen and Sword. Extract from *Even More Submarine Memories* used by kind permission of Gatwick Submarine Archive. Extracts from *Corvette and Submarine* used by kind permission of the author. Extracts from *Take Her Deep!* by Admiral I. J. Galantin, USN, Retd. © 1987 by Admiral I. J. Galantin, USN, Retd. Reprinted by permission of Algonquin Books of Chapel Hill. Extracts from *War in the Boats* used by kind permission of Potomac Books, Inc. (formerly Brassey's, Inc). Extracts from *Submarine!* used by kind permission of Naval Institute Press. Extracts from *Diary of a Submariner* used by kind permission of John de Majnik and Juanita Ironside. Extracts from *One of Our Submarines* used by kind permission of Pen and Sword Military Classics. Transcribed extracts of interviews held by the Sound Archive of the IWM published by kind permission of the Imperial War Museum. Extracts from the diary and final letter of Lieutenant Ian Anderson used by kind permission of Mrs H. Clark. Extracts from the papers of Commander P. Bartlett used by kind permission of his estate. Extracts from the papers of J. C. Brighton used by kind permission of his estate. Jan Biesemaat's memoir used by kind permission of Ton Biesemaat. Extracts from *Aria Alla Rapida* published by kind permission of Associazione Nazionale Marinai d'Italia di Milano. Extracts from *In Depth* and *All Round Look* used by kind permission of their editor. Transcript of Hartwig Looks' interview for *The World At War*, Thames Television, 1972, used by kind permission of Fremantle Media. Extracts from *Plongée* used by the kind offices of the Association Génerale Amicale des Anciens des Sous-Marins. Extracts from *Sea Devils* published by kind permission of Don Andrea Scirè dei Principi Borghese

Full details of all the books and documents can be found in the Bibliography.

# Index